Information Retrieval Methods for Multidisciplinary Applications

Zhongyu (Joan) Lu
University of Huddersfield, UK

Information Science
REFERENCE

Managing Director: Lindsay Johnston
Editorial Director: Joel Gamon
Book Production Manager: Jennifer Yoder
Publishing Systems Analyst: Adrienne Freeland
Development Editor: Joel Gamon
Assistant Acquisitions Editor: Kayla Wolfe
Typesetter: Lisandro Gonzalez
Cover Design: Jason Mull

Published in the United States of America by
Information Science Reference (an imprint of IGI Global)
701 E. Chocolate Avenue
Hershey PA 17033
Tel: 717-533-8845
Fax: 717-533-8661
E-mail: cust@igi-global.com
Web site: http://www.igi-global.com

Library of Congress Cataloging-in-Publication Data

Information retrieval methods for multidisciplinary applications / Zhongyu (Joan) Lu, editor.
pages cm
Includes bibliographical references and index.
Summary: "This book provides innovative research on information gathering, web data mining, and automation systems, addressing multidisciplinary applications and focusing on theories and methods with an enterprise-wide perspective"-- Provided by publisher.
ISBN 978-1-4666-3898-3 (hardcover) -- ISBN 978-1-4666-3899-0 (ebook) -- ISBN 978-1-4666-3900-3 (print & perpetual access) 1. Data mining. 2. Querying (Computer science) 3. Information storage and retrieval systems. I. Lu, Zhongyu, 1955-
QA76.9.D343I546 2013
006.3'12--dc23
2012048660

British Cataloguing in Publication Data
A Cataloguing in Publication record for this book is available from the British Library.

Associate Editors

List of Reviewers

Table of Contents

Detailed Table of Contents

Most existing XML stream processing systems adopt full structured query languages, such as XPath or XQuery, but they are difficult for ordinary users to learn and use. Keyword search is a user-friendly information discovery technique that has been extensively studied for text documents. This paper presents an XML stream filter system called XKFilter, which is the first system for supporting keyword search over XML stream. In XKFilter, the concepts of XLCA (eXclusive Lowest Common Ancestor) and XLCA Connecting Tree (XLCACT) are used to define the search semantic and results of keywords, and present an approach to filter XML stream according to keywords. The prototype XKFilter is implemented in the experiments.

This paper describes issues and challenges in the design and implementation of interactive client-server applications where program logic is expressed in terms of an extensible markup language (XML) document. Although the technique was originally developed for creating interactive short message service (SMS) applications, it has expanded and is used for developing interactive web applications. XML-Interactive (or XML-I) defines the program states and corresponding actions. Because many interactive applications require sustained communication between the client and the underlying information service, XML-I has support for session management. This allows state information to be managed in a dynamic way. The paper describes several applications that are implemented using XML-I and discusses design issues. The software framework has been implemented in a Java environment.

The World Wide Web is a large distributed digital information space. The ability to search and retrieve information from the Web efficiently and effectively is an enabling technology for realizing its full potential. Information Retrieval (IR) plays an important role in search engines. Today's most advanced engines use the keyword-based ("bag of words") paradigm, which has inherent disadvantages. Organizing web search results into clusters facilitates the user's quick browsing of search results. Traditional clustering techniques are inadequate because they do not generate clusters with highly readable names. This paper proposes an approach for web search results in clustering based on a phrase based clustering algorithm. It is an alternative to a single ordered result of search engines. This approach presents a list of clusters to the user. Experimental results verify the method's feasibility and effectiveness.

As web contents grow, the importance of search engines become more critical and at the same time user satisfaction decreases. Query recommendation is a new approach to improve search results in web. In this paper a method is proposed that, given a query submitted to a search engine, suggests a list of queries that are related to the user input query. The related queries are based on previously issued queries, and can be issued by the user to the search engine to tune or redirect the search process. The proposed method is based on clustering processes in which groups of semantically similar queries are detected. The clustering process uses the content of historical preferences of users registered in the query log of the search engine. This facility provides queries that are related to the ones submitted by users in order to direct them toward their required information. This method not only discovers the related queries but also ranks them according to a similarity measure. The method has been evaluated using real data sets from the search engine query log.

Designing a well-structured XML document is important for the sake of readability, maintainability and more importantly to avoid both data redundancies and update anomalies. This paper proposes to improve and simplify XML structural design using a normalization process. To achieve this, Graphical Notation for Document Type Definition (GN-DTD) is used to describe the structure of XML document at the schema level. Multiple levels of normal forms for GN-DTD are proposed and the corresponding normalization rules to transform from poorly designed into well-designed XML documents. A case study is presented to show the application of these normal forms and normalization algorithm.

In the age of information the rise in development of (ICT) Information Communication Technology and Internet, the format of documents has changed to digital. Electronic information sources have become an important part for today's library and users. Electronic information is gaining more importance in academic activities with an extreme change in the pattern of dissemination of knowledge. Web technology provides dynamism to the electronic documents that were note possible in the essentially sequential style of presentation of printed documents. Interactive hyperlinks to related resources, links to full range of multimedia, traditional indexing, and abstracting services, etc., are some of the novelties that are common in a web document. Faculty has a vital role in providing up-to-date information with the latest technologies, so they must be skilled users of electronic information through online journals. Hence, it is worth studying the use of online journals. Suggestions have been given to strengthen existing online journals subscription, the availability of full text online journals, and accessibility, e.g., system speed and maximizing the use of online journals among science faculty members at the University of Pune.

In this paper, the authors discuss the MapReduce implementation of crawler, indexer and ranking algorithms in search engines. The proposed algorithms are used in search engines to retrieve results from the World Wide Web. A crawler and an indexer in a MapReduce environment are used to improve the speed of crawling and indexing. The proposed ranking algorithm is an iterative method that makes use of the link structure of the Web and is developed using MapReduce framework to improve the speed of convergence of ranking the WebPages. Categorization is used to retrieve and order the results according to the user choice to personalize the search. A new score is introduced in this paper that is associated with each WebPage and is calculated using user's query and number of occurrences of the terms in the query in the document corpus. The experiments are conducted on Web graph datasets and the results are compared with the serial versions of crawler, indexer and ranking algorithms.

Soft-set theory proposed by Molodstov is a general mathematic tool for dealing with uncertainty. Recently, several algorithms have been proposed for decision making using soft-set theory. However, these algorithms still concern on Boolean-valued information system. In this paper, Support Attribute Representative (SAR), a soft-set based technique for decision making in categorical-valued information system is proposed. The proposed technique has been tested on three datasets to select the best partition-

Preface

AN OVERVIEW OF THE SUBJECT MATTER

Information retrieval is ubiquitous. It is directly linked to multidisciplinary and interdisciplinary applications. Discovery of findings from scientific research requires it. Analysis of experiment results in engineering and technology requires it. Obtaining arguments and opinions in social science requires it. Dealing with large dataset in healthcare requires it. Improving learning and teaching in education requires it. Observing the market trends in business requires it. Predicting financial profits requires it. It follows that as long as information exists, information retrieval is pervasive.

The methodologies of information retrieval are moving from traditional document engineering, static data, text, and images to dynamic multimedia audio video systems, from simple database management system to complex spatial datasets, from PC desktop to Smartphone technologies. It integrates emerging technologies to speed up the modernization of information retrieval.

Information retrieval involves fields beyond the word "retrieval" itself. Data search-ability, security, integrity, confidentiality, and accessibility are the same important as efficiency and accuracy. Advanced hardware improves retrieval efficiency and storage capacity for large datasets. Advanced software system services like web pages, emails, music, and videos add additional meanings and contents in today's information retrieval. Service oriented framework such as cloud computing enhances the facilities and environments for the information retrieval but brings new challenges to the subject area. It follows that the topic involves in this book significantly fits the demanding in the world today.

Emerging technologies, such as XML technologies, has strong impact on information retrieval. XML related research on the data integrity, confidentiality, authentication and other security issues becomes an immediate task for the scientists and researchers in the subject area. XML related database mapping delivered a convenient tool for users who are familiar with traditional applications but willing to accept new challenges. XML related e-resources, e-reading, e-journals or other e-platforms are next moves in next generations' information retrieval.

In the light of above, this book will open a conversation to the audience about what happened in today's information retrieval.

THE TARGET AUDIENCE

Immediate audiences for this book are from the area of information retrieval communities around world. The book targets at the readers from learner/trainers in educational institutes, industrial, commercial or non-commercial associations. Researchers in science and social science can be also benefited from the book. Professors, lecturers, and teachers from a wide range of subject areas can be benefited from the book if they are interested in information retrieval. The book can be an inspiration for research initiatives, and reading materials for educationists and students, and a library collection for this fast developing subject area with emerging cutting age technologies.

THE IMPORTANCE OF EACH OF THE CHAPTER

This book is organized in 17 chapters with different topics in the subject area. The importance of each chapter are introduced as follows.

Chapter 1 is to introduce a popular search technology: XML keyword filter, especially used on XML Stream. The authors argued that keyword search technology in XML stream is user friendly in comparison with most existing XML stream processing systems that are difficult for ordinary users to apply. This chapter claims that the system XKFilter is innovative as it is the first system for supporting keyword search over XML stream. In XKFilter, the concepts of XLCA (eXclusive Lowest Common Ancestor) and XLCA Connecting Tree (XLCACT) are used to define the search semantic and results of keywords, and present an approach to filter XML stream according to keywords. The prototype XKFilter is implemented in the experiments.

Chapter 2 describes a study based on XML related client server applications, particularly for the interactive web applications. The work discussed the key methods and technologies used in the research. Meanwhile, authors also discussed the state of the art technology, implementation for the developed system, and finally, contributions to the management of dynamic information management systems.

Chapter 3 addresses a topic related to the technology in document engineering in information retrieval research. The authors argued that keyword search did have inherent disadvantages. Traditional clustering techniques are inadequate in search efficiency for web documents. Finally the research proposes an alternative method based on the phrase based clustering algorithm. The research demonstrates that experimental results verify the method's feasibility and effectiveness.

Chapter 4 introduces a new query method that is based on clustering processes in which groups of semantically similar queries are detected. The clustering process uses the content of historical preferences of users registered in the query log of the search engine. This facility provides queries that are related to the ones submitted by users in order to direct them toward their required information. This method not only discovers the related queries but also ranks them according to a similarity measure. The method has been evaluated using real data sets from the search engine query log.

Chapter 5 presents XML documents normalization using GN-DTD. The research approached a fundamental problem in XML technology, i.e. designing well structured XML documents. The techniques of graphic notation for Document type definition are used in the investigation. Case study demonstrated the developed normal forms and normalization algorithm.

Chapter 6 provides mining Product Reviews in Web Forums. The research revealed information retrieval research on social impact. Opinion mining techniques have been used to analyze user-reviews. Finally the research has provided a recommendation to the products available on the web by analyzing the context to score the sentences for each review by identifying the opinion and feature words using a novel algorithm.

Chapter 7 talks about Schema Independent XML Compressor. XML has become the standard way for representing and transforming data over the World Wide Web. The problem with XML documents is that they have a very high ratio of redundancy, which makes these documents demanding a large storage capacity and large network band-width for transmission. This study designs a system for compressing and querying XML documents (XMLCQ) which compresses the XML document without the need to its schema or DTD to minimize the amount of technologies associated with these documents. XMLCQ first compressed the XML document by separating its data into containers according to the path of these data from the root to the leaf, and then it compressed these containers using a back-end compression technique. The compressed file then could be retrieved with any kind of queries applied. Only the required information is decompressed and submitted to the user. Depending on several experiments, the query processor part of the system showed the ability to answer different kinds of queries ranging from simple exact match queries to complex ones. Furthermore, this paper introduced the idea of retrieving information from more than one compressed XML documents.

Chapter 8 describes predictive modeling techniques in Determination of Algorithms Making Balance between Accuracy and Comprehensibility in Churn Prediction Setting. The research provides some detailed comparisons of rule based classifiers in churn prediction context. Key techniques in logistic regression (LR) and additive logistic regression (ALR) are used in the investigation. The research has developed eight distinctive algorithms, namely C4.5, C4.5 CP, RIPPER, RIPPER CP, PART, PART CP, LR, and ALR.

Chapter 9 presents a new model in Virtual Community of Practice Ontocop: Towards a New Model of Information Science Ontology (ISO). Information Science (IS) is an ambiguous field as its boundaries overlap with other domains such as Archive Science, Library Science and Computing Science which requires defined clear definition. This study creates a systematic and comprehensive ontology targeted to explore IS boundaries and foundations. This paper uses Mereotopolgy theory to describe classes, instances, and their relations. The classes are created based on taxonomy of IS to create an asserted model of Information Science Ontology (ISO) that can be as a skeletal foundation for knowledge base. The main classes are actors, method, practice, studies, mediate, kinds, domains, resources, legislation, philosophy & theories, societal, time, and space. The design is based on Methontology to create ISO from scratch. Its framework facilitates the construction of ontology at the knowledge levels. It is found that identifying the IS boundaries through implementation ontology workflow is encoded using Protégé and Web Ontology Language (OWL) for formalizing and representation of the ISO. ISO is an effective way to represent knowledge and overcome semantic heterogeneity, ISO is a fundamental integration between semantic that realizes the interoperability information of the domain.

Chapter 10 studied Improved Parameterless K-Means: Auto-Generation Centroids and Distance Data Point Clusters. The research presents a new approach and an improved method for effective and efficient clustering process evidenced by an improved version of K-means algorithm with auto-generate an initial number of clusters (k) and a new approach of defining initial Centroid for effective and efficient clustering process. The efficiency and effectiveness are analyzed, evaluated and discussed within the context.

Chapter 11 presents a research into the Ranking Tagged Resources Using Social Semantic Relevance. The research addresses the information retrieval research in web information environment. Ontology and web technology are discussed in the context. A questionnaire was designed to assess the crawled web pages for their graded relevance on a topic. Experiment studies have been conducted during investigation.

Chapter 12 introduces a Model of E-Reading Process for E-School Book in Libya. E-resources are factors that provide significant insights into actual reading behaviors and cognitive processes of readers. Two different samples of students, who study in Libyan primary schools, aged 9 to 12, were selected to investigate how students use and interact with both print and digital school books, identify the e-reading process, outline the aims of using the internet and technology, and define what students like and dislike in both versions. Furthermore, students found using the e-textbook to be more difficult than paper book and a significant difference is found in the reading process between paper books and electronic books. In addition, two reading strategies were used to read school book in both versions (electronic and paper): (1) view the text then answer the questions, or (2) view the questions than search for the correct answers.

Chapter 13 describes The Effect of Stemming on Arabic Text Classification: An Empirical Study. The research applies techniques of text classification for Arabic text documents. The results achieved an accuracy using the test modes up to 87.79% and 88.54%. Experiments and evaluation have been discussed in the chapter.

Chapter 14 presents a research in Electronic Resources Management in Jaykar Library. The research involves in the electronic document transformation through Internet. The research provides some suggestions on ICT enhanced management of electronic resources and speeding up the use of online journals among scientific department in the university.

Chapter 15 introduces a research in the MapReduce Based Information Retrieval Algorithms for Efficient Ranking of Webpages. The authors discuss the MapReduce implementation of crawler, indexer, and ranking algorithms in search engines. The algorithms are used in search engines to retrieve results from the World Wide Web. Tools like the crawler and an indexer in a MapReduce environment are used to improve the speed of crawling and indexing. Categorization is used to retrieve and order the results according to the user choice to personalize the search. A new score is introduced in this investigation. The experiments are conducted on Web graph datasets and the results are compared with the serial versions of crawler, indexer and ranking algorithms.

Chapter 16 presents a study in SAR: An Algorithm for Selecting a Partition Attribute in Categorical-Valued Information System Using Soft Set Theory. A soft-set based technique for decision making in categorical-valued information system is investigated, tested and evaluated. The results of this research will provide useful information for decision makers to handle categorical datasets.

Chapter 17 introduces a research in the area of XML and database: XRecursive: Connecting XML with Relational Databases. The research proposes an alternative method named *Xrecursive* for mapping XML (eXtensible Markup Language) documents to RDB (Relational Databases). The authors described the algorithms developed in the investigation and experiment results have been analyzed and evaluated.

CONCLUSION

In conclusion, this book presents a general picture for the latest concepts and the state of the art technology in information retrieval research. In particular, it addresses that:

1. Information retrieval is moving from traditional concepts, theories, and technologies in document engineering, text stream and language translation into an advanced level in both hardware facilities and software systems.
2. Information retrieval is pervasively working with interdisciplinary and multidisciplinary applications. The driving force is the emerging technologies, such as XML that is machine readable and human readable language to enable the applications ubiquitously on the common ground.
3. New challenges in the modernization of information retrieval are discussed throughout this classical field.

Zhongyu (Joan) Lu
University of Huddersfield, UK

Chapter 1
XKFilter: A Keyword Filter on XML Stream

Weidong Yang
Fudan University, China

Nan Li
Fudan University, China

Fei Fang
Fudan University, China

Zhongyu (Joan) Lu
University of Huddersfield, UK

ABSTRACT

Most existing XML stream processing systems adopt full structured query languages, such as XPath or XQuery, but they are difficult for ordinary users to learn and use. Keyword search is a user-friendly information discovery technique that has been extensively studied for text documents. This paper presents an XML stream filter system called XKFilter, which is the first system for supporting keyword search over XML stream. In XKFilter, the concepts of XLCA (eXclusive Lowest Common Ancestor) and XLCA Connecting Tree (XLCACT) are used to define the search semantic and results of keywords, and present an approach to filter XML stream according to keywords. The prototype XKFilter is implemented in the experiments.

INTRODUCTION

Stream-based continuous query processing (Babcock, Babu, Datar, Motwani, & Widom, 2002; Madden, Shah, Hellerstein, & Raman, 2002) fits a large class of new applications, such as sensor networks, location tracking, network management, publish-subscribe systems. As eXtensible markup language – XML is a standard for information exchange, the problem of processing streaming XML data is gaining widespread attention from the research community (Babcock et al., 2002; Diao, Altinel, Franklin, Zhang, & Fischer, 2003; Peng & Chawathe, 2005). An XML stream system (XSS) aims to provide fast and on-the-fly matching of XML-encoded data to user's query, which is different from traditional XML database management systems (Lu & Rahman, 2007). The XSS usually involves handling the XML stream coming online at any moment and any order, and requiring timely response without incurring more memory cost. Therefore, the numbering schemes like Dewey numbers and XML indexing techniques

DOI: 10.4018/978-1-4666-3898-3.ch001

for accelerating query process in XML databases don't apply to XML data streams processing generally. For XML stream systems, currently, most existing researches adopt full structured query languages such as XPath or XQuery. These query languages can convey complex meaning in the query specifications containing constraints on both structure and content of an XML document, thus, can precisely retrieve the desired results. However, for an ordinary user, especially for a web user, it is difficult to learn the complex query languages, it is also impossible to write a correct query without knowing the exact structure of an XML document.

Keyword search is a user-friendly information retrieval technique that has been extensively studied for text documents. Unlike structured queries on database which adopts exact match approach, the keyword search adopts best match approach which has to "guess" the best search results and provide an appropriate rank model; different from traditional information retrieval systems, keyword search on database, instead of retrieving whole documents, aim at retrieving content components of the whole database, i.e. joined tuples (for relational database) or XML elements (for XML database) of varying granularity that fulfill the user's query. Recently, many researchers in database field extended this technique into relational database (Liu, Yu, Meng, & Chowdhury, 2006) and XML database (Cohen, Mamou, Kanza, & Sagiv, 2003; Guo, Shao, Botev, & Shanmugasundaram, 2003; Hristidis, Papakonstantinou, & Balmin, 2003; Hristidis, Koudas, Papakonstantinou, & Srivastava, 2006; Liu, Walker, & Yichen, 2007; Xu & Papakonstantinou, 2005) by combining information retrieval techniques and database techniques, and proposing various approaches to define and rank the keyword search results, and developing algorithms to accelerate the execution of keyword search. It is noted that keyword search is also well-suited to some applications under streams data processing environment such as publish-subscribe systems, web monitoring systems. Alexander et al. (Markowetz, Yang, & Papadias, 2007) presented a system called "S-KWS" for keyword search on relational data streams.

XML technology has its reputation in semantic representation of information and knowledge in the subject areas, because of its underpinned theory: ontology, which could define or constrain the unique feature of DTD and schema (Lu, 2005; Lu & Rahman, 2007). The purpose to Integrate Keyword search technology into semantically oriented XML system is to increase the simplicity, efficiency and effectiveness during retrieval process (Lu & Fox, 2007).

In this paper, we focus on keyword search on XML Stream. The main contributions made in the paper are:

1. We present a new software system: XKFilter, to the best of our knowledge, the first system for keyword search on XML Stream. XKFilter can process XML streams with or without schemas.
2. In this system, unlike relational data streams, XML streams are self-described, with its content and multilevel structure which can be recursive mixed together. When XML DTD is not available, we let users register their queries by writing several keywords simply (called pure keyword search), and we define the search results as eXclusive Lowest Common Ancestor Connecting Tree (XLCACT) based on our previous work (Josifovski, Fontoura, & Barta, 2005). Also, we design an algorithm "S-XSF" based on stack to process XML stream and buffering return results efficiently in a single pass.
3. XKFilter provides a user-friendly search interface based on both keyword search and DTD, if the XML DTD is available. This search interface is a simple expansion of pure keyword search syntax which contains a list of search terms. Each search term is composed of a keyword and the label containing keyword directly. By using the search

terms of users and XML DTD, the keyword search can be refined to a Keyword Query Graph (KQG). As a result, the XML fragment unrelated to the keywords search will be ignored. It has two benefits: (1) effectively reducing the search space of XML streams; (2) effectively reducing the parsing amount of XML streams. In order to process XML stream in a single pass, base on the KQG, the Keyword Query State Machine (KQSM) is built. The KQSM supports state forward transition and backward transition, and use a run-time stack to process the XML stream and buffering return results effectively.

METHOD

Participants

Keyword search is a user-friendly information retrieval technique that has been extensively studied for text documents. However, it is often difficult, even sometimes impossible to convey precise meaning in the keyword proximity search. Therefore, one of the key techniques of keyword search is defining the search semantics and results of a set of keywords. Many current researches regard XML document as a tree, definite the XML keyword search semantic base on the Lowest Common Ancestor (LCA) of all keywords (Cohen, Mamou, Kanza, & Sagiv, 2003; Guo, Shao, Botev, & Shanmugasundaram, 2003; Hristidis, Papakonstantinou, & Balmin, 2003; Hristidis, Koudas, Papakonstantinou, & Srivastava, 2006; Liu, Walker, & Yichen, 2007; Xu & Papakonstantinou, 2005). For example, XKSearch (Xu & Papakonstantinou, 2005) defines the keyword search as the search for Smallest Lowest Common Ancestor (SLCA) of an XML document tree. According to the SLCA semantics, the result of a keyword query is the set of nodes that (1) contain the keywords either in their labels or in the labels of their descendent nodes and (2) they have no descendant node that also contains all keywords. XKSearch proposed two algorithms, Indexed Lookup Eager and Scan Eager, for keyword search in XML documents according to the SLCA semantic by using Dewey numbers. Li et al. (2004) define XML keyword search semantic as Meaningful Lowest Common Ancestor, which is essentially similar to SLCA. Vagelis et al. (2006) regard Minimum Connecting Tree that contains all keywords as a significant query result.

However, if the concept of SLCA is applied to an XML document that has recursive structure or there is some element names shared by a node of same type, it may lose some meaningful information. For instance, as the XML fragment shown in Figure 1, if a user give a query including

Figure 1. Sample XML document 1

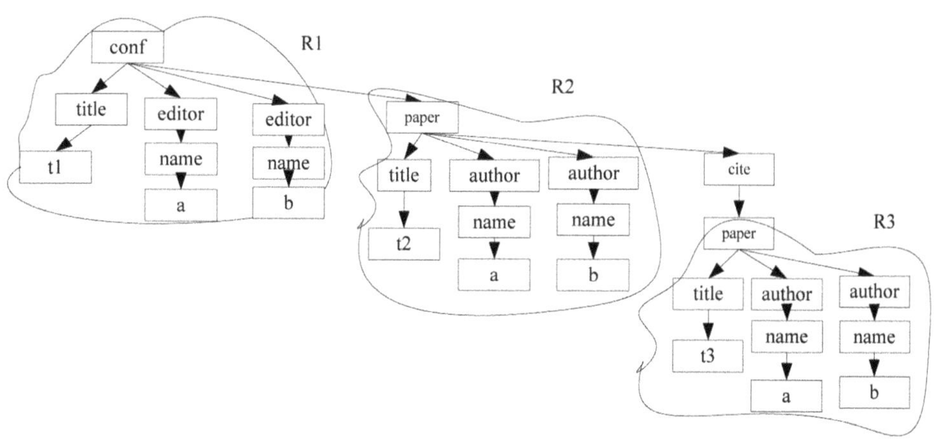

keywords: "a", "b", "title". Then, the information he expects possibly is 1) The paper with its title "t2" and with its author "a" and "b". 2) The paper "t3" cited by "t2" with the same author "a" and "b". 3) The conference "t1" with its editor "a" and "b". However, according to the concept of SLCA, the information of paper "t2" and conference "t1" will be lost even if they exist.

To solve the above-mentioned problem, our previous work (Gong, Qian, Yan, & Zhou, 2005) defined the concept of XLCA (eXclusive Lowest Common Ancestor) based on SLCA as follows: first of all, find out all the SLCAs in XML document tree T; these SLCAs are just XLCAs; second, remove from T the fragments rooted at these SLCA nodes, and then find out again all the SLCAs of T; these SLCAs are also XLCAs; the second step repeats until there is no SLCA in T. It can be seen that all the XLCAs are exclusive, i.e. non-overlapped. Based on XLCA, we define the results of a set of keywords over XML stream as XLCA Connecting Tree (XLCACT), which is the minimum subtrees that rooted at the XLCAs of the nodes that contain the keywords.

Materials and Procedure

Stack based algorithms are used in some research work for processing XML keyword search, for instance, stack based sort-merge algorithm (DIL) in XRANK (Guo, Shao, Botev, & Shanmugasundaram, 2003) and Stack Algorithm (Xu & Papakonstantinou, 2005) for finding SLCAs in XML document. In these work, Dewey numbers are used for locating the LCA of two nodes. But under the XML stream processing environment, for processing XML streams in a single pass, these techniques are not suitable. Therefore, by modifying the above-mentioned algorithms, we design an algorithm (called S-XSF) based on stack to process the pure keyword search over XML stream and return the XLCACTs to users

S-XSF algorithm accepts the SAX events of an XML stream produced by parsing the input document in a pre-order traversal of the XML tree and transforms the SAX events into the form of (tagName, type), where tagName is the node being tested and type is the event type, which can be "Start Element", "End Element", etc. We use a runtime stack to buffer the processed node and potential results. The data structure of each entry in stack contains three components (N, B=<$flag_1$,... ,$flag_n$>, RT), where N indicate the node name being processed. B is an array containing a series of flags (TRUE or FALSE) corresponding to a list of keywords of a query, the number of elements in array B is equal to the number of inputting keywords, the flags are initialized as FALSE. RT is the candidate output of the query, which is implemented as a tree structure. RT is a subtree of XML document tree maintained by S-XSF algorithm dynamically.

S-XSF algorithm is shown in the Table 1. It consists of two parts corresponding to the SAX event handlers of "Start Element" and "End Element", and the "Attribute" events are produced by iterating over the attributes in the "Start Element"

Table 1. Search algorithm 1 for S-XSF

Algorithm 1. S-XSF

Input: XML stream data;
An array KWS(kw_1, kw_2, …, kw_n) that contains the keywords of query;
Output: XML fragments rooted at XLCAs of keywords (XLCACTs).
Method startElement(n)
1 push new entry *en* as (N=n, B=<F,…,F>,R=n) into S; // S is the runtime stack
2 for each keyword kw_i in the query
3 if v matches kw_i; // v represents the content, tagName, or attribute value of current element.
4 set en.B_i to TRUE;
5 link v to en.R as its child branch;
Method endElement (n)
6 pop the top entry en_{pop} form S;
7 if all the flags of en_{pop}.B are TRUE then // n is a XLCA
8 output en_{pop}.R as an answer;
9 else // n is not a XLCA
10 for each TRUE flags B_i in the en_{pop}
11 set the flag top(S).B_i to TRUE; // keep information in its parent node
12 link en_{pop}.R to the top(S).R as its child branch;
13 drop en;

SAX handler. When a “Start Element” event or an “Attribute” event is encountered, the stack entry corresponding to the node being processed is pushed onto the stack, the node pushed into the stack becomes an active node. An active node is an XML node whose start tag has been processed but end tag has not yet been processed by the SAX parser. If a keyword match occurs, which means the node name (the element name, the content of an element, or the attribute value) and the keyword are the same, we set the corresponding flag in B to TRUE, and add the node into RT. When an “End Element” event is encountered, if all flags of the top entry in the stack are TRUE, the stack item is popped and the node is added to the RT. At this point in time, the node is a XLCA, and the buffered result in RT of the popped entry is a XLCACT, which should be returned to users. Otherwise, if there are some TRUE flags in this entry, the entry is popped from the stack, and then the corresponding flags of the current top item in the stack are set to TRUE. If there are no any TRUE flags in this entry, just pop it from the stack.

To illustrate the processing of the algorithm S-XSF, we use a sample document shown in Figure 1 and a simple query Q (“a”, “b”, “title”). The state of its runtime stack after each event is represented in the Figure 2. Firstly, when the startElement (conf) is encountered, since no keywords match occurs, the entry (conf, <F,F,F>,”conf”) is just pushed into the stack. When the startElement (title) is encountered, the entry (title,<F,F,F>,”title”) is pushed, and the first flag of array B is set to TRUE due to a keyword match is found, then the “title” and its content “t1” are added into the R. Next, when the endElement (title) is encountered, the entry is popped from the stack and the corresponding flag of current top entry of the stack is set to TRUE, and its result is linked to the R of current top entry of the stack (Figure 2(3)). When the endElement of last “paper” is encountered, the entry (paper,<T,T,T>,R3) is pop from stack, and its R is an answer of query (Figure 2(4)) due to all the flags of the entry are TRUE (For clarity, the results are represented as R1, R2, R3 respectively). When the close tag of “conf” is encountered, entry (conf,<T,T,T>,R1) is pop and its R is another and last answer of query(Figure 2(6)). Then we will get three answers of Q Q(“a”, “b”, “title”): R1,R2,R3 (Figure 1).

Figure 2. A running example of S-XSF

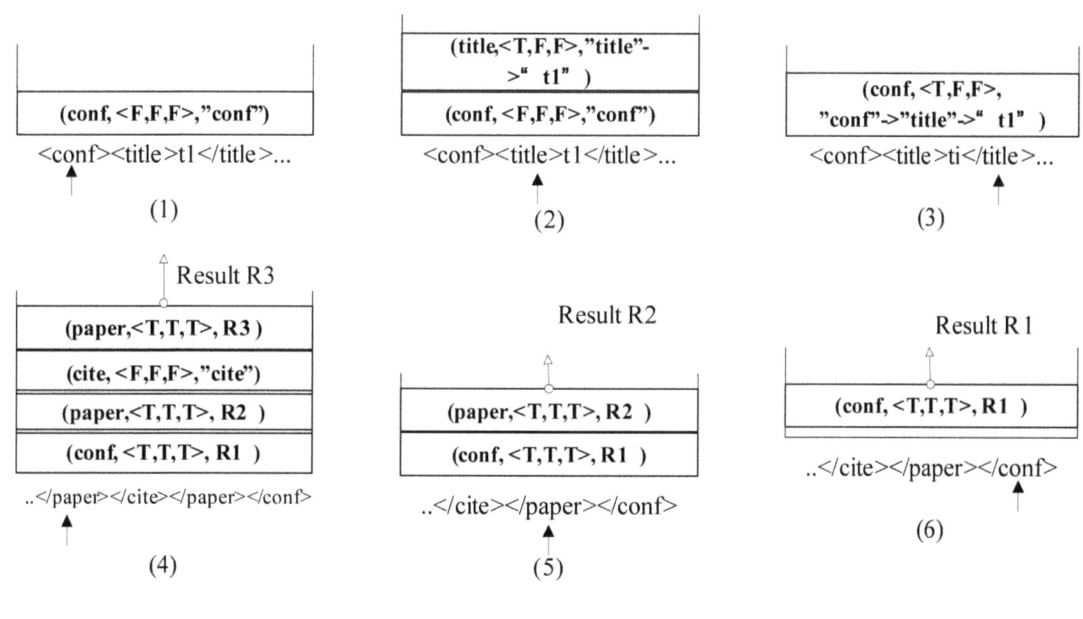

Theorem 1: For the given XML Document Tree D and a set of keywords Q(kw_1, kw_2, …, kw_n), the outputs of algorithm S-XSF are a set of XLCACTs of KW, where KW={kw_i|i∈1…k}.

To prove the correctness of S-XSF, we define N as the set of nodes of D, RS as the output set of S-XSF, and give the following propositions.

- **Proposition 1:** In the processing of "End Element" events in the algorithm S-XSF, the first node n ∈ N, which all the flags in its stack entry are TRUE, is a SLCA of KW.
    - **Proof Sketch:** S-XSF algorithm processes the "Start Element" events of an XML stream in a pre-order traversal of the XML tree and processes the "End Element" events in a post-order traversal. When an "End Element" event is encountered, the "first" means until the processing of "End Element" event of n, there are no other nodes have all true flags. Since all the flags are true, it means (1) n contains all the keywords in its descendent nodes. (2) There is no descendant node of n that also contains all keywords. As n is the first node with all true flags and descendant nodes of n has been processed but none of them has all true flags. According to the definition of SLCA, n is a SLCA of KW. A SLCA must be a XLCA, therefore, the first node n with all true flags in the processing of "End Element" events is a SLCA of KW.
- **Proposition 2:** In the processing of "End Element" events in the algorithm S-XSF, any node n ∈ N, which all the flags in its stack entry are TRUE, is a XLCA of KW.
    - **Proof Sketch:** According to the S-XSF algorithm, when an "End Element" event of a node n is encountered and the flags of the n are all TRUE, its stack entry is popped and its result is returned to users, any information of the node n and its descendents (including its flag states) is not kept in the runtime stack. It just likes that the subtree rooted at the node n is removed from the XML document. On the basis of proposition 1, in the processing of "End Element" events, the first node with all TRUE flags is a XLCA, because of the post-order processing of "End Element" events, all the remainder nodes with all TRUE flags are also XLCAs in turn.

On the basis of proposition 1 and proposition 2, we can prove the correctness of Theorem 1 straightforward. Initially, the output set RS is empty. When the first XLCA is met, we can get the first XLCACT in RS; Repeat these steps until the whole document has been processed, we can get all the XLCACTs of KW.

- **Schema-Awared Keyword Search Over XML Streams:** By using the algorithm S-XSF, users just need to input a list of keywords simply with pure keyword search approach and do not need to know any information for XML Schema. Nevertheless, this makes the pure keyword search approach of XML Stream has to parse the whole document, then its processing time will be directly proportional to the size of the XML document. An XML document can optionally have a schema. In many applications of XML stream processing, service providers know the Schema of XML document in advance if it is available, therefore, we expand the pure keyword search approach to a schema-aware approach in order to reduce the search space and optimize the performance of XML stream process.

- **Simplified DTD Entity-Attribute Graph:** Besides XML Schema, Document Type Description (DTD) is a commonly used method to describe the structure of an XML document and acts like a schema. A DTD specifies the structure of an XML element by specifying the names of its sub-elements and attributes. Sub-element structure is specified using the operators * (set with zero or more elements), + (set with one or more elements), ? (optional), and | (or). There is a special attribute, id, which can occur once for each element.

To decide what information should be returned to users, XSeek (Liu, Walker, & Chen, 2007) mimics the Entity-Relationship model in relational databases, which recognized XML documents as a set of real world entities, each of which has attributes. What users really want is the information related entities of the real world, similar to XSeek, we classify the nodes (a node means an element, a sub-element, or an attribute) in DTD into entities, entity attributes and connection nodes according to their node relationships by using the following classifying rules:

1. If a node with name n1 has a one-to-many relationship ("*" operator, or "+" operator) with nodes with name n2, then n2 represents an entity;
2. If a node with name n has only one child which is a value, then the node n denotes an entity attribute;
3. If a node has attributes, then the node represents an entity;
4. if a node with name n represents neither an entity nor an attribute, then the node n is a connection node. A connection node can have a child that is an entity, an attribute or another connection node.

To filter XML stream effectively based on keywords by using DTD, what we only need to consider is the possible paths containing the keywords. The operator "*" implies many relation, "+" implies one-to-many relation, "#" implies requirement relation, "?" implies optional relation, "|" implies exclusive or relations. As all the operators imply there is a possible path at least between two nodes, we ignore the difference among operators of DTD and treat them as a contain relations between the elements and its sub-elements uniformly.

Therefore, we use a graph called Simplified DTD Entity-Attribute Graph (SDEAG) to describe a DTD of an XML document.

Definition 1: A Simplified DTD Entity-Attribute Graph. SDEAG is a pair (V, E), where nodes V is a finite set, and edges E is a binary relation on V: $E \subseteq V \times V$. The set V consists of elements and attributes in a DTD, each edge $e \in E$ represents the relation of an element contains a sub-element or an element has an attributes. In addition, the set V is divided into four categories:

- $r \in V$ is the designated root of SDEAG.
- $VE \subseteq V$ represents the set of the entity nodes of SDEAG.
- $VA \subseteq V$ represents the set of the entity attribute nodes of SDEAG.
- $VC \subseteq V$ represents the set of the connection nodes of SDEAG.

The DTD fragment of Figure 1 is shown in Figure 3. The SDEAG of Figure 3 is shown in Figure 4, where the entity node is shown as a rectangle (for example, "paper"), the entity attribute node is shown as a circle (for example, "title"), and the connection node is shown as a triangle (for example, "editor").

According to the classifying rules and the definition of SDEAG aforementioned, we known that a same entity node can only occur once in a SDEG (for example, the entity nodes "author",

Figure 3. A DTD fragment of Figure 1

```
<!ELEMENT conf    (title, editor*, paper*)>
<!ELEMENT title    (#PCDATA)>
<!ELEMENT editor  (name)>
<!ELEMENT name  (#PCDATA)>
<!ELEMENT paper  (title, author+, cite?)>
<!ATTLIST   paper  id   ID #REQUIRED>
<!ELEMENT author (name, (email|phone)?)>
<!ELEMENT email  (#PCDATA)>
<!ELEMENT phone  (#PCDATA)>
<!ELEMENT cite (paper*)>
```

Figure 4. The SDEAG of Figure 3

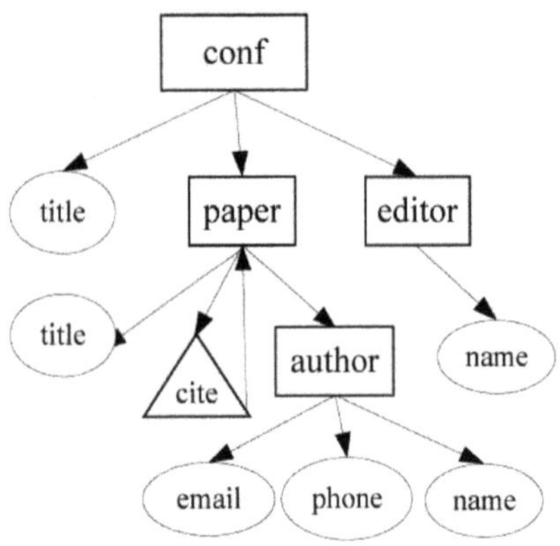

"paper", etc in Figure 4.), a same attribute node can occur more than once due to belonging to different entity nodes (for example, the attribute node "name" Figure 4).

- **Entity Search Term:** If the DTD of an XML document is available, XSEarch (Cohen, Mamou, Kanza, & Sagiv, 2003) uses a simple extension of the pure keyword search approach to search XML documents, which allows a user to specify labels and keyword-label combinations that must or may appear in a satisfying document in addition to specifying keywords. A keyword-label combination is called a search term, which has the form l: k formally, where l is a label and k is a keyword.

In order to filter XML stream based on keywords effectively by using DTD, we adopt the similar idea in our approach, but here comes another problem: there are too many labels in the DTD due to a large and complex document structure possibly, and many of them are not meaningful for users (for example, label "cite" in Figure 1) or represent more than one meaning due to different contexts (for example, label "title" in Figure 1 may can mean a paper's title or a conference's title). For giving a meaningful selection and provide a concise interface for the user, we combine the concepts of search term and entity.

Definition 2: An Entity Search Term (EST) has the form e: a: k, where "e" is a entity label defined in SDEAG, "a" is the attribute of the entity and "k" is a keyword which is the value of the attribute. The query Q(S) submitted by user is a set of entity search terms S={ e_1: a_1: k_1, e_2:a_2: k_2, ..., e_n: a_n: k_n}.

In the user search interface, we list the entity nodes in the DTD for users, and users can choose one or more entities they interest in, and then select the attribute of the entity, finally, input the keywords they want to search. If a user selects an entity and an attribute of the entity, but the inputted keyword is empty, then it means that the user wants to get the value of the attribute. Figure 5 is the user registration interface of XKFilter, where user can select an entity in drop list box and an attribute of the entity, and then input a keyword in the text field. A user can add an EST by clicking the "add" button and register his keyword search by clicking the "submit" button.

Revise the Keyword Search Results. Each entity node in SDEAG may have multiple entity instances (i.e. XML elements) in its corresponding XML document. As aforementioned, what the users really want is the information related to entities. In order to reflect this idea, we revise the keyword search results by using entities.

Definition 3: Most Related Entity Instance (MREI) of XLCA. Given an XML document tree D and a list of entity search terms S={

Figure 5. Keyword Search Interface of XKFilter

e_1: a_1: k_1, e_2:a_2: k_2, …, e_n: a_n: k_n}. X is the set of XLCAs of keywords in S. If $x_i \in X$ is an entity instance, then x_i is a most related entity instance; If $x_i \in X$ is not an entity instance, then the nearest ancestor entity instance of x_i is the most related entity instance. e is the nearest ancestor entity instance of x_i means: e is an ancestor of x_i and e is an entity instance, and e has no descendant node that is both an ancestor and an entity instance of x_i.

According to the definition above, we revise the search results as a Most Related Entity Instance Connecting Tree (MREIMCT), which is a minimum connecting tree rooted at the MREI that contains the keywords.

- **Refining Keyword Search by Using DTD:** In the pure keyword search over XML streams, the filter system has to parse and process the whole XML document due to lacking the structured information of the XML document. By using the DTD of an XML document and a set of EST submitted by users, we can constraint the keyword search to a restricted space of the XML document, therefore, the filter system can ignore the unrelated portions of an XML document to the submitted keywords.

Given an input XML tree T, the SDEAG of T, and a query Q(S) containing a list of EST, where S={ e_1: a_1: k_1, e_2: a_2: k_2, …, e_n: a_n: k_n}. A=a_1,…,a_2 is called matched attribute nodes in the SDEAG which contain keyword directly. We refine the keyword search Q(s) by taking the following steps roughly:

- Mark the matched attribute nodes a_1,…,a_2 in the SDEAG, and link the keywords to the corresponding matched attribute node.
- For each node that has been marked, mark its parent nodes and the edges between them if they are unmarked.
- Delete the unmarked nodes and edges in the graph.

For example, given a sample XML document shown Figure 1, the SDEAG of Figure 1 is shown in Figure 4. Suppose a user submits a list of EST: S={author: name: a, author: name: b, paper: title}, its matched attribute nodes in the SDEAG are "title" and "name". After the refining process abovementioned, we get a structure called Keyword Query Graph (KQG) shown in Figure 6. Now we give the definition of Keyword Query Graph formally.

Definition 4: (Keyword Query Graph, KQG). Keyword Query Graph is a ten-tuple, kQG = (V, E, ∑, λ, ψ, ρ, τ, r, K, A)

- V represents a finite set of nodes, E is a binary relation on V: E⊆V×V.
- ∑ represents a finite set of node labels
- **λ:** V→∑ is a label function, λ(n) returns the name of label of node n.
- ψ(n) returns the type of the node n. The types include entity, attribute and connection.
- **ρ:** V→∑∪ε is a parent function, ρ(n) returns the parent nodes of node n.
- **τ:** V→∑∪ε is a child function, τ (n) returns the child nodes of node n.
- r∈V is the designated root of KQG.
- K=$k_1,\ldots,k_n$ is the list of keywords.
- A= $a_1,\ldots,a_m$ is the attribute nodes containing K directly.

Figure 6. A sample keyword query graph

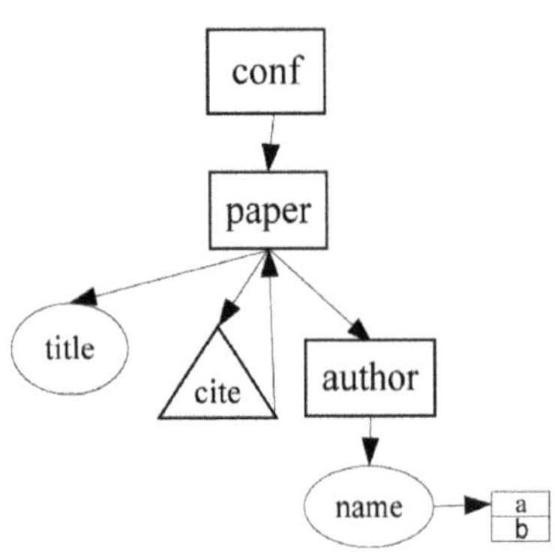

- **XML Stream Filtering by Using Schema:** By using KQG, we can reduce the search space due to ignoring the irrelevant parts of a coming XML document. In the process of filtering the XML document, we consider the KQG as a finite state machine, called Keyword Query State Machine (KQSM). The nodes in KQG become the states of KQSM, meantime, the root node r of KQG is treated as the initial state of KQSM. The system accepts the SAX events of an XML stream and computes the solutions for keyword search driven by KQSM. The SAX events are transformed into the state transition function of KQSM. The child function τ(n) and parent function ρ(n) in KQG can be used as the transition functions in KQS, separately corresponding to the "Start Element" and "End Element" event. For clarity, we define KQSM formally below:

Definition 5: (Keyword Query State Machine, KQSM). Keyword Query State Machine KQSM(Q, q_0, F, I, δ_s, δ_e, ∑', λ', **κ,** QA) is constructed from KQG, where

- Q is the state identity corresponding to the nodes V in KQG.
- q_0 ∈ Q is the initial state of KQSM.
- F is a sub set of Q, represents the accepting state of KQSM corresponding to the entity nodes in KQG.
- I is the SAX event (tagName, type), tagName represents name of current parsing tag, type represents event type, include "Start Element", "End Element" etc.
- δ_s and δe represents the state transition function separately corresponding to the parent function ρ and child function τ in KQG. δs is a forward transition function which means it only reacts to the "Start Element" event, and δe is a backward transition function which means it only reacts to the "End Element" event.

- $\sum$' represents finite input symbol, corresponds to the $\sum$ in KQG.
- **λ':** Q→$\sum$' is a name function, returns the label name of the state corresponding to the λ function in KQG.
- ψ' corresponds to the type function ψ in KQG. q_0 is a special state ψ'(q_0)=0. Given q∈ Q, If q's type is Entity, then ψ'(q)=1; If q's type is Connection node, then ψ'(q)=2; If q's type is Attribute, then ψ'(q)=2.
- QA ⊆ Q, corresponds to the attribute nodes containing the list of keywords K=k_1,…,k_n in KQG
- **κ:** QA→K, is a keyword function, returns the contained keywords.

Similar to S-XSF, the process of filtering XML stream based on KQG (called Schema-XSF) also uses a run-time stack, but each entry in the stack contains four components (ID, Type, B = <$flag_1$, …, $flag_n$>, RT), where ID indicates the state identify of a state in KQSM; the Type indicates the type of a state node (1 represents Entity type, 2 represents Connection type, 3 represents Attribute type). The execution process of Schema-XSF is similar to the process of S-XSF, but there are some main differences:

- Schema-XSF is driven by KQSM, which means only matched incoming XML document nodes with KQSM states can be pushed into the runtime stack. When an element's open tag matches with a state in KQSM (denoted as a state match occurs), then invokes δ_s transition function; when a state match occurs in an element's close tag, the δ_e function will be invoked.
- When a state's flags are all TRUE and state's corresponding node is an entity, an accepting state of KQSM is reached, we call a query matching occurs. Noted that if an accepting state is reached, the KQSM doesn't stop, but keep running until the entire XML stream has been processed.

For making out the difference between Schema-XSF and S-XSF, we use the same sample XML document and query to illustrate the process of Schema-XSF. Suppose a query registered by a user is a list of ESTs: S={author: name: a, author: name: b, paper: title}. Its corresponding KQG is shown in Figure 6. Its KQSM constructed from Figure 6 is shown in Figure 7, where an arrow indicates a forward state transition, for clarity, all backward state transitions (corresponding to the "End Element" event) are omitted.

The processing is illustrated in Figure 8. Firstly, the initial state q_0 is pushed in the stack, when the startElement(conf) is encountered, a state match occurs, the state of KQSM is transformed from q_0 to q_1, i.e. δ_s (conf, q_0) →q_1.Likewise, when the startElement(title) is encountered, δ_s (title, q_2) →q_3, in the same time, the flag of title is set to true due to a keyword match occurs. When the endElement(title) is encountered, δ_e (title, q_3) →q_2, the entry of q_3 is popped up and its true flag is set to corresponding flag of q_2. When the first endElement(paper) is encountered (shown in Figure 8(4)), δ_e(paper, q_2) →q_4, the (q_2,1,<T,T,T>,R3) is pop from stack as an answer of the query due to all the flags of the entry are TRUE and it is a Entity type. Note that by using the list of ESTs as the user's query, the results can reflect the user's intent more accurately. In this example, the results of Schema-XSF are R2 and R2.

Figure 7. The KQSM of Figure 6

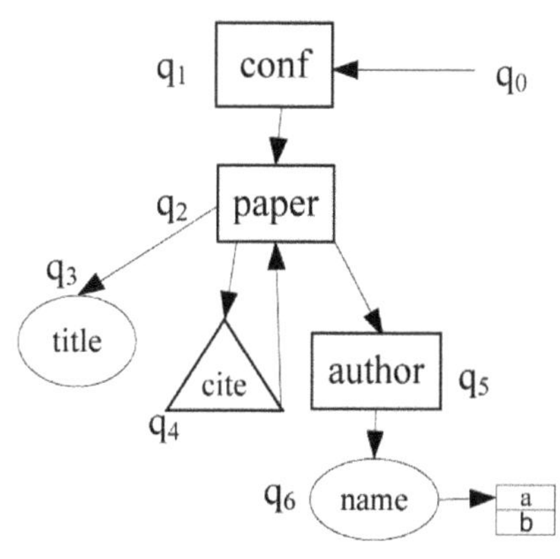

Figure 8. A running example of schema-XSF

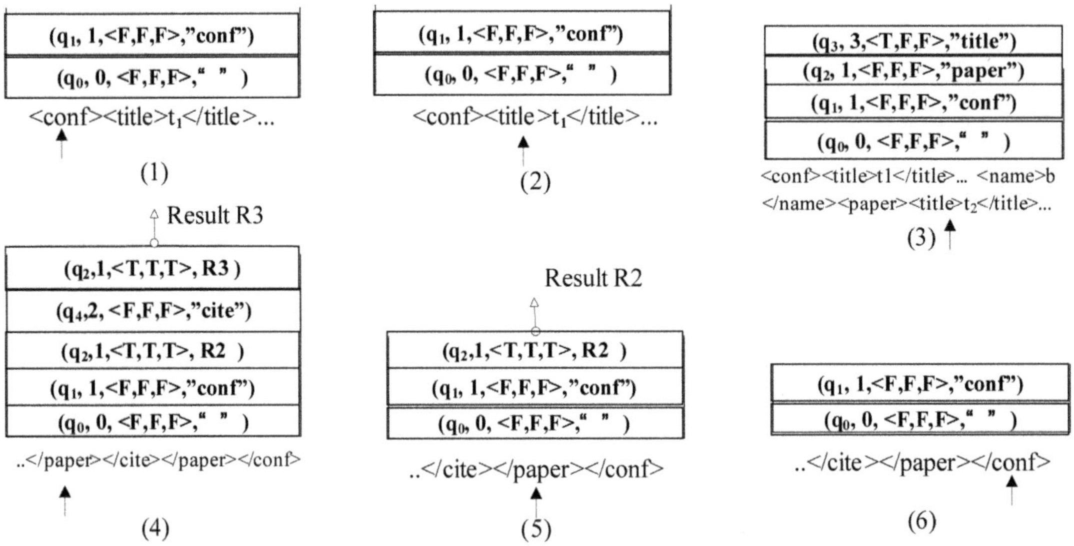

Theorem 2: For the given XML Document Tree D and a set of keywords $Q(kw_1, kw_2, \ldots, kw_n)$, the outputs of algorithm S-XSF are a set of XLCACTs of KW, where $KW=\{kw_i|i\in 1\ldots k\}$.

THE OVERVIEW OF SYSTEM ARCHITECTURE

The whole system architecture is shown in Figure 9.The component of XML parser is event-based and based on the SAX interface: when an XML

Figure 9. The architecture of XKFilter

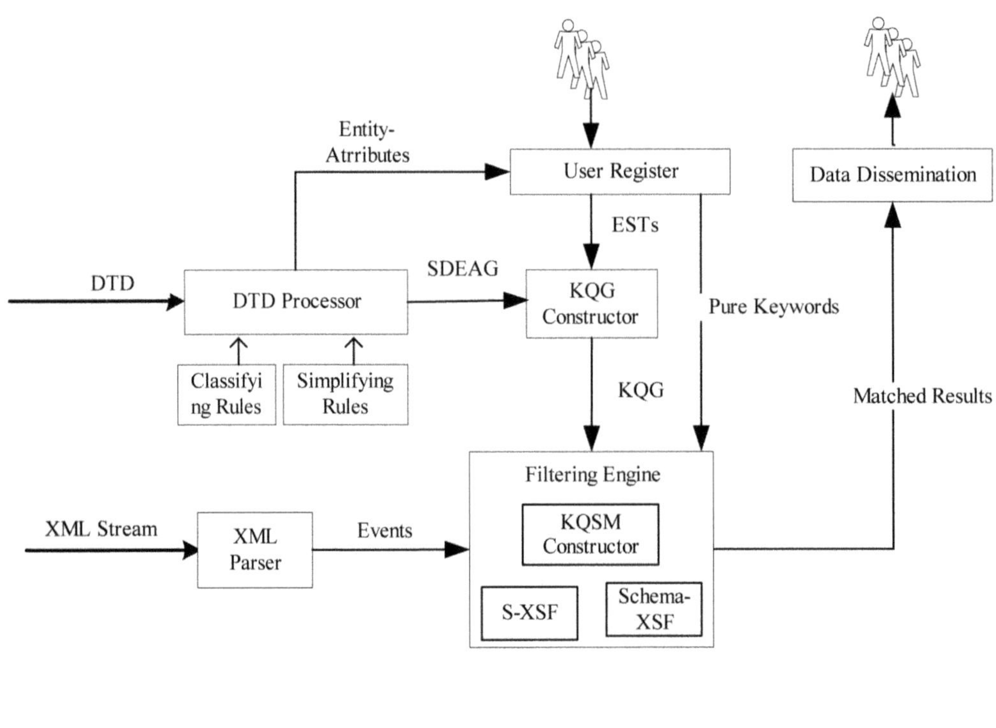

document arrives at the system, it is run through the XML parser and treated as a linear sequence of events mark the beginning and the end of the parse of a document and its elements. For examples, “Start Document” and “End Document” events mark the beginning and the end of the parse of a document; A “Start Element” event carries information such as the name of the element, its attributes, etc; An “End Element” event corresponds to an earlier “Start Element” event by specifying the element name and marks the close of that element in the document.

The component of DTD Processor is implemented based on an automaton for parsing the DTD of an XML document, extracting entities and attributes, and constructing the SDEAG. During the processing, the DTD Processor also simplifies the DTD by using the simplifying rules shown in Table 2, and extracts the entities and attributes by using the rules mentioned. In general, DTDs can be very complex and most of the complexity stems from the complex specification of the type of an element and is not useful in XKFilter. So, we can simplify the details of a DTD and just remains the possible containing relations, the example simplifying rules are shown in Table 2. The component of user register accepts the lists of entities and attributes of the DTD outputted from the component and present the lists to the users, then, the users can submit the keywords for getting useful information. The component of KQG Constructor accepts the SDEAG from the DTD processor and the ESTs from the user register, and then constructs the KQG.

The component of filtering engine is at the heart of the system. It takes the KQG as its input

Table 2. Simplifying rules of DTD

<table>
<tr><td>(e1, e2)*→ e1, e2</td><td>e1** → e1</td><td>..., a*, ..., a*, ... →a, ...</td></tr>
<tr><td>(e1, e2)?→e1, e2</td><td>e1*? → e1</td><td>..., a*, ..., a?, ... →a, ...</td></tr>
<tr><td>(e1|e2)→ e1, e2</td><td>e1?* → e1</td><td>..., a?, ..., a*, ... →a, ...</td></tr>
<tr><td></td><td>e1?? → e1</td><td>..., a?, ..., a?, ... → a, ...</td></tr>
<tr><td></td><td></td><td>..., a, ..., a, ...→ a,</td></tr>
</table>

and converts it to the KQSM by using the KQSM Constructor component. It also receives and reacts to events from the XML parser. These events call back the corresponding handlers implemented by the filtering engine, which perform the matching of documents against keywords registered by users. When the input of the filtering engine is the pure keywords from the user register, the S-XSF algorithm is used; when the input is the KQG from the KQG constructor, the Schema-XSF is used. The implementation of KQSM in Schema-XSF adopts the way based on state transition table. The Strategy Pattern is used to organize the algorithms for adapting XKFilter to the future changes.

Once the matching results have been identified for a document, the results must be sent to the appropriate users by using the data dissemination component. Our current implementations simply send the matched results to each interested user. As for the effective delivery mechanisms are beyond the scope of this current paper, so they are not addressed further here.

RESULTS

XKFilter is implemented by using Java 1.5, with the IDE Eclipse Platform 3.3.0 and SAX XML parser (Xerces2-Java XML Parser 2.9.1).

We run all the experiments on a machine with 2GHz *2 CPU and 2GB memory, Windows XP professional. XKFilter can process XML streams with or without schema by using pure keyword search approach (S-XSF) and schema-aware keyword search approach (Schema-XSF). To the best of our knowledge, XKFilter is the first system filtering XML streams based on keywords. So, we have evaluated XKFilter by comparing the performance between S-XSF and Schema-XSF.

We used the synthetic XMark and DBLP data for our experiments. The datasets were used generated by an XML generator from IBM. We generated XML documents of different sizes by using the DTD of XMark and DBLP. S-XSF and Schema-XSF were evaluated in two different aspects: (a) by varying the size of input documents; (b) by varying the number of input keywords.

First, we used small document for the experiments. The size of document varies from 500K to 8000K, the number of keywords is 3, and the frequency of keywords in document is 1000,1000,1000 (it means each keyword occurs 1000 times in the document). The result is shown in Figure 10, which illustrates that, Schema-XSF is more efficient than S-XSF. The execution time of S-XSF is increasing with the increase of document size, while The execution time of Schema-XSF is increasing more slowly. Second, we test the execution time of large document. The size of document varies from 11MB to 56MB and other parameters remain the same. The result is shown as Figure 11. Similar to the smaller document, S-XSF grows much faster than Schema-XSF. Therefore, we can conclude that no matter the document size is small or large our algorithm based on DTD has better performances than pure keyword search in time. Finally, we vary the number of keywords from one to five and let the size of document be 22.8MB. The experiment result is shown in Figure 12. We can see that the processing time of S-XSF is going up with the increase of the number of keywords obviously, but Schema-XSF is not sensitive to the number of keywords, it's process time is almost constant while the number of keywords is increasing from 1 to 5.

S-XSF includes startElement and endElement method. For each node in an input XML document, the startElement method is invoked when the node's open tag is encountered, it's entry is pushed into the runtime's stack, and each keyword match is computed; when the node's close tag is encountered, the endElement method is invoked to do necessary process. Therefore, the processing time of S-XSF is increasing proportional to the size of input XML document and more sensitive to the number of keywords. Schema-XSF refines a list of keywords to the KQG by using DTD and constructs its KQSM from KQG, then the execution process of Schema-XSF is driven by the KQSM. Then, only the nodes of input document matched to the states of KQSM will be pushed into the runtime stack and the keywords match will be computed, the unrelated parts of input document to the KQSM are ignored. Therefore, the process time of Schema-XSF is not sensitive to the size of entire document, but only to the related parts to the KQSM.

Figure 10. Experiments for small document

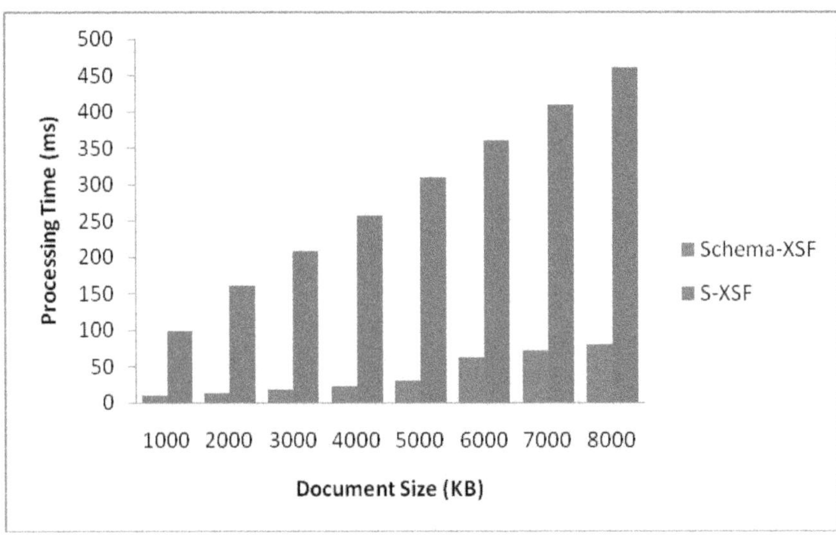

Figure 11. Experiment for large document

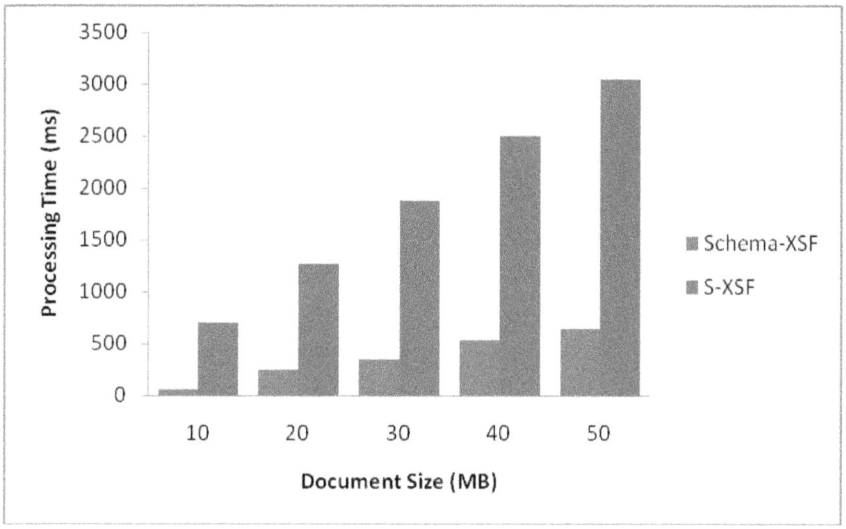

Figure 12. Experiment results for varying the number of keywords

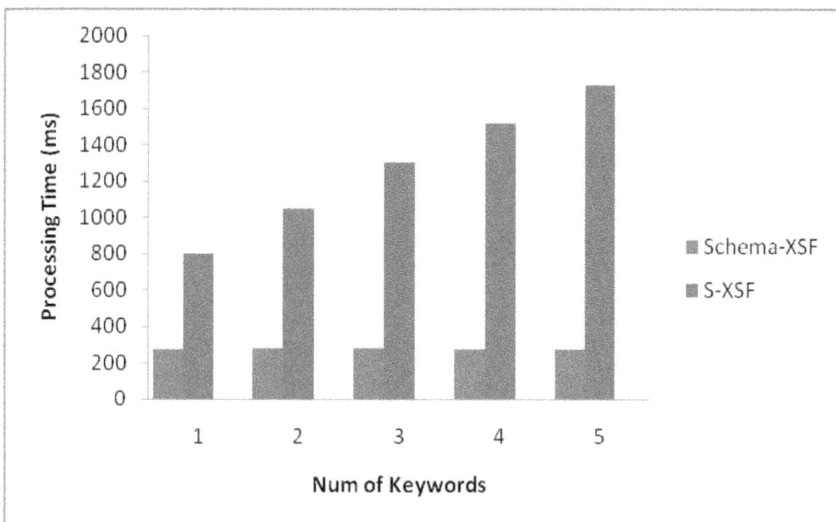

DISCUSSION

A lot of researches about XML keyword search are proposed in last few years such as XKeyword (Hristidis, Papakonstantinou, & Balmin, 2003), XKSearch (Xu & Papakonstantinou, 2005), XSearch (Cohen, Mamou, Kanza, & Sagiv, 2003), XRANK (Guo, Shao, Botev, & Shanmugasundaram, 2003) etc. Keyword search adopts the best match approach, which means that the most related results to the list of keywords should be selected. Most existing researches regard VLCA (Variation of LCA) as the meaningful XML fragment to the keywords. For example, XKSearch (Xu & Papakonstantinou, 2005) defines the keyword search as the search for Smallest Lowest Common Ancestor (SLCA) of an XML document tree. Because the SLCA approach may lose some meaningful information, our previous work (Josifovski, Fontoura, & Barta, 2005) extended the concept of SLCA to XLCA (eXclusive Lowest Common Ancestor). XML keyword search also focus on finding more efficient algorithms to search the XML documents. XKSearch proposed two algorithms, Indexed Lookup Eager and Scan Eager, for keyword search in XML documents according to the SLCA semantic by using Dewey numbers as the index XRANK (Guo, Shao, Botev, & Shanmugasundaram, 2003) presented stack based sort-merge algorithm (DIL). Because these works need to build the index (often use Dewey numbers) before searching the documents, they are not suitable for the environment of processing XML streams.

Stream-based continuous query fits a large class of new applications, such as sensor networks, location tracking, network management and financial data analysis (Babcock, Babu, Datar, Motwani, & Widom, 2002). As extensible markup language XML is a standard for information exchange, the problem of processing streaming XML data is gaining widespread attention from the research community (Altinel, Franklin, 2000; Diao et al., 2003; Gong et al., 2005; Josifovski et al., 2005; Peng & Chawathe, 2005). XML stream systems aim to provide fast, on-the-fly matching of XML-encoded data to large numbers of queries. Since that XML stream systems have to process the incoming stream instantly, and it is not allowed to store documents persistently and build an index on documents in advance, therefore, it needs an algorithm to process streams in a single pass with incurring a small memory cost. It is now well accepted that approaches using event-based parsing and Finite State Machines (FSMs) can provide the basis for highly scalable XML stream process systems, for example, the XFilter system (Altinel & Franklin, 2000) was the first published FSM-based XML filtering approach and used a separate FSM per path query to allow all of the FSMs to be executed simultaneously during the processing of a document; based on XFilter, YFilter (Diao et al., 2003) combines all of the path queries into a single Nondeterministic Finite Automaton (NFA). So far, almost all XML stream systems adopted structured query languages to represent user's profiles (such as XQuery, XPath) which can convey complex meaning by containing constraints on both structure and content but is difficult to learn for an ordinary user, it is also impossible to write a correct query without knowing the exact structure of a document.

XKFilter combines keyword search techniques and stream processing techniques to provide the abilities of filtering XML streams by using keywords. XKFilter defines the results of keyword search based on the concept of XLCA and proposes an algorithm named S-XSF based on runtime stack for pure keyword filtering over XML streams. Different from the stack based sort-merge algorithm presented in XRANK (Guo, Shao, Botev, & Shanmugasundaram, 2003), S-XSF uses event-based parsing to filter an input XML document in a single pass without building document index in advance, which can be fit for stream processing systems. XKFilter also proposes schema-aware approach called Schema-XSF for filtering XML streams if the DTD of the input documents is available. By using the DTD, XKFilter refines the keyword search to a constrained query structure named KQG and constructs a state machine named KQSM to drive the execution process of document filtering. Like YFilter, Schema-XSF also adopts the approach using FSM, but different from YFilter, KQSM of Schema-XSF is deterministic (the nondeterminability of finite state machine in YFilter is due to containing the "//" axes in its XPath). In addition, as the KQSM supports forward transition and backward transition, Schema-XSF can process the stream in a single pass, but when a query containing nested paths is parsed in YFilter, it is decomposed into a list of absolute paths: the main path and any extended nested paths, and then joins the intermedial results.

This research has achieved that XKFilter can support both pure keyword search and schema-aware keyword search. For the pure keyword search approach, we presented a stack based algorithm S-XSF to process the input document in a single pass and return the results to the users; for the schema-aware keyword search approach, we presented Schema-XSF to refine the keyword search to a constrained query structure KQG. For processing streams efficiently, the special finite state machine KQSM was constructed from the KQG to drive the execution process of document filtering. We conducted a series of experiments for the evaluation of S-XSF and Schema-XSF. The experiments showed that Schema-XSF was more efficient than S-XSF if the DTD of the input document is available. Essentially, the process of S-XSF is similar to the process of Schema-XSF, the main difference is that Schema-XSF is driven by the KQSM.

XKFilter is the first system for XML keyword filtering. In the future, we will extend our system to include more rich features, for example, extending the XKFilter to the ability of processing multiple lists of keywords submitted by large numbers of users simultaneously. We will also use ontology to support keyword search on heterogeneous data sources in order to increase the accuracy of the search outcome. Furthermore, security issue will be introduced to future research approach (Lu & Cripps, 2005).

ACKNOWLEDGMENT

This research was supported in part by the grants from National Natural Science Foundation of China (No. 60773076), National High Technology-Research and Development Program of China under Grant 2008AA121706, the Key Research of Shanghai under Grant 08JC1402500, Xiao-34-1.

REFERENCES

Altinel, M., & Franklin, M. J. (2000). Efficient filtering of XML documents for selective dissemination of information. In *Proceedings of the 26th International Conference on Very Large Databases* (pp. 53-64).

Babcock, B., Babu, S., Datar, M., Motwani, R., & Widom, J. (2002). Models and issues in data stream systems. In *Proceedings of the International Conference on Management of Data and Symposium on Principles of Database Systems* (pp. 1-16).

Cohen, S., Mamou, J., Kanza, Y., & Sagiv, Y. (2003). XSEarch: A semantic search engine for XML. In *Proceedings of the 29th International Conference on Very Large Databases* (pp. 45-56).

Diao, Y., Altinel, M., Franklin, M., Zhang, H., & Fischer, P. (2003). Path sharing and predicate evaluation for high-performance XML filtering. *ACM Transactions on Database Systems*, *28*(4), 467–516. doi:10.1145/958942.958947

Gong, X., Qian, W., Yan, Y., & Zhou, A. (2005). Bloom filter-based XML packets filtering for millions of path queries. In *Proceedings of the 21st International Conference on Data Engineering* (pp. 890-901).

Guo, L., Shao, F., Botev, C., & Shanmugasundaram, J. (2003). XRANK: Ranked keyword search over XML documents. In *Proceedings of the ACM SIGMOD International Conference on Management of Data* (pp. 16-27).

Hristidis, V., Koudas, N., Papakonstantinou, Y., & Srivastava, D. (2006). Keyword proximity search in XML trees. *IEEE Transactions on Knowledge and Data Engineering*, *18*(4), 525–539. doi:10.1109/TKDE.2006.1599390

Hristidis, V., Papakonstantinou, Y., & Balmin, A. (2003). Keyword proximity search on XML graphs. In *Proceedings of the 19th International Conference on Data Engineering* (pp. 367-378).

Josifovski, V., Fontoura, M., & Barta, A. (2005). Querying XML streams. *International Journal on Very Large Data Bases*, *14*(2), 197–210. doi:10.1007/s00778-004-0123-7

Li, Y., Yu, C., & Jagadish, H. V. (2004). Schema-free Xquery. In *Proceedings of the 30th International Conference on Very Large Databases* (Vol. 30, pp. 72-83).

Liu, F., Yu, C., Meng, W., & Chowdhury, A. (2006). Effective keyword search in relational databases. In *Proceedings of the ACM SIGMOD International Conference on Management of Data* (pp. 563-574).

Liu, Z., Walker, J., & Yichen, Y. (2007). Xseek: A semantic XML search engine using keywords. In *Proceedings of the 33rd International Conference on Very Large Databases* (pp. 1330-1333).

Lu, J. (2005). A survey of XML applications on scientific technology. *International Journal of Software Engineering and Knowledge Engineering*, *1*, 1–33. doi:10.1142/S0218194005001902

Lu, J., & Cripps, N. (2005). *Impact of XML applications on interdisciplinary and multidisciplinary applications.* Paper presented at the International Conference on Systemics, Cybernetics and Informatics.

Lu, J., & Fox, R. (2007). Effectively storing and querying XML. In *Proceedings of International Conference on Internet Computing and Conference on Computer Games Development* (pp. 311-317).

Lu, J., & Rahman, U. (2007). Semantic search technology for information retrieval on the web. *International Internet Journal of Agent Oriented Software Engineering*, *1*(2), 225–243. doi:10.1504/IJAOSE.2007.014408

Madden, S., Shah, M., Hellerstein, J., & Raman, V. (2002). Continuously adaptive continuous queries over streams. In *Proceedings of the ACM SIGMOD International Conference on Management of Data* (pp. 49-60).

Markowetz, A., Yang, Y., & Papadias, D. (2007). Keyword search on relational data streams. In *Proceedings of the ACM SIGMOD International Conference on Management of Data* (pp. 605-616).

Peng, F., & Chawathe, S. (2005). XSQ: A streaming XPath engine. *ACM Transactions on Database Systems*, *30*(2), 577–623. doi:10.1145/1071610.1071617

Tatarinov, I., Viglas, S., Beyer, K., Shanmugasundaram, J., Shekita, E., & Zhang, C. (2002). Storing and querying ordered XML using a relational database system. In *Proceedings of the ACM SIGMOD International Conference on Management of Data* (pp. 204-215).

Xu, Y., & Papakonstantinou, Y. (2005). Efficient keyword search for smallest LCAs in XML databases. In *Proceedings of the ACM SIGMOD International Conference on Management of Data* (pp. 527-538).

This work was previously published in the International Journal of Information Retrieval Research, Volume 1, Issue 1, edited by Zhongyu (Joan) Lu, pp. 1-18, copyright 2011 by IGI Publishing (an imprint of IGI Global).

Chapter 2
On the Design and Implementation of Interactive XML Applications

Jeff Brown
University of North Carolina Wilmington, USA

Rebecca Brown
University of North Carolina Chapel Hill, USA

Chris Velado
University of North Carolina Wilmington, USA

Ron Vetter
University of North Carolina Wilmington, USA

ABSTRACT

This paper describes issues and challenges in the design and implementation of interactive client-server applications where program logic is expressed in terms of an extensible markup language (XML) document. Although the technique was originally developed for creating interactive short message service (SMS) applications, it has expanded and is used for developing interactive web applications. XML-Interactive (or XML-I) defines the program states and corresponding actions. Because many interactive applications require sustained communication between the client and the underlying information service, XML-I has support for session management. This allows state information to be managed in a dynamic way. The paper describes several applications that are implemented using XML-I and discusses design issues. The software framework has been implemented in a Java environment.

INTRODUCTION

Client-server applications are often written as customized software that is dedicated to providing the information service desired. Each new service is a new application (or procedure) that implements the service. Like the basic web protocol (http), the client-server environment is often stateless – meaning that the environment won't do anything to preserve the session state. Each request and response is a new one and not related to any other. Therefore when writing interactive client-server applications, session management is a major part of the effort since one must implement stateful sessions in a stateless environment.

Multi-tier web development architectures have become commonplace in modern web applications. A multi-tier, or more specifically a 3-tier, architecture refers to a client-server architecture in which the presentation, application processing,

DOI: 10.4018/978-1-4666-3898-3.ch002

and the data management layers are logically separate processes (Wikipedia, n.d.). The idea is to modularize the software application into functional units with well-defined interfaces so that changes and upgrades to any software layer (tier) can be made independently. Web application frameworks, such as Java Enterprise Edition (J2EE) and Ruby on Rails, are often used to support the development of dynamic web sites, web applications, and web services. These frameworks help alleviate the overhead associated with common activities performed in web development, such as providing libraries for data access, security, and session management (Wikipedia, n.d.).

In a recent article, a flexible framework for developing interactive short message service (SMS) applications was presented (Brown et al., 2010). This framework was called XML Interactive or XML-I. In this paper, we show how XML-I can be used not just for creating interactive SMS applications but also for creating any interactive client-server web application that requires state information and state control. Although this work is a relatively new, it builds upon the established work of more general web application frameworks. With XML-I, program logic is expressed in terms of an XML document which contains the program states and corresponding actions. Because many interactive applications require sustained communication between the client and the underlying information service, XML-I also has support for session management. This allows state information to be managed in a dynamic way. This paper describes several applications that have been implemented using XML-I and discusses design issues. The software framework has been implemented in a Java environment.

WHAT IS XML-I

XML Interactive is a specification, in XML format, of a software application. Thus, XML-I can be used for both the conceptual and the actual design of interactive SMS and web applications. The software framework of XML-I contains properties that can be easily implemented by simple programs in a web server environment, using Java's application programming interface (API). By establishing XML-I in a multi-tier architecture, web services can be extended to create complex client-server conversations based on the input received from a mobile originated (MO) SMS message or more traditional web (HTTP) request.

Before the introduction of XML-I, many interactive SMS services were implemented by responding to a single and specific keyword contained in the MO message. The SMS applications would generate mobile terminated (MT) messages based upon the specific keyword received. With XML-I, users are able to carry out multifaceted conversations with the underlying information service without the need to specify a keyword for each client-server interaction. For example, a user might navigate through several menu options (responding via SMS messages) in order to request more specific information from a large data set.

Just as standard XML is based on tree structures, XML-I code contains specific nodes and attributes that control the navigation within the XML along with key commands to enable client interaction. When a user sends a message, the content within that message determines the new "state" of the application. Moving to a new state will determine what actions will take place. Basic functionality such as switching state or terminating conversations is also part of this system. Changing an existing application is easy – one simply updates the states and actions in the XML document.

SMS APPLICATION: DRUG TRIAL PRESCREENING

Mobile Education LLC has established the hardware and software infrastructure needed for implementing interactive SMS applications (Brown & Vetter, 2010). One of these applications involves prescreening applicants who are interested in participating in experimental drug trials. The basic idea behind this application can be described as follows.

Participants are sought for an upcoming drug trial. Ads say "*Text TRIAL to 90947*" to see if you qualify. In this simple example, we are going to look for participants who are females between 18 and 24 years of age. However, we have an upcoming trial for which we want males in the same age range. The user sends an MO with the word TRIAL to 90947.

The system sends an MT with the text, "*Welcome to the drug prescreening system. First, you need to answer some basic questions. How old are you? a) Under 18 b) 18-24 c) Over 24.*" If the response is 'a' or 'c', the user is thanked for their interest and told that they are not in the right age range and the conversation is over. If the response is 'b', the system responds with the text, "*What is your gender? a) Female or b) Male.*"

If the response is 'a', then the system sends the text: "*Thank you for your interest. You will be contacted shortly.*" There are also three additional actions taken:

1. A text is sent to a company representative with a message that includes that user's phone number.
2. An email is sent to a company representative with a message that includes that user's phone number.
3. The user's phone is associated with a text message group to whom broadcast messages can be sent.

If the response is 'b', the user is told that they are not needed for the current trial, but they might be suitable for an upcoming trial. In this case the action is to associate the phone number with a text message group for future contact. Figure 1 shows the XML-I for the drug trial application.

Figure 1. XML-I for drug trial prescreening application

```
<xmlInteractive id='root' message = 'Welcome to the pre-screening system.  How old are you? a)
under 18 b) 18-24 c) over 24'  error='Reply a, b, or c.  a) for under 18 years, b) for 18-24, or c)
for over 24'>

<state id='age1' route = 'a' message = 'Sorry, you are not old enough to participate.' />

<state id='age3' route = 'c' message = 'Sorry, you are not in the required age range' />

<state id='age2' route = 'b' message = 'What is your gender? a) female b) male' error='Please
reply a or b. a) female b) male'>

   <state id='female' route = 'a' message = 'Thank you for your interest.  You will be contacted
shortly.'>
        <action type='text' to='910xxxxxxx' message = ' needs to be contacted about trial'/>
        <action type='register' to = 'current_trial'/>
        <action type='email' to='who@where.edu' message = 'needs to be contacted about trial'/>
   </state>

   <state id='male' route = 'b' message = 'The current trial is for women, although we may
contact you
                   about a trial in the near future.'>
        <action type='register' to = 'future_trial'/>
   </state>

</state>
</xmlInteractive>
```

WEB APPLICATION: LEARNING TREES

A learning tree depicts a series of choices or decisions that are possible by structuring learning content into the form of a tree (Wikipedia, n.d.). Leaves denote final answers and the branches represent the choices that lead to those answers. Although the composition of learning content into a learning tree is an active area of research (Woda, 2006; Witten & MacDonald, 1998), one simple strategy for developing a learning tree might be described as follows:

- Start with a series of questions on one topic.
- For each question choose two or more answers.
- Each wrong answer corresponds to a new question sequence which, when completed successfully, leads to the same place you would have reached with the right answer.

For example, a learning tree that depicts several mathematical problems for elementary school students is shown in Figure 2. Each question in the tree has two edges below it, and the edges are labeled with numbers. This means that the question is stated as multiple-choice with two answers. The question at the root node might be stated as "Fill in the blank: 3 + 28 = __ . Answer either 25 or 31." If the student answers something other than 25 or 31, then the application can be set so that it either states the problem in another way, or it sends the same question again.

The three initial questions are the root node, the root's right child, and that child's right child. So answering the three initial questions correctly

Figure 2. Learning tree for mathematics

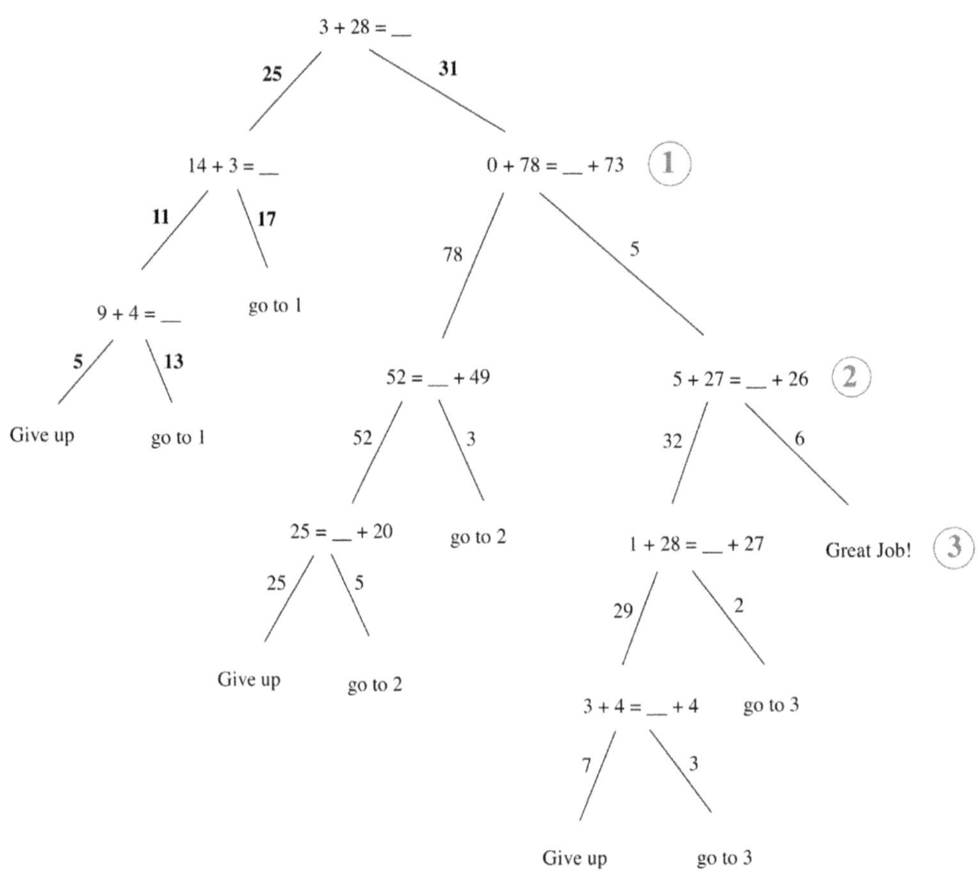

takes you down the right side of the tree to the node labeled 3. This tree is binary – every non-leaf node has two children. It is likely that a real example would have questions with more than two answers, but it is easier to see the overall scheme with a binary tree.

It is also likely that a real-world example might require more than one right answer to correct a series of wrong answers. For example, suppose your answers are 25, then 11, then 13. This leads you to a node labeled "go to 1", which means you go to the node labeled with the 1 corresponding to getting the first answer right. Having missed two and gotten one right, at this point there might be another question that would have to be answered correctly before jumping to node 1.

The nodes labeled 'Give up' indicate that you have three wrong in a row, and that you might need to be directed to another place. Figure 3 shows partial XML-I code for the mathematics learning tree.

To implement learning trees, there must be a simple way to put a set of questions into production, that is, construct the tree and generate the XML-I code. The example above was started by drawing a tree on paper. Real-world examples will probably contain enough branching that drawing the tree by hand will be difficult. Thus, there is a need for software that guides the input of questions and answers. Having a clear strategy will make it easier to design applications that let pedagogy experts build trees in a wizard-like environment. It is also important to note that the introduction of wildcard route attributes in XML-I allow us to create learning trees with questions that are not multiple choice questions. This is explained in more detail in the section on Design and Implementation Issues.

The strategy used for this learning tree resulted in one leaf node being the desired goal, and there is only one path through a tree leading to that goal. The jump feature in XML-I essentially turns the XML tree into a graph. This means that a learning tree (or graph) can describe complex navigation schemes, and hence complex applications can be specified.

The text message context is sufficient for the very basic mathematics in the learning tree example, but it is not suitable for more advanced mathematics. This is what led us to start thinking about extending XML-I to support web applications. In the web version of XML-I, the message attribute is replaced by the URL of a page to display. Links and text inputs are used in place of MO text messages. We have implemented a simple maze as a web XML-I application that can be seen at http://mymobed.com/xmli. Each page of the maze application contains the name of a room and links to adjacent rooms. The goal is the make it to the room called "You made it to the

Figure 3. Partial XML-I code for math learning tree

```
<xmlInteractive id='root' message=' 3 + 28 = _  Reply either 25 or 31'>

  <state id='w1' route='25' message='14 + 3 = _  Reply 11 or 17' >

     <state id='w2' route=11' ...>
       ...
     </state>

     <state id='r2' route='17' jump='r1'/>

  <state id='r1' route='31' message='Right!  0 + 78 = _ + 73  Reply 78 or 5'>

     ...
```

End!" Note that this maze uses the jump feature of XML-I, and the link called "Back" takes you to the parent of the current node.

INTEGRATED SMS/ WEB APPLICATION

The flexibility of XML-I allows for the development of comprehensive interactive applications. For example, we have developed a fully functional SMS/Web application, called TakeTextPoll (Brown et. al., 2010b), which uses SMS technology to deliver interactive text message surveys and polls to clients on their cell phone. Users text a keyword and receive questions as a series of text messages. As users respond to messages the system tallies the responses and results are made available in real-time on a secure web site. Text message based surveys and polls can be used for market research, call-to-action campaigns, electronic voting, and more.

TakeTextPoll is set up to be a web application that requires prior approval before its services are available. Once a client registers through the web site and is approved by the administrator, he or she is able to log in and start creating original polls. The *Create a Poll* page (Figure 4), allows the user to select a poll title, visibility (public or private), keyword, and a multiple choice question. With the use of JavaScript, a live count of the number of characters entered is automatically updated and displayed. This is a key issue for creating SMS polls since a text message has a limit of 160 characters

Figure 4. Create a poll web page

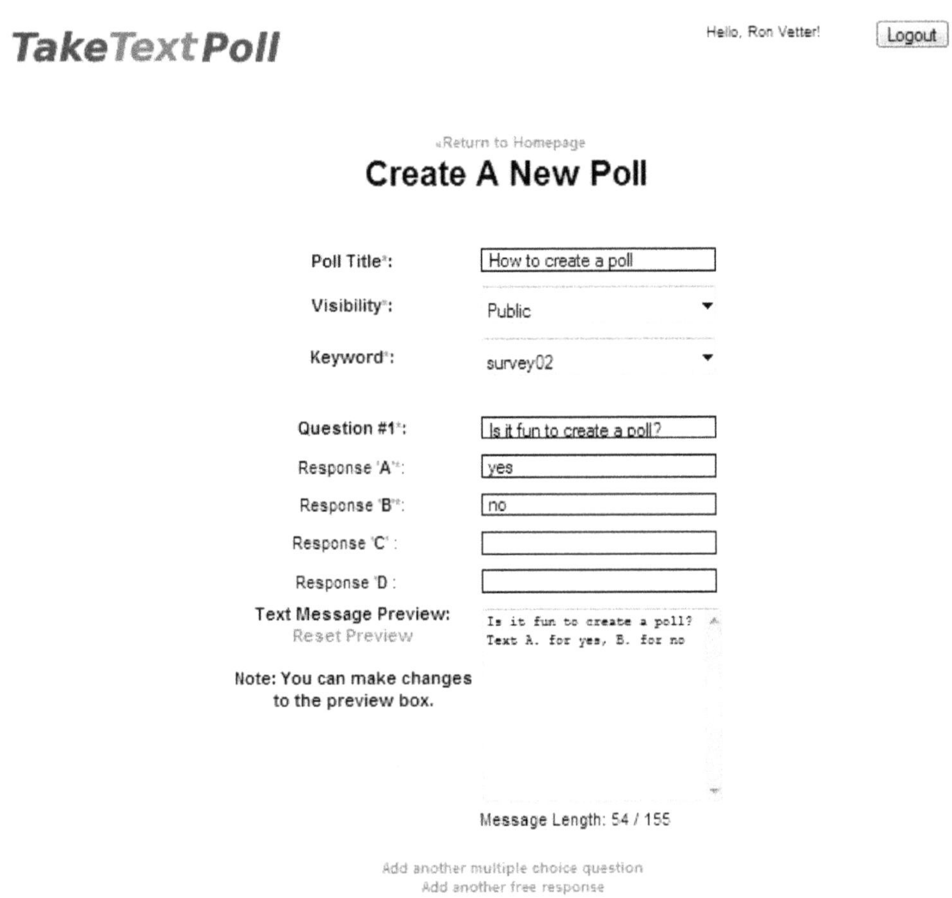

(we limit the maximum number of characters to 155 to allow for question number to be sent in the text message as well).

Once the user has completed the first question, they can proceed to add either another multiple choice question or a free response question. A free response question is one that allows the poll taker to respond with an open response (any text) for the answer to the question. The application currently allows for up to five questions per poll.

Users can deploy and un-deploy polls. When a user presses the deploy button, the poll is translated into XML-I, and sent to Mobile Education server. Mobile Education's server executes the XML-I application and relays responses back to the TakeTextPoll web application. Figure 5 shows an example of the XMI-I generated from a typical poll application.

The TakeTextPoll application is implemented as a multi-tier web application (Figure 6). The presentation tier consists of two main user interfaces: a web page and a SMS interface. The web page represents the portion where clients are able to visually create and manage their polls through web forms. Within that same tier, a mobile user is able to send a keyword to begin a SMS poll. The logic tier includes communication functionality. One computer server performs operations that include communicating between the web page and poll database, and between the poll web site and Mobile Education's server. The Mobile Education server performs operations that include communication between a poll taker's mobile device and web server. Finally, the data tier contains a database that stores account, poll, and poll response information.

An alternative view of the TakeTextPoll application is depicted by an activity diagram shown in Figure 7. An activity diagram is a graphical representation of workflows of the stepwise activities and actions of a system (Wikipedia, n.d.).

In the learning tree example the jump feature was used to provide multiple paths to the same node, in effect turning the tree into a graph. The XML-I

Figure 5. XML-I code for a TakeTextPoll application

```
<xmlInteractive id='root' message='(1/3) Which do you think TakeTextPoll could be of use? Text
A. for Business use, B. for Scientific use, C. for Education use, D. for None of the above'
error='reply A. Business use B. Scientific use C. Education use D. None of the above '>

<action type='relay' to='http://TakeTextPoll.com/...'/>

<state id='q2' route='a' message='(2/3) Please give an example of what you could see using
TakeTextPoll in the future. ' >
  <action type='relay' to='http://TakeTextPoll.com/...'/>
  <state id='q3' route='*' message='(3/3) How has this experience been? Text A. for Great, B. for
Ok, C. for Bad' error='reply A. Great B. Ok C. Bad '>
    <action type='relay' to='http://TakeTextPoll.com/...'/>
    <state id='q4' route='a' message='Thank you for your input.  For results, check
www.TakeTextPoll.com!'>
      <action type='relay' to='http://TakeTextPoll.com/...'/>
    </state>
    <state id='1a3' route='b' jump='q4'/>
    <state id='2a3' route='c' jump='q4'/>
  </state>
</state>

<state id='1a1' route='b' jump='q2'/>
<state id='2a1' route='c' jump='q2'/>
<state id='3a1' route='d' jump='q2'/>

</xmlInteractive>
```

Figure 6. Multi-tier architectural design

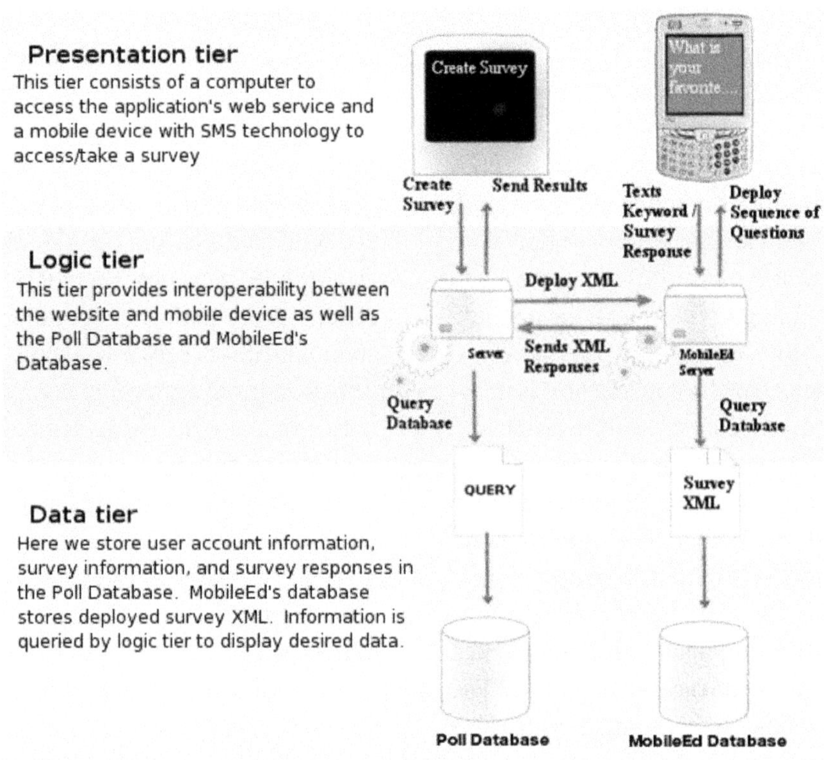

code produced by TakeTextPoll uses jump to avoid duplicating material in the XML document.

DESIGN AND IMPLEMENTATION ISSUES

Mobile Education's SMS system is based on keywords. When a user sends a text message to the short code 90947, the first word of the message identifies the program that will process the message. An important feature of XML-I is that the user does not have to use the keyword after the initial MO message. This feature makes XML-I more user-friendly and more robust. Consider, for example, the gender question from the drug trial prescreening application, "*What is your gender? a) Female or b) Male.*" If the response needed to begin with the keyword TRIAL, it would be awkward to state the options, and user input errors would be much more common. Mobile Education's SMS system implements sessions with a program called the Interceptor (Figure 8). When a user starts an XML-I conversation, the user's phone number, the identifier of the XML-I application, the timeout for that application, and the current time are stored in a database. When a message enters the system, the Interceptor checks the database to see if the phone number is in a session that has not timed out. If so, it appends the appropriate keyword to the front of the message and continues processing.

XML is the natural choice for holding the hierarchical data needed by XML-I applications. Another reason for having the application specified by XML is that other applications can create XML-I applications simply by writing XML. TakeTextPoll is one example of this kind of application and we expect to create more examples in the future.

Figure 7. Activity diagram for TakeTextPoll application

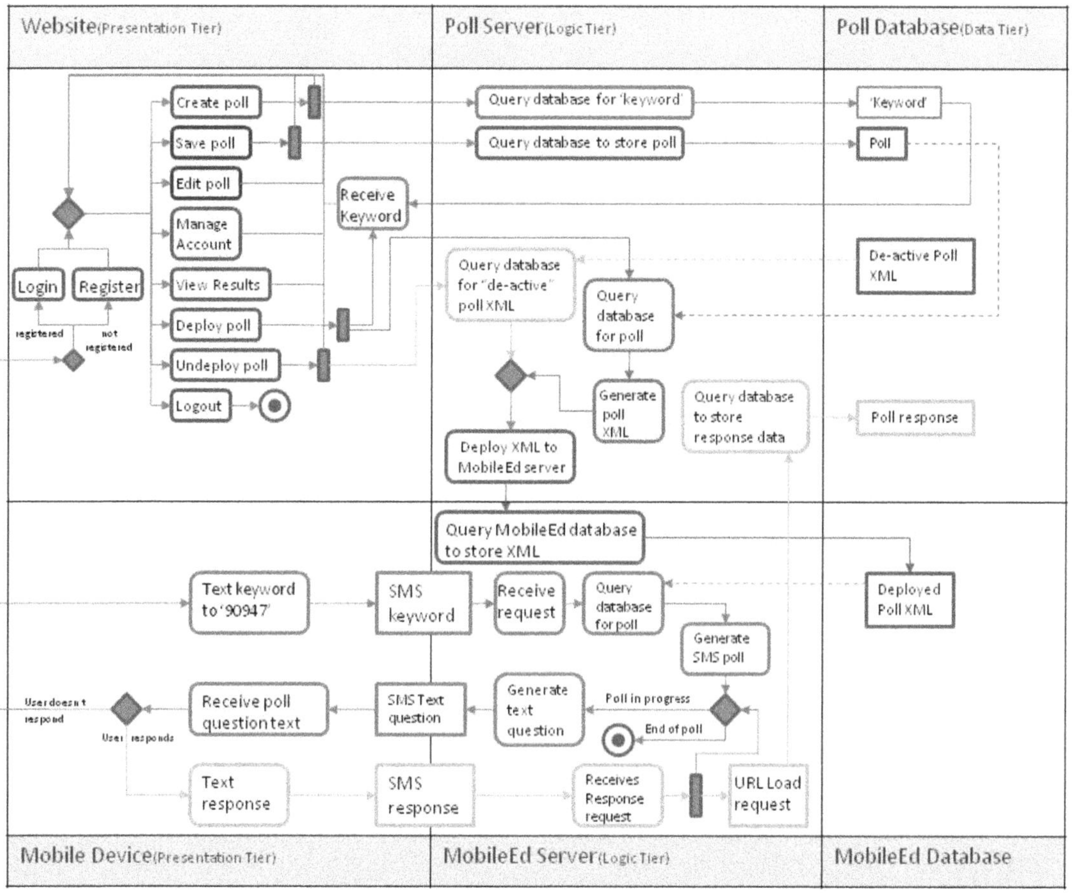

The tree structure of XML also fits well with the question/answer nature of XML-I applications. We have seen in the learning tree and TakeTextPoll applications that it can be necessary to go from the current state to another state that is not a child the current one. The jump feature of XML-I makes it much more flexible.

The current XML Schema used to validate XML-I applications is shown in Figure 9. The schema requires the root element to be named xmlinteractive and to have an attribute named id with value 'root'. All other elements in the document are either state tags or action tags. State tags must have unique id attributes. As the user interacts with the application, the id of their current state is stored in a database.

State tags also need an attribute named route, which is used to determine the next state for the user. If the expected response to a question is either a or b, then the current state tag should have a child with route attribute a, and another with route attribute b. A state's optional error attribute is used as a message to the user when they send an unexpected response. For example, look again at the drug trial prescreening application. The root element's message attribute is "*Welcome to the drug prescreening system. First, you need to answer some basic questions. How old are you? a) under 18 b) 18-24 c) over 24,*" so we expect to receive a response starting with either a, b, or c, and there are child nodes with those route attributes. If we receive any response other than a, b, or c, the optional error attribute is sent to the user.

Figure 8. Flow of control and data

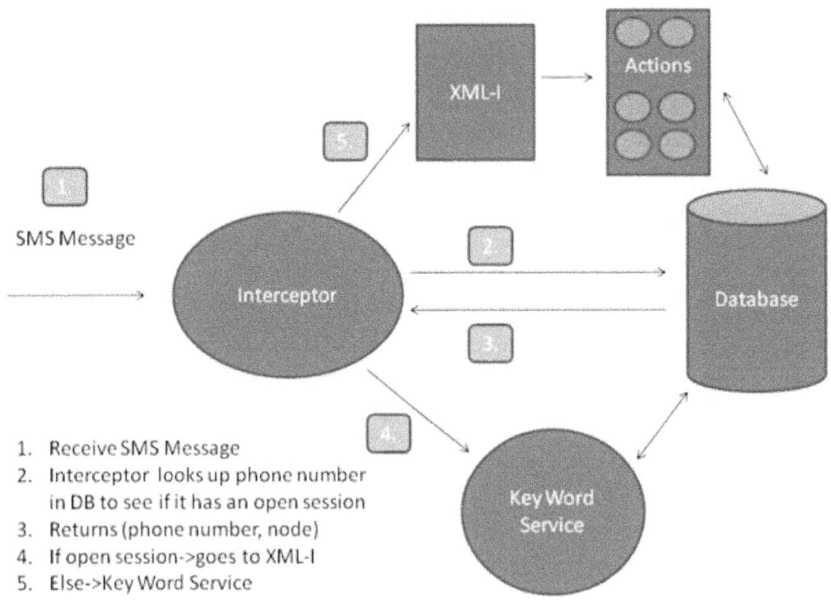

The idea is to restate the required response in a way that might be clearer. In this example the error attribute is "Reply a, b, or c. a) for under 18 years, b) for 18-24, or c) for over 24."

The route attribute of a state node can also be the wildcard character *. If the current node has a child with route = '*', and the response does not match the route attribute of any other child, then the child with the wildcard route becomes the current node. For an example of how this can be used, consider the learning tree application for mathematics. Suppose the question is "Fill in the blank: 3 + 11 = __ + 12." There are three child nodes with route attributes 2, 14, and *. The correct answer is 2. The instructor expects some children to answer 14, because they think of the equal sign as an instruction to do a calculation, not as part of an equation. So, 14 is an expected incorrect answer. All other answers result in the user being sent to the node with wildcard route. Wildcard routes are also used in polls and surveys where a free response is solicited.

One way to extend the capabilities of XML-I is to add new actions, and we have done that after discussing application requirements with new user groups. Another means of extension is to use the relay action, which sends the user input and phone number to another server. TakeTextPoll uses the relay action to process user input. TakeTextPoll uses XML-I to handle navigation, but it also needs to process user input to tally the survey results. So relay actions are used to transmit all users input to a second server for processing.

Another issue involves the creation of learning trees. We can use XML editing software (Wikipedia, n.d.) to guide the input of questions and answers, and to take care of syntax details. XML editors also ensure the data supplied is consistent with the document type definition or schema provided. Using an XML editor is also faster and more convenient than entering the XML by-hand. However, because most XML editors are designed to edit documents with very general tags and structures, they do not provide a good solution for creating XML-I applications with a very limited set of tags. What is needed is an XML authoring tool that shows the XML-I states and branches in a graphical interface and that lets pedagogy experts build graphs in a wizard-like environment. The development of such a tool is part of our on-going work.

Figure 9. XML-I schema: actions, message types, and states

```
<xs:schema xmlns:xs="http://www.w3.org/2001/XMLSchema">
 <xs:simpleType name="actionType">
  <xs:restriction base="xs:string">
    <xs:enumeration value="email"/>
    <xs:enumeration value="text"/>
    <xs:enumeration value="register"/>
    <xs:enumeration value="emailUser"/>
    <xs:enumeration value="relay"/>
  </xs:restriction>
 </xs:simpleType>
 <xs:simpleType name="msgType">
  <xs:restriction base="xs:string">
   <xs:minLength value="1"/>
   <xs:maxLength value="140"/>
  </xs:restriction>
 </xs:simpleType>
 <xs:element name="xmlInteractive">
  <xs:complexType>
   <xs:sequence>
    <xs:element ref="state" minOccurs="0" maxOccurs="unbounded"/>
    <xs:element ref="action" minOccurs="0" maxOccurs="unbounded"/>
   </xs:sequence>
   <xs:attribute name="id" type="xs:string" use="required" fixed="root"/>
   <xs:attribute name="message" type="msgType" use="required"/>
   <xs:attribute name="error" type="msgType"/>
  </xs:complexType>
  <xs:unique name="uniqueId">
   <xs:selector xpath=".//state"/>
   <xs:field xpath="@id"/>
  </xs:unique>
 </xs:element>
 <xs:element name="state">
  <xs:complexType>
   <xs:sequence>
    <xs:element ref="state" minOccurs="0" maxOccurs="unbounded"/>
    <xs:element ref="action" minOccurs="0" maxOccurs="unbounded"/>
   </xs:sequence>
   <xs:attribute name="id" type="xs:string" use="required"/>
   <xs:attribute name="message" type="msgType"/>
   <xs:attribute name="route" type="xs:string" use="required"/>
   <xs:attribute name="error" type="msgType"/>
   <xs:attribute name="jump" type="xs:string"/>
  </xs:complexType>
 </xs:element>
 <xs:element name="action">
  <xs:complexType>
   <xs:attribute name="type" type="actionType" use="required"/>
   <xs:attribute name="to" type="xs:string" use="required"/>
   <xs:attribute name="subject" type="xs:string"/>
   <xs:attribute name="message" type="msgType"/>
   <xs:attribute name="includePhone" type="xs:string"/>
```

CONCLUSION AND FUTURE WORK

The XML-I framework is implemented in Java and deployed in Tomcat 6, an open source JSP/Servlet engine. It also uses a mySQL 5 database to store application configuration and session state. The use of the Java platform worked well because its web components, JSP and servlets, are well suited for service-oriented applications that process requests and construct responses. JSP pages not only allow text-based documents to be rendered as servlets but also allow a more natural approach to creating content. As in many modern applications, XML proved to be an excellent way to package and exchange data. XPath was also an obvious choice since it follows the industry standard way to parse and locate information in XML documents.

The XML-I engine is continually being enhanced to allow for new actions and program states. We are currently working on the development of an XML authoring tool that shows the XML-I states and branches in a graphical interface and that lets pedagogy experts build educational applications in a wizard-like environment. We are also investigating software support tools to help automate the addition of new actions and element types.

REFERENCES

Brown, J., Shipman, B., & Vetter, R. (2007). SMS: The short message service. *Computer*, *40*(12), 106–110. doi:10.1109/MC.2007.440

Brown, J., Velado, C., & Vetter, R. (2010a, July 12-15). XML Interactive: A software framework for developing interactive SMS applications. In *Proceedings of the International Conference on Internet Computing*, Las Vegas, NV (pp. 216-224).

Brown, J., Velado, C., & Vetter, R. (2010b). *Take text poll home page*. Retrieved from http://www.taketextpoll.com/

Brown, J., & Vetter, R. (2010). *Mobile education home page*. Retrieved from http://www.mymobed.com/

Wikipedia. (n.d.). *Activity diagram*. Retrieved from http://en.wikipedia.org/wiki/Activity_diagram

Wikipedia. (n.d.). *Decision tree learning*. Retrieved from http://en.wikipedia.org/wiki/Decision_tree_learning

Wikipedia. (n.d.). *Multitier architecture*. Retrieved from http://en.wikipedia.org/wiki/Three-tier_(computing)#Three-tier_architecture

Wikipedia. (n.d.). *Web application framework*. Retrieved from http://en.wikipedia.org/wiki/Web_application_framework

Wikipedia. (n.d.). *XML editor*. Retrieved from http://en.wikipedia.org/wiki/XML_editor

Witten, I., & MacDonald, B. (1998). Using concept learning for knowledge acquisition. *International Journal of Man-Machine Studies*, *29*(2), 171–196. doi:10.1016/S0020-7373(88)80045-2

Woda, M. (2006, May 25-27). Conception of composing learning content into learning tree to ensure reliability of learning material. In *Proceedings of the International Conference on Dependability of Computer Systems*, Szklarska Poreba, Poland (pp. 374-381).

This work was previously published in the International Journal of Information Retrieval Research, Volume 1, Issue 1, edited by Zhongyu (Joan) Lu, pp. 19-30, copyright 2011 by IGI Publishing (an imprint of IGI Global).

Chapter 3
A Roadmap to Integrate Document Clustering in Information Retrieval

R. Subhashini
Sathyabama University, India

V. Jawahar Senthil Kumar
Anna University, India

ABSTRACT

The World Wide Web is a large distributed digital information space. The ability to search and retrieve information from the Web efficiently and effectively is an enabling technology for realizing its full potential. Information Retrieval (IR) plays an important role in search engines. Today's most advanced engines use the keyword-based ("bag of words") paradigm, which has inherent disadvantages. Organizing web search results into clusters facilitates the user's quick browsing of search results. Traditional clustering techniques are inadequate because they do not generate clusters with highly readable names. This paper proposes an approach for web search results in clustering based on a phrase based clustering algorithm. It is an alternative to a single ordered result of search engines. This approach presents a list of clusters to the user. Experimental results verify the method's feasibility and effectiveness.

INTRODUCTION

Since large information is available in an unstructured manner, retrieving out relevant documents containing the required information is the primary goal of research. This task is known as Information Retrieval. Most of the information retrieval systems are limited to the query processing based on keywords and key phrases. In Vector space model (VSM) (Khaled et al., 2004) a document is represented as a vector of index terms. In information retrieval system (Manning et al., 2008) the matching of the query against a set of text record is the core of the system. Any IR (Information Retrieval) system defines four basic elements:

- A collection profile,
- A document and query representation,
- A matching function,
- A ranking criteria.

DOI: 10.4018/978-1-4666-3898-3.ch003

Retrieval of the relevant natural language text document is a great challenge. The ability to search and retrieve information from the Web (Jansen, 2000; Page, & Brin, 1998) efficiently and effectively is an enabling technology for realizing its full potential.

The IR community has explored document clustering as an alternative method of organizing retrieval results (Branson & Greenberg, 2002). Document clustering is widely applicable in areas such as search engines, web mining, information retrieval, and topological analysis. Document clustering is an automatic grouping of text documents into clusters so that documents within a cluster have high similarity, but are dissimilar to documents in other clusters. Existing search engines such as Google, Yahoo and MSN often return a long list of search results, ranked by their relevancies to the given query. Most of the web search engines (Cutting et al., 1992) are also characterized by extremely low precision. Clustering algorithms, attempt to group documents together based on their similarities; thus documents relating to a certain topic will hopefully be placed in a single cluster. Clustering technique relies on four concepts: data representation model, similarity measure, clustering model and clustering algorithm that generates the clusters using the data model and the similarity measure. This can help users both in locating interesting documents more easily and in getting an overview of the retrieved document set. Moreover, most traditional clustering algorithms cannot be directly used for search result clustering, because of some practical issues. Zamir and Etzioni (1999) gave a good analysis on these issues. The algorithm should take the document snippets instead of the whole documents as input, because of the downloading time of original documents; the clustering algorithm should be fast enough for online calculation; and also the generated clusters should have readable descriptions for quick browsing by users, etc. We also follow these requirements to design our algorithm.

In this algorithm, several properties for each phrase such as phrase frequencies, document frequencies, phrase length, etc are considered and score of the phrase is calculated. The phrases are ranked according to the score, and the top-ranked phrases are taken as base clusters, which are further merged according to their corresponding documents. Our method is more suitable for Web search results clustering because we emphasize the efficiency of identifying relevant clusters for Web users. Furthermore, the clusters are ranked according to their scores, thus the more likely clusters required by users are ranked higher. It generates shorter and more readable cluster names, which enable users to quickly identify the topics of a specified cluster.

RELATED WORKS

The vector space model, VSM, provides a baseline for the purpose of ranking documents based on a query (Baeza-Yates & Ribeiro-Neto, 1999). The similarity between the terms or keywords of the document and the terms of the query are determined based on the frequency of the occurrence of the terms in the document. The higher the frequency of the occurrence of query terms, the higher the document will be ranked. This method has the advantage of not depending on the order of the keywords. Automatically extracting key phrases from documents is a task with many applications in information retrieval and natural language processing. Turney's Extractor (1999) extracts a small number of key phrases from documents. The research on clustering search results has been investigated in a number of previous works. Agglomerative Hierarchical Clustering (AHC) algorithms are probably the most commonly used. These algorithms are typically slow when applied to large document collections. Single-link and group-average methods typically take O (n2) time, while complete-link methods typically take O(n3) time (Zamir & Etzioni, 1998). Lee et al. (1997) described how using index terms and keywords alone generally causes poor retrieval performance. The methods such as K-Means, AHC will improve the clustering quality, but they are suitable for "off-line" clustering situation due to time efficiency.

Phrase searching enables users to find documents containing the full text that a user seeks. Search engines, allow users to provide exact phrases to search for and will only return documents containing the phrase as it appears. The more unique the phrase is, the more likely the correct document will appear in the highly ranked documents. Phrase searching is a very efficient way to achieve the desired result than performing a keyword search (Jansen, 2000). Phrase searching can however fail, if in correct words are used or they appear in the wrong order. In this case, no results will be found and irrelevant results will be retrieved. Another related work is the DIG (Khaled et al., 2004), which allows for the incremental construction of a phrase based index for a document set. Some of them (Cutting, 1992; Hearst, & Pedersen, 1996; Leuski & Allan, 2000) apply traditional clustering algorithms which first cluster documents into topically-coherent groups according to content similarity. They generate descriptive summaries for clusters and are often unreadable, which make it difficult for Web users to identify relevant clusters. Zamir and Etzioni (1998, 1997) presented a Suffix Tree Clustering (STC) which first identifies sets of documents that share common phrases, and then create clusters according to these phrases as base clusters. Zamir (1998) has shown that STC outperforms other algorithms. The main advantages of STC over other clustering algorithms are that it uses phrases rather than words, and that it allows clusters to overlap. Hau Jun Zeng et al. (2004) introduced an improved suffix tree with n-gram to deal with the problem of the original suffix tree. But STC with n-gram give too many base clusters. Chim and Deng (2007) have proposed a new clustering algorithm combine the advantages of two document models in document clustering. The research on document clustering has been stared over the past several years. Our method of phrase clustering is almost similar to STC but we shall further calculate several important properties to identify the score of the phrases and base clusters before merging the similar clusters. Some topic finding (Liu et al., 2003) works are also related to our method. The difference is that we are given titles and short snippets rather than whole documents. The new document clustering algorithm we proposed is to improve the quality in clustering web page snippets, and the clustering speed can meet the demand of "on the fly" mode.

Background Knowledge

Overview of IR

Information retrieval (IR) is the science of searching for documents in the internet, for information within documents, and for metadata about documents and the World Wide Web. The following major models have been developed to retrieve information: the Boolean model, the Statistical model, which includes the vector space and the probabilistic retrieval model, and the Linguistic and Knowledge-based models. The first model is often referred to as the "exact match" model; the latter one as the "best match" models. In a collection of heterogeneous topics, the number of unique terms will be quite large. This results in document vectors of high dimensionality also called as curse of dimensionality. A number of pre processing steps are described next that can help address this issue.

Pre-Processing

Pre processing consists of steps that take as input a plain text document and output a set of tokens (which can be single terms or phrases) to be included in the vector model.

- **Filtering:** The process of removing special characters and punctuation that are not thought to hold any discriminative power under the vector model. This is more critical in the case of formatted documents, such as web pages, where formatting tags can either be discarded or identified and their constituent terms attributed different weights.
- **Tokenization:** The goal of the tokenization process is to determine sentence boundaries, and to separate the text into a stream of individual tokens (words). More sophisticated methods, drawn from the NLP, parse the grammatical structure of the text to pick significant terms. Single spaces are used to delimit tokens, while double spaces delimit sentences. Document texts must be tokenized correctly in order for the noun phrase extractor to parse the text efficiently.
- **Stemming:** The process of reducing words to their base form, or stem. For example, the words \connected," \connection", \ connections" are all reduced to the stem \ connect." Porter's algorithm is the de facto standard stemming algorithm.
- **Stop Word Removal:** A stop word is defined as a term which is not thought to convey any meaning as a dimension in the vector space (i.e. without context). A typical method to remove stop words is to compare each term with a compilation of known stop words such as "I", "am", "and" etc. are removed
- **Pruning:** Removes words that appear with very low frequency throughout the corpus. The underlying assumption is that these words, even if they had any discriminating power, would form too small clusters to be useful. A pre-specified threshold is typically used, e.g. a small fraction of the number of words in the corpus. Sometimes words which occur too frequently (e.g. in 40% or more of the documents) are also removed.

The vector space model, VSM (Supreethi & Prasad, 2003) also called the bag of words or dictionary model, provides a baseline for the purpose of ranking documents based on a query. The similarity between the terms (keywords or phrases) of the document and the terms of the query are determined based on the frequency of the occurrence of the terms in the document. The higher the frequency of the occurrence of query terms, the higher the document will be ranked. The vector model was originally developed for automatic indexing.

Feature Selection

Under the vector model, a collection of n documents and queries with m unique terms is represented as an m X n term-document matrix (where each document and query is a vector of m dimensions).

In this model, each text document d is represented by a vector of frequencies of the remaining m terms:

$$d = (tf1, tf2, \ldots\ldots\ldots\ldots tfm) \quad (1)$$

The document vectors are composed of weights i.e., the frequency of the terms in the document multiplied by the inverse of their frequency in the entire collection (tf _ idf). Salton and Buckley (1988) review the use of statistical information for weighting document terms and query terms, and discuss various ways of defining and combining TF and IDF. TF is the frequency of a term in the document. The more often a term occurs in the document, the more likely it is to be important for that document. The standard TF of a term T in a document D is calculated by:

$$\text{Standard TF} = \text{no. of occurrences of T in D} \quad (2)$$

The normalized TF is calculated by normalizing the standard TF factor by the maximum.

$$Normalized\ TF = 0.5 + 0.5\frac{TF}{\max\ \text{TF}} \quad (3)$$

A term (Salton, 1989) that occurs in only a few documents is often more valuable than a term that occurs in many documents. The assumption is that words which occur frequently in a document but rarely in the entire collection are of highly discriminative power. IDF is the rarity of a term across the collection.

$$IDF = \log\frac{No.\text{ of documents in collection}}{No.\text{ of documents T occurs in}} \quad (4)$$

The weight W_{ik} of term ti in document dk can be calculated as
follows:

$$W_{ik} = \text{Normalized } TF_{ik} \text{ X } IDF_i \quad (5)$$

where TF_{ik} denotes the frequency of term ti in document dk and

Similarity

When documents and queries are represented as term vectors, the similarity between the document and the query corresponds to the correlation between the vectors. This is quantified as the cosine of the angle between vectors, that is, the so-called cosine similarity. Cosine similarity is one of the most popular similarity measure applied to text documents, such as in numerous information retrieval applications and clustering too. The cosine similarity is non-negative and bounded between [0,1].An important property of the cosine similarity is its independence of document length. For a document D and query Q, the cosine similarity measure is given by:

$$Sim(D,Q) = \frac{\sum_i (d_i * q_i)}{\sqrt{\sum_i d_i^Z * \sum_i q_i^Z}} \quad (6)$$

where d, q are m-dimensional vectors over the term set T = {t1, . . ., tm}. Each dimension represents a term with its weight in the document, which is non-negative.

Overview of STC (Document Clustering)

Document clustering is a more specific technique for unsupervised document organization, that puts all the related documents in to groups and is useful for categorizing, organizing, refining search results, automatic topic extraction and fast information retrieval or filtering. A web search engine often returns thousands of pages in response to a broad query, making it difficult for users to browse and identify relevant information. Clustering methods can be used to automatically group the retrieved documents into a list of meaningful categories, as is achieved by Enterprise Search engines such as Vivisimo.

Firstly the key requirements of web document clustering pointed out by Zamir (1999) is discussed below.

Key Requirements for Web Document Clustering

1. **Relevance:** The method ought to produce clusters that group documents relevant to the user's query.
2. **Browsable Summaries:** The user needs to determine at a glance whether a cluster's contents are of interest. We do not want to replace sifting through ranked lists with sifting through clusters. Therefore the method has to provide concise and accurate descriptions of the clusters.
3. **Overlap:** Since documents have multiple topics, it is important to avoid confining each document to only one cluster.
4. **Snippet-Tolerance:** The method ought to produce high quality clusters even when it only has access to the snippets returned by

the search engines, as most users are unwilling to wait while the system downloads the original documents off the Web.

5. **Speed:** A very patient user might sift through 100 documents in a ranked list presentation. We want clustering to allow the user to browse through at least an order of magnitude more documents. Therefore the clustering method ought to be able to cluster up to one thousand snippets in a few seconds. For the impatient user, each second counts.
6. **Incrementality:** To save time, the method should start processing each snippet as soon as it is received over the Web.

Most of the clustering algorithms are based one of these two document models: the vector space document (VSD) model and the suffix tree document model. Clustering method base on VSD model such as K-Means and agglomerative hierarchical clustering (AHC) cluster the document according to the similarity of vectors which represent documents in the defined vector space. There methods can improve the clustering quality, but they are suitable for "off-line" clustering situation due to time efficiency.

To achieve a more accurate document clustering, a more informative feature term, phrase ordered sequence of one or more words is used in Suffix Tree Document (STD) model and was proposed by Zamir et al. It also allows clusters to overlap. In this the existing Keywords or bag of words are replaced by phrases to find the similarity and for creating clusters on the fly.

STC Algorithm

This algorithm was developed by Zamir and Etzioni (1998). Based on this algorithm they have developed the clustering engine named Grouper. Suffix Tree Clustering (STC) is a linear time clustering algorithm that is based on identifying the phrases that are common to groups of documents. A phrase is an ordered sequence of one or more words. The base cluster is a set of documents that share a common phrase.STC has three logical steps: (1) document "cleaning", (2) identifying base clusters using a suffix tree, and (3) combining these base clusters into clusters.

Step 1: Document "Cleaning".

In this step, the string of text representing each document is transformed using a light stemming algorithm (delete word prefixes and suffixes and reducing plural to singular).Sentence boundaries (identified via punctuation and HTML tags) are marked and non word tokens such as numbers, HTML tags and most punctuation are stripped.

Step 2: Identifying Base Clusters.

The identification of base clusters can be viewed as the creation of an inverted index of phrases for the document collection. This is done efficiently using a data structure called a suffix tree. This structure can be constructed in time linear with the size of the collection, and can be constructed incrementally as the documents are being read. The idea of using a suffix tree for document clustering was first introduced in 1997. Each node of the suffix tree represents a group of documents and a phrase that is common to all of them. Therefore, each node represents a base cluster. Furthermore, all possible base clusters (containing 2 or more documents) appear as nodes in our suffix tree. Each base cluster is assigned a score that is a function of the number of documents it contains and the words that make up its phrase.

Step 3: Combining Base Clusters.

Documents may share more than one phrase. As a result, the document sets of distinct base clusters may overlap and may even be identical. To avoid the proliferation of nearly identical clusters, the third step of the algorithm merges base clusters with a high overlap in their document sets, phrases are not considered in this step. The STC algorithm is incremental and order independent. As each document arrives from the Web, we 'clean' it and add it to the suffix tree. Each node that is updated (or created) as a result of this is tagged. We then update the relevant base clusters and recalculate the similarity of these base clusters to the rest of the base clusters. The final clusters are scored and sorted based on the scores of their base clusters and their overlap. As the final number of clusters can vary, the top few clusters need to be reported. Typically, only the top 10 clusters are of interest. For each cluster reported, the number of documents it contains, and the phrases of its base clusters. In STC, as documents may share more than one phrase with other documents, each document might appear in a number of base clusters. Therefore a document can appear in more than one cluster. Note that the overlap between clusters cannot be too high, otherwise they would have been merged into a single cluster.

Yahoo's API

Yahoo! (the company) provides many online services, most important of which is Yahoo! the search engine. BOSS (Build your Own Search Service) is Yahoo open search web services platform. The application is written in c# and is used to retrieve the top n results. This engine is useful for our system because it:

- Advertises a free API (over REST/XML), allowing it to be remotely queried from many programming languages and environments.
- Provides the title, URL and snippet of matched documents, which serve as a synopsis.
- Queries per Day is unlimited
- No Restrictions on Presentation
- Re-Ordering is allowed
- Blending of Proprietary and Yahoo! Search Content Allowed
- Key Terms / Query Suggestions

Some limitations of the API are that a maximum of 100 results per search and limitation is Per-IP query. Developers have expressed interest in altering the result order, removing results they do not want, and blending in their own data. All of these activities are allowed and encouraged with BOSS but not in the existing search API.

System Overview

In this framework, Information Retrieval System (IRS) and phrase based document clustering are combined together. Our system is active at the beginning and end of the search session and we follow a typical Service Oriented Architecture, with a consumer (our system) and provider (Yahoo!). Clustering techniques play an important role in searching and organization of web pages. In this paper we proposed an approach for web search results clustering based on a new document clustering algorithm. It is an alternative to a single ordered result of search engines. This approach presents a list of clusters to the user. This algorithm is used to generate the clusters to the users based on the shared phrases and is also used to re rank the clusters based on the score of the clusters. The proposed system is shown in Figure 1.

NOVEL DOCUMENT CLUSTERING

This method has three logical steps: (1) Search result fetching (2) Document pre processing (3) Build the suffix tree and selection of Base cluster (4) Merging base clusters (5) Scoring final clusters

1. Search result fetching.

The first step is to get the snippets of search results returned by a certain Web search engine.

Figure 1. Proposed system

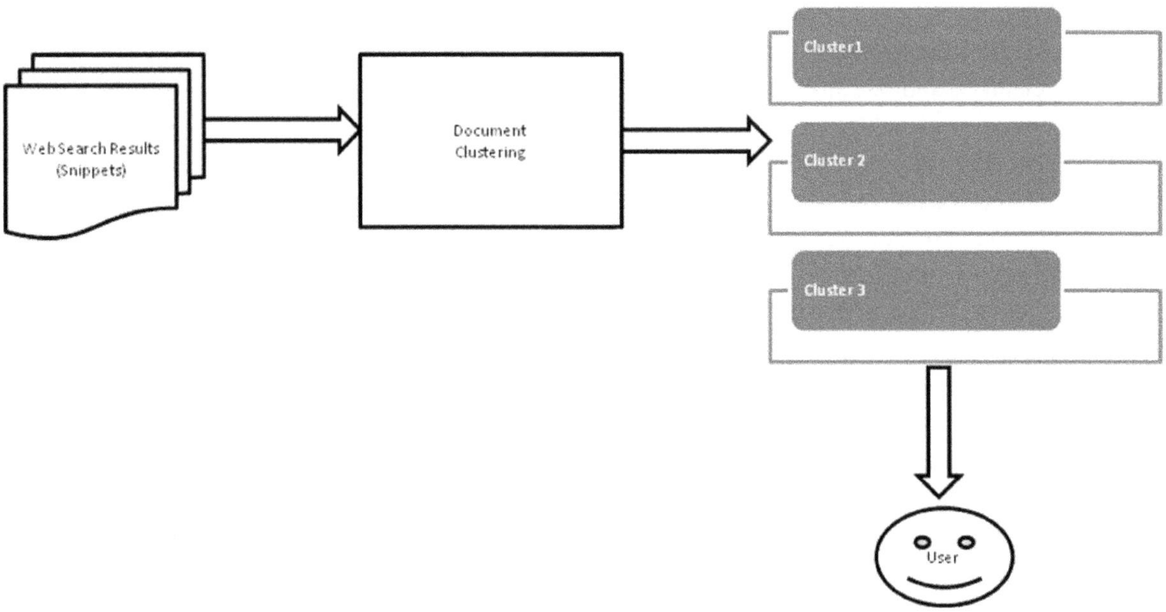

These snippets are analyzed and result items are extracted. We assume these contents are informative enough because most search engines are well designed to facilitate user's relevance judgment only snippet, thus it is able to present the most relevant contents for a given query. Each extracted phrase is in fact the name of a candidate cluster, which corresponds to a set of documents that contain the phrase.

2. Pre processing.

Pre-processing is selecting the most suitable terms that describe better content. The terms are transformed using stemming algorithm. Non-word tokens, such as articles, pronouns, prepositions, etc., are eliminated (Porter, 1980). The snippets are given to stop word removal module. As mentioned in the "document cleaning", stop words are removed from the given data. Extracted snippet information is given to STC module for insertion. The suffix tree data structure has been introduced as an efficient string processing technique. A suffix tree allows us to insert a string into the suffix tree incrementally.STC is available as a DLL here. The given snippets are splitted as mentioned in the STC algorithm and formed Suffix tree along with cluster information that also will be updated.

Stop words Lists and stemming algorithms are two commonly used information retrieval techniques for preparing text document. Stop words are useless to index or use in search engines or other search indexes because they are insignificant words and frequently occurring in the documents. There are some commonly occurring words slightly affecting the precision of the suffix tree similarity measures. Almost all popular document clustering algorithms including STC algorithm still prefer to consider these words as new stop words, and ignore them in their document similarity measure. Since the stopwords are stripped in the pre processing stage, that improves not only the veracity of the algorithm but also the speed of the algorithm for reducing the units of document.

Chim and Deng (2007) also proposed a new definition "stopnode", which applies the same idea of stopwords in the suffix tree similarity measure computation. A node with a high document frequency df can be ignored in the similarity measure, but the corresponding phrase and its words might be kept by other nodes in the suffix tree. In this paper, we adopt the same idea of "stopnode" instead of stopwords, which also prove to be efficient. For example, STC algorithm maintains a stoplist that is supplemented with Internet specific words in computing the score of each base cluster, e.g. \previous", \java", \frames" and \mail". Words appearing in the stoplist, or that appear in too few or too many documents receives a score of zero in computing the score S(B) of a base cluster. The main aim of pre processing is feature selection. The feature selection is included as an optimization is that it has a significant impact on clustering quality, larger than any other parameter described in this section.

3. Selection of base clusters.

Once the STC formation is completed, we evaluate the phrase importance by statistical method which is usually applied in VSD model. In this paper, the equation for computing an interesting score, shown in Equation 10, is modified from Chim and Deng (2007).

In Zamir's (1998) STC the score of the base cluster is calculated by:

$$S(B)= |B| * f(|P|) \quad (7)$$

where $|B|$ is the number of documents in B, and $|P|$ is the number of words in P. Then all base clusters are sorted by the scores, and the top k base clusters are selected for cluster merging. In this the properties of the phrases are not considered, hence it produces more number of base clusters.

According to Chim and Deng (2007), all the nodes n of the common suffix tree are mapped to a M dimensional space of VSD model (n = 1,2..........M), each document d can be represented as a feature vector of the weights of M nodes, d = {w(1,d),w(2,d),............w(M, d)}.

When we represent each document as a feature vector in the M dimensional space, it's very easy to understand that the document frequency of each node df(n) is the number of the different documents that have traversed node n; the term frequency tf(n; d) of a node n with respect to a document d is the total traversed times of document d through node n. The suffix tree constructed from documents usually contains lots of internal nodes (phrases). Not all internal nodes (phrases) are useful for document clustering, and some of the nodes (phrases) may give irrelevant results. So selecting a subset of original nodes as document features can reduce the high dimensionality of the feature space and also improve the accuracy of clustering results. For each internal node $n_{i,}$, the phrase designated by n_i is p_i. When we are constructing the suffix tree, use variable tf (p_i) accumulate the times traverse through the node n_i by the suffix in the documents corpus, then $tf(p_i)$ is the term frequency of phrase p_i ; the times of different documents that traverses through the node n_i is $df(p_i)$, then $df(p_i)$ is the document frequency. Therefore the weight of phrase p_i in documents corpus i.e., the weight w(n,d) of node n in document d can be calculated using the classic tf / idf scheme in formula (7), where N is the total number of documents in corpus.

$$tf / idf = \log(tf(p_i)) \cdot \log(N/df(p_i)) \quad (8)$$

These phrase frequency and inverse document frequency properties are supposed to be relative to the salience score of phrases. Intuitively, more frequent phrases are more likely to be better candidates of salient phrases; while phrases with higher document frequency might be less informative to represent a distinct topic.

A phrase is an ordered sequence of one or more words. The more number of words a phrase contains, the richer meaning it can express. Therefore, the importance of a phrase should incorporate a factor about the length of phrase $p_{i,}$ which designated by $|p_i|$. The phrase length property is simply the count of words in a phrase. For example, LEN("Computer")=1 and LEN("Information Retrieval Systems")=3. Generally, a longer name is preferred for users' browsing. We calculate the factor using a heuristic utility function in following formula:

$$f(|p_i|) = \log_2 |p_i| \quad (9)$$

The time cost for finding all nodes traversed by a suffix tree is decided by the length of its longest common prefix (LCP) in the suffix tree. The maximum length of LCPs in the suffix tree of standard documents is only 4 in our experimental data sets.

The score $s(n_i)$ of node n_i (phrase p_i) is given by formula(10).

$$S(n_i) = tf / idf \bullet f(|p_i|) . |d| \quad (10)$$

Where $|d|$ is the number of snippets in cluster $n_{i.}$ Then the base clusters containing the highest scoring phrases i.e., top n ranked base clusters should be selected for merging. The initial time complexity of cluster merging process is $O(n^2)$. To keep this cost as constant, the similarity is not calculated for all base clusters but only for top 'n' ranked base clusters. Here, the value of n= 500 was sufficient to ensure better performance.

4. Merging base Clusters.

For merging the base clusters, Zamir's STC defines a binary similarity measure between base clusters based on the overlap of their document sets. Given two base clusters Bm and Bn, with sizes $|Bm|$ and $|Bn|$ respectively, and representing the number of documents common to both base clusters. The similarity of Bm and Bn to be 1 if:

$$|Bm \cap Bn| / |Bm| > 0.5 \text{ and} \quad (11)$$

$$|Bm \cap Bn| / |Bn| > 0.5$$

Otherwise, their similarity is defined to be 0.

It is found that the "and" Boolean operator is not suitable in the following condition if one base cluster is the subset of the other i.e., Bm c Bn. So the "and" operator is changed to "or" operator:

$$|Bm \cap Bn| / |Bm| > \alpha \text{ or} \quad (12)$$

$$|Bm \cap Bn| / |Bn| > \alpha$$

This is essentially identical to Yang's (2004) improvement. Here the α varies from 0.4 to 0.9 and it shows better performance at α =0.6. A smaller α can result in a large number of merged clusters, but the similarity between the documents in the merged cluster is not strong. A bigger α can generate very similar documents in the same merged cluster, however, the number of the merged clusters is usually less. Since it uses the top n ranked base clusters for merging, only less number of clusters are formed than the existing method.

5. Scoring final clusters.

The score of the final cluster is calculated by

$$S(C) = \sum S_{ni} \quad (13)$$

ni € C

where ni is the base cluster belonging to final cluster(C).

The salience phrases are then ranked by the score. Then based on the scores of these base clusters, the final clusters are ranked. After salient phrases are ranked, the corresponding document lists constitute the candidate clusters, with the salient phrases being cluster names. Meanwhile, the cluster names are adjusted according to the new generated cluster i.e., any label or combination of labels in the merged cluster should be a good general description of the documents in the cluster. However, it is noted that some labels are the subsets of one another, which may be merged into the same clusters. We do not want to double count them. Labels created are based on these shared phrases and are more easily readable and understandable to the user. More specially, we choose the longest label first, and then choose the labels which are not the subsets of any selected labels. Finally, the topmost clusters are shown to user. When a user selects a cluster, the corresponding document list is shown to the user.

Experiments

In this section, we evaluate the effectiveness and efficiency of our algorithm by comparing it with the existing STC. The Standard test collections and also our own web documents dataset are also used to evaluate the performance. BOSS (Build your Own Search Service) is Yahoo's open search web services platform. The optimized query is given to yahoo API and it returns the top n documents i.e., the xml documents and it contains the URL's and snippets. Here, the value of n is set to 100 i.e., it represents the first 100 documents retrieved by the search engine.

The performance of the results are calculated for different values of similarity constant and it provides better performance at α =0.6. The STC algorithm does not require the user to specify the required number of clusters. However, we found that the performance of STC is not very sensitive to this threshold, unlike AHC algorithms that showed extreme sensitivity to the number of clusters required. We use C # to implement the algorithm, and use Excel to plot all figures.

Evaluation Measures

Performance measures of Information retrieval are precision and recall. Precision (P) is the fraction of retrieved documents that are relevant.

Precision = Relevant Items Retrieved / Retrieved Items (14)

Recall = Relevant Items Retrieved / Relevant Items (15)

We commonly used F-measure for evaluating and comparing different clustering results. F-measure combines the Precision and Recall ideas from the Information Retrieval literature. The precision and recall of a cluster j with respect to a "correct" class i are defined as:

P = Precision(i,j)= Nij / Nj (16)

R = Recall(i,j)= Nij / Ni (17)

where Nij: is the number of members of class i in cluster j,

- **Nj:** is the number of members of cluster j, and
- **Nj:** is the number of members of class i.

The standard F-measure F is used as an overall measure of how well the clustering matches the ideal clustering:

F = 2(P*R) / P+R (18)

Dataset Preparation

Due to lacks of standard dataset for testing web search results clustering, a small test dataset is built. For this purpose, we have been defined a set of queries such as computer, Internet, Database and so on, for which search results were collected from the search engine. We manually assigned a relevance judgement (relevant or not) to each document in these collections.

Web documents dataset are collected with the help of Yahoo API. Yahoo! Search BOSS (Build your Own Search Service) is an initiative in Yahoo! Search to open up Yahoo!'s search infrastructure and enable third parties to build revolutionary search products leveraging their own data, content, technology, social graph, or other assets. This release includes Web, News, and Image Search as well as Spelling Suggestions. Developers have expressed interest in altering the result order, removing results they do not want, and blending in their own data. All of these activities are allowed and encouraged with BOSS but not in the existing search API.

```
SYNTAX
http://boss.yahooapis.com/ysearch/
web/v1/{query}?appid={yourBOSSappid}
[&param1=val1&param2=val2&etc]
EX
http://boss.yahooapis.com/ysearch/
web/v1/animals?appid=12345&format=xml
&start=1&count=10
```

Where the parameter start represents the ordinal position of first result where first position is zero. The parameter count represents the total number of results to return; maximum value is 100. This API returns the XML, that dump the search results and it contains the URL, Title, Snippet, Description.

Results

In Figure 2 the average precision values of the existing STC and proposed STC are compared and it shows better precision value for the proposed system. These precision values are calculated for the web document datasets collected by the queries specified in Table 1.

Table 1. Queries used for evaluation

Query	No. of clusters
Anatomy of Computer Architecture	7
Why Computer Security is important	6
Advantages of Database Management System over File System	8
Uses of Internet	9
Various Programming Languages	5
Importance of Networking in an Organization	6
Advantages of Firewall Software	4
Data mining and Data warehousing	7
Multimedia Applications in Mobile Wireless	6
What is cloud computing	

Figure 2. Average precision of web document datasets

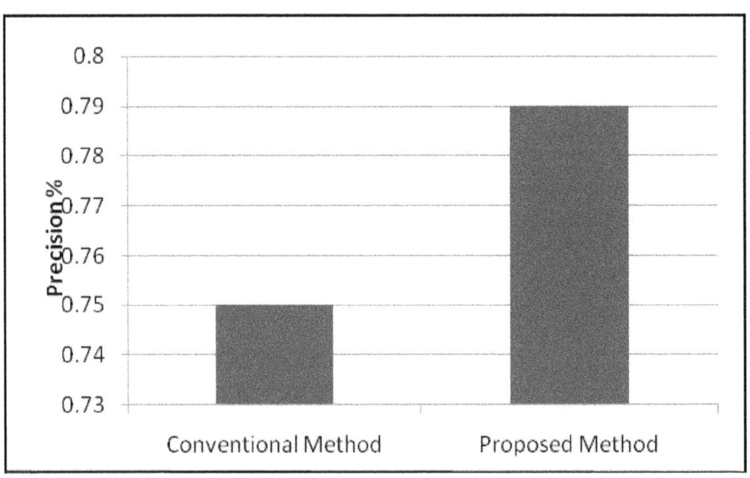

In this experiment, we submitted 10 different queries to the Google search engine and the search results of 100 snippets are collected for each query. After that, we created a suffix tree and merge the base clusters to get the final clusters of the query that is displayed to the user. While merging, the base clusters are merged with different values of α. This is essentially identical to Yang's (2004) improvement. Here the α varies from 0.4 to 0.9 and it shows better performance at α =0.6. And identified the documents which are not in any of the merged clusters, those are listed in a new cluster.

Figure 3 shows the average number of merged clusters for the similarity constant of different α values. This is given in detail under the subtopic "Merging Base Clusters". In "Equation (11)" the α is a threshold value for the similarity constant. The top n base clusters returned by the algorithm were evaluated with six different values of the similarity constant and it is good for α =0.6.

Table 1 shows the various 10 queries used to generate the web document datasets and the corresponding clusters generated for each query by using the proposed phrase clustering algorithm. The Figure 4 indicates the time taken to cluster

Figure 3. Comparison of similarity constant for the Query "computer"

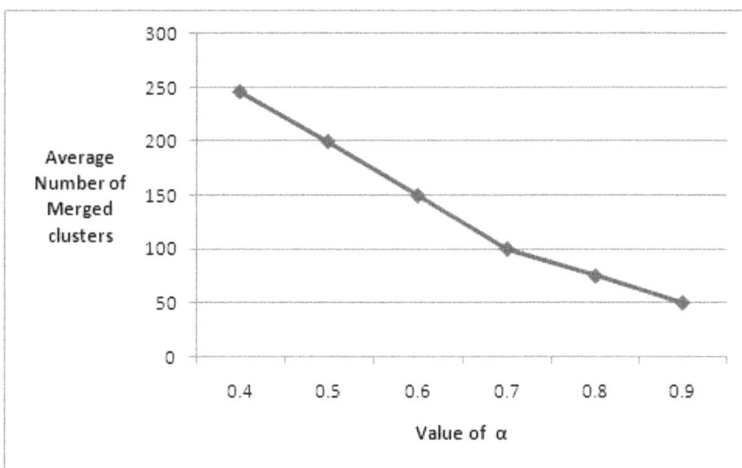

Figure 4.Time cost for cluster generation

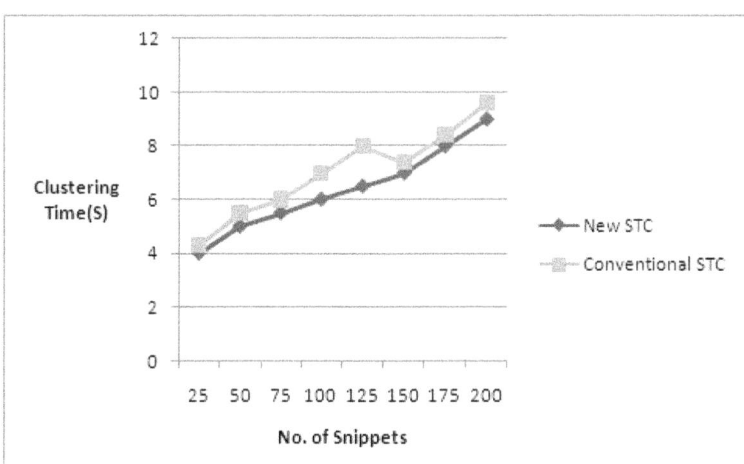

the number of documents and it is linearly increasing with the number of documents. In Figure 4 the time taken to cluster the snippets is comparatively less for the proposed method.

CONCLUSION

In this work we have shown a novel document clustering algorithm. We modified the STC by the new definition of cluster score. This method is mainly focused on improving the effectiveness of document clustering. As a synchronous wrapper around yahoo, the proposed system is inherently slower than Yahoo! According to the preliminary experiment results, the new approach provides smaller clusters and more readable cluster label than that approach using the previous STC algorithms. Further experiments are also necessary to confirm modified STC's apparent advantage over existing clustering algorithms. This is the enhanced experimental evaluation of clustering algorithms on Web search engine results.

REFERENCES

Baeza-Yates, R., & Ribeiro-Neto, B. (1999). *Modern information retrieval.* New York, NY: ACM Press.

Branson, S., & Greenberg, A. (2002). *Clustering web search results using suffix tree methods.* Retrieved from http://www.stanford.edu/class/cs276a/projects/reports/arigreen-sbranson.pdf

Chim, H., & Deng, X. (2007). A new suffix tree similarity measure for document clustering. In *Proceedings of the 16th International Conference on World Wide Web*, Banff, AB, Canada (pp. 121-130).

Cutting, D. R., Karger, D. R., Pedersen, J. O., & Tukey, J. W. (1992). Scatter/Gather: A cluster-based approach to browsing large document collections. In *Proceedings of the 15th International ACM SIGIR Conference on Research and Development in Information Retrieval* (pp. 318-329).

Hammouda, K. M., & Kamel, M. S. (2004). Efficient phrase-based document indexing for web document clustering. *IEEE Transactions on Knowledge and Data Engineering, 16*(10), 1279–1296. doi:10.1109/TKDE.2004.58

Hearst, M. A., & Pedersen, J. O. (1996). Reexamining the cluster hypothesis: Scatter/Gather on retrieval results. In *Proceedings of the 19th Annual International ACM SIGIR Conference on Research and Development in Information Retrieval,* Zurich, Switzerland (pp. 76-84).

Jansen, B. J. (2000). The effect of query complexity on web searching results. *Information Research, 6*(1).

Lee, D. L., Chuang, H., & Seamons, K. (1997). Documents ranking and the vector space model. *IEEE Software, 14*(2), 67–75. doi:10.1109/52.582976

Leuski, A., & Allan, J. (2000). Improving interactive retrieval by combining ranked list and clustering. In *Proceedings of the RIAO Conference,* Paris, France (pp. 665-681).

Liu, B., Chin, C. W., & Ng, H. T. (2003). Mining topic-specific concepts and definitions on the web. In *Proceedings of the Twelfth International World Wide Web Conference*, Budapest, Hungary (pp. 251-260).

Manning, C. D., Raghavan, P., & Schütze, H. (2008). *Introduction to information retrieval.* Cambridge, UK: Cambridge University Press.

Page, L., & Brin, S. (1998). The anatomy of a search engine. In *Proceedings of the 7th International WWW Conference*, Brisbane, Australia.

Porter, M. F. (1980). An algorithm for suffix stripping. *Program*, *14*(3), 130–137.

Salton, G. (1989). *Automatic text processing*. New York, NY: Addison-Wesley.

Salton, G., & Buckley, C. (1988). Term-weighting approaches in automatic text retrieval. *Information Processing & Management*, *24*(5), 513–523. doi:10.1016/0306-4573(88)90021-0

Supreethi, K. P., & Prasad, E. V. (2007). Web document clustering technique using case grammar structure. In *Proceedings of the International Conference on Computational Intelligence and Multimedia Applications* (pp. 98-102).

Turney, P. (1999). *Learning to extract keyphrases from text* (Tech. Rep. No. ERB-1057). Ottawa, ON, Canada: National Research Council of Canada.

Yang, J. W. (2004). A Chinese web page clustering algorithm based on the suffix tree. *Journal of National Sciences*, *9*(5), 817–822.

Zamir, O., & Etzioni, O. (1998). Web document clustering: A feasibility demonstration. In *Proceedings of the 19th International ACM SIGIR Conference on Research and Development of Information Retrieval* (pp. 46-54).

Zamir, O., & Etzioni, O. (1999). Grouper: A dynamic clustering interface to web search results. In *Proceedings of the Eighth International World Wide Web Conference*, Toronto, ON, Canada (pp. 1361-1374).

Zeng, H.-J., He, Q.-C., Chen, Z., Ma, W.-Y., & Ma, J. (2004). Learning to cluster web search results. In *Proceedings of the 27th Annual International ACM SIGIR Conference on Research and Development in Information Retrieval* (pp. 210-217).

This work was previously published in the International Journal of Information Retrieval Research, Volume 1, Issue 1, edited by Zhongyu (Joan) Lu, pp. 31-44, copyright 2011 by IGI Publishing (an imprint of IGI Global).

Chapter 4
Query Recommendation for Improving Search Engine Results

Hamada M. Zahera
Menoufiya University, Egypt

Gamal F. El-Hady
Menoufiya University, Egypt

W. F. Abd El-Wahed
Menoufiya University, Egypt

ABSTRACT

As web contents grow, the importance of search engines become more critical and at the same time user satisfaction decreases. Query recommendation is a new approach to improve search results in web. In this paper a method is proposed that, given a query submitted to a search engine, suggests a list of queries that are related to the user input query. The related queries are based on previously issued queries, and can be issued by the user to the search engine to tune or redirect the search process. The proposed method is based on clustering processes in which groups of semantically similar queries are detected. The clustering process uses the content of historical preferences of users registered in the query log of the search engine. This facility provides queries that are related to the ones submitted by users in order to direct them toward their required information. This method not only discovers the related queries but also ranks them according to a similarity measure. The method has been evaluated using real data sets from the search engine query log.

INTRODUCTION

With the increase of size and popularity of the World Wide Web, many users find it's difficult to get the desired information, although they use most efficient search engines (e.g. Google, Yahoo), (Tjondronegoro & Spink, 2008). Actually theses search engines allow users to specify queries simply as lists of keywords, following the approach of traditional information systems (Baeza-Yates & Ribeiro-Neto, 1999; Cambazoglu, 2010). But this list of keywords is not always a good descriptor of the needed information, therefore it was important to achieve user's stratification of

DOI: 10.4018/978-1-4666-3898-3.ch004

search engine results and make it easy to retrieve the required information (Hong, Siew, & Egerton, 2010; Höchstötter & Lewandowski, 2009). The problem of improving search engine results and obtaining the desired information from this huge amount of web contents has been processed by different ways such as clustering the search engine results in specific topics so the user can find the required results in selected category of search results (Chen, 2010; Caramia & Pezzoli, 2004). Although, the user doesn't use the proper search words or search query while searching so this leads to a problem of getting un-required results and the user have to be familiar with specific terminology in a knowledge domain (Baeza-Yates, Hurtado, & Mendoza, 2004). This is not always the case of many users; they have only a little background about the information they are searching and unfortunately they didn't get the required results. In order to overcome this problem, it's not enough to use clustering search results method because the problem is not in obtaining the huge results but it's in the keywords used in searching are not strongly related (Baeza-Yates, Hurtado, & Mendoza, 2004). Query recommendation suggests related queries for search engine users when they are not satisfied with the results of an initial input query, thus assisting users in improving search quality (Giacometti, Marcel, & Negre, 2009). Conventional approaches to query recommendation have been focused on expanding a query by terms extracted from various information sources such as a thesaurus like WordNet (Li, Otsuka, & Kitsuregawa, 2008; Chatzopoulou, Eirinaki, & Polyzotis, 2009).

The previous queries stored in query logs can be a source of additional evidence to help future users. A query recommendation system based on large-scale Web access logs and web page archive, and evaluate three query recommendation strategies based on different feature spaces (i.e., noun, URL, and Web community) has been presented (Li, Otsuka, & Kitsuregawa, 2008). The suggested Method aimed to help search engine users in finding their required results easily and quickly, this method suggests related queries beside the input query while the user searches so he can build a proper search query with the knowledge domain terminology which is important for search engine to get the related results. Also the additional time for improving the results must be unnoticeable by the user.

This paper discuses in details the proposed method for recommending list of queries are related to input query user which based on clustering process over web queries extracted from search engine query log file.

RELATED WORK

Yates (2004) has done a survey in to show the different improvements of search engine aspects (Wen, Nie, & Zhang, 2001) presented an algorithm for clustering search engine queries according to four notions according to: first, the context of the query; second, common clicked URLs between queries; third, Similar strings between the queries and fourth, the distance of the clicked documents in some pre-defined hierarchy. Beeferman and Berger (2000) suggested a technique for query clustering based on the third notion. Fonseca, Golgher, De Moura, and Ziviani (2003) presented a new method to discover the related queries which are based on association rules .The queries represent items in tradition association rules. The query log file is considered as a collection of transactions which represent a session in which the user submit all related queries in a specific time .The method showed good results, nevertheless arising of two problems .The first problem is the difficulty of determining which sessions of these queries that are belong to the same search process. The second problem the related queries which are submitted by different users can't be discovered .This is because the support of a rule increases only of its queries are in the same session and they must by submitted by the same user.

Hosseini and Abolhassani (2008) have described a method for recommending associated queries according to clustering process over web queries from search engines query log. Zaiane and Strilets (2002) presented a method for recommending queries according to seven aspects of query similarity, Three of them are moderated variations of the first and second notions .In addition our method recommend the related queries to the input query but my search for different issues like the previous information from query log file (Gayo-Avello, 2009). There is anther approach to suggest related queries by query expansion. The researchers show that average query terms are near two (Jansen, Spink, Bateman, & Saracevic, 1998). So most of the time, queries are ambiguous. One possible solution for this problem is to expand a query with new terms. Query clustering helps to find relevant terms for this expansion which can be applied in two ways: First Query expansion in terms of similar queries. Scand expansion in terms of selected pages of similar queries.

DESCRIPTION OF THE METHOD

In this section, we will describe the proposed method, in order to compute the similarity between queries, we first build a term-weighted vector for each query. Each term is weighted according to the number of occurrences and the number of clicks of the documents in which the term appears. All previous queries stored in the query file are considered with their clicked URLs to recommend the users with the related queries to the input query. Scand we consider Queries and URLs clicked as a bipartite graph, the nodes of one side for queries and the nodes on the other side for clicked URLs. Figure 1, for example, shows a sample of such graph when the left nodes denote queries and the right nodes denote URLs, so that it will be clear which are the URLs clicked with the query submitted by the users (Hosseini, M., Abolhassani, H, 2007). We symbolize the graph by *G (V, E)* where *V* is the set of all vertices of queries (*Q*) and URLs *(U), E* is the set of edges between *Q* and *U*. The graph *G (V, E)* is a bipartite graph among two vertex classes such *Q* and *U* while $Q \cup U = V$ and $Q \cap U = \varphi$, and each edge in *E* connects between the query issued by user and the clicked URLs has one endpoint in *Q* and one endpoint in *U*.

Figure 1. Query-URL representation as bipartite graph

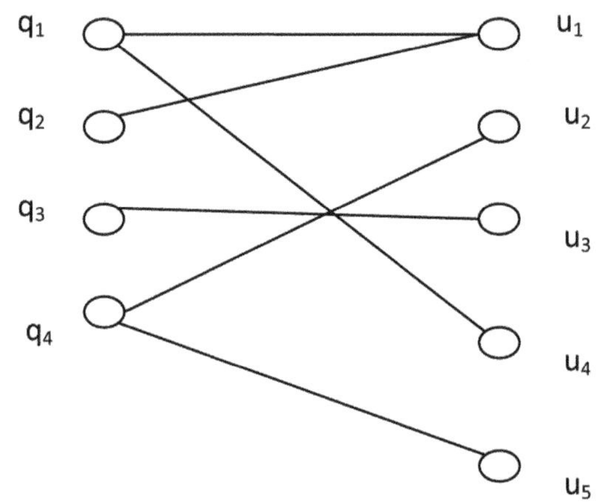

It's important to set a weight for every edge between *Q* and *U* to show the importance of this edge and distinguish between other edges.

We considered weighted bipartite graph as *G (V, E, W)* where *W* is number of clicked on the link *U* when the query *Q* is submitted by the user, and $W_{ij} > 0$ when there is edge between vertex *i* and *j* otherwise $W_i = 0$. Queries along with the clicked URLs extracted from Query log are clustered. This is a preprocessing phase before applying query recommendation algorithm which queries are similar and also to determine which the most similar cluster to the input query is. We compute the clusters by k-mean algorithm because of its simplicity and it's more appreciated for document clustering (Zhao & Karypis, 2002) compared with other algorithms for document clustering (Li, Chung, & Holt, 2008).

QUERY RECOMMENDING ALGORITHM

In our research work, we applied an algorithm to recommend related queries to a query submitted by the user.

The clustering process aims to categorize all related queries into groups based on all information in the query log file. When the user submit a query, the algorithm finds the proper group of related queries and ranks them according to it's relevance to the user input query and finally it suggests all previous related queries to the user. The Query Recommendation Algorithm works as the following steps:

1. Queries and Their clicked URLs extracted from the search engine query log file are clustered by k-mean algorithm.
2. While the user submit an input query, the algorithm finds the similar cluster to the input query ;how it's close the centroied of which cluster
3. **Query Vectorization:** In which each query is represented as a vector where j^{th} element represent between the query and URL j. a query vector is shown in (1)

$$\vec{q}_i = [r_1, r_2, r_3, ...r_j] \quad (1)$$

where r_i the relation value between Q and URLj, it's computed as shown in (2)

$$r_j = \frac{w_{i_j}}{\sum_{k=1}^{n} w_{kj}} \times \log\left(\frac{|L|}{\sum_{k=1}^{m} connect(q_i, l_j)}\right) \quad (2)$$

where n is the total number of unique queries and m is the total number of distinct URLs. The first part of (2) is the ration between w_{ij} (number of click times) and total number of w_{ij} for all queries with the URL j. The second part is the logarithm of the ration between $|L|$ (total number of distinct URLs) to the number of URLs which $connect(q_i, l_j)$ is a Boolean function as shown in (3)

$$connect(q_i, l_j) = \begin{cases} 1 & ; w_{ii} > 0 \\ 0 & ; w_{ij} = 0 \end{cases} \quad (3)$$

4. **Similarity of the Query:** Measuring the similarity of the query to the input query is depend on the relation between Queries and URLs. Each query is considered as a vector, depicted in equation (1), which the features are relation between the Query and URLs computed with equation (2), so we measure the similarity by using Tanimoto coefficient similarity measure to show how two queries are similar together as shown in (4)

$$T(q_i, q_j) = \frac{\vec{q}_i \cdot \vec{q}_j}{|\vec{q}_i|^2 + |\vec{q}_j|^2 - \vec{q}_i \cdot \vec{q}_j} \quad (4)$$

5. **Support of the Query:** This is a measure of how the query is relevant in the cluster. The support of the query is measured as the ratio of the number of clicked URLs returned by the query that captured the attention of users (clicked URLs). It is estimated from the query log and computed as equation (5), where |Li| is the number of clicked URLs for q_i that is member of cluster C.

$$Sup(q_i) = \frac{|L_i|}{\sum_{j \in C} |L_i|} \quad (5)$$

Finally, the queries in the selected cluster are ranked base on linear combined between similarity and support; the rank score is measured as shown in equation (6) where the similarity between all queries in the cluster q_i and the input query q. The term constants α and β used for normalization .

$$Rank(q_i) = \alpha \times T(q_i, q) + \beta \times Sup(q_i) \quad (6)$$

EXPERIMENTAL RESULTS

In our experiments, a query log of the America OnLine's (AOL) search engine was used for collecting click through data. A record on this query log represents the visit to a result for a query or the submission of a query (if no result is visited), (Brenes & Gayo-Avello, 2009; Bhargava, & Feng, 2005).

Each record store:

- An anonymous ID that allows to group queries from the same user without revealing the AOL user's nickname
- Query submitted by the user.
- Date and time of the submission of the query
- Rank position of the result visited by the user on each record.

Examples of this record can be found in Table 1 and a full description of the AOL query log is illustrated in (Pass, Chowdhury, & Torgeson, 2006).

In order to evaluate our similarity measure, we compared it with the Cosine similarity which has been used by Mehdi and Hassan [8]. We extracted 10,000 queries from AOL dataset for clustering. After constructing the clusters we select ten queries of the clustered dataset: (1) weather; (2) newspaper; (3) computer Software; (4) airline flights; (5) scholarships; (6) Nobel award; (7) five star hotels; (8) human development books; (9) MIT universities; (10) migrations. All the selected queries are sent to the recommendation algorithm in order to suggest useful queries for the user. In addition to that, the suggest queries are ranked according to rank score which is calculated by Eq.6 with parameters α =0.8 and β =0.2.

Table 2, shows the quality of ranking based on two different similarity measure: Cosine similarity used by (Hosseini & Abolhassani, 2008) and our similarity measure (Tanimoto coefficient measure).In this example, the algorithm recommend 6 related queries to the input query "scholarship".

In Figure 2, we compared the ranking of results based on cosine similarity measure (Hosseini & Abolhassani, 2008), and Tanimoto coefficient similarity measure to show the efficiency of ranking. Cosine similarity has overestimate measure-

Table 1. Example of AOL log queries

User ID	Query	Time	Visited URLs
123	Computer virus	2006-03-08 12:21:23	http://www.microsoft.com/security/antivirus/whatis.aspx http://www.howstuffworks.com/virus.htm http://www.snopes.com/computer/virus/virus.asp .....
154	Funny videos	2006-05-12 02:12:32	http://www.break.com/ http://www.funnyordie.com/ http://www.dailyhaha.com/ .....
217	Albert Einstein	2006-08-17 05:19:05	http://www.westegg.com/einstein/ http://www.albert-einstein.org/

Table 2. Recommended queries for "scholarship"

Query	Recommended Query	Similarity by Tanimoto	Similarity by Cosine	Rank Score by Tanimoto	Rank Score by Cosine
Q1	International scholarship	0.958	0.98	0.791	0.808
Q2	Grants and fellowships	0.921	0.989	0.765	0.82
Q3	Fulbright Scholarship	0.651	0.987	0.549	0.818
Q4	Study abroad chances	0.117	0.257	0.122	0.234
Q5	Scholarship programs	0.62	0.794	0.525	0.664
Q6	Full funded scholarship	0.422	0.743	0.366	0.623

Figure 2. Ranking efficiency between Tanimoto and Cosine Similarity

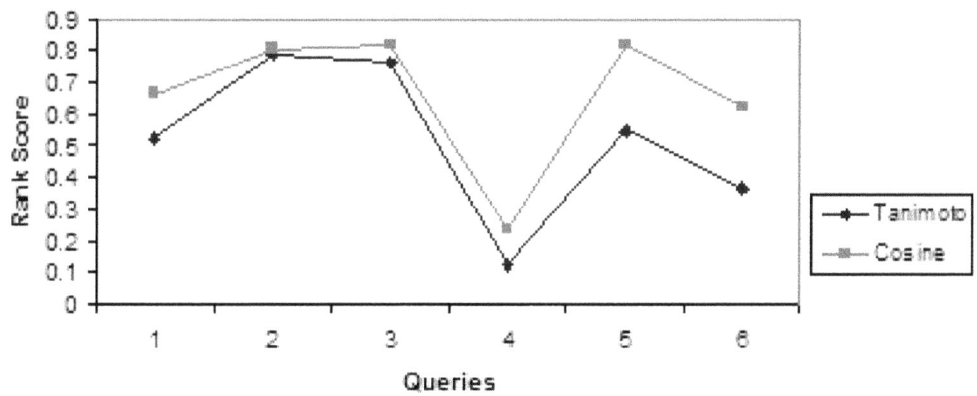

ments of query similarity as we see query 2 "Grants and fellowships" is more similar to user query "Scholarships" rather than query1 "International scholarships". Although query 2 is semantically equal to the user query, but query 1 is much better because it has the most similar string and mean to the user query. Therefore this measure affect on result ranking of search engine by using Tanimoto coefficient in similarity measurement has more precision and accuracy in ranking the search engine results.

CONCLUSION AND FUTURE WORK

We have presented a method for recommending the related queries to the input based on clustering process over the web queries extracted from a search engine query log. We are doing the experimentations with larger logs more than used and considering more queries to improve the evaluations of our approach. In addition, we are trying to expand the queries using the keywords related to the cluster Also we consider the improvement of Similarity by considering the clicks in query answer to documents that are similar to the input query

As future work, we consider to improve the notion of attention of the suggested queries and to expand other notions of interest for the recommendation algorithm. For example finding the queries which share words but not have common clicked URLs, this might involve the same words but have different meanings if the text of the URLs also is not share. Hence we can know polysomic words.

REFERENCES

Baeza-Yates, R., Hurtado, C., & Mendoza, M. (2004). Query recommendation using query logs in search engines. In W. Lindner, M. Mesiti, C. Turker, Y. Tzitzikas, & A. Vakali (Eds.), *Proceedings of International Workshop on Current Trends in Database Technology* (LNCS 3268, pp. 395-397).

Baeza-Yates, R., & Ribeiro-Neto, B. (1999). *Modern information retrieval*. New York, NY: Addison-Wesley.

Beeferman, D., & Berger, A. (2000). Agglomerative clustering of a search engine query log. In *Proceedings of the Sixth ACM SIGKDD International Conference on Knowledge Discovery and Data Mining* (pp. 407-416).

Bhargava, H. K., & Feng, J. (2005). America OnLine's Internet access service: How to deter unwanted customers. *Electronic Commerce Research and Applications*, *4*(1), 35–48. doi:10.1016/j.elerap.2004.10.008

Brenes, D., & Gayo-Avello, D. (2009). Stratified analysis of AOL query log. *Information Sciences*, *179*, 1844–1858. doi:10.1016/j.ins.2009.01.027

Cambazoglu, B. B. (2010). Review of search engines: Information retrieval in practice by Croft, Metzler And Strohman. *Information Processing & Management*, *46*, 377–379. doi:10.1016/j.ipm.2009.12.009

Caramia, G. F., & Pezzoli, A. (2004). Improving search results with data mining in a thematic search engine. *Computers & Operations Research*, *31*, 2387–2404. doi:10.1016/S0305-0548(03)00194-1

Chatzopoulou, G., Eirinaki, M., & Polyzotis, N. (2009). Query recommendations for interactive database exploration. In *Proceedings of the 21st International Conference on Scientific and Statistical Database Management*, New Orleans, LA (pp. 3-18).

Chen, L.-C. (2010). Using a new relational concept to improve the clustering performance of search engines. *Information Processing & Management*, 1–13.

Fonseca, B., Golgher, P., De Moura, E., & Ziviani, N. (2003, November). Using association rules to discovery search engines related queries. *In Proceedings of the First Latin American Web Congress*, Santiago, Chile (p. 66). Washington, DC: IEEE Computer Society.

Gayo-Avello, D. (2009). A survey on session detection methods in query log and a proposal for future evaluation. *Information Sciences*, *179*(12), 1822–1843. doi:10.1016/j.ins.2009.01.026

Giacometti, A., Marcel, P., & Negre, E. (2009). Recommending multidimensional queries. In T. Pedersen, M. Mohania, & A. M. Tjoa (Eds.), *Proceedings* of *the 11th International Conference on Data Warehousing and Knowledge Discovery,* Linz, Austria (LNCS 5691, pp. 453-466).

Höchstötter, N., & Lewandowski, D. (2009). What users see – structures in search engine results pages. *Information Sciences*, *179*, 1796–1812. doi:10.1016/j.ins.2009.01.028

Hong, J. L., Siew, E.-G., & Egerton, S. (2010). Information extraction for search engines using fast heuristic techniques. *Data & Knowledge Engineering*, *69*, 169–196. doi:10.1016/j.datak.2009.10.002

Hosseini, M., & Abolhassani, H. (2007). Hierarchical co-clustering for web queries and selected URLs. In B. Benatallah, F. Casati, D. Georgakopoulos, C. Bartolini, W. Sadiq, & C. Godart (Eds.), *Proceedings of the 8th International Conference on Web Information Systems Engineering* (LNCS 4831, pp. 653-662).

Hosseini, M., & Abolhassani, H. (2008). Clustering search engines log for query recommendation. In Sarbazi-Azad, H., Parhami, B., Miremadi, S.-G., & Hessabi, S. (Eds.), *Advances in computer science and engineering* (*Vol. 6*, pp. 380–387). Berlin, Germany: Springer-Verlag. doi:10.1007/978-3-540-89985-3_47

Jansen, D., Spink, A., Bateman, J., & Saracevic, T. (1998). Real life information retrieval: A study of user queries on the web. *ACM SIGIR Forum*, *32*(1), 5–17. doi:10.1145/281250.281253

Li, L., Otsuka, S., & Kitsuregawa, M. (2008). Query recommendation using large-scale web access logs and web page archive. In S. Bhowmick, J. Kung, & R. Wagner (Eds.), *Proceedings of the 19th International Conference on Database and Expert Systems Applications* (LNCS 5181, pp.134-141).

Li, Y., Chung, S. M., & Holt, J. D. (2008). Text document clustering based on frequent word meaning sequences. *Data & Knowledge Engineering*, *64*(1), 381–404. doi:10.1016/j.datak.2007.08.001

Pass, G., Chowdhury, A., & Torgeson, C. (2006). A picture of search. In *Proceedings of the First International Conference on Scalable Information Systems* (pp. 1-7).

Tjondronegoro, D., & Spink, A. (2008). Multimedia search engine functionality: An exploratory study. *Information Processing & Management*, *44*(1), 340–357. doi:10.1016/j.ipm.2007.03.004

Wen, J., Nie, J., & Zhang, H. (2001). Clustering user queries of a search engine. In *Proceedings of the 10th International World Wide Web Conference* (pp. 162-168).

Yates, R. (2004). Query usage mining in search engines. In Scime, A. (Ed.), *Web mining: applications and techniques*. Hershey, PA: IGI Global. doi:10.4018/9781591404149.ch014

Zaiane, O., & Strilets, A. (2002). Finding similar queries to satisfy searches based on query traces. In J.-M. Bruel & Z. Bellahsene (Eds.), *Proceedings of the International Workshop on Advances in Object-Oriented Information Systems,* Montpellier, France (LNCS 2426, pp. 349-359).

Zhao, Y., & Karypis, G. (2002). Comparison of agglomerative and partitional document clustering algorithms. In *Proceedings of the SIAM Workshop on Clustering High-dimensional Data and its Applications.*

This work was previously published in the International Journal of Information Retrieval Research, Volume 1, Issue 1, edited by Zhongyu (Joan) Lu, pp. 45-52, copyright 2011 by IGI Publishing (an imprint of IGI Global).

Chapter 5
XML Documents Normalization Using GN-DTD

Zurinahni Zainol
University of Hull, UK, & Universiti Sains Malaysia, Malaysia

Bing Wang
University of Hull, UK

ABSTRACT

Designing a well-structured XML document is important for the sake of readability, maintainability and more importantly to avoid both data redundancies and update anomalies. This paper proposes to improve and simplify XML structural design using a normalization process. To achieve this, Graphical Notation for Document Type Definition (GN-DTD) is used to describe the structure of XML document at the schema level. Multiple levels of normal forms for GN-DTD are proposed and the corresponding normalization rules to transform from poorly designed into well-designed XML documents. A case study is presented to show the application of these normal forms and normalization algorithm.

1. INTRODUCTION

Like managing traditional database, the management of XML documents require capabilities to handle with integrity, consistency, data dependency, data redundancy and anomalies (Arenas & Libkin, 2004; Dobbie et al., 2000; Embley & Mok, 2001; Vincent et al., 2004, 2007; Wang & Topor, 2005; Yu & Jagadish, 2008). Amongst the important problem related to XML design that needed to be looked into are data redundancy and update anomalies (Arenas & Libkin, 2004; Yu & Jagadish, 2008). Data redundancy and anomalies can happen in XML document if the schemas: DTD (Document Type Definitions) (Powell, 2007) or XML schema (Tompson et al., 2008), are not well-designed. These schemas allow one to define the structure, the content and the semantic of XML document. In this work, we consider only DTD since it is expressive enough for a large variety of applications and has been widely studied in database theory (Arenas & Libkin, 2004).

The design problem for XML document has recently been a subject of interest for database researchers, and a number of normal forms have been proposed to reduce data redundancies

DOI: 10.4018/978-1-4666-3898-3.ch005

caused by functional or multi-valued dependencies (Arenas & Libkin, 2004; Feng et al., 2002; Mani et al., 2001;Vincent et al., 2004; Wang & Topor, 2005; Yu & Jagadish, 2008). However, XML normal form XNF, proposed by (Arenas & Libkin, 2004) achieves the best possible design form the point of view of eliminating redundancies in XML documents (Kolahi, 2007). But, there are problems with this definition of normal forms and normalization process. Firstly, the notions of XML normal forms are presented in a difficult term to be understood and hard to be implemented practically because of the lack of graphical notations for the proposed theories. Secondly; the current approach of XML normal form did not show the tremendous benefit to practitioners and thirdly; the normalization algorithms only works for the existing normal form which has a very limited semantic expressiveness.

In this paper, we propose to improve and simplify XML structural design and normalization process using graphical model called GN-DTD (Zainol & Wang, 2010). We define multi levels normal forms for GN-DTD to allow users to find an 'optimal' structure of XML elements/attributes and to produce a correct, complete and consistent representation of the real world XML data which may interest to the user.

GN-DTD is a graphical modelling approach for describing XML documents. For GN-DTD itself, we define a complete set of syntax and structure which incorporate of attribute identity, simple data type, complex data type and relationship types among elements. Furthermore, semantic constraints are also precisely defined in order to capture semantic meaning among those defined objects. The significance of using GN-DTD model is that, it helps user to arrange the content of XML document in order to give a better understanding of its corresponding DTD structures. DTD commonly represented as textual representation, hence it is particularly difficult to be analysed and understood. In practise, it often causes difficulties when even designing a simple DTD. This is partly due to textual form of the grammar itself. Because of using these GN-DTD's notations, we found it is particularly easily to improve XML structural design and more importantly, make the XML normalization procedure simpler and practical.

The rest of the paper is organized as follows. Section 2 provides a brief overview of GN-DTD's syntax and semantic. Section 3 presents multiple levels of normal forms for GN-DTD. The normalization procedure of XML document based on GN-DTD is presented in section 4. A case study is given in section 5 to illustrate the application of normal forms and normalization rules. Section 6 and 7 discuss the related work.

2. BACKGROUND

Some of the notations of GN-DTD have been adopted and improved from the current data model ORA-SS (Dobbie et al., 2000) notations and conventional ER model (Chen, 1976). The significant difference between GN-DTD and the other models is complex element, simple element, and attribute nodes are explicitly distinguished. This is because such distinction is crucial for clarifying the semantics of the data. More importantly, GN-DTD provides an explicit semantic relationships definition to allow the user to define semantic relationship between nodes. The GN-DTD allows users to define the structure of nodes in a hierarchical way. We have made the ordering of sub-elements significant by treating them as a set, sequence (list) or disjunction. The GN-DTD model is briefly discussed in the following section. The details of the GN-DTD specification can be found in (Zainol & Wang, 2010).

2.1. Syntax and Semantics of GN-DTD

Graphical Notation for Data Type Definition (GN-DTD) graphical modelling (Zainol & Wang, 2010) consists of six basic components:

Complex Element Nodes

A complex element node is used to represent a set of elements which have another sub element and attribute. The complex element node is illustrated as labelled rectangle box. This notation is adopted from the ER model (Chen, 1976) which is similar to entity. The label is written in the rectangle box as a tuple *<name,level>*, where *name* represents the name of the node and *level* represent the depth of the node in GN-DTD. The name is mandatory.

Simple Element Nodes

A simple element node is used to represent an element associated with #PCDATA or #CDATA. It is illustrated as a labeled rounded rectangle box with the form *<name,level,type>* where *name* is the name of the simple element, *level* is the depth of the node in the GN-DTD and *type* represents PCDATA or CDATA or string 'S' . All simple element nodes are assumed to be mandatory and single valued, unless the node contains the symbol ? which signifies it is single value and optional, or + which signifies that it is multi-valued and required, or an * which shows that it is optional and multi-valued. This notation is similar to ORA-SS (Dobbie et al., 2000). The symbol is written in front of the tuple *<name,level,type>* to differentiate among them accordingly.

Attribute Nodes

Attribute nodes are used to represent attributes defined in *ATTLIST*, which describe the properties of a complex element node. An attribute node is an identifier for a complex element node. It is represented as ID which is unique and mandatory among the instances of complex element. Attributes can be classified as single attributes and composite attributes. A single identifier attribute has an atomic value and composite attributes have more than one identifier attributes. A single identifier attribute is represented as an oval and a composite attribute as a double oval.

Set Relationship Type

Two types of link exist in GN-DTD: Inheritance link and Part- of Link

Inheritance link

The inheritance link is a relationship between complex element node and another complex element node. This link shows inheritance between parent nodes to child nodes or ancestor node to descendant node. For inheritance relationships, a semantic meaning, which is indicated by the connectivity between complex element occurrences, is important. The connectivity of a relationship specifies the mapping of the associated complex element occurrence in a relationship. Basic constructs for connectivity are: one-to-one (unary or binary relationship), one-to-many (unary or binary relationship), and many-to-one, many-to-many (unary or binary relationship). All these type of relationships are indicated by directional arrows. To differentiate among them, both cardinality constraint and degree are attached to the arrow. The notation as presented as (name, d, cp,cc) where name represents the name of the relationship, d is the degree of relationship, cp and cc are cardinality constraints for parent and child respectively. This notation is similar to ORA-SS (Dobbie et al., 2000).

- **Degree of Relationship:** Degree of relationship is the number of complex elements associated with the relationship. An n-ary relationship is of degree n. Unary, binary and ternary relationships are special cases in which the degree is 1, 2, and 3, respectively.
- **Cardinality Constraint for Complex Element:** To reveal more semantics in their relationship, the cardinality constraint is associated with the inheritance link. The same rule applies for cardinality constraints for both parent node (cp) and child node (cc). Here cardinality of com-

plex elements in a relationship is represented as a 2 tuple (min:max). The constraint (0:N), (0:1)and (1:N) is represent as the operators *, respectively except cardinality constraint (1:1) is presented as 1. This relationship cardinality constraint is indicated using a directional arrow: For instance, the diagram in Figure 1 illustrates a binary inheritance relationship between complex element student and complex element courses where a student can take zero or many courses while many courses can be taken by zero or many students.

Part-of Link

Part-of link is divided into two types: Part-of link attribute is a relationship between a complex element node and attribute node. This is a mandatory relationship. It is illustrated as a bold double arrow. Part-of link simple element is a relationship between a complex element node and a simple element node. It is illustrated as a single double arrow. For instance, attribute identifier for a complex element is linked as a one-to-one relationship.

Semantic Constraint Between Set Relationships.

There are two types of set relationships: First, sequence between a set of child elements nodes. We emphasise in our notation that the attribute node(s) must be located in the first position in the sequence. For instance, the notation *sequence* is used to capture the list of the first author and the second author of a book. To express such ordering in a GN-DTD, we draw a directed upwardly curving arrow labelled with {sequence} across all the set of relationships involved. Second, disjunction between the set of sibling nodes. To illustrate this, we draw a line labelled with {XOR} across all the set of relationships involved.

Figure 1. Many-to-many binary relationship

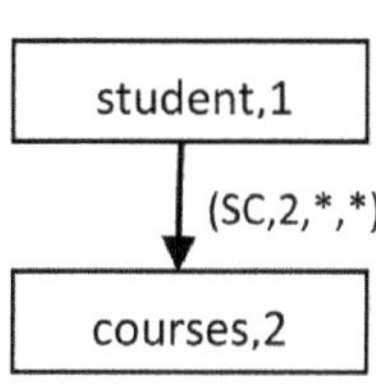

A Root Node

Root node notation is similar to complex element notation where it is a special case of a complex element node and its level is always zero.

A Last Node

A last node notation is similar to attribute and simple elements notation where their level is at n-1.

Let us consider a DTD in Figure 2 which describes a university database. This DTD specifies the set of elements allowed in the XML document, and for each element it specifies the set of sub elements and attributes. For example, the text segment *<!ELEMENT department(course*)>* is an element declaration that represent the subelement of each element of type *department* has a grammar regular expression of *course**. If an element structure is desribed as *#PCDATA*, it means that the elements of this type contain string data. The attributes of each element are represented using *ATTLIST* declaration. A *DOCTYPE* declaration

Figure 2. A DTD for the university database

```
<!DOCTYPE department[
    <!ELEMENT department(course*)>
    <!ELEMENT course(title, student*)>
      <!ATTLIST course cno ID #REQUIRED>
    <!ELEMENT title (#PCDATA)>
    <!ELEMENT student(fname|lname?,lecturer)>
        <!ATTLIST student  Sno ID #REQUIRED
    <!ELEMENT fname(#PCDATA) >
    <!ELEMENT lname(#PCDATA) >
    <!ELEMENT lecturer (tname)>
        <!ATTLIST lecturer  tno ID #REQUIRED>
    <!ELEMENT tname (#PCDATA)>
]>
```

represents the root element of the XML document. More specifically, this DTD has the following information:

- Each department offers many courses indicated by the notation *.
- Every course is described by the attribute course no (cno), title and numbers of students taking the course.
- Each student has a student number (sno), first name or last name as optional and an assigned lecturer.
- Each lecturer has his/her number (tno), and name (tname).

Figure 3 shows GN-DTD describing the structure of an XML document corresponding to DTD in Figure 2. Root node Department has a binary inheritance relationship with the complex element node course. The semantic relationship between them reveals that the Department can have one-to-many courses at one time. The complex element course has a sequence of attribute cno, simple element node title and complex element node student. The part-of link attribute is a mandatory relationship where the attribute node cno is required and unique for every course in the XML document. The simple element node title is part-of the complex element courses. One course can be taken by many students while the complex element student consists of a sequence of attribute node sno, simple elements fname, lname and complex element lecturer. Attribute node sno is required for the complex element student. Complex element node student requires only one of its subelements either fname or lname to appear in the XML document while the simple element lname is optional. The semantic relationship between course, student and lecturer is indicated as a ternary relationship since each student is assigned to a lecturer who is teaching the course.

Attribute *tno* is required while simple element *tname* is mandatory and string S denotes a node is a type PCDTA. Attribute key *tno* and simple element *tname* are the last node in GN-DTD. The level of each node is indicated explicitly in the model.

The XML document in Figure 4 is an instance of GN-DTD in Figure 3. However, this XML document is likely to contain data redundancies which may lead to update anomalies. As shown in Figure 4, *student* name "David Grey" and both *lecturer* name "Bing" and "Bottaci" have appeared twice in the document. This means that, if we want to

Figure 3. GN-DTD

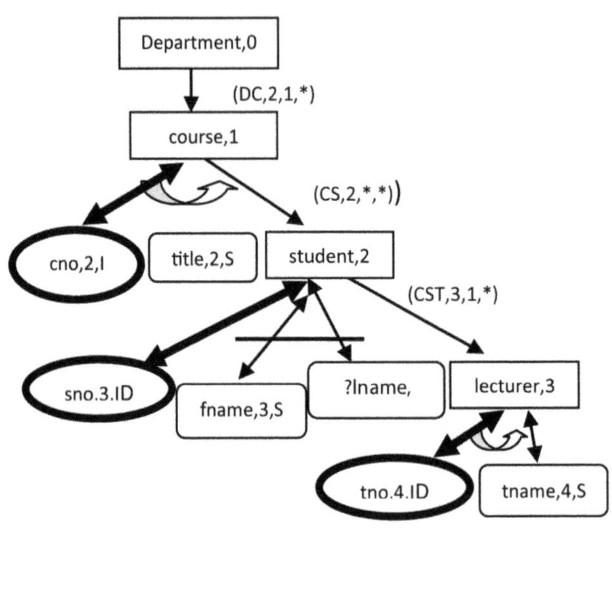

Figure 4. XML document conforms to GN-DTD in Figure 3

```
<!DOCTYPE Department [
  <course>
    <course cno = “csc101”>
    < title > XML database </title>
    < student >
        <student sno = “112344”>
        <fname> David</fname>
        <lname> Grey </lname>
        <lecturer>
           <lecturer tno = “123”>
           <tname>Bing </tname>
         </lecturer>
    </student>
    < student >
        <student sno = “112345”>
        <fname>Helen</fname>
         <lecturer>
           <lecturer tno = “123”>
           <tname> Bing </tname>
        </lecturer>
     </student>
 </course>
 <course>
    <course cno = “csc102”>
    < title > Z formal methods </title>
     < student >
        <student sno = “112344”>
        <fname> David</fname>
        <lname>Grey </lname>
        <lecturer>
           <lecturer tno = “123”>
           <tname> Bottaci </tname>
         </lecturer>
     </student>
    < student >
        <student sno = “112345”>
        <fname>Helen </fname>
         <lecturer>
           <lecturer tno = “123”>
           <tname> Bottaci </tname>
        </lecturer>
     </student>
 </course>
</Department>]
```

update the information about Bing and Bottaci, we have to update them twice. This is because *one-to-many* ternary inheritance relationship between *course*, *student* and *lecturer* exist in GN-DTD. Therefore to achieve a redundancy-free XML document, a set of normal form rules should be provided to a designer to help them to design a good XML documents.

2.2. Data Dependencies

Data dependencies are part of the real world semantics (Arenas & Libkin, 2004; Ling et al., 2005; Vincent et al., 2007; Lv et al., 2004; Wang & Topor, 2005). They represent the semantic information in the form of relationships between different attributes in the XML documents. In Ling et al. (2005), it is stated that "*data dependencies should be modelled precisely early in the design stage for a correct and complete database representation of semantic*". There are various types of structural properties in GN-DTD model, which should be analysed in the normalization process. We consider here two types of data dependencies: functional dependency and key dependency.

2.2.1. Key Dependency

We define a key attribute as a unique attribute that can determine uniquely other simple element in the whole XML document. For instance course number (cno), student number (sno) and lecturer number (tno) are unique and mandatory, because they are represented as one-to-one relationships between complex element and attribute node. We define this in GN-DTD as a key dependency similar to (Buneman et al., 2002).

cno → *course* and *tno* → *teacher*

2.2.2. Functional Dependency

Functional dependency models real world constraints, showing that some of the complex elements or simple elements/attributes depend on other complex elements or attributes/simple elements. Based on the GN-DTD model, we define four types of functional dependencies: relationship dependency, global dependency, transitive dependency and partial dependency.

2.2.2.1. Relationship Dependency

The relationship dependencies are presented clearly in the GN-DTD diagram using a directed arrow. Our XML relationship dependency is defined in terms of a uniqueness constraint in the relationship between complex element nodes in GN-DTD. These types of relationships could cause data redundancy and should be eliminated from GN-DTD. The categories are:

- One-to-many binary inheritance relationship dependency
- Many-to-many binary inheritance relationship dependency
- Many-to-one binary or ternary inheritance relationship dependency
- Many-to-many ternary inheritance relationship dependency

2.2.2.2 Global Functional Dependency

Global functional dependency occurs based on a few reasonable constraints (dependency) that a database designer may specify for his/her application. Global functional dependency holds in GN-DTD if a dependency exists between the attribute and simple element of the corresponding complex element under a binary or n-ary many-to-many inheritance relationship at the last node of GN-DTD. We adopted this definition from Arenas and Libkin (2004) with some modification to suit the hierarchical structure of XML documents.

Definition 1: Let CE be a set of complex elements under binary or n-ary one-to-many/many-to-many inheritance relationship, Let ATT be an identifier attribute of CE and SE is a simple element of CE. The global functional dependency of GN-DTD is defined as follows:

1. For each part-of-link simple element $<SE,l_{n-1}>$ of $<CE,l_{n-2}>$, where $<SE,l_{n-1}>$ and ATT are last nodes in GN-DTD

$<ATT,l_{n-1}> \rightarrow <SE,l_{n-1}>$ is a global dependency in GN-DTD. $<SE,l_{n-1}>$ can be a set of simple element, list of simple elements or single value of a simple element.

2. For each last node attribute ATT_1 of CE which is not the attribute identifier of CE, $ATT \rightarrow ATT_1$ and $ATT_1 \rightarrow ATT$ is also a global dependency.

For instance, in Figure 3, the possible global dependency (GFD) of the complex element lecturer is as follows:

$$<tno,4> \rightarrow <tname,4> \quad (1)$$

This above *GFD(1)* represents the constraint, whenever two nodes agree on the value of all attributes *tno*, they also agree on the value of all attributes in *tname*. This GFD can be viewed as a function from one set of attributes/simple elements to another set of attributes/simple elements. This GFD is similar to XFD defined by Arenas and Libkin (2004) but we put it in a different way without using the path notation.

2.2.2.3 Functional Transitive Dependency

We adopted the definition of transitive dependence from the relation model (Codd, 1972) and nested relation (Ling, 1985). Transitive functional dependencies between complex elements occur if theirs attribute or simple element node has dependency with another simple element node from a different level.

Definition 2:

- **Case 1:** Let ATT be a key identifier for complex element(CE) and $\{SE_a, SE_b\}$ are simple elements for CE
  - If there exist two constraints $<ATT,l_i> \rightarrow <SE_a,l_i>$ and $<SE_a,l_i \rightarrow <SE_b,l_i>$, then we say that attribute $<SE_b,l_i>$ is transitively dependent on $<ATT,l_i>$
- **Case 2:** Let ATT_a be a key identifier for CE_a, ATT_b is a key identifier to CE_b and SE_c is a simple element for CE_c and they are located in different levels.
  - If there exist two constraints $<ATT_a,l_i> \rightarrow <ATT_b,l_{i+1}>$ and $<ATT_b,l_{i+1}> \rightarrow <SE_c, l_{i+1}>$, then we say that $<SE_c, l_{i+1}>$ is transitively dependent on $<ATT,l_i>$

2.2.2.4. Functional Partial Dependency

We adopted the definition of functional partial dependency (PFD) from Lv et al(2004).

Definition 3:

- Let ATT_a, ATT_b, $ATT_{c,}$ ATT_d be a key identifier for CE_a, $CE_{b,}$ CE_c and CE_d respectively. These CE have a binary or tenary relationship with each other and are located in different levels.
- If there exist two constraints
- **PFD1:** $\{<ATT_a,l_i>,<ATT_b,l_{i+1}>,<ATT_c,l_{i+2}>\} \rightarrow <ATT_d,l_{i+3}>$
- **PFD2:** $<ATT_a,li> \rightarrow <ATT_d,l_{i+3}>$

then constraint *PFD2* is called functional partial dependency because it is a subset of *PFD1* where attribute $<ATT_a,l_i>$ alone can be used to determine $<ATT_d,l_{i+3}>$. Functional partial dependencies involve composite attribute keys. The composite key attribute could be from the same level or from a different level. The subset of composite key attribute can functionally determine the simple element node.

3. NORMAL FORM FOR GN-DTD

A normal form specifies a set of syntactic conditions that a well-designed schema should satisfy. Normal form usually deal with removing redundancies from a database to avoid possible anomalies during updates or insertion of data. Like relational model (Codd, 1972), we next define a multi level of normal form for GN-DTD. These normal forms are based on notion of data dependencies and semantic relationship of GN-DTD.

3.1. First Normal Form GN-DTD (1XNF GN-DTD)

The first normal form for GN-DTD is about finding unique identifier attributes for the complex elements set, and to check that no node (complex element, simple element or attribute) actually represents multiple values. Only one value for each simple element node or attribute node of GN-DTD can be stored. If there is more than one value, we must add some new simple elements node or attributes node to store them. For instance, consider Figure 3, if a complex element courses has two titles, we need two title simple elements node for each courses to store the two title names. This is equivalent as there is 'no repeating group' in relational schema (Codd, 1972). More importantly, the primary key (unique identifier) for complex element must be defined. To be precise, we propose the following rules.

GN-DTD is in first normal if and only if:

1. Given a GN-DTD, XML documents must *satisfy* to corresponding GN-DTD.
2. All the attributes, complex element or simple element are not NULL and have single label.

3. The root element of a GN-DTD model should be located at level 0 and cardinality of root element node must be one.
4. Each set of complex element node in the GN-DTD has at least one attribute node key.

3.2. Second Normal Form GN-DTD (2XNF GN-DTD)

If a relationship between a parent node (Complex element node) and child node (complex element node) is one-to-many (such as *department* and *course*, as shown in Figure 3) the potency of data duplication might exist. Some nodes need to be restructured however they can then still be in a single document. This is possible in XML because XML supports hierarchies in a single document, while relational databases do not support hierarchies in a single row. This is different from the relational second normal form (2NF), which requires one-to-many relationships to be in separate tables.

The GN-DTD is in second normal form if and only if:

1. GN - DTD is in IXNF.
2. XML documents must *conform* and *satisfy* to corresponding 2XNF GN -DTD.
3. There is no nested binary inheritance relationship or ternary inheritance relationship under many-to-many or one-to-many inheritance relationships with the following condition:

For each nested set of complex element <CE, *l+1*> of <CE, *l*>, and any key attribute (ATT) of <CE, *l*>, the key attribute and simple element of <CE, *l+1*> is not *partial dependent* on ATT of complex element

<CE ,*l*>

3.3. Third Normal Form GN-DTD (3XNF GN-DTD)

In the third normal form of GN-DTD, making a change to one unique complex element node set would not affect the integrity of another complex element node set. If needed, a complex elements node set would be divided into two separate complex element node sets. This is similar to the relational third normal form.

GN- DTD is in third normal form if and only if:

1. GN-DTD is in 2XNF.
2. There exists no nested inheritance relationship type of *n*-ary many-to-many or one-to-many under a one-to-many inheritance relationship set in GN-DTD and the following conditions are satisfied:
   a. For each nested set of complex elements $<CE_b, l+1>$ of set of complex element $<CE_a, l>$, any key attribute and simple element of $<CE_b, l+1>$ is not transitively dependent on attribute node key of complex element $<CE_a, l>$
   b. Any key attribute node of any complex element node located in a different level are disjoint (ATT $<CE, l> \cap$ ATT $<CE, l+1> \cap$ ATT $<CE, n>$ =0)

3.4. Normal Form GN-DTD (NF GN-DTD)

GN- DTD is in Normal Form if and only if:

1. GN-DTD is in 3XNF.
2. For nested one-to-many or many-to-many inheritance relationship in GN-DTD, the following condition satisfied:

There are no global dependencies among attribute nodes or simple element nodes of complex element node at last node of GN-DTD.

4. TRANSFORMATION FORM UN-NORMAL FORM GN-DTD TO THE NORMAL FORM GN-DTD

The common feature of normalization procedure is to convert an initial schema into one in a normal form to reduce the anomalies and redundancies in XML document. In this section, we propose rules to transform the un-normal form GN-DTD into a normal form one. This transformation based on our proposed normalization rules to remove data redundancy in XML documents caused by relationship dependency, global functional dependency, partial and transitive functional dependency. Generally, in these rules, we first restructure the GN-DTD by creating a new complex element node, moving up node and moving sub-tree node. We subsequently adjust the semantic relationship between simple element nodes or attribute nodes in GN-DTD. We next define the normalization rules.

4.1. Normalization Rules

Data dependency presented in this section similar to previous notion however to be more general, we add new notations in representation such as shown in Box 1.

4.2. Normalization Algorithm

Normalization is a process that analyses and restructures the schema of an XML document to minimize redundancies with the help of data dependencies in the data. The normalization algorithm takes GN-DTD and set of data dependencies specified by the user as an input, and returns the normal form GN-DTD as output. These algorithms apply to normalization rules presented in the previous section. We propose three algorithms to transform a GN-DTD into 2XNF, 3XNF and XNF, respectively.

5. CASE STUDY

In this section, we present a simple case study to design a university database presented in XML which describes in Figure 4. To show how the XML document can be designed using GN-DTD, we illustrate it in the following section. We present the transformation of GN-DTD according to 1XNF, 2XNF, 3XNF and XNF respectively. We assume a set of data dependencies presented in the following section with the GN-DTD in Figure 3 are used as input.

The following constraints are given based on the database designer's requirements:

Constraint 1: Each set course, student and lecturer has unique identifier.
Constraint 2: In the department, a student number (sno) determines fname and lname
Constraint 3: In the department, course number (cno) and student number(sno) determines lecturer number (tno)
Constraint 4: In the department, course number (cno) determines lecturer number(tno)
Constraint 5: In the department, course number (cno) and lecturer number (tno) determines lecturer name(tname).
Constraint 6: In the department, lecturer number (tno) determines lecturer name(tname)

Using definition given in section 2.2, the above constraints are categorized and represented as follows respectively.

- **Key Dependency:** Constraint 1 is considered as key dependency since key attribute can determine their complex element: <cno,2>→<course,1>, <sno,3>→<student,2>, and <tno,4>→ <lecturer,3>
- **Global Functional Dependency:** Constraint 2 and constraint 6 are classified

Box 1.

r represents root element
ATT represents attribute
SE represents simple element
CE represents set of complex elements
$\rightarrow^{R}$ represents relationship
l represents level of node where (0 ≤ l ≤ n-1), n is a finite positive number

Rule 1. Eliminate redundancy through global functional dependencies

Let *ATT→{SE} is a global functional dependency… (1)*

1.1. Create a new set complex element name *<CE_new,1>*

1.2. Locate node *<CE_new, 1>* at level one *(1=1)* at the right most position of GN-DTD

1.3. Create new relationship type of binary one-to-many *inheritance link* between root and new set complex element name *<CE_new,1>*

1.4. Replicate attribute node *ATT* and simple node *SE*.

1.4.1 Make them as a children to node *<CE_new,1>*

1.4.2 Let new attribute node ATT of *<CE_new, 1>* be a key node

1.5. Create a new relationship type of *part-of link* between attribute node *ATT* and simple element node *SE* with *<CE-new, 1>*

1.6. Delete simple element node *{SE}* from original location and its relationship

1.7. Eliminate global functional dependency *(1)* from set of data dependency

Rule 2. Eliminate n-ary many-to-many or one-or-many inheritance relationship with partial transitive

To eliminate n-ary many-to-many or one-or-many relationship we must avoid multi - hierarchy. For each, n-ary relationship *R* (n>2), many-to-many or one-to-many relationship dependency type

(<CE_a, *l* > $\rightarrow^{R}$<CE_b, *l+1*>)

2.1. Create a new set complex element name

<CE_b *_new,l*>

2.2. Locate node <CE_b*_new,l*> at the same level of level <CE_a, *l* > at the rightmost position of GN-DTD

2.3. Create a new relationship type of binary one-to-many binary *inheritance link* between parent of <CE_a, *l* > and new set complex element name <CE_b*_new,l*>

2.4. If partial dependency exists in the <CE_b, *l+1*> then replicate all children of <CE_b, *l+1*> to be children of the set complex element <CE_b*_new,l*>

2.5. Delete all children of <CE_b, *l+1*> except the key attribute node

Rule 3. Eliminate binary many-to-many/many-to-one/one-to-many inheritance relationship with transitive dependency

For each, binary many-to-one relationship type

(<CE_a, *l* > $\rightarrow^{R}$<CE_b, *l+1*>)

If exist, <CE_a,l> with attribute ATT_a and <CE_b,l+1> with attribute ATT_b, with

continued on following page

Box 1. Continued

and simple element SE_b

Where $ATT_a \rightarrow ATT_b$

$ATT_b \rightarrow SE_b$

$ATT_a \rightarrow SE_b$ is a transitive dependency

3.1. Move up the set complex element <CE_b, *l+1*> along with its children to the same level <$CE_{a,}$ *l* >

3.2. If parent of <$CE_{a,}$ *l* > is a root node

then create a new relationship type of one-to-many *inheritance link* between parent of <$CE_{a,}$,*l*> with set complex element node < CE_b,*l+1* >

else create new relationship type of many-to-many *inheritance link* between parent of <$CE_{a,}$ *l* >

3.3. Eliminate transitive dependency ATTa $\rightarrow$ SE_b from set of complex element <$CE_{a,}$ *l* > and <CE_b, *l+1*>

Algorithm 2. Algorithm 2XNF GN-DTD

Input: The GN-DTD D in 1XNF-DTD and set of specified dependencies constraint.
Output: The GN- DTD in 2XNF-DTD

Let D be GN-DTD
If D is 2XNF GN-DTD, then output D
Else
Search all inheritance relationships in GN-DTD from root node to last node
If there exist
n-ary many-to-many inheritance relationship or one-to-many inheritance relationship under many-to-many inheritance relationship
Then take the last inheritance relationship in the GN-DTD
Restructure D by applying rule 2
Update set of data dependencies
Repeat until no more partial functional dependency in the semantic relationship
Output D

Algorithm 3. Algorithm 3XNF GN-DTD

Input: A GN-DTD D in 2XNF GN-DTD and given set of data dependencies.
Output: A GN-DTD in 3XNF GN-DTD

Let D be GN-DTD
If D is 3XNF GN-DTD, then output D
Else
If there exist many-to-many or many-to-one or one-to-many inheritance relationship with transitive functional dependency
Then
Restructure D by applying rule 3
Update set of data dependencies
Repeat until no more transitive functional dependency in semantic relationship
Output D

Algorithm 4. Algorithm XNF GN-DTD

```
Input: A GN-DTD D in 3XNF GN-DTD and given set of data
dependencies.
Output: A GN-DTD in XNF GN-DTD

        Let D be GN-DTD
 If D is XNF GN-DTD, then output D
 Else
        Get all the dependency constraint
 If there exist constraint with global functional dependency
 Then apply rule 1
 Update set of data dependencies
 Repeat until no more global functional dependency in seman-
 tic relationship
 Output D
```

as global functional dependencies because they involve attribute and simple elements.
  - <sno,3>→{<fname,3>,<lname,3>}
  - <tno,4>→ <tname,4>
- **Transitive Functional Dependency**
  - **Constraint 4:** < cno,2> → <tno,4>
  - **Constraint 6:** <tno,4> →<tname,4>

Simple element *<tname,4>* is transitively dependent on attribute node key *< cno,2>* which derive the following transitive functional dependency.

Constraint 7: < cno,2> →<tname,4>

- **Partial Functional Dependency**
  - **Constraint 5:** <cno,2>,<tno,3>→ <tname,4>
  - **Constraint 6:** < tno,3> → <tname,4>

Constraint 6 is called partial functional dependency because the attribute node key, course number < *tno,3*> alone can be used to determine teacher name *<tname,4>*.

- **Relationship Dependency:** Based on GN-DTD given, there exist binary many-to-many relationship between course and student which represented as *<course,1>*$\rightarrow^{R}$*<student,2>* and ternary one-to-many relationship between course, student and lecturer node which is represented as *(<course,1>, <student,2>*$\rightarrow^{R}$*<lecturer,3>)*.

5.1. IXNF GN-DTD

The GN-DTD illustrated in Figure 3 shows that it is in first normal form (1XNF) because each set of complex element nodes *course*, *student* and *lecturer* has *cno, sno* and *tno* as a unique key identifier respectively, while all simple element nodes and attribute nodes have one unique label. The *department* node is a root element since it is located at level 0. Moreover, the XML documents shown in Figure 4 satisfy and conform to GN-DTD in Figure 3.

5.2. 2XNF GN-DTD

GN- DTD of Figure 3 is not in 2XNF because

- There exists a ternary inheritance relationship type nested under many-to-many inheritance relationship type, <co urse,1>,<student,2>$\rightarrow^{(cst,3,1,*)}$*<lectur er,3>*. This dependency relationship involves complex element *course*, *student* and *lecturer* nodes. As a consequence information about *lecturer* is stored redundantly in the XML document and can cause update anomaly. If the information about the *lecturer* is changed, then it must be updated in all subtree *students* who are taking the same *course*.
- There exists a partial functional dependency < *tno,3*> → *<tname,4>* where the attribute and simple element are children of complex element *lecturer.*

To be in 2XNF GN-DTD, the structure of GN-DTD needs to restructure using algorithm 2XNF. Based on this algorithm, the new set complex element *lecturernew* along with its children is created at the same level as complex element *student* node. A one-to-many inheritance link between *course* and *lecturernew node* is created. All children from the original complex element *lecturer* are deleted except key attribute node *tno*. In this way, the original semantic relationship is preserved in GN-DTD. Figure 5 presents 2XNF GN-DTD. Having this structure, partial functional dependency under ternary one-to-many inheritance relationship is eliminated in complex element lecturer, but still preserved in complex element *lecturernew,* which denoted as *<tno,3>→<tname,3>*. Finally, all constraints in set of data dependencies that involve the constraint *<tno,3>→<tname,3>* need to be updated. As consequence, the new version of set data dependencies will be as follows:

- **Key Dependency**
  - **Constraint 1:** <cno,2>→<course,1>, <sno,3>→<student,2>, and <tno,4>→ <lecturer,3>, <tno,3>→ <lecturernew,2>
- **Global Functional Dependency**
  - **Constraint 2:** *< sno,3> {<fname,3>,<lname,3>}*
  - **Constraint 6:** *<tno,3>→<tname,3>*
- **Transitive Functional Dependency**
  - **Constraint 4:** *< cno,2> → <tno,3>*
  - **Constraint 6:** *< tno,3> →<tname,3>*
  - **Constraint 7:** *< cno,2> →<tname,3> is TFD*
- **Partial Functional Dependency**
  - **Constraint 5:** *< cno,2>,<tno,3> →<tname,3>*
  - **Constraint 6:** *< no,3> →<tname,3> is a PFD*
- **Relationship Dependency:** In 2XNF GN-DTD, there exists binary one-to-many relationship between complex element node *course* and complex element node *lecturernew* student which represented as *<course,1>*$\rightarrow^{R}$*<lecturernew,2>,* binary many-to-many relationship between complex element *course* and complex ele-

Figure 5. GN-DTD in a second normal form

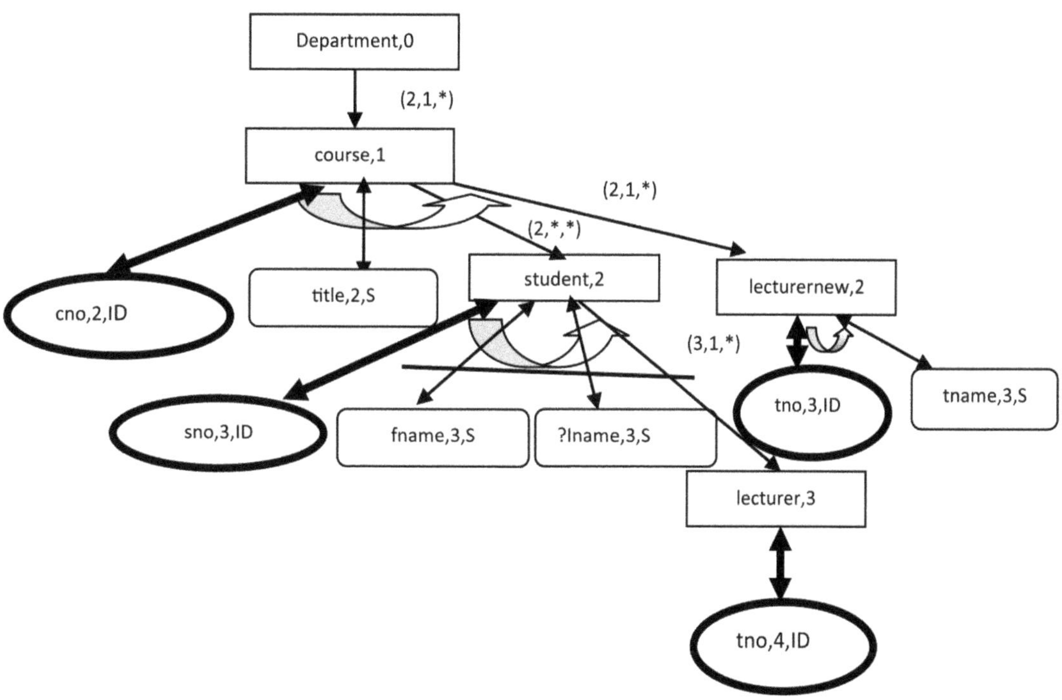

ment *student*, *<course,1>→^{R}<student,2>* and ternary one-to-many relationship between course, student and lecturer node which is represented as (*<course,1>, <student,2>→^{R}<lecturer,3>).*

5.3. 3XNF GN-DTD

GN-DTD of Figure 5 is not in 3XNF because

- There exist one-to-many inheritance relationships between element *lecturernew* and *course* node under one-to-many inheritance relationship.
- There exists TFP caused by *Constraint 4* and *constraint 6* which involve complex element *course* and complex element *lecturernew* with < cno,2> →<tname,3>.

To be in 3XNF GN-DTD, the inheritance link between the set of complex element node *course* and complex element *lecturernew* node needs to be restructured and transitive functional dependency eliminated within *course* node and complex element *lecturernew*. The set of complex element node *lecturernew* along with its children is moved up and linked with *department* node. Because department is a root, a binary one-to-many hierarchical link is created. Figure 6 presents a new structure of 3XNF GN-DTD after eliminating the above constraints.

Having this structure, transitive functional dependency under ternary one-to-many inheritance relationship is eliminated in complex element lecturer, but still preserved in between complex element *course* and *lecturernew,* which denoted as *<cno,2>→<tname,2>*. Finally, all constraints in set of data dependencies that involve the constraint *<cno,2>→<tname,2>* need to be updated. As consequence, the new version of set data dependencies will be as follows:

Figure 6. GN-DTD in a third normal form

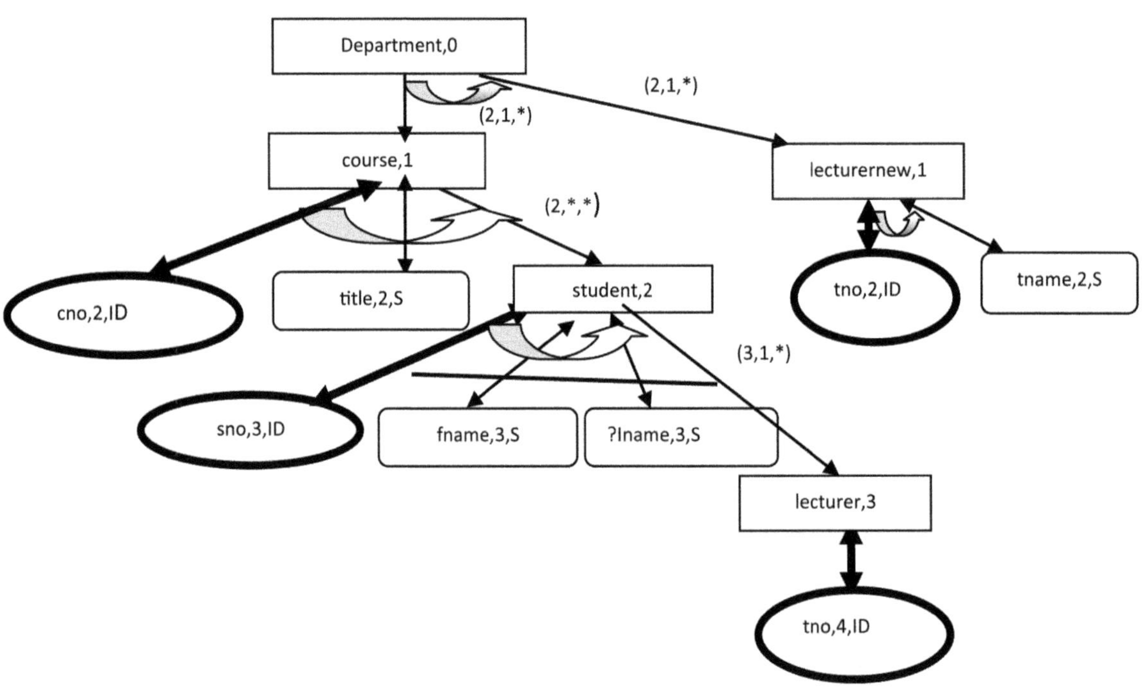

- **Key Dependency**
  - **Constraint 1***:* <cno,2>→<course,1>, <sno,3>→<student,2>, and <tno,4>→ <lecturer,3>, <tno,2>→ <lecturernew1>
- **Global functional dependency(GFD)**
  - **Constraint 2***:* *<sno,3> {<fname,3>,<lname,3>}*
  - **Constraint 6***:* *<tno,2>→<tname,2>*
- **Transitive functional dependency(TFP)**
  - **Constraint 4***:* *< cno,2> → <tno,2>*
  - **Constraint 6***:* *<tno,2> →<tname,2>*
  - **Constraint 7***:* *< cno,2> →<tname,2> is TFD*
- **Partial functional dependency(PFD)**
  - **Constraint 5***:* *<cno,2>,<tno,2>→<tname,2>*
  - **Constraint 6***:* *<tno,2> →<tname,2> is a PFD*
- **Relationship Dependency:** In 3XNF GN-DTD, there exists binary one-to-many relationship between complex element node *department* and complex element node *lecturernew* student which represented as *<department,0>→^{R}<lecturernew,1>,* binary many-to-many relationship between complex element *course* and complex element *student, <course,1>→^{R}<student,2>*and ternary one-to-many relationship between course, student and lecturer node which is represented as *(<course,1>, <student,2>→^{R}<lecturer,3>).*

5.4. XNF GN-DTD

3XNF GN- DTD of Figure 6 is not in XNF because

1. There exists GFD *sno →{fname,lname}* for set complex element *student* node and *course* node under many-to-many relationship. If the information about the *fname and lname* is changed, then it must be updated in the whole document.

To remove redundancies caused by GFD, a new *set* of complex element node *studentnew* is created. The attribute node *sno* and simple element node *fname* and *lname* are replicated and they become children of set complex element *studentnew*. The *part of link* is created between them accordingly. Both of simple element node *fname and lname* are deleted from *student* node but key attribute node *sno* is remained as a child for complex element *student* node.

Figure 7 illustrates new structure of XNF GN-DTD has similar result to the XNF defined by Arenas and Libkin (2004). More importantly, as shown, all data dependencies are still preserved in XNF GN-DTD. Figure 8 is an XML document conforming to XNF GN-DTD with free redundancy.

- **Key Dependency**
  - **Constraint 1:** <cno,2>→<course,1>,<sno,3>→<student,2>,<sno,2>→<studentnew,1>,<tno,4>→<lecturer,3>, <tno,2>→ <lecturernew1>
- **Global Functional Dependency**
  - **Constraint 2***:* *<sno,2> {<fname,2>,<lname,2>}*
  - **Constraint 6***:* *<tno,2>→<tname,2>*
- **Transitive Functional Dependency**
  - **Constraint 4:** *< cno,2> → <tno,2>*
  - **Constraint 6:** *<tno,2> →<tname,2>*
  - **Constraint 7:** *< cno,2> →<tname,2> is TFD*
- **Partial Functional Dependency**
  - **Constraint 5:** *<cno,2>,<tno,2>→ <tname,2>*
  - **Constraint 6:** *<tno,2> →<tname,2> is a PFD*
- **Relationship Dependency:** Based on XNF GN-DTD given, there exists binary one-to-many relationship between complex element node *department* with complex element node *lecturernew, course* and *studentnew* which represented as *<department,0>→^{R}<lecturernew,1>,<*

Figure 7. GN-DTD in a normal form

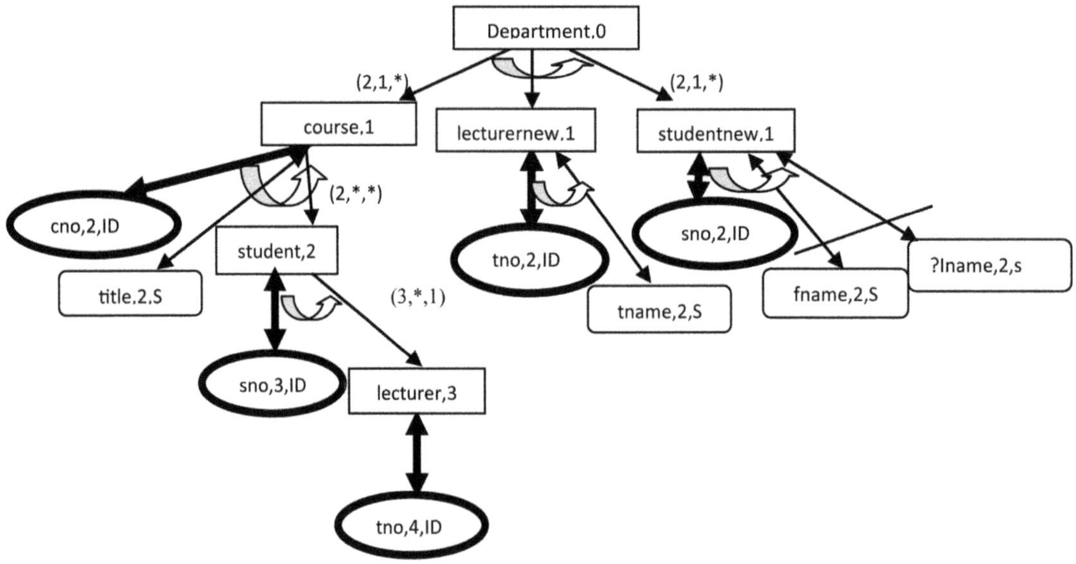

department,0>→^{R}<studentnew,1>and <department,0>→^{R}<course>, binary many-to-many relationship between complex element *course* and complex element *student, <course,1>→^{R}<student,2>,* ternary one-to-many relationship between course, student and lecturer node which is represented as *(<course,1>, <student,2>→^{R}<lecturer,3>).*

6. COMPARISONS WITH RELATED WORK

To evaluate this paper, a comparison of our work with related approaches is discussed. The comparison based on the number of criteria, specifically:

- **Expression of DTD Structure:** In Arenas and Libkin's work, they used mathematical notations to represent the DTD structure, which is hardly to be understood by a normal designer. For instance, we present here their formal definition of DTD as follows:

A DTD is defined to be $D = (E, A, P, R, r)$ (Arenas & Libkin, 2004), where:

1. E⊆ El is a finite set of element types.
2. A⊆ Att is a finite set of attributes.
3. P is a mapping form E to element type definition defined in a regular expression $\alpha := \varepsilon \mid \tau' \mid \alpha|\alpha \mid \alpha, \mid \alpha^*$ where ε is the empty sequence, $\tau' \in E$, and "|", "," and "*" denote union, concatenation, and Kleene closure, respectively.
4. R is a mapping from E to the power set of value of R: P(A)
5. r ∊ E *and is* called the root element type

The symbols ε and S represent element type declaration EMPTY and #PCDATA, respectively.

For example, reconsider the DTD in Figure 2 which is presented by Arenas and Libkin (2004) as follows:

- E = {*D*epartment, Course, Student, Teacher},

Figure 8. Redundancy-free XML document conforms to GN-DTD in Figure 7

```
<!DOCTYPE Department [
  <course>
     <course cno = "csc101">
     < title > XML database </title>
      < student >
         <student sno = "112344">
        <lecturer>
          <lecturer tno = "123">
        </lecturer>
      </ student >
      < student >
         <student sno = "112345">
       <lecturer>
         <lecturer tno = "123">
       </lecturer>
    </student >
  </course>
 <course>
    <course cno = "csc201">
    < title > Database technique </title>
    < student >
        <student sno = "112344">
       <lecturer>
         <lecturer tno = "123">
      </lecturer
    </ student >
     < student >
        <student sno = "112346">
       <lecturer>
         <lecturer tno = "123">
      </lecturer
     </student >
 </course>
<course>
    <course cno = "csc102">
    < title > Z formal methods </title>
     < student >
        <student sno = "112344">
        <lecturer>
          <lecturer  tno = "124">
      </lecturer>
    </student>
      < student >
        <student sno = "112345">
        <lecturer>
          <lecturer  tno = "124">
        </lecturer>
      </student>
   </course>
 <lecturernew>
     <tinfo tno = "123">
     <tname> bing </tname>
</lecturernew>
<lecturernew>
      <tinfo tno = "124">
      <tname> bottaci</tname>
```

- A = *{*cno,sno,tno,}
- r = Department

Furthermore, P *and* R *are* defined as follows:

- P (Department) = {course*}, P*(*course) = {title, Student*}, P*(*student) ={fname, lname, teacher*}, P*(*tname) = S,
- *P* (fname)= S, *P(lname) = S, P*(title) = S.
- *R(* Department) = ∅, *R(*course*) = cno, R* (student) = sno, *R*(teacher) = tno.

From the above the definition, it clearly shows that textual of grammar representation make it difficult to be analysed and understood. In practise, it often causes difficulties when even designing a simple DTD. More importantly, the semantic constraint and relationship between the element in the XML document cannot be represented precise and clearly. For instance the relation between *course* and *student* is not defined explicitly. The semantic relation between the elements present only one-to-many relationships by notation *, while other relationship such as many -to-many or many-to-one relationships is not defined.

However, compare to our work, a graphical notation is used to visually represent a DTD structure which is used to describe XML document. By having this way, we believe the user can have better understanding of DTD structure. Representation of GN-DTD slightly difference from the Arenas and Libkin's DTD. Firstly, we distinguish explicitly the difference between complex elements, simple element and attribute. We emphasise the simple element is element with no children element while attribute is a key or candidate key of complex element. The reason is, to avoid using *S* as text representation and it will make easier to visualise during normalization process. Secondly, we present the GN-DTD structure as hierarchical structure of elements which is similar to XML document structure to illustrate the real picture of XML document. For

GN-DTD's notation itself, we adopt some of notation from (Chen, 1976; Dobbie et al, 2000; Feng et al, 2002) but we add few semantic such as sequence, disjunction, hierarchical link, part-of link between the nodes to reveal more semantic between the element nodes.

XML Normal Forms

XML normal form has been introduced by Arenas and Libkin (2004), Wang and Topor (2005), Vincent et al (2004), and Yu and Jagadish (2008). However, XML normal form XNF, proposed by Arenas and Libkin (2004) achieves the best possible design (Kolahi, 2007). A defined normal form for XML documents (XNF) is based on XML functional dependency which is used to avoid update anomalies and redundancies. They define XML document as a tree called 'XML tree' which consist of nodes, edges to represent a relation between parent and child node, and a root node. In XML tree, they use paths to represent element nodes stating form the root node until last child node. The same path definition also applies to the path in DTD denoted as *path (D)*. The child node is normally an attribute node or a string (denoted as symbol @ and *S* respectively). Every path in XML tree will contain at least one element node type. For example,

Department.course.student.lecturer@tno and *Department.course.student.lecturer.tname.S* are all paths in XML document.

In Arenas and Libkin (2004), XML functional dependency (XFD) is used to represent the semantic constraint which could cause data redundancy. They defined XFD as a path based on the idea from relational schema (Codd, 1976) and nested relational schema (Ling, 1985). For example, the constraint that two lecturer elements with same lecturer number (tno) must have the same name is expressed as follows:

Department.course.student.lecturer.@ tno, →*Department.course.student.lecturer. tname.S* (2)

Where *Department.course.student.lecturer.@ tno* is a left hand side(LHS) of paths and *Department.course.student.lecturer.tname.S* is a Right Hand Side(RHS)paths. Using this XFD definition, the following XML normal form is presented.

- **Definition XNF:** Given a DTD and a set of $\sum$ of XFDs over D, (D, $\sum$) is in XML normal form (XNF) if and only if for every nontrivial XFD p →q.@l or p →q.S or, the XFD p→q is also in (D, $\sum$)$^+$. Where p and q is a set of path(D) (Arenas & Libkin, 2004).

Generally, the above definition means that a DTD is in a normal form (XNF) if every functional dependency defined over DTD is in XNF. The XFD is XNF if every LHS path can determine a unique value of RHS path. In other words, XNF does not allow any redundancy in data values occurring in the leaves of the XML tree. Intuitively, this XNF ensures the value of *q.@l* or *q.S* will not repeated in two different locations of the XML tree. For instance, XFD in (2) is not in XNF since the value for the element *lecturer* name is not unique for the attribute given, as *lecturer* name Bing appears twice in the XML document as shown in Figure 2. Because of this XFD (2), DTD is not in XNF.

Based on Arenas and Libkin's definition, recently, Kolahi (2007) has proposed a third normal form for XML by extends 3NF to XML. Kolahi adopted the notion of XML tree and DTD from Arenas and Libkin (2004) but extended the notion of prime attribute from relational database to case of paths to XML tree. We present here the definition of prime attribute path in order to present X3NF:

- **Definition X3NF:** XML specification (D, $\sum$) is in X3NF if and only if for every non-trivial XFD p→ q.@l ∈(D, $\sum$)$^+$, we have that p→q ∈(D, $\sum$)$^+$ or q.@l is a prime path (Kolahi, 2007).

As a relational counterpart, a prime path is a path that uniquely determine path element of a 'tree tuple' from the root. Like the 3NF, X3NF try to achieve a schema that can preserve the functional dependency and at the same time reduced data redundancy in XML documents. However, to date there is no normalization algorithm has been developed based on X3NF definition.

Other than that, based on Arenas and Libkin's work, Lv et al. (2004) also proposed first, second and third normal which considered partial functional dependency and transitive functional dependency respectively. They defined second and third normal form as follows:

- **Definition 2XNF:** XML specification (D, $\sum$) is in X2NF if and only if for every XFD $p_1.p_2.@l_1$→ $p_1.p_2$.p3.@l∈(D, $\sum$), if there is another XFD' $p_1.@l_2$→ $p_1.p_2.p_3$@l ∈(D, $\sum$), there is no partial dependency p_1.@l →p_1. $p_2.p_3$@l and $p_1 \neq$ r. Where p_i is a set of path(D).(Lv et al, 2004)
- **Definition 3XNF:** XML specification (D, $\sum$) is in X3NF if and only if for every XFD p_1.@l→ p_1. p_2.@l ∈(D, $\sum$), if there is another XFD' $p_1.p_2$.@l→ p_1. p_2. p_3@l ∈(D, $\sum$), there is no transitive dependency p_1.@l →$p_1.p_2.p_3$@l. Where p_i is a set of path(D). (Lv et al, 2004)

We refer the reader to Lv et al(2004) for further reading.

Our work is similar with (Arenas & Libkin, 2004; Lv et al., 2004) but we simplify these definitions so that it is more practical, easy to be understood and implemented and give the same result. As shown in section 3, we propose normal form for GN-DTD (XNF GN-DTD) at the schema level based from Arenas and Libkin's definition. Furthermore, we present also other normal forms such as 1XNF, 2XNF and 3XNF which are generalise from definition given by Kolahi (2007) and Vincent et al. (2007). Generally, the nature of definition of the normal form GN-DTD depends on a number of conditions. First, except root node, each of complex element nodes must have attribute node key. Second, there should not exist any nested hierarchical relationship between complex elements node starting from root element node until last complex element node with global, transitive and partial functional dependency. The significant differences between our normal form and the one presented in (Arenas & Libkin, 2004; Kolahi, 2007; Lv et al., 2004) are:

1. Firstly, GN-DTD model is proposed to assist in XML document design at the conceptual model. Our normal forms are based on combination of different types of functional dependencies such as relationship dependency, transitive dependency, partial dependency, and global dependency definitions. We define these functional dependencies based on GN-DTD structure without consider the path; which is simpler than in Arenas and Libkin's approach. However in (Arenas & Libkin, 2004; Kolahi, 2007; Lv et al., 2004), they totally defines their normal form based on the XFD definitions. XFD is formally defined on the concept 'tree-tuple' and path (Arenas & Libkin, 2004). As we know, functional dependency is already the area where designer have the most problem specifying in relational models, so making them more complicated an unfamiliar to designer make XML document design more difficult.
2. Second, we apply our defined functional dependencies based on the structure of GN-DTD at the schema level to present explicitly the position and level of complex elements, simple elements, attribute node and the se-

mantic relationship. Based upon the analysis of these structural properties, the GN-DTD schema is iteratively transformed into refined normal form preserving the data dependencies. To preserve data dependencies, all the data dependencies are updated iteratively to match with the current GN-DTD structure.

Normalization Algorithm

Arenas and Libkin (2004) have proposed a normalization algorithm to transform XML design into XNF design. This algorithm performs iteratively two rules to produce XNF design.

1. **Moving Attributes:** The rule is used to eliminate global dependency. Consider global XFD: $\boldsymbol{p \to q.@l}$. To eliminate this XFD, the attribute $@l$ is moved from its original location to a new location of the last element of p
2. **Creating New Element Type:** The rule is used to eliminate local dependency. Consider XFD: $p, q_1.@l_1,..,q_n.@l_n \to \boldsymbol{q.@l}$. To eliminate this type of XFD, a new element type e is created as a child of last p *and attribute* @ $l_{1,...,}$ $@l_n$ are copied for τ and $@l$ is moved from its original location to become an attribute of τ.

We present this algorithm next (Figure 9):

Algorithm proposed by Arenas and Libkin (2004) (Figure 9), only consider for the case of local and global functional dependency. To make this algorithm more flexible, we enhance the rules from (Arenas & Libkin, 2004; Lv et al, 2004) with some modification to suit to our normal forms definition. As presented in section 4.2, we next explain it in a more general way.

1. Given the initial DTD, it will be analysed and carefully investigated. The recognition of complex element, simple element, attribute and semantic relationship depends on depth of the information requirement analysis to establish a better GN-DTD.
2. Based on user requirement, refine the GN-DTD, by supplementing the additional properties and data dependencies such as functional dependency, transitive functional dependency, partial functional dependency and relationship dependency.
3. Transform the initial GN-DTD into the equivalent target GN-DTD which is in normalised and simplified i.e 1XNF, 2XNF, 3XNF or XNF. This procedure is iteratively implemented by taking the previous refined GN-DTD until it becomes normal form. In order to establish a systematic approach to

Figure 9. XNF Normalization Algorithm (Arenas & Libkin, 2004)

(1) IF $(D, \sum)$ is in XNF then return $((D, \sum)$, otherwise go to step (2).
(2) / * moving attribute*/
    If there is an anomalous XFD $q \to p.@l$ and $q \in paths(D)$ *such that* $q \to X \in (D, \sum)^+$ then:
    2.1 Choose an attribute @m
    2.2 $D := D[p.@l := q.@m]$
    2.3 $\sum := \sum[p.@l := q.@m]$
    2.4 Go to step (1)
(3)/ * create new element types*/
    Choose a $(D, \sum)$ – *minimal anomalous XFD* $\{q, p_1.@l1, ..., p_n.@l_n\} \to p.@l$
    (3.1) Create fresh element types $\tau, \tau_1, .., \tau_n$
    (3.2) $D := D[p.@l := q.\tau[\tau_1.@l_1, ..., \tau_n.@l_n, @l]]$
    (3.3) $\sum := \sum[p.@l := q.\tau[\tau_1.@l_1, ..., \tau_n.@l_n, @l]]$
(3.4) Go to step (1)

obtain better GN-DTD schema, we propose the normalization rules. As shown in section 4, we add another rule which is moving up complex element together with it children to another location and level. This rule is used to eliminate transitive functional dependency in the GN-DTD by considering one-to-many, many-to-many or many-to-one inheritance relationship between complex element nodes in GN-DTD.

4. Based upon the analysis of these structural semantic relationships, the GN-DTD schema is iteratively transformed into refined normal form preserving the data dependencies as well. It is basically required the data dependency should be preserved throughout the transformation of GN-DTD model. To preserve the data dependencies, each of data dependencies is updated to match with the new location of associated complex element, simple elements and attribute in GN-DTD. By the analysis of the data dependencies, the initial GN-DTD schema may be transformed into a better schema which is normalised and simplified.

7. DISCUSSION

Arenas and Libkin's (2004) approach have a remarkable impact on principle of XML document normalization. But we have found that XML database designer expects a bit difference and more practical technique:

1. It has to be very simple, precise, and understandable and should work with minimum of abstract concepts, similarly as "the classical relational model normalization". We suppose that introduction of difficult introduction distinctively exceeding over classical normal forms by having a lots of types of concepts, is not a right way.
2. It should be focused concretely on graphical view of XML schema model rather than the text representation. This is because, graphical modelling language is widely accepted as a more visually effective means of specifying and communicating data requirement user and suitable who has no technical background (Gustas, 2010; Halpin, 2010).
3. We need to model structures and semantic of element, attributes of the XML documents schema (DTD) used for data storage and data manipulation. As stated by Feng et al. (2002), "*To enable efficient business application development in large-scale electronic commerce environment, it is necessary to describe and model real world semantics and their complex interrelationship*".
4. It has to be flexible to a designer to choose which normal form better to their application requirements and the same time preserve the data constraints.

Our propose method is complement to Arenas and Libkin (2004) approach. In our approach, we consider all the requirements that have been discussed above when designing an XML document. Besides that, we found that the main feature of GN-DTD's notations is particularly easily to improve XML structural design and more importantly, make the XML normalization procedure simpler and practical. Since the semantic relationships represented in this approach is not complicated, it is thus easy to use GN-DTD to maintain XML document as well.

8. CONCLUSION AND FUTURE WORK

Multiple levels of normal forms such as IXNF, 2XNF, 3XNF and XNF for GN-DTD have been defined to eliminate data redundancy and update anomalies in XML documents. A normalization rules have been proposed to transform from one normal form to another level of normal form. The transformation steps from one normal form to the next can be described as series of transformations on the GN-DTD model. Particularly, these algorithms have restructured the original GN-DTD by considering the hierarchical structure, the level of nodes and relationship types between nodes associated to a given set of data dependencies.

To prove the concept, we provide a simple case study to illustrate the application of our propose GN-DTD normal forms and normalization rules to achieve a free redundancy XML document design. We show through case study, having GN-DTD as a conceptual model simplifies the complex procedure of XML document design and normalization. Even though the length of XML document is longer than the original document, but structure is free from data redundancy and update anomalies.

The normal form GN-DTD presented in this paper has shown three advantages. First, the designer can indentify complex elements, simple elements, attributes graphically and can add the relationship types between the nodes from user specification. Hence, this will give more control to the designer to evaluate each successive normal form GN- DTD. Second, normalizing the GN-DTD can effectively removes redundancies and anomalies at a schema level. More importantly, able to preserve both DTD hierarchical structure and XML document structure and satisfy user requirement. As ongoing work, we are defining formally the GN-DTD and presenting the prototype system using formal specification method. For future work, we will develop more complex and comprehensive case study to show the application of GN-DTD normal forms and normalization algorithm.

ACKNOWLEDGMENT

The authors thank and also gratefully acknowledge anonymous reviewers for the valuable comments.

REFERENCES

Arenas, M., & Libkin, L. (2004). A normal form for XML documents. *ACM Transactions on Database Systems*, *29*(1), 195–232. doi:10.1145/974750.974757

Buneman, P., Davidson, S., Fan, W., Hara, C. S., & Tan, W. C. (2002). Keys for XML. *Computer Networks*, *39*(5), 473–487. doi:10.1016/S1389-1286(02)00223-2

Chen, P. P. (1976). The entity-relational model: Towards a unified view of data. *ACM Transactions on Database Systems*, *1*(1), 9–36. doi:10.1145/320434.320440

Codd, E. (1972). A relational model of data for large shared data banks. *Communications of the ACM*, *13*(6), 377–387. doi:10.1145/362384.362685

Dobbie, G., & Xiaoying, W. Ling. T. W., & Lee, M. L. (2000). *ORA-SS: An object-relationship-attribute model for semi-strucured data*. Unpublished doctoral dissertation, National University of Singapore, Pulau Bukom.

Embley, D., & Mok, W. Y. (2001). Developing XML documents with guaranteed "good" properties, In *Proceedings of the 20th International Conference on Conceptual Modeling* (pp. 426-441).

Feng, L., Chang, E., & Dillon, T. (2002). A semantic network-based design methodology for XML documents. *ACM Transactions on Information Systems*, *20*(4), 390–421. doi:10.1145/582415.582417

Gustas, R. (2010). A look behind conceptual modelling constructs in information system, analysis and design. *International Journal of Information System Modeling and Design*, *1*(1), 79–108. doi:10.4018/jismd.2010092304

Halpin, T. (2010). Object role modelling: Principle and benefit. *International Journal of Information System Modeling and Design*, *1*(1), 33–55. doi:10.4018/jismd.2010092302

Kolahi, S. (2007). Dependency-preserving normalization of relational and XML data. *Journal of Computer and System Sciences*, 636–647. doi:10.1016/j.jcss.2006.10.014

Lee, S. Y., Lee, M. L., Ling, T. W., & Kalinichenko, L. A. (1999). Designing good semi-strucutred databases. In J. Akoka, M. Bouzeghoub, I. Comyn-Wattiau, & E. Metais (Eds.), *Proceedings of the 18th International Conference on Coneptual Modeling* (LNCS 1728, p. 767).

Ling, T. W. (1985). A normal form for entity-relationship diagram. In *Proceedings of the 4th International Conference on Entity-Relationship Approach* (pp. 24-35).

Ling, T. W., Lee, M. L., & Dobbie, G. (2005). *Semi structured database design*. New York, NY: Springer.

Lv, T., Gu, N., & Yan, P. (2004). Normal forms for XML documents. *Information and Software Technology*, 839–846.

Mani, M., Lee, D., & Muntz, R. R. (2001). Semantic data modeling using XML schemas. In H. Kunii, S. Jajodia, & A. Solvberg (Eds.), *Proceedings of 20th International Conference on Conceptual Modeling,* Yokohama, Japan (LNCS 2224, pp. 149-163).

Powell, G. (2007). *Beginning XML databases*. Inidianapolis, IN: Wiley Publishing.

Tompson, H. S., Beech, D., Moloney, M., & Meldensohn, N. (2004). *XML schema part 1: Structures second edition.* Retrieved from http://www.w3.org/TR/xmlschema-1

Vincent, M., Liu, J., & Liu, C. (2004). Strong functional dependencies and their application to normal form in XML. *ACM Transactions on Database Systems*, *29*(3), 445–462. doi:10.1145/1016028.1016029

Vincent, M., Liu, J., & Mohania, M. (2007). On the equivalence between FDs in XML and FDs in relations. *Acta Infomatica*, 230-247.

Wang, J., & Topor, R. (2005). Removing XML data redundancies using functional and equality-generating dependencies. In *Proceedings of the 16th Australian Database Conference* (Vol. 39, pp. 65-74).

Yu, C., & Jagadish, J. H. (2008). XML schema refinement through redundancy detection and normalization. *International Journal on Very Large Data Base*, *17*(2), 203–223. doi:10.1007/s00778-007-0063-0

Zainol, Z., & Wang, B. (2010). GN-DTD: Graphical notations for describing XML documents. In *Proceedings of the 2nd International Conference on Advances in Databases, Knowledge, and Data Applications* (pp. 214-221).

This work was previously published in the International Journal of Information Retrieval Research, Volume 1, Issue 1, edited by Zhongyu (Joan) Lu, pp. 53-76, copyright 2011 by IGI Publishing (an imprint of IGI Global).

Chapter 6
Mining Product Reviews in Web Forums

S. Hariharan
Pavendar Bharathidasan College of Engineering and Technology, India

T. Ramkumar
A.V.C. College of Engineering, India

ABSTRACT

Internet has brought a major drift in user community. Apart from its well-known usage, it also promotes social networking. Research on such social networking has advanced significantly in recent years which have been highly influenced by the online social websites. People perceive the web as a social medium that allows larger interaction among people, sharing of knowledge, or experiences. Internet or social web forums act as an agent to reproduce some general information that would benefit the users. A product review by the user is a more accurate representation of its real-world performance and web-forums are generally used to post such reviews. Though commercial review websites allow users to express their opinions in whatever way they feel, the number of reviews that a product receives could be very high. Hence, opinion mining techniques can be used to analyze the user-reviews, classify the content as positive or negative, and thereby find out how the product fares. This paper focuses its attention on providing a recommendation to the products available on the web by analyzing the context to score the sentences for each review by identifying the opinion and feature words using a novel algorithm.

1. INTRODUCTION

Internet has been considered as a medium to exchange information or knowledge. Due to the rapid growth of information online, almost every activity in human life has become automated. For instance consider a user, who wishes to purchase a music system or digital camera. The user can sit comfortably in his place and browse for the best products through online websites which provides about each products. Such commercial sites allow people to express their opinions on the products that they have purchased. Hearst (1992) and Wiebe (1994) originally proposed the idea of mining direction-based text, namely, text containing opinions, sentiments, affects, and biases.

The current scenario is that, social web-forums allows each individual to post review which may be a discussion groups or blogs which enables the new user to buy product based on the views

DOI: 10.4018/978-1-4666-3898-3.ch006

of expressed by different users. These reviews are useful for both customers and manufacturers. Opinions or sentiments about the products can be analyzed about these products and their performances can be analyzed effectively. Opinions are hidden in long forum posts and blogs, which allows human to find relevant sources, summarize them and organize them into usable forms. Sun et al. (2009) proposed the system for sentimental classification and comparison of products from both subjective and objective perspective on various feature levels.

To make decisions about online reviews, opinions are so important and we should take some special interest in mine such positive and negative opinions. Review comments from the sites are considered as valuable because they cover a lot more products than those formal review sites. Facts and opinions are the categories of textual information. All entities and events in the world have objective statements that are called facts. On contrary subjective statements that reflect people's sentiments or perceptions are called opinion. Recent research on such opinion mining and sentimental analysis have been performed based on unsupervised learning approach (Popescu & Etzioni, 2005), analyzing lexical features and their relationships (Riloff et al., 2006), sentimental word based scheme (Cai et al., 2008) and frequency of occurrence of product features (Wong & Lam, 2005).

Opinion or sentiment bearing words (e.g., great, amazing, wonderful, bad, and poor) are mainly used in the research on opinion mining. As per the review, work on mining such opinion bearing words and to identify their semantic orientations (i.e., positive or negative) helps both merchants and buyers (Su et al., 2008). Since a product may have hundreds or even thousands of reviews it is difficult for buyers to choose right decision and also for manufacturer to keep track of change if products of different kinds are produced. Hu and Liu (2004) aimed to mine and to summarize all the customer reviews of a product in a system. Only those opinions that are given by customers as positive or negative for each product is summarized; this makes the task different from traditional text summarization.

User generated contents are created and published by the end users who surf the web on a daily basis. Examples of such online documents are blogs, newsgroup postings and discussion forums. There are two types of textual information available on the web namely facts and opinions. Facts are objective expressions about entities, events and their properties. Facts can be expressed with topic keywords. Currently available search engines search only for facts and they are not appropriate for opinion retrieval or search. But the user generated content on the web such as personal experiences and opinions about a product or a movie in the form of reviews play a very important role in business, education, e-commerce, etc. Online review websites allow users to express their opinions for the information they are interested in. So there is a huge amount of information available online, however they fail to provide the knowledge about the products.

Customers could assess a product by reading opinions of other customers, which will help them to decide whether to purchase the product or not. On the other hand, the manufacturers can improve their products by tracking the feedback from the customers. With the emergence of e-commerce, the number of reviews that a product receives is quite high and many reviews are lengthy with only few sentences containing the actual opinions on the product. It is not easy for a customer to read all the reviews in order to decide on whether to buy the product or not. If the customer reads only a few reviews, then the opinion might be biased. Manufacturers also find it difficult to analyze all the reviews and to interpret the customer opinions. This paper attempts to provide a methodology to mine the reviews available in web forums and to express the opinions from them

The rest of this paper is organized as follows: In Section 1 we have exposed the web as a medium of information gathering. Section 2 focuses on the related research carried out, while Section 3 focuses on opinion mining detailing the pros and cons of the existing system. Section 4 presents the proposed system for mining the user reviews and in Section 5 experiments and discussions were elaborated with a sample review and the output. Finally Section 6 provides the conclusion and the future works.

2. RELATED WORK

Hu and Liu (2004) developed a feature-based opinion summarization system that mines and summarizes all the customer reviews of a product. This system differs from other text summarization systems in number of ways. It mines only the features of the product that customers have expressed their opinions on and the summary generated is structured rather than a free text document as generated by other text summarization systems. The summarization is performed by the system in three steps: (1) Finding the features on which the customers have expressed their opinions. (2) Identifying opinion sentences in each review and analyzing the polarity of the sentence (3) Producing a summary.

Lu et al. (2009) focused on the problem of generating a rated aspect summary of short comments. The input is a large number of short comments about a target entity. Each comment is associated with an overall comment. The solution to the problem involved three steps namely aspect discovery and clustering, aspect rating prediction and representative phrases extraction. The effectiveness of this method was demonstrated using eBay sellers' feedback comments.

A classification based approach was developed for detecting low quality product reviews (Lin et al., 2007). A set of specifications for judging the quality of reviews are defined. Based on the specifications the low-quality reviews are separated from high-quality ones then summarization is done.

Feldman et al. (2008) have presented a set of techniques for analyzing how consumers view product markets. They have extracted relative sentiment analysis and comparisons between products, to understand what attributes users compare products on, and which products they prefer on each dimension. This system also compares state-of-the-art machine learning methods against simple hand-coded patterns. The key steps in extraction of the product mentions are information extraction and snippet extraction. Snippet extraction involves pattern extraction and pattern filtering. They have used a fast algorithm that finds all matches of all patterns with complexity logarithmic in the number of patterns and linear in the corpus size. Finally summary of the results is generated.

Cui, Mittal, and Datar (2006) classified online product reviews into positive and negative classes. This paper employs three algorithms: (1) Winnow (Nigam & Hurst, 2004) (2) a generative model based on language modeling and (3) a discriminative classifier that employs projection based learning (Shwartz et al., 2004). Three classifiers and n-grams as linguistic features are used to classify sentences. Classifier combined with high order n-grams as features can achieve better performance.

Prabowo and Thelwall (2009) evaluated the effectiveness of different classifiers, and shows that the use of multiple classifiers in a hybrid manner can improve the effectiveness of sentiment analysis in terms of micro and macro-averaged than any individual classifier. This paper combines rule-based classification, supervised learning and machine learning into a new combined method. This method reviews number of automatic document classification techniques. This also includes semi-automatic, complementary approach in which each classifier can contribute to other classifiers to achieve a good level of effectiveness.

Wong and Lam (2005) developed a technique for mining and summarizing hot items from multiple auction Web sites. In the auction Web sites, the items with high number of bids are automatically regarded as hot items. This approach is a two phase framework for mining and summarizing hot items. The first phase is to extract the product features and product feature values of the items and the second phase is to mine and summarize hot items. Hidden Markov model (HMM) is used to reliably extract the product features since the format of the description is greatly different ranging from regular format such as tables to unstructured free texts.

Melville, Gryc, and Lawrence (2009) designed the explosion of user-generated content on the Web to focus the attention about monitoring the discussion around companies' products with new opportunities and significant challenges. As per the sentiment expressed in blogs, specific brands and products of such analysis is characterized .The author focused on the task of automatically identifying whether a piece of text expresses a positive or negative opinion about the subject matter. A text classification problem, where sentiments are classified based on training data that is labeled is treated. Background lexical information with associations and specific domain refinement in a unified framework is considered. The author found that better approach is to use Empirical results on diverse domains than using background knowledge or training data in isolation, as well as alternative approaches to using lexical knowledge with text classification.

Prabowo and Thelwall (2009) proposed a new method by combination of rule-based classification, supervised learning and machine learning. Movie reviews, product reviews and MySpace comments is tested using this method. The author found that the classification effectiveness in terms of micro- and macro-averaged $F1$ can be improved by a hybrid classification where both the precision and recall of a classifier's effectiveness is taken into account. A good level of effectiveness can also be achieved by using a semi-automatic, Complementary approach in which each classifier can contribute to other classifiers.

Ahmed, Chen, and Salem (2008) focused their attention on the use of sentiment analysis methodologies for classification of Web forum opinions in multiple languages. For sentiment classification of English and Arabic content stylistic and syntactic features is evaluated. To account for the linguistic characteristics of Arabic Specific feature extraction components are integrated and a hybridized entropy weighted genetic algorithm (EWGA) is also developed, which will be used for feature selection by incorporating the information-gain heuristic. The author found that better performance and assessment can be achieved by using EWGA that are evaluated on a benchmark movie review dataset and U.S. and Middle Eastern Web forum postings. For document-level classification of sentiments EWGA and Stylistic features outperformed better than other techniques.

Whitelaw, Garg, and Argamon (2005) have introduced sentiment classification based on the use of fine-grained semantic distinctions in features. Based on extraction and analyzing appraisal groups such as "very good" or "not terribly funny", a new method was developed. As per Appraisal Theory, a set of attribute values in several task-independent semantic taxonomies represent an appraisal group. A lexicon of appraising adjectives and their modifiers were built by methods that are semi-automated. It was reported that state-of-the-art accuracy of 90.2% for review by using the combined features of taxonomies with standard "bag- of-words". The author also found sentiment classification is more significant by using some types of appraisal than others.

Feldman et al. (2008) analyzed the technique that results the most sentiment analysis for various views of products by the customers. The results also extracted relative sentiment analysis and comparisons between products based on attributes and dimensions and include the case study of analyzing the sedan car markets.

Cai, Spangler, Chen, and Zhang (2008) designed a sentiment analysis system that included a sentiment classification component and sentiment topic words recognition component. The authors found that sentiment classification alone was insufficient because sentiment classification summarizes customer's opinions but does not reveal the implicit root cause of the sentiments. Such reasons were called the "sentiment topics" linked with the sentiments. Sentiment topic words recognition component detects the topics hidden behind the positive or negative opinions based on a combined PMI (Point wise Mutual Information) and word support metrics. The sentiment classification process is based on a semantic based approach that mainly depends on opinion word collection in the form of knowledge base or sentiment dictionary. Using real-world usage cases the authors verified the effectiveness of their technique on reviews posted on blogs, message boards, etc.

3. OPINION MINING

Opinion Mining is a technique which analyzes opinions on various products expressed in the form of reviews in online review websites and to classify the reviews as positive or negative. This section elaborates the basics of opinion mining, challenges, formats of the reviews available and sentiment analysis. Each of these was discussed in the subsections that follow.

3.1. Challenges

Opinion mining also known as sentiment classification or opinion extraction is a challenging task. In human language there are many ways to express the same opinion. Although the overall opinion about a topic is useful, it is only a part of the information of interest. Document level sentiment classification fails to detect sentiment about individual aspects of the topic since it considers the whole document as the basic information unit. Existing research on sentiment classification assumes that the opinionated document 'D' (e.g., a product review) expresses opinions on a single object 'o' and the opinions are from a single opinion holder 'H'. This assumption holds for customer reviews of products and services. However, it may not hold for a forum and blog post because in such a post the author may express opinions on multiple products and compare those using comparative and superlative sentences. Hence we focus on to classify the reviews based on sentence level approach discussed in the next section.

3.2. Sentence-Level Subjectivity and Sentiment Classification

Sentiment classification can also be applied to individual sentences. The task of classifying a sentence as opinionated or not opinionated is called subjectivity classification. The resulting opinionated sentences are also classified as expressing positive or negative opinions, which is called the sentence level sentiment classification.

Given a sentence 'S', two sub-tasks are performed:

- **Subjectivity Classification:** Determine whether 'S' is a subjective sentence or an objective sentence.
- **Sentence-Level Sentiment Classification:** If 'S' is subjective, determine whether it expresses a positive or negative opinion.

Sentence-level sentiment classification assumes that the sentence expresses a single opinion from a single opinion holder. This assumption is only appropriate for simple sentences with a single opinion. For example, "*The picture quality of this camera is amazing.*"

However, for compound sentences, a single sentence may express more than one opinion. For example, the sentence, "*The picture quality of this camera is amazing and so is the battery life, but the viewfinder is too small for such a great camera*", expresses both positive and negative opinions (one may say that it has a mixed opinion). For "picture quality" and "battery life", the sentence is positive, but for "viewfinder", it is negative. It is also positive for the camera as a whole.

3.3. Formats of User Reviews

Though there are two common review formats on the web for the expressing product reviews, the technique for extracting the opinions from them vary significantly.

- **Format 1 – Pros, Cons and the Detailed Review:** The reviewer is asked to describe Pros and Cons separately and also write a detailed or full review. Figure 1 shows a sample review of format 1.
- **Format 2 – Free Format:** The reviewer can write his comments freely, i.e., no differentiation of Pros and Cons. Figure 2 shows a sample review of format 2. Experiments in this paper were carried for reviews of format 2 only.

3.4. Feature-Based Sentiment Analysis

Although classifying opinionated texts at the document level or at the sentence level is useful in many cases, they do not provide the necessary detail needed for some other applications. A positive opinionated document on a particular object does not mean that the author has positive opinions on all aspects or features of the object. Likewise, a negative opinionated document does not mean that the author dislikes everything. In a typical opinionated text, the author writes both positive and negative aspects of the object, although the general sentiment on the object may be positive or negative. Document-level and sentence-level

Figure 1. Sample review of format 1

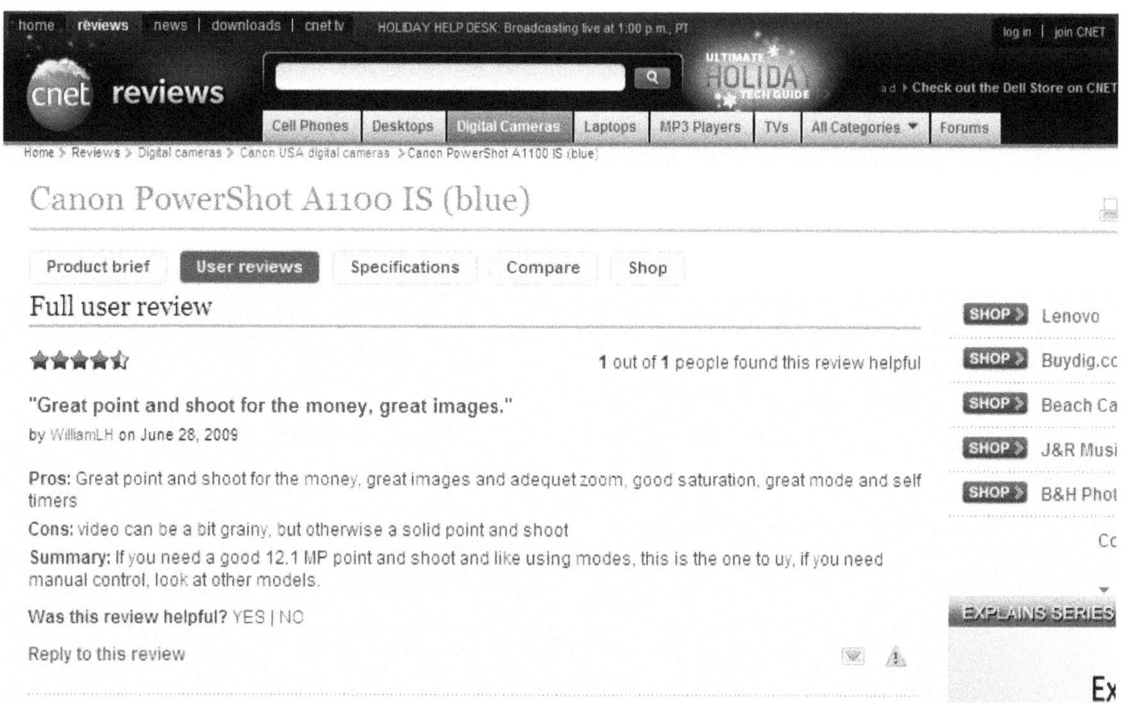

Figure 2. Sample review of format 2

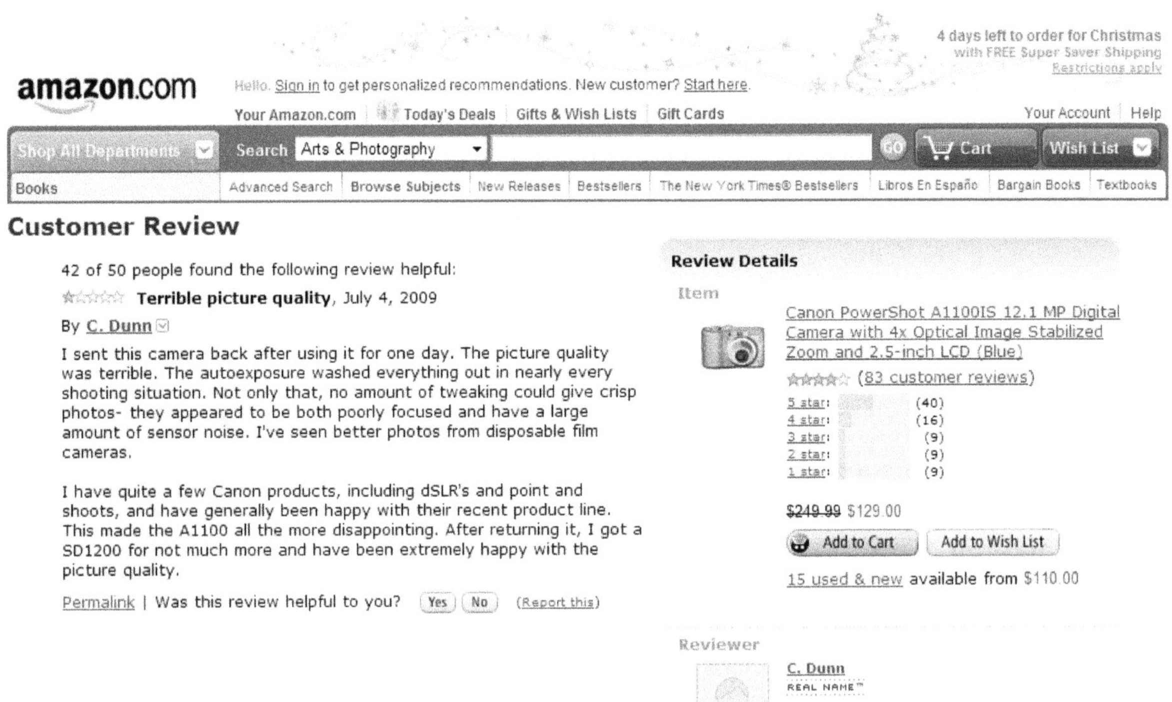

classification does not provide such information. To obtain such details, we need to go to the object feature level analysis.

At the feature level, the mining task is to discover every occurrence of a set of an object 'o', a feature of the object 'f', and 'oo' the orientation or polarity of the opinion on feature 'f' of object 'o'. In this section, we mainly focus on two key mining tasks:

- Identify object features that have been commented on. For instance, in the sentence, "*The picture quality of this camera is amazing*," the object feature is "picture quality".
- Determine whether the opinions on the features are positive, negative or neutral. In the above sentence, the opinion on the feature "picture quality" is positive as denoted by the opinion word "amazing".

In product reviews, the reviewed objects are usually known. However, this is not the case for opinions expressed in blogs and discussion posts. For example, in the post, "*I have a Canon S50 camera purchased from Amazon. It takes great photos*," two interesting questions can be asked: (1) what object does the post praise and (2) what "it" means in the second sentence? Clearly, we humans know that the post praises "Canon S50 camera", which is the problem of object extraction, and we also know that "it" here means "Canon S50 camera", which is the problem of coreference resolution. Coreference resolution is a major challenge.

3.5. Opinion Orientation Identification

The lexicon-based approach basically uses opinion words and phrases in a sentence to determine the orientation of the opinion. Apart from the opinion lexicon, negations, intensifiers and conjunctions in a sentence are also crucial and need to be handled.

Negations are terms that reverse the sentiment of a certain word. For example consider the sentence. While analyzing negations the words like none, not, no, never, hardly, seldom, or little, are all considered.

For example, consider the sentence *"The picture quality of this camera is not good."* Because of the presence of not the sentence is negative.

Intensifiers are terms that change the degree of the expressed sentiment. For example, in the sentence *"This camera is very nice"*, the terms *very* and *nice* are more positive together than just *nice* alone. Another example of an intensifier is *deeply* from the phrase *"deeply suspicious"*, which increases the intensity of the word *suspicious*. On the other hand, in the sentence *"This camera is barely any good"*, the term *barely* makes the sentence less positive.

A conjunction is a word that links words, phrases, or clauses, and it may be used to indicate the relationship between the ideas expressed in a clause and the ideas expressed in the rest of a sentence.

Conjunctions such as *however, yet* and *but* plays a vital role in deciding the overall polarity of a sentence. These types of words often change the sentiment into the opposition orientation or add in the strength of the sentiment.

- **Example:** *"The picture quality of this camera is excellent but the battery life is not good".*

This sentence contains the word *but*. If we consider the word *excellent* alone, the sentence conveys a positive opinion. However, the word *but* in the sentence changes its sentiment orientation, actually the sentence conveys a negative opinion.

3.6. Existing Solution

Existing works are mostly context insensitive and provide inaccurate results. An example is given below to illustrate the present scenario.

- **Example:** *"The time taken to focus is long"*

The word 'long' is considered to be a positive opinion word. Hence the sentence would be scored as a positive sentence. But the sentence expresses a negative opinion indirectly about the camera's zoom feature. Most of the existing algorithms do not analyze the context in which the words occur and perform scoring blindly.

Even the few existing context-sensitive algorithms are not capable of handling various review formats like the Pros-cons format and the freeform format. Different formats may need different techniques to perform the feature and opinion extraction task.

Analysis based on comparative study of reviews is often biased and inaccurate. A comparison is used to state that one object has more of a certain quantity than another object. Hence one can obtain the comparative information with respect to two or more products rather than the outright opinion about an individual product.

Also, most of the algorithms perform 'stemming' – the process for reducing inflected words to their root form, which often leads to losing the much important detail of the opinion word.

- **Example:** *"iPhone is **light**, but MotoRAZR is even **lighter**."*

In the above example, if stemming was performed, the word 'lighter' would be reduced to 'light'. The word 'lighter' is the higher degree superlative form of the adjective 'light'. Hence the word 'lighter' carries higher value than the word 'light'. But most of the existing algorithms would give the same score for both of these words if stemming is performed.

4. PROPOSED SOLUTION

Crawled user-review from online review web sites is obtained as input through the user interface. Such reviews are called as unstructured reviews, since they are of free form expressed by users. The overall system architecture is shown in Figure 4. Each of the tasks involved in the proposed system is explained in this section in a detailed manner with appropriate examples and illustrations.

4.1. Extraction

Extraction involves splitting the review into units of sentences by considering the punctuation marks and conjunctions present in the review. The first step involves extracting the text neglecting the formatting and breaking them into units of sentences. This is done taking into account the punctuations like '.', '!', '?', ';' and conjunctions like 'but', 'yet', etc. At the end of this step we are left with sentence units, chopped down from the given text of a user-review. Figure 3 shows a sample list of punctuations and conjunctions. A sample review is given and the results are shown in Section 5.

4.2. Pre-Processing

In pre-processing, the non-informative words called stop words and special characters present in the review sentences are removed. The preprocessing task and the obtained output is shown in Figure 11.

4.2.1. Stop-Words Removal

Stop words are those words which rarely contribute useful information in terms of document relevance. Most stop words are functional words which do not carry any meaning, including articles, prepositions and some other high-frequency words, such as *a, the, of, and, I, it* and *you*. Such a list of acceptable

Figure 3. Sample list of punctuations and conjunctions

.	;	!	?	but	yet	whereas

stop words are compiled from the web**. There is no definite list of stop words which all Natural Language Processing (NLP) tools incorporate. The assumption of stop words removal is that, when assessing the contents of natural language, the meaning can be conveyed more clearly, or interpreted more easily, by ignoring the functional words. Removal of non-informative stop words reduces the noisy information and it is found to improve the performance of the system in tasks like summarization, question answering systems etc. In specific it is found to have a significant effect in text processing. We eliminate such unwanted words from user-review text. Figure 5 shows a sample list of stop words.

4.2.2. Special Characters Removal

Plaintext reviews usually contain special characters (-, $, ',:,<,>,@, =, #, %, &, etc). Hence it is essential to remove these special characters from the input review.

4.3. Opinion Mining

Opinion mining identifies the feature words, negations, intensifiers, opinion words, neutral words in the review sentences. An appropriate score is assigned to each word. Each sentence is scored and the overall scores for all the sentences in the review are calculated.

4.3.1. Opinion and Feature Words Identification

This step analyzes the pre-processed review sentences for the presence of feature words. A sample list of feature words is shown in Table 1. Feature words such as *image quality, video quality, clarity, sharpness, etc* are replaced by a common word *performance*.

Then the review sentences are checked for the presence of inverters. Figure 6 shows a sample list of inverters.

Figure 4. Proposed system for mining the reviews

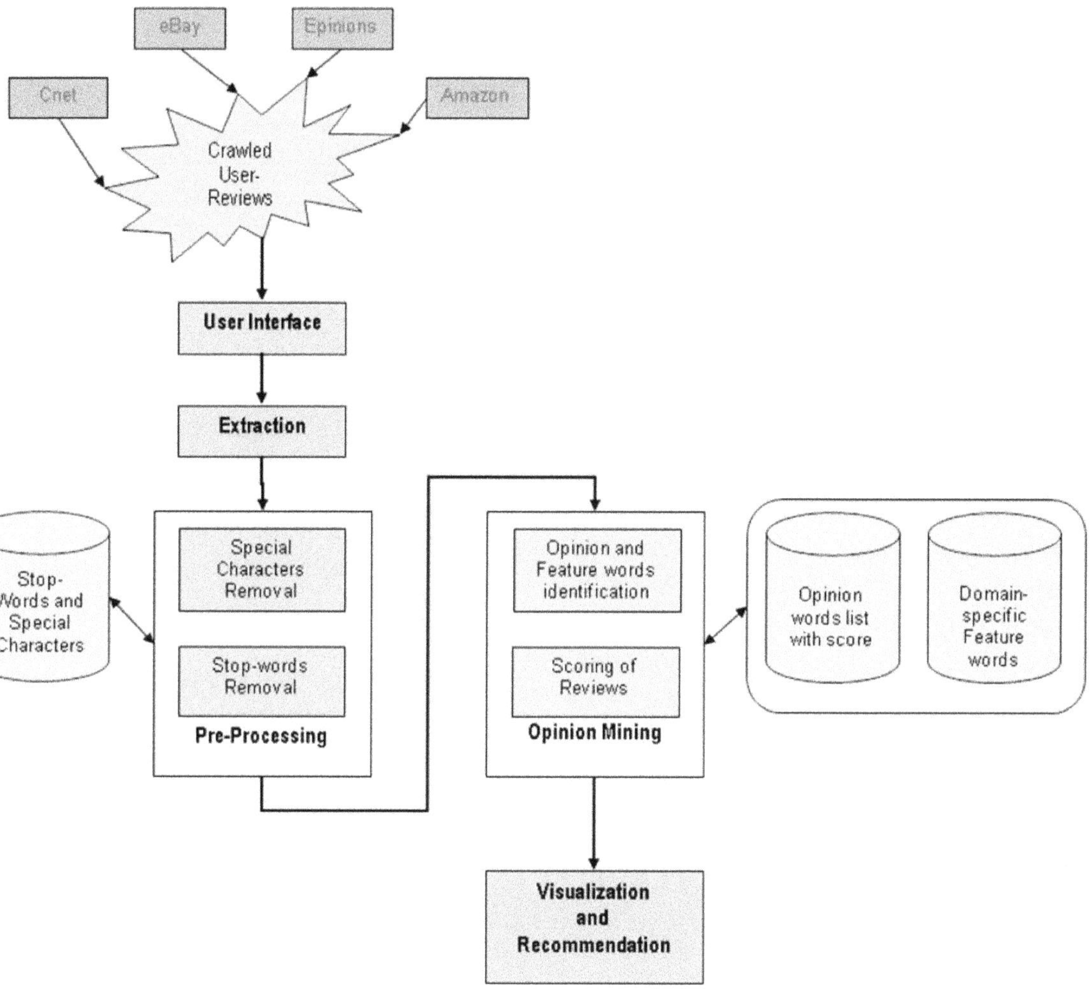

Figure 5. Sample list of stop words

a, every, hereafter, now, among, except, him , often, be, face, her, on, before, for, in, over, could, from, is, off, despite, further, inside, put, does, forever, many, per, during, has, meanwhile , perhaps, ever, hence, neither, past

Figure 6. Sample list of inverters

Cannot, hardly, aren't, not, seldom, couldn't, nor, don't, daren't, neither, cant, maynt, never, no, mightnt, nothing, wont, wouldn't, don't, not, non, nor, hardly, hasn't, seldom, haven't, didn't

Table 1. Sample list of feature words

Features			
performance	**features**	**value**	**ergonomics**
pictures picture quality video quality image quality colors Clarity sharpness	image stabilization lens resolution focus optical zoom zoom memory	price cost value money add-ons	weight size grip ease design

The intensifiers and opinion words present in the review are identified. Table 2 shows a sample list of intensifiers. Intense factor is a value which when multiplied by the score of the opinion word following the intensifier changes the degree of the expressed sentiment (Feldman et al., 2008). Feature words identified in the review should be associated with the corresponding opinion word.

For instance consider the sentence, *"video quality quite good"*. Here video quality will be identified as feature word, quite as intensifier and good as opinion word. Subsequently, the feature word "video quality" will be replaced by the word "performance". The output will be *"performance quite good"*.

4.3.2. Scoring

The opinion words are classified according to their intensity as strongly negative, moderately negative, lightly negative, strongly positive, moderately positive and lightly positive as shown in Table 3. They are given a score of -15, -10, -5, +15, +10 and +5 respectively. The words which do not belong to any of these categories are considered as neutral words and they are given a score of +1 or -1 depending upon the orientation of the opinion in the review sentence. The presence of any intensifier words (quite, very, etc.) or inverter words (not, doesn't, etc.) are also considered while calculating. Then the overall score for each sentence is calculated based on these conditions and the pattern of occurrence of the words listed.

Table 2. Sample list of intensifiers and corresponding intense factors

INTENSIFIERS	INTENSE FACTOR
least	0.5
just, bit, little, minor	0.6
quite	0.8
relatively	0.9
really	1.1
very	1.2
much, more	1.3
too, ultra	1.4
most, mostly, extremely	1.5

Generally a feature word (F) will be followed or preceded by an intensifier-opinion word (IO) combination/ opinion word (O). So there are different patterns of review sentences based on the order of occurrence of feature words, intensifiers, opinion words, inverter words (Inv) and neutral words (N). They are FIO, FO, OF, IOF, FNIO, FNO, IO and O. The feature score for feature (F) is the score that is assigned to the intensifier-opinion word (IO) combination/ opinion word (O) following or preceding the feature word. In the absence of a feature word, any Intensifier-Opinion word pair (IO) or Opinion Word(O) occurring by themselves are also scored and the corresponding score is added up to the overall score alone. After scoring each sentence, the feature scores for each feature (performance, features, ergonomics and value) are calculated. This score is also added up to the overall score of the product.

The sentence *"performance quite good"* (FIO pattern) is scored as follows. *"Good"* is a lightly positive opinion word and it is given a score of +5. *"Quite"* is an intensifier (intense factor=0.8).

Quite good= 0.8*5=4.0

Table 3. Sample list of opinion words

Negative words			Neutral	Positive Words		
Strongly -ve -15	**Moderately -ve -10**	**Lightly -ve -5**	**± 1**	**Lightly +ve +5**	**Moderately +ve +10**	**Strongly +ve +15**
Worst Pathetic Abysmal Terrible Awful	Worse Expensive Heavy Slow Sluggish Hate Skip Overhyped Expensive Restrictions	Bad Inferior Stale Ordinary Poor Ugly Small Hard		Good Fine Nice Able Available Ok Okay Care Beautiful Pretty Possible Exceeded Large Easy Simple	Better Fast Light Compact Reliable Love Buy Long Great	Excellent Awesome Marvelous Best Fastest Superb

So the sentence *"The video quality is quite good"* is given a score of 4.0 and the feature score for the feature *"performance"* is 4.0. The scoring is performed for all the sentences in the review and a % of recommendation is calculated using the formula shown in Figure 7.

The industry average values are updated taking into account the scores generated for all the reviews processed so far and by calculating the average of those values with the currently generated value. The industry average values are calculated using the formula shown in Figure 8.

4.4. Visualization and Recommendation

In visualization and recommendation, graphs are displayed with industry average. A recommendation verdict is given to the user. If the recommendation percentage is above 50%, then the product is recommended. A bar graph is generated based on score data. Score for each feature along with the industry average and the overall score with its industry average are displayed. The product recommendation verdict is chosen based on the constraints below:

Figure 7. Calculation of recommendation percentage

$$\text{Recommendation \%} = \frac{(\text{Positive Score}) * 100}{(\text{Positive score}) + (\ |\text{Negative Score}|\ )}$$

Figure 8. Calculation of industry average

$$\text{Industry Average \%} = \frac{(\text{Prev. Industry Avg.}) * (\text{No. of Reviews}) + \text{Current Score}}{(\text{No. of Reviews}) + 1}$$

- **Highly Recommended:** If the recommendation percentage is greater than or equal to 75%.
- **Recommended:** If the recommendation percentage is greater than or equal to 50% and less than 75%.
- **Not Recommended:** If the recommendation percentage is greater than or equal to 25% and less than 50%.
- **Strictly not Recommended:** If the recommendation percentage is less than 25%.

5. EXPERIMENTS AND DISCUSSION

The data set is created by gathering customer reviews of products from online review sites. Table 4 provides the data set constituted for the experiments.

Table 4. Sample of the dataset used for the experiment

Product Name	Number of reviews collected	Source
Digital Camera	200	www.ebay.com
	150	www.epinions.com
	175	www.cnet.com
	250	www.amazon.com

Figure 9. Sample user-review

"This is the best digital camera that I have ever used. The camera exhibits good image quality. The pictures are clear. It has a decent battery life (200-280 shots) and the LCD is too good. The cost is quite expensive ($225). The weight is bit bulky; the 10x zoom in this camera is amazing. The video quality is nice but it is not possible to zoom while recording. Sometimes focusing is sluggish but it depends on the settings. The screen size is comfortable enough to display photos effortlessly. The placement of the cord on the bottom of the camera is very strange. Offers great value for money you pay!!"

5.1. Sample Review

Figure 9 presents a sample user review expressed in free format.

5.2. Extraction Output

The sample review shown in Figure 9 is broken into units of sentences taking into account the punctuation marks and conjunctions present in Figure 3. Figure 10 presents the results after extracting the sentences and Figure 11 shows the output after pre-processing task.

5.3. Opinion Mining Output

From the pre-processed review sentences (shown in Figure 11), inverters, feature words, intensifiers, opinion words are identified and score is calculated for each review sentence. The recommendation percentage is calculated using the formula shown in Figure 7. The feature scores are calculated and the scores for each sentence in the review is shown in Tables 5 and 6.

Table 6 illustrates the feature score assigned to each sentence of the review. Figure 12 presents the visual screens by providing recommendations in bar chart format. Earlier approaches discussed in Section 2 fails to capture the legends mentioned in tables 1, 2 and 3. Hence for the same example presented in Table 5, the recommendation for the product is "REJECTED". Hence, the approaches existing already are contrary to the method pro-

Figure 10. Review in sentence format for the sample shown in Figure 9

1. *This is the* best digital camera *that I have ever* used.
2. *The* camera *exhibits* good image quality.
3. *The* pictures *are* clear.
4. *It has a* decent battery life *(*200-280 shots*) and the* LCD *is* too good.
5. *The* cost *is* quite expensive *($225).*
6. *The* weight *is* bit bulky.
7. *the* 10x zoom *in this* camera *is* amazing.
8. *The* video quality *is* nice.
9. *it is* not possible *to* zoom *while* recording.
10. *Sometimes* focusing *is* sluggish.
11. *it* depends *on the* settings.
12. *The* screen size *is* comfortable *enough to* display photos effortlessly.
13. *The* placement *of the* cord *on the* bottom *of the* camera *is* very strange.

Figure 11. Sentences after preprocessing

1. best digital camera used.
2. camera exhibits good image quality.
3. pictures clear.
4. decent battery life 200 280 shots lcd too good.
5. cost quite expensive 225.
6. weight bit bulky.
7. 10x zoom camera amazing.
8. video quality nice.
9. not possible zoom recording.
10. focusing sluggish.
11. depends settings.
12. screen size comfortable display photos effortlessly.
13. placement cord bottom camera very strange.

Table 5. Scoring of the reviews presented in Figure 9

Sentence No.	Review	Positive Score	Negative Score
1	**best** digital camera used	+15+1+1+1=18	
2	camera exhibits **good performance**	+1+1+5+0=7	
3	**performance clear**	0+5=5	
4	**decent features** 200 280 shots lcd **<u>too</u> good**	+10+0+1+1+1+1+1.4(+5)=21	
5	**value <u>quite</u> expensive** 225		0+0.8(-10)-1= -9
6	**ergo <u>bit</u> bulky**		0+0.6(-10)= -6
7	10x **features** camera **amazing**	+1+0+1+15=17	
8	**performance nice**	0+5=5	
9	**not possible features** recording		-1(+5+0+1)= -6
10	**features sluggish**		0-15= -15
11	depends settings	1+1=2	
12	screen **ergo comfortable** display **performance effortlessly**	+1+0+10+1+0+5=17	
13	placement cord bottom camera **<u>very</u> strange**		-1-1-1-1-1.2(+5)= -10
14	offers **great value** pay	+1+10+0+1=12	
Recommend % = (104/(104+46))*100 = 69.333336% (Above 50% < 75%) PRODUCT RECOMMENDED		**104**	**-46**

LEGEND: Positive opinion word, Negative opinion word, Feature word, Intensifier, Inverter

Table 6. Feature scores for the sample review shown in Figure 9

Sentence No.	Review Sentence	Sentence Pattern	Feature score			
			Performance	Features	Ergonomics	Value
1	best digital camera used	ONNN	0	0	0	0
2	camera exhibits good performance	NNOF	5	0	0	0
3	performance clear	FO	5	0	0	0
4	decent features 200 280 shots lcd too good	OFNNNNIO	0	10	0	0
5	value quite expensive 225	FION	0	0	0	-8
6	ergo bit bulky	FIO	0	0	-6	0
7	10x features camera amazing	NFNO	0	15	0	0
8	performance nice	FO	5	0	0	0
9	not possible features recording	InvOFN	0	-5	0	0
10	features sluggish	FO	0	-15	0	0
11	depends settings	NN	0	0	0	0
12	screen ergo comfortable display performance effortlessly	NFONFO	5	0	10	0
13	placement cord bottom camera very strange	NNNNIO	0	0	0	0
14	offers great value pay	NOFN	0	0	0	10

LEGEND: Positive opinion word, Negative opinion word, Feature word, Intensifier, Inverter

Figure 12. Visualization and recommendation for the sample review

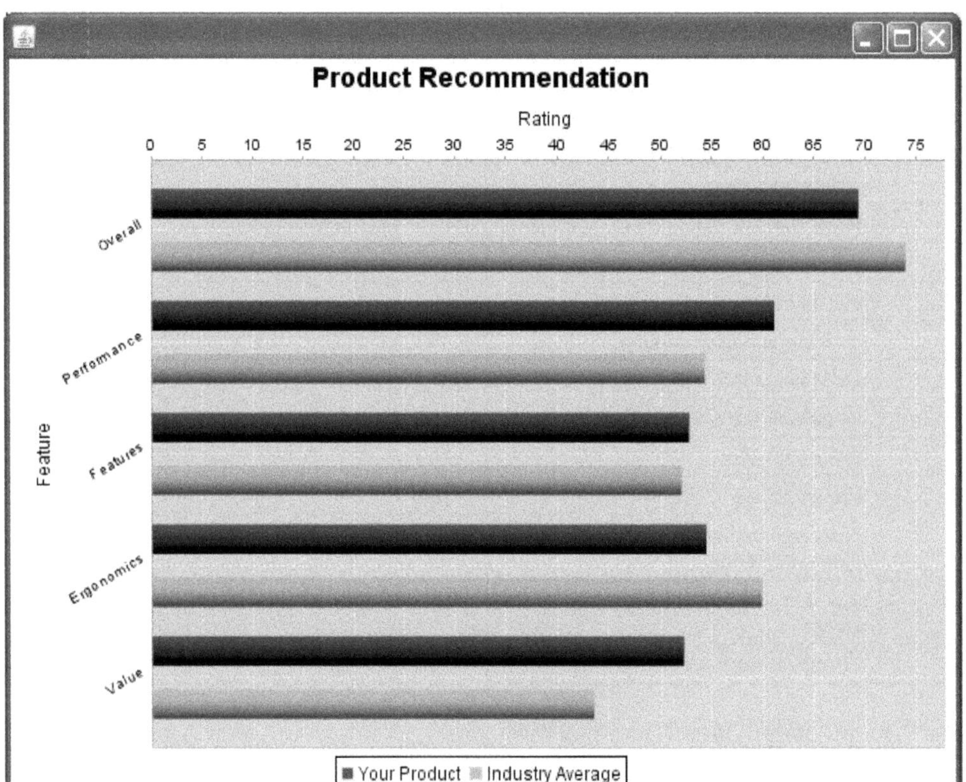

posed here. Hence the proposed system is reasonable. The paper has provided a strong justification or validation on the results obtained, instead it has shown the need for the proposed system. The evaluation part is considered for future extension.

6. CONCLUSION AND FUTURE WORK

In this paper, we have developed an automated system to analyze the user reviews for a product available in the commercial websites. The system proposed recommends the product to the user based on the recommendations obtained. Apart from the product recommendation verdict, it also displays the feature scores for each feature discussed about in the user-review, in the form of a bar graph. We have classified the opinion words into six classes to make scoring more sensitive to varying levels of usage of opinion words. This method is domain independent and can be applied to any domain. Moreover this method is context sensitive and can be applied to any review format and the verdict remains to be independent of the length of the sentences. Our experimental results indicate that this method produces more accurate results.

In the future work, we focus on to classify the sentences as subjective (opinions) or objective (facts) and then we analyze the subjective sentences thereby improving performance. Work is in progress for spell checker to pre-process the reviews. Also, we have attempted to design a smart crawler that fetches the relevant information from various web pages in a website is automatically.

REFERENCES

Abbasi, A., Chen, H., & Salem, A. (2008). Sentiment analysis in multiple languages: Feature selection for opinion classification in web forums. *ACM Transactions on Information Systems*, *26*(3), 12.

Cai, K., Spangler, S., Chen, Y., & Zhang, L. (2008). Leveraging sentiment analysis for topic detection. In *Proceedings of the International Conference on Web Intelligence and Intelligent Agent Technology*, Sydney, Australia (pp. 265-271).

Cui, H., Mittal, V., & Datar, M. (2006). Comparative experiments on sentiment classification for online product reviews. In *Proceedings of the 21st National Conference on Artificial Intelligence* (Vol. 2, pp. 1265-1270).

Feldman, R., Fresko, M., Goldenberg, J., Netzer, O., & Ungar, L. (2008). Using text mining to analyze user forums. In *Proceedings of the International Conference on Service Systems and Service Management*, Melbourne, Australia (pp. 1-5).

Hearst, M. A. (1992). Direction-based text interpretation as an information access refinement. In Jacobs, P. (Ed.), *Text-based intelligent systems: Current research and practice in information extraction and retrieval*. Mahwah, NJ: Lawrence Erlbaum.

Hu, M., & Liu, B. (2004). Mining and summarizing customer reviews. In *Proceedings of the Tenth ACM Conference on Knowledge Discovery and Data Mining*, Seattle, WA (pp. 168-171).

Lin, C. Y., Liu, J., Cao, Y., Huang, Y., & Zhou, M. (2007). Low-quality product review detection in opinion summarization. In *Proceedings of the Joint Conference on Empirical Methods in Natural Language Processing and Computational Natural Language Learning* (pp. 334-342).

Lu, Y., Zhai, C. X., & Sundaresan, N. (2009). Rated aspect summarization of short comments. In *Proceedings of the 18th International Conference on World Wide Web*, Madrid, Spain, (pp. 131-140).

Melville, P., Gryc, W., & Lawrence, R. D. (2009). Sentiment analysis of blogs by combining lexical knowledge with text classification. In *Proceedings of the 15th ACM SIGKDD International Conference on Knowledge Discovery and Data Mining* (pp. 1275-1284).

Nigam, K., & Hurst, M. (2004). Towards a robust metric of opinion. In *Proceedings of the AAAI Spring Symposium on Exploring Attitude and Affect in Text: Theories and Applications*.

Popescu, A. M., & Etzioni, O. (2005). Extracting product features and opinions from reviews. In *Proceedings of the Conference on Human Language Technology and Empirical Methods in Natural Language Processing*, Vancouver, BC, Canada (pp. 339-346).

Prabowo, R., & Thelwall, M. (2009). Sentiment analysis: A combined approach. *Journal of Informatrics*, *3*(2), 143–157. doi:10.1016/j.joi.2009.01.003

Riloff, E., Patwardhan, S., & Wiebe, J. (2006). Feature subsumption for opinion analysis. In *Proceedings of the Conference on Empirical Methods in Natural Language Processing*, Sydney, Australia (pp. 440-448).

Shwartz, S., Crammer, K., Dekel, O., & Singer, Y. (2004). Online passive-aggressive algorithms. In Thrun, S., Saul, L., & Scholkopf, B. (Eds.), *Advances in neural information processing systems* (p. 16). Cambridge, MA: MIT Press.

Su, Q., Xu, X., Guo, H., Guo, Z., Wu, X., Zhang, X., et al. (2008). Hidden sentiment association in Chinese web opinion mining. In *Proceedings of the ACM Conference on World Wide Web*, Beijing, China (pp. 959-968).

Sun, J., Long, C., Zhu, X., & Huang, M. (2009). Mining reviews for product comparison and recommendation. *Research Journal on Computer Science and Computer Engineering with Applications*, *39*, 33–40.

Whitelaw, C., Garg, N., & Argamon, S. (2005). Using appraisal groups for sentiment analysis. In *Proceedings of the 14th ACM International Conference on Information and Knowledge Management*, Bremen, Germany (pp. 625-631).

Wiebe, J. (1994). Tracking point of view in narrative. *Computational Linguistics*, *20*(2), 233–287.

Wong, T. L., & Lam, W. (2005). Hot item mining and summarization from multiple auction web sites. In *Proceedings of the Fifth IEEE International Conference on Data Mining* (pp. 797-800).

Wong, T. L., & Lam, W. (2008). Learning to extract and summarize hot item features from multiple auction web sites. *Knowledge and Information Systems*, *14*(2), 143–160. doi:10.1007/s10115-007-0078-2

Yi, J., Nasukawa, T., Bunescu, R., & Niblack, W. (2003). *Sentiment analyzer: Extracting sentiments about a given topic using natural language processing techniques* (pp. 427–434). Almaden, CA: IBM Almaden Research Center.

This work was previously published in the International Journal of Information Retrieval Research, Volume 1, Issue 2, edited by Zhongyu (Joan) Lu, pp. 1-17, copyright 2011 by IGI Publishing (an imprint of IGI Global).

Chapter 7
Schema Independent XML Compressor

Baydaa Al-Hamadani
University of Huddersfield, UK

Zhongyu (Joan) Lu
University of Huddersfield, UK

Raad F. Alwan
Philadelphia University, Jordan

ABSTRACT

XML has become the standard way for representing and transforming data over the World Wide Web. The problem with XML documents is that they have a very high ratio of redundancy, which makes these documents demanding a large storage capacity and large network band-width for transmission. This study designs a system for compressing and querying XML documents (XMLCQ) which compresses the XML document without the need to its schema or DTD to minimize the amount of technologies associated with these documents. XMLCQ first compressed the XML document by separating its data into containers according to the path of these data from the root to the leaf, then it compressed these containers using a back-end compression technique. The compressed file then could be retrieved with any kind of queries applied. Only the required information is decompressed and submitted to the user. Depending on several experiments, the query processor part of the system showed the ability to answer different kinds of queries ranging from simple exact match queries to complex ones. Furthermore, this paper introduced the idea of retrieving information from more than one compressed XML documents.

1. INTRODUCTION

The eXtensible Markup Language (XML) is a W3C standard which has been widely used by both the commercials and the researchers. In the recent years, we have witnessed an increasing volume of XML digital information that either created directly as an XML document or converted from another type of data representation. The importance of XML comes from different factors, its ability to represent different data types in one document, solving the problem of long-term accessibility, and to becoming the solutions to interoperability problem (Al-Hamadani et al., 2009).

DOI: 10.4018/978-1-4666-3898-3.ch007

Due to the replication of the XML schema in each record, XML document is considered to be one of the self-describing data files, which means that these kinds of files have a lot of data redundancy in both of its tags and attributes (Ray, 2001). For the above reason the need to compress XML documents becoming increasingly dramatic. Furthermore, an extensive need evolved to retrieve information directly from the compressed documents and then decompress only the retrieved information (Ferragina et al., 2006).

Because of the wide range of XML documents usage and with different kinds of users, there are many issues should be taken into consideration. One issue is to deal with all kinds of queries to cover the entire user's needs from a querying system. It is also important to minimize the amount of technologies associated with XML documents, such as Schema and Document Type Definition (DTD), in order to ease the use of retrieving information from them.

Although the XML documents' schema or their DTD are very important in the design of these documents, they add more complexity to the retrieving process from the user's point of view. Moreover, sometimes the schema cannot be seen by the user or there is one schema that describes two or more different documents.

The remedy to the previous dilemmas is to design a compression technique that has the capability to compress the XML document without any reference to the schema or the DTD of this document. This compressor has the ability to retrieve information from the compressed version and decompress only the relevant information.

This study reveals a new technique called "*XMLCQ*" which consists of two stages. In the first stage, it separates the data part of the XML document into several containers according to the path of that data within the document. Then each of the containers is compressed separately using a back-end compressor. The compressed file is added into a database which can be used as a reference to get the compressed document in the retrieval stage. The second stage is to process different kinds of XPath queries. The compression ratio was compared with other queriable XML compressors and the XPath queries were tested against XPathMark benchmark.

Collecting the compressed files in a database gives an expansion to the XPath query, if the user does not know the exact XML document that contains the required information. Moreover, if the information is disseminated within several documents, then the user can take advantage of retrieving all the relevant information from all these documents.

2. RELATED WORKS

Recently, large numbers of XML compression techniques have been proposed. Each of which has different characteristics. This section discusses the differences between these compressors and their main features.

XML compressors can be classified into two classes either to be XML-blind or XML-conscious compressors. XML-blind or general purpose compressors deal with the XML document as a traditional text document ignoring its structure and apply the general purpose text compression techniques to compress them. These techniques can be classified into two main classes (Salomon, 2007), either to be statistical or dictionary based compressors (Augeri et al., 2007; Augeri, 2008). The statistical or the arithmetic compressors represent each string of characters using a fixed number of bits per character. PPM, CACM3, and PAQ are examples of this kind of compressors (Cleary & Witten, 1984; Moffat, 1990; Alistair et al., 1998). On the other hand, dictionary compression techniques substitute each string in the input by its reference in a dictionary maintained by the encoder. WinZip (http://www.winzip.com/), GZIP (http://www.gzip.org/), and BZIP2 (http://www.bzip.org/) are examples of this compression class.

On the other hand, XML-conscious compressors try to utilize the structural behaviour of XML documents in order to achieve better compression ratio and less time in comparative with the XML-blind type. Table 1 sets the main differences between the two aforementioned compressors types. XML-conscious compressors can be classified according to their ability to querying the compressed documents into two main sub-classes; these are queriable and non-queriable compressors.

The main theory of data compression, which described in Shannon (1948), is the formulation of the entropy rate *(H)* which indicates the limit to lossless data compression. The value of *(H)* depends on the probability of each symbol in the information source. The most popular entropy value is:

$$H = \sum_{i=1}^{n} P_i log \frac{1}{P_i} \quad (1)$$

where, P_i is the probability of the symbol a_i.

In this paper, Shannon proved that the compression ration cannot exceed the value of *(aH)*, where *(a)* is the number of symbols in the source.

Since XML are heterogeneous data, the theory of XML compressors is to separate the data from the structure, separate the data into containers according to the type of the data, and apply a general purpose compressor for each container. This process can lead to produce an optimal compressor over heterogeneous data. Liefke and Suciu (2000) developed the entropy value for XML compression to be:

$$H = \frac{1}{2}\left(H_0 + p_1 H_1 + \ldots + p_k H_k\right) \quad (2)$$

where, $H_0, H_1, \ldots, H_k$ are the entropies for the sources, and $p_1, p_2, \ldots, p_k$ are the probabilities of these sources.

A. Non Queriable XML Compressors

This kind of compressors showed good compression performance but the resulting document cannot be queried without decompressing it. The main purpose of these compressors is to achieve highest compression ratio for archival purposes. The following sections discuss the relationship between examples of these techniques.

XMill (Liefke & Suciu, 2000) is the first XML-conscious compressor. It depends on compressing the structure (i.e., elements and attribute names) of the XML document separately from its data by encoding the structure using a dictionary-based compressor and then passing the results to a back-end compressor. All elements and attribute names are assigned with an integer number to be considered as a key to the dictionary. The data part grouped into containers depending on the type of that data and its path from the root. Before subtle in a container, the data value could be compressed if the user specifies one of the eight semantic compressors used by XMill. If not, the data value will go without being compressed to

Table 1. The main differences between XML-conscious and MXL-blind compressors

XML-conscious compressors	MXL-blind compressors
Information about XML documents is usually available which can be optimized by XML-conscious compressors to get better compression.	Cannot take advantage of the previous information about the file.
They utilize the structure of XML document and the type of the data inside.	They do not take in consideration the entire file structure or data types.
Some of them abridge the original XML tree in a summary or compact tree for better ratio.	Cannot exploit redundancies in the XML tree structure.
Most of them are powerful in compressing small or large files.	Do not efficiently compress small files that can be in transactions for e-business (Hung, 2009).

an appropriate container. Each container then, is compressed using *gzip* compressor. Although XMill achieve good compression ratio, it need the user to define the back-end compressor.

In the same year, Girardot and Sundaresan (2000) produced *Millau* as a new compression technique to compress business to business XML documents. Millau encodes the contents of the documents into tokens and split these tokens into different code spaces. This technique depends on the DTD of the XML document in order to specify these code spaces and to determine the type of each attribute value.

While XMill uses static dictionary to represent tags and attribute names only, *XWRT* (Skibinski et al., 2007) uses semi-dynamic dictionary to encode tags, attribute names, ordinary words within the data part, emails, URL address prefixes, and sequence of spaces. All the entries of the dictionary should be of length greater than a given threshold and should have occurrence exceed a given threshold.

RNGzip compressor (League & Eng, 2007) induces tree automaton from the Relax NG schema by Clark and Makoto (2001) for the XML document need to be transmitted. After the schema agreement by both the sender and the receiver, RNGZip uses the tree automaton to transmit only little information and the receiver then reconstructs the complete XML document. It acts as a key in the encryption and decryption process. This technique shows bad compression ratio on data-centric documents.

In Bonifati et al. (2009) paper, the authors produced a new lossy XML compression which depends on the words abbreviation technique by removing or eliminating some characters from the data, tags, and formatting according to specific rules for each part.

B. Queriable XML Compressors

The main goal of this type of compressors is to provide the ability to the compressed version of the XML document to be queried without complete decompression them. The compression ratio for these compression techniques is lower than the blind-XML or the non-queriable techniques. However, these techniques are important when dealing with resource-limited applications and with mobiles. Some of these techniques are homomorphic compressors, which mean that the compressed file is a semi-structure file. In the next section a brief description to some of these techniques will be given.

The first queriable compressor is *XGrind* by Tolani and Haritsa (2000). This technique replaces the tags and attribute names with the letters *"T"* and *"A"* respectively, followed by a unique identifier. Moreover, it replaces the end tags with *"/"* sign. The data part of the document is encoded using Huffman encoding. For the purpose of querying the compressed document, XGrind's query processor finds the simple path to check whether it satisfies the path in the given query. The main drawback with XGrind is that it has the ability to process exact-match and prefix match queries on the compressed documents while range or partial-match queries requires partial decompression to be handled.

In order to solve XGrind's partial decompression problem, *Xpress* (Min et al., 2003) uses the reverse arithmetic encoding method to encode the label paths of the XML document as a distinct interval in [0.0, 1.0) . Using the relationships between these intervals will give the ability to evaluate path expressions more efficiently on the compressed XML document. Furthermore, by using this method, Xpress uses path-by-path matching instead of element-by-element matching that has been used in XGrind. To encode the data part of the XML document, Xpress uses different compression techniques depending on the type of the data and without the need to the human interference (Min et al., 2009) although it has the ability to handled exact-match, partial-match, and range queries, it fails in handling other query types.

Because XGrind and Xpress are homomorphic, the relationship between the size of the compressed document and the size of the original one is linear. To solve this problem Cheng and Ng (2004) proposed a new technique (XQzip) that depends on extracting the Structure Index Tree (SIT) from the tree structure of the original document. The SIT depth is non-linear to the structure tree which makes this technique accomplishes higher compression ratio and faster query evaluation.

Instead of using (SIT), XQueC (Arion et al., 2007) uses the structure summery tree in order to efficiently stores the XML documents. The space needed to store the structure summary (*SS*) is:

$$CSaux = \sum_{n \in SS} \left(|tag(n)| + \log_2(|SS|) \right) \quad (3)$$

This represents the summation of the space needed to store a tag node plus the space needed to store all its successive nodes. The space needed to store the containers using the structure summary is:

$$CScont = \sum_{c} \left(|c| * \log_2 \left(|seq_c| \right) + \sum_{i=1,\ldots,|c|} size\left(c_i\right) \right) \quad (4)$$

Furthermore, instead of using hash table to store the tags and attribute names, XQueC used the structural identifiers, which has been used in some querying techniques (Al-Khalif et al., 2002; Grust, 2002; Halverson et al., 2003; Paparizos et al., 2003) in order to uniquely identify a node in the XML tree. This technique considered to be the first one that uses XQuery as a query language.

Finally, Arroyuelo et al. (2010) proved in their proposed *SXSI* compressor that the XPath queries can be performed better when using indexing technique to compressed XML document. This technique depends on producing a labelled tree from the XML Tree structure and then indexing this tree into small matrix using (BWT) transformation. Although the compression ratio of SXSI is not competitive but the querying time and the retrieving quality is better than traditional retrieving techniques.

Table 2 shows the main differences between the compression techniques mentioned above and our XQPoint technique. It is clear that the compression of all XML-conscious compressors are better than traditional blind-compressors.

3. *XMLCQ* ARCHITECTURE

As illustrated in Figure 1, the *XMLCQ* system consists of two main stages. The first one is designing a new XML compression technique which converts the normal XML documents to

Table 2. A comparison between different compression techniques

Compression technique	queriable	Compression technique	Back-end compressor	Average compression ratio
XMill (Liefke & Suciu, 2000)	No	Dictionary-based	Gzip, Bzip2, PPM	0.55
Millau (Girardot & Sundaresan, 2000)	No	Dictionary-based	GZip, deflate	0.59
XWRT (Skibinski et al., 2007)	No	Dictionary-based	Gzip, LZMA, PPM	0.54
RNGzip (League & Eng, 2007)	No	Deterministic automaton Tree	Gzip	0.58
XGrind (Tolani & Haritsa, 2000)	Yes	Dictionary-based	Huffman	0.39
Xpress (Min et al., 2003)	Yes	Dictionary-based	Reverse encoding	0.42
XQZip (Cheng and Ng, 2004)	Yes	Dictionary-based	Gzip	0.54
XQueC (Arion et al., 2007)	Yes	Binary encoding	Depending on the type of the data	0.54
SZSI (Arroyuelo et al., 2010)	Yes	FM indexing	BWT	n/t

a compressed version. The second is designing a retrieving technique that processes the XPath vague queries type in order to retrieve the relevant information from the compressed document accordingly.

The design of the *XMLCVQ* does not depend on the XML schema or the DTD of the document. This due to several reasons:

1. Since the main purpose of any compressor is to save as much memory usage as it can, *XMLCQ* saves the amount of memory required to store the schema.
2. Even if the schema for a document exists, it could not be accessed by the user.
3. It is important to eliminate the technologies related with XML document to ease their use.

The following sections illustrate the design of each part of the system starting with XMLCQ-Compressor (XMLCQ-C), passing by XMLCQ-Decompressor (XMLCQ-D), and ending with XMLCQ-Query Processor (XMLCQ-QP).

Figure 1. XMLCQ system stages

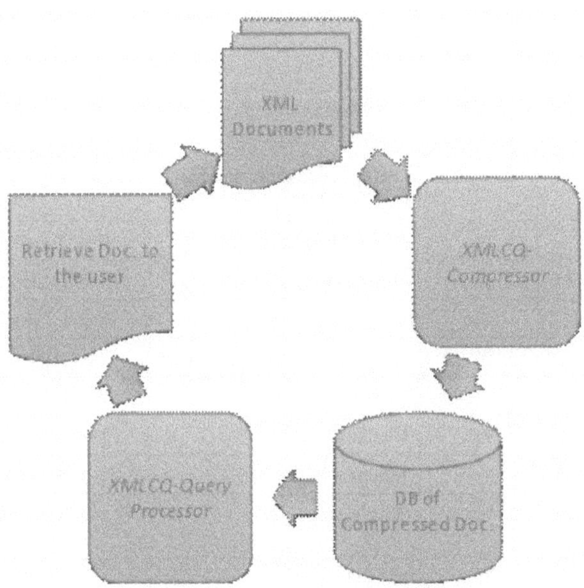

3.1. The Compressing Methodology

XMLCQ-C compressor takes an XML document as an input and creates the compressed version from this document by passing through several steps. An example in Figure 2(a) from (W3schools, 2006) is going to be used during the following sections in order to simplify the exact process of each step:

1. **Create the Structured-Tree:** In this step *XMLCQ*-C scans the document to generate the structured tree from it. The structured-tree for the running example is shown in Figure 2. The data under each root-leaf path were stored in containers linked to that path. Each data item is accompanied with a number ID_{order} that represent the order of this item within the document (the number between the brackets in Figure 2(a)). ID_{order} counts each start element, attribute name, attribute value and end element. According to this number, each node is uniquely identified for the purposes of decompression process and in the querying process. Previous XML compressors used two numbers for each node

Figure 2. An XML Example (a) and its IST (b)

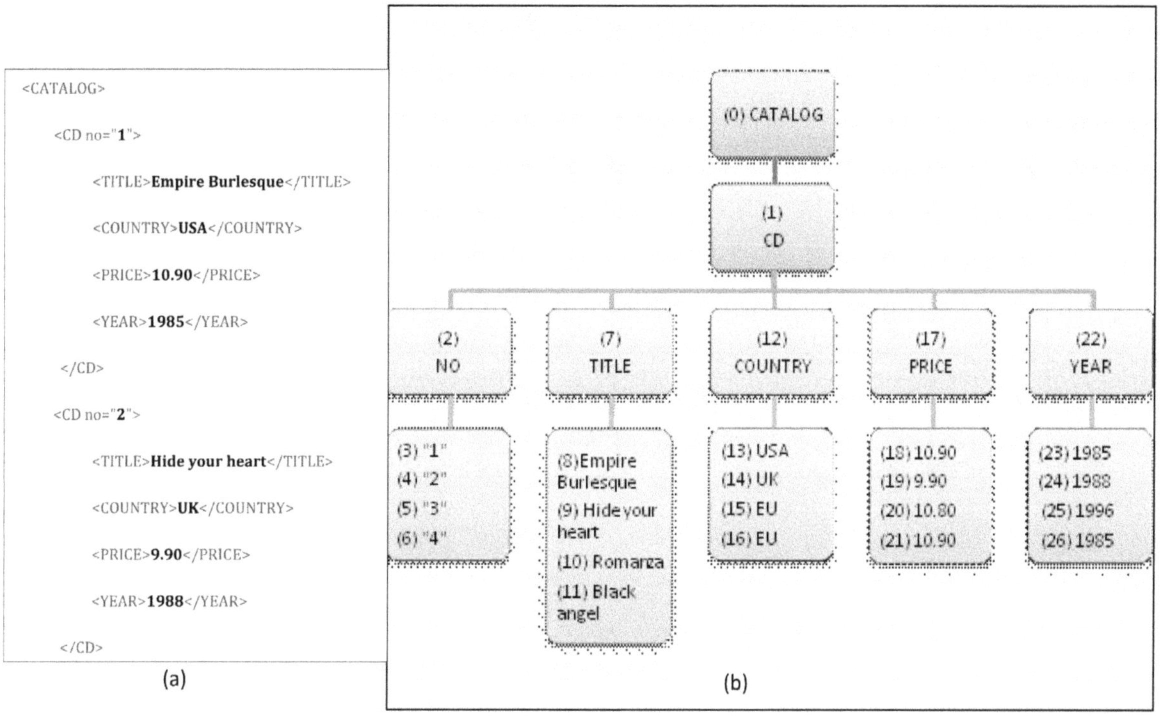

in the structured-tree to identify this node uniquely. This number represented by the pre-order and post-order traversal of that node $[ID_{pre}, ID_{post}]$ (Cheng & Ng, 2004; Arion et al., 2007; Arroyuelo et al., 2010).

The number of bits required to store the structured-tree with N nodes in the previous works is shown in equation 0:

$$S_{SIT} = 2(N * \log_2 N) \quad (5)$$

While the number of bits required to store the same structured-tree in *XMLCQ-C* is shown in Equation 6

$$S_{SIT} = (N * \log_2 N) \quad (6)$$

In this stage *XMLCQ-C* saves half the number of bits required to store the structured-tree.

2. **Creating the Containers:** *XMLCQ-C* creates the containers from the structured tree. First each node is replaces with a number represents the entry of that node's name in the *path-Dictionary*. The structured-tree is traversed to create the containers. Each path from the root to a leaf is used as index to the container and the contents of that containers were the data values under that path.

For the running example, the path-Dictionary and the containers are illustrated in Figure 3(a) and 3(b) respectively. The complete algorithm to create the containers is in Figure 4.

4. **Compressing the Containers:** After preparing all the containers and replacing the element's names in the containers with their entry in the *pathDictionary*, now the contents of the containers should be compressed. To do this, *XMLCQ-C* uses LZW compressor.

Figure 3. Creating containers process. (a) The path-Dictionary. (b) The container

0	CATALOG
1	CD
2	NO
3	TITLE
4	COUNTRY
5	PRICE
6	YEAR

(a)

/0/1/@2	(3) "1"(4) "2" (5) "3" (6) "4"
/0/1/3	(8)Empire Burlesque (9) Hide your heart (10) Romanza (11) Black angel
/0/1/4	(13) USA (14) UK (15) EU (16) EU
/0/1/5	(18) 10.90 (19) 9.90 (20) 10.80 (21) 10.90
/0/1/6	(23) 1985 (24) 1988 (25) 1996 (26) 1985

(b)

Figure 4. An algorithm for creating the containers

```
Algorithm creatContainers(String Q, attributes attribList)
let pathDictionary=[i_0, i_1, ..., i_n]
let structured-Tree=[j_0, j_1, ..., j_m]
let pathStack=[k_p, k_p-1, ..., k_0]
let containers=[c_1, c_2, ..., c_q]
For (Q and all attribList)
  if (Q ∈ attribList)
     Q'='@'+Q
  if !(Q|Q' ∈ pathDictionary)
     Q|Q' → i_n+1 → pathDictionary
  Q"=n+1
  currentPath ← k_0 + k_1 + ...+ k_p
  if (currentPath ⊄ [j_0, j_1, ..., j_m]
     structured-Tree ← [j_0, j_1, ..., j_m] ∪ ([j_0, j_1, ..., j_m] ∩ [k_p,k_p-1, ...,k_0])
  pathStack=[k_p, k_p-1, ..., k_0] ∪ [Q"]
  if (Q ∈ attribList)  {
     currentPath ← k_0 + k_1 + ...+ k_p
     if (currentPath ⊄ [c_1, c_2, ..., c_q]{
         containers ← [c_1, c_2, ..., c_q] ∪ currentPath
         currentPath.value+= Q'.value
         pathStack=[k_p-1, ..., k_0]
     }
  }
End.
```

While previous related works depend on different granularity to compress parts of the XML document, as illustrated in Table 3, *XMLCQ-C* granularity is the highest one since it depends on compressing the content of each container as one unit. This will affect the query processing in which it increase the amount of data needed to be decompressed in order to retrieve the relevant information.

3.2. The Decompressor Design

To decompress the compressed file, *XMLCQ-D* first applies the LZW Decompression technique to decompress the contents of all the containers to get the data shown in Figure 3(b) for the running example. The second step is to reconstruct the XML document from the container's indexes and contents. The main operation here is to determine the order of each element, attribute, and data value within the XML document. This order is the ID_{order} which is accompanied with the data in the containers but it should be checked for its consistency with the new XML document. To check the consistency of the order, *XMLCQ-D* uses Equation 7 such that:

*If XMLCQ-D has the piece of data [(ό)*D], where ό denotes the ID_{order} accompanied with the data in the container, then (C_{order}) can be calculated as shown in Equation 7:

Table 3. Compression granularity comparison

XML compression technique	Back-end compression technique used	Compression granules
XGrind	Huffman Coding	Value/tag
XPress	Huffman + reverse arithmetic	Value/path
XQZip	GZip	Blocks
XQueC	Cost driven	Container item/ tag
XMLCQ	LZW	Container item/ path

$$C_{order} = \left(\sigma - \mu_P - \left(\left[\mu_P\right] - \left[\mu_C\right]\right) - \left(\sigma' + 1\right)\right) / 2 \quad (7)$$

where:

- σ' **:** Represents the number of elements, attributes names, and data values written in the XML document so far.
- μ_P **:** The number of elements and attributes names written in the XML document so far.
- μ_C **:** The number of elements and attribute names in the index of the container of this data.

Then the value of C_{order} is checked and a performance made as shown in Equation 8.

$$if\, C_{order} \begin{cases} = 0 & newID_{order} = \sigma \\ \neq 0 & \sigma' = \sigma' \bigcup \left(\left[\mu_P\right] - \left[\mu_C\right]\right) \end{cases} \quad (8)$$

If C_{order} equals to (0) this means that the current ID_{order} is consistent with the number of elements and attribute names printed out to the XML document, otherwise, the difference between the current path and the index path for the current container should be added to the XML document before adding the required data.

The first step in the decompression algorithm in Figure 5 is to upload the *pathDictionary* and the containers from the compressed file to a predefined data structure in the memory. Since the first data value in each container always holds the minimum order within this container, the process of looking for the minimum order will check only *(n)* item, where *(n)* represents the number of containers of searching all the data in the containers.

If this piece of data is the first data value in the XML document (line 9) then, all the path's elements in the index of the container holding this data were pushed in a stack which represent

Figure 5. XMLCQ-Decompression algorithm

```
1.  Algorithm XMLCQ-D (pathDictionary [P0, P1, ...,Pm], containers [C0, C1, ...,Cn])
2.        let currentPathStack=[Sk, Sk-1, ...,S0]
3.        let dataOrder= number of elements, attribute names, and data values in the
    outputFile
4.        While (the containers are still having data) Do
5.           for i=0 to n
6.              let minDataSet[(O0,D0), (O1,D1),... (On,Dn)] ← first element in each
        container
7.              minOrder=min(O0, O1,..., On)
8.              minData ← Di from (minOrder, Di)
9.           if currentPathStack=∅
10.             currentPathStack ← Ci.index
11.             outputFile ← open tags of Ci.index
12.             update dataOrder
13.          }
14.          else
15.             currentPathStack ← [Ci.index]-[currentPathStack]
16.          dataCons=⌊(minOrder − Ci.indexSize − {[Ci.index] − [currentStackPath]} − dataOrder + 1)⌋
17.          if dataCons ≠ 0
18.             outputFile ← close tag {[Ci.index] − [currentStackPath]}
19.             update dataOrder
20.          }
21.          outputFile ← Di
22.          update dataOrder
23.          remove (minOrder, Di)
24.       }
25.       outputFile ← close tag [Sk, Sk-1, ...,S0]
26.  End.
```

the current working path and add these elements (or attribute names) in the new XML document as an open tags. Otherwise, a check is made (line 14) to determine the difference between the current working path (stack contents) and the index path of the current container. This difference is added to the output file either as closing tag (from stack) or as opening tag (from index).

Before adding the data to the output file, a consistency check is made by following the instructions in (line 16) where ({}) means set difference between the contents of the stack and the index path. If there is no consistency (line 17) then the difference between the stack content and the index path is added to the output file as losing tags and then the piece of data is added to the output file. In every addition to the output file, the value of (*dataOrder*) is updated (lines 12, 19, and 22) to check the consistency between the each time.

After adding the data to the output file, this data alongside with its order is deleted from the container. This process is done to keep the order of the first data items in all the containers in their minimum value and to release the memory storage used by this data value.

This process is continued until all the containers are empty, then all the content of the stack is added to the output file as closed tags to finish the new decompressed XML document.

3.3. The Query Processor Methodology

The design of the query processor, which illustrated in Figure 6, consists of different stages. The role of each stage and its design were discussed in this section using the same running example in Figure 2(a):

1. **XPath Query:** *XMLCQ-QP* uses XPath as a query language since it consider being the core of all other XML query languages. Each query is checked first against the XPath Extended Backus Naur Form (EBNF) (Berglund et al., 2007) to determine if it is a syntactically true XPath query.

XMLCQ-QP has the ability to retrieve information from more than one file if the user doesn't specify the exact XML documents that have the required information. As a simple example, if the user submits the query (title/year), then she/he might get information about the titles and years of some publications for CDs, movies, books or journals. Moreover, *XMLCQ-QP* has the ability to compare the results from one file with the data from another file and retrieve the results accordingly.

Figure 6. The architecture of the query processor

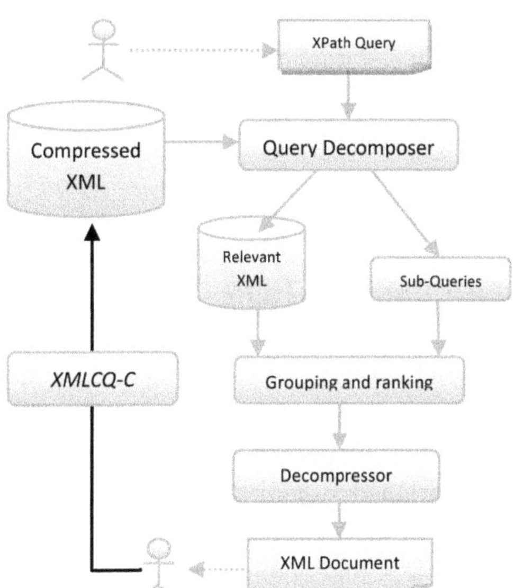

Example 1: Suppose the following user query: (catalog/book/author/bookstore/book[author="Erik Ray"). This query is considered to be a merged from two queries, (catalog/book/author="Erik Ray") and (bookstore/book/author="Erik Ray"). Each one is to retrieve all the books for the author's name ("Erik Ray") from a separate XML document.

Example 2: suppose the following user query: (cars/car/price lt carType/Ford[model eq 2008]/price)

In this query the user is interesting in looking for all the cars that their price is less than (*lt*) the *Ford 2009* car price. *XMLCQ-QP* first looks for the smallest price (*x*) in the path (carType/Ford[model eq 2008]/price) and then retrieve all the information from the path (cars/car/price) which are less than (*x*). Notice that the two paths are from two separate XML documents.

2. **Query Decomposer:** This part of the *XMLCQ-QP* is responsible of decomposing the XPath query into several sub-queries as shown in Figure 7. It passes either through only the second decomposition stage or through the first followed by the second stages, as follows:
   a. **Stage-1:** If the user's query doesn't specify the required XML document to retrieve information from, then the query should pass through this stage. During this stage, the retrieval engine scans the XML database to specify the relevant XML documents and decompose the user's query depending on the relevant document. The resulted queries then are passed to the second stage.
   b. **Stage-2:** In this stage the result sub-queries from the first stage or the

Figure 7. The design of XMLCQ-Query decomposer

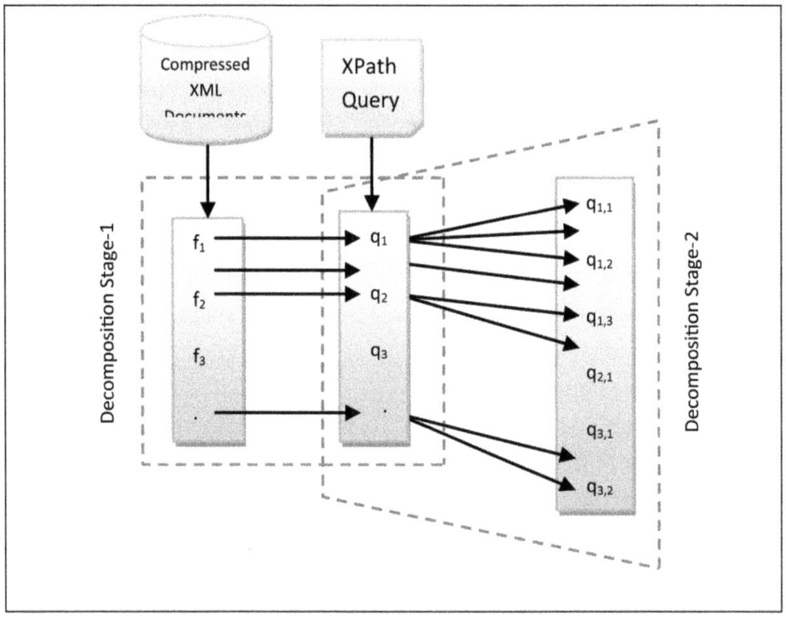

complete user's query (if the query specifies the required XML document) is decomposed according to the containers of the relevant document. Only the relevant compressed containers are loaded into the memory, each of which is accompanied by its relevant sub-query.

Definition 1: (Relevant container) To determine the relevant container, each element or attribute name (*x*) in the query is compared against the index of each container (*c*) in the document. If (*c*) contains (*x*) then the container is considered to be relevant (Figure 8).

3. **Grouping and Ranking:** Depending on the cost of transformation, the retrieved information from the sub-queries is ranked. Instead of retrieving more than one part on XML documents, all the relevant information were grouped together n one XML document to form a single tree instead of a forest.

4. **Decompression:** During all the previous stages no decompression required except in data value matching queries.

In this stage all the retrieved and ranked containers were decompressed to form a new XML document. If the user needs more queries to be processed on this document, then it should be compressed first to be within the XML data base and then it can be used in its compressed version. This feature is called composition and is borrowed from XQuery, in which the retrieved information is stored in a temporary XML file for further retrieving.

4. IMPLEMENTATION

The implementation of XMLCQ is done using java programming language under eclipse environment. Figure 9 demonstrates the class diagram for the designed system showing only the main classes. The design depends on implementing three packages: the compressor, the decompressor,

Figure 8. Processing an XPath query algorithm

```
Algorithm processXPathQuery(structure qNames)
   let qNames= [a1, a2, …, an] such that:
   ai consists of: ai.name, ai.type, ai.value, ai.operation
   let fileDB=[f1, f2, …, fm]
   let relevant=[r1, r2, …, rk]
   for all ai.name ∈ qNames
     for all fj ∈ fileDB
      if ai.name ∈ fj.pathDictionary
        relevant ← fj
        relevant ← ai
     }
   }
   for all ri ∈ relevant
     subQuery= Decpmpose(ri.query)
     cost=relax(ri.subQuery)
     if cost<threshold
       remove (ri) from relevant
     tree=retrieveData
      }
   allTrees=Combine all the retrieved trees
   decompress(allTrees)
End.
```

Figure 9. The class diagram for XMLCQ

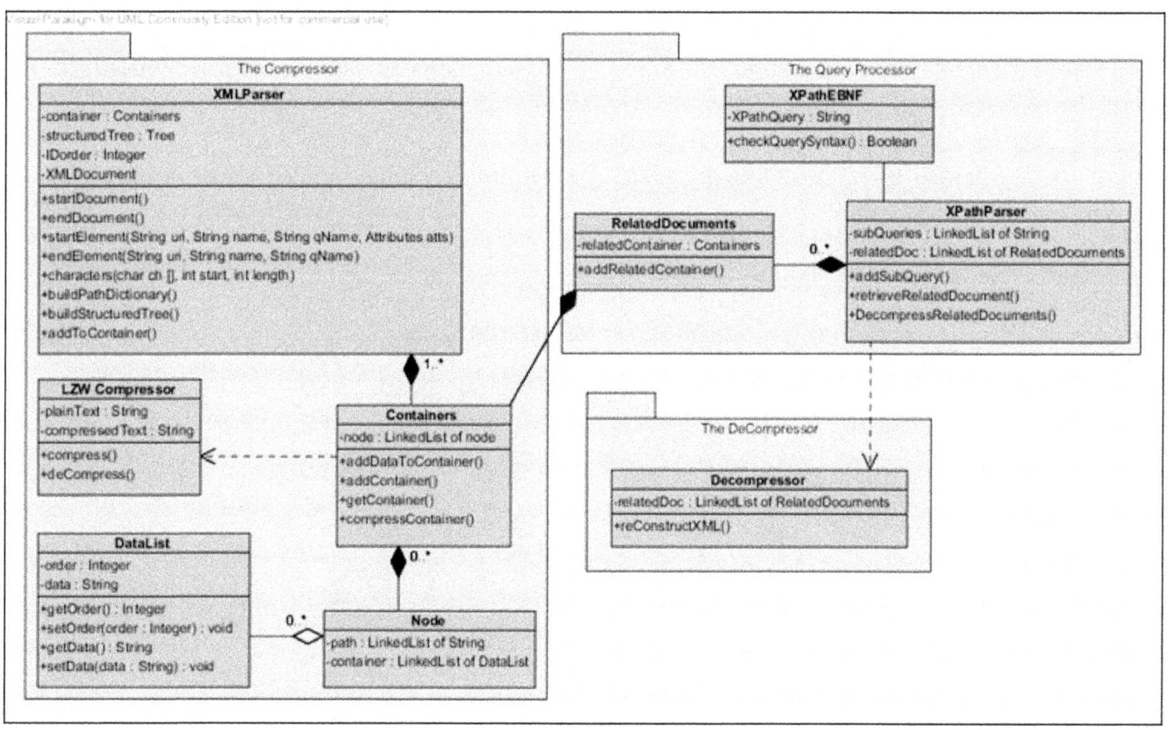

and the query processor packages. The first package contains all the classes that are responsible on accepting an XML document, implement the SAX parser on it, create its structures tree and the containers, and compress these containers.

On the other hand, the decompressor package has the class that responsible on decompressing a specific XML document or decompresses the XML document that is generated by the query processor which contains the relevant information to a given query. The last package (the query processor) contains all the classes that accepts the XPath query, check the query syntactic and semantic errors, decompose the query and collect the relevant XML documents, determine the relevant containers, and send the relevant information to the decompressor to be viewed to the user.

Figure 10 shows a snapshot from XMLCQ implementation, specifically for the compressor part. It specifies the results of an XML compression process and the shape of the structured tree for the compressed document.

Figure 11 shows the first step in the decompressing process when the user specifies the compressed file name to be decompressed. Note that all the compressed files have *.xcvq* as an extension to be distinguished from other files.

After the decompression process end, the user has the choice to open the decompressed file to see it, as shown in Figure 12.

A snapshot for the query processor window is shown in, which gives the ability to the user to write an XPath query and get the relevant results in a new XML document.

5. TESTING AND EVALUATION

5.1. Testing

This section determines the testing environment, testing strategies and testing results for both the *XMLCQ-Compressor* and the *XMLCQ-Query Processor*.

5.1.1. Testing Environment

In this section the testing of both the compressor and the query processor is made. The design was implemented under Eclipse environment for

Figure 10. The results of compressing an XML document

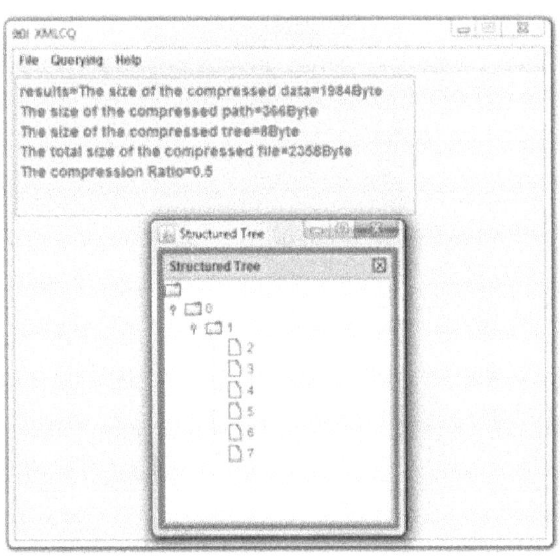

Figure 11. Choosing a file to be decompressed

Figure 12. The results from the decompression process

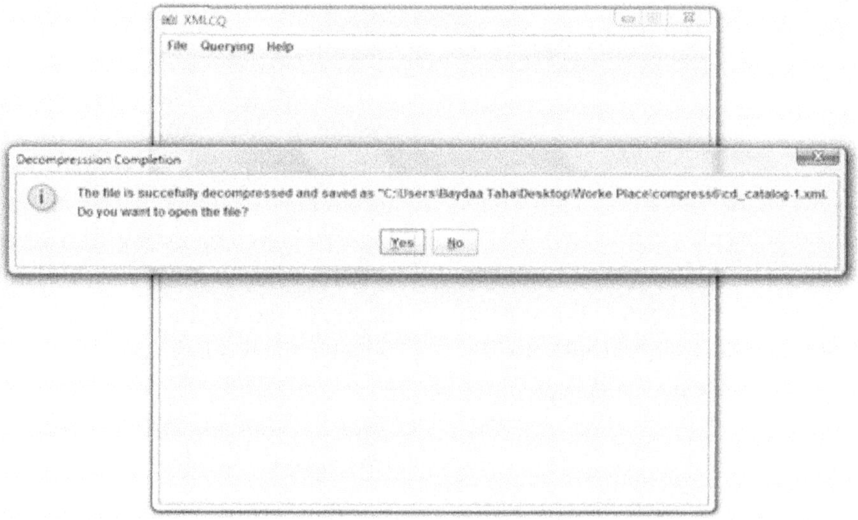

Figure 13. Query processor snapshot

Java using Intel(R) Core™2 Due processor with 3.00GHz speed. The API used to analyse the XML document was the Simple API for XML (SAX) parser, since it does not need to upload the entire document in the memory to be dealt with. Instead, it generates events to catch the start of the document and its end, and an element and data occurrences.

5.1.2. Testing Strategies and results

For the purpose of testing *XMLCQ-C*, we used the compression ratio factor as specified in (*Test-1*) spending on a corpus of data that includes different kinds of XML documents with different size and depth.

On the other hand, to test the *XMLCQ-QP*, we used XPath benchmark in its two faces, the functionality test (*Test-2*), and the performance test (*Test-3*).

Test-1: The Compression Ratio

To test *XMLCQ-C* technique, a set of different types of XML documents has been chosen. These documents should be in different sizes, number of tags, number of nodes, the depth of the longest path, and the data ratio (DR) which is (Sakr, 2009):

$$DR_d = (D_d / Si_d) / 100 \qquad (9)$$

such that DR_d is the data ratio for the XML document (*d*), (*D*) is the data, and (*Si*) represents the size of the XML document.

According to their main characteristics, XML documents can be categorized into three types (Maneth et al., 2008; Sakr, 2009):

1. **Textual Documents (TD):** The DR_d of this type of documents exceeds 70%. The structure of these documents is very simple. Books and articles are examples of this type.
2. **Structural Documents (SD):** In this type of XML documents, the DR_d is less than 30%. Baseball box score and line-item shipping are two examples of this type.
3. **Regular Documents (RD):** These documents have DR_d between 40 and 60 percent. Relational databases are examples of this type.

Table 4 shows the actual XML documents that are used to test *XMLCQ-C*. This list is chosen because it contains all XML types from different area of knowledge and of different sizes.

The last column of the table demonstrate the compression ratio (CR) for *XMLCQ* which calculated using equation 10 (Salomon, 2007).

$$CR = 1 - \left(\frac{Size\,of\ compressed\ file}{Size\,of\ original\ file} \right) \qquad (10)$$

The average compression ratio for the designed system is 0.65, which considered being comparative comparing with other XML compression techniques. It is clear that the compression ratio is higher when compressing (SD) documents, while it is lower when dealing with (TD) documents. This is due to the back-end compressor used (LZW) which creates a large dictionary.

Test-2: The Functional Test of the Query Processor

For the purpose of testing the performance of the *XMLCQ-QP*, a XPath benchmark is used from XPathMark (Franceschet, 2005) since it covers all types of XML queries. The queries in this benchmark is divided into two main categories either functional test (XPath-FT) or performance test (XPath-PT). XPath-FT queries are used to check the completeness and the correctness of the query processor and they are grouped into five aspects. Table 5 illustrates these aspects. *XMLCQ* passes all the query types in the functional test.

Test-3: The Performance Test of the Query Processor

On the other hand, the XPath-PT queries test the exact time required to answer a specific query. For this purpose, these queries are grouped into six fragments, listed in Table 6 alongside with their description, where each fragment extends the previous one by adding a new criterion to it.

Figure 14 (top) shows the average time for the tested XML documents needed to query the compressed database. It was impossible to compare the response time with other techniques since they are not using a specific benchmark that has all query types. All the tested queries do not mention the exact XML document that

Table 4. XML corpus used to test the compressor

XML file name	Description	Category	Size/bytes	XMLCQ CR
GB-meta Sweden-meta Turkey-meta (European, 2003)	Air and climate changes in GB, Sweden and Turkey	RD	51192952 3519488 6144	**0.72** **0.70** **0.71**
EnWikiNews EnWikiQuote EnWikiTionary EnWikiSource (Wikipedia, 2001)	Backup of Wikipedia (the free encyclopaedia) sources	TD	72794112 130305024 611298304 1061537792	**0.55** **0.56** **0.58** **0.50**
Henry IV, Part I Macbeth Richard II (Harold, 2000)	Shakespeare plays	TD	196608 163840 193536	**0.55** **0.59** **0.58**
Baseball (University of Washington, 2002)	The statistics of all players of each team that participated in the 1998 Major League.	SD	672768	**0.85**
DBLP (University of Washington, 2002)	Database of bibliographic information of computer science journals and conference proceedings.	RD	137539584	**0.70**
Mondial (University of Washington, 2002)	Database of statistical information of all the countries in the world.	SD	1864704	**0.88**
SwissPort (University of Washington, 2002)	Database describing DNA sequences	TD	118239232	**0.55**
Xbench-DCSD (Waterloo, 2003)	Transaction data and e-commerce catalogue	RD	110486528	**0.58**
LineItem (University of Washington, 2002)	transactional RDB benchmark	SD	32295936	**0.82**
NASA (University of Washington, 2002)	A catalogue represents the proper motions of stars in the zone catalogue	RD	25818112	**0.61**

Table 5. XPathMark-FT query benchmark

XPathMark-FT concept	Description
Axes	parent, descendant, preceding
Filters	predicates
Node Test	Comment(), text(), node()
Operators	Relational operators (<, =,...) and boolean operators (and, or)
Functions	String manipulating functions and mathematical functions

Table 6. XPathMark-PT query benchmark

XPathMark-PT concept	Description
XPath-A	child and descendant axes, no operators are allowed
XPath-B	All XPath axes+boolean operators
XPath-C	All relational operators
XPath-D	All arithmetic operators and functions
XPath-E	All types of functoions
XPath-F	idref() and closure() functions

has the required information. This means that the *XMLCQ-QP* should look for the relevant documents in the set of compressed documents in the database. This time was decreased when the XPath query specifies a single XML document to retrieve information from, as illustrated in Figure 14 (bottom).

Figure 14. Querying time. (Top) non specified document, (bottom) specified document

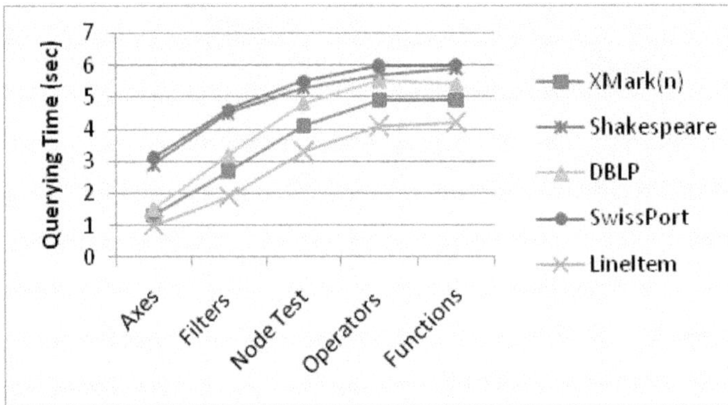

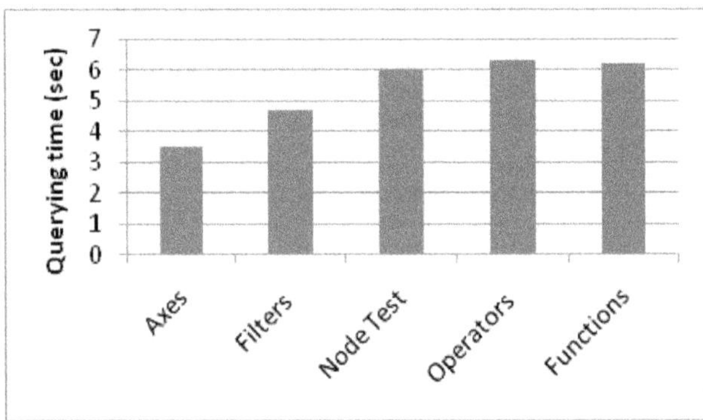

XMLCQ-QP spends more time when dealing with TD type, while it spends less time when querying SD types. This due to the need of decompressing the required containers in order to answer some query types such as *operators* and *functions* queries.

5.2. System Evaluation

To evaluate the *XMLCQ*-C, we compared it with other equivalent XML compressors. As shown in Figure 15, *XMLCQ* shows good compression ratio when dealing with RD and SD types such as

Figure 15. Comparing XMLQC with other compression techniques

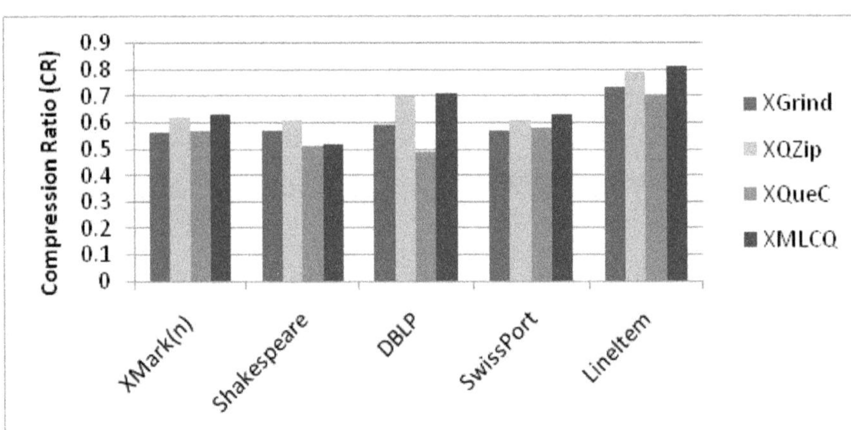

(LineItem), which is better than its dealing with TD type such as (Shakespeare). This is due to the huge dictionary generated by LZW back-end compressor.

6. CONCLUSION AND FUTURE WORK

This paper submits XMLCQ as a new compression technique with several abilities. The first ability is to compress the XML document without the need to its schema or DTD which decrease the amount of technologies associated with these documents. The paper introduce a new idea of retrieving information from more than one XML document by decomposing the user's query into several sub-queries, process each one separately, and combine the retrieved information in a new XML document.

In the compression side, the system shows an average compression ratio of 0.66 which considered to competitive according to other compression techniques. In the querying side, it answers all the types of queries in the XPathMark benchmark with 5.34sec as an average if the query didn't specify an exact XML file to retrieve information from and 4.09sec when the XML document was specified.

As a future work, *XMLCQ* could be developed to be a complete XML management system which has the ability to add, remove or update any part of the compressed document with as less as possible decompression.

REFERENCES

W3schools. (2006). *XML examples.* Retrieved from http://w3schools.com/

Al-Hamadani, B. T., Alwan, R. F., Lu, J., & Yip, J. (2009). Vague content and structure (VCAS) retrieval for XML electronic healthcare records (EHR). In *Proceedings of the International Conference on Internet Computing* (pp. 241-246).

Al-Khalifa, S., Jagadish, H., Patel, J., Wu, Y., Koudas, N., & Srivastava, D. (2002). Structural joins: A primitive for efficient XML query pattern matching. In *Proceedings of the 8th International Conference on Data Engineering*, San Jose, CA (pp. 414-152).

Alistair, M., Radford, M. N., & Ian, H. W. (1998). Arithmetic coding revisited. *ACM Transactions on Information Systems, 16*, 256–294. doi:10.1145/290159.290162

Arion, A., Bonifati, A., Manolescu, I., & Pugliese, A. (2007). XQueC: A query-conscious compressed XML database. *ACM Transactions on Internet Technology, 7*, 10. doi:10.1145/1239971.1239974

Arroyuelo, D., Claude, F., Maneth, S., Maakinen, V., Navarro, G., Nguyen, K., et al. (2010). Fast in-memory XPath search using compressed indexes. In *Proceedings of the IEEE Twenty-Sixth International Conference on Data Engineering* (pp. 417-428).

Augeri, C. J. (2008). *On some results in unmanned aerial vehicle swarms.* Unpublished doctoral dissertation, Air Force Institute of Technology, San Diego, CA.

Augeri, C. J., Bulutoglu, D. A., Mullins, B. E., Baldwin, R. O., Leemon, C., & Baird, I. (2007). An analysis of XML compression efficiency. In *Proceedings of the Workshop on Experimental Computer Science*, San Diego, CA (p. 7).

Berglund, A., Boag, S., Chamberlin, D., Fernández, M. F., Kay, M., Robie, J., & Siméon, J. (2007). *XML path language (XPath) 2.0.* Retrieved from http://www.w3.org/TR/xpath20/

Bonifati, A., Lorusso, M., & Sileo, D. (2009). XML lossy text compression: A preliminary study. In Z. Bellahsène, E. Hunt, M. Rys, & R. Unland (Eds.), *Proceedings of the International Symposium on Database and XML Technologies* (LNCS 5679, pp. 106-113).

Cheng, J., & Ng, W. (2004). XQZip: Querying compressed XML using structural indexing. In *Proceedings of the International Conference on Extending Data Base Technology* (pp. 219-236).

Clark, J., & Makoto, M. (2001). *RELAX NG specification.* Retrieved from http://relaxng.org/spec-20011203.html

Cleary, J., & Witten, I. (1984). Data compression using adaptive coding and partial string matching. *IEEE Transactions on Communications, 32*, 396–402. doi:10.1109/TCOM.1984.1096090

Ferragina, P., Luccio, F., Manzini, G., & Muthukrishnan, S. (2006). Compressing and searching XML data via two zips. In *Proceedings of the 15th International Conference on World Wide Web*, Edinburgh, Scotland (pp. 751-760).

Franceschet, M. (2005). XPathMark: Functional and performance tests for XPath. In S. Bressan, S. Ceri, E. Hunt, Z. G. Ives, Z. Bellahsène, M. Rys, & R. Unland (Eds.), *Proceedings of the Third International Conference on Database and XML Technologies* (LNCS 3671, pp. 129-143).

Girardot, M., & Sundaresan, N. (2000). Millau: An encoding format for efficient representation and exchange of XML over the web. *Computer Networks, 33*, 747–765. doi:10.1016/S1389-1286(00)00051-7

Grust, T. (2002). Accelerating XPath location steps. In *Proceedings of the ACM SIGMOD International Conference on Management of Data*, Madison, WI (pp. 109-120).

Halverson, A., Burger, J., Galanis, L., Kini, A., Krishnamurthy, R., Rao, A., et al. (2003). Mixed mode XML query processing. In *Proceedings of the 29th International Conference on Very Large Data Bases*, Berlin, Germany (pp. 225-236).

Harold, R. S. (2000). *Shakespeare*. Retrieved from http://www.cafeconleche.org/examples/shakespeare/

Hung, P. C. K. (2009). *Services and business computing solution with XML*. Hershey, PA: IGI Global. doi:10.4018/978-1-60566-330-2

League, C., & Eng, K. (2007). Schema-based compression of XML data with Relax NG. In *Proceedings of the IEEE Data Compression Conference* (pp. 9-17).

Liefke, H., & Suciu, D. (2000). XMill: An efficient compressor for XML data. *SIGMOD Record, 29*(2), 153–164. doi:10.1145/335191.335405

Maneth, S., Mihaylov, N., & Saker, S. (2008). XML tree structure compression. In *Proceedings of the 19th International Conference on Database and Expert Systems Application* (pp. 243-247).

Min, J.-K., Park, M.-J., & Chung, C.-W. (2003). XPRESS: A queriable compression for XML data. In *Proceedings of the ACM SIGMOD International Conference on Management of Data*, San Diego, CA (pp. 122-133).

Min, J.-K., Park, M.-J., & Chung, C.-W. (2009). *U.S. Patent No. 5956724: Method of performing queriable XML compression using reverse arithmetic encoding and type inference engine.* Washington, DC: United States Patent and Trademark Office.

Moffat, A. (1990). Implementing the PPM data compression scheme. *IEEE Transactions on Communications, 38*(11), 1917–1921. doi:10.1109/26.61469

Paparizos, S., Al-Khalifa, S., Chapman, A., Jagadish, H. V., Lakshmanan, L. V. S., Nierman, A., et al. (2003). TIMBER: A native system for querying XML. In *Proceedings of the ACM SIGMOD International Conference on Management of Data*, San Diego, CA.

Ray, E. T. (2001). *Learning XML guide to creating self-describing data*. Sebastopol, CA: O'Reilly Media.

Sakr, S. (2009). XML compression techniques: A survey and comparison. *Journal of Computer and System Sciences*, *75*, 303–322. doi:10.1016/j.jcss.2009.01.004

Salomon, D. (2007). *Data compression: The complete reference*. New York, NY: Springer.

Shannon, C. E. (1948). A mathematica theory of communication. *The Bell System Technical Journal*, *27*, 379–423.

Skibinski, P., Grabowski, S., & Swacha, J. (2007). Effective asymmertic XML compression. *Software, Practice & Experience*, *38*(10).

Tolani, P. M., & Haritsa, J. R. (2000). XGRIND: A query-friendly XML compressor. In *Proceedings of the IEEE 18th International Conference on Data Engineering*, University of Washington. (2002). *Index of research/xmldatasets/data*. Retrieved from http://www.cs.washington.edu/research/xmldatasets/data/

This work was previously published in the International Journal of Information Retrieval Research, Volume 1, Issue 2, edited by Zhongyu (Joan) Lu, pp. 18-38, copyright 2011 by IGI Publishing (an imprint of IGI Global).

Chapter 8
Determination of Algorithms Making Balance Between Accuracy and Comprehensibility in Churn Prediction Setting

Hossein Abbasimehr
K. N. Toosi University of Tech, Iran

Mohammad Jafar Tarokh
K. N. Toosi University of Tech, Iran

Mostafa Setak
K. N. Toosi University of Tech, Iran

ABSTRACT

Predictive modeling is a useful tool for identifying customers who are at risk of churn. An appropriate churn prediction model should be both accurate and comprehensible. However, reviewing the past researches in this context shows that much attention is paid to accuracy of churn prediction models than comprehensibility of them. This paper compares three different rule induction techniques from three categories of rule based classifiers in churn prediction context. Furthermore logistic regression (LR) and additive logistic regression (ALR) are used. After parameter setting, eight distinctive algorithms, namely C4.5, C4.5 CP, RIPPER, RIPPER CP, PART, PART CP, LR, and ALR, are obtained. These algorithms are applied on an original training set with the churn rate of 30% and another training set with the churn rate of 50%. Only the models built by applying these algorithms on a training set with the churn rate of 30% make balance between accuracy and comprehensibility. In addition, the results of this paper show that ALR can be an excellent alternative for LR, when models only from accuracy perspective are evaluated.

DOI: 10.4018/978-1-4666-3898-3.ch008

1. INTRODUCTION

The importance of Customer relationship management (CRM) is well known for firms in industries with high competitive and saturated market. One of the key components of CRM is customer retention. Customer retention is an important strategy to keep and satisfy existing customers. Existing customer is a valuable asset for most companies (Athanassopoulos, 2000; Jones, Mothersbaugh, & Beatty, 2000; Thomas, 2001). Acquisition of new customer costs more than keeping existing customers (Coussement & Van den Poel, 2008a). It is stated that attracting new customer costs 12 times more than retaining existing one (Coussement, Benoit, & Van den Poel, 2010).

Benefits of increasing customer loyalty or retention with in a current customer base are:

1. There is less need to offer incentive to loyal customers
2. Loyal customers are less price sensitive
3. Loyal customer will recommend the company to other people
4. Individual revenue of each customer grows as trust increase (Chaffey, Ellis-Chadwick, Mayer, & Johnston, 2006).

To keep existing customer, a company must identify likely churners (customers tend to stop their business with company). Churn prediction is a useful tool to predict customer at churn risk.

Finding churn drivers of customer churn or model building for customer churn prediction are the aims of researches in this field (Coussement & Van den Poel, 2009). In past researches, many modeling techniques had been used for customer churn prediction; however, in this regards, only the accuracy of the constructed models is considered and less attention has been paid to the comprehensibility of the developed model (Verbeke, Martens, Mues, & Baesens, 2010). Accuracy is not the only important criterion in evaluating a churn prediction model (Verbeke et al., 2010). Comprehensibility of model causes it to disclose some valuable knowledge about churn drivers of customers. Such knowledge can be extracted in the form of "if then" rules which allows marketing managers to develop right strategies for retaining the churners (Verbeke, Martens, Mues, & Baesens, 2010). Also, being accurate, a model can recognize churner and non-churner well. In this study, we have concentrated on both accuracy and comprehensibility of churn prediction models.

Data mining techniques had been used widely in churn prediction context. From data mining view point, churn prediction is a binary classification task. The aim of churn prediction model is classifying of customers into two classes as churner and non-churner (Coussement, Benoit, & Van den Poel, 2010).

Basic techniques of data classification are decision tree classifiers, Bayesian classifiers, Bayesian belief networks and rule based classifiers, k-nearest-neighbor classifiers, case-based reasoning, neural network technique and so on (Han & Kamber, 2006).

In this study, the main motivation is the comparison of three different algorithms from three categories of rule-based classifier in churn prediction context. These algorithms include: C4.5 decision tree (Han & Kamber, 2006; Tan, Steinbach, & Kumar, 2005; Witten & Frank, 2005) is belonging to divide-and-conquer algorithms category, RIPPER (Reduced Incremental Pruning to produce Error Reduction) (Han & Kamber, 2006; Tan, Steinbach, & Kumar, 2005; Witten & Frank, 2005) which is belonging to separate-and-conquer algorithms, PART (Witten & Frank, 2005) algorithm which is a combinational method of divide-and-conquer and separate-and-conquer algorithms. Although divide-and-conquer and separate-and-conquer strategies previously had been used by researchers in churn prediction setting, to the best of our knowledge this is the first study in a customer churn context that evaluates and uses algorithms, which are a combinational method of divide-and-conquer and separate-and-conquer algorithms. The performance of these algorithms is measured by both accuracy and comprehensibility metrics.

Moreover, we have used Logistic regression and additive logistic regression. Besides in this paper we have identified a good class distribution for mining churn data.

The reminder of this paper is organized as follows. Firstly, a literature review about churn prediction is presented in Section 2.Executed methods are described in Section 3. In Section 4, the evaluation metrics is illustrated. In Section 5 the data preprocessing, model building and results of a series of experiments are discussed. Conclusions are considered in Section 6.

2. CHURN PREDICTION: A LITERATURE REVIEW

Neslin et al. (2006) defined customer churn as" the tendency of customers to stop doing business with a company in a given time period". Customer churn can be categorized as: unavoidable churn, involuntary churn and voluntary churn (Lin, Tzeng, & Chin, 2011). This categorization is corresponding to Burez and Van den Poel (2008). Customer churn prediction has received a growing attention in recent years. Table 1 provides some of the recent researches in this area which used data mining techniques for building churn prediction models. The table summarizes the contribution, applied modeling techniques, evaluation metrics and features/variables for each research.

Before developing any model for customer-base analysis, such as churn prediction model, it is necessary to recognize the business setting for which we want to develop a model. Fader and Hardi (2009) made distinction of business setting from two aspects:

1. **Type of Relationship with Customer:** Contractual and non-contractual types
2. **Opportunities for Transaction:** Continuous and discrete types

As a result, the business setting can be classified into four categories: Contractual/ Discrete, Contractual /Continuous, Non-Contractual / Discrete and Non-Contractual/ Continuous. In contractual settings, customer churn can be predicted by simply looking at contract termination date and its non-renewal (e.g., newspaper subscription). However in non-contractual settings, prediction customer churn is not obvious (e.g., prepaid cellular phone) (Fader & Hardi, 2009).

As Verbeke et al. (2010) stressed in their paper, the accuracy measure is not sufficient in evaluating a churn prediction model, and measures related to comprehensibility of model should be considered. As can be seen from Table 1, only in Verbeke et al. (2010) the authors emphasized on the importance of comprehensibility of churn prediction models, and in this regard they presented two new data mining techniques that take in to account both comprehensibility and accuracy of churn prediction models . Being comprehensible, a model can reveal the rationales for customer churn, this knowledge help marketing managers in developing right retention measures (Verbeke et al., 2010). Consequently, in this paper, we have compared three categories of data mining techniques that allow building interpretable churn prediction models in terms of accuracy and comprehensibility points.

3. METHODS

3.1. Rule Based Classifier

Rules are a good way of representing information or bits of knowledge. A rule-based classifier uses a set of IF-THEN rules for classification. Rule Based classifier can be built by three different techniques (Han & Kamber, 2006).

3.1.1. Rule Induction Using a Divide-and-Conquer Algorithm

We can extract IF-THEN rules from a divide-and-conquer algorithm such as decision tree. To extract rules from a decision tree, one rule is created for

Table 1. Overview of churn prediction researches

Source	Contribution	Techniques	Evaluation metrics	Features/variables
Coussement & Van den Poel (2008)	Comparison of two parameter selection techniques for support vector machines in churn prediction context	Support Vector Machines (SVM), Logistic regression, Random forests	PCC, AUC, Top-decile lift	Client/company-interaction variables, Renewal-related variable, Socio-demographic variables, Subscription-describing variables
Burez & Van den Poel (2008)	The use of information from the internal database of a Pay-TV company for separating financial churn from commercial churn	random forests, survival analysis	Area under the receiving operating curve(AUC)	current subscription, socio-demographic information, previous bad-payment behavior history information, contact information
Coussement & Van den Poel (2008b)	Examination of the beneficial effect of adding variables related to the voice of customers through call center emails – i.e., textual information – to a churn-prediction system	Logistic regression	Lift, Area under the receiving operating curve (AUC).	All information sent by the subscriber via email, client/company interaction variables, subscription related variables, renewal specific variables and socio-demographics.
Pendharkar (2009)	Application of two genetic-algorithm (GA) based neural network (NN) models in churn prediction context	Genetic algorithm based neural network approaches	ROC curve	Service usage, subscription details
Xie, Li, Ngai, & Ying (2009)	Presentation of a novel classification technique, called improved balanced random forests (IBRF), to address some limitation of churn prediction problem such as data imbalance	Artificial neural network(ANN), Decision tree (DT), Support vector machines (SVM), Random forests, Improved Balanced Random forests(IRBF)	Accuracy, Top-decile lift	Personal demographics, Account level, Customer behavior
Tsai & Lu (2009)	Application of two hybrid models in customer churn prediction	Artificial neural networks(ANN), self-organizing maps (SOM)	Accuracy, Type I and II errors	No information
Glady, Baesens, & Croux (2009)	Utilization of customer lifetime value (CLV) as a basis concept for the modeling and prediction of churn in a financial service	Logistic regression, decision trees and neural networks, cost-sensitive classifiers (AdaCost), Cost-sensitive decision tree	Area under the profit curve(AUPROC), PCC, Area under the receiver operating curve (AUROC) AUROC, the percentage of true positives	Customers' transaction variables
Coussement & Van den Poel (2008a)	Application of Generalized Additive Models (GAM), in churn prediction context in a subscription service	Generalized Additive Models(GAM), Logistic Regression	AUC, Top-decile lift	Client/company-interaction variables, Renewal-related variable, Socio-demographic variables, Subscription-describing variables

continued on following page

Table 1. Continued

Source	Contribution	Techniques	Evaluation metrics	Features/variables
Huang, Buckley, & Kechadi (2010)	Application of ''nondominated genetic algorithm II (NSGA-II) to select optimal subsets of features for churn prediction	Decision Tree C4.5	The overall accuracy (OA), The accuracy of the true churn (TC), The accuracy of true nonchurn (TN)	Demographic profiles, Information of grants, Account information, Call details, Service orders, Henley segmentation, Payment and bill information, Telephone line information
Owczarczuk (2010)	Testing the usefulness of the popular data mining models to predict churn of the clients of the Polish cellular telecommunication company	Logistic regression, linear regression, Fisher linear discriminate analysis and decision trees	Lift curves	Usage data
Karahoca & Karahoca (2010)	Proposition of integrated system for churn management based on adaptive neuro fuzzy inference system with fuzzy C-means	Fuzzy C-means clustering and adaptive neuro fuzzy inference system (ANFIS)	Correctness, Specificity, Sensitivity, Precision	Demographic, usage data
Verbeke et al. (2010)	Presentation of two novel data mining techniques, called ALBA and Antminer+ in churn prediction that consider both accuracy and comprehensibility measures in evaluation of churn prediction models	Antminer+, Active Learning Based Approach (ALBA), RIPPER, SVM, Logit, C4.5	PCC, Sensitivity,Specificty, #rules	Usage data

each path from the root to a leaf node. Each splitting criterion along a given path is logically ANDed to form the rule antecedent ("IF" part). The leaf node holds the class prediction, forming the rule consequent ("THEN" part). The number leaves in each decision tree is equal to the number of rules that we can extract from it (Han & Kamber, 2006). For example, if we build a C4.5 decision tree, we can know the number of its rules by counting its leaf nodes (Han & Kamber, 2006). We selected the C4.5 decision tree algorithm as a representative of this category.

3.1.1.1. C4.5 Decision Tree

The C4.5 algorithm is the expanded version of ID3 algorithm which is developed by Quinlan (1993) for generating decision trees (Han & Kamber, 2006; Tan, Steinbach, & Kumar, 2005; Witten & Frank, 2005; Larose, 2005). It constructs decision trees in a top down recursive divide and conquer manner (Han & Kamber, 2006). The C4.5 algorithm recursively visits each decision node, selecting the optimal split using a splitting criterion, until no further splits are possible. It uses the concept of information gain or entropy reduction to select the optimal split (Han & Kamber, 2006; Tan, Steinbach, & Kumar, 2005; Witten & Frank, 2005; Larose, 2005).

Let D, the data partition, be a training set of class-labeled instances. As illustrated in Equation (1), information gain is defined as the difference between the original information requirement and the new requirement (Han & Kamber, 2006). That is,

$$\text{Gain (A)} = \text{Info (D)} - \text{Info}_A \text{(D)} \quad (1)$$

where Info (D) is the expected information needed to classify an instance in D:

$$\text{Info}\left(\text{D}\right) = -\sum_{i=1}^{m} \text{P}_i \log_2 \quad (2)$$

and $Info_A(D)$ is the expected information required to classify an instance from D based on the partitioning by A (Neslin, Gupta, Kamakura, Lu, & Mason, 2006):

$$Info_A\left(D\right) = \sum_{j=1}^{v} \frac{|Dj|}{|D|} * \text{Info}\left(Dj\right) \quad (3)$$

In other words, *Gain (A)* tells us how much would be gained by branching on the attribute *A* (Han & Kamber, 2006).

One limitation of Gain is that it tends to select attributes having a large number of values (Han & Kamber, 2006). To overcome for this, C4.5 uses an extension to information gain known as gain ratio (Han & Kamber, 2006).

3.1.2.1. Rule Induction Using a Sequential Covering Algorithm

By using a sequential covering algorithm, one can extract IF-THEN rules directly from the training data (Han & Kamber, 2006). This technique also called as separate-and-conquer algorithm (Witten & Frank, 2005).

There are many sequential covering algorithms. Popular types include AQ, CN2, and the more recent, RIPPER. The general strategy is as follows. Rules are learned one at a time. Each time a rule is learned, the instances covered by the rule are removed, and the process repeats on the remaining instances (Han & Kamber, 2006; Tan, Steinbach, & Kumar, 2005; (Witten & Frank, 2005). In this study, we selected RIPPER algorithm as a representative of this category.

3.1.2.2. RIPPER Algorithm

RIPPER algorithm is widely used direct method for rule induction (Han & Kamber, 2006; Tan, Steinbach, & Kumar, 2005; Witten & Frank, 2005). Suppose we have training data D { (x_1, y_1), …, (x_N, y_k) } with x_i a vector valued feature and $y_{i=}$ {y_1,…y_k}.Generally RIPPER orders the classes {y_1,…,y_k} according to their frequencies. Suppose y_1 be a least frequent class and y_k to be a most frequent class. RIPPER generates rules for each class starting with least frequent one to most frequent one. When generating rule for class y_i, all instances belong to y_i are labeled as positive instances while those belong to other classes are labeled as negative instances (Han & Kamber, 2006; Tan, Steinbach, & Kumar, 2005; Witten & Frank, 2005).

For each class $y_{i=}$ {y_1,…y_k} RIPPER executes three phases: Rule Growing, Rule Pruning and Building the Rule Set (Han & Kamber, 2006; Tan, Steinbach, & Kumar, 2005; Witten & Frank, 2005).

1. **Rule Growing:** RIPPER employs a general-to-specific strategy for growing rule and the FOIL's information gain measure for to choose the best conjunct to be added into rule antecedent. Adding conjunct to rule stops when the rule start covering negative instances.
2. **Pruning Phase:** Once the rule is induced, RIPPER tests the performance of it on validation set by computing the following metric to determine whether pruning is needed: (p-n)/(p+n), where p/n is the number of positive/negative instances in the validation set covered by rule. This metric shows the rule's accuracy on validation set. If the metric improves after pruning then the conjunct is removed from the rule. Pruning is done starting from last conjunct added to the rule. For example, given rule ABCD → y, RIPPER checks whether D should be pruned first, followed by CD, BCD and etc.

3. **Building the Rule Set:** After inducing a rule, all the positive and negative instances covered by the rule are removed. The rule is added into the Rule Set as long as it does not violate the stopping condition which is based on minimum description length (Han & Kamber, 2006; Tan, Steinbach, & Kumar, 2005; Witten & Frank, 2005).

3.1.2.3. Obtaining Rules from a Partial Decision Tree

There is an alternative method to rule induction that generates accurate, compact, rule sets. The method combines the divide-and-conquer strategy for decision tree learning with the separate-and-conquer one for rule learning. It adopts the separate-and-conquer strategy in that it constructs a rule, removes the instances it covers, and continues creating rules recursively for the remaining instances until no instance remains. However, it performs differently from the standard approach in the way that each rule is created. Mainly, for creating a single rule, a pruned decision tree is built for the current set of instances, the leaf with the largest coverage is made into a rule, and the tree is discarded (Witten & Frank, 2005).

We selected the PART (Witten & Frank, 2005) algorithm as representative for this category.

As we have mentioned in introduction section, the main contribution of this study is applying algorithms which combines divide-and-conquer and separate-and-conquer strategies.

3.1.2.4. PART Algorithm

PART (Witten & Frank, 2005) adopts the divide-and-conquer with separate-and-conquers strategy. More precisely, PART generates a set of rules according to the divide-and-conquer strategy, removes all instances from the training collection that are covered by this rule and proceeds recursively until no instance remains. To generate a single rule, PART builds a partial decision tree for the current set of instances and chooses the leaf with the largest coverage as the new rule. Subsequently, the partial decision tree is discarded. A partial decision tree is an ordinary decision tree that contains branches to undefined sub-trees (Witten & Frank, 2005).

3.2. Logistic Regression

Any regression technique, whether linear or nonlinear can be used for classification purpose (Witten & Frank, 2005). Logistic regression technique is used when the dependent variable is dichotomous (Witten & Frank, 2005). It uses a logit transformation to constrain the outcomes of the linear combination of the characteristics between 0 and 1 (Witten & Frank, 2005). Logistic regression is a commonly used data mining technique in marketing area and especially in churn prediction context.

3.3. Additive Logistic Regression

An alternative to Logistic Regression is Additive Logistic Regression. Additive regression can also be applied to classification just as linear regression (Witten & Frank, 2005). Suppose we have training data$(x_1, y_1), \ldots, (x_N, y_N)$ with x_i a vector valued feature and $y_i =$ -1 or 1, For this two-class problem, an additive logistic model has the form

$$\text{logit}\left\{P(X)\right\} \equiv \log\{\frac{P(y=1\mid x)}{P(y=-1\mid x)}\} = \sum_{j=m}^{M} f_m(x)$$

f_j is the jth regression model in the ensemble and $f_j(x)$ is its prediction for instance **x** (Witten & Frank, 2005).

Additive logistic regression performs classification using a regression scheme as the base learner (Witten & Frank, 2005).

4. EVALUATING THE PERFORMANCE OF MODELS

4.1. Evaluation Techniques

Holdout, random sub-sampling, cross-validation, and the bootstrap are common used techniques for assessing the accuracy of classifiers (Han & Kamber, 2006). In this paper, we have used the cross-validation technique to assess the constructed models.

In cross validation, the data D are divided into k non-overlapping sets, D_1, . . ., Dk. At each iteration *i* (from 1 to k), partition D_i is reserved as the test set, and the remaining partitions are collectively used to train the model (Burez & Van den Poel, 2009). In general, stratified 10-fold cross-validation is recommended (Han & Kamber, 2006). In this paper we have used 10-fold cross-validation.

4.2. Evaluation Metrics

Accuracy or PCC (percentage of correctly classified examples), specificity, sensitivity, and AUC (area under the curve) are commonly used metrics for evaluating a classifier (Han & Kamber, 2006). In this study, we have used these metrics for evaluating the classification models.

The PCC measure computes the ratio of correctly classified examples to the total number of examples to be classified. The sensitivity measure is the proportion of positive examples that are correctively classified. The specificity measure is the proportion of negative examples that are correctly identified.

ROC (Receiver Operating Characteristic) curves are a useful visual tool for comparing two classifiers (Han & Kamber, 2006). The area under the curve (AUC) is a measure to assess the accuracy of a model (Han & Kamber, 2006).

For testing a model from comprehensibly view point, we use the number of generated if- then rules (#R) for each model. Therefore, the comprehensibility of a churn prediction model is high if the number of generated rules from it is low and vice versa (Verbeke et al., 2010).

5. EMPIRICAL ANALYSIS

Research procedure is showed in Figure 1. The figure shows the techniques used in each phase of this research.

5.1. Data Set

All algorithms used in this paper are applied on a publicly available dataset downloaded from the UCI Repository of Machine Learning Databases at the University of California, Irvine (http://www.ics.uci.edu). The data set contains 20 variables worth of information about 5000 customers, along with an indication of whether or not that customer churned (left the company). The proportion of churner in the dataset is 14.3%.

5.2. Data Preprocessing

There are many incomplete, noisy, and inconsistent data in large real world databases. However, the data mining results will not be useful, if the quality of input data be low (Han & Kamber, 2006). Therefore, Data preprocessing step is an important step in data mining. There are a number of data preprocessing techniques such as data cleaning, data transformation, data integration, data reduction (Han & Kamber, 2006). In this paper we have done correlation analysis and feature subset selection to remove irrelevant attributes from our used dataset.

Figure 1. Research architecture

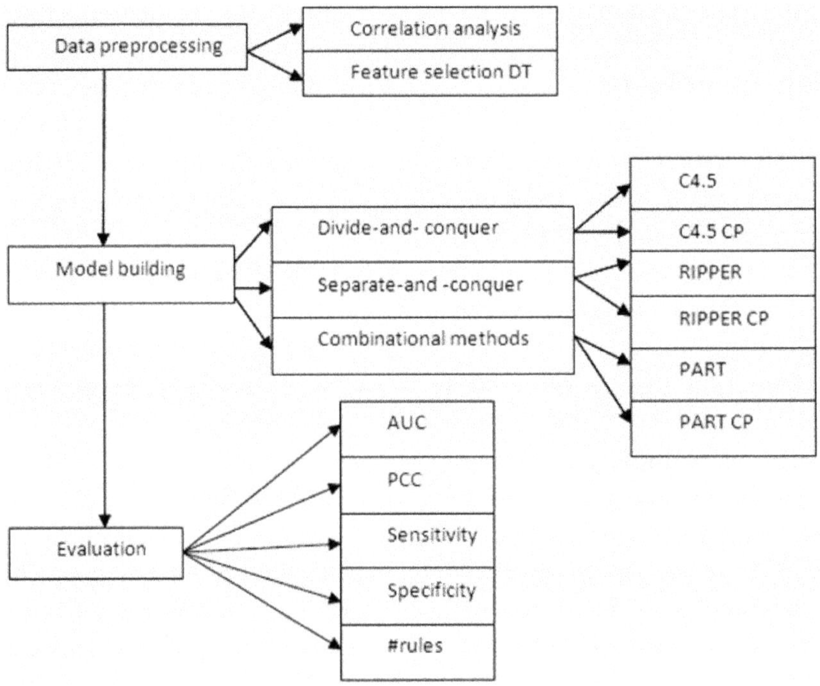

5.2.1. Feature Selection by Correlation Analysis

Feeding correlated variables to a data mining technique cause the resulted model to output unreliable results. So, correlation analysis should be done before entering to the model building step to prevent correlated data to be fed (Larose, 2005).

In this study we have done correlation analysis. After doing it, we have omitted three variables.

5.2.2. Feature Selection by Decision Tree Approach

We built C4.5 decision tree with remained features, then we traversed the tree to choose the features that is exist on the tree. In fact we have applied decision tree as a feature selection tool. Ultimately after performing data preprocessing phase, 11 features selected for data mining purpose. These features are shown in Table 2.

Table 2. Top eleven features selected during data processing phase

Feature	Type	What
InterPlan	Categorical	International Plan Subscriber(0=no, 1=yes)
VmailP	Categorical	VoiceMail Plan Subscriber(0=no, 1=yes)
TotalDayCharge	Continuous	Charge for day time usage
TotalEveCharge	Continuous	Charge for evening time usage
TotalEveCalls	Continuous	Total evening calls
TotalNightCharge	Continuous	Charge for night time usage
TotalNightCalls	Continuous	Total night calls
TotalInterCharge	Continuous	Charge for international calls
TotalInterCalls	Continuous	Total international calls
NumberofCalltoCS	Continuous	Number of calls to customer service
Churn	Categorical	1=churner, 1= nonchurner

5.2.3. Handling Class Imbalance

Customer churn event occurs seldom in service industries (Burez & Van den Poel, 2009). This means that real customer churn datasets have extremely skewed class distribution. For example the dataset used in this study has extremely skewed class distribution; such that the Class distribution of churners to non-churners is 14.3:85.7.

There are several data mining problems related to rarity along with some methods to address them (Burez & Van den Poel, 2009). The basic sampling methods include under-sampling and oversampling. Under-sampling eliminates majority-class examples whereas over-sampling duplicates minority-class examples. By using theses sampling techniques, the overall level of class imbalance is decreased (Weiss, 2004).

In this study, by applying oversampling technique on training data, we have obtained two new training sets: 1- training set with percentage of churner equal to 30%. 2- Training set with percentage of churner equal to 50%. We have done our research on three training sets: original, 30% churners and 50% churners. By doing so, we investigated the best training set that establishes a reasonable tradeoff between accuracy and comprehensibility.

5.4. Model Building

As previously mentioned, the aim of this research is to compare three algorithms from three different categories of rule-based classifiers in churn prediction context. Because the category of rule based classifiers, are interpretable, they can develop models that are not a black box one. We also have built churn prediction models by logistic regression and additive logistic regression. Also these two algorithms don't generate rules, but we have used their results in terms of accuracy to compare with the accuracy of rule-based classifiers. In addition by building models by logistic and additive logistic regression, we have compared the performance of them.

We have compared three interpretable algorithms in terms of comprehensibility and accuracy in churn prediction context. These algorithms include: C4.5 decision tree, RIPPER and PART (Partial decision tree). These algorithms correspond to three different categories of rule-based classifiers respectively divide-and-conquer, separate-and-conquer and algorithm that is a combination of first and second one.

The use of PART (Partial decision tree) algorithm is the first contribution of this paper.

For each of these algorithms, we have used two versions of them, one with standard parameters setting and the other with changed parameters that leads to complete pruning. For C4.5 and PART algorithms, we changed two parameters: The first parameter is Confidence factor which is the confidence threshold for pruning; and the second is minimum number of instances permissible at a leaf (Witten & Frank, 2005). For RIPPER algorithm, we have changed one parameter, which is the minimum total weight of instances in a rule.

By doing so we have built six algorithms namely as C4.5, C4.5 CP, RIPPER, RIPPER CP, PART, PART CP.

The parameters of C4.5 are "confidence factor" with value of 0.25 and "the minimum number of instances per leaf" with value of 2. The parameters of C4.5 CP are "confidence factor" with value of 0.001 and "the minimum number of instances per leaf" with value of 20. The parameters of PART are "confidence factor" with value of 0.25 and "the minimum number of instances per leaf" with value of 2. The parameters of PART CP are "confidence factor" with value of 0.001 and "the minimum number of instances per leaf" with value of 20.

We have also obtained the result of RIPPER and RIPPER CP with standard and complete pruning (minimum total weight of instances in a rule of respectively 2.0 and 12.0)

We have applied the above mentioned six algorithms along with logistic regression (LR) and additive logistic regression (ALR) on three training sets (the original training set with 14.3% churner, the one with 30% churner and the other one with 50% churner). In sum, we have built 24 churn prediction models. All the Experiments were conducted using WEKA (Waikato Environment for Knowledge Analysis) data mining software (Witten & Frank, 2005). As mentioned earlier, the experiments were carried out and validated with a 10-fold cross-validation in which the training sets are divided in 10-folds. Any nine of the ten segments is selected to perform training. The remaining part will be executed for testing the model. As a result, each part will be trained and tested ten times. At last, the average performance is calculated.

5.5. Results and Discussion

At first, we investigate the effect of oversampling on performance of churn prediction models. For this reason we have applied eight algorithms on three training sets.

The results of churn prediction experiments on Original training set, the second training set with the percentage of churner equal to 30% and the third training set with the percentage of churner equal to 50% are summarized respectively in Table 3, Table 4 and Table 5.

5.5.1. Comparison of Models from Accuracy and Comprehensibility Points

When looking at the results of experiments on three training sets, we see that in terms of AUC, PCC, sensitivity, and specificity, the additive logistic regression (ALR), outperforms all other algorithms, but as stressed in literature (Verbeke et al., 2010) accuracy of a churn prediction model is

Table 3. Performance of algorithms on original training set

Technique		AUC	PCC	Sensitivity	Specificity	#Rules
Original	RIPPER	0.866	95.11	0.741	0.987	13
	RIPPERCP	0.861	94.80	0.73	0.986	10
	C4.5	0.857	94.78	0.67	0.99	40
	C4.5CP	0.843	93.24	0.631	0.984	11
	PART	0.86	93.78	0.667	0.984	31
	PART CP	0.878	92.73	0.66	0.973	12
	LR	0.82	86.20	0.21	0.97	----
	ALR	0.91	94.78	0.72	0.99	----

Table 4. Performance of algorithms on training set with 30% churners

Technique		AUC	PCC	Sensitivity	Specificity	#Rules
30%	RIPPER	0.898	93.85	0.816	0.98	12
	RIPPERCP	0.897	93.75	0.808	0.981	11
	C4.5	0.925	93	0.83	0.967	124
	C4.5CP	0.896	90.1	0.75	0.96	18
	PART	0.94	92.6	0.785	0.97	48
	PART CP	0.899	91.46	0.741	0.97	14
	LR	0.82	79.5	0.39	0.94	----
	ALR	0.98	95.88	0.91	0.97	----

Table 5. Performance of algorithms on training set with 50% churners

		AUC	PCC	Sensitivity	Specificity	#Rules
50%	RIPPER	0.974	95.93	0.995	0.924	46
	RIPPERCP	0.961	93.09	0.962	0.90	24
	C4.5	0.976	97	0.999	0.941	180
	C4.5CP	0.906	88.6	0.85	0.93	23
	PART	0.98	97.6	1	0.95	78
	PART CP	0.96	90	0.90	0.91	45
	LR	0.823	76.32	0.76	0.77	----
	ALR	0.998	98.7895	0.999	0.976	----

not the only aspect. Another aspect of a good churn prediction model is its comprehensibility. A good customer churn prediction model should make balance between the accuracy and comprehensibility (Verbeke et al., 2010). However in reality both high accuracy and high comprehensibility may be not possible concurrently. As the accuracy of a model increases the comprehensibility of it decreases and vice versa. The results of Tables 3, 4, 5 confirm this issue. For example, as seen from Table 3 RIPPER CP (AUC=0.861, # Rules=10) is more comprehensible but less accurate; on the other hand, the result of C4.5 (AUC= 0.976, #Rules=180) as seen from Table 5 indicates that it is more accurate but less comprehensible. Since AUC is a more appropriate evaluation metric for assessing accuracy of a classification model and particularly a churn prediction model (Burez & Van den Poel, 2009) in analyzing the results, we use it.

As it is shown in the above Tables 3, 4, and 5, generally the AUC of all models increases as we move from original training set toward the training set with a 50/50 proportion. This shows that as the percentage of churners in the training set increases, the accuracy of built models also increases. This issue indicates that from the point of accuracy; the higher degree of oversampling results in a higher performance. This information is also shown in Figure 2.

Figure 2. AUC versus degree of oversampling

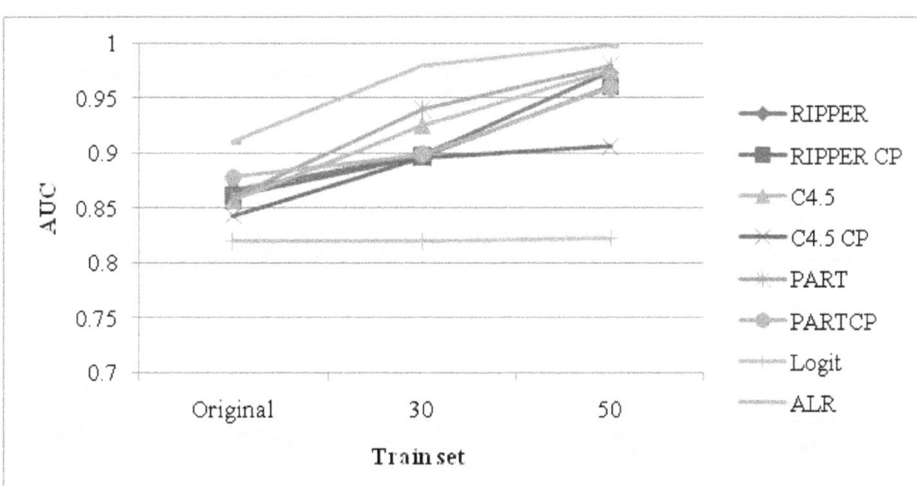

On the other hand, as seen from Tables 3, 4, and 5, generally the number of generated rules of all models increases as we move from original training set toward the training set with a 50/50 proportion. This indicates that as the degree of oversampling increases, the number of generated rules increases too. However, the higher number of generated rules results in the decrease in interpretability and comprehensibility of the resulting model. But as we discussed in previous sections, a churn prediction model should be both accurate and comprehensible. By these explanations, we concluded that the models built on original training set and training set with 50% churners cannot be an appropriate churn prediction models. The reason for this fact is that the accuracy (in terms of AUC and sensitivity) of models built on original training set is low where as the comprehensibility is high. In addition the accuracy of models built on training set with 50% churner is high while the comprehensibility of them is low. Figure 4 illustrates this finding. Notice that if the number of generated rules by an algorithm is high then the comprehensibility of it becomes low.

As Figure 4 shows, an appropriate tradeoff between accuracy (in terms of AUC) and comprehensibility (in terms of the number of generated rules) are established, when we apply the algorithms on the training set with the churn rate of 30%. Now we analyze the performance of built models from training set with 30% churners (RIPPER, RIPPER CP, C4.5, C4.5 CP, PART, PART CP, LR, and ALR) in terms of accuracy and comprehensibility. As can be seen from Table 3, the highest and lowest value of AUC is obtained respectively by using additive logistic regression (ALR) and logistic regression (LR).This shows that ALR performs far better that LR and is an attractive alternative to LR.

Since ALR and LR don't generate rules, we focus only on the remained algorithms (RIPPER, RIPPER CP, C4.5, C4.5 CP, PART, and PART CP). Among these algorithms, PART obtains the highest AUC, but with the number of rules equal to 48. This indicates that PART does not establish appropriate balance between the AUC and the number of rules metrics. In addition C4.5 algorithm, creates a model with a high accuracy (AUC=0.925), but the number of generated rules of it is very high (#rules=124), for this reason we conclude that the C4.5 model cannot be a proper choice. The AUC of the RIPPER, RIPPER CP, C4.5 CP and PART CP respectively are 0.898, 0.897, 0.896 and 0.899. These results indicate that in terms of AUC, their performances don't differ significantly, and the difference is minor that we can assume them equal. In other words in terms of accuracy, they are performing the same. Therefore, we compare them from comprehensibility point.

The number of rules (#rules) of the RIPPER, RIPPER CP, C4.5 CP and PART CP respectively are 12, 11, 18 and 14.

By analyzing these results, we notice that RIPPER CP (AUC=0.897, #Rules =11) outperforms RIPPER, C4.5 and PART CP from both accuracy and comprehensibility view points. It has nearly the same AUC when compared with other, but the lower number of generated rules.

Furthermore The RIPPER (AUC=0.898, #Rules =12) and PART CP (AUC=0.899, #Rules =14) show proper performance. Their performances don't significantly differ from the performance of RIPPER CP.

However the performance of C4.5 CP (AUC=0.896, #Rules =18) from the perspective of comprehensibility is worse and it is not an appropriate choice.

As we have mentioned above, the PART CP (AUC=0.899, #Rules =14) algorithm shows admirable performance in terms of both accuracy and comprehensibility. Researchers can use this algorithm in their study.

When looking at results, we see that parameter setting lead to appropriate performance for all algorithms. For example, C4.5 CP works better than C4.5; PART CP performs superior than PART and finally RIPPER CP performs better than RIPPER. This shows that parameter setting plays an important role in improving performance of algorithms (Figure 3).

Figure 3. Number of rules versus degree of oversampling

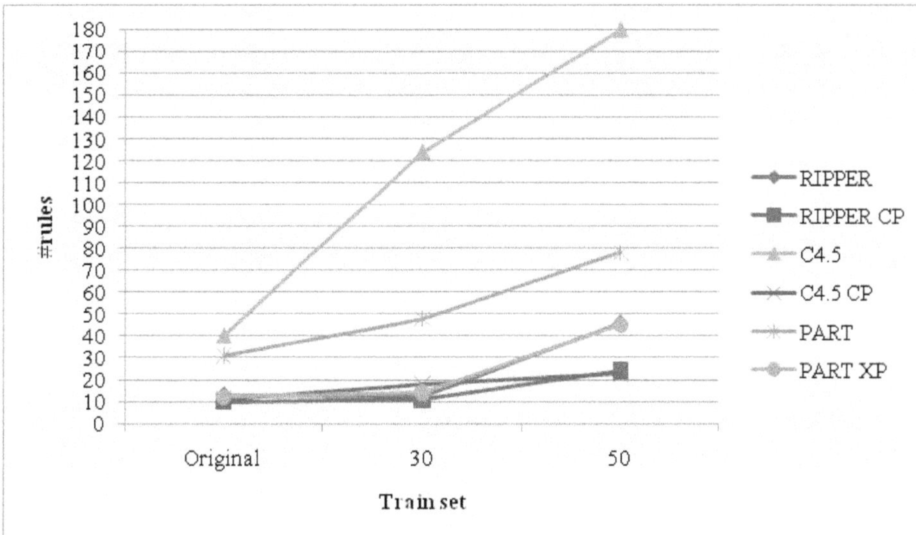

Figure 4. Tradeoff between accuracy and comprehensibility

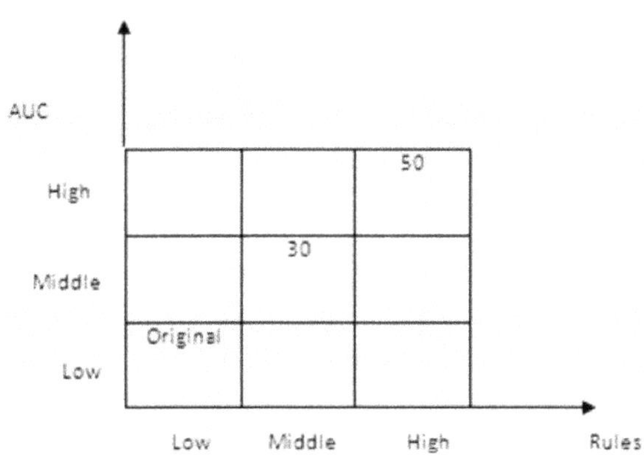

6. CONCLUSION

Customer churn is a focal concern of most firms in all industries. Churn prediction is a useful tool for to identify customers at risk of churn. As mentioned in the literature review, much attention is paid to accuracy of a churn prediction model in the past researches. Besides being accurate, a churn prediction model should be comprehensible to reveal the reason for customer churn.

In this paper, we have compared three different algorithms from three different categories (divide-and-conquer, separate-and-conquer, combination of first and second) of rule based classifiers. These algorithms are C4.5, RIPPER, and PART. Furthermore, we have applied additive logistic regression along with logistic regression. The first finding of this paper is that we should handle class imbalance to obtain a churn prediction model that makes balance between accuracy and comprehensibility. The results of this study showed that the performance of all algorithms from points of accuracy and comprehensibility are reasonable when these algorithms are applied to the training set with the churn rate of 30%. The second finding is that in terms of accuracy, additive logistic regression outperforms all other methods. The third finding is that RIPPER, RIPPER CP, C4.5 CP, PART CP performs the same in terms of AUC when applied to the training set with the churn rate of 30%, but among them RIPPER CP, from the category of separate-and-conquer algorithms outperforms them in terms of accuracy and comprehensibility. The fourth finding is that parameter selection plays an important role in improving performance of algorithms the results of RIPPER CP, C4.5 CP, PART CP confirms this issue. The final finding is that PART CP algorithm showed appropriate performance, and researchers can apply this algorithm in their researches in other areas.

REFERENCES

Athanassopoulos, A. D. (2000). Customer satisfaction cues to support market segmentation and explain switching behavior. *Journal of Business Research*, *47*(3), 191–207. doi:10.1016/S0148-2963(98)00060-5

Burez, J., & Van den Poel, D. (2008). Separating financial from commercial customer churn: A modeling step towards resolving the conflict between the sales and credit department. *Expert Systems with Applications*, *35*, 497–514. doi:10.1016/j.eswa.2007.07.036

Burez, J., & Van den Poel, D. (2009). Handling class imbalance in customer churn prediction. *Expert Systems with Applications*, *36*, 4626–4636. doi:10.1016/j.eswa.2008.05.027

Chaffey, D., Ellis-Chadwick, F., Mayer, R., & Johnston, K. (2006). *Internet marketing strategy, implementation and practice*. Upper Saddle River, NJ: Prentice Hall.

Coussement, K., & Van den Poel, D. (2008b). Integrating the voice of customers through call center emails into a decision support system for churn prediction. *Information & Management*, *45*, 164–174. doi:10.1016/j.im.2008.01.005

Coussement, K., & Van den Poel, D. (2009). Improving customer attrition prediction by integrating emotions from client/company interaction emails and evaluating multiple classifiers. *Expert Systems with Applications*, *36*, 6127–6134. doi:10.1016/j.eswa.2008.07.021

Coussement, K. F., Benoit, D., & Van den Poel, D. (2010). Improved marketing decision making in a customer churn prediction context using generalized additive models. *Expert Systems with Applications*, *37*, 2132–2143. doi:10.1016/j.eswa.2009.07.029

Coussement, K. F., & Van den Poel, D. (2008a). Churn prediction in subscription services: An application of support vector machines while comparing two parameter-selection techniques. *Expert Systems with Applications*, *34*, 313–327. doi:10.1016/j.eswa.2006.09.038

Fader, P. S., & Hardi, B. G. S. (2009). Probability models for customer-base analysis. *Journal of Interactive Marketing*, *23*, 61–69. doi:10.1016/j.intmar.2008.11.003

Glady, N., Baesens, B., & Croux, C. (2009). Modeling churn using customer lifetime value. *European Journal of Operational Research*, *197*, 402–411. doi:10.1016/j.ejor.2008.06.027

Han, J., & Kamber, M. (2006). *Data mining concepts and techniques*. San Francisco, CA: Morgan Kaufmann.

Huang, B., Buckley, B., & Kechadi, T. (2010). Multi-objective feature selection by using NSGA-II for customer churn prediction in telecommunications. *Expert Systems with Applications*, *37*, 3638–3646. doi:10.1016/j.eswa.2009.10.027

Jones, M. A., Mothersbaugh, D. L., & Beatty, S. E. (2000). Switching barriers and repurchase intentions in services. *Journal of Retailing*, *76*(2), 259–374. doi:10.1016/S0022-4359(00)00024-5

Karahoca, A., & Karahoca, D. (2011). GSM churn management by using fuzzy c-means clustering and adaptive neuro fuzzy inference system. *Expert Systems with Applications*, *38*(3).

Larose, D. (2005). *Discovering knowledge in data: An introduction to data mining*. Hoboken, NJ: John Wiley & Sons.

Lin, C. S., Tzeng, G. H., & Chin, Y. C. (2011). Combined rough set theory and flow network graph to predict customer churn in credit card accounts. *Expert Systems with Applications*, *38*, 8–15. doi:10.1016/j.eswa.2010.05.039

Neslin, S. A., Gupta, S., Kamakura, W., Lu, J., & Mason, C. (2006). Defection detection: Measuring and understanding the predictive accuracy of customer churn models. *JMR, Journal of Marketing Research*, *43*(2), 204–211. doi:10.1509/jmkr.43.2.204

Owczarczuk, M. (2010). Churn models for prepaid customers in the cellular telecommunication, industry using large data marts. *Expert Systems with Applications*, *37*, 4710–4712. doi:10.1016/j.eswa.2009.11.083

Pendharkar, P. (2009). Genetic algorithm based neural network approaches for predicting churn in cellular wireless network services. *Expert Systems with Applications*, *36*, 6714–6720. doi:10.1016/j.eswa.2008.08.050

Quinlan, J. R. (1993). *C4.5: Programs for machine learning*. San Francisco, CA: Morgan Kaufmann.

Tan, P.-N., Steinbach, M., & Kumar, V. (2005). *Introduction to data mining*. Upper Saddle River, NJ: Pearson Education.

Thomas, J. S. (2001). A methodology for linking customer acquisition to customer retention. *JMR, Journal of Marketing Research*, *38*(2), 262–268. doi:10.1509/jmkr.38.2.262.18848

Tsai, C., & Lu, Y. (2009). Customer churn prediction by hybrid neural networks. *Expert Systems with Applications*, *36*, 12547–12553. doi:10.1016/j.eswa.2009.05.032

Verbeke, W., Martens, D., Mues, C., & Baesens, B. (2011). Building comprehensible customer churn prediction models with advanced rule induction techniques. *Expert Systems with Applications*, *38*(3).

Weiss, G. M. (2004). Mining with rarity: A unifying framework. *SIGKDD Explorations*, *6*(1), 7–19. doi:10.1145/1007730.1007734

Witten, I. H., & Frank, E. (2005). *Data mining: Practical machine learning tools and techniques*. San Francisco, CA: Morgan Kaufmann.

Xie, Y., Li, X., Ngai, E., & Ying, W. (2009). Customer churn prediction using improved balanced random forests. *Expert Systems with Applications*, *36*, 5445–5449. doi:10.1016/j.eswa.2008.06.121

This work was previously published in the International Journal of Information Retrieval Research, Volume 1, Issue 2, edited by Zhongyu (Joan) Lu, pp. 39-54, copyright 2011 by IGI Publishing (an imprint of IGI Global).

Chapter 9
Virtual Community of Practice Ontocop:
Towards a New Model of Information Science Ontology (ISO)

Ahlam Sawsaa
University of Huddersfield, UK

Zhongyu (Joan) Lu
University of Huddersfield, UK

ABSTRACT

Information Science (IS) is an ambiguous field as its boundaries overlap with other domains such as Archive Science, Library Science and Computing Science which requires defined clear definition. This study creates a systematic and comprehensive ontology targeted to explore IS boundaries and foundations. This paper uses Mereotopolgy theory to describe classes, instances and their relations. The classes are created based on taxonomy of IS to create an asserted model of Information Science Ontology (ISO) that can be as a skeletal foundation for knowledge base. The main classes are Actors, Method, Practice, Studies, Mediate, Kinds, Domains, Resources, Legislation, Philosophy & Theories, Societal, Time, and Space. The design is based on Methontology to create ISO from scratch. Its framework facilitates the construction of ontology at the knowledge levels. It is found that identifying the IS boundaries through implementation ontology workflow is encoded using Protégé and Web Ontology Language (OWL) for formalizing and representation of the ISO. ISO is an effective way to represent knowledge and overcome semantic heterogeneity, ISO is a fundamental integration between semantic that realizes the interoperability information of the domain.

DOI: 10.4018/978-1-4666-3898-3.ch009

1. INTRODUCTION

Ontology is an important emerging discipline that has vast potential in the development of information organization, management and understanding. It has been vital in many different fields, particularly in the knowledge management area. Ontology describes concepts, terms and relations in a specific domain to create communication richness and provide a clear description of these concepts which are related to the domain knowledge. Ontology can be used from people and software agents as a knowledge base (Gòmez-Pérez et al., 2004; Gruber, 1993). However, the main motivation for building and developing ontology is to create potential for sharing knowledge and re-using it in many applications within a specific domain, it allows used this coding in efficient way.

Since community of practice (Cop) has been recognised as a knowledge management tool, many organisations have changed their direction to Cop as a solution for creating and sharing knowledge (Wenger, 2002; Schlemiel, 2008; Saint-Ongo, 2003).

Communities of Practice are an attempt by individuals, groups and organisations to share what they know and exchange ideas, concepts, perspectives, and expertise from various cultures (Gasevic et al., 2006).

The central focus of Cop is to improve the knowledge domain (Erat et al., 2006). Just as knowledge management has been widely discussed, so the issue of the Communities of Practice as part of an overall knowledge management strategy has been commonly discussed on in literature and by practitioners who implement them (Wenger, 1998).

The contribution of an Ontocop community can be developed in terms of asking the following questions:

- How members of IS domains share information?
- How they interact and learn from new experience?
- How they gain competence to enter into the community?

To answer the above questions, the overall objective of this research is proposed, i.e., to visualize the IS domain. In regard to knowledge acquisition; how Ontocop helps to create potential members who join together to develop the ontology process. This paper focuses on: 1). How virtual Communities of Practices are organised, evolved and managed; 2). How community members will share a common interest in the subject area, ongoing interaction among them to develop the ontology; 3). how Communities of practice (Cops) work, to find sources of knowledge; 4). How Cops use resources for improvement of innovation and productivity.

2. BACKGROUND

2.1. Virtual Communities of Practice (VCops)

2.1.1. Community of Practice (Cops)

Community of Practice is introduced by Lave and Wenger (1998) as a learning process within the Legitimate Peripheral Participation (LPP). LPP in his perspective is an important aspect of effective social learning. LPP is based on the idea that members of the community with less experience will learn from social interaction with experts in a specific domain. This initial definition relates the theory of situativity, situated learning within ethnographic study.

Community of Practice has developed when redefined by Wenger (1998) from use within a business environment, to be used in knowledge management as a location for successful knowledge sharing. The concept has received much attention from both participants and scholars in the knowledge management field. Community of Practice has been defined (Cox, 2005; Roberts, 2006).

The most definitions of Cops refer to the idea of the exchange of information and knowledge and shared concerns within groups of people.

Community of practice is not a formal structure for knowledge generation. The generation of knowledge accrues when people co-operate and communicate to seek solutions to problems or to develop a new product. Many studies conducted that community of practice is the best and strongest way to bind a team (Nirenberg, 1995; Stewart, 1997).

2.1.2 Virtual Community of Practice (VCops)

Development of technology has led to the emergence of virtual communities. In these communities people can meet virtually and exchange stories or chat via the internet or just to play games or build social relationships. Also, allowing transfer of knowledge across the world and cultural boundaries (Jansen, 2002; Wenger, 2002).

Virtual community has been defined by Licklider as computer networking. This term can be used for:

- Groups of people using comport, mediated as a social network to communicate.
- Online groups using chat rooms and listing services to share activity online (Gourlay, 2001).

A virtual community has been defined from different perspectives (Catherine et al., 2000; Gomez, 1998; Panteli & Duncan, 2004) .Virtual communities of practice are a crucial tool for knowledge acquisition. The reason for this is that tacit knowledge is embedded in people's mind. By exchanging stories and conversation between experts they share experience to gain skills. Since the world has become a global village and face- to face contact is limited for the exchange of ideas, with an increase of websites on the internet, virtual communities have become an alternative to a physical communities of practice with dispersed multinational organizations (Araujo, 1998; Ardichvili et al., 2003).

After examining many studies concerning virtual communities of Practice, we found that, there is no full agreement in defining it. The purpose of this study is to define some key features from literature reviews. Features for VCops are typically:

- The ability to meet in a virtual space and communicate via the Internet.
- People are brought together, by means of a technical platform, who might never meet in reality.
- VCop facilitates activities by using Information technology IT.
- The existence of the virtual community can aid identification of an idea or task.
- Groups can self-select.
- Member's interests are usually related to a specific Knowledge Domain.
- Members can establish social relationships or a sense of belonging to the group.
- Building trust.

However, VCops are teams of individuals who meet and communicate virtually with others; they are linked by a specific interest and emerging social relationships. However, their technical infrastructure is fundamentally for knowledge exchange within virtual communities. They have had a significant effect in enabling people to transfer tacit knowledge, which is difficult to articulate.

Many virtual communities are now based on social relationships on the internet. For example, YouTube, news group, wiki and Linked In. All of these focus on working as virtual groups. Not all virtual community VCs are VCoPs; in the former knowledge can be transferred from expert to inexpert, but in the latter knowledge can be exchanged from peer to peer, whether they are professionals or experts in a specific domain. Professionals codify tacit knowledge, which reduces vagueness in coding and analysis.

Regarding the presentation of knowledge we emphasise that, members of VCoPs should be professionals in a specific domain. A professional is a person who holds knowledge in a particular domain and has the ability to solve problems and the commitment to work efficiently. In other words VCops should be composed of experts in order to present knowledge as the knowledge base (KB). In real life many VCops exist. For instance, VCops in the educational domain such as Tapped In htpp://www.tappedin.org (TappedIn, 2010). Table 1 summarizes the differences between these communities of practice.

Table 1. Comparison between communities of practice

Category	Traditional Cops	Virtual VCops
Communication via the internet	☒	☑
Existence for an identification of an idea or task	☒	☑
Existence according to a place based	☑	☒
Norms	☑	☑
Groups self-selected	☒	☑
Groups emerge through task	☑	☑
leadership	☑	☑
boundaries	Evolving	Fluid
Transparency	Low	High
Knowledge Domain	Interest –related work	Interest –related knowledge
Trust	☑	☑
Membership criteria	☑	☑
Level of member participation	Limited	Widely

2.2. Ontology

Ontology emerged from the philosophical field as a study of being introduced by Aristotle. This term has been borrowed from computer science and become used to represent the knowledge to understand the world.

The concept of ontology has diversity of meaning within different fields such as philosophy, computing, linguistics, mathematics and social science. However, the definition of ontology came from a branch of philosophy. The philosophy defined ontology in relation to the study of human beings.

Smith (2003) asserted that ontology is a science of what is, and existence of beings which is related to the field of computer and information systems.

In current years ontology has become an area of attention for computer science. Hence, Computer science has defined ontology based on knowledge system (KMS), as classification of knowledge.

Gruber provides the most cited definition of ontology that seems as conceptual model "ontology is an explicit specification of conceptualisation".

Artificial intelligence communities have to be aware of the knowledge power and it is effect on IA systems. Ontology presents a formal specification that progressed by Artificial intelligence (AI) or could be an informal specification that deals with human relations. (AI) defined ontology:

"Ontology is a theory of what entities can exist in the mind of a knowledgeable agent".

Guarino and Giaretta pointed out terminological clarification to identify what ontology is; they asserted clarified the misunderstanding between ontology as a conceptual framework at the knowledge level and ontology as artefact at the symbol level, to be used for a particular purpose. Ontology constructs from these components are:

1. Classes – class hierarchy.
2. Instances.
3. Slots- values.
4. Inheritance (multiple? Defaults?).

5. Restrictions or slots (type, cardinality).
6. Properties of slots (symmetric, transitive).
7. Reasoning tasks (classification, subsumption) to make sure this ontology is built for specific purposes.

It is clear that developing ontologies has become increasingly important for knowledge level interoperation and information integration. It provides functional features for IA and knowledge representation. We shall seek to explain the needs of ontologies:

- To ask questions about a particular subject domain, that required conceptualization.
- Conceptualization domain describes its entities and the relations between them.
- Providing a vocabulary for representing knowledge about the domain.
- Support the system developer with a core of domain knowledge beside the vocabulary.
- It is vital for developing and using intelligent systems, also for the interoperation of heterogeneous systems.

Furthermore, Ontology has many common types and is classified according to the structure and the user's need and it is categorized from different approaches. We have compared these approaches in Table 2.

Table 2. Ontology categories

Approaches	Categorizations of ontologies
Mizoguchi et al. (1995)	• Content ontology • Communication ontology for shearing knowledge • Indexing ontology • Meta-ontology
Van Heijst et al. (1997)	Classify ontologies into two diminutions: 1. It has three categories: a. Terminological ontologies as lexicons. b. Information ontologies as database schemata c. Knowledge modelling 2. It has four categories: a. Representation b. Generic c. Domain d. Application ontology
Guarino (1998)	According to level of dependence: 1. Top level ontology 2. Domain ontology 3. Task ontology 4. Application ontology
Sowa (2000)	1. Informal ontology 2. Formal ontology 3. Domain ontology
Lassila and McGuinness (2001)	Based on the ontology needs and the richness of its structure 1. Controlled vocabularies 2. Glossaries 3. Thesaurus 4. Informal is-a relations. 5. Formal is-a hierarchy 6. Formal instance 7. Frames, value restriction 8. General logical constrains.
Happel and Seedorf (2006)	Categorized Ontologies in Software Engineering based on abstraction and their expressivity: 1. Ontology-driven development (ODD 2. Ontology-enabled development (OED) 3. Ontology-based architectures (OBA) 4. Ontology-based architectures (OBA)

However, categories can appear in different ways such as taxonomy (is-a superclass, subclass), to group the domain in classical taxonomical categories according to Aristotle's prospective, which is become now a matter particularly with the time.

3. RESEARCH APPROACH

3.1. Theoretical Model

3.1.1. Category Theory

A number of thinkers including Hartmann and Husserl asserted that ontology adopts a categorical framework which means, it searches for what is universal in both specific and general domains (Hartmann, 1952). The precise meaning of ontology relies on the theory of category as grounding on contemporary mathematics (Lawvere, 1969).

3.1.2. Mereology Theory

Husserl introduced the theory of Mereology as basic for formal ontology. Mereology is a formal theory concerned with wholes and part structures (Husserl, 1970). Whereas, topology is a theory of wholeness that defines the relations connected to its properties, and how to represent these components within the system (Varzi, 1996; Herre, 2010).

The basic metrological system is M= (E, ≤) in which E is domain entities, and ≤ is binary relations. The E, ≤ binary relations is denoted M can be considered as ground Mereology. The ground merelogy is the first order partial ordering theory as reflexive, ant symmetric, transitive relations, some relations can be axiomatised as following:

- (M1) $\forall x\ (x \leq x)$, (reflexive)
- (M2) $\forall xy\ (x \leq y\ \Lambda\ y \leq x \rightarrow x = y)$, (anti-symmetry)
- (M3) $\forall x\ y\ z\ (x \leq y\ \Lambda\ y \leq z \rightarrow\ \leq z)$, (transitivity).

3.1.3. Mereotoplogy Theory

The Mereology and topology theories together are integrated as Mereotoplogy theory due to the fact that they supplement each other. It has become a main tool for formal ontological analysis (Variz, 1998). Mereology is a theory of part and wholes and concerned with part to part structure. Topology is a theory of whole, and concerned with connecting these parts. The limitation of each one requires more ontological relations. "Mereotoplogy is built out of Mereology together with Topological component ….." (Barry, 1996, p. 287). As seen in Table 3 which presents the main features of both theories.

The axioms in Mereotoplogy are designed to serve a formal ontological system. The primitive relations of parthood or constituency are as follows: if *x* is a part of *y* '*x* P *y*' then y will be consistent with *x's* being identical to y:

- **x overlaps y xOy:** $= \exists z\ (zPx\ \Lambda\ zPy)$
- **x is discrete from y:** $xDy: = xOy$
- **x is a point Pt (x):** $= \forall y\ (yPx \rightarrow y = x)$

Table 3. The main features of Mereology and Topology theory

Category Theory	Mereology theory	Topology Theory
Fundamental theory of classification	Fundamental theory of identity	Fundamental base of Mereology
searches for what is universal in both specific and general domain	Theory of parthood	Is generalization of Mereology where the relations of joining and connection
to group the domain in classical taxonomical categories	Can seen as ground theory	Theory of whole
	Build supplying the necessary notions and principle	

Based on the above taxonomy of IS has a fundamental root of its theory emerged from other sciences such as: Library science, Computer science and Archival science. The IS classification basically is based on a faceted analytic-synthetic system. Ranganathan's contribution was got through in facet analysis; his approach was the creation of five categories, namely: Personality, Matter, Energy, Space and Time called PMEST. Our approach corresponds to CRG Research group classification which exteneds these categories to 13 faceted. Thus, we analyse IS and extension the domain into 13 categories. These categories are:

Actors, Method, Practice, Studies, Mediate, Kinds, Domains, Resources, Legislation, Philosophy & theories, Societal, Time, Space.

3.2. Ontology Construction of IS

Creating an ontology of Information science (IS) is bring together concepts and terms from varied disciplines such as library science, computer science, archive science and engineering, to build together the boundaries of Information Science.

Also, to avoid the ambiguity in the concepts of the whole domain. As shown in Figure 1.

Information Science still suffers from problem identification, but it is still a complex problem and controversial point. Information science has been defined as a system concerned with processes of storing and transferring information. Additionally, analysing, collecting, classifying, manipulating, storing, and retrieving the information.

Many perspectives consider that the nature of this science is one of these areas: Informatics, computer science and Information Technology. In fact, we need to analyze data to determine concepts for development and specifying them.

3.3. Ontology Building Method

Ontology of Information science (IS) provides classification structure and semantic relations between the classes and instances in the domain. The proposed approach is to offer a control vocabulary in information science (IS). This study follows Methontology which began at the specification stage to identify goals, scope, strategy and boundary, beside uses and users (Sawsaa & Lu, 2010). Therefore, to create the conceptual model of ontology, during the conceptualization stage from annotating ontocop's knowledge resources to create:

Figure 1. Ontology of information science (IS)

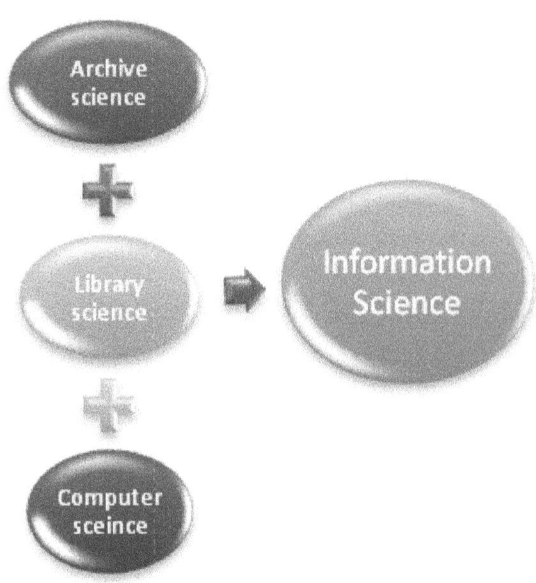

1. Glossary of terms, define each in natural language, e.g., data, Information, Knowledge, computer.
2. **Concept Taxonomy:** Classes, subclasses, partitions, disjoint.
3. The concept dictionary, e.g.,
   a. **Information Science:** Defined as: discipline that deals with the processes of storing and transferring information and organises all concepts and relations
4. **Rows List Relations between Concepts:** Concept name, Synonyms, Acronym, and Class attributes, Instance.
5. **Binary Relation:** To explain relationships between concepts.
6. Ontology formalisations in Protégé tool and OWL language.
7. Refinement, evaluation (feedback from experts in the domain).
8. Maintaining the ontology (Staab & Studer, 2001; Tatiana Gavrilova, 2008) as illustrated in Figure 2.

3.3.1. System Development

The Ontocop website is designed to support group interaction. For knowledge management, it allows communication through the community of Information Science (IS) to enable members to communicate and interact across diverse destinations. Ontocop is a tool to build the ontology of (IS) by extracting the main concepts and relations. The architecture of Ontocop consists of many layouts; the homepage contains the navigation icon to search on the Google or on the website itself. The News page provides the recent news about the developing ontology. Layout is a tool namely:

Figure 2. An approach to building ontology of IS (Sawsaa & Lu, 2009)

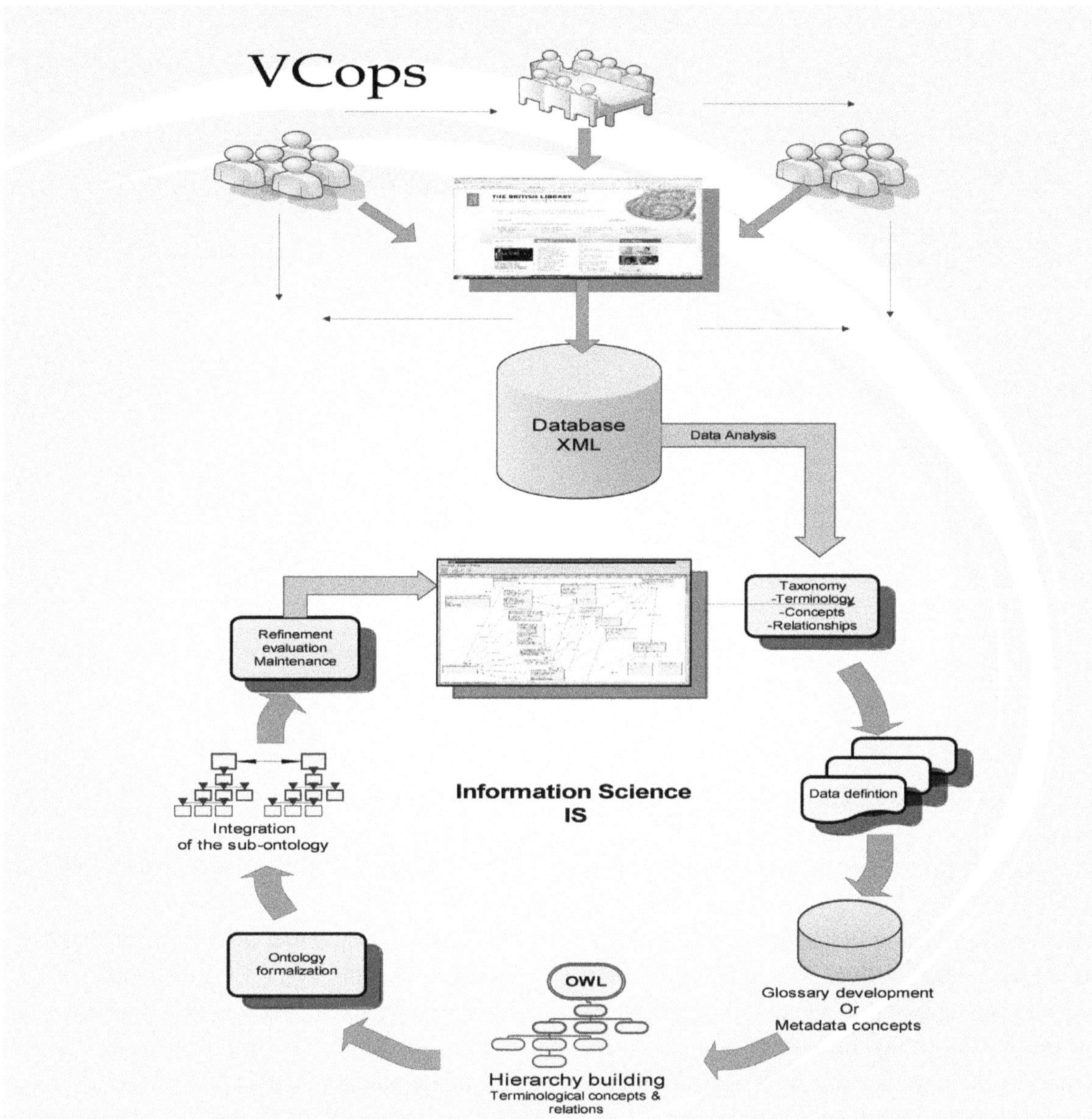

- To display Events of the website and to organize the discussion topics to be realised for participation.
- A Forum for debate and discussion of Information Science topics, as well as Chat and E- conferencing online.

Information pages explain and clarify some information about the Ontocop and the reasons for creating the ontology model, and shows frequently asked questions (FAQ), feedback, members profile, and the contact details. As depicted in Figure 3.

Figure 3. Website layout

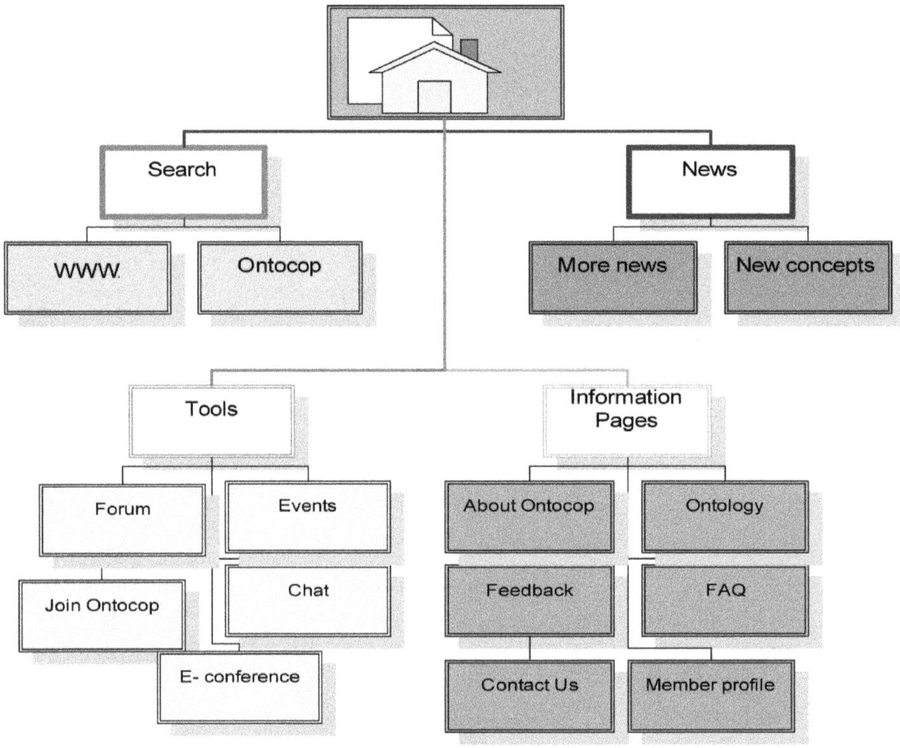

3.3.2. System Requirements

The system requires usability and sociability. The usability features include consistency between pages and words used in the web site such as the title of pages and headings. The members should be able to navigate easily and to follow the pages smoothly without any difficulty. Throughout the website, each page has the same navigation bar. Due to the lack of consistency between browsers, the main page has a common browser. If users find any problems with other browsers, they can view with Internet Explorer or Firefox.

However, for the integrity of the website there is a registration policy for new members to keep information in the data base and in other sites under control because this is a community for research purposes and is for experts in the domain of information science only.

3.4. Implementation

3.4.1. System Implementation

Ontocop was launched in November 2009. By invitation people were informed and encouraged to participate. The online community has been created by a research student as designer and moderator to support her research project. The designer of the web site has chosen to use the chat room features provided free by php free Chat Company and Forum features provided free by phpBB3. Additionally, it uses E- conference features (Koch, 2000).

3.4.2. Technical Features

Ontocop is hosted by Huddersfield server, which has proven suitable for this project and developed in this research, and has been tested on Mozilla Firefox and Microsoft Internet Explorer.

Most of the pages in Ontocop original Web-Pages use mark up languages such as: Hyper Text Mark-up Language (HTML) tag standards and Extensible Hypertext Mark up Language (XHTML). To gain excellent style, the Cascading Style Sheets (CSS) is used which is appropriate for the website theme as background. This style applied for the text, font, image provide a convenient mode for human sense. Additionally Java scripts, php and MySQL are used. The software has been successfully tested in the following hardware:

- Microsoft Windows XP Professional version 2002, Service pack3.Computer intel (R) core (TM) Duo CPU, E 7500@2.93 GHz, 2.96 GHz RAM Physical address.
- Microsoft Windows XP Professional version 2002,Service pack3.Computer intel (R) core (TM) Duot CPU, E 7500@2.93 GHz, 2.96 GHz RAM
- Physical address. Toshiba personal Rating: 1.0 Windows Experience 2 Dou CPU. E 7400@2.80 GHz 2.80 GHz. Memory (RAM) 4.00 GB system type 32-bit operating system, Windows Vista Home Premium, 2007.

3.4.3. Aesthetic Features

The format in Ontocop is designed to be appropriate for users.

Background colour is white with some bright colours like blue and yellow as appropriate for human interaction. Mixed colours and fonts are not used in the design. Yellow is to draw the visitor's attention to the main menu and left menu. Magenta is used for visited navigational links (Sawsaa & Lu, 2010).

Arial, helvetica, verdana and sans-serif, the family fonts, are the fonts used for the main body and also for different sized headings. The graphics sustain the web site theme. Modifications of the main picture are suitable for other pages such as ontology, contact us, FAQ pages and the forum and chat features (Sawsaa & Lu, 2010).

4. RESULTS

4.1. Ontocop a System of Visualisation IS Knowledge

The core function of VCop is generating ideas and elaborates tacit knowledge through problem solving and suggesting topics to be discussed. This knowledge could be stored in a multimedia database from where it is easier to extract knowledge. Tacit knowledge is shared in VCops through technology using several tools. VCops requires resources to operate its functions such as, space for members meetings, database to store discussions, information ideas, ways to share tacit knowledge and also, record activities. The designer decided to make the following resource available:

- **Member Meeting's Space:** Members of a community require a place to meet face to face or virtually, this space needs to be easy to access to enable members to interact and communicate asynchronously by leaving comments and ideas. The virtual space is provided online via software such as forums, online chat, and virtual meeting rooms and e- conferencing.

Figure 4 shows the Forum which is an essential part of the website infrastructure. A professional community should be restricted by rules such as initial registration for the ID and password. Access is just for the community member themselves; Ontocop is accessible by these criteria.

By inviting people after activation of their account. Pseudonyms are not permitted.

Obviously in a physical space members communicate face to face yet in the virtual community members can do it through technology using e

Figure 4. Ontocop forum

conferencing and chat. Figure 5 shows a Chatting page, which provides communication between members online to debate specific topics.

Figure 6 shows the Event management calendar which is the record of the community's activities. The Community needs software to record concepts to generate ideas for ongoing discussions. These general concepts help to suggest topics and future activity. As a calendar of events or activity it can be in electronic format to update frequently and also, as a record of the past events.

Figure 7 List of members of Ontocop: a community needs to identify their members. Members are identified by a list to clarify who are actually members of the community. Verifiable members in ontocop have profiles kept as a record in the database. A member profile helps to create a social network by linking members with the same interest.

Figure 8 shows the Ontology page, which allows members to follow the developments in building the ontology.

Figure 9 shows the feed back page, which helps to improve the ontocop for users.

Figure 10 illustrates Link of Questions and Answers FQA to give clarification about ambiguous points in the community.

Figure 11 illustrates Link to contact us, which contains a form to email the subject of issues to clarify or to contact the moderator. It Links to members of Ontocop: Trust is vital in the online community as well as in a virtual community of practice.

4.2. Ontology Life Cycle Model of IS

4.2.1. Specification

Building ontology followed many steps as mentioned above. We now attempt to describe each phase by representing the visual construction.

Analyzing the purposes and goals of building ontology from the beginning is very important to help in the development process and to avoid any inconsistency between classes of the ontology. Also, it is vital to identify why this ontology is being build and for what purpose.

Figure 5. Ontocop chatting page

Figure 6. Ontocop chatting page

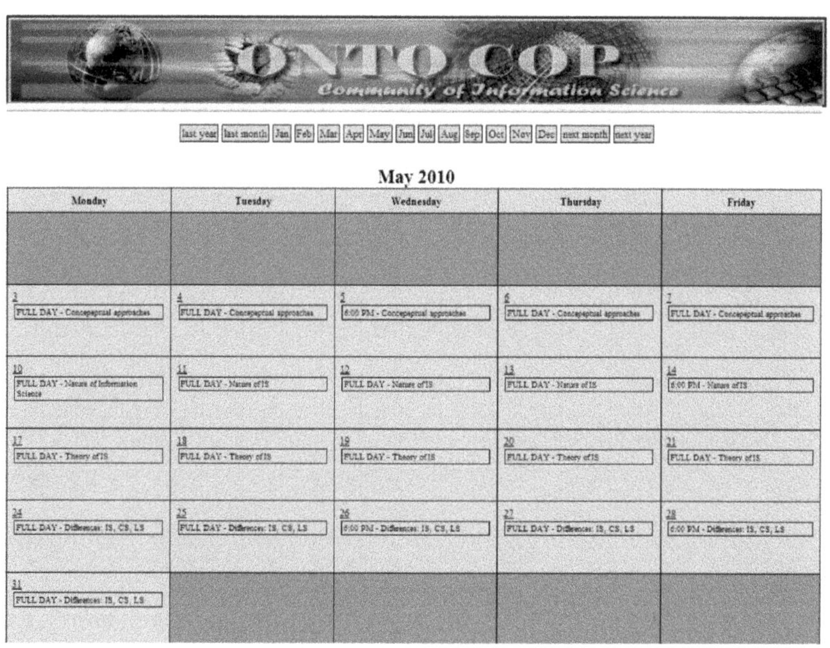

Figure 7. Ontocop members list

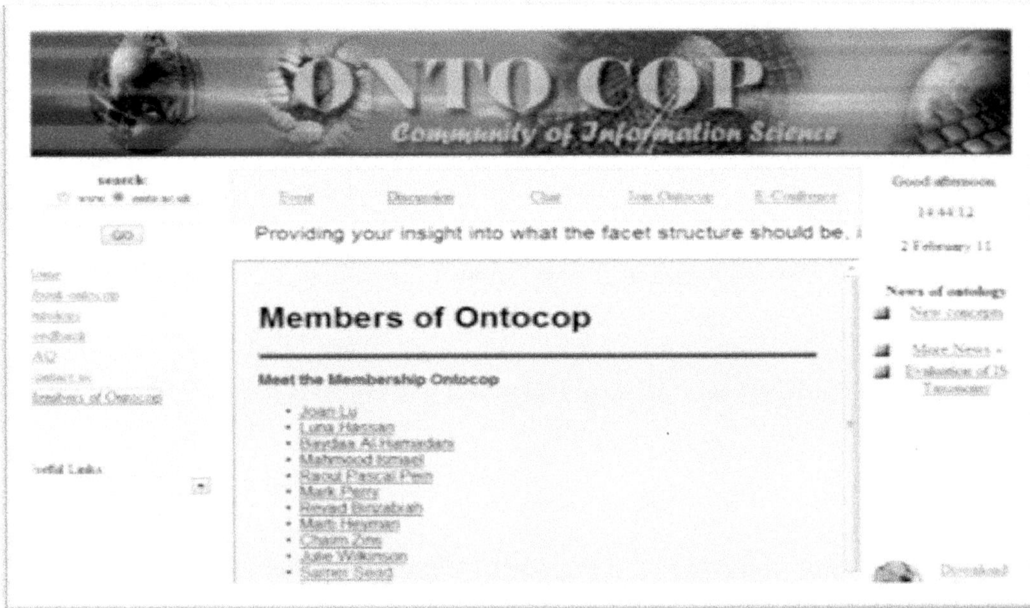

Figure 8. Ontology page

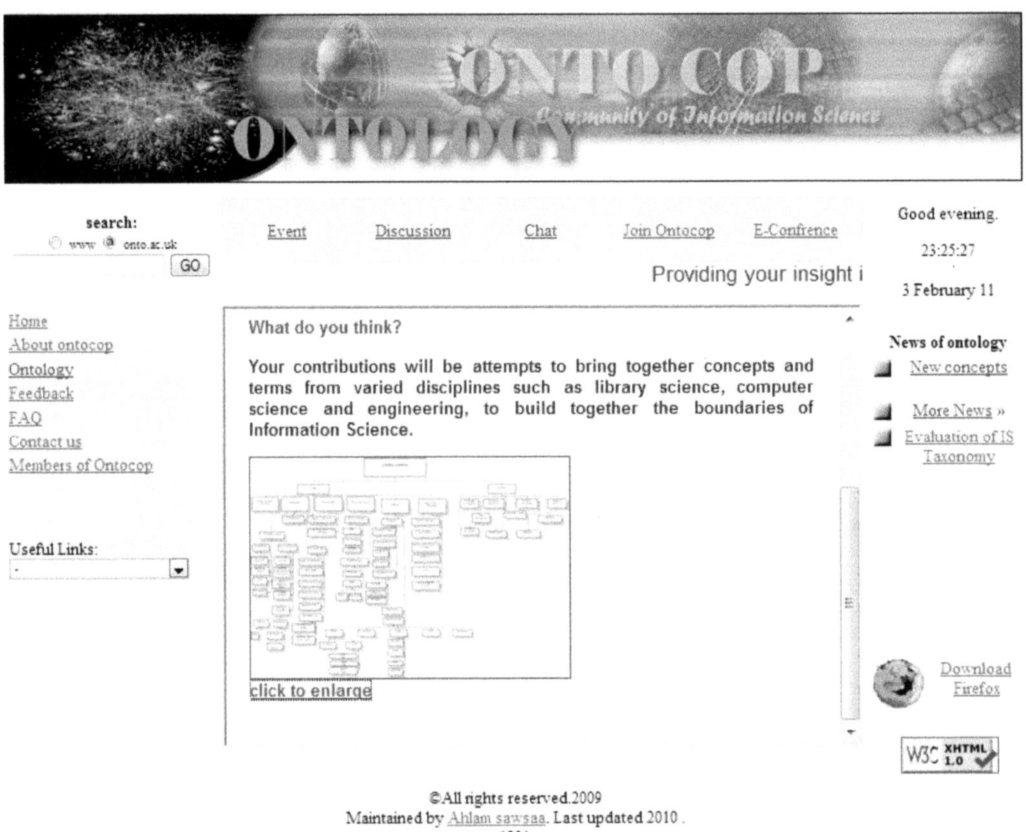

Figure 9. Feedback page

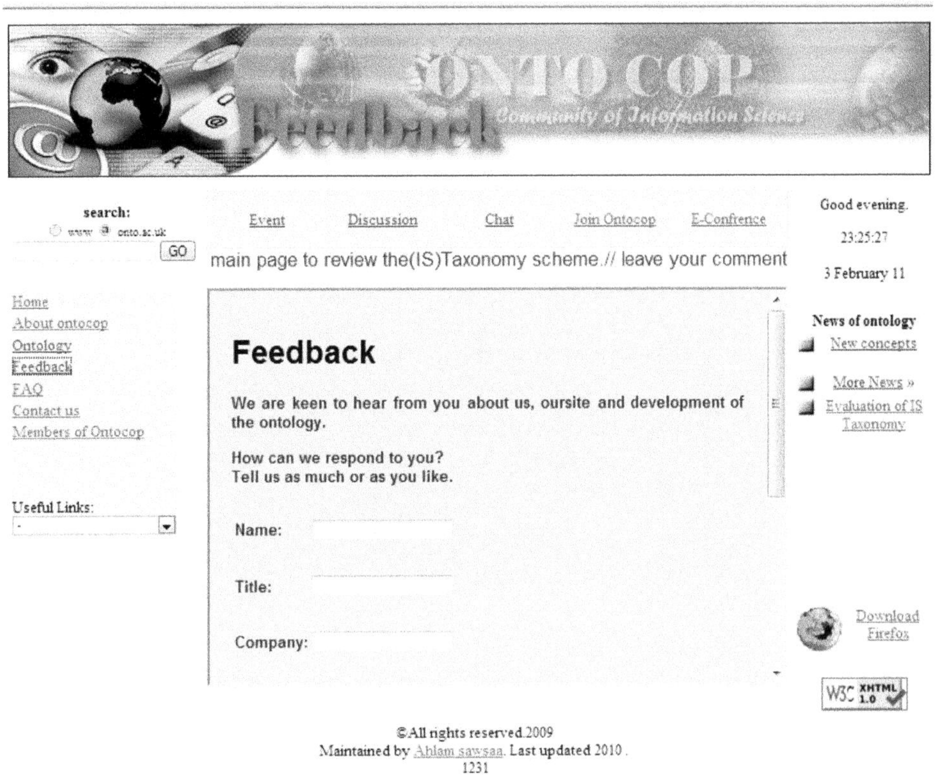

Figure 10. FQA page

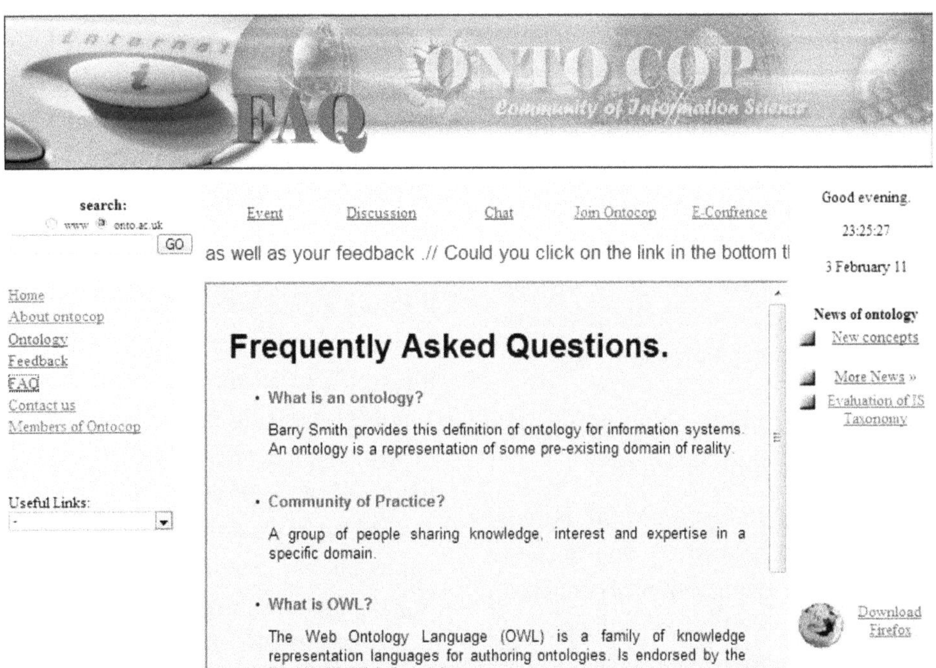

Figure 11. Contact page

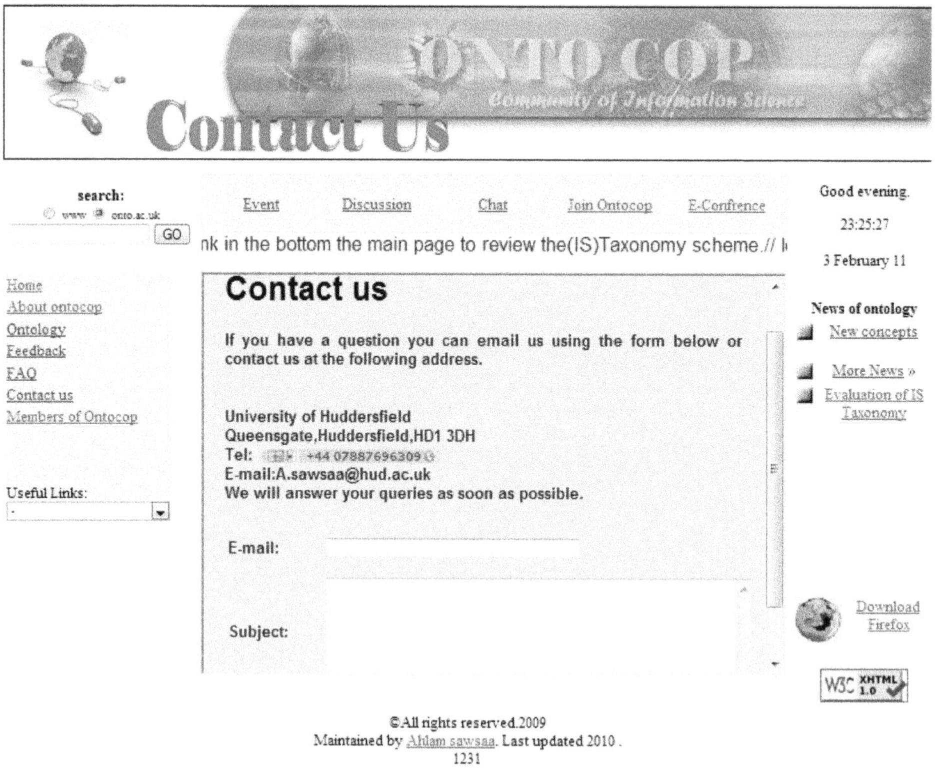

4.2.2. Conceptualization

4.2.2.1. Building the Glossary of IS:

The initial stage in building a conceptual model of ontology is creating a glossary of terms, which includes many terms that refer to the same concepts. The glossary contains main terms and all the related terms in the domain, synonym, acronyms and a simple description for each term that is included in the ontology. Also to build relations between them to avoid any ambiguity (Table 4).

4.2.2.2. Taxonomy of Classes and Hierarchy Building Of Concepts and Relations

The method s of creating a taxonomy are based on both Top- down and bottom- up approaches (Turk, 2006), to allow the identification of concepts to control the level of detail (class –subclass – partition-of). Top- down approach emphasises the planning and complete understanding of domain modelling which starts with modelling concepts and relationships in every generic level of knowledge, and specialized into specific concepts. The IBM researcher Harlan Mills and Nicklaus Wirth initially promoted this approach. The main feature of top—down strategy is to control the level of details.

To cover domain hierarchy building ontology information science followed methods of Top down to classify the concepts and instances. The method top down provides relations between concepts by using the information dictionary to express the meaning of each.(Fox, 1992; Gruninger & Fox, 1995) (Figure 12).

The main reason for adopting the bottom- up approach has been increased popularity since object oriented programming emerged in 1980. Also, the domain of Information Science is new so no ontology already exists. The bottom up ap-

Table 4. Glossary of terms and concepts of IS

Concept Name	Synonyms	Acronyms	Description	Type (class, instance)
Abstract	theoretical	-	Summarises contents of document, and it is usually accompanied by description and bibliography to give access to the original document[1]	class
Artificial Intelligent	Thinking machines	AI	An area of computer science focusing on mimic human ability. This device and applications is used to make decisions.	class
abstracting & indexing	-	-	Service provides bibliographic citation and abstracts of the literature in a specific subject.	class
abstracting			Process of extracting key information from the document. This process is complementary to the indexing	class
abstracting journal	abstracts of articles	-	A journal that specializes in providing summaries	class
abstracting service	-	-	A commercial indexing service that provides both a citation and a brief summary or abstract of the content of each document indexed	class

proach is more appropriate. The implementation of this approach is generalising individuals and instances to general concepts, as illustrated in Figure 13. The strategy is identifying the specific concepts to be generalized into abstract concepts, to compose a whole system.

4.2.2.3. Concepts Dictionary

Ontology identifies relations and instances attributes to each class; they should be well defined in the dictionary to organize all classes and their relations in the domain. The dictionary includes domain concepts and their meaning, and class attributes and instances. Table 5 shows the concepts dictionary of information science. This table provide concepts name, while class attributes present information that describes the classe itself and its value.

4.2.2.4. Building Binary Relation

Binary relations between concepts contained is in the concept dictionary as shown in the simple diagram of the binary relations in the IS ontology. If an information class has a fact as subclass the relation is named Has-A, the inverse relations will be Is- an elementOf. See Figure 14 the binary relations will sort it in a table to help identify the correct binary relations.

4.2.2.5. Formalization

This means to put the code of explicit conceptualization of the domain concepts captured in previous stages in to some formal language based on the conceptual model. The output of this system is IS Ontology. Implementation of IS ontology is encoded by using Protégé. The following classes were created; Actors, Method, practice, Studies, Mediate, Kinds, Domains, Resources, Legislation, Philosophy & theories, Societal, Time, space to create the asserted model of IS Ontology, as shown in Figures 15a and 15b. The attributes are created in properties tap and data tap. The relations are created in object properties tab.

4.2.2.6. Ontology Valuation

Valuation means that consideration guarantees the stability and accuracy of the ontology. Valuation of the ontology avoids concepts duplication,

Figure 12. Top down approach

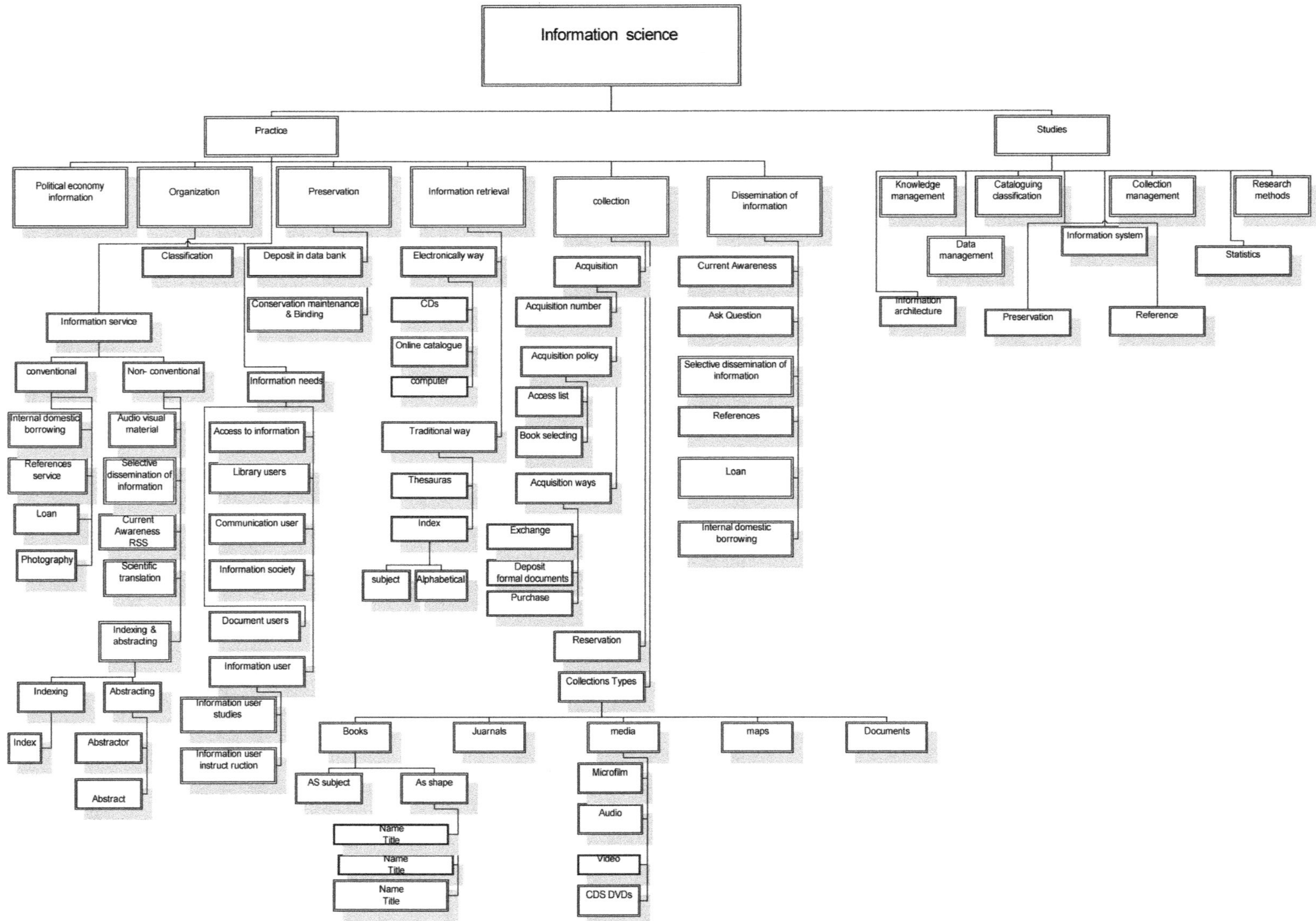

Figure 13. Bottom-up approach

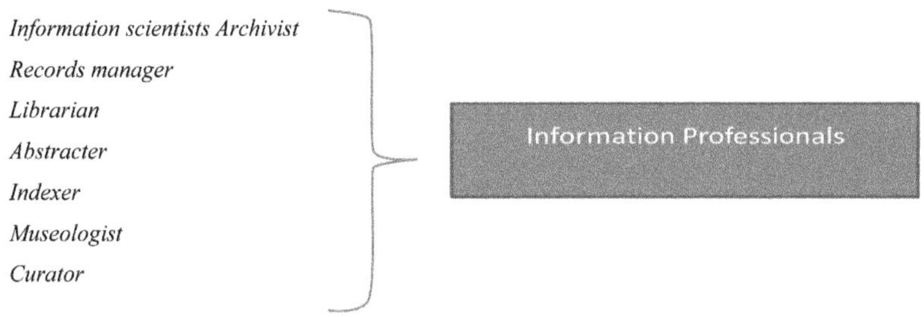

Figure 14. The binary relations

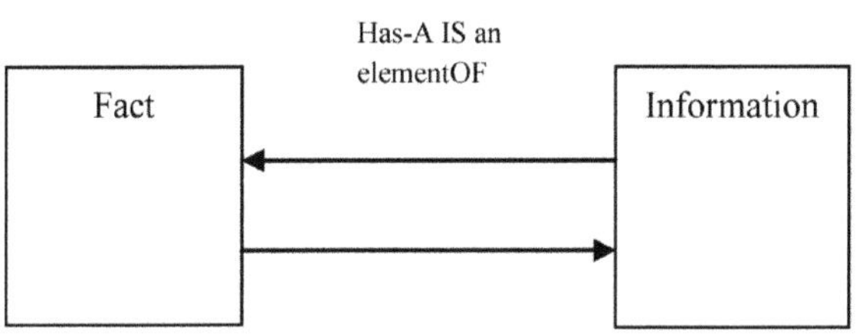

excessiveness and inconsistent relationships to make understanding simpler. Furthermore, Completeness ensures the ontology includes all concepts, relationships, and axioms relevant to the domain. Also, consistency to ensure it includes contradictory information.

Ontology needs to evaluate based on metrics of ontology quality. The metrics of ontology quality is based on a semiotic framework (Barrona et al., 1999), which is divided into these branches: Semantic quality, Syntactic quality, Pragmatic quality and Social quality.

- **Semantic Quality:** To know how the ontology is reflected its through universe of discussion. To ensure there is no confounding and contradictory concepts. Also, en-

Figure 15. Fragment of ISO classes(top); Fragment of IS ontology (bottom)

```
<?xml version="1.0"?>
<rdf:RDF
xmlns:rdf="http://www.information science.owl#"
xmlns:xsd="http://www.w3.org/2001/XMLSchema#"
xmlns:rdfs="http://www.w3.org/2000/01/rdf-schema#"
    xmlns:owl="http://www.w3.org/2002/07/owl#"
      xmlns="http://www.owl-ontologies.com/unnamed.owl#"
    xml:base="http://www.owl-ontologies.com/unnamed.owl">
<owl:Ontology rdf:about="Information science"/>
<owl:Class rdf:ID="Information science"/>
<owl:Class rdf:ID="Library science">
<rdfs:subClassOf>
   <owl:Class rdf:ID="library science studies"/>
</rdfs:subClassOf>
</owl:Class>
 <owl:Class rdf:ID="practical">
  <rdfs:subClassOf rdf: collection="/Book#"/>
 </owl:Class>
<owl:Restriction>
<owl : onProperty rdf:collection="/# title/>"/
<rdfs:subClassOf>
   <owl:Class rdf:ID="Author"/>
  </owl: Restriction> </owl:Class>


<!-- Created with Protégé - http://Protégé.stanford.edu-->
```

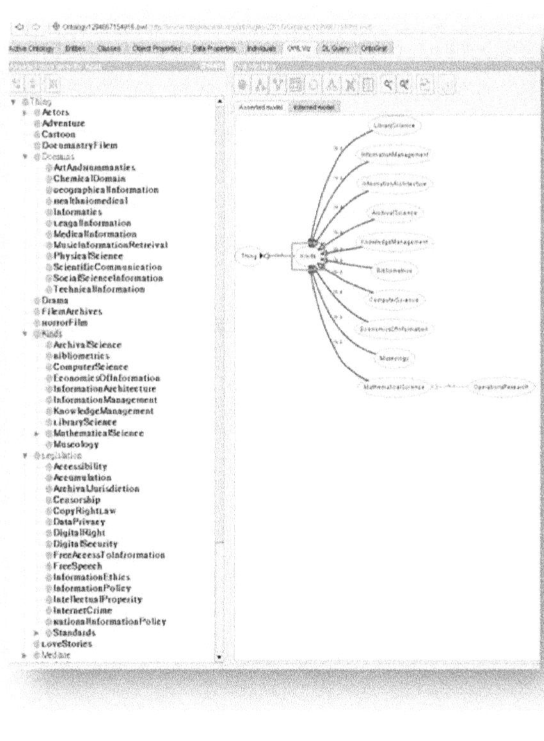

Table 5. Concepts dictionary of IS

Concept Name	Class attribute	Instance attribute	Relations
Public Library	Library type	Name, size, service	Is part of, has relation with
Anglo-American Cataloguing Rules	Roles name	standards	Is kind of
Digital Video Disc	-	size	Has A, Is A
digital library	Library type	Name, URL	Is part of, subclassOf

suring consistency of the terms with their meaning and clarity.

- **Syntactic Quality:** Checking how ontology is written to ensure ontology syntax does not contain any errors. Thus, ensure of richness and complexity of syntactic aspects of the ontology, not just correctness.
- **Pragmatic Quality:** To ensure the accuracy of information and relevance these information for the task. It also, guarantees a comprehensiveness of the ontology classes and properties and ensuring how it is easy to understand for end-users.
- **Social Quality:** Is related to the history of the ontology that measures how long and how much the ontology has been used.

Gomez-Perez and others (Gòmez-Pérez et al., 2004), provided two approaches to evaluate ontologies as follows:

- **Terminology Evaluation:** Can be done from a technical or expert's opinion of the ontology, to ensure terms are defined well and follow a particular method during the development process.
- **Taxonomy Evaluation:** Taxonomy is the backbone of the ontology and the main components. Taxonomy evaluation ensures that ontology is classified consistently and completely, If not the ontology will have many errors. If we say that *computer scientist* is a subclass of *Information professional*, and *Information professional* is a subclass of *computer scientist.* And if we say *public library* and *School library* have emerged from the partition of class (library). And the ontology indicated to the *public service* as common for both. It is called circularity.

6. ANALYSIS AND DISSECTION

To date, the members at Ontocop have already collaborated for some time. Thirty (30) participants responded and they have actively participated.

Figure 16. Errors in ontologies

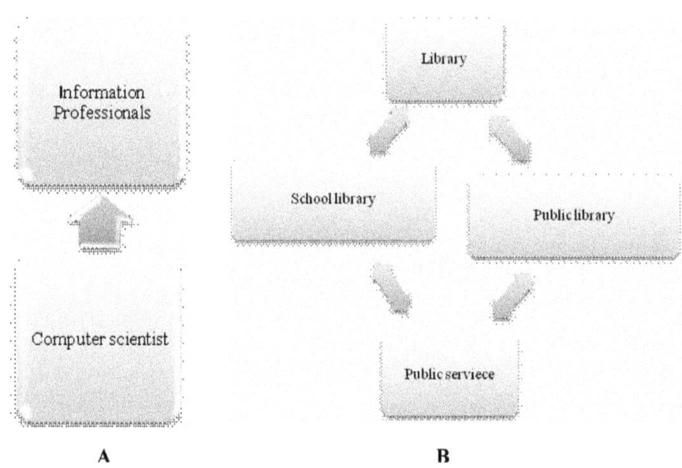

1. The core group review events and topics to be discussed from the calendar.
2. Some critical points have emerged to measure the success of Ontocop at this stage. As widely known, creating a social network is a big challenge:
   a. **Trust:** Members need to know each other. Interview potential members of Ontocop by arranged virtual meeting using chat tools, to introduce themselves and to get to know existing members. Furthermore, creating a members profile page to display their information.
   b. **Education:** To provide some information about the website to educate people, since people do not know how to contribute they will not get involved. Creating a section in Home page covering simple guidelines for these criteria e.g., "Getting Started" to explain how to register.
   c. **Guide & Template:** There is an assumption that people panic when they view an empty page. Prepared examples in the forum help members participate effectively by writing down some definitions and argument issues, following the templates.
   d. **Refreshing:** Encourage the community to keep the content up to date and interesting for everybody.
   e. **Easy Access:** Ontocop is not commercial website, but it could be accessed using search engines.
   f. **Authentic and Personal:** Present the developer of ontocop in "About" to let people know the person behind Ontocop.

The great challenge in this community is to know how it will develop over time. I will outline a potential future and some intention of Ontocop:

- **Potential:** As a beginning it is essential to find out who will participate in the community and be a member of it, to share common background and experience. This helps to make it less challenging.

The initiative stage started with inviting people to be a core group in Ontocop, which began as follows:

1. Collecting information about people who work in the Information science (IS) field into the database to make sure that the potential numbers of members of Ontocop are likely to join the project, and preparing the database to be ready at the time of invitation. The total number of people is (1633) from (58) universities around the world.
2. Collected data is requested: first name, last name, full address, email address, picture and their WebPages and interests; thereafter, sending an invitation letter including URL of website. This stage helps to determine whether or not they are willing to share in the community, by sending an email to prepare them before starting.

The core group is professionals involved in Library & Information studies- computer science departments at universities around the world, in different geographical locations. As illustrated in Figure 17.

On the other hand, it is important to ensure members feel that they are participating at a voluntary level and that their participation will keep them up-to-date in their field.

Community members share a common interest in the subject area. They discuss and provide feedback on ongoing process such as evaluating the preliminary conceptual model of the ISO by display graphs on the website. The feedback improves innovation and productivity (Figure 18).

To take Ontocop a step forward, I have outlined some stages that have been taken place:

Figure 17. Illustrates percentage of participants& countries

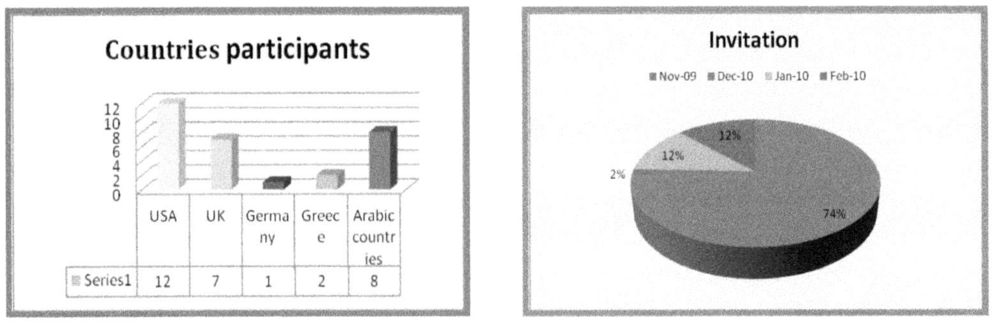

Figure 18. Display the preliminary conceptual model of the ISO on ontocop

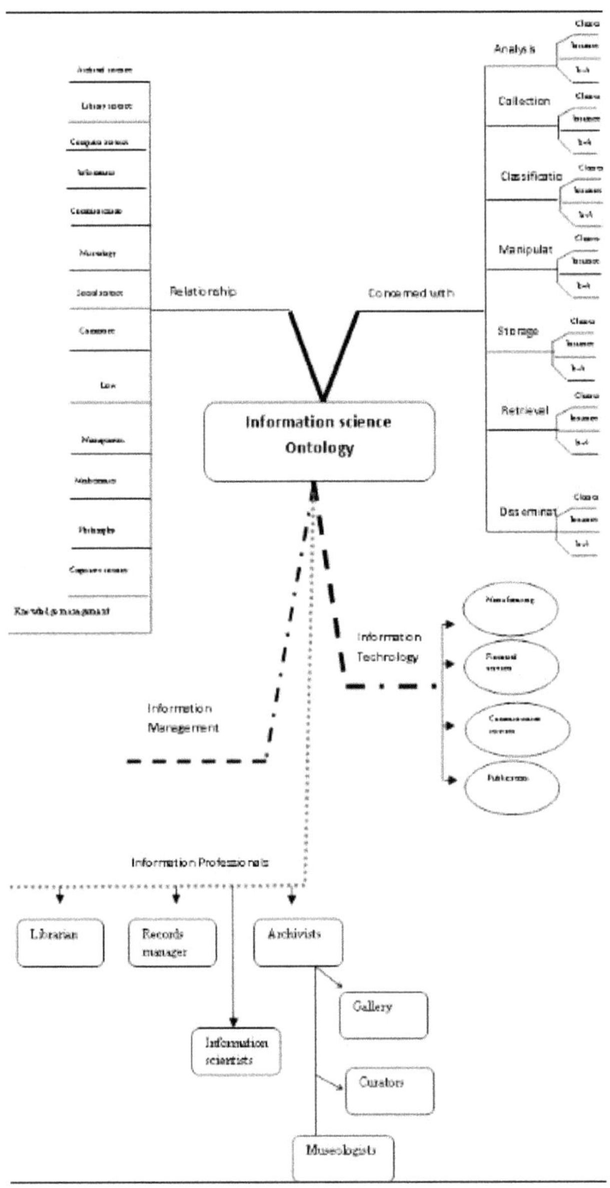

1. Launch the Ontocop with a kick-off.
2. (1633) emails sentin November and December, 2009 respectively. (15) People responded offering their support. While, (112) emails failed through a mistake in the mailing address. By January and February 2010 the number had increased to (30) active participants. Overall, the most emails sent were in November 2009 about (74%) while in January and February 2010 approximately (12%).

The result of participations on the community is derived from the website analysis tool Piwiki. Piwiki provides details on the Ontocop website for visitors. Using this tool helps to assess how and when users have been visiting the website. Visitors started visiting the community and participating in January 2010, and the number increased in Feb., Mar, and April respectively as illustrated in Figure 19.

7. CONCLUSION AND FUTURE WORK

To conclude, a virtual community of practice is potentially the ultimate learning atmosphere within collaborative cultures. This paper presents a small part of the theory that is behind VCops to make clear the positive effects which are included in the ISO. Thereafter, however it discusses a variety of aspects for transferring the concept of community of practice from the physical to the virtual. Therefore, this paper presents the Ontocop Information Science community as a system and tool to visualise the domain knowledge of IS, and demonstrate how it will be a basis for the future of VCops, for Information specialists to develop their professional knowledge.

- Ontology of information science helps to identify the features of this science which mainly consists of an overlapping set of sciences which made it difficult to determine its boundaries, such as Library science, Computer science and archival science.

For furthers research the ISO ontology needs to integrate with other ontologies to provide a basic knowledge for a semantic web to leverage information retrieval, for instance Social science, Cognitive science, philosophy, law management and mathematics. Any science has the same basic concepts generated in ISO which is Actors, Method, practice, Studies, Mediate, Kinds, Domains, Resources, Legislation, Philosophy & theories, Societal, Time, space. These general concepts could be linked with other sciences to create top level ontologies.

Figure 19. Ontocop visitors website analysis

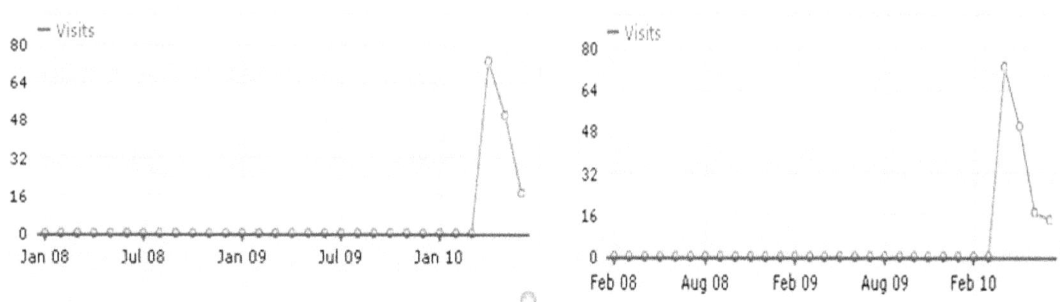

REFERENCES

Araujo, L. (1998). Knowing and learning as networking. *Management Learning*, *29*, 317–336. doi:10.1177/1350507698293004

Ardichvili, A., Page, V., & Wentling, T. (2003). Motivation and barriers to participation in virtual knowledge -sharing communities of practice. *Knowledge Management*, *7*, 64–77. doi:10.1108/13673270310463626

Barrona, T. M., Chiang, R. H. L., & Storey, V. C. (1999). A semiotics framework for information systems classification and development. *Decision Support Systems*, *25*, 1–17. doi:10.1016/S0167-9236(98)00088-8

Barry, S. (1996). Mereotopology: A theory of parts and boundaries. *Data & Knowledge Engineering*, *20*, 287–303. doi:10.1016/S0169-023X(96)00015-8

Catherine, C. M., Shipman, F. M. III, & Raymond, J. M. (2000). Making large-scale information resources serve communities of practice. *Journal of Management Information Systems*, *11*, 65–86.

Cox, A. (2005). What are communities of practice? A comparative review of four seminal works. *Journal of Information Science*, *31*, 527–540. doi:10.1177/0165551505057016

Erat, P., Desouza, K. C., Schäfer-Jugel, A., & Kurzawa, M. (2006). Business customer communities and knowledge sharing: Exploratory study of critical issues. *European Journal of Information Systems*, *15*, 511–524. doi:10.1057/palgrave.ejis.3000643

Fox, M. S. (1992). The Tove project: Towards a common-sense model of the enterprise. In *Proceedings of the 5th International Conference on Industrial and Engineering Applications of Artificial Intelligence and Expert Systems* (pp. 25-34).

Gasevic, D., Devedzic, V., & Djuric, D. (2006). *Model driven architecture and ontology development*. Berlin, Germany: Springer-Verlag.

Gomez, R. (1998). The nostalgia of virtual community: A study of computer- mediated communications use in Colombian non- governmental organisation. *Information Technology & People*, *11*, 217–234. doi:10.1108/09593849810228020

Gòmez-Pérez, A., Fernandez-Lopez, M., & Corcho, O. (2004). *Ontological engineering: With examples from the areas of knowledge management, e-commerce and the semantic web*. New York, NY: Springer.

Gourlay, S. (2001). Knowledge management and Hrd. *Human Resource Development International*, *4*, 27–46. doi:10.1080/13678860121778

Gruber, T. R. (1993). Toward principles for the design of ontologies used for knowledge sharing. In Guarino, N., & Poli, R. (Eds.), *Formal ontology*. Boston, MA: Kluwer Academic.

Guruninger, M., & Fox, M. S. (1995). Methodology for the design and evaluation of ontologies. In *Proceedings of the Workshop on Basic Ontological Issues in Knowledge Sharing*, Montreal, QC, Canada (pp. 6.1-6.10).

Hartmann, N. (1952). *The new ways of ontlogy*. Westport, CT: Greenwood Press.

Herre, H. (2010). The ontology of mereological systems: A logical approach. In Poli, R., & Seibt, J. (Eds.), *Theory and applications of ontology: Philosophical perspectives*. London, UK: Springer. doi:10.1007/978-90-481-8845-1_3

Husserl, E. (1970). *Logical investigations*. London, UK: Routledge and Kegan Paul.

Jansen, W., & Jagers, H. P. M. (2002). Knowledge management and virtual communities. In White, S. (Ed.), *Knowledge mapping and management*. Hershey, PA: Irma Press.

Koch, M. (2000). *Learning from civilization.* Retrieved from http://www.linezine.com/3.1/features/mklic.htm

Lawvere, W. (1969). Adjointness in foundations. *Dialectica, 23*, 281–296. doi:10.1111/j.1746-8361.1969.tb01194.x

Nirenberg, J. (1995). From team building to community building. *National Productivity Review*, 51-62.

Panteli, N., & Duncan, E. (2004). Trust and temporary virtual teams: Alternative explanations dramaturgical relationships. *Information Technology & People, 17*, 423–441. doi:10.1108/09593840410570276

Roberts, J. (2006). Limits to communities of practice. *Journal of Management Studies, 43*, 624–639. doi:10.1111/j.1467-6486.2006.00618.x

Saint-Ongo, H. W. (2003). *Leveraging cops for strategic advantage*. Waltham, MA: Elsevier Science.

Sawsaa, A., & Lu, J. (2009). A generic model of knowledge mapping through virtual communities of practice in information science. In *Proceedings of the International Conference on Internet Computing* (pp. 234-240).

Sawsaa, A., & Lu, J. (2010). Ontocop: A virtual community of practice to create ontology of information science. In *Proceedings of the International Conference on Internet Computing.*

Schlemiel, A., & Teigland, R. (2008). Improved organizational performance through communities of practice. *Journal of Knowledge Management, 12*, 106–118. doi:10.1108/13673270810852421

Smith, B. (2003). *Ontology: An introduction: How to build an ontology.* Retrieved from http://ontology.buffalo.edu/smith/

Staab, S., & Studer, R. (2001). Knowledge processes and ontologies. *Knowledge Management*, 26-34.

Stewart, T. (1997). The invisible key to success. *Fortune*, 173–176.

Tappedin. (2010). *Community of educational domain*. Retrieved from http://tappedin.org/tappedin/

Tatiana Gavrilova, H. J. (2008). One approach to knowledge mapping for international student portal. In *Proceedings of the International Conference on Knowledge-Dialogue-Solution*, Varna, Bulgaria.

Variz, A. (1998). Basic problems of mereotopology. In Guarino, N. (Ed.), *Formal ontology in information systems*. Amsterdam, The Netherlands: IOS Press.

Varzi, A. (1996). Parts, wholes, and part-whole relations: The prospects of mereotopology. *Data & Knowledge Engineering, 20*, 259–286. doi:10.1016/S0169-023X(96)00017-1

Wenger, E. (1998). *Communities of practice: Learning, meaning, identity*. Cambridge, UK: Cambridge University Press.

Wenger, R. M., & Snyder, W. (2002). *Cultivating communities of practice: A guide to managing knowledge*. Boston, MA: Harvard Business School Press.

This work was previously published in the International Journal of Information Retrieval Research, Volume 1, Issue 2, edited by Zhongyu (Joan) Lu, pp. 55-78, copyright 2011 by IGI Publishing (an imprint of IGI Global).

Chapter 10
Improved Parameterless K-Means:
Auto-Generation Centroids and Distance Data Point Clusters

Wan Maseri Binti Wan Mohd
University Malaysia Pahang, Malaysia

Tutut Herawan
University Malaysia Pahang, Malaysia

A.H. Beg
University Malaysia Pahang, Malaysia

A. Noraziah
University Malaysia Pahang, Malaysia

K. F. Rabbi
University Malaysia Pahang, Malaysia

ABSTRACT

K-means is an unsupervised learning and partitioning clustering algorithm. It is popular and widely used for its simplicity and fastness. K-means clustering produce a number of separate flat (non-hierarchical) clusters and suitable for generating globular clusters. The main drawback of the k-means algorithm is that the user must specify the number of clusters in advance. This paper presents an improved version of K-means algorithm with auto-generate an initial number of clusters (k) and a new approach of defining initial Centroid for effective and efficient clustering process. The underlined mechanism has been analyzed and experimented. The experimental results show that the number of iteration is reduced to 50% and the run time is lower and constantly based on maximum distance of data points, regardless of how many data points.

INTRODUCTION

Data clustering is often used in a variety of applications, such as Vector Quantization (VQ) (Lai et al., 2002), pattern recognition (Theodoridis & Koutroumbas, 2003), knowledge discovery (Fayyad et al., 1996), pattern recognition (Liu & Kubala, 2004), debugging and web / data mining. Among the clustering formulations that minimize a cost function, k-means algorithm is possibly the most widely used and studied (Kanungo et al., 2002). It is also known as the Generalized Lloyd Algorithm (GLA) is a special case of a generalized hard clustering scheme, when representatives

DOI: 10.4018/978-1-4666-3898-3.ch010

of section are adopted and squared Euclidean distances are used to measure the distortion (the difference) between a vector X and its representative cluster (cluster center) C (Lai & Huang, 2010).

Existing clustering algorithms can be merely divided into two categories: hierarchical clustering and partional clustering. Classic algorithm K-Means (KM) clustering algorithm is the most popular for its simplicity and efficiency. Although the k-means algorithm is widely used to solve problems in many areas and very sensitive to initialize, the better centers have been chosen, the better results have found. Furthermore, it is easily trapped in local optimal. Recently, various work has been done to overcome these problems (Khan & Ahmad, 2004; Jiang et al., 2010).

Different approaches have been proposed for improving k-means algorithm, which gradually are more successful. These progressive approaches to the cluster are calculated by solving all the problems of intermediate clustering (Bagirov, 2008; Hansen et al., 2005; Likas et al., 2003). The global k-means algorithm has been proposed in Likas et al. (2003) and modified global k-means algorithm has been proposed in Bagirov (2008) and Bagirov and Mardaneh (2006) are gradually clustering algorithms. Bagirov (2008) presented a new version of the global k-means algorithm. The numerical experimental result shown that these algorithms allowed to find a global or near global clusters minimize (or error) function. These algorithms are memory intensive because they require storage of the affinity matrix. Alternatively, this matrix can be calculated each iteration, but would extend the computing time significantly (Bagirov et al., 2011).

K-Means (MacQueen, 1967) is one of the simplest unsupervised learning algorithms to solve the well-known clustering problem. The procedure is simple and easy to classify a data set through a certain number of clusters (assume k clusters) fixed a priority. The main objective is to define k centroids, one for each cluster. These centroids should be placed strategically because different location causes different results. So the best option is to place them as much as possible from each other. The next step is to take each data point and assign it to the nearest center centroid. When all points are assigned, the first step has been completed. At this point have to re-calculate k new centroids of the clusters resulting from the previous step. After that it has these k new centroids, a new binding has to done between the same set of data sets and the newest centroid. The process has been repeated. As a result of this loop, it notes that k Centroid change their location step by step until centroid does not move. Finally, this algorithm is to minimize an objective function, in this case, a-squared error function. The objective function, J is defined as in formula (1).

$$J = \sum_{j-1}^{k}\sum_{i-1}^{n} || x_i^{(j)} - c_j ||^2 \qquad (1)$$

The algorithm is composed of the following steps:

1. Place *K* points into the space represented by the objects that are being clustered. These points represent initial group centroids.
2. Assign each object to the group that has the closest centroid.
3. When all objects have been assigned, recalculate the positions of the *K* centroids.
4. Repeat Steps 2 and 3 until the centroids no longer move. This produces a separation of the objects into groups from which the metric to be minimized can be calculated.

The Pseudo-code of the Lloyd's K-Means algorithm has shown in Algorithm 1 (Dunham, 2003).

K-Means is a simple algorithm that has adapted to areas with many problems. Similar to other algorithm, K-Means clustering has several limitations (Ming et al., 2011; Pelleg & Moore, 2000; Xu & Wunsch, 2005; Jain & Dubes, 1988; Jain et al., 1999).

Algorithm 1. Lloyd's K-Means algorithm

```
Input:
  D= {t1, t2,.... Tn } // Set of elements
  K // Number of desired clusters
Output:
  K // Set of clusters
K-Means algorithm:
  Assign initial values for m1, m2,.... mk
  repeat
    assign each item ti to the clusters which has the closest
mean;
    calculate new mean for each cluster;
  until convergence criteria is met;
```

1. **Scalability:** It scales poorly computational.
2. **Initial Means:** The clustering result is extremely sensitive to initial condition. Different initial condition may produce different result of cluster.
3. **Number of Clusters:** The number of clusters, k must be determined before the k-means clustering begins. If the numbers are not so many, the initial group will determine the cluster significantly.
4. **Local Minima:** The algorithm converges to local minima.
5. It is never known the real cluster, using the same data, if inputted in a different order can produce different cluster if the number of data are few.
6. It is also never known which attribute contributes more to the grouping process since we assume that each attribute has the same weight.
7. It is not realistic with respect to outliers. Very far data from the centroid can pull the centroid away from the real one.

In our previous work (Mohd et al., 2007), has been proposed new parameterless k-means algorithm and were implemented. In this paper has been improved the parameterless k-means algorithm. The Lloyd's algorithm (Jones & Beltramo, 1991) has been used to compare with the new algorithm introduced in this paper. Lloyd algorithm is based on the optimal placement center, which is at the centroid of the cluster (Krishna & Murty, 1999; Babu & Murty, 1993). Since the P set of n data points in real-time d-dimensional space, _d, and an integer k, the problem is to determine the number of K points in _d, called *centers*, so as to minimize the average distance to Euclidean squared between each data point to its nearest center. This measure is frequently called the *squared-error distortion* (Jones & Beltramo, 1991). The objective is to minimize the sum of the distances to the nearest center and the Euclidean k- *center* problem, where the goal is to minimize the maximum distance.

RELATED WORK

K-means algorithm is very sensitive to the choice of initial centers and a poor choice of centers may lead to a local optimum that is far below the global optimum (Babu & Murty, 1993; Bradley & Fayyad 1998; Selim & Ismail, 1984). The Genetic Algorithm (GA) has been designed to find good sets of centers that lead to higher partitions on k-means (Laszlo & Mukherjee, 2007).

Some GA-based approaches have been developed to increase the probability of finding globally optimal partitions. It notes that the first cluster of the GA-based methods (Bhuyan et al., 1991; Jones & Beltramo, 1991) are impractical, because of the prohibitive cost of computing functions and conditions of chromosome repair. Krishna and Murty (1999) suggested that GA uses k-means rather than to identify local optima crossover and mutation prevented operator to expand the search beyond local optima. Babu and Murty (1993) presented a center-based GA for the selection of the k-means. Their method used a string of bits representing a number of centers and employs the traditional crossover operation, in which both parents for the exchange of random subsets of centers (Bandyopadhyay & Maulik, 2001a, 2001b; Maulik & Bandyopadhyay, 2000) coordinates of the centers of floating-point vectors, which represent the candidate vectors, elements of the springs and replace randomly selected strings during crossover.

Since past 30 years, many researchers have focused to improve the KM. Some focus on creating better presentation skills, while others try to find the optimal values of K and others to find the optimal solutions globally. Gungo and Alper (2008) proposed a K-harmonic means clustering algorithm with tabu search method, which is known as TabuKHM. The algorithm was implemented and tested in some well-known data sets. They presented experiments with the algorithm (TabuKHM) outperforms KM, FKM and KHM from the point of view, in most cases. On the other hand, KHM softened the harsh nature of the algorithm of KM, such as FKM.

In order to improve the performance of k-means algorithm various methods has been proposed (Kanungo et al., 2002; Likas et al., 2003; Charalampidis, 2005). In one method it can be find that the k-means algorithm is one of the most widely used algorithms. However, it is known that the K-means algorithm is sensitive to the initial cluster centers and easy to get stuck in local optimal solutions (Selim & Ismail, 1984). In addition, when the number of data points is large, it takes an enormous amount of time to find an optimal global solution (Späth, 1989). Chang et al. (2009) combines the K-means algorithm for Genetic Algorithms (GA) to obtain better performance.

Partitioned clustering involves the sharing of data in a series of different groups, called clusters. Redmond and Heneghan (2007) described a method for initializing the K-means clustering algorithm using kd-trees. In their research, they referred N data points extends to the m-dimensional space and entered the k when the number of clusters in the data is partitioned. Partitioned clustering tries to partition data points into clusters so that the similarity of points in each cluster is at a maximum of about a global measure. So, if the points in each cluster are similar at most K, then change the point to another cluster. Only serves to reduce the selected global measure.

Likas et al. (2003) presented comprehensive K-means algorithm which can gradually increase the number of seeds until K are found. They compare their method with multiple tracks of K-means algorithms. They use a variation of the kd-tree to initialize each run of this method of comparison. They only use the kd-k tree to create K buckets and used the centroid of each bucket as seeds. The change in the kd-tree they used was to divide each bucket along the direction of maximum variance, as defined in the principal component analysis.

Ming et al. (2011) presented an efficient algorithm, known as Pattern Reduction (PR), for reducing the computation time of k-means and k-means-based clustering algorithms. Their algorithm worked by compressing and removing the iteration of the patterns will change its composition in the future. It can also be applied to many other iterative algorithms such as the kernel-based and population-based clustering. The experiments from 2 to 1000 dimensions and 150-10000000 patterns indicate that, with little loss of quality. The algorithm significantly reduced the computation time of the entire state of-the-art clustering algorithms evaluated, particularly for large and high-dimensional data sets.

Kalyani and Swarup (2011) presented a modified K-means algorithm (PSOKM) using particle swarm optimization technique for the evaluation of static security, transient. Training set of vectors generated from offline simulations are presented as input to the PSO algorithm based K-means classification using supervised active learning to adjust its weight vectors (cluster centers). The algorithm was implemented in IEEE 30 bus, 57 bus, 118 bus and 300 bus standards of test cases and its performance was compared with other K-means algorithm. Their results show that the high-accuracy classifiers with lower rate of misclassification can be exchanged with the classification PSOKM.

Bradley and Fayyad (1998) presented the refinement algorithm to define initial parameter of K-means by initially selects J of small random sub-samples of data, $Si, i = 1, \ldots, J$. The subsamples are clustered via k-means with assumed that the termination of the empty cluster will have their initial centers re-assigned and sub-sample will be re-clustered. Set the $CMi, i = 1, \ldots, J$ are these clustering solutions over the sub-samples that form the set CM. CM is then clustered via K-Means initialized with CMi produced a solution FMi. The refined initial point is then chosen as the FMi having minimal distortion over the set CM.

This paper has presented another refinement of defining the initial parameter of K-Means through the auto generation of the number of clusters using the maximum distance of data points and a novel approach of defining initial centroid for effective and efficient clustering process. This algorithm can help the user in estimating the number of clusters which is highly dependent on the domain knowledge that is not so desirable.

Definitions and Notations

The following terms and notations have been used:

1. A pattern (*or feature vector, observation or datum*) x is a single data item used by the clustering algorithm. It generally consists of a vector of *d* measurements:

$x = (x_1, \ldots, x_d)$

2. The individual scalar components x_i of a pattern x are called (*features or attributes*).
3. *d* is the dimensionality of the pattern or of the pattern space.
4. A pattern set is denoted $X = (x_1, \ldots, x_n)$. The *i*th pattern in X is denoted $x_i = (x_{i1}, \ldots, x_{id})$.

Improved Parameterless K-Means Algorithm: MaxD K-Means

This section presents the improved k-means algorithm MaxD, auto-generation of the initial number of cluster and effective centroids. MaxD K-means consists of two parts, one of the pre-processing parameters and another is Lloyd's k-means algorithm. The pre-processing parameters consist of two parts, which are auto-generation of the original number of clusters and determining the centroids of the clusters.

In the pre-processing algorithm, centroids are defined from the centers of two points starting from the maximum and minimum value of the data points. The rational of generating centroids from maximum and minimum data points and subsequently sort them is that the probability of binding all items in the dataset to the nearest centroid is high since the generated centroids is near to all respective items. The algorithm starts with setting maximum and minimum values of data points as centroids, then the center of this two values is set as a new centroid. Then, from the generated centroids, new centroids are further generated by reassigning the new maximum and minimum from the new centroids. The process of generating centroids will end when the maximum number of iteration is reached. The maximum iteration is defined as follows:

$$c\_iteration = 2^{\sqrt{(((X_{Max} - X_{Min})/2) + X_{Min})}+1} \quad (2)$$

where, $x = (x_{i,} \ldots x_d)$ be a point in $R^{d.}$ and x_i is the individual item in x.

Afterword the centroids are sorted in ascending order before the Lloyd's K-means algorithm starts. The rational of sorting the centroids is to converge the items into sorted order and thus the processing time in the next iteration is reduced. Finally, the initial number of clusters (k) is defined as the total number of centroids generated by the above process. By setting the initial number of clusters based on the total number of centroids, allows the binding process to be faster since the seeking of the nearest centroid of each element is very fast.

The preprocessing algorithm is shown in Algorithm 2.

Definition 1: (Centroids of Clusters): The centroids of the clusters are defined as the maximum, minimum and mean of the partitioning points starting from the maximum and minimum values of data points until to reach the maximum iteration which is defined in algorithm (2).

Rational 1: The rational of having the maximum number of centroids and sorted in ascending order is to ensure that the number of itera-

Algorithm 2. Preprocessing algorithm

Input: **x** = (*x*1, . . . *xd*) // Set of elements (data points)

Output: Set of Clusters

Let C_i represent new centroids where $C = (C_1, \dots C_n)$ be the list of centroids and C_i is the individual item in C

1. Get the first minimum and maximum value of data point, as the first 2 centroids.
   $XMax = \text{Max}(C_1, \dots Cn)$
   $XMin = \text{Min}(C_1, \dots Cn)$
2. Calculate the new centroids from the min and max
$C3 = ((X_{Max} - X_{Min})/2) + X_{Min}$
$C4 = ((C3 - X_{Min})/2) + X_{Min}$
$C5 = ((X_{Max} - C_3)/2) + C_3;$
5. Repeat for c_iteration
   $(X_{Max} - NC_3)/2) + NC_{3;}$
3. Insert the first 5 centroids into the centroids table
4. Calculate maximum number of iteration for the next centroids Generation.
   c_iteration = $2\sqrt{(((X_{Max} - X_{Min}/2) + X_{Min})+1}$
For j = 1 to c_iteration
6. Read existing centroids from centroids table
7. Set first record as the new Minimum (X_{Min}) and second record as a new Maximum (X_{Max})

8. ***Repeat until end of record***
9. Calculate the new centroids for all existing centroids in the centroid table

$C3 = ((X_{Max} - X_{Min})/2) + X_{Min}$
$C4 = ((C_3 - X_{Min})/2) + X_{Min}$
$C5 = ((X_{Max} - C_3)/2) + C_{3;}$
10. Save new centroids into temporary table
11. Set the current maximum as the new Minimum
   $X_{Min} = X_{Max}$
12. ***Next Record***

13. Transfer new centroids from temporary table into centroid table and flush the temporary table
14. *Next j*
15. Get the initial numbers of clusters (k)
K=count(total records in centroids table)
16. Get initial values for centroids from centroid table and sorted in ascending order
   $(C_1, C_2, \dots C_k)$= ***Read all records from centroids table where k is the number of centroids***
17. **K-Means Algorithm:**
   repeat
      assign each item Xi to the cluster which has the closest mean;
      calculate new mean for each cluster;
   until convergence criteria is met
18. Remove the clusters with zero items
19. Display the final clusters

tions needed to get the best clusters for all data points is faster compared to the Llyod's algorithm where the centroids are defined as random selection of the data points with no special sorting order.

Definition 2: (Number of Initial Clusters): The number of initial clusters is defined as the total number of centroids generated from definition 1.

Rational 2: Since there is no initial setting of number of clusters, the algorithm seeking the maximum possible clusters for the data points. The rational of partitioning the value of data points into the maximum partitions is to ensure that the probability of all data points to be assigned to the most appropriate cluster is high. However, at the end of the processing, there will be empty clusters which shall be removed. Through this algorithm ensures that all data points fall into their most appropriate clusters, compared to the existing algorithm where the data points are forced to be assigned to the nearest cluster which is not always the most appropriate cluster for the item

EXPERIMENT AND RESULT

In order to study the effectiveness of the proposed approach for setting the parameters of K-Means algorithm, the first phase experiment is conducted using synthetic data which is taken from the Llyod's K-Means experiments (Dunham, 2003).

- **Experimental Data:** To show the significant improvement of the new algorithm, the experiment was divided into several cycles. The first cycle of this experiment, compared the result of using the new approach of defining centroids, while maintaining the same approach of setting the number of desired clusters. The comparison is shown in Table 5 and Table 6.

Cycle 1

Llyod's K-Means Algorithm

- Input – k - number of desired clusters.
- Initial values for centroids - $c_1, c_2, \ldots c_k$.
- Given the following items to cluster:
- {3, 5, 11, 13, 4, 21, 31, 12, 26}
- Suppose, $k = 2$ *and* $c_1 = 2$, $c_2 = 4$

The Llyod's K-Means algorithm has been used to obtain the results in Table 1.

MaxD K-Means Algorithm

- Input – k - number of desired clusters.
- Initial values for centroids- $c_1, c_2, \ldots c_k$ using new approach of defining centroids as in Algorithm 1.
- Given the following items to cluster:
- {3, 5, 11, 13, 4, 21, 31, 12, 26}
- And suppose k = 2 and $c_1 = 2$, $c_2 = 30$ (using new approach of defining centroids)

Using the new K-Means algorithm, we obtain the results in Table 2.

- **Observations:** The result in Table 1 and Table 2 shows that the use of new approach

Table 1. Result of Llyod's K-means algorithm

Iteration	Clusters (k)	Cluster's Members
1	1	{3,4}
	2	{5,11,13,21,31,12,26}
2	1	{3,4,5}
	2	{11,13,21,31,12,26}
3	1	{3,4,5,11}
	2	{13,21,31,12,26}
4	1	{3,4,5,11,12,13}
	2	{21,31,26}
5	1	{3,4,5,11,12,13}
	2	{21,31,26}

Total number of Iterations = 5

Table 2. Result of new K-means algorithm (new approach of defining centroids)

Iteration	Clusters (k)	Cluster's Members
1	1	{3,5,11,13,4,12}
	2	{21,26,31}
2	1	{3,5,11,13,4,12}
	2	{21,26,31}

Total number of Iterations = 2

for defining the centroids, the number of iterations is reduced from 5 to 2, which is 60% improvement.

In the second cycle of the experiment, has been generated the number of clusters (k) and defining the centroids by using the new approach. The data set is maintained as in cycle 1.

Cycle 2

- **MaxD K-Means Algorithm:** Given the following items to cluster: {3, 5, 11, 13, 4, 21, 31, 12, 26}

K and m_1, m_2,... m_k are generated from the pre-processing Algorithm 1.

The result of pre-processing algorithm is shown below:

k =17

m_1=3.0, m_2=4.75, m_3=6.5, m_4=8.25, m_5=10.0, m_6=11.75, m_7=13.5, m_8=15.25, m_9=17.0, m_{10}=18.75 m_{11}=20.5, m_{12}=24.0, m_{13}=17.0, m_{14}=25.75 m_{15}=27.5, m_{16}=29.25, m_{17}=31.0

Using the MaxD K-Means algorithm, we obtain the results in Table 3 (after removing empty cluster).

To compare the performance of the new algorithm with the Llyod's K-Means algorithm, has been used the same number of clusters generated from the new algorithm as desired clusters *(k)* and define the centroids using the Llyod's approach.

Table 3. Result of new K-means algorithm (new approach of defining number of clusters and centroids)

Iteration	Clusters (k)	Cluster's Members
1	1	{3}
	2	{4,5}
	6	{11,12}
	7	{13}
	11	{21}
	14	{26}
	17	{31}
2	1	{3}
	2	{4,5}
	6	{11,12}
	11	{13}
	14	{21}
	17	{26,31}
3	1	{3}
	2	{4,5}
	6	{11,12}
	14	{13}
	17	{21,26,31}
4	1	{3}
	2	{4,5}
	6	{11,12}
	14	{13}
	17	{21,22,31}

Llyod's K-Means Algorithm

$k = 5$ (as generated by the new algorithm) and

Centroids: $c_1 = 3$, $c_2 = 5$, $c_3 = 11$, $c_4 = 13$,

$c_5 = 4$ (using the Llyod's approach)

Using the Llyod's K-Means algorithm, we obtain the results in Table 4.

- **Observations:** The results in Table 3 and Table 4 show that by using the new approach of defining the number of clusters and centroids, the number of iterations is reduced from 6 to 4, which is 33% improvement We also found that the appropriateness of the cluster's members is better by using new K-Means algorithm compared to the Llyod's K-Means algorithm. This is shown in Table 4 where the members of cluster 3 and 5 are not so appropriate since 11 is nearer to 10 rather than 12, but it has been assigned into different clusters.

Table 4. Results of Llyod's k-means algorithm (number of clusters as an input (k) and randomly generated centroids)

Iteration	Cluster s (k)	Cluster's Members
1	1	-
	2	-
	3	{11,12}
	4	{13,21,26,31}
	5	{3,4,5}
2	1	-
	2	-
	3	{11,12,13}
	4	{21,26,31}
	5	{3,4,5}
3	1	-
	2	-
	3	{11,12}
	4	{21,26,31}
	5	{3,4,5,12}
4	1	{3}
	2	-
	3	{11,13}
	4	{21,26,31}
	5	{4,5,12}
5	1	{3,4,5}
	2	-
	3	{11,13}
	4	{21,26,31}
	5	{12}
6	1	{3,4,5}
	2	-
	3	{11,13}
	4	{21,26,31}
	5	{12}

Table 5. Comparison between new K-means and Llyod's K-means using N=80

Algorithm	Clusters	Number of Members in Cluster
New K-Means N= 80 K = 17 Number of iteration= 4 Total Cluster=10	1	2
	2	9
	3	9
	4	8
	5	6
	6	8
	7	16
	8	18
	11	3
	17	2
Llyod's K-Means N=80 K=10 Number of Iteration=18 Total Cluster =10	1	2
	2	12
	3	0
	4	12
	5	11
	6	8
	7	10
	8	13
	9	3
	10	9

In the third cycle of the experiment, the number of data points is increased.

Cycle 3

Suppose the total number of data points (N) is 80 and the minimum and maximum values of data points is maintained as in the above experiments which is 1 and 30, respectively

- **Observations:** The results from Table 5 show that with the new algorithm, the number of iteration improves tremendously when N is larger. It shows that the number of iterations is reduced from 18 to 4, which is an improvement of 78%.

Table 6 shows the percentage of improvements of the new algorithm compared to the Llyod's K-Means algorithm, derived from the results from the three (3) cycles of the experiments.

- Let k = number of desired clusters
- And c = centroids of the clusters

- **Observations:** Results from Table 6 show that as the number of data points increased, the new algorithm shows the tremendous increase in the performance, in terms of processing time or number of iterations needed to process the data.

Table 6. Improvement analysis of the new algorithm

Cycle	Algorithm	N(number of data points)	Improveme nts (in terms of number of iterations)
1	k as input, c is generated from the system using new technique	9	60%
2	k and c are auto generated from the system using new techniques	9	33%
3	k and c are auto generated from the system using new techniques	80	78%

CONCLUSION

This paper has addressed problems with Lloyd K-means clustering algorithms which requires the number of clusters k, must be determined beforehand, which is not desirable as the number of cluster configuration needs domain knowledge. It has also another problem with Lloyd k-means in regards to setting of centroids. In addition, it proposed a clustering method called MaxD K-means clustering algorithm. MaxD k-means algorithm auto generates initial k (the desired number of clusters) without asking for input from the user. MaxD also uses new technique to set the initial centroids. Setting the centroid is divided from the maximum distance of data points. From the number of generated centroids, it derives the initial number of clusters. Because the new algorithm deals only with the maximum distance of data points, it works very efficient with large data sets. The performance of the algorithm is only affected when the distance of maximum data points is large or outlier. The new approach to determine initial centroid also can be used when k is fixed. The performance of the new technique of setting the centroids by using the maximum distance of data points is also tremendous.

FUTURE WORK

The future work of this research shall be continued to experiment and improve the algorithm with larger N and higher dimension of data points. The application of the new technique will be in clustering (time, complexity, memory) the educational data.

ACKNOWLEDGMENT

Appreciation conveyed to Ministry of Higher Education Malaysia for project financing under Fundamental Research Grant Scheme RDU110104.

REFERENCES

Babu, G. P., & Murty, M. N. (1993). A near-optimal initial seed value selection for k-means algorithm using genetic algorithm. *Pattern Recognition Letters*, *14*, 763–769. doi:10.1016/0167-8655(93)90058-L

Bagirov, A. M. (2008). Modified global k-means algorithm for sum-of-squares clustering problem. *Pattern Recognition*, *41*, 3192–3199. doi:10.1016/j.patcog.2008.04.004

Bagirov, A. M., & Mardaneh, K. (2006). Modified global k-means algorithm for clustering in gene expression datasets. In *Proceedings of the AI Workshop on Intelligent Systems of Bioinformatics*, Hobart, Australia (pp. 23-28).

Bagirov, A. M., Ugon, J., & Dean, W. (2011). Fast modified global k-means algorithm for incremental cluster construction. *Pattern Recognition*, *44*, 866–876. doi:10.1016/j.patcog.2010.10.018

Bandyopadhyay, S., & Maulik, U. (2001a). Non-parametric genetic clustering: Comparison of validity indices. *IEEE Transactions on Systems, Man and Cybernetics. Part C, Applications and Reviews*, *31*, 120–125. doi:10.1109/5326.923275

Bandyopadhyay, S., & Maulik, U. (2001b). An evolutionary technique based on k-means algorithm for optimal clustering in RN. *Information Sciences--Applications, 146*, 221-237.

Bhuyan, J. N., Raghavan, V. V., & Venkatesh, K. E. (1991). Genetic algorithm for clustering with an ordered representation. In *Proceedings of the 4th International Conference on Genetic Algorithms* (pp. 408-415).

Bradley, P., & Fayyad, U. (1998). Refining initial points for k-means clustering. In *Proceedings of the 15th International Conference on Machine Learning*.

Chang, D., Xian, D., & Chang, W. Z. (2009). A genetic algorithm with gene rearrangement for K-means clustering. *Pattern Recognition*, *42*, 1210–1222. doi:10.1016/j.patcog.2008.11.006

Charalampidis, D. (2005). A modified K-means algorithm for circular invariant clustering. *IEEE Transactions on Pattern Analysis and Machine Intelligence*, *27*(12), 1856–1865. doi:10.1109/TPAMI.2005.230

Dunham, M. H. (2003). *Data mining: Introductory and advance topics*. Upper Saddle River, NJ: Prentice Hall.

Fayyad, U. M., Piatetsky, G., Smyth, P., & Uthurusamy, R. (1996). *Advances in knowledge discovery and data mining*. Cambridge, MA: MIT.

Gungo, Z., & Alper, U. (2008). K-Harmonic means data clustering with tabu-search method. *Applied Mathematical Modelling*, *32*, 1115–1125. doi:10.1016/j.apm.2007.03.011

Hansen, P., Ngai, E., Cheung, B. K., & Mladenovic, N. (2005). Analysis of global k-means, an incremental heuristic for minimum sum-of-squares clustering. *Journal of Classification*, *22*(2), 287–310. doi:10.1007/s00357-005-0018-3

Jain, A. K., & Dubes, R. C. (1988). *Algorithms for clustering data*. Upper Saddle River, NJ: Prentice Hall.

Jain, A. K., Murty, M. N., & Flynn, P. J. (1999). Data clustering: a review. *ACM Computing Surveys*, *31*(3). doi:10.1145/331499.331504

Jiang, H., Yi, S., Li, J., Yang, F., & Hu, X. (2010). Ant clustering algorithm with K-harmonic means clustering. *Expert Systems with Applications*, *37*, 8679–8684. doi:10.1016/j.eswa.2010.06.061

Jones, D., & Beltramo, M. A. (1991). Solving partitioning problems with genetic algorithms. In *Proceedings of the 4th International Conference on Genetic Algorithms* (pp. 442-449).

Kalyani, S., & Swarup, K. S. (2011). Particle swarm optimization based K-means clustering approach for security assessment in power systems. *Expert Systems with Applications*, *38*, 1083–10846. doi:10.1016/j.eswa.2011.02.086

Kanungo, T., Mount, D., Netanyahu, N. S., Piatko, C., Silverman, R., & Wu, A. (2002). An efficient K-means clustering algorithm: analysis and implementation. *IEEE Transactions on Pattern Analysis and Machine Intelligence*, *24*(7), 881–892. doi:10.1109/TPAMI.2002.1017616

Khan, S. S., & Ahmad, A. (2004). Cluster center initialization algorithm for K-means clustering. *Pattern Recognition Letters*, *25*, 1293–1302. doi:10.1016/j.patrec.2004.04.007

Krishna, K., & Murty, M. N. (1999). Genetic k-means algorithm. *IEEE Transactions on Systems, Man, and Cybernetics*, *29*(3), 433–439. doi:10.1109/3477.764879

Lai, J. Z. C., & Huang, T.-J. (2010). Fast global k-means clustering using cluster membership and inequality. *Pattern Recognition*, *43*, 1954–1963. doi:10.1016/j.patcog.2009.11.021

Lai, J. Z. C., Liaw, Y. C., & Lo, W. (2002). Artifact reduction of JPEG coded images using mean-removed classified vector quantization. *Signal Processing*, *82*(10), 1375–1388. doi:10.1016/S0165-1684(02)00277-3

Laszlo, M., & Mukherjee, S. (2007). A genetic algorithm that exchanges neighboring centers for k-means clustering. *Pattern Recognition Letters*, *28*, 2359–2366. doi:10.1016/j.patrec.2007.08.006

Likas, A., Vlassis, M., & Verbeek, J. (2003). The global k-means clustering algorithm. *Pattern Recognition*, *36*, 451–461. doi:10.1016/S0031-3203(02)00060-2

Liu, D., & Kubala, F. (2004). Online speaker clustering. In *Proceedings of the IEEE Conference on Acoustics, Speech, and Signal Processing* (Vol. 1, pp. 333-336).

MacQueen, J. B. (1967). Some methods for classification and analysis of multivariate observations. In *Proceedings of the 5th Berkeley Symposium on Mathematical Statistics and Probability*, Berkeley, CA (pp. 281-297).

Maulik, U., & Bandyopadhyay, S. (2000). Genetic algorithm-based clustering technique. *Pattern Recognition*, *33*, 1455–1465. doi:10.1016/S0031-3203(99)00137-5

Ming, C. C., Tsai, C. W., & Yang, C. S. (2011). A time-efficient pattern reduction algorithm for k-means clustering. *Information Sciences*, *181*, 716–731. doi:10.1016/j.ins.2010.10.008

Mohd, W. M. W., Mohd Zain, J., & Embong, A. (2007, November 12-15). Parameterless K-Means: Auto-generation of centroids and initial number of cluster based on distance of data points. In *Proceedings of the Malaysia-Japan International Symposium on Advanced Technology*, Kuala Lumpur, Malaysia.

Pelleg, D., & Moore, A. W. (2000). X-means: extending k-means with efficient estimation of the number of clusters. In *Proceedings of the Seventeenth International Conference on Machine Learning* (pp. 727-734).

Redmond, S. J., & Heneghan, C. (2007). A method for initializing the K-means clustering algorithm using kd-trees. *Pattern Recognition Letters*, *28*, 965–973. doi:10.1016/j.patrec.2007.01.001

Selim, S. Z., & Ismail, M. A. (1984). K-means type algorithms: a generalized convergence theorem and characterization of local optimality. *IEEE Transactions on Pattern Analysis and Machine Intelligence*, *6*, 81–87. doi:10.1109/TPAMI.1984.4767478

Späth, H. (1989). *Cluster analysis algorithms*. Chichester, UK: Ellis Horwood.

Theodoridis, S., & Koutroumbas, K. (2003). *Pattern recognition* (2nd ed.). New York, NY: Academic Press.

Xu, R., & Wunsch, D. (2005). Survey of clustering algorithms. *IEEE Transactions on Neural Networks*, *16*(3), 645–678. doi:10.1109/TNN.2005.845141

This work was previously published in the International Journal of Information Retrieval Research, Volume 1, Issue 3, edited by Zhongyu (Joan) Lu, pp. 1-14, copyright 2011 by IGI Publishing (an imprint of IGI Global).

Chapter 11
Ranking Tagged Resources Using Social Semantic Relevance

Anjali Thukral
University of Delhi, India

Hema Banati
University of Delhi, India

Punam Bedi
University of Delhi, India

ABSTRACT

The WWW today is overwhelmed with information on almost every topic. Therefore, relevance ranking of web pages to a user's expectations is a challenge, rather than retrieving a collection of thousands of web pages selected by keyword matching. This paper presents an approach to rank tagged web pages retrieved from a Social Bookmarking Site for a learner who needs web resources containing content on a given topic. Besides the popularity of the web page in the community, the relevance of a web page for ranking is computed based on the semantic distance between tags and a given topic using domain ontology. An experimental study has been conducted to evaluate the ranks generated by the proposed approach. The test collection was created using a questionnaire which was designed to judge the crawled web pages for their graded relevance on a topic.

1. INTRODUCTION

The World Wide Web has evolved as a unanimous powerful information portal that allows a learner to retrieve and access available resources or documents on any subject or topic. Various search engines, with their rational design and organizational efficiency retrieve web pages on a user's query or search topic. However, the resulted web pages are usually very large in number which consequently leaves the user with the only option to search required content by visiting each web page. Such large volume of search results therefore needs a ranking according to the user's information requirements. The ranking algorithms used to rank search results often relay on the formation of user's query, and its Boolean and syntactic keyword matching in the web pages' content. This means that the document / resource or web page relevance is determined by using the words

DOI: 10.4018/978-1-4666-3898-3.ch011

in the topic or the query which is matched (keyword based) with the content of the web pages. The web page retrieval and ranking algorithms (Yi, Liangjie, Ruihua, Jian-Yun, & Ji-Rong, 2009; Chawla & Bedi, 2008; Greg, Chowdhury, & Torgeson) based on classification, clustering of queries and documents, click logs, terms co-occurrence (Matsuo and Ishizuka 2003), etc., are the few used by many search engines. Apart from these, the algorithms based on the term frequency (TF, IDF) (Salton and Buckley 1987), internal, external links, and clickthrough of HIT count methods (Kleinberg, 1999; Kazunari, Kenji, Masatoshi, & Shunsuke, 2003) with their various modified versions, that uses syntactic keyword matching (Agrahri, Anand, & Riedl, 2008) are also used to search and rank relevant documents. These algorithms work best for a well formed query with specific keywords because of their syntactic searching potential. However, the ranking criterion built on the algorithms like clickthrough usually gets biased interpretations in selecting links. This is apparent from the study (Chi and Mytkowicz 2008) that shows more than 90% of search sessions do not go beyond the first result page. As the result, most of the time, the users click links available only on first few pages, ignoring various links that exist at the end pages. Moreover, people have also been found biased in the selection of search engines and their search activities (Shenghua, et al. 2007). Besides this, many links that exist at end pages never get a chance to get their HIT. All above studies infer that the users' clicks are biased in nature and are influenced by many factors like placing few links at the top on the first page of search results, selection of search engine and placing popular keywords in the web pages. However while computing relevance to rank resources, if semantically related terms to the search topic or query and some sort of the community's feedback regarding web resources are incorporated, the ranking order of resources can be improved.

This paper proposes Social Semantic Ranking (SSR) to rank tagged web resource using Social Semantic Relevance (S2R) which is based on Vector Space Model. It uses tags which are bookmarked in Social Bookmarking Site (SBS), and pre-existing semantic knowledge from ontologies for computing Semantic Relevance of the crawled web resources on a search topic.

The rest of the paper is organized as follows: In Section 2 the related work and some basic features used in the approach have been discussed. The proposed approach for Social Semantic Relevance ranking of tagged resources with respect to a search topic is explained in Section 3. Section 4 presents the implementation of the approach and evaluation of its ranked results in the experimental study. Finally Section 5 concludes the paper.

2. RELATED WORK

Tagging is a very powerful source of information which emerges from a collaborative effort of numerous users of similar community. These tags are usually placed by users after analyzing the content of web resources and therefore can be considered as a useful feedback. This implicit feedback in the form of tags given by the users can be considered more appropriate than the computational based classification approaches where the attempt is made to compute the meaning of a resource. Besides, a collaborative bookmarking system facilitates to locate many relevant resources, which a normal crawler in a search engine is usually unable to find. Using tags as the base for deciding which URL fits best for a concept makes the decision more fruitful. Research on Social annotation (Bischoff, et al. 2008) has shown promising results in this direction. Experimental results (Firan, Nejdl and Paiu 2007) have also shown that the tag based search algorithms yield improved results and faster recommendations, which consequently can improve the effectiveness of web search engine (Agrahri, Anand, & Riedl, 2008). Adding semantics among resources in a collaborative system, results in the collection of more analyzed and categorized structure (Jovanović, et al. 2009).

The machine learning algorithms based on gradient boosting technique, developed in recent times (Mohan, Chen and Weinberger 2011) were produced to predict ranking of documents with the available dataset consisting of document, query and relevance value (called labels) triples. These algorithms use query terms and their term occurrence frequency in the document to compute their basic weights. The ranking algorithm proposed by Vadrevu and Velipasaoglu (2011), called PASCAL (PAge Segment Content quALity) is also based on gradient boosting technique but uses an effective method that make use of web page segments to determine content quality. The web page in this algorithm is treated as a structure consisting of various segments where each segment is evaluated separately to determine the relevance and quality of the web page with respect to a query term. Incorporating semantically relevant terms to compute basic weights of the documents, as proposed in this paper may further enhance these algorithms. However, the same has not been still tested.

Another method (Yeung, et al. 2011) called SPEAR (spamming-resistant expertise analysis and ranking) which first rank users of collaborative tagging system as experts of a topic and after that based on the findings, it presumes that the resources tagged by experts should be useful and of interest to the community. Their vibrant method also takes care of spammers. Similar to other algorithms our method of using ontology to determine the relevance of tagged resources can be applied here also to enhance the prediction of resource ranking.

Evaluation of the ranks generated using the proposed approach is one of the important factors taken care in this paper. There exist various standard test collections like Cranfield, TREC, and CLEF, etc. (Baeza-Yates and Ribeiro-Neto 1999). They consist of a set of documents and their corresponding dichotomous relevance judgments (Kekalainen and Jarvelin 2002). However, the data present in these test collections are insufficient to work upon especially for the dynamic systems like SBS that intent to produce ranked resources instead of the dichotomous relevance. The corpuses in TREC datasets belong to certain domains. In order to compute semantic relevance of these documents through the proposed approach, a pre-existing domain ontology consisting of all important terms is required in addition to the associated tags to the documents. Unfortunately, neither the ontology, nor the tags for the documents collection are available in the dataset. Indeed, different searching situations require different approaches to build a test collection as also suggested by Sanderson and Braschler (2009).

The other traditional evaluation metric Precision-Recall (Vaughan 2004) is usually used as the standard since the Cranfield tests (Ellis 1996). However, due to the following shortcomings, they could not be applied to evaluate the results presented in this paper.

- The rank order of documents could not be evaluated efficiently using Precision-Recall as it uses dichotomous relevance only, i.e., relevant or not relevant, whereas the documents need to be evaluated for relevance in a range to determine a rank order.
- Determining total number of relevant web resources or exact number of web resources in the WWW, at a given time is not feasible, which are actually required in order to calculate the 'recall'. Precision-Recall therefore can only be applied to a subset of web resources as it is there in the case of standard test collections.

The Social Semantic Ranks computed by the proposed approach have been evaluated to measure the effectiveness of the proposed system using normalized Discounted Cumulative Gain DCG(n) metric, instead the Precision-Recall metric. DCG(n) has been found particularly useful in evaluating the ranks generated by the system.

3. SOCIAL SEMANTIC RANKING OF TAGGED WEB RESOURCE: A PROPOSED APPROACH

The proposed approach Social Semantic Ranking (SSR) generates a rank order of web resources that are expected to be relevant to the stated needs of a web user. As a pre process, the approach requires domain ontology that contains the search topic as one of its nodes, and a set of bookmarks downloaded from a SBS (Figure 1). For this purpose, taxonomy consisting of few domains needs to be constructed which can be expressed in ontology (Bedi, Banati, & Thukral, 2010a, 2010b). The

Figure 1. Framework for Social Semantic Ranking (SSR)

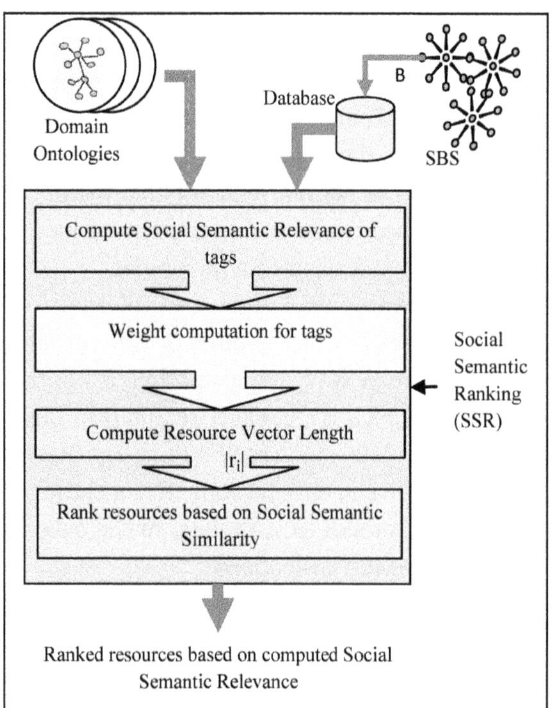

concept ontologies like SKOS (Simple Knowledge Organization System) (Allemang and Hendler 2011, 207-220) on Semantic Web, which is also a W3C recommendation suits best for our application. In near future the semantically relevant terms to a query can also be extracted using these Semantic Web ontologies. The ontology used for the approach has been structured mainly with sub-concept, super-concept properties besides many other properties to represent association among various concepts specifically designed for semantic information retrieval. Each concept or a domain related term is represented as a node in ontology, where two nodes are linked with a property (or relation) which together forms a triple. This link or edge between two nodes represents the semantic distance between two concepts. This means that if two nodes consisting of concepts are three edges apart in ontology then those two concepts (nodes) are said to have a semantic distance of 3. Semantic Relevance between two concepts is inversely proportional to the semantic distance, i.e., more the semantic distance, less will be the semantic relevance. Semantic Relevance thus acts as a basic unit to compute relevance among concepts which has been later used to compute relevance among resources. A structure, called expanded list, of semantically relevant terms to the search topic is created such that it includes concepts from the ontology according to the depth of content required by a user. That is, if a user requires some basic information on a topic, then the list would include super-concepts of a topic and only few sub-concepts. This is because as we go down in the taxonomy, we would get more specific concepts than the one which is at the top. This suggests that if more deep information on a topic is required then the expanded list of the topic should include more sub-concepts linked below the topic in the taxonomy.

A SBS can be viewed as a set of bookmarks, B, where each bookmark, $b \quad B\, b \in B$, is a set of triples:

$\{r, u, t_1\}, \{r, u, t_2\} \ldots \{r, u, t_k\}$

Thus a single triple consists of three data units, $< r_i, u_j, t_k >$, signifies resource r_i being tagged by user u_j with tag t_k. Each bookmark b represents a single web resource with a URL. This resource is further tagged by multiple users with multiple tags. Potentially relevant bookmarks have been downloaded from a SBS using a crawler called FCHC (Focused Crawling based on Human Cognition) crawler (Thukral, Mendiratta, et al. 2011) as a part of pre-process task. The crawler is designed to download those bookmarks which contain tags that are semantically relevant terms to the search topic or the query term. Thus by filtering out the potentially relevant bookmarks from the SBS during download, the crawler reduces the sparseness in social data and minimizes disk storage as well. However, the web resources which are not bookmarked, or if they are bookmarked but not tagged at all (a very rare case), they are not considered by the crawler at present and hence by the SSR algorithm. A resource is usually bookmarked and tagged by a number of users. Thus if a particular resource is not being tagged by few of the users, it does not put much impact on the resource relevance computation.

The proposed approach Social Semantic Rank (SSR) has been applied on these documents to rank them according to the computed semantic relevance. Disambiguation of a query term is handled by the proposed approach through analysing the co-existing tags with the query term, for a resource. This has been explained here with an example. Consider the following bookmarks from the social site:

Example 1

- **URL:** http://dmlcentral.net/conference2011
- **Tags:** Conference, learning, education, digital media, 2011, dml, technology

Example 2

- **URL:** http://www.orafaq.com/faq/what_are_the_difference_between_ddl_dml_and_dcl_commands
- **Tags:** Sql, oracle, database, ddl, dml, dcl, tcl, computer dbms

Above two examples of the bookmarks represent tag 'dml' in two different contexts, one as 'data manipulation language' from database domain and another as 'digital media and learning' representing conference. In order to disambiguate the query term we analyze collection of all tags given to a particular resource, and match it with the semantically expanded list on the query term using domain ontology. The domain is assumed to be provided with the query term by the searcher. The resource vector computed on all the resource associated tags, given by the users produces the semantic similarity to the query term. If 'dml' query is searched in database context, the former bookmark would compute to very small relevance, perhaps less than 0.01, whereas the latter bookmark would give relevance more than 0.7. The ranking algorithm that computes the semantic relevance of each resource to a given query term and its domain is explained below and shown in Figure 2.

Each tag tg_k assigned by a SBS user is viewed as a concept from ontology in the approach. A resource r_i is described by a set of tags, collaboratively tagged by the users for the resource. The ranks are computed based on the similarity measures, achieved using the four steps as explained in the following subsections, and illustrated in Figure 1.

1. Computing Semantic Relevance of Tags

The Semantic Relevance (SR) of each unique tag t_k of a resource r_i to a query term Q_0 Q_o is cal-

Figure 2. The social semantic rank algorithm

```
/* Social Semantic Rank (SSR) Algorithm
   Input: Expanded query, Q and Set R consisting of N+a resources (web pages)
   Output: ordered list of ranked resources, R
*/

SSR(Q, R ) {
    // Query vector computation
    for each q ∈ Q   {              // Q consists of 0..n semantically relevant terms to the query q[0] fetched
                                        from ontology
        q[t] = semRelv( )           // function returns SR from Q if term exist otherwise read ontology
        sigmaSRqt = sigmaSRqt + q[t]
    }
    // normalization and weight computation of semantically expanded term
    for each   q ∈ Q    {
        Wt_q[t] = q[t]/ sigmaSRqt
        sigmaWtsq_qt =  sigmaWtsq_qt  + sq(Wt_q[t])
    }
    // Query vector length
    Q_vector = sqrt(sigmaWtsq_qt)

    // Resource vector computation
    for each resource  r ∈ R {
        for each unique and relevant tag,  tgk   {
            compute count_tg[k]
            S2R_tg[k] = semRelv( ) * count_tg[k]
            sigmaS2R_tgk += S2R_tg[k]
        }
    // normalization and weight computation of tags associated with a resource
        for each unique and relevant tag,  tgk   {
            Wt_tg[k] =  tg[k]/sigmaS2R_tgk
            sigmaWtsq_rt = sigmaWtsq_rt + sq(Wt_tg[k])
        }
    // Resource vector length
        r_vector[j] = sqrt(sigma_SR_tg)
    // Compute cosine similarity, theta
        theta_Qr[i] = dot_product(Q, r[j].tg[k])/(Q_vector * r_vector)
    }
    // ordered list of ranked resources
    R = sort theta_Qr
```

```
/* Computes dot product of Query and Resource to determine similarity between them
   The function is used by the SSR algorithm */

dot_product(Q, r[j].tg) {
    for each similar tag term, tgk  and query term, qt {
        Wt_prod = Wt_q[t] * Wt_tg[k]              // product of similar query term weight and tag weight
        sigma_qt_tgk = sigma_qt_tgk + Wt_prod
    }
    return sigma_qt_tgk
}
```

culated using the domain ontology through following equation.

$$SR_{Q_o, t_k} = \frac{1}{|d|_{Q_o, t_k} + 1} \quad (1)$$

Here, |d| is the absolute distance between Q_0 (query term) and t_k (tag) in the ontology. As mentioned earlier each edge between the two concepts represents one unit of the semantic distance. The two concepts are thus are said to be semantically more relevant if they exist at a smaller distance in ontology. It may further be noted that Semantic Relevance for all tags relevant to the query term were computed as a pre-process task. Therefore, the algorithm does not require any re-computation at this stage, which consequently reduces the over head computational expense of accessing ontology for computing Semantic Relevance again. Next we calculate the tags weight.

2. Weight Computation for Tags

The social aspect can be calculated using the crawled data from SBS which gives the Social Semantic Relevance (S2R) of each tag. It can be obtained by counting similar terms tagged by SBS users for the resource. Tag weight includes the popularity of associated resource and thus represents the measure of usefulness. It is proportional to the number of times a resource has been tagged with the same term by different users. Thus, more the number of users visited and tagged a resource with same term; more will be the weight of the tag. That is, if Count_{t_k} is the number of times, a tag t_k has been used for a resource r_i by all users who have bookmarked a resource r_i, then the Social Semantic Relevance, S2R of each tag for a resource is computed as

$$\mathrm{S2R}_{Q_o,t_k}(r_i) = \frac{\mathrm{Count}_{t_k}}{|d|_{Q_o,t_k} + 1} \qquad (2)$$

The tag weight $Wt_{t_k r_i}$ $t_k \mathrm{Wt}_{t_k r_i}$, of a tag t_k is determined by normalizing all tags (their S2R from eq. (2)) of a resource r_i, thus we obtain, tag weight, $Wt_{t_k r_i}$ as

$$\mathrm{Wt}_{t_k r_i} = \frac{\mathrm{S2R}_{Q_o,t_k}(r_i)}{\sum_{k=1}^{n2} \mathrm{S2R}_{Q_o,t_k}(r_i)} \qquad (3)$$

The tags weight formulated using above method does not only determines empirical measure for resource usefulness as reviewed by the community, but also determines the Semantic Relevance of tags with the implicit weighted feedback.

3. Combining Tags Weight to Compute Resource Vector Length

The relevance of a resource is enumerated by its tags weight. Therefore, resource vector for each resource in R, a set of all retrieved web resources, is computed as a square root of the sum of resource's tags weight that are greater than zero using Vector Space Model (Salton & Buckley, 1987; Garcia, 2006b). Mathematically, for each resource r_i we calculate the resource vector length (magnitude) as,

$$|r_i| = \sqrt{\sum_k \mathrm{Wt}^2_{t_k,r_i}} \qquad (4)$$

A resource vector is computed for each relevant resource. A resource is considered relevant to a search query term if it contains relevant tags with sufficient weight in SBS. The tags for a resource usually occur as a collection of many contextually related terms representing a domain. A resource that belongs to a different context while sharing the same query term due to the term ambiguity would not have other tags from the searching domain. Therefore, the resource as whole would show very small relevance which would not be greater than 0.1 in most of the cases.

4. Ranking Resources Based on the Social Semantic Similarity

The query vector length |Q| is computed similarly as resource vector length has been computed, using the semantically expanded list of a given search topic. The similarity between a resource and a query has been measured as the angular distance between the resource vector lengths $|r_i|$ and the query vector length $|Q|$ using the Vector Space Model. The significance of the proposed approach is that the term weights here have been computed using the semantic distance between terms which is in contrast to other approaches that have used Vector Space Model for similar purpose. The social semantic similarity between each resource and a given query term can be determined using the widely accepted cosine similarity measure (Garcia 2006a). The normalized cosine similarity between a query Q_o , and a resource r_i is defined as,

$$\text{Cosine}_{\,Q_o, r_i} = \frac{Q \cdot r_i}{|Q| * |r_i|} \quad (5)$$

where, $Q \cdot r_i$ is the dot product, determined by the following equation,

$$Q \cdot r_i = \sum_{q_t = t_k} (Wt_{Q_o, q_t} \cdot Wt_{t_k r_i}) \quad (6)$$

Wt_{Q_o, q_t} in eq. (6) represents the weight of a term from semantically expanded query list corresponding to a query term Q_0. By substituting eq. (4), (6) and $|Q|$, in eq. (5), we get cosine similarity between the resource and the query term as

$$\text{Cosine } \theta_{Q_o, r_i} = \frac{\sum_{q_t = t_k} (Wt_{Q_o, q_t} \cdot Wt_{t_k r_i})}{\sqrt{\sum_{q_t} Wt^2_{Q_o, q_t}} \sqrt{\sum_{k} Wt^2_{t_k, r_i}}} \quad (7)$$

Cosine similarity $\grave{e}_{Q_o, r_i}$ (eq. (7)) is computed for all (N+a) resources (i.e., top N resources as crawling seeds fetched from a search engine and additional 'a' '*a*' resources filtered from SBS, using the FCHC crawler). These resources are then ranked by sorting them on the computed values of Cos è θ in descending order. It can further be noticed that, the value of similarity measure(Cosθθ) is maximum for the most relevant resource, and the relevance of a resource to a query term decreases with the decreasing Cosθθ.

4. EXPERIMENTAL STUDY

The experimental study is carried in two parts. The first part (Implementation of SSR) consists of the implementation of the proposed approach SSR and the second part (Evaluation of SSR Results) evaluates the ranks of the results obtained from the first part of the experimental study.

Implementation of SSR

Setup

Most of the coding on the proposed approach has been written using java programming language, and ProtégéOWL APIs to access ontologies. The knowledgebase consisting of ontologies has been developed using Protégé (Thukral, Bedi, & Banati, 2011a, 2011b). The SBS crawler was coded using java. MySql has been used to store crawled relevant resources. The experiment was conducted on Intel core 2 Duo processor with 1.67 GHz, 2 GB RAM and 32-bit OS.

Implementation

The experiment was conducted on sets of queries from three domains (Table 1). Depth of the content required by a user in a resource was assumed as 'Basic level', which means all super-concepts and single level sub-concepts of the topic would be added to the expanded list from the domain ontologies. However, the approach can be implemented for any topic, provided the ontology on the query domain exists. Three domain ontologies were constructed to conduct the experiment, and therefore the queries were purposely chosen from these domains.

Table 1. Set of queries used for experiment

Domains	Query terms
java programming language	java, datatype, variable, loop, applets, event handling, recursion
database	dml, sql, insert into, set operators, group by
computer network	transmission media, integrated circuits, coaxial cable, topologies, TCP/IP, protocols, modem, subnet

The crawler FCHC was used to download bookmarks from the SBS, delicious.com. The top 10 search results from the search engine (Google) on the query terms were fed as seeds to initiate crawl in SBS. Finally, the proposed approach SSR was executed on the potentially relevant bookmarks downloaded by the crawler. It computed the social semantic relevance between each of the downloaded resource and the search query using similarity measure cosine θ as explained in the previous section. The resources were then arranged in the descending order according to their computed relevance (Cos θ) in order to rank them.

Evaluation of SSR Results

Any IR technique is evaluated by measuring its effectiveness (Sanderson and Braschler 2009), i.e., by determining the relevance of retrieved items, relative to a user's information need. The results produced after executing the proposed approach on the potentially relevant documents crawled from SBS corresponding to various queries, were evaluated majorly by the experts (teachers or research scholars) of the domains selected for the experiments. An exhaustive evaluation was carried out with the help of 31 non probabilistic purposive respondents, on randomly chosen three queries from database domain. The reason for choosing database domain was that the group of respondents had some basic knowledge on database subject, similar to the intent assumed to semantically expand the query terms from ontology. For rest of the queries, experts from the respective domains were approached to evaluate the system generated ranks, as carrying evaluation process with such large groups is expensive in terms of time and resources. Nevertheless, the similarities in the evaluated results for select query terms by both types of the judges justify the evaluations done on other queries by experts.

More specifically, here we evaluate the results to check/ measure:

1. Whether the approach has retrieved relevant web resources from SBS and whether it shows any benefit of using collaborative tagging?
2. Whether the rank order generated by SSR on retrieved web resources correlates with the user's relevance judgment?
3. Whether the learners are satisfied with the ranking order generated by the proposed approach?

The experimental setup for creating test collection, and evaluate the effectiveness of the proposed system is described in the remaining part of this section.

Setup for Creating Test Collection

For creating the test collection, a questionnaire was designed to judge 15 web resources for their graded relevance to the query term. These web resources consist of top 15 resources ranked by SSR. The sample population was taken purposively consisting of 31 undergraduate students who were studying 'Databases' in their course and were beginners for the concept 'dml', which was also the query topic in the experimental study. The work in this paper is intended for the eLearning domain, therefore to an extent the user's intension while searching is assumed as the need for some basic understanding about the topic. This assumption led us to precisely define the relevance using a concrete structure of domain knowledge. The assumption also supports the judges to be represented as the real searchers to an extent. After face to face introduction with respondents and training them regarding the search requirements and procedure to fill questionnaire, the communication was done through email. Each respondent was instructed to open web resources one by one which were represented by their URLs. They were suggested to browse and analyze each resource and then select one option from a four point scale, where each point represents most relevant, fairly relevant, marginally relevant or irrelevant respectively, similar to the criterion considered by Jarvelin and Kekalainen (2002).

Relevance Judgments

Quality of the relevance judgment by humans variably differs by their capability. If they are given a set of web resources to rank them in some order, they would be able to do that correctly, possibly up to 5 or 6 ranks, after that the quality of their judgment deteriorate due to a number of reasons. They might not remember the contents of early resources while comparing them with later resources. In general, one is able to remember the contents up to a few numbers of initial resources only to put them in some order; beyond that, the chances of ranking them with wrong decisions increases. Alternatively, the judges can be asked to assign individual web resources a degree of relevance, e.g., 3, 2, 1, or 0 for highly relevant, fairly relevant, marginally relevant or irrelevant respectively. This type of a 4 point scale assessment allows a respondent to judge web resource relevance independent of other web resources in the list and allows the assessment of more number of web resources; without the need to relatively assess all resources. However, the assessment of results, in the presented experiment is conducted with both of the methods. An expert's relevance feedback consisting of ranked web resources to the query relevance has been used in the first method; whereas the later assessment method uses the relevance judgment of 31 purposive respondents.

Moreover, the web resources are judged on the stated topical relevance, in the presented experiment. The term 'stated relevance' was originally given by Cleverdon and Keen (as cited in Ellis, 1996). It indicates that the resource relevance is judged by a respondent other than the actual searcher while considering the given search conditions.

Evaluation Metric DCG(n): Discounted Cumulative Gain

DCG and nDCG (Jarvelin and Kekalainen 2002) are useful metrics to measure the effectiveness of IR techniques as they combine the degree of web resources relevance and their ranks in a coherent way. It computes cumulated gain as a single measure at any number of retrieved web resources, irrespective of the recall base size. It is an improved measure over Cumulated Gain, motivated by the facts that:

- Highly relevant documents are more valuable than marginally relevant documents, and
- The greater the ranked position of the relevant document, the less valuable it is for the user, because less likely it is that the user will ever examine the document.

Accordingly, the discounted function progressively reduces the document score by the log of its rank, as its rank increases. Consecutively, for a greater rank, a smaller share of the document score is added to the cumulated gain. The cumulated gain vector with discount DCG is defined recursively as the vector DCG, where

$$DCG\left[i\right] = \begin{cases} CG\left[i\right], & if\, i < b \\ DCG\left[i-1\right] + G[i] / \log_b i, & if\, i \geq b \end{cases}$$

Base of the logarithm is selected to make the discounts sharper or smoother. For example, $\log_2 2 \log_2 2 = 1$ and $\log_2 1024\,1024 = 10$, which means that the document at the position 1024 would get one tenth of its gain value; whereas with base 10, i.e., $\log_{10} 10 \ \log_{10} 10 = 1$ and $\log_{10} 1000 \ \log_{10} 1000 \ \log_{10} 10 = 3$ would get one third of its gain value while documents positioned from 1 to 9 would get their usual cumulative gain.

- **Gain vector, GG:** Gain vector is the ordered list of relevance score called gain value for each document assigned by a judge. The gain values are arranged in order to the ranks obtained by the IR ranking technique. In this evaluation, relevance scores ranges from 0 to 3, where 0 represents irrelevant or no value and 3 represents highly relevant or high value.
- **Cumulated Gain, CG:** Cumulated Gain vector is defined recursively as the vector CG CG where:

$$CG[i] = \begin{cases} G[i], if\ i = 1 \\ CG[i-1] + G[i], otherwise \end{cases}$$

Thus, the cumulative gain at ranked position i is computed by summing from position 1 to *i* when *i* ranges from 1 to *n* (where *n* is the last rank in the list of relevant documents).

- **Ideal DCG(n):** This vector represents theoretically best possible vector. It is constructed using the best possible score vector BV for kk, l, and mm relevant documents at the relevance levels 1, 2, and 3. The method of the construction is as follows.

$$BV[i] = \begin{cases} 3, & if\ i \le m, \\ 2, & if\, m < i \le m + l, \\ 1, & if\, m + l < i \le m + l + k, \\ 0, & otherwise. \end{cases}$$

An ideal gain vector obtained is a sorted descending order of an actual gain vector. Ideal DCG vector is then computed in the same way as DCG(n) using the ideal gain vector.

- **Normalized DCG(n):** The DCG vectors are normalized by dividing them by the corresponding ideal DCG vectors, component by component. Therefore for any vector position, the normalized value 1 represents ideal performance, and lies in the range (0, 1). Thus, formally we get the normalized DCG vector as,

$$nDCG(n)[i] = DCG(i) \,/\, IDCG(i)$$

The normalized DCG, nDCG is used to compare the results up to a given rank generated by different IR techniques, over a set of queries and thus gives a measure to analyze their performance differences.

Results Analysis

This section presents a detailed analysis and evaluation of ranked results, their comparisons with the resources retrieved by the search engine, and rankings given by human judges. The output of SSR on various queries showed overall a satisfactory performance. However, very few relevant documents were found for advanced concepts from almost all domains. On the other hand, a significantly large number of relevant documents were retrieved when queried on broader concepts. Out of three domains, java_programming_language and database showed comparatively better retrieval of documents as compared to the Computer_Network domain. This observation infers that the concepts for which the community participation is active at a large scale, a larger set of very relevant documents are retrieved on those concepts. Nevertheless, the documents on even advanced concepts, though small in number, have been found very relevant to the search topics.

The SSR generated ranked results on the queries listed in Table 1 were evaluated by human judges. Results of 'DML', 'SQL' and 'Group_by' queries were evaluated by purposely selected respondents who were beginners in the database subject. Other queries were evaluated by 3 to 8 experts in each domain for each query. A detailed analysis is however presented for 'dml' query with few results on 'sql' and 'group_by' queries. Almost similar results were observed for queries from other domains.

Retrieval of Web Resources from SBS

In reference to the above sited question for the evaluation of the presented approach, that whether the approach has retrieved additional relevant web resources from SBS and whether it shows any benefit of using collaborative tagging, the answer is yes. Table 2 shows the comparison among ranks computed by SSR, search engine and the expert (from the field of the topic chosen for the experiment). Although in the presented experiment, Google is chosen as the search engine, however it can be replaced by any other search engine also. Following observations have been inferred (Figure 3):

1. The result generated by SSR consists of 18 relevant resources out of 25 retrieved web resources (10 from search engine's top result and rest from SBS),
2. 4 resources being not bookmarked in SBS could not be evaluated by SSR; although among these 4 resources, 3 were not relevant from the expert's view and one got the rank 16 from the expert, which shows comparatively very little relevance to the query topic,
3. Resources marked relevant by SSR approach were also found relevant by the expert and same was the case with irrelevant resources, except those 4 resources that were not found by the proposed approach, and
4. Ranks 4 to 18 of resources, generated by SSR, were all relevant and were bookmarked in SBS. These were the additional resources that did not exist in at least top 30 results produced by the search engine at the time of evaluation. The graph in Figure 4 shows the improved results generated by SSR approach consisting of seed resources from the search engine and the filtered resources from SBS ranked according to their relevance to the search query. On comparing results with the originally select resources from the search engine, it is apparent that the crawler downloaded additional web resources which are not seen in the search engine's result graph line (lying on x-axis). Hence the benefit of using SBS to rank and retrieve resources is also evident.

Comparison of SSR with Expert's Ranking Order

Figure 5 shows the comparison between the ranks of web resources generated by SSR approach and the ranks given by an expert in the similar field of query topic. One may analyze a reasonable similarity between the two results in the graph with Pearson correlation coefficient of 0.73. This answers the second problem posed previously, i.e., the rank order generated by SSR on retrieved web resources is in correlation with the user's relevance judgment.

Frequency Distribution for Graded Relevance Judgment

Figure 6 shows the frequency distribution for graded relevance judgment made by the respondents. The non-probabilistic purposive judgment was carried on a four point scale: 3, 2, 1 and 0 representing most relevant, marginally relevant, fairly relevant and irrelevant respectively. In the graph, x-axis represents the resources ranked by SSR. Each bar represents the resources relevance distribution made by 31 respondents for an individual document. It shows that most of the choice has been made between 2 (marginally relevant)

Table 2. Social semantic relevance and ranks generated by SSR compared with ranks given by other sources

Web Resources (URLs)	Social Semantic Relevance	SSR Ranks	Google order	Expert Ranks
http://en.wikipedia.org/wiki/Data_Manipulation_Language	0.805085	1	1	1
http://www.tomjewett.com/dbdesign/dbdesign.php?page=ddldml.php	0.801896	2	4	2
http://www.orafaq.com/faq/what_are_the_difference_between_ddl_dml_and_dcl_commands	0.769261	3	2	5
http://www.cs.sfu.ca/CC/354/zaiane/material/notes/Chapter1/node17.html	0.698888	4	*	3
http://www2.aao.gov.au/2dFGRS/Public/Release/Database/sql_intro.pdf	0.698888	5	*	4
databases.about.com/od/sql/a/sqlfundamentals_3.htm	0.646596	6	*	6
dev.mysql.com/doc/refman/5.0/en/insert.html	0.432221	7	*	8
dev.mysql.com/doc/refman/5.0/en/create-table.html	0.415603	8	*	14
http://en.wikipedia.org/wiki/Data_Definition_Language	0.415314	9	*	12
en.wikipedia.org/wiki/Join_(SQL)	0.406125	10	*	17
http://sqlzoo.net/	0.404035	11	*	7
www.stylusstudio.com/sqlxml_tutorial.html	0.403724	12	*	11
www.ssmstoolspack.com/Features.aspx	0.393837	13	*	20
dev.mysql.com/doc/refman/5.0/en/alter-table.html	0.388677	14	*	13
en.wikipedia.org/wiki/Data_Control_Language	0.372111	15	*	15
http://www.ibm.com/developerworks/db2/library/techarticle/dm-0608cao/	0.186055	16	*	10
www.postgresql.org/	0.122978	17	*	18
en.wikipedia.org/wiki/SQL	0.048087	18	*	9
http://www.geekinterview.com/question_details/12782	not found in SBS	NF	3	NR
http://www.dmlgroup.in/	not found in SBS	NF	6	NR
http://www.wiziq.com/tutorials/data-manipulation-language-dml	not found in SBS	NF	7	16
http://www.discogs.com/artist/DML	not found in SBS	NF	10	NR
http://www.dragon-models.com/	0	NR	5	NR
http://www.dmlonline.com/	0	NR	8	NR
http://finance.yahoo.com/q?s=DML.TO	0	NR	9	NR

*: not in top 30 google results
NF: URL not found in SBS
NR: Non relevant to query at all

and 3(most relevant) by the respondents and 0 (irrelevant) has been at the minimum. The observation clearly shows that most of the retrieved resources are relevant.

Comparing DCG with its Idealist DCG to Determine User Satisfaction

Figure 7 and Figure 8 shows the comparison between ranked resources as expected by the

Figure 3. Description of web documents used by SSR approach for one of the queries

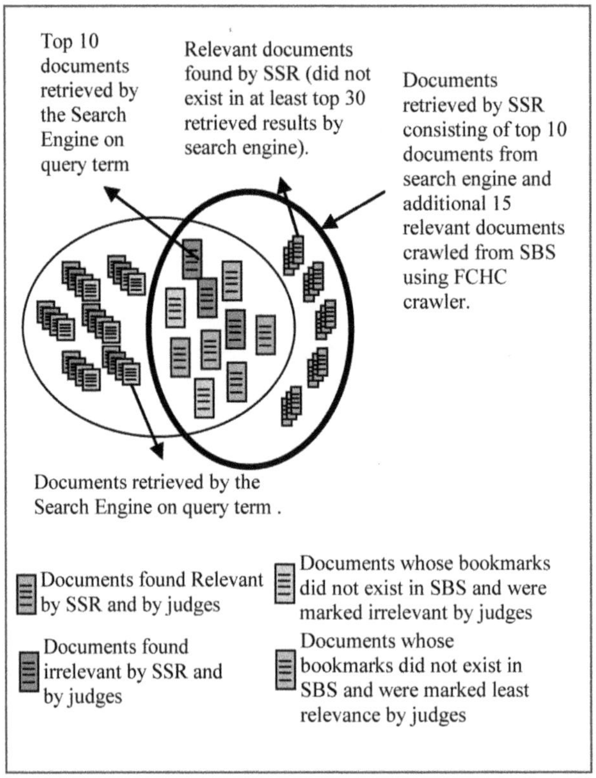

Figure 4. Results analysis of the proposed approach SSR: Web resources retrieved from SBS

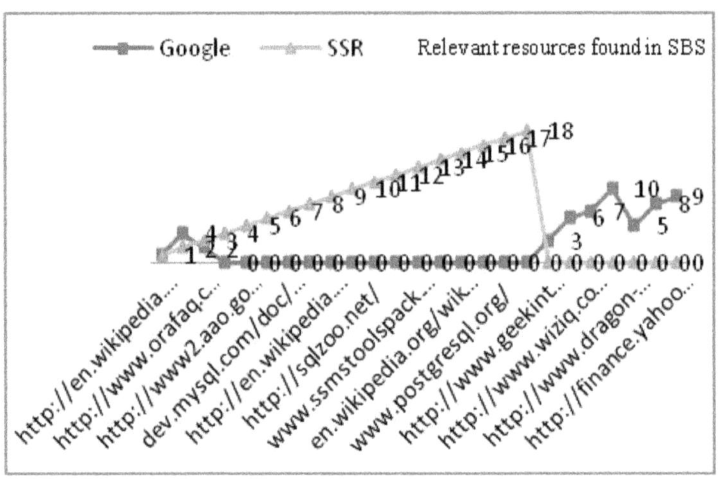

learner in idealistic situation (IDCG(n) vector) and ranks as generated by SSR for that learner (DCG(n) vector), for the most satisfied user data and the least satisfied user data respectively. User satisfaction can be considered as inverse of the area between two curves formed by DCG(n) and IDCG(n). More the area between these two curves less will be the user satisfaction. Thus,

Figure 5. Results analysis of the proposed approach SSR: Rank comparison of retrieved Web resources for a sample query

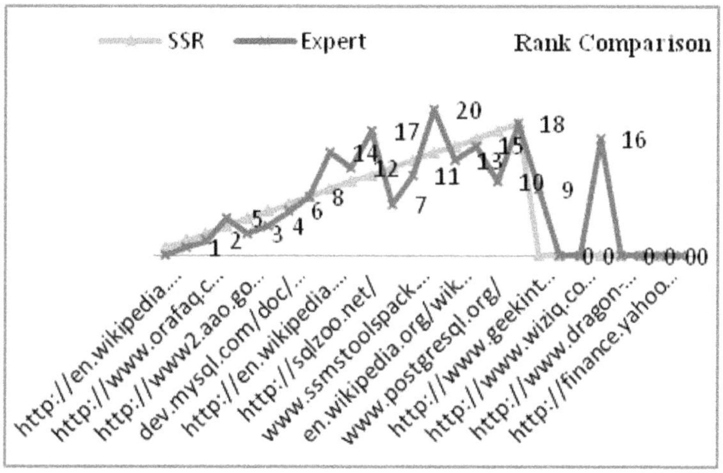

Figure 6. Results analysis of the proposed approach SSR: Frequency distribution for graded relevance judgment

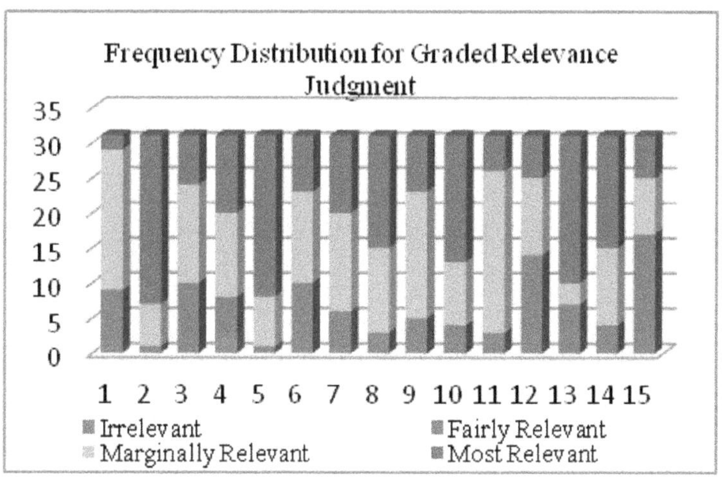

Figure 7 and Figure 8 show the upper and lower bound of the user satisfaction for retrieved results. A small area between the curves shows high-quality of user satisfaction, which answers the third question related to the user's satisfaction. Figure 7 and Figure 8 show the results of query term 'dml' while Figure 9 and Figure 10 shows the results for query terms 'sql' and 'group_by' respectively.

nDCG(n) Vectors Over a Set of Test Collection for Best, Average and Worst Cases

The graph (Figure 11) shows the normalized DCG(n) (for n=15) for two respondents' judgment data with maximum and minimum nDCG(15) measure. The curve with the blue color (upper curve) shows the best result obtained among all

Figure 7. Results analysis of the proposed approach SSR: User satisfaction (best case) –for query term 'dml'

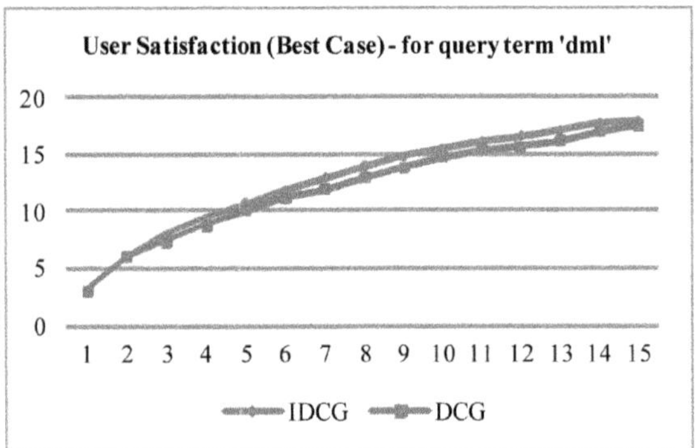

Figure 8. Results analysis of the proposed approach SSR: User satisfaction (worst case)

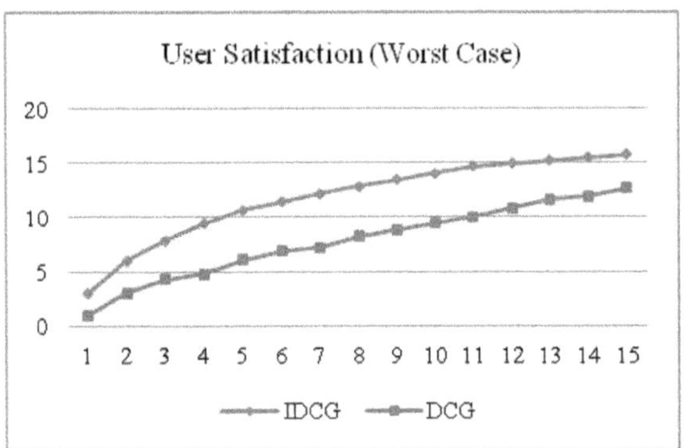

Figure 9. Results analysis of the proposed approach SSR: User satisfaction (Avg) –for query term 'sql'

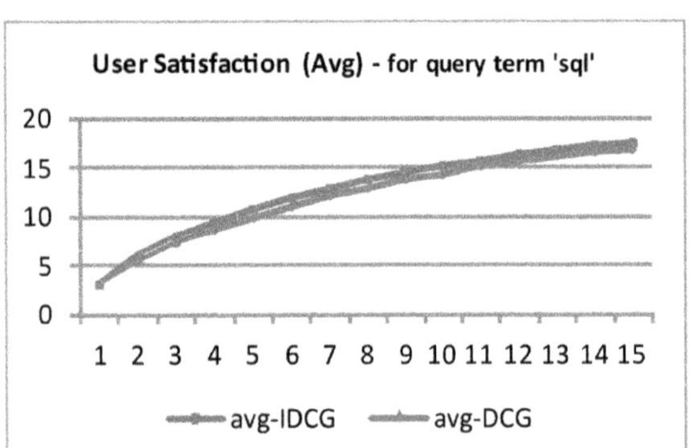

Figure 10. Results analysis of the proposed approach SSR: User Satisfaction (Avg) –for query term 'group_by'

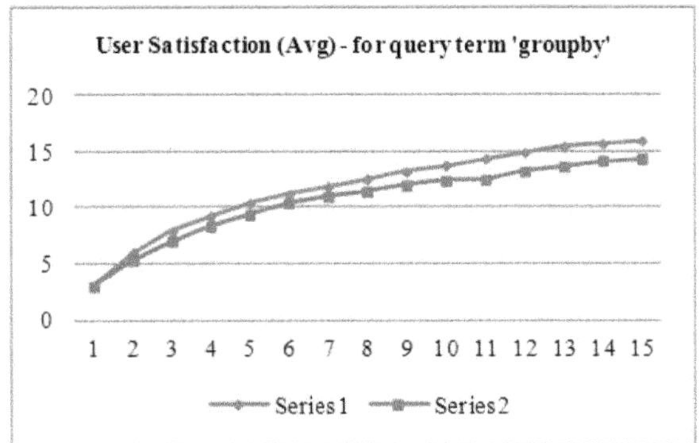

Figure 11. Results analysis of the proposed approach SSR: nDCG(n) Vectors over a set of test collection

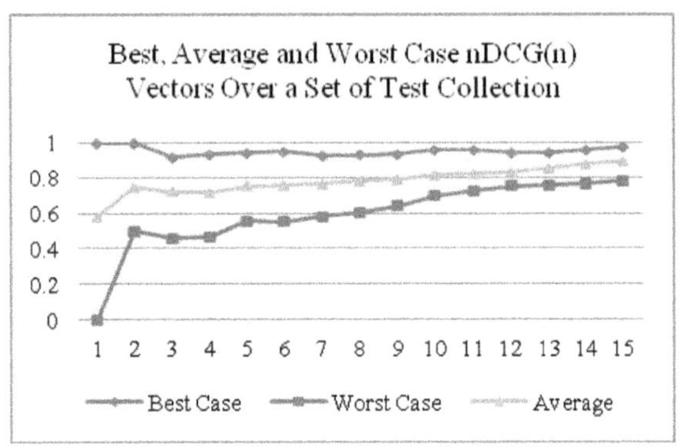

judgments which exist in close proximity to the idealistic case. Other one with red color shows the worst case lying below the best case. All other nDCG(n) values lies within these two curves. The curve with green color in Figure 11 shows avg-vect(nDCG) over the set of test collection. The average normalized DCG vector shows the average performance of a particular IR technique over a set of test queries. The curve shows that the proposed approach SSR gradually improves in ranking, although few of the initial ranks have comparatively low gain on an average.

5. CONCLUSION

An approach called Social Semantic Ranking (SSR) has been presented in this paper. It was used to rank the tagged web resources which were retrieved using a crawler as a pre-process task. It was designed to retrieve the web pages through a SBS using few seed URLs which in this case were taken from a search engine's search results. The ranks for these web resources were computed based on their Social Semantic Relevance (S2R) to the given search topic. The technique S2R has been modeled on VSM which uses domain based taxonomies expressed in ontology, and social tagging information from the downloaded web pages. These web pages were downloaded using a specially designed focused crawler called FCHC (Focus Crawling Based on Human Cognition) for crawling potentially relevant documents intended to reduce sparseness in the dataset and disk storage space as well. SSR based on S2R thus utilizes both the social and semantic information to determine the two fold relevance of web pages.

The experimental study to evaluate the ranks generated by the approach SSR was conducted on sets of queries from three domains. Seed URLs from the Google search engine and dataset downloaded from delicious.com were fed as input to the approach. The ranked web resources were then evaluated partially on a self created test collection, and rest from the experts of each domain. The self created test collection was processed using a questionnaire which was designed to judge web resources for their graded relevance with a search topic. The sample population was taken purposively consisting of 31 undergraduate students who were studying 'Databases' in their course and were beginners for the subject, which was one of the domains for experimental study. The effectiveness of SSR was measured using normalized DCG(n) (Discounted Cumulative Gain) metric. It showed average nDCG(n) above 0.8 for most of the queries used in the experimental study. On comparing the ranks computed by SSR with those given by the expert (of the query term topic) showed a remarkable Pearson correlation coefficient of 0.73 for a sample query, which shows an improvement in the ranking order.

ACKNOWLEDGMENT

Authors would like to acknowledge the Editor-in-Chief and the anonymous reviewers for their valuable suggestions to improve this paper.

REFERENCES

Agrahri, A. K., Divya, A. T. M., & Riedl, J. (2008). Can people collaborate to improve the relevance of search results? *Second ACM International Conference on Recommender Systems*. Switzerland: ACM, 283-286.

Allemang, D., & Hendler, J. (2011). *Semantic Web for the Working Ontologist. Second*. USA: Morgan Kaufmann, Elsevier.

Baeza-Yates, R., & Ribeiro-Neto, B. (1999). *Modern Information Retrieval*. Boston, MA: Addison-Wesley Longman.

Bedi, P., Hema, B., & Anjali, Thukral (2010). Social semantic retrieval and ranking of eResources. *Second International Conference on Advances in Recent Technologies in Communication and Computing*, Kerela, India: ACEEE. 343-347.

Bedi, P., Banati, H., & Thukral, A. (2010). Use of ontology for reusing web repositories for eLearning. Edited by Khaled Elleithy et al. *Technological Developments in Networking, Education and Automation*. Netherlands: Springer Netherlands. 97-101.

Bischoff, K., Firan, C. S., Nejdl, W., & Paiu, R. (2008). Can all tags be used for search? *Seventeenth ACM Conference on Information and Knowledge Management.* New York, USA: ACM, 193–202.

Chawla, S., & Bedi, P. (2008). Query expansion using Information Scent. *International Symposium on Information Technology.* Kuala Lumpur, Malaysia: IEEE Press, 1-8.

Chi, E. H., & Mytkowicz, T. (2008). Understanding the efficiency of social tagging systems using information theory. In *Nineteenth ACM Cconference on Hypertext and Hypermedia* (pp. 81–88). Pittsburgh, PA, USA: ACM. doi:10.1145/1379092.1379110

Ellis, D. (2008). The dilemma of measurement in information retrieval research. *Journal of the American Society for Information Science- Special issue: evaluation of information retrieval systems* (John Wiley & Sons, Inc) 47, no. 1: 23-36.

Firan, C. S., Nejdl, W., & Paiu, R. (2007). The benefit of using tag-based profiles. *Latin American Web Conference.* Santiago de Chile: IEEE, 32-41.

Garcia, E. (2006a). Cosine similarity and term weight. *Information Retrieval Tutorials.* http://www.miislita.com/information-retrieval-tutorial/cosine-similarity-tutorial.html

Garcia, E. (2006b). The classical vector space model. *Term Vector Theory and Keyword Weights Tutorial.* http://www.miislita.com/term-vector/term-vector-3.html

Jarvelin, K., & Kekalainen, J. (2002). Cumulated gain-based evaluation of IR techniques. *ACM Transactions on Information Systems, 20*(4), 422–446. doi:10.1145/582415.582418

Jovanović, J., Gašević, D., Torniai, C., Bateman, S., & Hatala, M. (2009). The social semantic web in intelligent learning environments: state of the art and future challenges. [Roughtledge]. *Interactive Learning Environments, 17*(4), 273–309. doi:10.1080/10494820903195140

Kazunari, S., Kenji, H., Masatoshi, Y., & Shunsuke, U. (2003). Refinement of TF-IDF schemes for web pages using their hyperlinked neighboring pages. *Fourteenth ACM conference on Hypertext and hypermedia.* Nottingham, United Kingdom: ACM, 198-207.

Kekalainen, J., & Kalervo, J. (2002). Using graded relevance assessments in IR evaluation. *Journal of the American Society for Information Science and Technology* (John Wiley & Sons) 53, no. 13: 1120–1129.

Kleinberg, J. M. (1999). Authoritative sources in a hyperlinked environment. *Journal of the ACM, 46*(5), 604–632. doi:10.1145/324133.324140

Matsuo, Y., & Ishizuka, M. (2003). Keyword extraction from a single document using word co-occurrence statistical information. *Sixteenth Interational Florida AI Research Society Conference.* St. Augustine, Florida: AAAI, 392-396.

Mohan, A., Chen, Z., & Weinberger, K. (2011). Web-search ranking with initialized gradient boosted regression trees. Edited by Olivier Chapelle, Yi Chang and Tie-Yan Liu. *JMLR: Workshop and Conference Proceedings of the Yahoo! Learning to Rank Challenge.* Haifa, Israel: Microtome Publishing, 77-89.

Pass, G., Chowdhury, A., & Torgeson, C. (2006). A picture of search. *1st international conference on Scalable information systems.* Hong Kong Spink: ACM, Article No.: 1.

Salton, G., & Buckley, C. (1987). *Term-weighting approaches in automatic text retrieval. Tech. Rep* (pp. 513–523). Ithaca, NY, USA: Cornell University.

Sanderson, M., & Braschler, M. (2009). *Best practices for test collection creation and information retrieval system evaluation. Technical Report.* Pisa, Italy: TrebleCLEF.

Shenghua, B., Guirong, X., Xiaoyuan, W., Yong, Y., Ben, F., & Zhong, S. (2007). Optimizing web search using social annotations. *Sixteenth international conference on World Wide Web, May 08-12, 2007.* Banff, Alberta, Canada: ACM, 501-510.

Thukral, A., Bedi, P., & Banati, H. (2011). Automatic organization of web resources in ontologies for lLearning purpose. *Second International Conference on e-Education, e-Business, e-Management and E-Learning (IC4E).* Mumbai, India.: IEEE, 2011. 38-44.

Thukral, A., Bedi, P., & Banati, H. (2011, April). Architecture to organize social semantic relevant web resources in a knowledge base. *International Journal of e-Education, e-Business, e-. Management Learning, 1*(1), 45–51.

Thukral, A., Mendiratta, V., Behl, A., Banati, H., & Bedi, P. (2011). FCHC: a social semantic focused crawler. *International Conference on Advances in Computing and Communications.* Kochi, India: Springer, 273-284.

Vadrevu, S., & Velipasaoglu, E. (2011). Identifying primary content from web pages and its application to web search ranking. In *WWW 2011* (pp. 135–136). Hyderabad, India: ACM. doi:10.1145/1963192.1963261

Vaughan, L. (2004). New measurements for search engine evaluation proposed and tested. [Pergamon Press]. *Information Processing and Management: an International Journal, 40*(4), 677–691. doi:10.1016/S0306-4573(03)00043-8

Yeung, C.-M., Au, M. G., Noll, N., Gibbins, C., Meinel, & Shadbolt, N. (2011). SPEAR: spamming-resistant expertise analysis and ranking in collaborative tagging systems. *International Journal of Computational Intelligence* (Wiley-Blackwell) 27, no. 3: 458-488.

Yi, L., Liangjie, Z., Ruihua, S., Jian-Yun, N., & Ji-Rong, W. "Clustering queries for better document ranking." *Eighteenth ACM conference on Information and Knowledge Management.* Hong Kong, China: ACM, 2009. 1569-1572.

This work was previously published in the International Journal of Information Retrieval Research, Volume 1, Issue 3, edited by Zhongyu (Joan) Lu, pp. 15-34, copyright 2011 by IGI Publishing (an imprint of IGI Global).

Chapter 12
Model of E-Reading Process for E-School Book in Libya

Azza Abubaker
University of Huddersfield, UK

Joan Lu
University of Huddersfield, UK

ABSTRACT

Defining the stages which the reader follows when reading e-resources is one of several factors which can provide significant insights into actual reading behaviours and cognitive processes of readers. Two different samples of students who study in Libyan primary schools, aged 9 to 12, were selected to investigate how students use and interact with both print and digital school books, identify the e-reading process, outline the aims of using the internet and technology, and define what students like and dislike in both versions. Furthermore, students found using the e-textbook to be more difficult than paper book and a significant difference is found in the reading process between paper books and electronic books. In addition, two reading strategies were used to read school book in both versions (electronic and paper): (1) view the text then answer the questions, or (2) view the questions than search for the correct answers.

1. INTRODUCTION

Reading e-texts brings several challenges to readers, such as the difficulty of reading on the screen in the case of long lines, difficulty browsing and moving from page to page, and the inability of the search tools to satisfy the needs and requirements of the reader. These aspects have drawn the attention in many research areas, such as information science, computing science, and human science. Thus, there are three categories of digital reading research:

DOI: 10.4018/978-1-4666-3898-3.ch012

1. Research focused on the usability of e-text, e.g., comparing reading on-screen to paper reading; measuring the legibility and comprehension of text (Davis, Tierney, & Chang, 2005; Dillon, 2001); and examining user behaviours in digital environments.
2. Research presented the 'new approach of technologies support reading on screen' which concentrated on new software and hardware, hypertext, and interface design (Godoy, Schiaffino, & Amandi, 2004; Scane, 2003; Thissen, 2004).
3. Finally, research focused on the phenomenology of reading, such as studying human

interaction with e-resources and the reading process in both linear text and hypertext (Carusi, 2006; Miall & Dobson, 2001).

Generally, reading is a complex activity. It requires different skills according to the purpose of reading. Furthermore, the reading scenario changes based on the type of e- materials, starting from short text reading (i.e., e-mail) to long text reading (i.e., e-books). For instance, scholarly articles are not similar to books. In the first case, readers usually skip the abstract of an article, skim the introduction, read the research problem, and subsequently read various paragraphs for the theoretical perspective. These differences in actions lead to the creation of several functions and tools to meet all reading requirements.

The aim of this study is to observe how students read school books in e-format, to accordingly investigate reading behaviours adopted by students so as to examine how students' reading behaviours change in both versions. However, understanding these changes in the reading process would support designers in their effort to design an effective computer-based learning environment.

In this work, we will attempt to build an e-reading strategy based on users' cognitive and behavioural processes. The remainder of this paper is organised as follows. First, we illustrate related work in reading e- resources behaviours. Second, we define the methodology of research and dataset for analysis. Third, we provide two reading strategy models. Finally, we summarise findings and make generalisations and recommendations for the reading process.

2. RELATED WORKS

With the increase in the number of students who read e- text for pleasure or learning, there are still deficiencies in studies that seek to understand how people deal with the digital text as previous studies have shown, i.e., most researchers in e-reading are just focused on comparing issues without having a clear idea about how readers deal with e-text or if this technology has affected the way that readers read e-text (Livingstone, 2003; Anuradha, 2006; Cavanaugh, 2006; Han, 2008; Hines, 2009; Segal-Drori, Korat et al., 2009; Shin, 2011).

Thus, researches in the field of usability are concentrated on addressing questions such as why, what and how do people read a document to be used in the first stage with any research interest, in reading generally and e-reading specifically. Also, research is focusing on cognitive and behavioural aspects of the reader by asking questions that bring issues related to the context which appears in certain factors affecting the presentation of the medium such as text layout (Hartley, 2004; Wastlund, Norlander et al., 2008; Yao-Ting Sung, 2010) and text size (Feely, Rubin et al., 2005; Alotaibi, 2006; Haboubi, Maddouri et al., 2006; Lee, Shieh et al., 2008).

Otherwise, the reading process differs according to the purpose of reading and the type of material, where Kol and Schcolink (2000) argued that understanding reading strategy and teaching students how to deal with e-text could help students read effectively from screen. This argument was supported by several empirical researchers in the reading process. For instance, Dillon (2001) built two models of the reading process, one for reading academic journals and the second manual can be seen in Figures 1 and 2. Researchers noted that there was a distinction between text types in the characterisation of usage which led to the use of various techniques when using these materials. In Dillon's case, the difference becomes clear in terms of searching the text, e.g., when reading a journal the reader starts with the title and the abstract using skim strategy, whereas in the manual the reader uses the scan technique to scan the index then select the section that contains the information required.

Moreover, Terras (2005) suggested a model relating to the process of reading ancient texts by experts through understanding a complex process

Figure 1. Generic model of journal usage (adapted from Dillon, 2001)

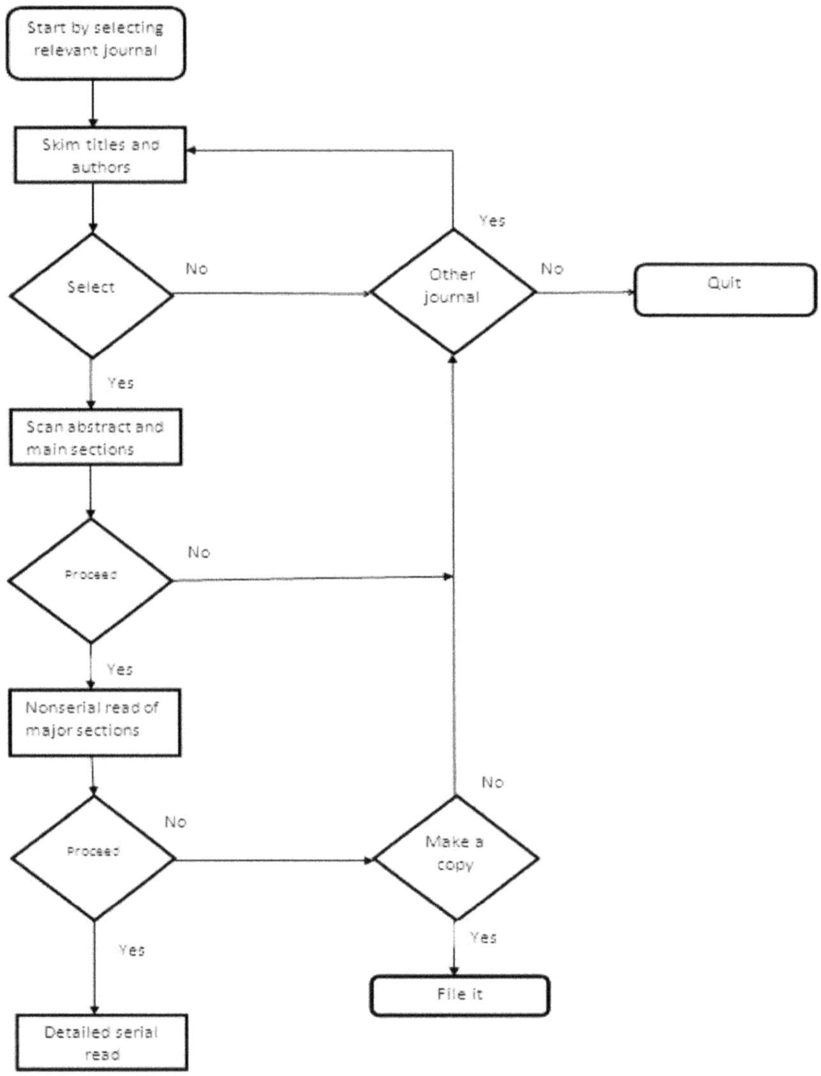

in the humanities. Based on content analysis, focused interviews and think-aloud protocols, the model were built. In addition, studies reported that three experts use different methods to examine the document; they spent a lengthy period of time checking the text and the words in different orders. In addition, they deal with visual features and then build up knowledge about the document. Additionally, the reading process is not linear and it also based on the communication of different aspects from the expert's understanding as can be seen in Figure 3. Terras implemented these findings to design a computer system that can work in several approaches, although the results are still not clear enough for building an optimal system.

In the same perspective, Harrison (2000) defined several reading behaviours, which can be classified into two types: comprehensive reading such as reading to learn and reading to critique or edit; the other type is skim reading such as reading to support listing, cross-references or to answer questions. Therefore, the reading style was added as a new variable which led to differences in reading strategies.

Figure 2. Generic model of manual usage (adapted from Dillon, 2001)

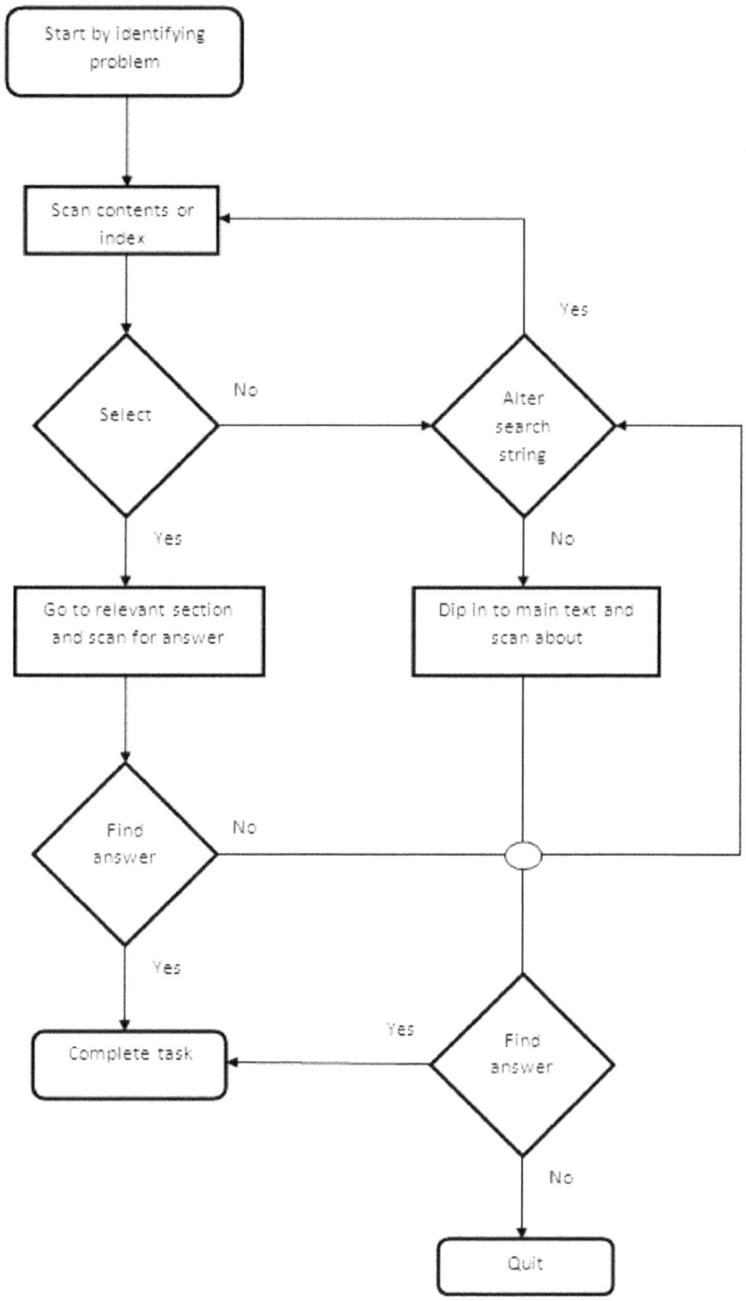

In addition, Sun (2003) discussed the effect of learning reading strategy in reading online to students with English as a second language. The researcher presented a flowchart illustrating the reading process in the system. The flowchart summarized the reading process in three stages: the pre-reading stage, the reading strategy which is divided into four steps (skimming for the gist, cultivating vocabulary, summarising and reading comprehension), and the final stage is

Figure 3. The model explains how experts read ancient texts (adapted from Terras, 2005)

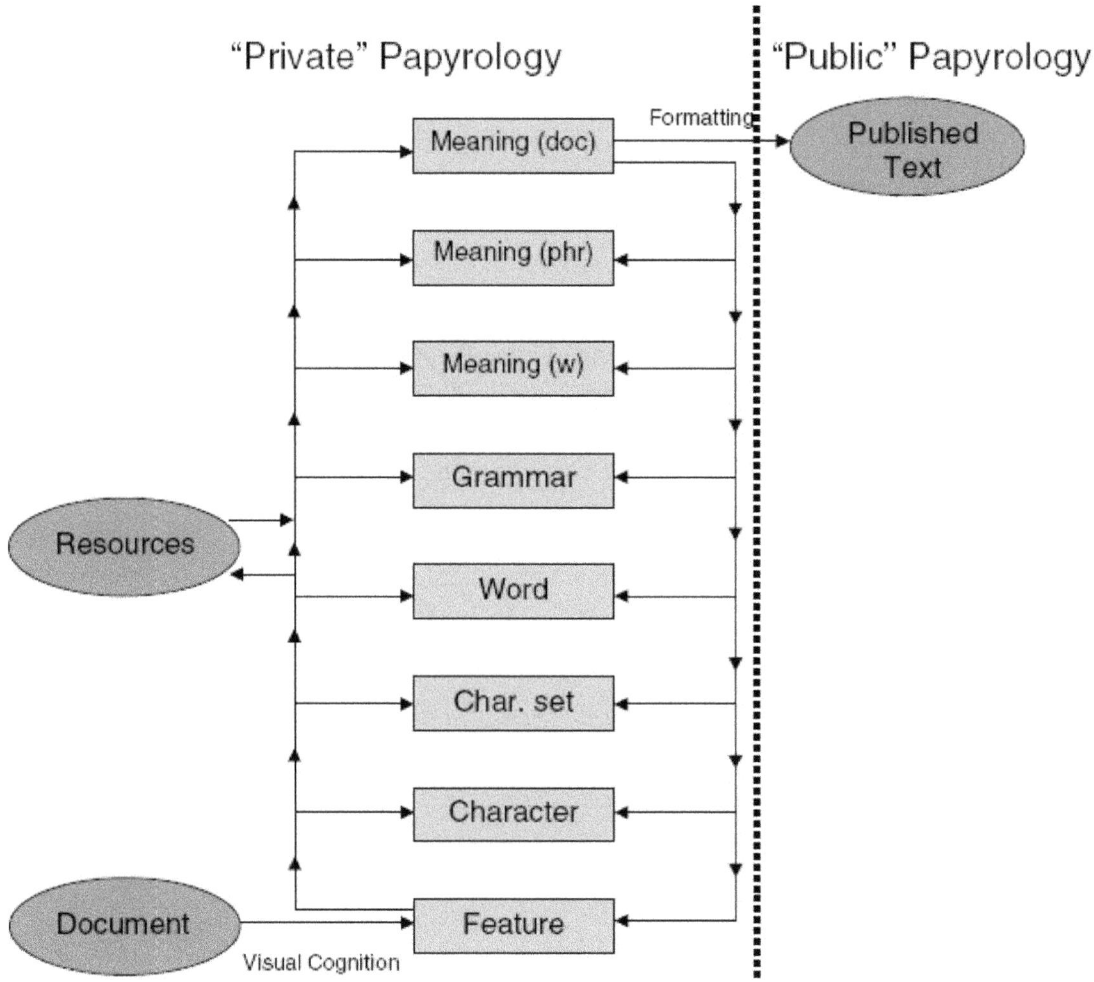

post-reading. These stages cannot be applied to all types of reading where the reading process is different depending on the information resources and the aim of reading. Therefore, these stages will help design an e-text that aims to develop rapid reading skills.

3. READING DEFINITION

From the history of research on reading topics, researchers have put forward a set of definitions to reading, but it is noteworthy that the majority focused on one side without providing a clear definition or explaining the outline of the concept of reading. One of these definitions classified reading as an active process, self-directed by the reader in many ways and for various purposes (Gibson & Levin, 1976). Others believe it is a difficult activity with a rule-based structure that must be compulsory for biological systems planned or developed for other reasons. Others consider reading as extracting information from the text. Children's reading is usually defined according to the brain structure (Frey & Fisher, 2010), where the brain is divided into three areas in the early stages of learning: the prefrontal cortex, the parietal cortex, and the cerebellum (Frey & Fisher, 2010). Therefore, reading happens only across the intentional appropriation of existing structure within the brain (Tomasello, 2008).

Generally, reading aims to create a comprehensive understanding of the text. This requires from the designer of the text a good textual organization, a clear structure, and a clear relation between words.

Based on the above, reading is both a bodily and mental process, and it is difficult to describe because it is one of those deep and difficult phenomena. Moreover, it is a complex communication between the script and the reader which is molded by the reader's previous knowledge, skills, approach, and language community which is socially located. The complexity of the process of reading can be attributed to the absence of a comprehensive definition.

4. READING PROCESS THROUGH E-TEXT

The other issue that drew the attention of researchers in the field of e-reading is the reading process of hypertext. Using hypertexts raises several issues relating to their impacts and ability to improve the accessibility of information in e-environments and reading processes.

For example, De Stefano and LeFevre (2007) presented a model showing the order of the steps that the reader follows when reading hypertext (Figure 4) where the model appears according to the amount of nodes and how the reading process is distinct when reading in a hypertext structure.

Alternatively, the construction integration model received much attention among researchers on hypertext comprehension. The model pointed to several elements that affect the text comprehension, with an emphasis on prior knowledge and coherence as key elements affecting comprehension (Yoh, Damhorst et al., 2003). However, most research used these two models to define reading stages on hypertext by analysing navigation path, order of reading, the number of nodes that the reader followed to access the information showing the effect of prior knowledge, and reader skills and education level in the path of reading. For instance, the impact of hypertext on academic reading remains unclear, although there are several researchers who argue that reading in an e-environment becomes more and more an interac-

Figure 4. The process model of hypertext reading (adapted from De Stefano & LeFebvre, 2005)

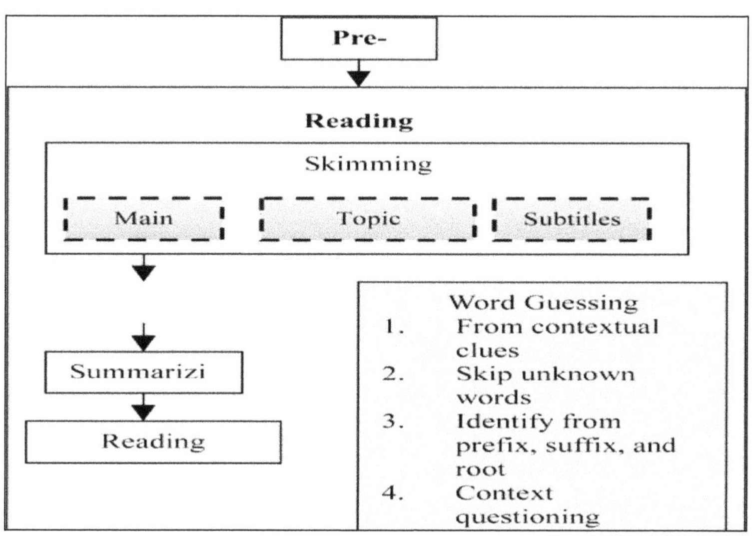

tive process (Patterson, 2000) which can engage a reader in having a further authorial role and which ultimately induces decision-making processes (De Stefano & LeFevre, 2007).

However, the design of hypertext in e-learning materials requires a good understanding of human cognition features, such as previous knowledge, memory structure, and the ability to impress in terms of the organisation of information.

In addition, numerous studies in visual research investigating the influence of the total number of nods on the process of browsing, reading and learning by measuring the speed of the search for information or word, concluded that there is an inverse relationship between the number of links and cognitive loads (Ajen, 1985; Amin, 2000; Clinton, Branch et al., 2003; Ni, Branch et al., 2004; De Stefano & LeFevre, 2007).

Alternatively, learners are more positive with fewer nodes in comprehension reading (Ajen, 2002). On the other hand, the reading time is not affected by the number of links. For instance, this requires from the designer creating a map that illustrates the path of the reader in the text or determining the strength of the relationship between the text and links.

Finally, there are different types of hypertext: (1) hierarchical hypertext; (2) additional links; (3) semantic links; and (4) networked hypertext. Each of these types has a different effect according to the type of text and the reason for reading. For example, hierarchical is better for readers' memory than network.

5. COMPARISON BETWEEN READING ONLINE AND FROM PAPER

There are two thoughts on the field of reading. The first thought believes that paper will never be replaced by e-text. This might be due to the ease and flexibility of using the p-book. For instance, controlling paper book is achieved by physical ability, by using fingers to turn a piece of paper, holding one finger in a unit as a location support, or flicking over tens of sections, whereas browsing the contents of a text is hard to activate or unachievable for lack of electronic support. Although developing the electronic manuscript might include using a mouse and scroll bar in one application, one might require menu selection and page numbers whilst another supports touch-sensitive buttons. Hypertext manipulation of large electronic text can be quick and easy while other systems might take longer to refresh the display after the execution of the next sheet (Dillon, 2001).

Alternatively, the second thought believes that e-book will be replaced by the p-version, and they build their thought based on several advantages of the e-book such as ease of storage and retrieval (Liu, 2005; Tenopir, King, Edwards, & Wu, 2009). Also, it has the ability to use several features such as sound, animations, and hotspots.

However, it can be observed that the arguments provided by each team to support this point of view differ. For instance, defenders of p-book see that the p-book is better in terms of ease of handling and taking notes, but it is not as good in terms of search or storage as the e-book. Otherwise, supporters of the e-book see that the e-book is easy to navigate especially when using it for academic purposes. Therefore, there must be a third approach, which should propose that the e-book would not replace the p-book but the two versions will complement each other in order to satisfy the needs of readers. The evidence that supports this belief are many, e.g., when university students search for specific information they prefer using e-text but they will read it as p-version (Nicholas et al., 2008). But, it should also be working to improve the way of displaying text on screen through defining the barriers that effect legibility on screen.

On the other hand, Dillon (2001) draws a clear mark in the field, by providing a comprehensive view on the empirical literature on reading from paper against screens. This was followed by Muter (1996) and Dyson (2004) who examined the relation between the layout of the text and reading from screen.

Even though reading online offers clear advantages to readers, there are still a lot of challenges facing the reader when using e- media. Examining most of the studies comparing reading in both versions show mixed results. Most research findings in this area (Crestani, Landoni, & Melucci, 2006; Landoni, 1997; Truong, 2009; Wilson, Landoni, & Gibb, 2003) showed that reading from screen takes more time, without giving any explanations about the reasons behind it.

Consequently, the online reading environment has specific characteristics that make it different from reading papers. Some researchers such as Clarke (2001) reported that presenting text on a screen is broadly similar to displaying it on a page with a number of differences such as quality, size, and orientation. This might be the main cause of poor reading on screen. Therefore, using the structure of paper book to display on screen failed for three reasons: (1) technical aspects such as less space in screen than a page and the difficulty of displaying a large quantity of texts on screen; (2) users aspect is related to human aspects which affect reading on a screen such as previous knowledge on the topic, age, memory structure and stages; (3) content: this factor relates to the size and type of information where computer–based learning is not suitable for displaying large quantities of texts (Clarke, 2001).

Alternatively, reviewing the empirical evidence and theory on reading online shows that there are distinctions between paper and PC reading processes (Dillon, 2001; Wright, 1988). In addition, study on optimization of reading has been done with paper and then circulated on the electronic version (Frenckner, 1990). Therefore, comparison between conventional view of the text and e-text has been used as a starting point to examine reading on screen (Dyson, 2004). These researchers almost focused on comparisons in their research without investigating the variables that effect reading from screen. At the same time, M.C. Dyson focused on the typographic variables related to text formats on paper and screen such as line length, columns, and window size.

Consistent with prior research, it is notable that these researchers had been unable to provide answers to many questions such as how children read and use e-textbooks, what affective factors impact e-reading, and how children feel about the e-textbook. To consider such questions, in this research we will examine e-reading strategies that use reading e- textbook in Libyan schools to build an e-reading model and investigate the format factors that impact reading Arabic text from screen by examining the effect of font size and type in accuracy and reading speed. We also look at defining readable font size to build guidelines to help designers design effective e-learning materials using the Arabic language which can enhance e-textbook reading.

6. FOLLOW-UP SURVEY

6.1. Methods

This survey explores online reading practices of the students while using electronic and paper school text books where the main aim is to investigate students' interactions with e-books.

Qualitative approaches were used to investigate the causes of the phenomenon and the way it occurs. On the other hand, deductive and inductive approach is used in this research as a strategy, because it provides more flexibility to weaving back and forth between data and theory for linking theory with research.

6.1.1. Objectives of the Follow-Up Study

The main objectives of this follow- up survey could be summarised as follows:

- Investigate how easy or difficult it is to use e-books by observing how students interact with school books in the two versions [electronic and print].

- Measure participants' achievements in both versions by investigating how students use and interact with both print and digital school books.
- Examine if any differences existed in terms of preferences over book formats.
- Explore students' perceptions and impressions of certain features, such as a browsable and searchable book in the two versions.
- Define what students like and dislike in both versions; and
- Identify the e-reading process.

6.1.2. Focus of Observation

In order to ensure that all data needed to achieve the aims of survey was collected, the observation schedule was designed to guide the observation process (Table 1). The main point considered in this observation was defining how students interact with school books through examining three different scenarios: prepare the lesson; discuss the lesson; and read the lesson to extract the answer.

- Observing the way that students follow the lesson and the time it takes for each method that they used.

Table 1. Presented observation schedule to collecting data

Observing targets	Method	Time	Notes
Access to lessons			
Browsing the text			
Extract the words or answer			
Tools support reading			

- Observing procedures that students follow when browsing the text in different versions.
- Noting the techniques used to extract the word or concept from the lesson.
- Detecting the tools that students use to support reading steps and examine their effect in each steps of the reading.

6.1.3. Data Collection Methods

As mentioned earlier, the explanatory sequential design is used to answer research questions. The qualitative approach has been chosen as the research approach for this survey, for this approach mainly focuses on the phenomenological perspective that can be detected, described, measured, and statistically studied (Remenyi, Williams, Money, & Swartz, 1998).

6.1.3.1. Design Collecting Method

The participants carried out three different observations, which required dividing the participants into eight groups, each of which comprised 10 participants. Four groups used e-books (http://skooollibya.com/), while the other four groups used paper versions. During the first observations, participants were asked to prepare a lesson for discussion in class. They were given an open time to complete the task. The next day, teachers discussed the lesson with students and provided explanations, which lasted 45 minutes. Finally, the students were asked to search the text, answer the questions, and take a small quiz. Figure 5 shows the steps involved in the follow-up study.

The talk-aloud technique was used in order to identify users' cognitive and behavioural processes, and to collect quantitative data, which could not be obtained via any other method. It was also used to obtain more in-depth details from participants, such as describing their actions and reactions to the book interface, and where students were asked to describe whatever they are reacting

Figure 5. Showing the follow-up survey stages

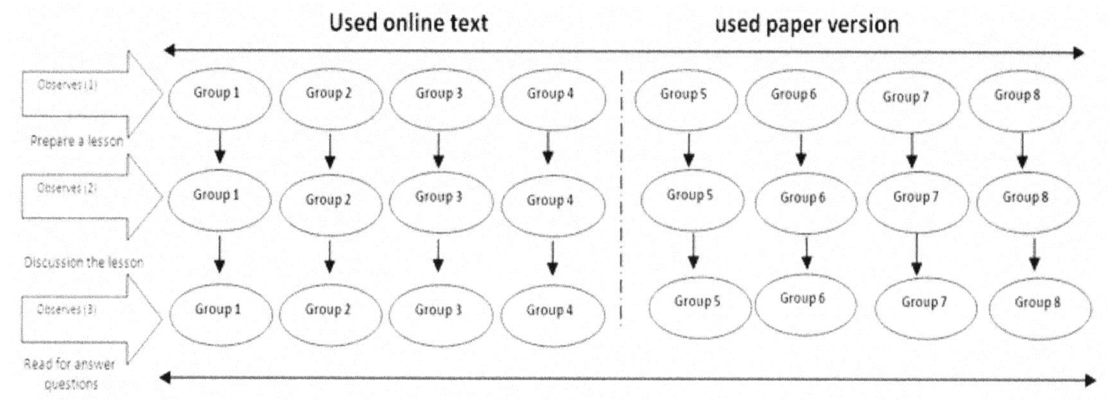

to, acting out, thinking about without trying to interpret their actions. In addition, students in each group sit in a straight line to facilitate the observation process.

6.1.4. Sampling

In order to follow-up and investigate in-depth users' cognitive behaviours with e-books, a sample of 80 participants—all of whom were considered more confident with e-books and who answered the questionnaire—was selected and distributed as follows:

- 46 males, thereby representing 57.5%; and 34 females, thereby representing 42.5%;
- The age of participants was between 9 and 13 years;
- The sample was distributed across the three studying stages: level 4 comprised 20 students; level 5 comprised 40 students; and level 6 comprised 20 students. These distributions are shown in Table 2.

Table 2. Presenting samples by gender and education levels

Education levels	Male	Female	Total
Level 4	13	7	20
Level 5	21	19	40
Level 6	12	8	20

6.1.5. Material Selection

The survey concerned the use of primary school books within Libya, which has been examined in order to recognise the main characteristics of such books and the overall structure of the text so as to obtain a clearer picture from the analysis of the content of the books and to accordingly highlight the aims of the education system. Table 3 shows the distribution of school books at each level. The e- version of the school books is available at http://skooollibya.com/.

6.1.6. Analysis of Structure of School Book

School books differ from other types of resources by way of presentation of information, the amount of information, and the structure of the content.

The author has examined a random sample from the school book in order to identify the main combination of school books, and has provided a document model, as shown in Figure 6, which illustrates the document in a top-down method, complete with independent descriptions of the

Table 3. Distribution of subjects studied at each level

School levels	Models									
	Math	Science	Reading	Grammar	History	English	Geographic	Religion	Computer		
Level 1	/	/	/					/			4
Level 2	/	/	/					/			4
Level 3	/	/	/					/			4
Level 4	/	/	/	/	/	/	/	/	/	/	10
Level 5	/	/	/	/	/	/	/	/	/	/	10
Level 6	/	/	/	/	/	/	/	/	/	/	10
Total											42

document elements. The document's content is expressed in a set of parts. The document's contents are divided into many parts. The text part is divided into many sections, such as the Table of Contents and Lessons. Each lesson component comprises several sections, and each section breaks down into paragraphs, with each paragraph combining sentences which are broken down into words. Each lesson ends with questions that summarized a whole lesson. In addition, each document then comprises a hierarchical structure of abstraction levels, with each level representing elements in the document. However, the analysis of the school books shows the following:

- The majority of the books' content in the first three levels comprises images, limited exercises, which mean the focus is on colour dynamics and flexibility.
- The books of levels 4, 5 and 6 are completely different to those of other levels in many aspects, such as the technique in which information is offered and organised, the structure, and the amount and types of information—all of which require the use

Figure 6. Structure of textbook

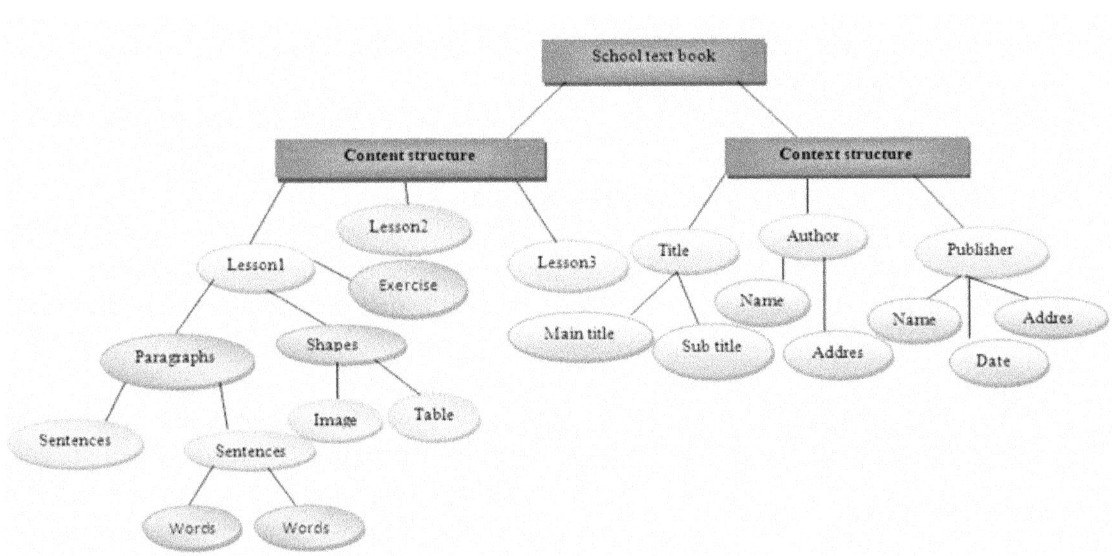

of different software, such as HTML and PDF. In addition, using links to other lessons helps students to review information from lower or higher level.

Generally, there is no particular order or rules to follow when designing e-text which is usually dependent on the subject, purpose of the text, age of reader, size of the text and screen size. Alternatively, the structure of e-learning material usually depends on what the education system is aiming to achieve. In many cases, learning material is presented as a package and mainly relies on itself to transmit understanding to the learner. This special structure of the educational material requires from designers the creation of a method for displaying the content which can help the learner to access and define the relation between content of learning packages.

Table 4. Showing participants' opinions about e-version of school book compared to paper version

	E- book		P- book	
	yes	No	yes	No
Easy to use	25%	75%	88%	12%
Can use it without any help	44%	66%	93%	7%
Easy to search	9%	91%	67%	43%
Easy to find answers	12%	88%	67%	33%
Sound helps to learn	19%	81%	-	-
Easy to extract information	26%	74%	55%	45%

7. DATASET ANALYSIS

7.1. Using E-Books and Paper Books in Primary Education

The use of paper versions is still the first choice for readers. For instance, Perry reports that 84% of participants preferred using a paper version. Alternatively, students in primary schools in Libya are also more confident when using paper school books, as can be seen in Table 4 and Figure 7. Furthermore, 75% of participants found using the e-version very difficult, whilst 88% of participants could not deal with the paper book easily. Navigation is another challenge which participants face with the e-versions, with 91% of respondents finding the transition from one page to another difficult, which in turn influences the communication between students and teachers. On the other hand, 67% of participants found browsing the lessons easier in the paper version. Moreover, identifying the location of information in both versions was not easy, but was more difficult with the e-book (74%) compared to the paper book (45%).

Figure 7. Participants' opinions about e-version of school book compared to paper version

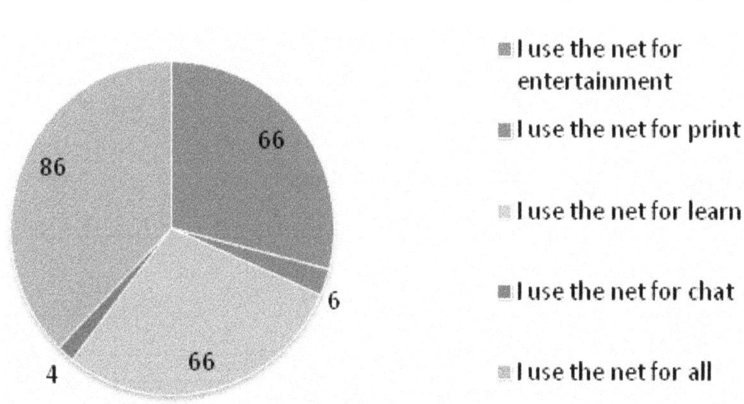

Moreover, there are several factors contributing to students' performance when reading paper versions of school books, some of which relate to technical aspects such as cohesion of content, linking, navigation, screen layout, segmentation of data, interface design, and location of data. On the other hand, there are personal or human aspects which affect reading on a screen such as previous knowledge on the topic, age, memory structure and stages.

However, paper books usually have a good structure and use the same structure to design e-materials, which are not the most suitable method for several reasons: the printed method has a long history, and was improved over time to become more efficient for readers by taking into account many different aspects such as reader behaviour, reading process, and types of reading.

In order to improve reading on-screen, student behaviours need to be studied at the first stage in order to define their reading process. This requires clarification of the reading stages which the student follows, and accordingly could define the reading strategy used.

In order to investigate the strategies of reading used by students, two questions were asked: 'Do you read the lesson first? Or do you read the questions first?' Table 5 presents the reading strategy used by students in Libyan primary schools. 65.8% of participants always read the lesson first and then answer the questions, whereas 34.1% read the questions first. Usually, both strategies are used by students based on the purpose of reading, e.g., if the student is reading for an exam, he/she will read the questions first, whereas if reading for understanding, they would then read the lesson first.

7.2. Reading Process

The survey reports that there are several scenarios used when reading a school book. These scenarios are built based upon the purpose of using the school book: the school book is always used at school or home. In each case, the purpose of use is different.

- **Use at School:** At school, the teacher also directs students by telling them the page number, the lesson title, the number of questions, and so forth. These stages, in this case, were controlled by the teacher.
- **Use at Home:** At home, some students get support from their parents, whilst others do not. In both cases, students use reading for two purposes: firstly, to memorise the lessons taught at school; or for preparing the next lesson. In the case of the latter, the teacher prefers comprehensive reading. Notably, 34.1% of students simply read the questions when they have an exam.

Thus, how the students use the school book changes according to where the book is read (at

Table 5. Reading strategy used by students

Strategies	Read the lesson first			Read the question first								
levels												
	Always	usually	Sometimes	Always	usually	Sometimes						
	N	P	N	P	N	P	N	P	N	P	N	P
Level 4	92	18.2	22	4.3	20	3.9	16	3.1	32	6.3	44	8.7
Level 5	104	20.6	50	9.9	26	5.1	88	17.4	60	11.9	32	6.3
Level 6	136	26.9	36	7.1	18	3.5	68	13.4	48	9.5	64	12.6
total	332	65.8	108	21.4	64	12.6	172	34.1	140	27.7	140	27.7

school or home), and why they read it (extract information or read to learn).

The survey reported that students use three strategies when reading the school book: comprehensive strategy; skimming strategy; and scanning strategy. Using these strategies differ according to two elements: the aim of reading and the book type (electronic or paper). For example, scanning strategy in both versions is preferred when reading to extract information to answer questions (47%), whereas 80% of participants who use the e-book and 87.5% of participants who use the paper version prefer using comprehensive strategy when reading the lesson for the first time.

In addition, participants who used the e-book record a higher average in terms of time compared to students who used the paper book. This may be due to using a paper structured book without applying the tools to support the reading, e.g., the average comprehensive reading for the whole lesson in an e-book was 25 min., while to do the same task in a paper book would take just 15 min.

Furthermore, it is notable that using a comprehensive strategy was difficult in the case of reading an online text where the text is divided into various segments which make for browsing back and forward and thus takes a longer time than the paper version. On the other hand, there are no different records between the two versions when scanning or skimming the text. Table 6 shows the percentage of using each strategy by students and the average time taken to read according to the selected approach.

Finally, during the reading it is noted that students used different techniques such as take notes, highlight text, write the answers on the same page, or ask questions. These techniques are affected by the reading scenario, e.g., participants using paper tended to take notes in the book when they read the lesson for the sake of preparing the lesson or reading for discussion as seen in Table

Table 6. Presenting the strategy used in different reading scenarios and the medium time

Reading strategies	e-book group						P-book group					
	Prepare lesson		Reading for discussion		Reading for answering questions		Prepare lesson		Reading for discussion		Reading for answering questions	
	P	T	P	T	P	T	P	T	P	T	P	T
Comprehensive strategy	80%	25M	25%	21M	10%	29M	87.5%	15M	7.5%	6M	-	-
Skimming strategy	7.5%	24M	32.5%	20M	42.5%	20M	2.5%	10M	37.5%	4M	32.5%	4M
Scanning strategy	12.5%	20M	42.5%	22M	47.5%	25M	10%	9M	55%	3M	67.5%	3M

Table 7. Illustrating the techniques used by students during reading

Reading strategies	e-book group			P-book group		
	Prepare lesson	Reading for discussion	Reading for answering questions	Prepare lesson	Reading for discussion	Reading for answering questions
	P	P	P	P	P	P
Taking notes in the book	-	-	-	73%	80%	3%
Highlight words	-	-	-	89%	89%	1%
Write the answer in the school book	-	-	-	10%	13%	93%
Taking notes in note book	-	54%	72%	-	9%	5%

Figure 8. Reading strategies of paper school book

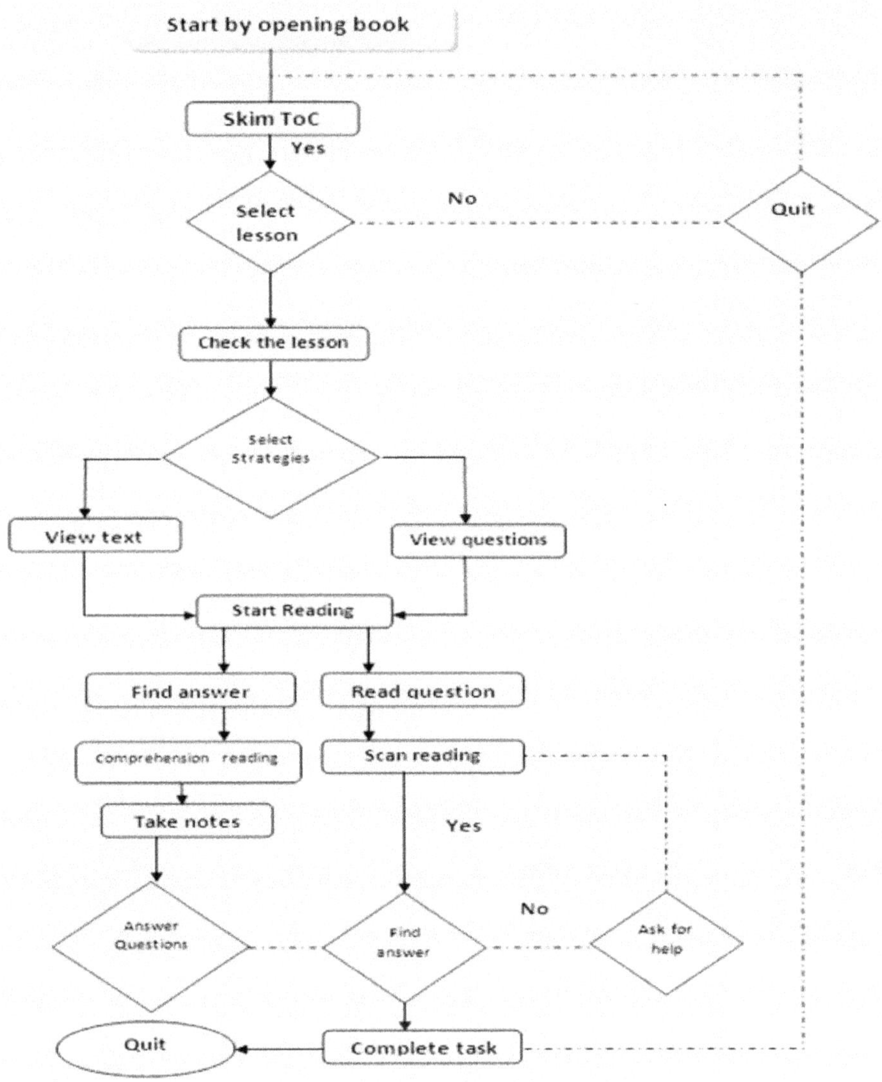

7. In addition, highlighting words or concepts in the text is preferred by students where 89% of participants use this technique during reading. On the other hand, students who used the e-book version were not able to use this technique in spite of the students who would prefer that. Also, the teacher tended not to let students use Microsoft Word for taking notes because this will not lead to improvement in handwriting or spelling which are necessary for students at this level of education. Table 7. Illustrating the techniques used by students during reading

7.2.1. Flow Chart of Reading Process

Figure 8 summarises the school book reading stage used by students at school or at home, which starts with opening the book and skimming the Table of Contents. 54.7% of participants always use the ToC to access the lesson, whereas 11% of participants access the lesson using the page

Figure 9. E-reading strategy model for e- school book

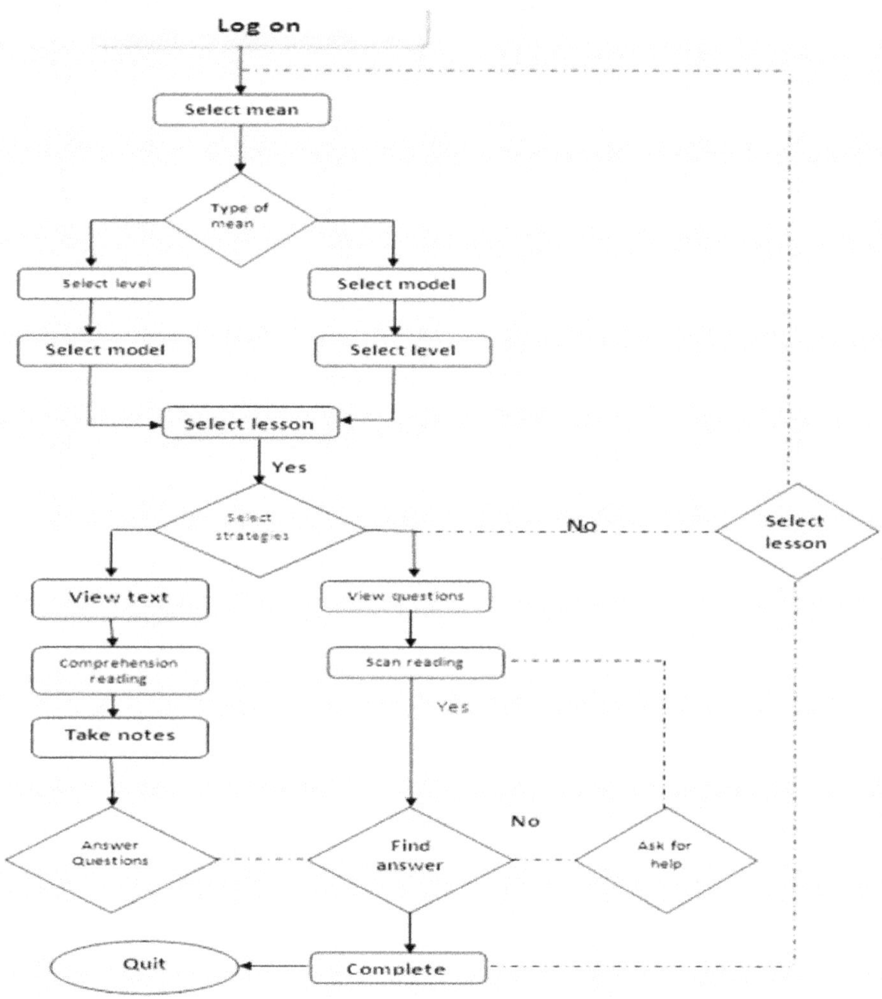

numbers when using the book at home. In the case of using the book at school, usually the teacher tells the students the number of the page where 85% of students did not use the TOC. Subsequently, students usually check lessons by identifying the subtitle, how long it is, and the number of questions before starting to read. This technique is also used when students read the lesson for the first time. In addition, when students decide to read the lesson, there are two ways to view the text, as the survey reports: either by viewing the text or viewing the questions. In each case, students use different reading methods.

On the other hand, based on qualitative feedback, the e-reading strategy for the school books was built. Figure 9 shows a generic description of the e-school book reading strategy, which starts by viewing the homepage of the system. Subsequently, students can access the book by viewing the models and then selecting the level, or by otherwise viewing the education levels and then selecting the model. The first action will be opening the book. At this point, the student has two options: to view the text or to view the questions. In the case of viewing the questions, the students will access the questions which link to the parts that include the answer rather than answering the questions, simply because the aim is to encourage students to read. Notably, if students select and view the text, they will then start with the introduction to the lesson before going through the lesson and learning the main bulk. Students can make notes and save those notes. This function was not available in the book used in this test where students used paper for taking some notes during reading which confused them.

Finally, there are no changes required in user needs when students read either the paper version of school books or e-versions, but the change appears in the way that students interact with the material. However, the student reading action changes in each version; this makes a difference in the overall reading process. For example, the page number is the main tool used by students to access the book content in the paper version, and just 54% of participants use ToC while in e-book the number of page does not support the reading process. On the other hand, in the case of the e-version, students access the lesson by means of lessons. Thus, defining the reading process can help define searching and reading steps. In the searching steps, students frequently search for a title or subtitle, or question and answer; this requires searching the content for concepts and titles. In the reading stage, students exploit two reading strategies: scanning and comprehension strategies.

8. DISCUSSION

As can be noted here, there are two reading strategies used to read the school book in both versions (electronic and paper): (1) view the text and then answer the questions; or (2) view the questions and then search for the correct answer. In the first case, students made a comprehensive reading of the whole text, during which he/she took some notes (where the kind and amount of notes differ according to the education levels) using different techniques, and when he/she is done with reading the text, he/she then turns to the questions. During this process, the student needs to check the notes that he/she took through reading the text to see if it includes the answer to the question which requires taking notes and saving these notes. In some cases, they may check the text to make sure of some information. Therefore, the text in this case should be presented in a way that allows the student to view the text quickly and simply which requires from designer taking care about the layout and the amount of text that should be displayed on the screen.

On the other hand, the findings of this research support the idea that the reading process is different according to the readers' characters and education level, e.g., the reading process was completely different to that presented by Dillon for using text in journal and manual (Dillon, 2001) or to that presented by Terras for reading ancient texts (Terras, 2005). Moreover, taking notes through reading was the common element between all academic reading processes except that the teachers in the first stage of education prefer using paper for taking notes to improve students' handwriting and spelling skills. On the other hand, in the school book reading process, students in both versions used various reading strategies, which should be considered when designing an e- school book by applying tools and structures that can support all the reading strategies.

In addition, presenting the text and questions in different windows should be avoided since browsing up and down has a negative effect on reading speed and distracts the attention among students.

On the other hand, several negative remarks regarding students' performance have been recorded when using the e-text school book:

- Fear and caution when browsing the e-book while the group who used the paper version are more confident when turning the pages.
- Students who used e-book take a longer time than those who used the paper version.

- Teachers in the e-book group spent more time to complete the lesson where students need help to find their path through the lesson.

9. CONCLUSION

The two styles of reading presented in this work are based on the usability theories that focus on understanding and analysing the attitudes and behaviours of the users. The general conclusion is that the reading process changes according to the reading purpose and type of recourse. In this study, students usually use two strategies when reading a school book: scanning and comprehension reading strategies. Each strategy requires specific tools and techniques, such as highlighting the sentence, taking notes, or using a finger when reading the text. However, these models will not only help to define the interaction amongst users and e-books, but will also help the designer to understand user behaviour of e-books and thereby to establish the most appropriate functions when building an e-book interface. Reading e-texts takes longer than reading the same text on paper which effectively means more research to determine the weaknesses that lead to the slowness in reading an online text. In addition, the survey reported differences in the reading process between e-book and p-book, which seem to have resulted from the difference in the designing of the text and the tools that are used.

FURTHER WORK

In the next stage of the research, the following questions will be asked:

1. What are the key elements to consider when designing an e-school book interface?
2. How should e-school books be designed to improve satisfaction, information recall, levels of confusion, and mental overload?
3. Measuring the factors that affect reading an e-text.
4. What are the factors that slow down reading an online text?

REFERENCES

Carusi, A. (2006). A comparison of hypertext theory and phenomenology of reading. *Arts and Humanities in Higher Education*, *5*(2), 163–180. doi:10.1177/1474022206063652

Clarke, A. (2001). *Designing computer- based learning materials*. London, UK: Gower.

Crestani, F., Landoni, M., & Melucci, M. (2006). Appearance and functionality of electronic books. *International Journal on Digital Libraries*, *6*(2), 192–209. doi:10.1007/s00799-004-0113-9

Davis, J., Tierney, A., & Chang, E. (2005). *A user adaptable user interface model to support ubiquitous user access to EIS style applications.* Paper presented at the Computer Software and Applications Conference

De Stefano, D., & LeFevre, J. (2007). Cognitive load in hypertext reading: A review. *Computers in Human Behavior*, *23*, 1616–1641. doi:10.1016/j.chb.2005.08.012

Dillon, A. (2001). *Designing usable electronic text: ergonomic aspects of human information usage*. London, UK: Taylor & Francis.

Dyson, M. C. (2004). How physical text layout affects reading from screen. *Behaviour & Information Technology*, *23*(6), 377–393. doi:10.1080/01449290410001715714

Frenckner, K. (1990). *Legibility of continuous text on computer screens -- a guide to the literature* (Tech. Rep. No. TRITA-NA-P9010). Stockholm, Sweden: Royal Institute of Technology.

Godoy, D., Schiaffino, S., & Amandi, A. (2004). Interface agents personalizing web-based tasks – special issue on intelligent agents and data mining for cognitive systems. *Cognitive Systems Research*, *5*, 207–222. doi:10.1016/j.cogsys.2004.03.003

Landoni, M. (1997). *The visual book system: a study of the use of visual rhetoric in the design of electronic books*. Glasgow, UK: University of Strathclyde.

Liu, X. (2005). Reading behaviour in the digital environment: changes in reading behaviour over the past ten years. *The Journal of Documentation*, *61*(6), 700–712. doi:10.1108/00220410510632040

Miall, D. S., & Dobson, T. S. (2001). Reading hypertext and the experience of literature. *Journal of Digital Information*, *2*(1).

Muter, P. (1996). *Interface design and optimization of reading of continuous text*. Retrieved from http://www.psych.utoronto.ca/users/muter/pmuter1.htm

Nicholas, D., Rowlands, I., Clark, D., Huntington, P., Jamali, H. R., & Olle, C. (2008). UK scholarly e-book usage: A landmark survey. *Aslib Proceedings*, *60*(4), 311–334. doi:10.1108/00012530810887962

Remenyi, D., Williams, B., Money, A., & Swartz, E. (1998). *Doing research in business and management: an introduction to process and method*. London, UK: Sage.

Scane, J. L. P. R. (2003). *User interface design*. London, UK: Crucial, a division of Learning Matters.

Sun, Y. C. (2003). Extensive reading online: an overview and evaluation. *Journal of Computer Assisted Learning*, *19*, 438–446. doi:10.1046/j.0266-4909.2003.00048.x

Tenopir, C., King, D. W., Edwards, S., & Wu, L. (2009). Electronic journals and changes in scholarly article: seeking and reading patterns. *Aslib Proceedings*, *61*, 5–32. doi:10.1108/00012530910932267

Terras, M. (2005). Reading the readers: Modelling complex humanities processes to build cognitive system. *Literary and Linguistic Computing*, *20*(1), 41–59. doi:10.1093/llc/fqh042

Thissen, F. (2004). *Screen design manual: communicating effectively through multimedia*. New York, NY: Springer.

Truong, Y. (2009). An evaluation of the theory of planned behaviour in consumer acceptance of online video and television services. *Electronic Journal Information Systems Evaluation*, *12*(2), 177–186.

Wilson, R., Landoni, M., & Gibb, F. (2003). The WEB Book experiments in electronic textbook design. *The Journal of Documentation*, *59*(4), 454–476. doi:10.1108/00220410310485721

Wright, P., & Lickorish, A. (1988). Colour cues as location aids in lengthy texts on screen and paper. *Behaviour & Information Technology*, *7*, 11–30. doi:10.1080/01449298808901860

This work was previously published in the International Journal of Information Retrieval Research, Volume 1, Issue 3, edited by Zhongyu (Joan) Lu, pp. 35-53, copyright 2011 by IGI Publishing (an imprint of IGI Global).

Chapter 13
The Effect of Stemming on Arabic Text Classification:
An Empirical Study

Abdullah Wahbeh
Dakota State University, USA

Qasem Al-Radaideh
Yarmouk University, Jordan

Mohammed Al-Kabi
Yarmouk University, Jordan

Emad Al-Shawakfa
Yarmouk University, Jordan

Izzat Alsmadi
Yarmouk University, Jordan

ABSTRACT

The information world is rich of documents in different formats or applications, such as databases, digital libraries, and the Web. Text classification is used for aiding search functionality offered by search engines and information retrieval systems to deal with the large number of documents on the web. Many research papers, conducted within the field of text classification, were applied to English, Dutch, Chinese, and other languages, whereas fewer were applied to Arabic language. This paper addresses the issue of automatic classification or classification of Arabic text documents. It applies text classification to Arabic language text documents using stemming as part of the preprocessing steps. Results have showed that applying text classification without using stemming; the support vector machine (SVM) classifier has achieved the highest classification accuracy using the two test modes with 87.79% and 88.54%. On the other hand, stemming has negatively affected the accuracy, where the SVM accuracy using the two test modes dropped down to 84.49% and 86.35%.

1. INTRODUCTION

The tremendous growth of available Arabic text documents on the Web and databases have posed a major challenge on researchers to find better ways to deal with such huge amount of information in order to enable search engines and information retrieval systems to provide relevant information accurately, which has become a crucial task to satisfy the needs of different end users.

Text classifications, and its techniques, have become a major tool for dealing with the large amount of available data on the Web and databases. Text classification is the task of automatically as-

DOI: 10.4018/978-1-4666-3898-3.ch013

signing text documents to one or more predefined categories based on content and linguistic features (Gharib et al., 2009; Mesleh et al., 2007; Rahman et al., 2003; Zubi, 2009; Al-Harbi et al., 2008). Several researches applied text classification and its techniques to English and other European languages. On the other hand, few researchers have addressed the issue of Arabic text classification.

Text preprocessing and preparation; especially for Arabic, is a crucial task in several applications including; information retrieval, text mining, and natural language processing where the processing tasks include different stages such as: stop word removal and stemming. Stemming tries to reduce a word to its stem (Al-Shammari et al., 2008), stemming process uses word morphological analysis in order to get the word's stems (Sembok et al., 2011).

Stemming is a very important technique that is usually used in information retrieval and data mining as well as many other NLP applications. Stemming is important for some natural languages and unimportant in others. As reported by Sembok et al. (2011) and Al-Shammari (2008), stemming has the following benefits:

- Stemming helps in reducing the size of the index terms.
- Stemming is used in information retrieval systems to reduce variant word forms to common roots in order to improve retrieval effectiveness.

Arabic is a language used by millions of people around the world in more than 25 countries. Arabic consists of 28 letters, three vowels and the remaining letters are consonants. Each letter has a different style depending on its position in the word (Duwari, 2007; Kadri et al., 2006) Arabic is a highly inflectional and derivative language which makes morphological analysis a very complex task. Moreover, Arabic do not use capitalizations in order to differentiate nouns form other words in documents (El-Halees, 2010). Arabic words have two distinctive genders, feminine and masculine; three numbers, singular, dual, and plural; and three grammatical cases, nominative, accusative, and genitive (Omer et al., 2010). Finally, the Arabic language consists of three types of words; nouns, verbs and particles; where nouns and verbs are derived from a limited set of about 10,000 roots (Said et al., 2009). All these characteristics make Arabic text classification a difficult task when comparing it with other text classification tasks that deal with English and other languages.

Many text classification techniques used in data mining and machine learning exist in literature such as: Support Vector Machine (SVM) (Gharib et al., 2009; Mesleh et al., 2007; Zhuang et al., 2005), Naïve Bayes (NB) (Gharib et al., 2009; Zubi, 2009; Duwari, 2007; El-Kourdi et al., 2004), K-Nearest Neighbor (KNN) (Zubi, 2009; Duwari, 2007; Zhou et al., 2003), Rocchio (Gharib et al., 2009), and Decision Tree (Al-Harbi et al., 2008). However, in this work we addressed three of those classifiers namely, Support Vector Machine (SVM), Naïve Bayes, and Decision Tree.

The main aim of the paper is to determine the effect of applying stemming as a preprocessing step on the classification performance of the three selected classifiers. All tests are done with the idea that stemming improves the classification accuracy for the classifiers under test as well as reducing the time required for building the model for testing purposes.

1.1. Research Questions

The problem statement or the research questions that this paper is trying to tackle are largely two questions:

- What is the impact of stemming on the text classification process? Will the stemming process always improve the accuracy of classification?

- What is the best text classification algorithm that can be used particularly for Arabic language classification?

The rest of the paper is organized as follows. Section 2 gives related works in the field of text classification. Section 3 demonstrates the methodology used to achieve the required goals. In Section 4 we demonstrate our conclusions and future works.

2. RELATED WORK

Text classification is one of the important and widely known applications in data mining field. A lot of research addressed the problem of text classification for many languages, including English (Zaghloul, Lee, & Trimi, 2009), Chinese (He, Tan, & Tan, 2000), Arabic (Al-Harbi et al., 2008; Al-Shargabi et al., 2011; Kanaan et al., 2009). The goal of text classification is achieving a high accuracy in classification documents to predefined categories, this accuracy is affected by different issues related to text classification, these issues include the usage of stemming algorithms and techniques, the features of the data set used, and the algorithms used for the task of text classification.

2.1. Text Classification Challenges

Text classification in Arabic and non-Arabic text has many challenges for machine learning techniques because there can be millions of word features (Dumais et al., 1998). However, challenges that are faced when dealing with the task Arabic text classification are more than those for non-Arabic.

2.2. Classifiers

Almost all research in text classification followed the same methodology, which consists of collecting the data, preprocessing the data, and finally conducts the classification task. However, these methodologies differ in terms of the nature of the data sets, preprocessing steps, evaluation techniques and measure, and algorithms used.

Many classification algorithm discussed in literature exist for conducting the task of text classification. These algorithms include Support Vector Machine (SVM) or Sequential Minimal Optimization (SMO) (Al-Harbi et al., 2008; Duwairi, 2007; Gharib et al., 2009; Qiu et al., 2008; Shang et al., 2007), Naïve Bayes (NB) (Duwairi, 2007; Kanaan et al., 2009; Shang et al., 2007), the Decision Tree (DT) algorithm including J48, C4.5 and C5 versions (Al-Harbi et al., 2008; Shang et al., 2007), k-Nearest Neighbor (k-NN) (Duwairi, 2007; Kanaan et al., 2009; Shang et al., 2007), Rocchio (Gharib et al., 2009; Kanaan et al., 2009; Shang et al., 2007), Neural Network (Duwairi, 2007; Shang et al., 2007), generalized instance set (Duwairi, 2007), linear least square fit (Shang et al., 2007), and many other algorithms. No text classification algorithm is better than the others; each of them has its own strength and weaknesses. However, according to Wu et al. (2007), the top ten data mining algorithms identified by the IEEE International Conference on Data Mining (ICDM) include the C4.5 decision tree, SVM, k-NN, Naive Bayes algorithms which are used for text classification.

2.3. Data Sets

A data set or a corpus is a collection of text documents that fall into many categories or classes is required for conducting the task of text classification. Different corpuses are used in text classification research for non-Arabic text. These corpuses differ from on research to another in term of the number of documents, number of classes or categories in which these documents falls, distribution of documents among classes or categories, length of text in the document, and type of classes or categories.

Mitra, Wang, and Banerjee (2007) use the Penrose library document collection which consists of 91,229 documents classified into six categories. Zaghloul, Lee, and Trimi (2009) use a data set consists of abstracts of 728 articles collected from the Management Information System Quarterly (MISQ) journal. The documents are categorized to nine MISQ categories, where experiments are done using just the top five categories. Shang et al. (2007), Lee and Lee (2004), Pomikálek and Rehurek (2007), and Largeron, Moulin, and Gery (2011) use the well-known Reuters-21578 document collection which contains 21,578 documents with an average of 137 words per document. Documents in the collection fall in 114 categories collected mainly from the Reuters newswire. Only the top ten classes from reuters-21578 with about 9779 documents are used by Shang et al. (2007). Lee and Lee (2004) also use another data set collected from universities websites consist of 8,282 pages classified into seven categories, Largeron et al. (2011) use another data set collected mainly from Wikipedia consisting of 114,366 documents classified into 15 categories. Pomikálek and Rehurek (2007) use two data sets; the 20Newsgroups data set that consists of 6,000 documents that falls into twenty categories, where every document contains on average 868 words; and the Springer data set which consists of 2,700 documents falls into nine categories where each document contains on average 4,285 words. Table 1 summarizes different characteristics about some of the non-Arabic data sets used in text classification task.

2.4. Arabic Text Classification

2.4.1. Arabic Language in Text Classification (How Arabic Classification Differs from Other Languages)

Developing text classification systems for Arabic documents is a challenging task due to the complex and rich nature of the Arabic language. The Arabic language consists of 28 letters. The language is written from right to left and it has a very complex morphology (Khreisat, 2006). Not like English and other languages, Arabic exhibits two genders: masculine and feminine, three number categories: singular, dual, and plural. Whereas singular and plural are familiar categories to most Western learners, the dual is less familiar. The dual in Arabic is used whenever the category of "two" applies, whether it be in nouns, adjectives, pronouns, or verbs. A noun has three cases, the nominative, accu-

Table 1. Non-Arabic data sets used in text classification

Article	Data sets	No. of doc.	Classes	Avg. words/doc	No. of doc. in class
Pomikálek and Rehurek (2007)	Reuters-21578	1800	6	167	300
	20Newsgroups	6000	20	868	300
	Springer	2700	9	4285	300
Largeron et al. (2011)	Reuters-21578	21578	114	173	Unknown
	INEX XML	114366	15	423	Unknown
Lee and Lee (2004)	Reuters-21578	21578	114	Unknown	Not Equal
	WebKB	8282	7	Unknown	Not Equal
Shang et al. (2007)	Reuters-21578	9779	10	Unknown	Not Equal
Zaghloul et al. (2009)	MISQ Articles	728	9	Unknown	Not Equal
Mitra et al. (2007)	Pensora Library	91229	6	Unknown	Not Equal

sative, and genitive (Ryding, 2005). Also, Arabic language is a Semitic language that is very inflectional and derivational language which makes monophonical analysis very difficult (El-Haless, 2010; Gharib et al., 2009). Arabic scripts contain vowels that are represented by diacritics which are left out in the text leading to some ambiguity (El-Haless, 2010; Duwairi, 2007). In addition, Capitalization is not used for proper nouns which are necessary in classifying documents classification (El-Haless, 2010). Arabic letters have different style depending on its location in the word, whether it is in the beginning (تائه), in the middle (ملتزم), or at the end of the word (صمت) (Duwairi, 2007).

2.4.2. Data Sets

Arabic data sets are exactly the same as those data sets used in other languages for the task of text classification except they are written in Arabic. They shared some characteristics with other non-Arabic datasets in terms of number of documents, number of classes or categories, distribution of documents among classes or categories, length of text in the document, and type of classes or categories.

Al-Harbi et al. (2008) use a data set collected from different newspaper websites. The data set consist of 17,658 documents falls in seven categories that differs in term of the number of documents. Mesleh and Kanaan (2008) and Kanaan et al. (2009) use a data set consists of 1,445 documents with nine categories that are collected from different news websites, where each category contains different number of document. Al-Shargabi, Al-Romimah, and Olayah (2011) use a corpus that consists of 1,132 documents with an average of 84 words per document that falls into six categories collected mainly from Egyptian newspapers websites. Duwairi (2007) use a corpus consisting of 1,000 documents that falls within 10 categories with a 100 document per category; the corpus is collected from online newspapers and magazine. Finally, El-Kourdi et al. (2004) use a corpus consisting of 300 documents that are fall in 5 categories or classes. Table 2 summarizes different characteristics about some of the Arabic data sets used in text classification task.

2.5. Stemming Techniques

Stemming is a technique that helps in reducing the high dimensionality of the feature space in text classification. Several Stemming approach exist for Arabic language each which produces a different set of roots. In Arabic the most known stemming approaches used are the light and the root-based stemmers (Thabet, 2004).

Root-based Stemming is based on removing all attached prefixes and suffixes in an attempt to

Table 2. Arabic data sets used in text classification

Article	Data sets	No. of doc.	Classes	Avg. words/doc	No. of doc. in class
Mesleh and Kanaan (2008)	Newspapers	1445	9	Unknown	Not Equal
Duwairi (2007)	Newspapers	1000	10	Unknown	100
Al-Shargabi et al. (2011)	Web	2363	6	Unknown	Not Equal
Gharib, Habib, and Fayed (2009)	Newspapers	1132	6	84	Not Equal
Al-Harbi et al. (2008)	Newspapers	17658	7	Unknown	Not Equal
Kanaan et al. (2009)	Newspapers	1445	9	Unknown	Not Equal
El-Kourdi et al., (2004)	Newspapers	300	5	Unknown	Not Equal

extract the root of a given Arabic surface word. Several stemmers are based on such approach like the Khoja stemmer. On the other hand, Light Stemming is used not to produce the linguistic root of a given Arabic surface form, but to remove the most frequent suffixes and prefixes. The most common suffixation includes duals and plurals for masculine and feminine, possessive forms, definite articles, and pronouns. These stemmers follow the same steps and differ in terms of the number of prefixes and suffixes removed (Thabet, 2004). There are some other trials of stemming or improving the stemming process. For example, Diab (2009) proposed AMIRA tool to process standard Arabic language. AMIRA language processing toolkit contained a clitic tokenizer, part of speech tagger, base phrase chunker, and shallow syntactic parser.

Different kinds of stemming algorithms exist in literature, each which can deal with different language such as Porter stemmer for English and Khoja stemmer for Arabic. Kanaan et al. (2009) use a light stemming approach for preprocessing the text document collection, light stemming is based on removing the suffixes and prefixes from the word if the removal results in three or more characters long, which gives better results when compared with root extraction and morphological analysis. Gharib et al. (2009) adopt a stemming approach that uses the light and trigram stemming, the approach show an improvement in the accuracy of classification algorithm under the test. Duwairi (2007) extracts word roots by assigning weight from 0-5, and ranks to the letters in a word. These letters weight are then multiplied by the rank, and the letters with the smallest product values represent the root of the word. Mesleh and Kanaan (2008) does not use any stemming algorithm in their works because they stated that stemming does not always improve classification performance because many words are stemmed to the same root which affect the classification process.

3. METHODOLOGY AND APPROACHES

Figure 1 demonstrates the methodology followed to classify Arabic text documents in this research.

As Figure 1 demonstrates, the first step in the methodology which consists of collecting Arabic text documents required to accomplish the task of classification.

3.1. The Corpus

1100 text documents were collected from different trusted websites; which fall into 9 categories: Agriculture, art, economics, health and medicine, law, politics, religion, science, and sports. Those 9 categories will be the class labels in the classification process.

Figure 1. Arabic text classification aided by stemming

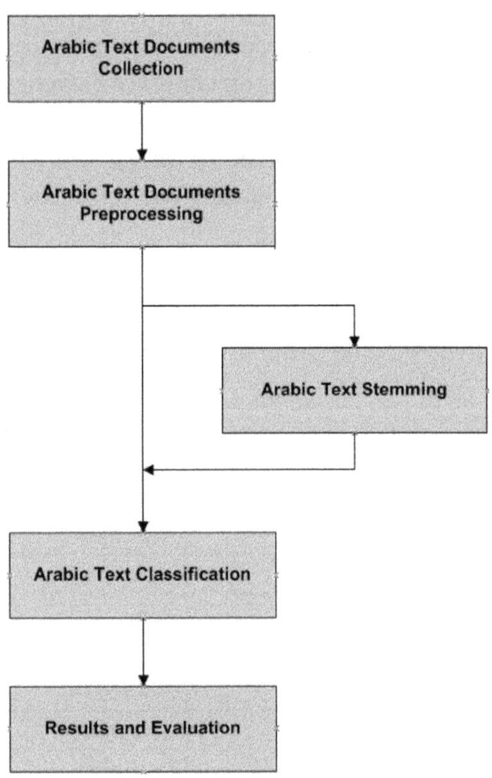

- **N:** Is the total number of documents in the collection.
- **n_i:** Is number of documents in the collection that contain term i.

After the term frequency and inverse documents frequency are computed for each term, the term weight is obtained using Equation (2).

$$W_{i,j} = TF_{i,j} \times IDF_{i,j} \quad (2)$$

where:

- **$TF_{i,j}$:** Term Frequency of term i in document j.
- **$IDF_{i,j}$:** Inverse Documents Frequency of term i in document j.

Classification of documents is then calculated based on IDF to decide what is the class of the document from the 9 evaluated classes based on the distance of IDF of the subject document relative to documents in all 9 classes.

3.2.4. Data Preparation

Once the documents are ready to be used with WEKA they are prepared to be converted to a suitable WEKA format. Different formats are available for presenting the data in the WEKA such as: ARRF, C4.5, CSV, XRRF data files, and ARFF file format. The most well-known format for defining the data are: ARFF and CSV file format. In this research the ARFF format is used. The ARFF file is constructed by using the core converters that are available in WEKA toolkit (Witten et al., 2005).

The final step in the process is conducting the experiments; after data has been processed and stored in a format that is appropriate for classification on WEKA toolkit. Three classification algorithms were used; SVM, C4.5, and NB algorithms.

3.3. The Used Classifiers

3.3.1. Classifying Documents Using SVM Algorithm

The collected dataset was used to assess the performance and efficiency of the Sequential Minimal Optimization (SMO); which is the WEKA version of SVM algorithm. SMO implements the sequential minimal optimization algorithm for training a support vector classifier, using polynomial or Gaussian kernels (Witten et al., 2005). One advantage of using this implementation is the fact that the amount of memory required by SMO is linear to the size of the data (Naughton et al., 2010). SVM tends to perform well on classification problems (Wu et al., 2006). The SVM is also able to handle hundreds and thousands of input values with great ease due to its ability to deal well with noisy data (Abbasi et al., 2005).

3.3.2. Classifying Documents Using C4.5 Algorithm

The dataset was also tested using the C4.5 algorithm. This algorithm was implemented under the J48 algorithm in WEKA. C4.5 builds decision trees from a set of training data using the concept of information entropy. C4.5 splits the attribute values into two partitions based on the selected threshold such that all the values above the threshold as one child and the remaining as another child. It also handles missing attribute values. C4.5 uses Gain Ratio as an attribute selection measure to build a decision tree and it removes the biasness of information gain when there are many outcome values of an attribute (Lavanya et al., 2011). Decision tree algorithm is used to categorize the types of examples; which may come in negative or positive forms. In addition, we can insert more than two types of examples. This means that, instead of having just positive and negative examples, we can have many other types as well (Wongpun et al., 2008). Decision tree models are widely used in machine learning and data mining, since they can be easily converted into a set of humanly readable if-then rules (Last et al., 2008).

3.3.3. Classifying Documents Using Naive Bayes Algorithm

The final algorithm that was tested using the data-set was the Naïve Bayes. A Naïve Bayes classifier is a well-known and practical probabilistic classifier that has been employed in many applications (Kim et al., 2006). This algorithm is based on Bayes' rule of conditional probability. In many works it has been proven that Naïve Bayesian classifiers are one of the most computationally efficient, effective, and simple algorithms for data mining applications (Cufloglu et al., 2008). Naïve Bayes works very well when tested on a dataset; particularly, when combined with some attribute features techniques (Witten et al., 2005). The basic idea in Naïve Bayes methods is to use the joint probabilities of words and categories to estimate the probabilities of categories in a document. The Naïve aspect of the method has to deal with the fact that the dependencies between words are ignored, i.e., the conditional probability of a word given a category is assumed to be independent from the conditional probabilities of other words given that same category. This assumption is necessary for efficiency reasons (Fang et al., 2001).

3.4. Experimental Setup

Once the text documents are processed, they are stemmed and converted to a suitable format to make them ready for the classification tasks. For evaluation purposes, the document collection is classified twice; the first time the document collection is classified before stemming is applied to documents (which is referred to as PC) while the second time after stemming is applied to the document collection (referred to as PSC).

Two test modes were used; the k-fold Cross Validation (k-fold CV) mode and the Percentage Split (PS) (also called Holdout method) mode. The k-fold CV refers to a widely used experimental testing procedure where the data set is randomly divided into k disjoint blocks of objects. The data mining algorithm is then trained using k-1 blocks and the remaining blocks are used to test the performance of the algorithm; this process is repeated k times. At the end, an average is taken for the recorded measures. It is common to choose k = 10 or any other size depending mainly on the size of the original dataset.

In percentage split method, the data set is randomly split into two disjoint datasets. The first set; the training set is from which the data mining algorithms try to extract knowledge. . The extracted knowledge can be tested against the second set; which is called the test set. In machine learning, to have the training and test sets, it is common to randomly split a dataset under the mining task into two parts. It is common to have 66% of the objects of the original database as a training set and the rest of objects as a test set.

3.5. Evaluation Measures

In general, classification is usually measured in terms of the classic information retrieval notions of precision and recall, adapted to the case of text categorization (Omer et al., 2010). As an evaluation metrics we use the accuracy measure which is the percentage of correctly classified documents. Also, R (Recall) measure is the value of recalling as a ratio of the number of data that has been correctly classified of any class from all data of the classes and is given by Zhuang et al. (2005) and Wongpun et al. (2008).

$$R = \frac{\text{\# of correctly classified positive examples}}{\text{\# of real positive examples and precision}} \quad (3)$$

Another measure is P (Precision) is the value of precision which is a ratio of the number of correctly classified data of any class from all the classified data in all the classes and is given by Zhuang et al. (2005) and Wongpun et al. (2008).

$$P = \frac{\#\text{ of correctly classified positive examples}}{\#\text{ of classifier predicted positive examples}} \quad (4)$$

Precision and Recall are generally accepted ways of measuring system's performance in this field. Another measure is the F-measure, which is a standard statistical measure that is used to measure the performance of a classifier system. The F-measure is an average parameter based on precision and recall (Wongpun et al., 2008). It is given by:

$$F = \frac{2PR}{P+R} \quad (5)$$

3.6. Experiments and Evaluation

Results are collected from applying three different classification methods: NB, SMO and J48. In the next section, we will summarize experimental results.

3.6.1. Classification Effectiveness

Figure 2 shows the results that were obtained when running the selected classification algorithms on the processed corpus using the two testing modes.

Figure 2 shows that SMO classifier has achieved the highest classification accuracy using the PS and CV test modes with 93.8% and 89.6% respectively. On the other hand, the NB classifier has achieved the second highest accuracy using the PS and CV modes with 83.9% and 83.5% respectively. Finally; the J48 classifier has achieved the lowest classification accuracy for both PS and CV modes with 78.3% and 75.3% respectively. Comparing the performance for the test modes themselves; the figure reveals that the CV test mode has either achieved almost the same accuracy as the PS mode, as shown for the NB classifier, or achieved lower accuracy than the PS mode, as shown for both the SMO and J48 Classifiers.

Figure 3 shows the results obtained when running the selected classification algorithms on the processed and stemmed corpus using the two test modes. As shown in Figure 3 the SMO classifier has achieved the highest classification

Figure 2. Classification performance using processed corpus

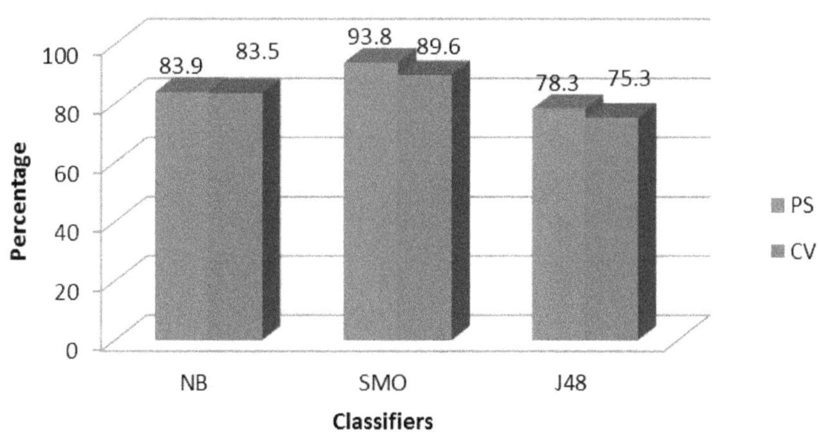

Figure 3. Classification performance using processed and stemmed corpus

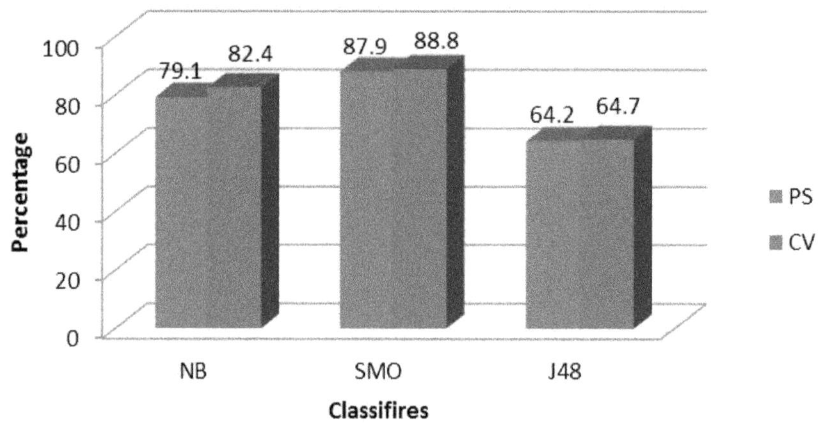

accuracy using the PS and CV test modes with 87.9% and 88.8% respectively. On the other hand, the NB classifier has achieved the second highest classification accuracy using the PS and CV test modes with 79.1% and 82.4% respectively. Finally; the J48 classifier has achieved the lowest accuracy using the PS and CV modes with 64.2% and 64.7% respectively. Comparing the performance of the test modes themselves, the CV mode has achieved the highest classification accuracy than the PS mode, for all classifiers.

Figure 4 shows the performance of the classifiers under test using the Processed Corpus (PC) and the Processed Stemmed Corpus (PSC) under the PS test mode. As the figure reveals; stemming affects the classification accuracy for all classifiers under test using the PS test mode. The accuracy of the NB classifier has dropped down when using the PSC instead of the PC where the accuracy has dropped from 83.9% to 79.1%. For the SMO classifier, the accuracy has also dropped down from 93.8% to 87.9%, when using the PSC instead of the PC. Finally; the J48 classifier has achieved an accuracy of 76.3% using the PC and has dropped down to 64.2% when using the PSC.

Figure 5 shows the performance of the classifiers using the processed corpus (PC) and the processed stemmed corpus (PSC) under the CV

Figure 4. Processed corpus vs. processed, stemmed corpus using PS test mode

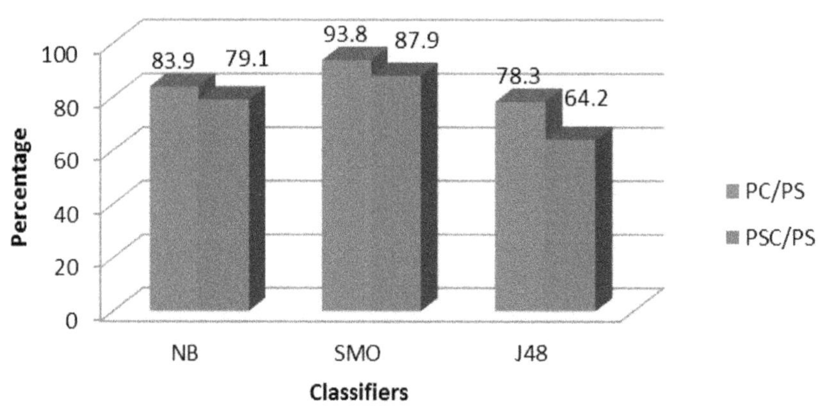

Figure 5. Processed corpus vs. processed, stemmed corpus using CV test mode

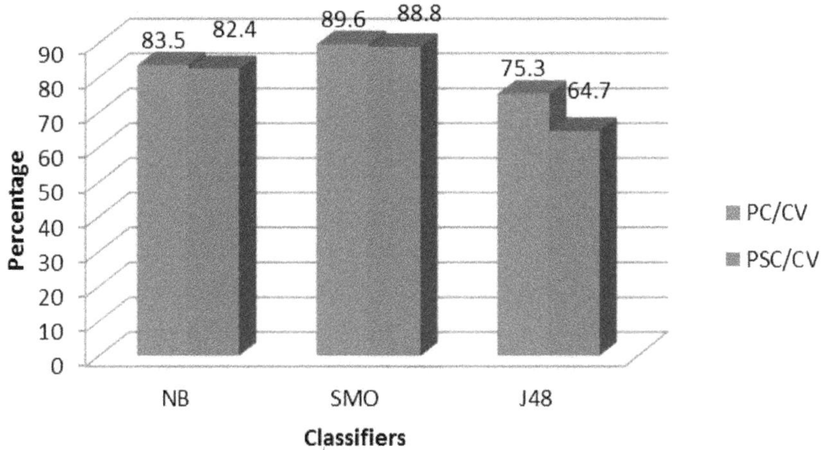

test mode. It can be seen that using the CV test mode, the stemming also affects the classification accuracy. Results have showed that accuracy of the NB classifier has dropped down from 77.89% to 75.79%, when using the PSC instead of the PC. For the SMO classifier, the accuracy has dropped down from 88.54% to 86.35%, when using the PSC instead of the PC. Finally; the J48 classifier has achieved an accuracy of 69.69% using the PC and has dropped down to 62.6% when, using the PSC.

In order to determine the reason behind the idea that stemming affect the classification performance negatively, we analyze the obtained results on the class level using the F-measure using all combination of test for classifiers under the test. Table 3 shows the summary of the results for the F-measure using the percentage split method.

Comparing the results for the F-measure for all classes under the test using the percentage split method for both the PC and PSC we can see that some of the classes achieved lower value for the F-measure when moving from the PC to the PSC and other classes have an improved F-measure when moving from the PC to the OSC. As we can see, the most affected classes when moving from the PC to the PSC (those that are highlighted) are: the Art class when using the NB classifiers, the Religion class for the SMO classifier, and the Economic, Politics, and Religion classes for the J48 classifier. Other classes for all of the classifier shows either an improvement for the F-measure or a little decrement in the value of the F-measure. Table 4 shows the summary of the results for the F-measure using cross validation method.

Comparing the results for the F-measure for all classes under the test using the cross validation method for both the PC and PSC we can see that some of the classes achieved lower value for the F-measure when moving from the PC to the PSC and other classes have an improved F-measure when moving from the PC to the OSC. As we can see, the most affected classes when moving from the PC to the PSC are the Science and Sport class when using the NB classifiers, the Religion and Economic classes for the SMO classifier, and the Economic, Politics, Sports, Law and Religion classes for the J48 classifier. Other classes for all of the classifier shows either some kind little improvement for the F-measure or decrement in the F-measure.

Table 3. F-measure for all algorithms' results using the percentage split method

Class	PC-NB	PSC-NB	PC-SMO	PSC-SMO	PC-J48	PSC-J48
Agriculture	1	0.992	1	0.967	0.974	0.842
Art	0.816	0.597	0.914	0.836	0.682	0.75
Economics	0.716	0.74	0.913	0.826	0.705	0.5
Health_medicin	0.946	0.944	0.933	0.946	0.827	0.667
Law	0.635	0.706	0.943	0.88	0.773	0.658
Politics	0.861	0.744	0.914	0.889	0.707	0.447
Religion	0.769	0.786	0.912	0.786	0.87	0.473
Science	0.814	0.757	0.885	0.844	0.509	0.545
Sport	0.966	0.785	0.989	0.881	0.857	0.756

Table 4. F-measure for all algorithms' results using cross validation

Class	PC-NB	PSC-NB	PC-SMO	PSC-SMO	PC-J48	PSC-J48
Agriculture	0.984	0.981	0.987	0.981	0.928	0.869
Art	0.793	0.828	0.904	0.896	0.684	0.73
Economics	0.732	0.735	0.873	0.829	0.611	0.4
Health_medicin	0.961	0.938	0.929	0.935	0.772	0.667
Law	0.639	0.761	0.761	0.831	0.805	0.613
Politics	0.817	0.788	0.872	0.897	0.701	0.56
Religion	0.765	0.749	0.89	0.804	0.77	0.558
Science	0.824	0.728	0.851	0.848	0.548	0.638
Sport	0.961	0.86	0.966	0.936	0.911	0.751

4. CONCLUSION

In this paper, we have addressed the effect of applying stemming, as a preprocessing step, on the classification efficiency and effectiveness of three well known classifiers namely; Naïve Bayes (NB), Sequential Minimal Optimization (SMO), and Decision Tree (J48). Two test modes were used; the k-fold Cross Validation (k-fold CV) mode and the Percentage Split (PS). The accuracy measure; which refers to the percentage of documents that are correctly classified by the classifier, was used to compare the performance of the algorithms under test. For evaluation purposes, the document collection was classified twice, the first time the document collection was classified before stemming is applied to documents (referred to as PC) while the second time after stemming was applied on the document collection (referred to as PSC). 1100 text documents were collected from different trusted websites. These 1100 text documents fall into 9 categories. Khoja stemmer was used in this study to accomplish the stemming task.

The obtained results have showed that using the Processed Corpus (PC), the SMO classifier has achieved the highest classification accuracy using the PS with 93.8% followed by the Naïve Bayes and J48 with 83.9% and 78.3% respectively. On the other hand, using CV test, SMO has achieved the highest classification accuracy of 89.6% followed by the Naïve Bayes and J48 with 83.5% and 75.3% respectively. Using the Processed Stemmed

Corpus (PSC), the SMO classifier has achieved the highest classification accuracy, using the PS, with an 87.9% followed by the Naïve Bayes and J48 with 79.1% and 64.2% respectively. On the other hand, using CV test, SMO has achieved the highest classification accuracy of 88.8% followed by the Naïve Bayes and J48 with 82.4% and 64.7% respectively.

Also, results showed that the reason behind the idea that stemming did not improve the classification accuracy for the classifiers under the test is that some of the classes achieved poor performance when using stemming and these classes affect the overall classifiers performance at the corpus level.

Obtained results have showed that stemming affects negatively the performance of the classification accuracy of the three classifiers, where the accuracy has decreased when using stemming comparing it without using stemming using the PS and CV test modes. However, we believe that the process depends on the nature of the stemming process, the nature of the classes and the documents that are inside those classes. In future, we are planning to mix automatic classification with user tagging. Several activities in the process can be improved with user intervention. For example, terms' weight accuracy can be also improved if users' were involved in giving weights to the terms based on their relevancy and importance to the subject class.

REFERENCES

Abbasi, A., & Chen, H. (2005). Applying authorship analysis to Arabic Web content. In P. Kantor, G. Muresan, F. Roberts, D. D. Zeng, F.-Y. Wang, H. Chen, & R. C. Merkle (Eds.), *Proceedings of the IEEE International Conference on Intelligence and Security Informatics*, Atlanta, GA (LNCS 3495, pp. 75-93).

Al-Harbi, S., Almuhareb, A., Al-Thubaity, A., Khorsheed, S., & Al-Rajeh, A. (2008). Automatic Arabic text classification. In *Proceedings of the 9th International Conference on Statistical Analysis of Textual Data* (pp. 77-83).

Al-Kabi, M., & Al-Mustafa, R. (2006). Arabic root based stemmer. In *Proceedings of the International Arab Conference on Information Technology*, Jordan.

Al-Kabi, M., Al-Radaideh, Q., & Akawi, K. (2011). Benchmarking and assessing the performance of Arabic Stemmers. *Journal of Information Science, 37*(2), 1–12. doi:10.1177/0165551510392305

Al-Radaideh, Q. (2008). The impact of classification evaluation methods on rough sets based classifiers. In *Proceedings of the International Arab Conference on Information Technology*, Sfax, Tunisia.

Al-Shammari, E. (2008). Towards an error free stemming. In *Proceedings of the International Conference on Data Mining*, Amsterdam, The Netherlands.

Al-Shammari, E. T., & Lin, J. (2008). A new Arabic stemming algorithm. In *Proceedings of the 2nd ISCA Workshop on Experimental Linguistics*, Athens, Greece.

Al-Shargabi, B., Al-Romimah, W., & Olayah, F. (2011). A comparative study for Arabic text classification algorithms based on stop words elimination. In *Proceedings of the International Conference on Intelligent Semantic Web-Services and Applications*, Amman, Jordan.

Al-Shawakfa, E., Al-Badarneh, A., Shatnawi, S., Al-Rabab'ah, K., & Bani-Ismail, B. (2010). A comparison study of some Arabic root finding algorithms. *Journal of the American Society for Information Science and Technology, 6*(5), 1015–1024. doi:10.1002/asi.21301

Cufoglu, A., Lohi, M., & Madani, K. (2008). A comparative study of selected classifiers with classification accuracy in user profiling. In *Proceedings of the 7th International Conference on Machine Learning and Application*, San Diego, CA (pp. 787-791).

Diab, M. (2009). Second generation tools (amira 2.0): Fast and robust tokenization, pos tagging, and base phrase chunking. In *Proceedings of the Second International Conference on Arabic Language Resources and Tools* (pp. 285-288).

Dumais, S., Platt, J., Heckerman, D., & Sahami, M. (1998). Inductive learning algorithms and representations for text categorization. In *Proceedings of the Seventh International Conference on Information and Knowledge Management*, Bethesda, MD.

Duwairi, R. (2007). Arabic text categorization. *International Arab Journal of Information Technology*, *4*(2), 125–132.

Duwairi, R., Al-Refai, M., & Khasawneh, N. (2007). Stemming versus light stemming as feature selection techniques for Arabic text categorization. In *Proceedings of the 4th International Conference on Innovations in Information Technology*, Dubai, UAE.

El-Halees, A. (2006). Mining Arabic association rules for text classification. In *Proceedings of the First International Conference on Mathematical Sciences*, Gaza, Palestine.

El-Halees, A. M. (2010). Arabic text classification using maximum entropy. [Series of Natural Studies and Engineering]. *The Islamic University Journal*, *15*(1), 157–167.

El-Kourdi, M., Bensaid, A., & Rachidi, T. (2004). Automatic Arabic document categorization based on the Naïve Bayes Algorithm. In *Proceedings of the 20th Workshop on Computational Approaches to Arabic Script-based Languages*, Geneva, Switzerland.

Fang, Y., Parthasarathy, S., & Schwartz, F. (2001). Using clustering to boost text classification. In *Proceedings of the IEEE International Conference on Data Mining* (pp. 123-127).

Gharib, T. F., Habib, M. B., & Fayed, Z. T. (2009). Arabic text classification using support vector machines. *International Journal of Computers and their Applications, 16*(4), 192-199.

Ghawanmeh, S., Al-Shalabi, R., Kanaan, G., Khanfar, K., & Rabab'ah, S. (2005). An algorithm for extracting the root for the Arabic Language. In *Proceedings of the 5th International Business Information Management Association Conference*, Cairo, Egypt.

Ghawanmeh, S., Al-Shalabi, R., Kanaan, G., Khanfar, K., & Rabab'ah, S. (2009). Enhanced algorithm for extracting the root of Arabic words. In *Proceedings of the Sixth International Conference on Computer Graphics, Imaging and Visualization*, China (pp. 388-391).

He, J., Tan, A. H., & Tan, C. L. (2000). A comparative study on Chinese text categorization methods. In *Proceedings of the PRICAI International Workshop on Text and Web Mining*.

Kadri, Y., & Nie, J. Y. (2006). Effective stemming for Arabic information retrieval. The challenge of Arabic for NLP/MT. In *Proceedings of the International Conference at the British Computer Society* (pp. 68-74).

Kanaan, G., Al Shalabi, R., Ghwanmeh, S., & Al Ma'adeed, H. (2009). A comparison of text classification techniques applied to Arabic text. *Journal of the American Society for Information Science and Technology*, *60*(9), 1836–1844. doi:10.1002/asi.20832

Khoja, S. (2011). *Personal web page.* Retrieved May 15, 2011, from http://zeus.cs.pacificu.edu/shereen/research.htm

Khoja, S., & Garside, R. (1999). *Stemming Arabic text.* Lancaster, UK: Lancaster University. Retrieved September 22, 1999, from http://www.comp.lancs.ac.uk/computing/users/khoja/stemmer.ps

Khreisat, L. (2006). Arabic text classification using N-gram frequency statistics a comparative study. In *Proceedings of the International Conference on Data Mining*, Las Vegas, NV.

Kim, S., Han, K., Rim, H., & Myaeng, S. (2006). Some effective techniques for Naive Bayes text classification. *IEEE Transactions on Knowledge and Data Engineering*, *18*(11), 1457–1466. doi:10.1109/TKDE.2006.180

Largeron, C., Moulin, C., & Gery, M. (2011). Entropy based feature selection for text categorization. In *Proceedings of the ACM Symposium on Applied Computing*, TaiChung, Taiwan.

Larkey, L. S., & Connell, M. E. (2001). Arabic information retrieval at UMass in TREC-10. In *Proceedings of the Text Retrieval Conference*, Gaithersburg, MA.

Last, M., Markov, A., & Kandel, A. (2008). Multi-lingual detection of Web terrorist content. In H. Chen, F.-Y. Wang, C. C. Yang, D. Zeng, M. Chau, & K. Chang (Ed.), *Proceedings of the International Conference on Intelligence and Security Informatics* (LNCS 3917, pp. 16-30).

Lavanya, D., & Usha, K. R. (2011). Performance evaluation of decision tree classifiers on medical datasets. *International Journal of Computers and Applications*, *26*(4).

Lee, G., & Lee, G. G. (2004). MMR-based feature selection for text categorization. In *Proceedings of the HLT-NAACL: Short Papers*, Boston, MA.

Mesleh, A. (2007, December 29-31). Support vector machines based Arabic language text classification system: feature selection comparative study. In *Proceedings of the 12th WSEAS International Conference on Applied Mathematics*, Cairo, Egypt.

Mesleh, A. M., & Kanaan, G. (2008). Support vector machine text classification system: Using ant colony optimization based feature subset selection. In *Proceedings of the International Conference on Computer Engineering & Systems* (pp. 143-148).

Mitra, V., Wang, C.-J., & Banerjee, S. (2007). Text classification: A least square support vector machine approach. *Applied Soft Computing*, *7*(3), 908–914. doi:10.1016/j.asoc.2006.04.002

Mustafa, S., & Al-Radaideh, Q. (2001, November 13-15). Arabic word stemming using letter successor and predecessor variety. In *Proceedings of the International Arab Conference on Information Technology*, Jordan (pp. 216-222).

Naughton, M., Stokes, N., & Carthy, J. (2010). Sentence-level event classification in unstructured texts. *Information Retrieval*, *13*(2), 132–156. doi:10.1007/s10791-009-9113-0

Nwesri, A. F. A., Tahaghoghi, S. M. M., & Scholer, F. (2006, July 22-23). Capturing out-of-vocabulary words in Arabic text. In *Proceedings of the Conference on Empirical Methods in Natural Language Processing*, Sydney, Australia (pp. 258-266).

Omer, M. A. H., & Ma, S. (2010). Stemming algorithm to classify Arabic documents. *Journal of Communication and Computer*, *7*(9).

Peng, J., Yang, D., Tang, S., Gao, J., Zhang, P., & Fu, Y. (2007). A concept similarity based text classification algorithm. In *Proceedings of the Fourth International Conference on Fuzzy Systems and Knowledge Discovery* (pp. 535-539).

Pomikálek, J., & Rehurek, R. (2007). The influence of preprocessing parameters on text categorization. *International Journal of Applied Science Engineering and Technology*, *1*(4), 430–434.

Qiu, L. Q., Zhao, R. Y., Zhou, G., & Yi, S. W. (2008). An extensive empirical study of feature selection for text categorization. In *Proceedings of the 7th IEEE/ACIS International Conference on computer and Information Science.*

Rahman, C. N., Sohel, F. A., Naushad, P., & Kamruzzaman, S. M. (2003). Text classification using the concept of association rule of data mining. In *Proceedings of the International Conference on Information Technology*, Kathmandu, Nepal (pp. 234-241).

Ryding, K. C. (2005). *A reference grammar of modern standard Arabic*. Cambridge, UK: Cambridge University Press.

Said, D. A., Wanas, N. M., & Darwish, N. M. (2009). A study of text preprocessing tools for Arabic text categorization. In *Proceedings of the Second International Conference on Arabic Language* (pp. 230-236).

Sawaf, H., Zaplo, J., & Ney, H. (2001). Statistical classification methods for Arabic news articles. In *Proceedings of the Arabic Natural Language Processing*, Toulouse, France.

Sembok, T. M. T., Abu Ata, B. M., & Abu Bakar, Z. (2011). A rule-based Arabic stemming algorithm. In *Proceedings of the 5th European Conference on European Computing Conference.*

Shang, W., Huang, H., Zhu, H., Lin, Y., Qu, Y., & Wang, Z. (2007). A novel feature selection algorithm for text categorization. *Expert Systems with Applications*, *33*(1), 1–5. doi:10.1016/j.eswa.2006.04.001

Taghva, K., Elkhoury, R., & Coombs, J. (2005). *Arabic stemming without a root dictionary.* Paper presented at the International Conference on Information Technology: Coding and Computing.

Thabet, N. (2004). Stemming the Qur'an. In *Proceedings of the Workshop on Computational Approaches to Arabic Script-based Languages*, Geneva, Switzerland.

Witten, H., & Frank, E. (2005). *Data mining: Practical machine learning tools and techniques* (2nd ed.). San Francisco, CA: Morgan Kaufmann.

Wongpun, S., & Srivihok, A. (2008). Comparison of attribute selection techniques and algorithms in classifying bad behaviors of vocational education students. In *Proceedings of the 2nd IEEE International Conference on Digital Ecosystems and Technologies*, Australia (pp. 526-531).

Wu, X., Kumar, V., Quinlan, J., Ghosh, J., Yang, Q., & Motoda, H. (2007). Top 10 algorithms in data mining. *Knowledge and Information Systems*, *14*(1), 1–37. doi:10.1007/s10115-007-0114-2

Wu, Y., Chang, C., & Lee, Y. (2006). A general and multi-lingual phrase chunking model based on masking method. In *Proceedings of the 7th International Conference on Intelligent Text Processing and Computational Linguistics*, Mexico City, Mexico (pp. 144-155).

Zaghloul, W., Lee, S. M., & Trimi, S. (2009). Text classification: Neural networks vs. support vector machines. *Industrial Management & Data Systems*, *109*(5), 708–717. doi:10.1108/02635570910957669

Zhou, S., Ling, T. W., Guan, J., Hu, J., & Zhou, A. (2003). Fast text classification: A training-corpus pruning based approach. In *Proceedings of the Eighth International Conference on Database Systems for Advanced Applications.*

Zhuang, D., Zhang, B., Yang, Q., Yan, J., Chen, Z., & Chen, Y. (2005). Efficient text classification by weighted proximal SVM. In *Proceedings of the Fifth IEEE International Conference on Data Mining* (pp. 538-545).

Zubi, Z. S. (2009). Using some web content mining techniques for Arabic text classification. In *Proceedings of the 8th WSEAS International Conference on Data Networks, Communications, Computers*, Baltimore, MD (pp. 73-84).

This work was previously published in the International Journal of Information Retrieval Research, Volume 1, Issue 3, edited by Zhongyu (Joan) Lu, pp. 54-70, copyright 2011 by IGI Publishing (an imprint of IGI Global).

Chapter 14

Biometrics:
Electronic Resources Management in Jaykar Library, University of Pune, India

Prakash Dongardive
University of Mekelle, Ethiopia

Neela Deshpande
University of Pune, India

ABSTRACT

In the age of information the rise in development of (ICT) Information Communication Technology and Internet, the format of documents has changed to digital. Electronic information sources have become an important part for today's library and users. Electronic information is gaining more importance in academic activities with an extreme change in the pattern of dissemination of knowledge. Web technology provides dynamism to the electronic documents that were note possible in the essentially sequential style of presentation of printed documents. Interactive hyperlinks to related resources, links to full range of multimedia, traditional indexing, and abstracting services, etc., are some of the novelties that are common in a web document. Faculty has a vital role in providing up-to-date information with the latest technologies, so they must be skilled users of electronic information through online journals. Hence, it is worth studying the use of online journals. Suggestions have been given to strengthen existing online journals subscription, the availability of full text online journals, and accessibility, e.g., system speed and maximizing the use of online journals among science faculty members at the University of Pune.

1. INTRODUCTION

The purpose of this study is to examine the attitude behaviors, perceptions and preferences of the faculty members of science stream in University of Pune. The importance of present research study is useful to know the parallel and electronic methods of online journals for knowledge dissemination among users and faculty members of science stream in University of Pune. Information needed by science faculty and student is increasing exponentially in the science. Interdisciplinary research; new fields of research has increased in science field therefore scientists need always new information. With the new technologies, academics, can distribute their own material more effectively

DOI: 10.4018/978-1-4666-3898-3.ch014

than the traditional sources. The rising cost of the general publication, coupled with the explosive growth in research and concomitant explosion of paper journal in various discipline for science libraries to maintain a comprehensive selection of literature. Significant increase in the speed of academic discourse can be achieved via electronic publication. Therefore there is a vibrant need to know the usability of online journals with their obstacle while having online journals through faculty members and research scholars. Online journals are the signal of future. Online journals in the scientific world, much like online newspaper, are an attempt to harness the power of computer-immediate communication networks to scientific communication and discourse. E-journals in the broader context of information technology and the electronic age competitive cultural perspectives form the past twenty years.

2. MATERIALS AND METHODS

The study was conducted on a sample of 181 full time science faculty members of University of Pune, from 17 science departments of which 122 responded positively. Pre-structured questionnaires were used to get the opinion about the use of online journals use and had distributed to the all of the faculty members of science stream in University of Pune.

3. REVIEW OF LITERATURE

Cochenour and Moothart's (2003) study present the study of a user survey which aimed in particular to determine whether all faculties, administrative professional and graduate student at Colorado state university supported canceling print subscriptions when they are duplicated by electronic equivalents. They sent a printed questionnaire in spring 2001 to a sample of 6968. The response rate was 10.4%. The result of this study demonstrated that although overall, 95.6% supported or strongly supported dual print/electronic subscriptions, only 74.3% supported canceling print subscriptions when they are duplicated by electronic equivalents; 25.7% opposed or strongly opposed canceling print; 77.4% supported the move electronic only subscriptions under the condition that the publisher guarantees perpetual access.

Atilgan and Bayram's (2006) articles reports the result of a survey on the use of e-databases at Ankara University. They surveyed faculty in 2002 to determine level of awareness of digital library resources, particularly journals articles, along with their use rate, and to evaluate the preference of the faculty for specific electronic databases. They distributed a questionnaire to a sample of 3800 researchers at Ankara University, out of which 1996 (53%) usable questionnaires were returned to the investigators. The main findings were that the majority of respondents (86.5%) indicated that they knew that digital library resources exist in Ankara University. Many of the faculty members (88%) use electronic databases. Full professors (53.8%) and research assistants (55.4%) place second after associate (67.8%) and assistant (63.4%) professors in the use of electronic journals although they place first in level of awareness of the Digital library. The most preferred databases have been Web of Science, Science Direct, and EBSCO. "It seems possible that there is a positive impact of newly subscribed databases on this increased in publishing. The extent to which the use of databases can influence productivity in Ankara University might be a topic for further study," they conclude.

Raza and Upadhyay's (2006) study measures the usage of e-journals by researchers at Aligarh Muslim University (AMU, Aligarh, India) They distributed a questionnaire to a sample of 72 researchers at AMU, out of which only 52 filled questionnaires were returned to the investigator. The overall response rate was 72%. The finding of the study, briefly, is as follows: the researchers were aware of e-journals in AMU; many research scholars access e-journals from their departmental labs and computer centre, for research and to update their own knowledge; most of the researchers used both printed journals and e-journals; a large number of researchers were storing e-journals articles by downloading them onto discs; and lack of training and slow downloading were the problems faced by the researchers while using e-journals. This study ends with the statement that e-journals will not replace the traditional print format but rather compliment it as a new medium of communication.

Borrego et al. (2007) reports the result of a survey o the use of print and e-journals by the academic staff of the University belonging to the consortium of academic libraries of Catalonia (CBUC). Between May and June 2005, a questionnaire was distributed to the population consisting of a total of 14,855researchers mainly by post. The 2682 replies received represented a response rate of 18.05%. The major results can be summarized as follows: more than 95% of the respondents are aware of the e-journals; electronic journals are used exclusively or predominantly by 52% of the respondents; use of the e-journal collection shows a statistically significant relationship with the discipline, the age of the respondents and their academic status; and 76% of the respondents prefer the electronic format over the printed format when both formats are accessible the acceptance of the format change is also related to the discipline and age and academic states of the respondents and 53.6% of respondents consult e-journals for both research and teaching.

Kurata, Keiko et al. (2007) present a study that seeks to identify changes in the place of e-journals, using factual data on Japanese researchers' usage and view of them. Their mainly focus on distinguishing between the function of scholarly journals and the electronic forms. They sent a questionnaire to 1427 physicists, 1026 chemists, and 1276 pathologists in universities and other research institute all over Japan, of whom 775 (54.3%), 494 (48.1%), and 541 (42.4%), respectively, supplied answers. The finding indicates that scholarly communication is gradually changing but at different speeds in different research fields. Other major finding of the study includes the following: only age was statistically significantly related with the frequency of use: about 70% of the respondents read articles in an electronic form; but also, 92.5% of the chemist and 91.6% of the pathologists were reader of print journals; the most frequent pattern after the introduction of e-journals was downloading and printing out PDF file (68% of the physicists, 60.1% of the chemist and 55.4% of the pathologists); an increase in the number of articles read was reported by 33.8% of the physicist, 35.9% of the chemists, and 41% of the pathologists; and semi permanent accessibility to back issues was regarded as the most important aspect of journals to be maintained in the future.

The Stanford University Library conducted a two-year research project investigating attitudes towards electronic journals published in Internet editions by High Wire Press, the Libraries' online service bureau for scholarly publishers. This domain of online scholarly communication is poorly understood and poorly researched. Moreover, competition among the profit and non-profit scholarly journal publishers has generated various claims regarding efficacy and efficiency of communication. Little data is available to support such claims. While the study benefited in particular more than 60 scholarly societies whose publication in Internet editions are associated with High Wire Others got benefit as well. This study is to assist scholars, librarians, and administrators in higher education and research making individual and collective choices in how they contribute to scholarly communication.

Super Journal is a research project (1999) and the main objective was to identify the features that deliver real value, and to explore the implications with stakeholders in the publishing process: readers, authors, libraries, and publishers. The research was conducted over three years (1996-1998) and the project ended in December 1998. The project aimed to use electronic journal application and made clusters of journals available to university test sites via the World Wide Web. At the start of the project readers were asked about their expectations for electronic journals. For two years their usage was recorded and analyzed. Users consider the back file to be an important feature of an electronic journal service, and most would like a back file of 5-10 years. Responses to user survey varied from 1 to 50 years, with Science users averaging 7 years, and Social Science users averaging 11 years. Users in the Social Sciences made wider use of the journals than users in the Sciences. Averaged over all journal users, the majority (82%) of Social Science users used 1-6 journals, where the majority of Science users used 1-3 journals. The survey indicates that over 90% user used journals first time. Use of journal issues in the current year was greater in the Sciences than in the Social Sciences. User's value abstracts. Most users (72%) said they would like publishers to publish abstracts in both print and electronic versions of their journals. Five of the Social Science journals included in Super Journal did not contain abstracts, and another four did not have abstracts for all articles. The Science users viewed abstracts less frequently than the Social Science users. Science users more often browsed at the Table of Contents level, or went direct from the TOC to the article itself. Typically users in the Sciences were using Super Journal to get specific articles and to keep up to date with specific journals. Surveys at the end of the project suggest that listing electronic journals on the library web site is the most successful technique overall. 24.5% of repeat users and 37.1% of non-repeat users found out about Super Journal in this way.

Mounissamy and Swaroop Rani (2005) have conducted a survey to know the usage and usability of electronic journals of National Institute of Technology, Tiruhcirapalli. The study carried out at the NIT, Tiruchirapalli revealed that 67% of students and 33% of faculty use the electronic journals. 25% of the respondents access electronic journals daily. 45.4% access once in a week. 14.8% access electronic journals once in a month and 14.8% access as and when they feel like it. 53.4% of the respondents access 1-3 journals in a month. 26.1% access 3-6 electronic journals in a month. 12.5% access 6-10 electronic journals in a month and 8% access above 10 journals.

4. OBJECTIVES OF THE STUDY

To carry out the present research study systematically, the investigator laid down the following objectives,

1. To find out the awareness and the use of online journals among faculty members in science stream of University of Pune.
2. To find out the opinions of science faculty members about the adequacy of available online journals on the library web portal of University of Pune.
3. To identify the features, functionality and development of electronic journals.
4. To trace the problems in the use of online journals.
5. To suggest ways and means to overcome problems faced by the faculty members.

5. RESULTS AND DISCUSSION

5.1. Perceived Level of Computer Literacy

A computer literate user is expected to benefit from effectively use online service and confidently explore the amazing world of internet. Effective use of these online databases/journals for retrieving needed information would be cumbersome without proper computing and information retrieval skill. Hence the Respondents were asked to indicate their skill in the use of compute. According to their own assessments, a majority 72% Respondents reported that they are having 'average skill' in the use of computers. 21% of the Respondents opined to have 'above average skills' and least 7.4% Respondents stated to have 'below average skill' (Figure 1).

5.2. Perceived Level of Using the Kinds of Library Resources

Faculty members of science stream use various library resources, in this context Respondents were asked about their preference of library resources. According to their responses the large majority of 92.62% Respondents reported that they use online/electronic resources, 63.93% of the Respondents use print resources from the library, and 24.59% Respondent use CD ROM resources, and 24.59% Respondents were using parallel resources like electronic, print, and CD ROM. In the present research study it was found that the highest 92.62% Respondents use online resources than those Respondents who use print and CD ROM resources (Figure 2).

5.3. Links of Online Journals Access

The Respondents were accessing online journals since last decade from different sites e. g. through publishers URLs, through search engine, through the link internet facility' created on university library home page. And through Jayakar library web portal which created through Jayakar library staff, on 1st august 2008 at the Jayakar library home page. It is beneficial to follow the link of every U.G.C InfoNet publisher wise full text databases for accessing online journals in various areas of subjects. In this regard Respondents were asked to give the response about accessing online journals. The result are summarized in Figure 2 that the large majority of 68.03 Respondents were access online journals through the link 'internet facility' created on the University of Pune home page, 56.55% responded that they were use search engine for accessing online journals, and only 43.44% Respondents were use Jayakar library Web Portal to access online journals and remaining 31.14% of the Respondents were accessing online journals through directly from publishers URLs (Figure 3).

5.4. Frequency of Library Visit

The Respondents were requested to mark all the modes by which they visit library. According to their responses, the 39.34% Respondents opined

Figure 1. Perceived level of computer literacy

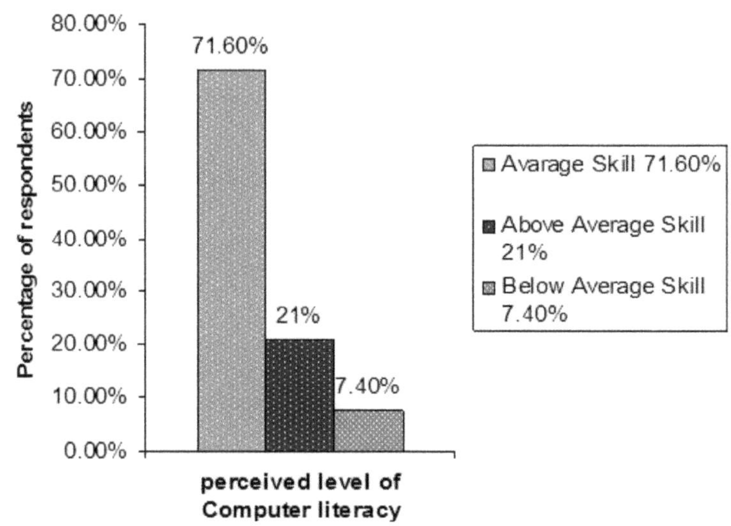

Figure 2. Use of library resources

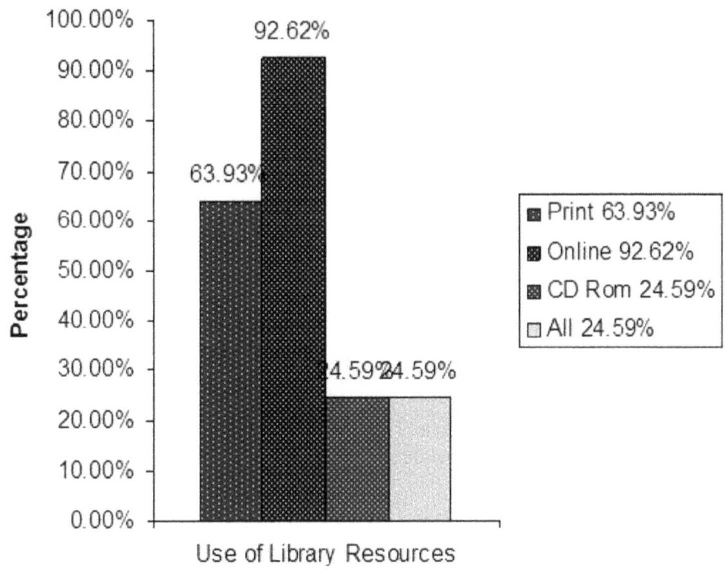

Figure 3. Perceived links of online journal access

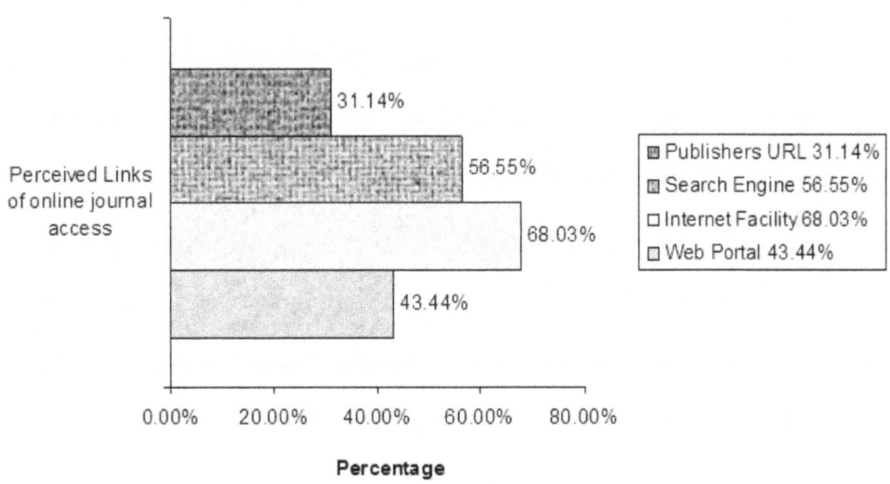

that they were visited library once a month, 19.67% Respondent were visit library in twice a week as well as more 19.67% Respondents were visit library once a fortnight, the ratio of the daily visiting library were just 4.91% out of total number of Respondents. 4.09% Respondents were visiting library trice a week and 12.29% Respondents had not visited to their university library (Figure 4).

5.5. Location of Accessing Online Journals

The large majority, 100% of the Respondents indicate that they have access to online journals from their individual department in the University campus while 7.37% Respondents opined that they were access online journals from their residence,

Figure 4. Frequency of library visits

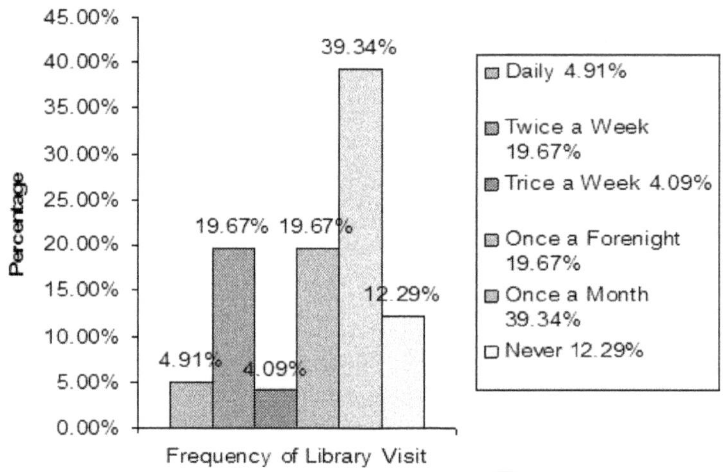

and there were no response for accessing online journals from university library building out of total numbers of Respondents (Figure 5).

5.6. Perceived Level of Online Journals Search

Respondents were requested to mark the entire mode by which they search the online journals from library Web portal. Generally online journals are search by subject, by title, by author, and other, e.g., by publisher, ISBN no., etc., according to their responses. It was found that the large majority of 77.04% Respondents were search online journals by subject, 62.92% Respondents were search the online journal by title search, 42.62% Respondents search their required online journals by authors search, and at least 7.37% Respondents search their online journals by other type, e.g., by publishers name and ISBN no etc. (Figure 6).

5.7. Experience of Online Journals Use

Respondents were asked to indicate the number of years of experience they had in using the on-line journals. It is found that 38.52% respondents have been using online journals for last five years,

Figure 5. Location of online journal access

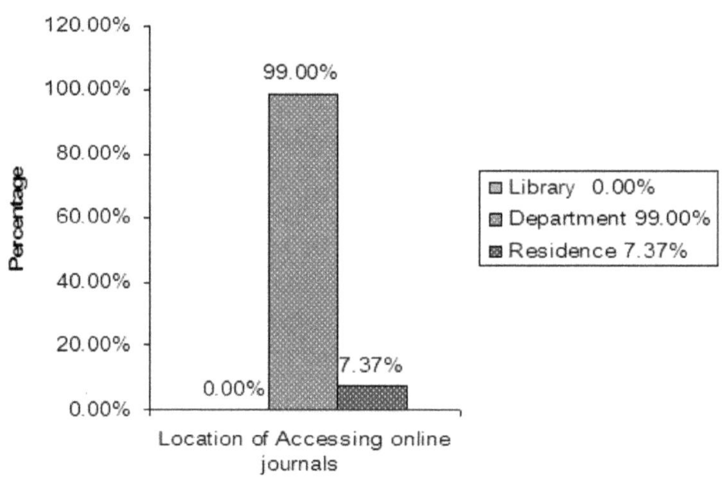

Figure 6. Preferred online journal search

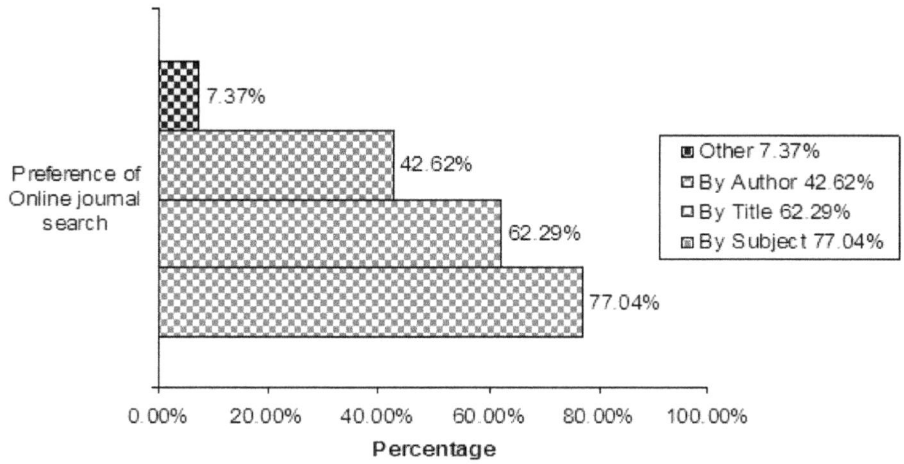

and 26.22% Respondents have been using online journals for last ten year, they have ten year experience in using online journals. The Figure 7 also depicts that only 13.11% Respondents started using online journals since 2 years, and few 21.31% Respondents' have less than a year of experience. Overall, Respondents had good amount of experience to exploit optimally the electronic journals and services.

5.8. Perceived Modes of Archival Collection for Online Journals Access

The Respondents were asked to indicate the opinion about archival collection of electronic journals provided by university library web portal available in which mode, e.g., CD ROM, online, hard copy of bound volumes/ back issue of electronic journals. According to their assessment, the large majority of 95.08% Respondents stated that archival collection of electronic journals available in online mode, 18.03% Respondents stated that the archival collection of online journal available in hard copy of bound volumes or back issue of online journals, and vary few 14.75% Respondents were stated that the archival collection of electronic journal available in both hard copy and online mode, and at least 1.63% Respondents opined that archival collection of online journals available in CD ROM mode. The majority of responses stated that online archival collection is available mostly online than CD ROM and hard copy of back issues (Figure 8).

Figure 7. Experience of online journal use

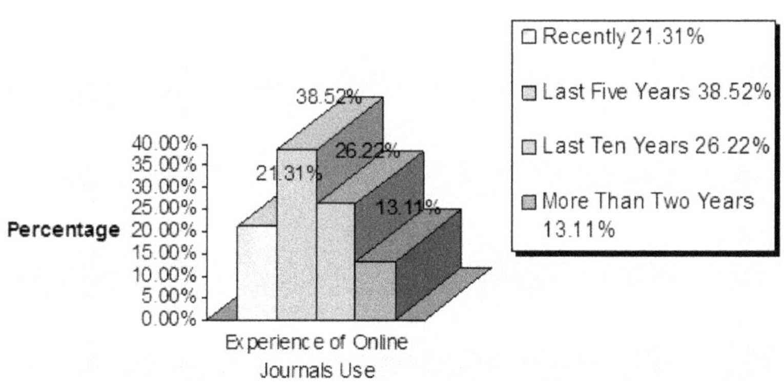

Figure 8. Archival collection of journals

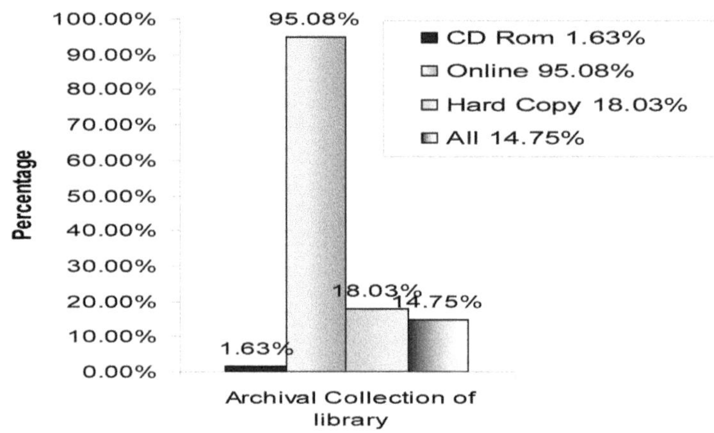

5.9. Library Alerting Services

The Respondents were asked to indicate their responses about the current issue of the electronic journals because the new issues of online journals always come in the library in the print and the online form, then the faculty member should be aware about the current information, in this regard the Respondents were asked to indicate their responses about the new issue of online journals, it is found that the majority of 48.36% Respondents state that they come to know about know journals through email alert service (provided by library staff), 36.06% Respondents indicate that they come to know about New journals through library Web page, and very few 11.47% Respondents indicate that they come to know about New issue through library user, and at least 9.83% of the Respondents state that they come to know about current issue through library bulletin (Internet) the majority of respondent indicate internet related alert service, those services must be update for better services through the library (Figure 9).

Figure 9. Library alert services

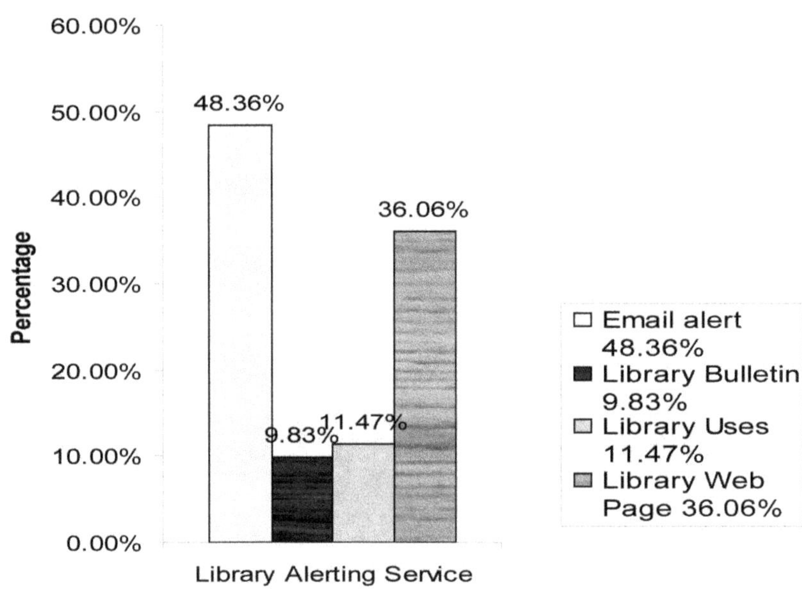

5.10. Internet Speed

Accessibility of online journals and its use rapidly depend on the internet speed. When internet speed is slow it take more time to accessing, downloading the articles then it is major problem for provision. In this regard Respondents were asked to indicate their opinions about the internet speed in the university campus; According to their assessment it was found that the large majority of 40.16% of the Respondents stated that the internet speed in the university campus was in average, 27.04% of the respondents opined that the speed was slow in University campus, 29.50% of the Respondents marked for the very slow about the speed of internet in university campus. And at least 0.81% responded that the internet speed was fast. Thus it seen that the internet speed is in average the university campus and it is a major problem in accessing online journals. The speed of internet must be increase (Figure 10).

5.11. Use of UGC INFONET Publisher Wise Full Text Databases

UGC INFONET E-journal consortia provide Full text and Full text com. Bibliographic databases to provide online journals access to 150 Universities in the country. Respondents were asked to mark about the awareness of UGC INFONET E-journals consortia according to their responses total majority of Respondents were aware about the availability of UGC INFONE E-journal consortia access at the university library and the large majority of 75.40% the responded that they could obtain required information from UGC INFONET journals. The percentage of Respondents about the use of publisher wise Full text databases at the Jayakar library web portal University of Pune. According to their assessment it was found that the large majority of 89.34% Respondents used Elsevier Science/Science Direct Publisher wise full text database to access online journals. 66.39% responded for Springer link, 42.62% of the Respondents indicated for Nature, 36.88%, and 36.88% Respondents marked for the use of American Chemical Society, and Blackwell Publishing. 35.24% for Oxford University Press, 25.40% for Annual Review, 23.77% for Institute of Physics, 22.95% for American Physical Society, 20.49% marked for JSTOR, 18.03% for American Institute of Physics 13.11 opined for IEEE Computer Society use, 4.09% for Project Euclid, 7.37% for EBSCO, 3.27% for Society for Industrial and Applied Mathematics (SIAM), 3.27% for Emerald, and at least 0.81% and the same 0.81% marked for the use of Portland Press and Project Muse at the University Library (Figure 11).

Figure 10. Internet speed rates

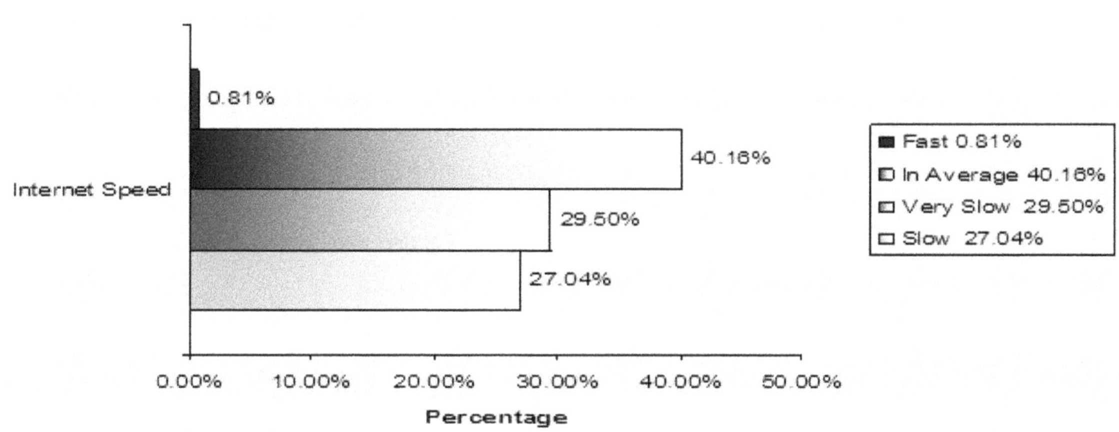

Figure 11. Database usage

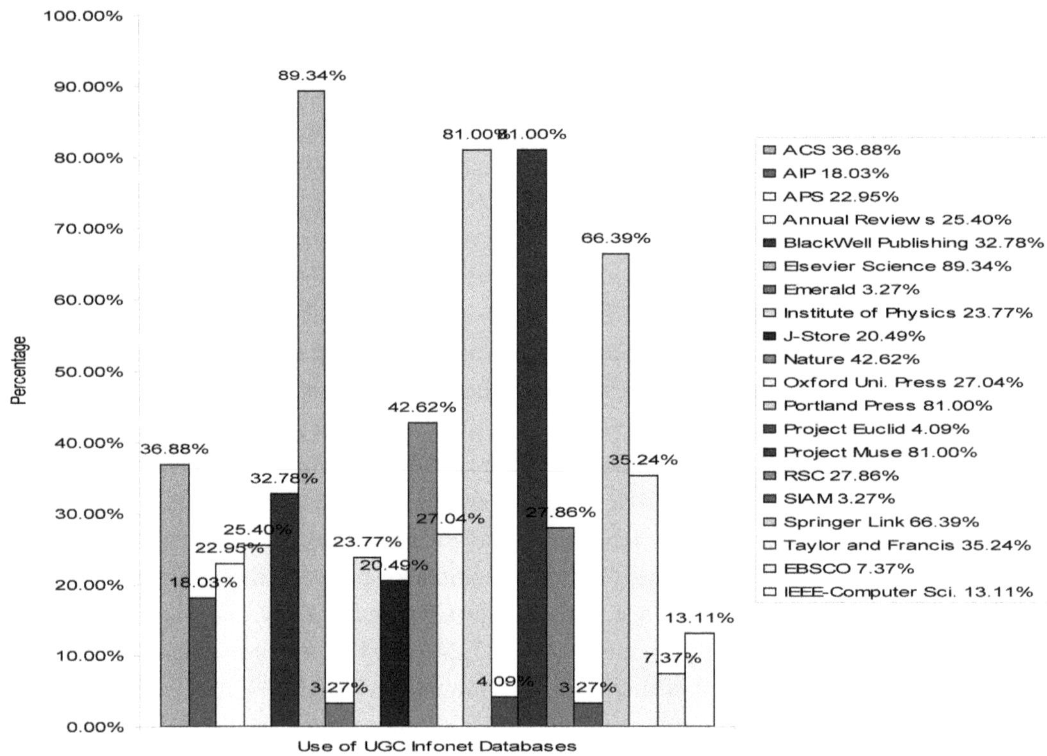

5.12. Use of Bibliographical Databases

Jayakar Library University of Pune has subscribed some bibliographical databases for accessing online journals and other useful services. Then it must be used in this regard Respondents were asked to indicate their opinion for their assessment of the use of Bibliographical databases. According to their opinions it was found that the majority of 35.24% Respondents marked for the use of Web of Science or Web of Knowledge. 33.60% were use Sci Finder Scholar, 14.75% responded for Royal Society of Chemistry (6 databases) 9.83% marked for the use of MathSciNet, 8.19% responded for the use of JCCC, and very few 1.63% Respondents indicate their opinion for the use of Institute for Studies in Industrial Development (ISDB) this all of this Bibliographical databases are very useful for the science community for their research and teaching (Figure 12).

5.13. Open Access Free Directories

Jayakar Library University of Pune provide open access free directory it is open for all Researcher and faculty members, it is also provider online journals. Directory of Open Access Journals (DOAJ), Open J-gate, Free Medical Journals Provides subject wise journals, Respondents asked to indicate their responses about the use of open access free directory. It was found that 14.75% Respondents were marked for open J-gate, 12.29% Respondents used Directory of Open Access Journals (DOAG), and 4.91% of the Respondents opined that they were using Free Medical Journals (Figure 13).

5.14. Open Access Journals

Jayakar Library University of Pune provides open access journals, these open access journals also provide useful information and online journals. Respondents were asked to mark their opinion

Figure 12. Bibliography database usage

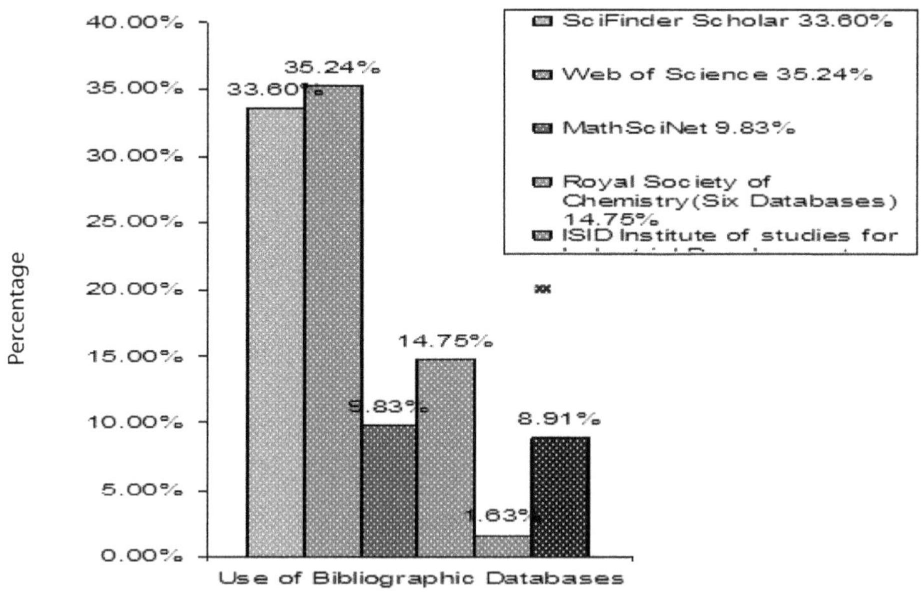

Figure 13. Open access to free directories

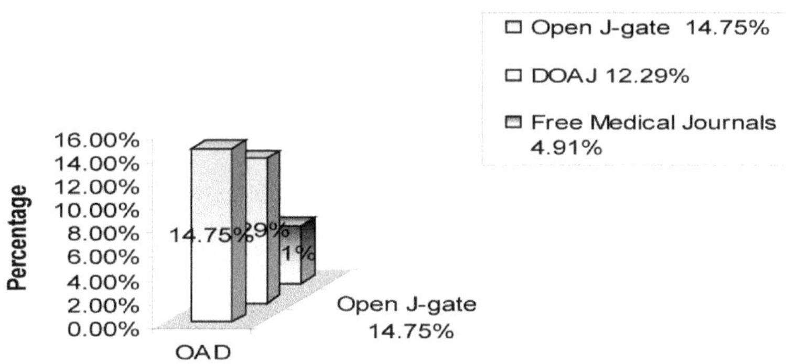

about the open access journals According to their assessment of use it was found that the majority of 27.86% respondents were use Indian academy of Science, 13.93% Respondents used Bio Med Central, 4.91% used Bio International, 22.99% of the Respondents used Indian journals, 19.97% Respondents used Pub Med Central, 4.91% of the Respondents were used journal of Pubic Library of Science (PloS), 3.27% of the Respondents used journals of Digital library of India, and at the least 0.81% Respondents used the journals of Digital Information, 0.81% used journal of Post Graduate Medicine, 0.81% used Med IND, 0.81% of the Respondents were used Med Know, 0.81% were used Molecular Diversity Preservation International (MDPI) and 0.81% responded that they used journals of Trials (Figure 14).

5.15. Components Online Journal

Respondents were asked to indicate their opined about the use of online journals components, the options table of contents, Journals Abstracts, Full text, Article reference, as an online journals component, with the Modes of use like, Most – A, Often – B, Sometimes – C, Somewhat – D, Least

Figure 14. Users of open access journal

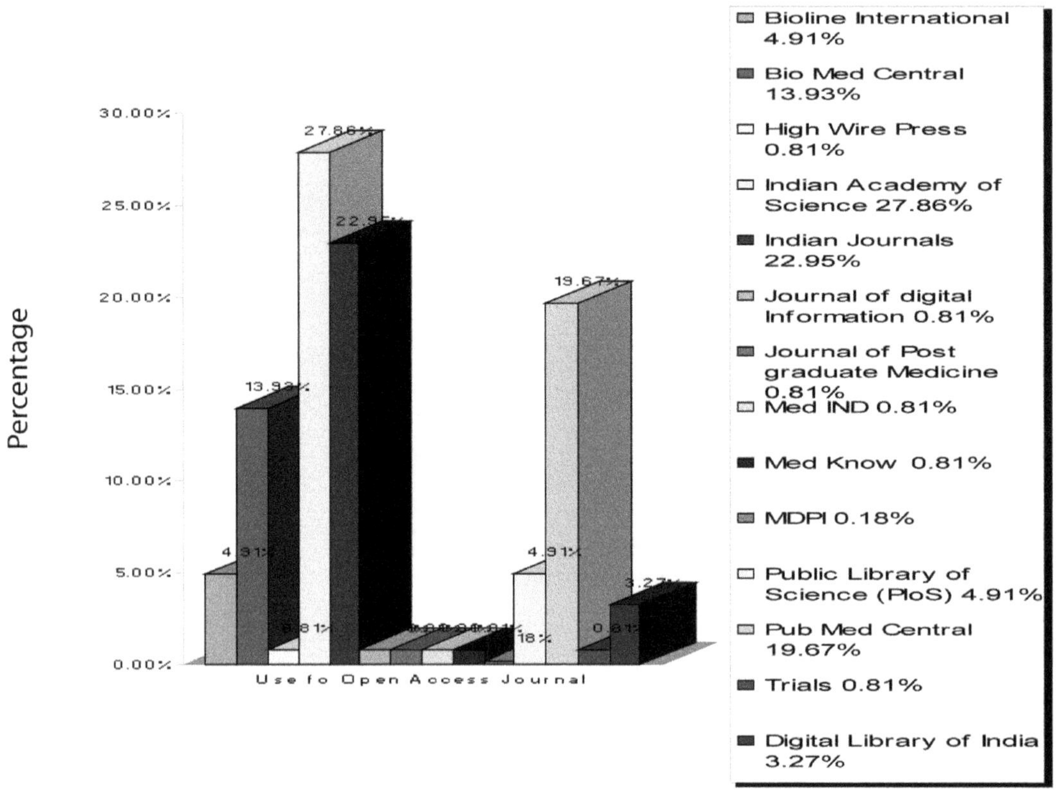

– E, were given to obtain the right perceived level of used online journal components. It was found that the table of contents used by Respondents in different level, that the majority of 35.24% of the Respondents use mostly table of contents, 20.49 responded often use of table of content, 15.57% used sometime (TOC), 3.27% marked for somewhat use of (TOC), and at least 3.37% Respondents use (TOC), Journals Abstracts. The majority of 56.55% Respondents were using Journals Abstracts. Mostly, 25.40% Respondents were using journals abstract often. 4.91% of the Respondents use journals abstracts sometime about the use of Journal Abstracts, 1.63% Respondents were use somewhat journal abstracts. Full text: Respondents were asked to mark their opinion about the use of Full text online journal component, after the survey it was found that the majority of 52.81% of the Respondents were using full text mostly, 36.06% Respondents responded that they used Full text often. 11.47% responded that they were using sometime full text component of online journals. Article reference: 19.67% Respondents were using the article reference mostly, 33.60% used Article reference often, and 21.31% Respondents were using Article reference sometimes, 5.73% Respondents were using article reference somewhat, and at least 1.63% of the Respondents were using article reference as a component of online journals. Figure 15 shows the percentage of Respondents with their use of online journal components.

5.16. Perceived Level of Using Online Journal Format

Online journals are published in various formats and different format provide different feature for

Figure 15. Online journal abstract use

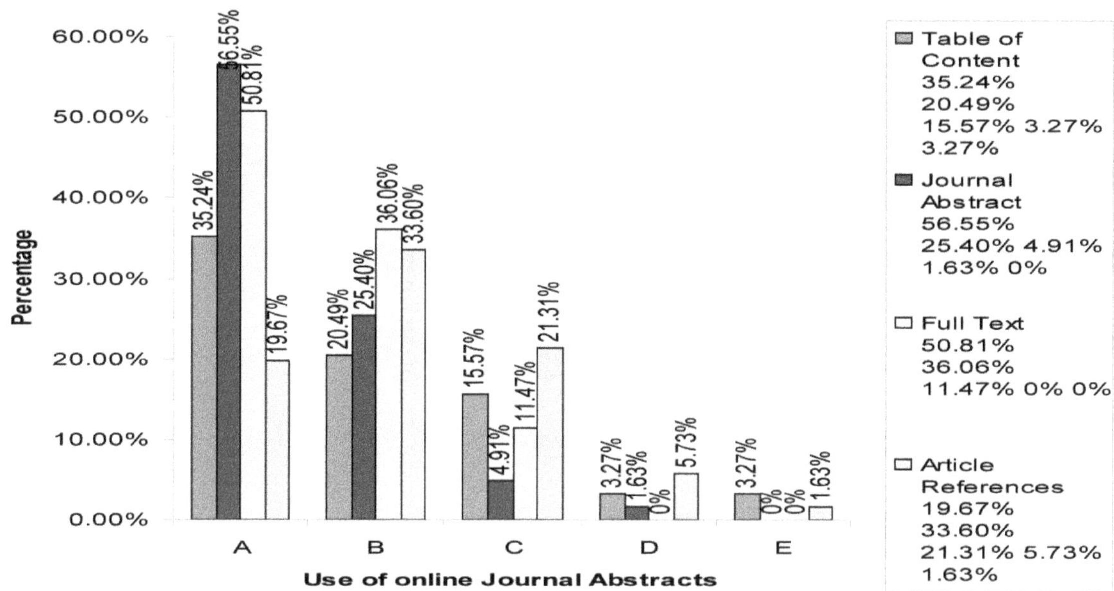

article, thus the user use different format for their use of online journals or other purpose. Respondents were asked to give their opinions about the online journal format. Respondents were using various formats with various modes like most, often, sometime, somewhat, and least. Portable Document Format (PDF) Respondents were asked to indicate their opinion about the PDF use. According to their survey it was found that the large majority of 95.90% Respondents marked for the mostly use of PDF, 4.09% Respondents marked for the often use of the PDF, Hypertext markup language (HTML) 10.65% of the Respondents marked for the mostly use of HTML, 17.21% of the Respondents used HTML often, 18.03% of the Respondents opined for somewhat HTML format, 2.45% of the Respondents were using HTML somewhat, and 7.37% of the Respondents were using HTML at least. Standard General Markup Language (SGML)- 3.27% of the Respondents were used SGML sometimes, 2.45% of the Respondents marked for the use of SGML somewhat, 15.57% of the Respondents used SGML format at least. ASCII- 3.27% of the Respondents were marked for the use of ASCII sometime, and the same 3.27% of the Respondents were use ASCII format somewhat, 15.57% opined that they using ASCII format at least. MSWord- 4.91% of the Respondents were use MS-Word mostly, 18.85% of the Respondents were using MS-Word often, 10.65% were using MS-Word sometime, 2.45% responded that they use MS-Word format somewhat, and 9.01% of the Respondents were use online format at least. Postscript- 1.63% of the Respondents were using Postscript Format mostly, 7.35% of the Respondents were use the postscript format often, and 8.19% of the Respondents using the postscript format sometimes for using online journals, 2.45% of the Respondents were using postscript format somewhat, and 13.11% of the Respondents were using postscript format at least (Figure 16).

5.17. Frequencies of Using Online Journals

Respondents were asked how frequently they used online journals. Options were Daily, Weekly,

Figure 16. Use of online journal format

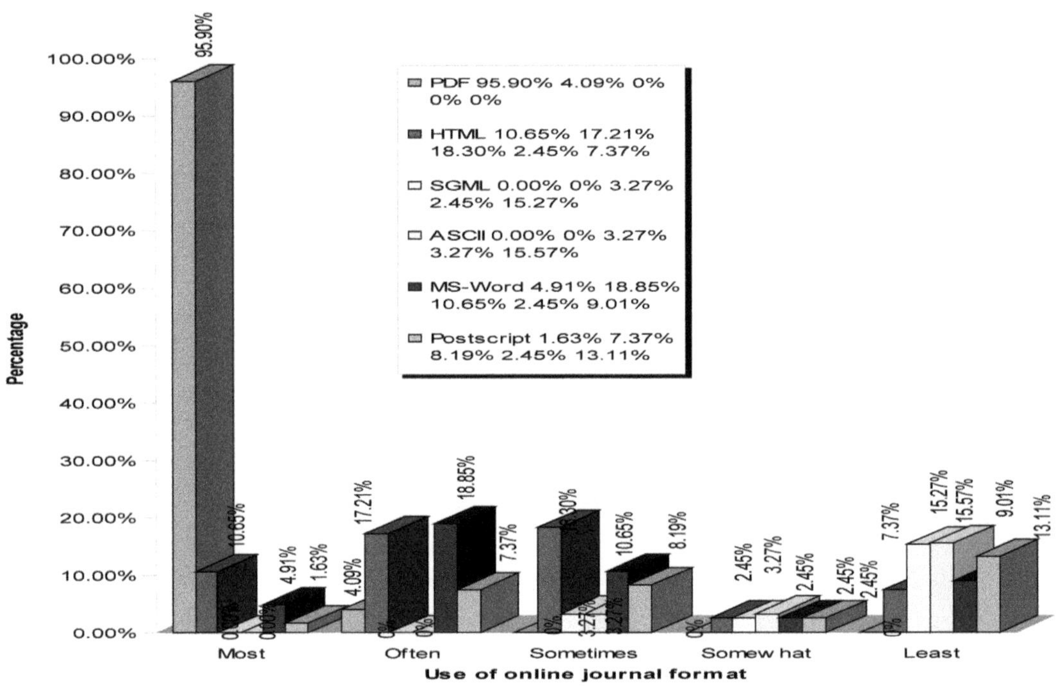

Figure 17. Frequency of online journal use

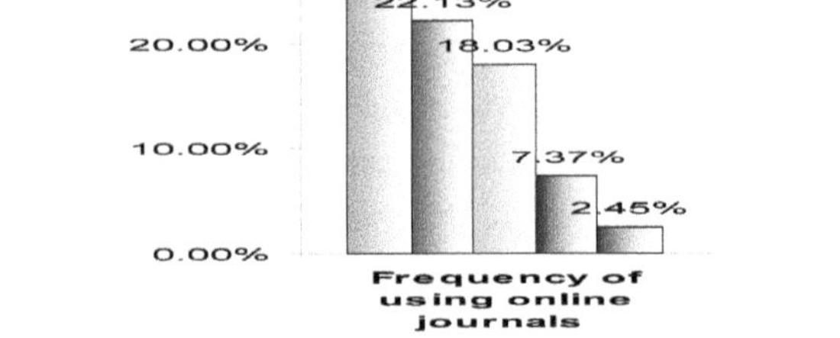

Monthly, Biweekly, and Bimonthly. Figure 17 shows that the large majority of 50.00% of the Respondents were accessing online journals Daily, 22.13% of the Respondents were accessing online journals Weekly, 7.37% of the Respondents were accessing online journals Monthly. 18.03% of the Respondents were accessing online journals Biweekly and 2.45% of the Respondents were accessing online journals Bimonthly.

5.18. Perceived Level of System Speed

Online journal article taka time to download online articles generally the time of downloading depends on the internet speed Respondents have their different opinion about the downloading time of the online articles with their daily working networked computer. The Respondents were asked to indicate their opined about the system speed; the options were less than 10 min, 10-20 min, 20-30 min, 30-40 min, 40-50 min, and more than 50 min. According to their responses, it was found that the 36.06% of the Respondents stated that it take less than 10 min, 40.98% reported that the system take 10-20 min, 9.83% opined that the system take 20-30 min time to download the online article, 4.91% respondent opined that it took 30-40 min to download one article, 2.45% responded that it took 40-50 min, and 2.45% of the Respondents stated that their networked computer at their Department it took more than 50 minutes to download one article. Overall opinions depend on the speed of the Internet; because of that Internet speed must be improved (Figure 18).

5.19. Time Spent for Reading Online Journals

Respondents were asked about the time which they spent weekly on reading online/off line journals it was found that the large majority of 43.44% of the Respondents state that they spent more than 120 min weekly on reading online journals. 4.91% spent 90-120 minutes for reading online journals, 22.55% Respondents spent 60-90 minutes, and 9.83% of the Respondents spent 30-60 minutes on reading online journals. 6.55% of the Respondents spent up to 30 minutes on reading online journals. It was found that 50.81% Respondents spent above 180 minutes weekly on offline reading articles. 22.95% of the respondent spent 120-180 minutes weekly on off reading. 4.91% of the Respondents state that they spent 60-120 minutes on off line reading. 4.91% of the Respondents were reported that they spent up to 60 minutes weekly (Figure 19).

5.20. Ratio of Reading Online Article

Respondents were asked to mark about the ratio of online article by weekly according to their assessment. It was found that the 13.93% of the Respondents read more than 15 articles online in a week. 13.11% of Respondents opined that they read 10-15 articles in a week, 47.75% Respondents read 5-10 articles in a week, and 26.2% of the Respondents read less than 5 articles in a week (Figure 20).

Figure 18. Perceived level of system speed

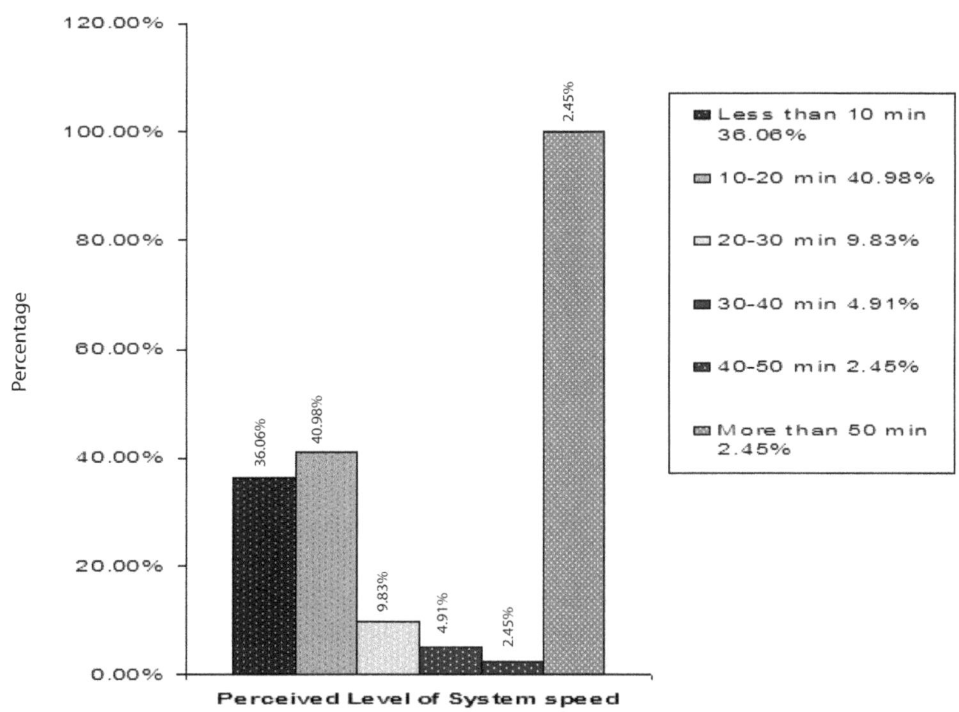

Figure 19. Frequency between online and offline reading

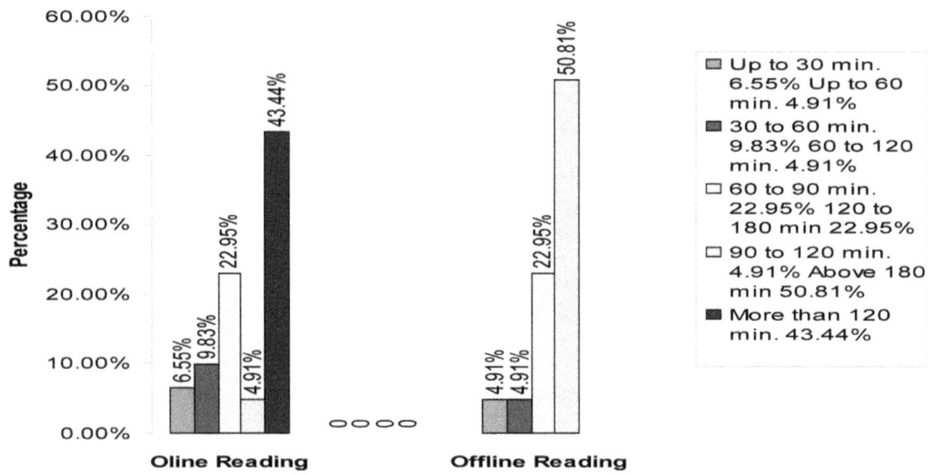

Figure 20. Ratio of reading online articles

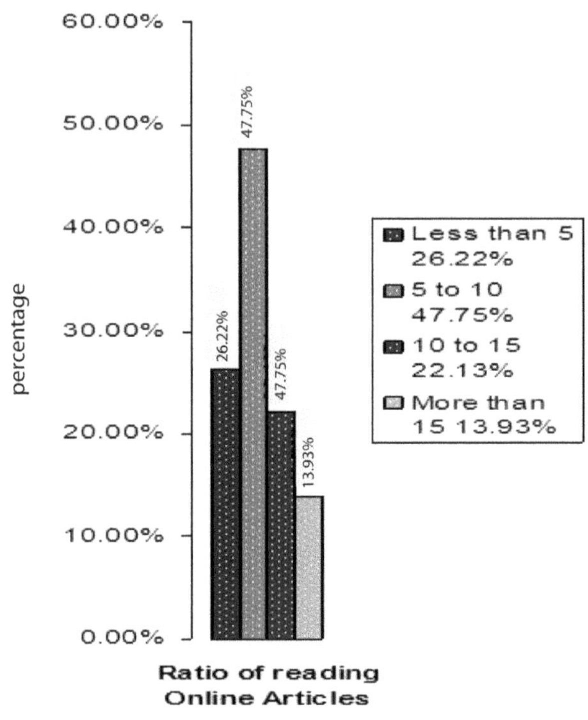

5.21. Perceived Level of Online Reading and on Print Reading

Respondents were asked to report their opinion about reading online articles. The options were read on monitor and read on print, indifferent modes like always, often, usually, sometimes, and never. It was found that the Respondents preferred to read on the monitor and on print. Read on monitor: it was found that the large majority of 45.08% Respondents always read their articles on the monitor, 28.68% of the Respondents were often read the journal on the monitors, 13.93% responded that they were usually reading articles on the monitor, 18.03% of the Respondents read somewhat their articles on the monitor, and 2.45% of the Respondents never read their articles on the monitor. Read on print: It was found that the large majority of 26.22% Respondents read their articles always on the print, 22.26% of the Respondents read their articles often on the print, 18.03% Respondents read articles usually on the print, 20.49% of the Respondents read their articles sometimes on the print, and 9.01% of the Respondents never read the articles on print (Figure 21).

5.22. Online Journals Browsing Features

The Respondents were asked indicate their opinions about online journals browsing features, in this regard several, specific statements were given and agreements and disagreements of the Respondents were recorded. Figure 22 shows that the 46.72% Respondents were agree strongly with the online journals browsing features, 44.26% were agree somewhat, and 7.37% were disagree somewhat about the content multimedia information as an online journal browsing feature. It was found that the large majority of 55.73% Respondents were agree strongly, 41.80% of the Respondents were agree somewhat, 0.81% Respondents were disagree somewhat, and 0.81% of the Respondents were disagree strongly about the 'content easy to understand' an online journals browsing feature. 68.85% Respondents were agree strongly, 30.32% Respondents were agree somewhat, 0.81% of the Respondents were disagree some somewhat, and 0.81% of the Respondents were disagree strongly about the 'user friendly interface' as a online journal browsing feature, as well as 40.10% Respondents were agree strongly, 47.54% Respondents were agree somewhat, 9.01% Respondents were disagree somewhat, and 2.45% Respondents were disagree strongly about the 'reading on monitor' a online journal browsing feature. Overall statement shows that the online journals were very beneficial for the Respondents (Figure 22).

Figure 21. Chart between reading from the computer or printed text

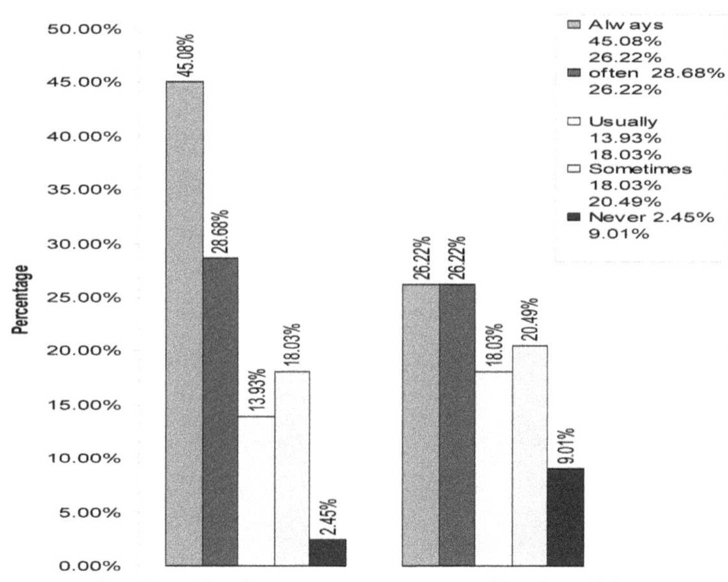

Figure 22. Graph on respondents opinion on browsing features

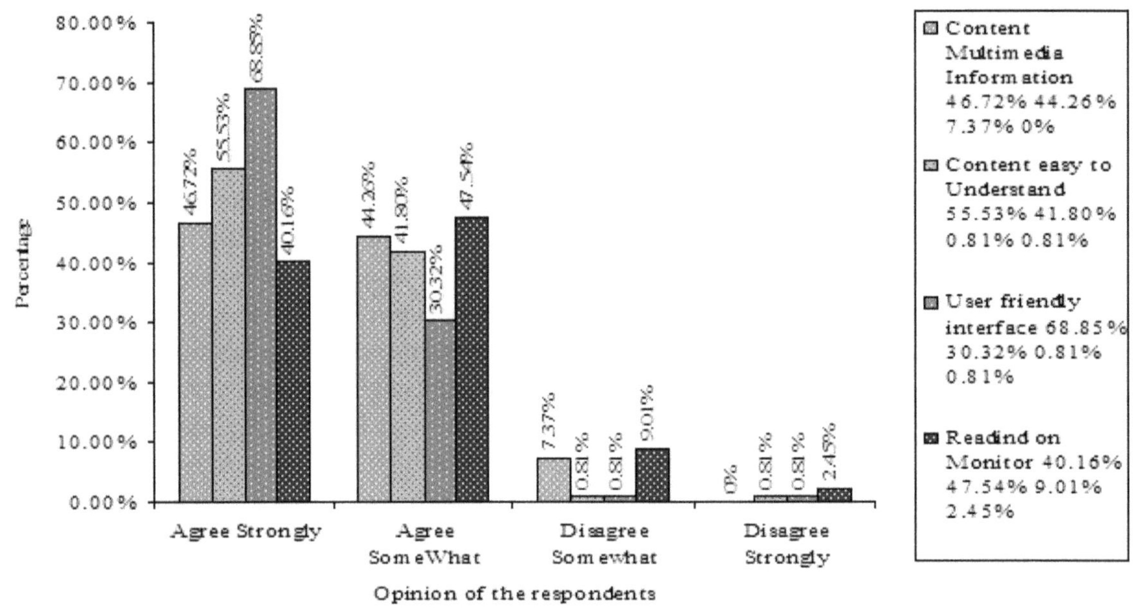

5.23. Purpose of Using Online Journals

Respondents were asked to indicate their opinion about the purpose of using online journals. It was found that the large majority of Respondents were using online journals for the for the purpose of research need, majority of 85.24% Respondents were using online journals for the purpose of teaching, 79.50% of the Respondent were using online journals for the purpose of updating knowledge, and 73.77% Respondents were using

Figure 23. Purpose of online journal use

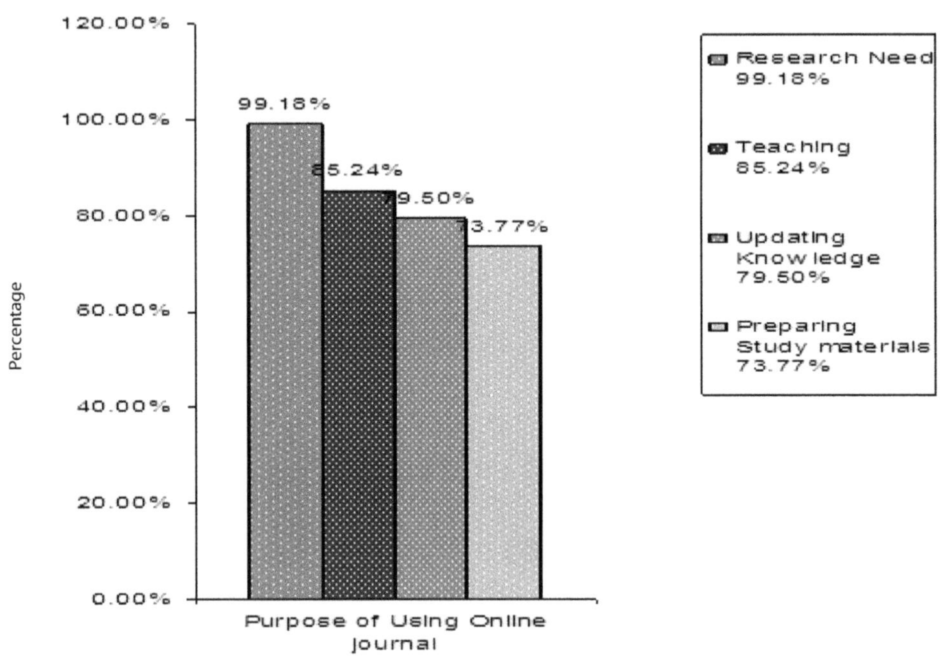

online journal for the purpose of preparing study materials. The most important purpose of the online journals is research reported by the majority of the Respondents (Figure 23).

5.24. Regularly Used Search Engines

The Respondents were requested to provide their opinions about the regularly used search engines. It was found that the majority of 99.18% Respondents were using Google, 19.67% Respondents were using SCIRUS, 4.09% were use Info seek, 70.49% Respondents use regularly Wikipedia, the free Encyclopedia, 9.83% Respondents were using Alta-Vista, and 29.50% Respondents use Yahoo search engine. The result is that about regularly using search engine among the Respondents are Google and the Wikipedia, The free Encyclopedia (Figure 24).

5.25. Barriers of Online Journals Use

Respondents were asked to indicate their opined about the barriers in using online journals use. The options were lack of time, cost, unawareness of the use, lack of facilities, inadequate working hours, lack of system speed, and difficulties in accessing non availability of Full text. According to their assessment, it was found that, the majority of 75.40% Respondents stated that they were facing lack of system speed, 76.22% of the Respondents were stated that they were facing the problem of non availability of Full text, 37.70% Respondents were facing the barrier of difficulties in accessing, 36.88% were stated that the lack of time, 8.09% Respondents were facing the barrier of lack of facilities, and 4.91% and the 4.91% Respondents were facing the difficulty of unawareness of use and inadequate working hours. After considering all the problems, it is seen that non availability of full text and the lack of system speed, difficulties of accessing, and lack of time were the major problems in the use of online journals (Figure 25).

Figure 24. Usage of search engines used by respondents

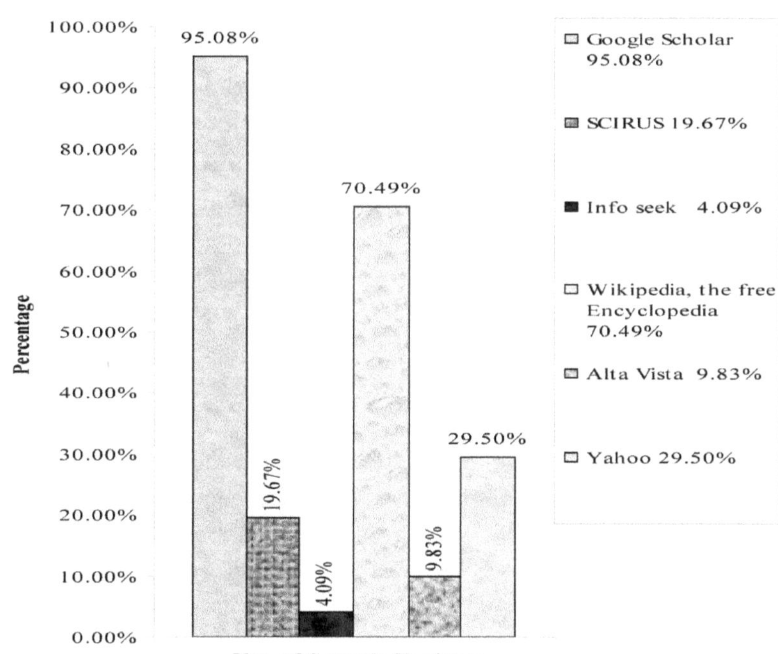

Figure 25. Graph on issues using online journals

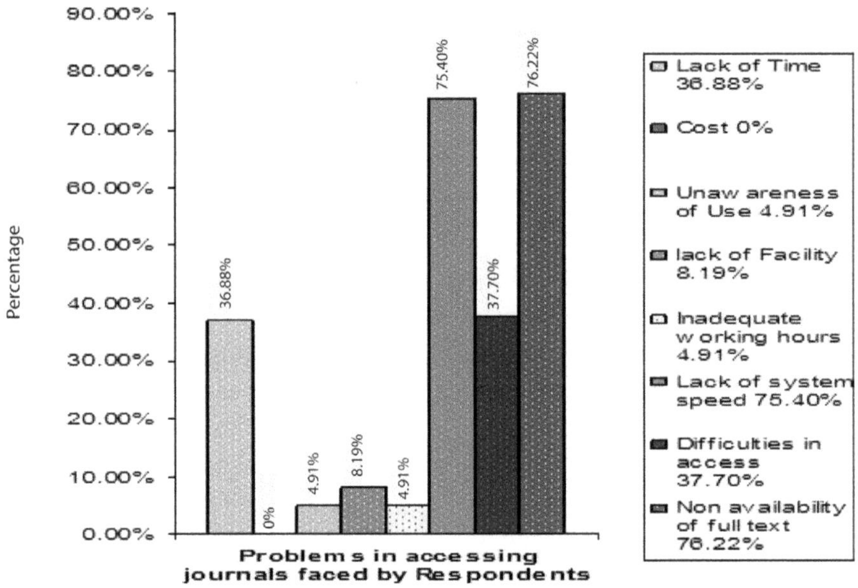

6. MAJOR FINDINGS

1. The majority of science faculty members use online journals for Research, teaching and for updating knowledge. The most important purpose among these is Research purpose.
2. The majority of 89.34% of the respondent were using science direct journals and the majority of 66.39% of the science faculty members responded that they access Springer link journals than other publisher wise full text databases. Thus it can be observed that the most preferred online journals of the science community are Springer journals and journals of science direct full text databases.
3. The majority of science faculty members were using Google and Wikipedia, the free Encyclopedia search engines regularly. 95.08% of the faculty members responded that they were using Google search engine regularly and 70.49% responded for the use of Wikipedia, the Free Encyclopedia search engines. The reveals that the most regularly used search engines among the science faculty members were Google and Wikipedia, the free Encyclopedia.
4. The majority of the science faculty members felt that the available online journals in science were moderately adequate.
5. The majority of science faculty member spent less than four hours weekly on reading online journals.
6. It is observed that the majority of 71.21% of the Respondents had not been getting the benefit of the orientation program through library staff to get familiar with the access to online journals.
7. It is observed that the majority of 26.22% of the Respondents have more than ten year experience and 38.52% of the Respondents have more than five years experience as well as 13.11% of the Respondents have more than two year experience and 21.31% or the Respondents were recently starting to access online journals.
8. It was observed that the large majority of 48.36% of the Respondents were using e-mail alert services to know the new issue in the library. As well as the large majority of 71.31% of the Respondents state that the

Jayakar library, University of Pune provided services are fairly well. It is found that the faculty members opined to provide independent net connection to each faculty members PC not through D-Link.

9. A great majority of the Respondents agreed that they were getting access to more information to and able to save their time considerably in addition to improve their professional competency due to the use of online journals.
10. It is observed that 'Retrieval of Irrelevant Information,' 'Poor Connectivity or Slow Access,' and 'Poor databases searching skill' are the major problems identified by the Respondents in the use of online journals.
11. It was also found that the non availability of full text, lack of time, and lack of system speed were the most important factors that hinder the use of electronic journals among the science faculty members at the University of Pune.

7. SUGGESTIONS

The suggestions are based on the finding of the study. The following suggestions are put forward to improve the use of online journals among the science faculty members in University of Pune:

1. At regular intervals, the University library should organize the orientation training program so that maximum number of user can learn how to use of online journals and other electronic resources.
2. In order to eliminate the slow pace of internet connectivity it may be suggested to the to increase Bandwidth and making available computers with latest processors as terminals for online journals and other electronic information sources use.
3. More number of computer terminals with electronic information resources accessibility should be instilled and repaired of the non working computers in every department as well as each PC of faculty members should be connected through individually to internet connection not with D-Link to get proper access and save the time of faculty members.
4. The emergence of different format of online journals. Necessitate the need of help, supports and explanation of appropriate time, hence the science community of University of Pune may be provide with on-going assistance through compilation, of manual and handbooks in the use of EIS, assistance via e-mail, personal assistance, and accessing quality information.
5. Also information regarding popular and latest website with their address should be displayed on the notice board on the library web page.
6. It is also suggested that university library should subscribe more useful databases e.g., 'review of scientific information,' American Scientific Publishers (ASP), and must increase the subscription of Web of Knowledge, Biological Abstracts, Nature, Royal Society of Chemistry (RSC), and Science Direct journals according to science community for their pursuit.

8. CONCLUSION

The emergence of electronic information and communication Environment has provide the academic science community of University of Pune. With wide opportunities to satisfy their information needs. The study state that the Jayakar library is switching over to electronic sources to electronic sources at on accelerated pace. Printed sources are supplemented by electronic databases, e-journals, and a variety of other media. The study state that according to the assessment of the respondents that the majority of 92.62% of the respondents were using online resources and the large majority of 100% Respondents were aware about the availability of the online journals at the Jayakar library Web Portal. As well as 98.36% of the respondent reported that the electronic journals were supported to their research and teaching. This study has put forth result that deserves a close and a careful scrutiny. The respondents were probed about the possible constraints, retrieval of irrelevant information, poor connectivity, poor databases searching skills, figure as significant pointers to the current state of affairs. The finding of this study has provided useful insight for the library management to take necessary steps to strengthen the existing electronic information sources and services. And to maximize the use of electronic journals among the faculty members of science stream in University of Pune.

REFERENCES

Atilgan, D., & Bayram, O. G. (2006). An evaluation of faculty use of the digital library at Ankara University, Turkey. *Journal of Academic Librarianship*, *32*, 86–93. doi:10.1016/j.acalib.2005.10.009

Baldwin, C. (1999). *Super journal project*. Retrieved from http://www.superjournal.ac.uk/sj

Borrego, A., Anglada, L., Barrios, M., & Comellas, N. (2007). Use and users of electronic journals at Catalan Universities: The result of a survey. *Journal of Academic Librarianship*, *33*(1), 67–75. doi:10.1016/j.acalib.2006.08.012

Cochenour, D., & Moothart, T. (2003). E-journal acceptance at Colorado State University: A case study. *Serials Review*, *29*, 16–25. doi:10.1016/S0098-7913(02)00267-8

Connell, T. H., Rogers, S. A., & Diedrichs, C. P. (2005). OhioLINK electronic journal use at Ohio State University. *Libraries and the Academy*, *5*, 371–390. doi:10.1353/pla.2005.0033

Curtis, D. (2005). *E-journals: A how-to-do-it manual for building managing, and supporting electronic journal collections*. London, UK: Facet.

Dilek-Kayaoglu, H. (2008). Use of electronic journals by faculty at Istanbul University, Turkey: The result of a survey. *Journal of Academic Librarianship*, *34*(3), 239–247. doi:10.1016/j.acalib.2008.03.007

Jamali, H. R., Nicholas, D., & Huntington, P. (2005). The use and the users of the scholarly e-journals: A review of log analysis studies. *Aslib Proceedings*, *57*, 554–571. doi:10.1108/00012530510634271

Kurata, K., Matsubayashi, M., Mine, S., Muranushi, T., & Ueda, S. (2007). Electronic journals and their unbundled functions in scholarly communication: View and utilization by scientific, technological and medical researchers in Japan. *Information Processing & Management*, *43*, 1402–1415. doi:10.1016/j.ipm.2006.01.006

Lad, A. (1995). *User study of Armament Research and Development Establishment (ARDE) library* (Unpublished master's thesis). University of Pune, Pune, India.

Masoom Raza, M., & Upadhyay, A. K. (2006). Usage of e-journals by researchers in Aligarh Muslim University: A study. *The International Information & Library Review*, *38*, 170–179. doi:10.1016/j.iilr.2006.06.009

Mounissamy, P., & Rani, S. (2005). Evaluation of usage and usability of electronic journals. *SRELS Journals of Information Management*, *42*(2), 189–205.

Murty, T. A. V., & Devi, T. S. (2008). Access of e-journals in the institute of higher education through UGC-info net e-journal consortium. In Nigam, B. S., & Kataria, S. (Eds.), *Digital libraries* (pp. 151–160). New Delhi, India: Mahamaya.

National Chemical Laboratory. (2007). *59th annual report (2006-2007)*. Pune, India: Author.

Rajeshwari, D. (2005). Use of information sources in digital environment: A case study. In *Proceedings of the 3rd International CALIBER INFLIBNET on Multilingual Computing and Information Networked Digital Environment*, Kochi, India (pp. 705-711).

Ramesh, D. B. (2008). Emergence of electronic journals. In Nigam, B. S., & Kataria, S. (Eds.), *Digital libraries* (pp. 259–268). New Delhi, India: Mahamaya.

Rusch-Feja, D., & Siebeky, U. (1999). Evaluation of usage of and acceptance of electronic journals. *D-Lib Magazine*, *5*(10).

Sujata, H. R., & Mudhol, M. V. (2008). Use of electronic information sources at the College of Fisheries, Mangalore, India. *Annals of Library and Information Studies*, *55*, 234–245.

University of North Dakota. (n.d.). *Cataloging electronic documents*. Retrieved from http://www.und.edu/dept/library/Departments/abc/Catedocs.html

Vinod, D. (2005). *Evaluation of the use of print and electronic journals in Central Library, I.I.T. Kharagpur*. Kharagpur, India: I.I.T. Kharagpur.

Voorbij, H., & Ongering, H. (2006). The use of electronic journals by Dutch researchers: A descriptive and exploratory study. *Journal of Academic Librarianship*, *32*, 223. doi:10.1016/j.acalib.2006.02.006

Zhang, X., & Haslam, M. (2005). Movement toward a predominantly electronic journal collection. *Library Hi Tech*, *23*(1), 82–89. doi:10.1108/07378830510586720

This work was previously published in the International Journal of Information Retrieval Research, Volume 1, Issue 4, edited by Zhongyu (Joan) Lu, pp. 1-22, copyright 2011 by IGI Publishing (an imprint of IGI Global).

Chapter 15
MapReduce Based Information Retrieval Algorithms for Efficient Ranking of Webpages

Srinivasa K.G.
M.S. Ramaiah Institute of Technology, India

Bharghava Varun A.
M.S. Ramaiah Institute of Technology, India

Anil Kumar Muppalla
M.S. Ramaiah Institute of Technology, India

Amulya M.
M.S. Ramaiah Institute of Technology, India

ABSTRACT

In this paper, the authors discuss the MapReduce implementation of crawler, indexer and ranking algorithms in search engines. The proposed algorithms are used in search engines to retrieve results from the World Wide Web. A crawler and an indexer in a MapReduce environment are used to improve the speed of crawling and indexing. The proposed ranking algorithm is an iterative method that makes use of the link structure of the Web and is developed using MapReduce framework to improve the speed of convergence of ranking the WebPages. Categorization is used to retrieve and order the results according to the user choice to personalize the search. A new score is introduced in this paper that is associated with each WebPage and is calculated using user's query and number of occurrences of the terms in the query in the document corpus. The experiments are conducted on Web graph datasets and the results are compared with the serial versions of crawler, indexer and ranking algorithms.

1. INTRODUCTION

World Wide Web is growing very rapidly from few thousand pages to more than two billion pages at present. The use of web has elevated significant social concerns in the fields of privacy, censorship and access to information (Pinkerton, 2000). Web data consists of enormous number of web pages and links connecting them. Due to its size and dynamic nature it becomes highly difficult to locate the information efficiently across the web. Hence search engines play a vital role in retrieving the relevant and accurate data from the web (Buttcher & Clarke, 2010) and they rely upon the huge collection of web pages obtained by the web

DOI: 10.4018/978-1-4666-3898-3.ch015

crawler, a computer program which browses the World Wide Web in a completely ordered and automated fashion.

Mining for specific data using sequential information retrieval algorithms is time consuming and inefficient. Hence there is a need to develop more parallel algorithms to search and retrieve the user specific data from the ever expanding World Wide Web. The aim of this paper is to utilize a MapReduce framework to build a crawler, indexer and ranking system to retrieve information from the Web and cater to the personalization of the data using Machine learning concepts. The problem with the retrieved results is the order in which they are displayed, as millions of results are obtained it becomes difficult for the user to locate the relevant one. Hence machine learning concept is used to identify the most popular items from the Web and rank them so that it becomes easier for the user to retrieve the popular and important information from the Web (Croft, Metzler, & Strohman, 2010).

PageRank (Brin & Page, 1998) is a link analysis algorithm that assigns a numerical weighting (Qin, Liu, Xu, & Li, 2007) to each element of a hyperlinked set of documents, such as the World Wide Web, with the purpose of "measuring" its relative importance within the set. PageRank hypothesizes that a link from page *A* to *B* implies the author of *A* recommends having a look at page *B*. A page is said to have a high PageRank value if there are many pages that point to it (Kim & Lee, 2002; Shenoy et al., 2004). The PageRank algorithm and implementation details are explained in detail in the later section. The algorithm represents the structure of the web as a matrix and PageRank as a vector. The PageRank vector is derived by computing matrix-vector multiplications repeatedly. The sum of all PageRank values should be one during computation. In this paper we use MapReduce framework to compute the ranks of the web pages correctly. Experimental evaluation is carried out and its results are briefly discussed.

The objective of this paper is to develop a web portal application with searching capability that runs as a website. As an outcome, the paper also aims at testing the performance of the proposed algorithms on various data sets. Parameters like retrieval time, computation time while ranking of web pages based on popularity and others are tested. The remainder of the paper is organised as follows. Section 2 discusses the related work and Section 3 gives the contributions of the paper. Sections 4 and 5 contain the details of the architectures of crawler, indexer and the ranking system proposed algorithms followed by the pseudocode of all the techniques used. An illustrative example is given in Section 6. Experimental results including timings of the iterative methods on graphs are discussed in Section 7 followed by conclusions.

2. BACKGROUND AND RELATED WORK

According to Google's MapReduce Programming Model (Lammel, 2008) follows the following five simple steps, i.e., (i) iteration over the input; (ii) computation of key/value pairs from each piece of input; (iii) grouping of all intermediate values by key; (iv) iteration over the resulting groups; and (*v*) reduction of each group. MapReduce framework is used to develop parallel algorithms. It is a programming model and an associated implementation for processing and generating large data sets. Users specify a map function that processes a key/value pair to generate a set of intermediate key/value pairs, and a reduce function that merges all intermediate values associated with the same intermediate key. In general the master node of the Map function takes the input, divides the work into smaller sub problems and assigns it to worker nodes. This is done repeatedly forming multi-level tree structure. The reduce function combines the results of all the sub-problems and obtains the solution to the original problem. Thus the MapReduce framework transforms a list of (key, value) pairs into a list of values. Many real world tasks are expressible in this model.

The architecture of serial web crawler is shown in Figure 1. It is used for crawling through a whole site on the Inter/Intranet. We specify a start-URL and the crawler follows all links found in that HTML page. Web crawler begins by parsing a specified web page, making a note of any hypertext links on that page that point to other web pages. They then parse those pages for new links, and so on recursively.

The web pages retrieved are checked for duplication, that is, a check is made to see if the web page is already indexed, if so the duplicate copy is eliminated. This is done by creating a data digest of a page then compared to the original signature for each successive visit. After the web page information is retrieved from the Internet, the information is stored in a database. The database is used to maintain web page information to index the web pages so that this database can be searched, for any search keyword, as in a search engine. But serial crawlers have drawbacks which can be overcome using distributed crawlers. It is possible to maximize download rate of documents and crawl the huge amounts of web pages on the World Wide Web faster. It is difficult to download the pages and then parse it in reasonable amount of time using serial crawlers as the size of the web has crossed 10 billion web pages. It becomes imperative to parallelize a crawling process to reduce and disperse network load.

In Cho and Garcia-Molina (2002) the design method of an effective parallel crawler is discussed. Due to the limitless nature of the web, it is very significant to parallelize the crawling process in order to finish downloading at a faster rate. The authors first propose several different architectures for parallel crawlers and discuss elementary issues related to parallel crawling. The following issues are taken care to examine the parallel crawler and make the study of it challenging:

- **Overlap:** When multiple web pages are downloaded in parallel, there is a possibility that different processes download the same page multiple times and the processes are not aware of it. This should be considerably minimized to increase the effectiveness of web crawler.
- **Quality:** Crawler has to first download all the important web pages relevant to the query in order to maximize the effectiveness. The quality of the downloaded pages should be as good for a parallel crawler as for a centralized one.
- **Communication Overhead:** In order to avoid overlap and improve the quality of the retrieved information the multiple pro-

Figure 1. Architecture of serial web crawler

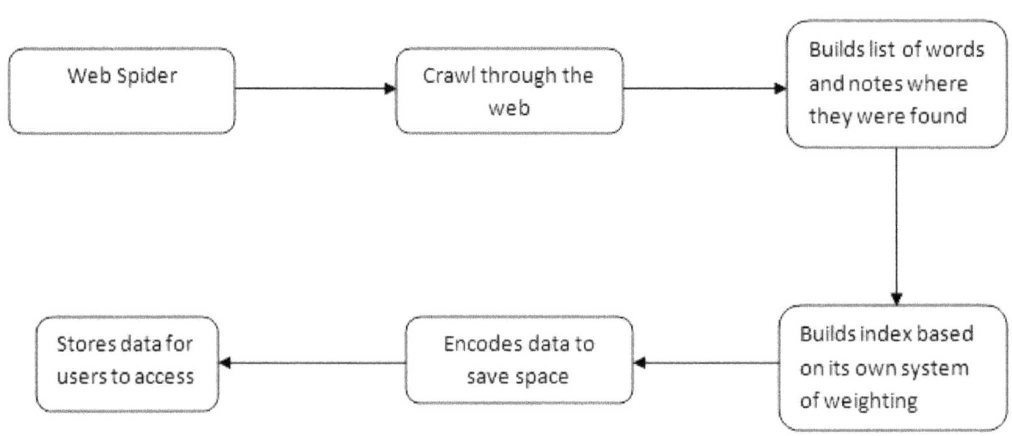

cesses should regularly communicate to co-ordinate with each other. What exactly the different processes need to communicate and how the significant overhead is avoided.

In Gleich, Zhukov, and Berkin (2004) a linear system approach is used to compute fast parallel PageRank. PageRank has become a very important tool used in all recent web search technologies. For each technology, the critical computation is the PageRank-like vector of interest. Thus, methods to accelerate and parallelize these computations are important. Various methods to accelerate the simple power iterations process have already been developed. Traditionally, PageRank has been computed as the principle eigenvector of a Markov chain probability transition matrix. In Haveliwala and Kamvar (2003) the PageRank linear system formulation and its iterative solution methods are discussed. It is well known that the random teleportation used in PageRank strongly affects the convergence of power iterations. To carry out several numerical experiments on real Web graph data, they have come up with a system which can compute results within no time on Web graphs with one billion or more links. They did not attempt to optimize each method and instead came up with an approach that is open to work with multiple methods in a consistent manner and it's easily adaptable to new methods.

3. CONTRIBUTION

This paper compares the efficiency of sequential and MapReduce implementations of the page ranking techniques of information retrieval. The performance issues of the MapReduce framework against sequential approaches with regard to crawling of the web and ranking the retrieved web pages has been explored. Various novel ideas such as result categorization based on various topics like Arts, Business, Computers and so on has been used to provide a personalised search for the users. Computation of page score based on user query using the frequency of the search terms on the web page is carried out and the same score is used on top of the rank calculated using the link structure, to provide a better ranking scheme. The concepts of Machine learning such as implicit, explicit and relevance feedback mechanism is also used to improve the search results.

4. ARCHITECTURE

The crawler has a global configuration state which is maintained in the database which contains the URLs column (list of URLs), visited column (binary 0 or 1, which corresponds to visited and not visited respectively) and Crawldatum (necessary information about that URL).The (URL, Crawldatum) pair forms the key-value pair. Unless the visited column is 1 for all the URLs, the workers in the map phase load the requested websites, extract their links and save them on local disk. The processed URLs and the links are collected in the reduce phase and database is updated after each reduce phase and this is continued until depth n is reached.

When the crawling is finished, which means the visited column is 1 for all the URLs, the indexer is started. It consists of another MapReduce program. The crawled URLs are given as input to the map function of the parser which parses the contents of each URL. The output is obtained in the form of key-value pair where key is the URL and the value is the content of the given URL. This is given as input to the reduce function which updates the contents to the database. The complete architecture of crawler and indexer is given Figure 2 (Schmidt, 2009; Schlatt, 2008).

The ranking algorithm uses iterative method. The proposed architecture has two MapReduce jobs. The input to the MapReduce jobs is the link structure of the web. The first MapReduce job handles the dangling pages and finds the sum of

Figure 2. Architecture of Crawler and Indexer

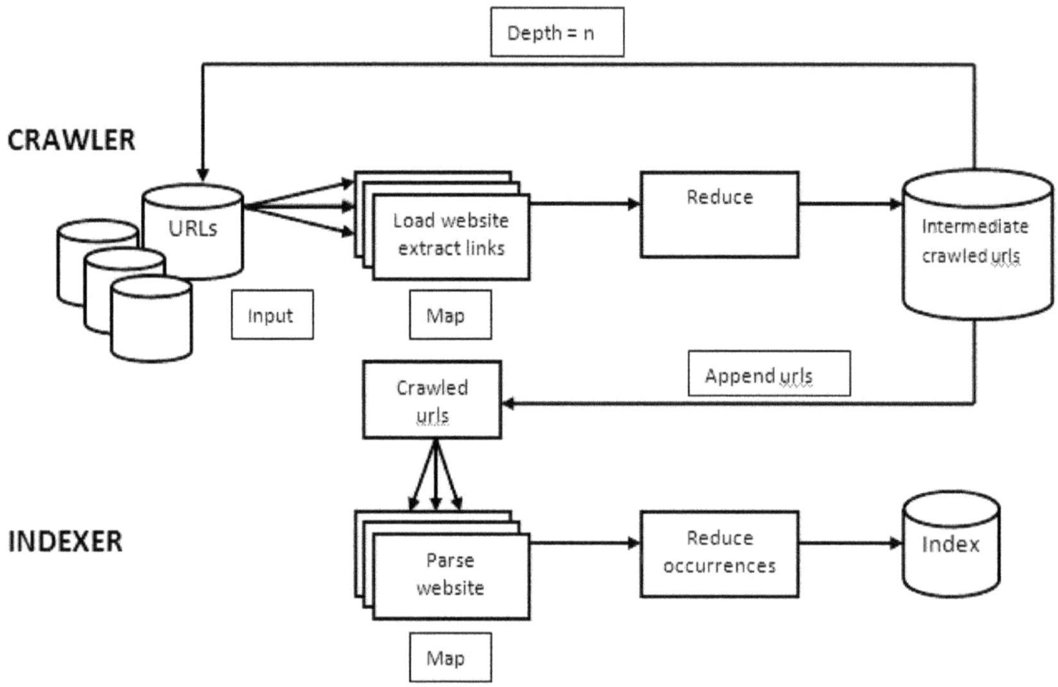

the ranks of each web page. This output is used in the second MapReduce job to compute the rank of all the web pages in the set. After each iteration, intermediate rank is obtained which is fed as input to second iteration and so on. The iteration is stopped once the ranks converge to a value. This is the final rank of the web page. The working principle of MapReduce based ranking system is depicted in Figure 3. The Algorithms (1) to (3) presents the serial implementation of Crawler,

Figure 3. Architecture of Ranking System

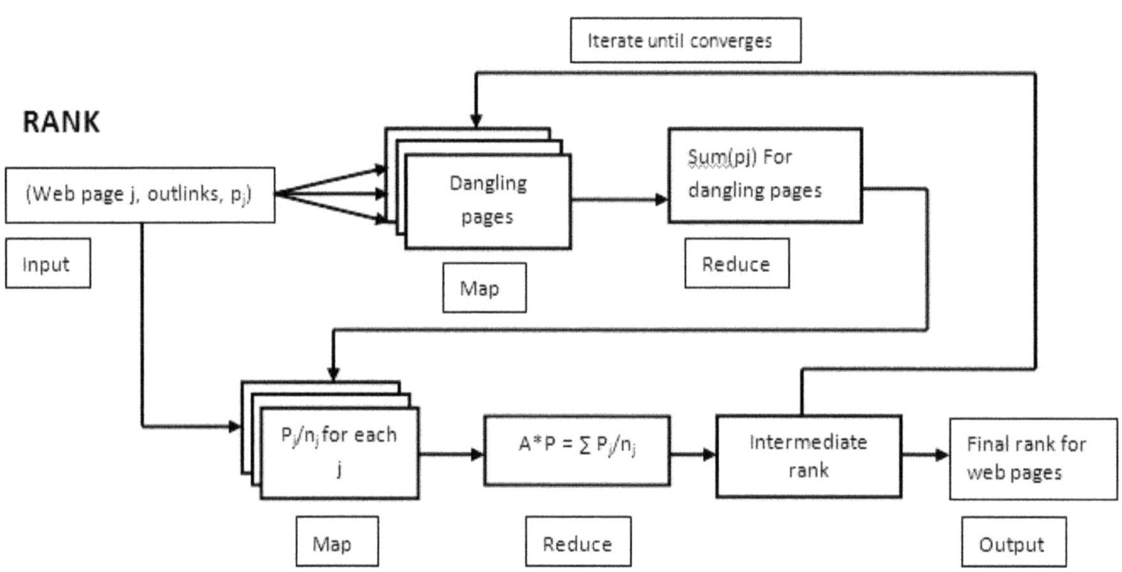

Parser and PageRank algorithms using iteration method and the corresponding MapReduce version of the page rank algorithm is given in Algorithm (4). The Algorithm (4) is iterated sequentially until the ranks of the web pages converge to a value.

5. ALGORITHMS

See Algorithms 1-4.

6. EXAMPLE

Let us consider a sample link graph with 10 nodes as shown in Figure 4. The computation of rank using the MapReduce approach is as follows. In Figure 4, the pages numbered 4 and 10 are dangling since there are no outlinks from them.

Consider the initial probability distribution as: P = (0.1, 0.1... 0.1). Now, when the function Mapper1 of Algorithm 4 is applied to the dataset corresponding to Figure 4, the output obtained is (1, 0.1) and (1, 0.1). In the next step, when the function Reducer1 of Algorithm 4 is applied to the output of Mapper1, we get the output as 0.2 and this value is stored as $ip = 0.2$.

The input for Mapper2 is the matrix form of the link structure of Figure 4 along with number of outlinks for each web page obtained from the matrix and the number of pages considered, say n (which is 10 with respect to Figure 4). For each webpage j, the rank is calculated as: For

Algorithm 1. Crawler

```
Input - A list of trusted feed URLs.
Output - Each URL is parsed to obtain the outlinks in that page, i.e., Hyper
links present in that page.
MapReduce Pseudo code

Function Mapper
Begin
        REPEAT
                url:=GET_FROM_FEED()
                page:=OPENURL(url)
                links[]:= PARSE(page)
                REPEAT
                        key:=hash(links[x])
                        OUTPUT key,links[x]
                UNTIL end of links
        UNTIL end of FEED
End

Function Reducer
Input - (input_key, input_value) where input_key represents hash of urls of
the page input_value URL
Output - (key, value) where value is the url
Begin
OUTPUT key,url
End
```

Algorithm 2. Parser

```
Function Mapper
Input: urls from crawled database
Output: url, contents, status where status represents whether URL is visited
or not
Begin
REPEAT
                url:= get each URL from crawled database
                data:= PARSE_CONTENTS(url)
                OUTPUT (url, data, visited)
        UNTIL status of all URLs is visited

Function Reducer
Input: url, data, status where status represents whether the URL is visited or
not.
Output: url, data, status into database
Begin
        UPDATE <url, data, status>
End
```

Algorithm 3. To find the Rank of the web page sequentially

```
Input - Given a Probability distribution P, link structure of the web A as a
matrix, a vector of dangling pages d, matrix E
representing teleportation to a random page, number of web pages n, and damp-
ing factor s.
Output - rank p of a page
Begin
        Initialize P:= (1/n, 1/n ...)
        IF page j links to page k THEN
                A_kj:= 1/n(j)
        ELSE
                A_kj:=0
        ENDIF
        D:= ed^T / n,  where e is a vector with entries 1
        E:= (1/n, 1/n, ...)
M:= sA + sD + tE, where t = 1 - s
REPEAT
Rank P_i+1:= M P_i
        UNTIL P converges to a value
End
```

Algorithm 4. MapReduce Pseudo Code for Ranking

```
Function Mapper1
Input - web page j, rank p, number of outlinks num_o, outlinks o
Begin
        IF num_o ==0 THEN
                OUTPUT (1, p_j)
        ELSE
                OUTPUT ()
        ENDIF
End

Function Reducer1
Input - (input_key, input_value) where input_key represents key of dangling
pages and input_value contains rank of dangling pages
Begin
        OUTPUT sum(input_value)
End

Function Mapper2
Input - web page j, rank p, number of outlinks num_o, outlinks o and number of
web pages n
Begin
        FOR EACH page j
Compute rank p_j:= p_j / n, for each outlink o in j
                OUTPUT (input_key, p_j for each page j)
        ENDFOR
End

Function Reducer2
Input - (input_key, input_value) where input_key represents the web page j,
input_value represents rank p_j computed in Mapper2, damping factor s, number of
web pages n and output of Reducer1 ip
Begin
        FOR EACH web page j
        Value:= s * sum(input_value) + s * ip / n + (1.0 - s) / n
        OUTPUT (web page j, Value)
End
```

Figure 4. Link graph with 10 nodes

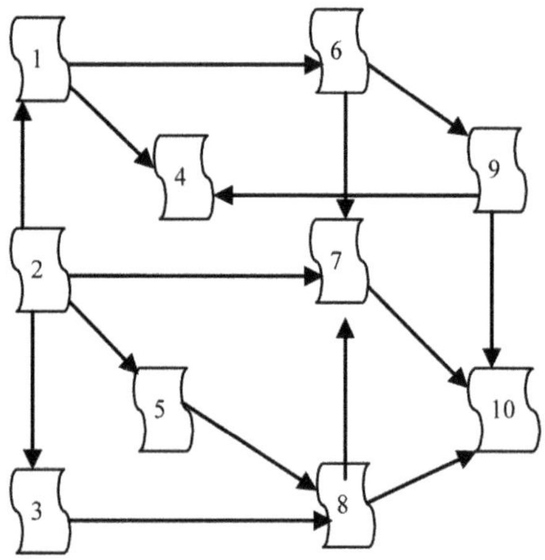

every j, $p_j = p_j / n$, i.e., When $j = 1$, $p_1 = p_1 / n$ = 0.1 / 10 = 0.01. Finally, the output of Mapper2 is <*key,value*> where *key* is page *j* and *value* is rank of page *j*.

Finally, the output obtained from Mapper2 is fed as input to Reducer2 of Algorithm 4, the following calculation is done for each web page *j*, and value is calculated as follows,

For $j = 1$, Value = 0.85 * (0.01 + 0.01) + 0.85 * 0.2/10 + 0.15/10 = 0.49. Similarly, the values are calculated for all j = 1 to 10 and the Reducer2 outputs <key, value> pair for every key (web page *j*) and value is *Value*. This process is repeated until the rank starts to converge.

6.1. Crawler

A spider (*aka* crawler or bot) that goes to every page or representative pages on every website that wants to be search-able and reads it, using hypertext links on each page to discover and read a site's other pages (Hawking, 2006). The most common use of a web crawler is in search engines. Web crawlers help search engines to gather information about available on the web which can then be processed to cater for user requests. The web spider traverses the web pages by following the hyperlinks and storing the web pages in a large database that is later indexed for efficient query execution. A crawler must satisfy two basic functionalities for ensuring this efficiency when subject to large scale implementation. It should have a good crawling technique, i.e., it must be able to figure out which page to download next and to able to provide a robust, manageable service (Olston & Najork, 2010). It is evident that all the search engines have highly optimised crawlers, although the details are proprietary. This paper discusses the implementation of web spider using the MapReduce model. The crawl procedure is divided in to map and reduce tasks. Several map and reduce tasks for a given feed of URLs are triggered which provides parallel computing and hence providing significant improvement in the speed with which the URLs are retrieved.

6.2. Computation of Rank

Ranking of web pages is achieved using link analysis concept which assigns a numerical weighting to each web page in the World Wide Web. The purpose of this is to measure the relative importance of a given web page in the overall set of web pages considered. This rank is basically a probability distribution which gives the chance of a random surfer ending up in a given web page. Pages with higher rank have more chance of appearing higher in the result set (Langville & Meyer, 2004).

The link structure of the web is used to pre-compute global rank of web pages and store it in the database. Let's say a web page j has an associated rank q_j which describes the popularity of that page j in the Web. This implementation uses the concept of crazy web-surfer who starts with a webpage. He can do one of the two things;

- Randomly follow the links in a page.
- Gets bored and teleports to another web-page randomly.

The rank q is computed as follows;

$q \leftarrow M^i P$

Here P represents initial probability distribution for the crazy web-surfer who makes i steps of "surfing", and M represents the change in the distribution in each step. Probability distribution P is an n-dimensional vector, and M is an $n \times n$ matrix whose entries reflect the link structure of the web. After i iterations the rank converges to a value q. The computation of matrix M is done using the following equation,

$M = sA + sD + tE$

where

- ***A***: Represents the web-surfer randomly picking links to follow;
- ***D***: Represents the web-surfer hitting a dangling page (one with no outbound links);
- ***E***: Represents the web-surfer getting bored and "teleporting" to a random webpage;
- ***s***: Represents damping factor and
- $t = 1 - s$.

Now the individual matrices and their entries are described as follows.

1. The matrix A encodes the link structure of the web. If suppose we define $n(j)$ to be the number of links outbound from page j. Then entries in the jth column of A are zero, except at locations corresponding to outgoing links, where they are $1/n(j)$. This represents the behaviour of a random web surfer who randomly chooses an outgoing link from page j.
2. The matrix D is introduced to deal with dangling pages. Dangling pages do not have outgoing links. Here we assume that the web-surfer randomly jumps to any other n pages considered in the experiment with equal probability. Therefore, if j is a dangling page, then the jth column of D should have all its entries 1/n, otherwise, all the entries should be zero. Thus D is calculated as: $D = ed^T/n$. Here d is the vector of dangling pages, i.e., if web page j is dangling then j^{th} entry in d is 1, otherwise it is zero. Vector e is a unit vector with all values equal to 1.
3. Finally, the matrix E describes a bored web-surfer who simply selects a link from the set of web pages randomly and teleports to that page. This matrix has all entries equal to $1/n$, representing a uniform probability of going to another webpage.

The above technique is used to develop a MapReduce code to compute rank. MapReduce code executed repeatedly where matrix M is multiplied with the vector P. Thus after repeated invocations of the MapReduce job, the rank of all web pages converges to a value P. Those invocations are done serially, but the individual MapReduce jobs are themselves all easily parallelized. Therefore MapReduce job includes multiplying M with P, that is: $P_{i+1} := MP_i$

To do this, we have considered two map-reduce jobs. First map-reduce job handles dangling pages and this output is used by second map-reduce job along with matrix A to compute the value of P in i iterations. The input to the first map-reduce job AP includes *(key, value)* pair where *key* is the webpage number j, and *value* includes several data describing the page like number of outbound links $n(j)$, list of pages that j links to and rank p_j.

Let's say $(k_1, k_2, k_3, \ldots)$ are the webpages that page j links to. Then for each page k_1 that page j links to, the mapper outputs intermediate key as k_1 and the *value* as $p_j/n(j)$. This is done by each node for each k_i, i = 1, 2, 3 and so on, during mapping phase. The reducer simply sums up these intermediate values thus giving the value of AP as output. In the same way, dangling pages and teleportation equation is dealt and thus the value MP_i is obtained. The same is iterated i times to get M^iP which will give the rank of the given web page based on link structure.

In the next step, to achieve Web Personalization we use the following technique. During teleportation, instead of going to a random page, the surfer goes to a random page chosen from a given set. This set includes pages that contain topics that the user is interested in. This data about what the user or surfer is interested in can be collected by basic feedback technique. In this case, *E will have repeated columns containing the personalized probability distribution P; and E = P.* This step increases the probability values of certain pages that the user is interested in.

6.3. Computation of Score: A Modified Approach

After the global ranks are computed, local ranks for the retrieved results are computed using a term context like occurrences of terms in the user query and web pages. This computation is done during query time by using the equations given:

pScore = score for web page *p*

Qtf = the square root of the frequency of term *t* in the query

Ptf = the square root of the frequency of term *t* in web page *p*

numPages = number of web pages in the set

pageFreq_t = number of web pages containing term *t*

idf_t = *log*(*numPages*/(*pageFreq_t* + 1.0)) + 1.0

pScore = *sum_t*(*Qtf* * *Ptf* * *idf_t*)

final_rank = *m* * (*rank*) + *n* * (*pScore*), where $m + n = 1$.

An appropriate ratio of m and n is chosen to get optimal rank. Computing global rank offline also helps to save time and retrieve results faster. The displayed results are categorized into 15 top level topics. The data for this categorization was obtained from Open Directory Project (http://www.dmoz.com). When using the search engine, the user can specify the order in which the categories are sorted and displayed, so that the category that the user is interested in is displayed first and the rest are displayed below them (Matthew & Pedro, 2001).

6.4. Machine Learning: Implicit and Explicit Feedback, Relevance Feedback

Implicit feedback is used to track the links clicked by the user for a given query (Thorsten, Laura, Bing, & Helene, 2007) and then it is stored in a log. If the user clicks on a link, we assume that the user is interested in that web page and finds it relevant. Explicit feedback can be given by the user by clicking on the relevant and irrelevant buttons provided along with each of the search result. If the result is relevant, then all the web pages similar to that web page are displayed. Along with this, a bonus score is given to results that are relevant while irrelevant result is penalised. Thus if a similar query is posed by other users, the result marked relevant appears higher in the result set while the result marked irrelevant appears comparatively lower in the result set (Liu, 2009).

Query expansion is used to retrieve similar documents. This is done by making use of synonyms of the important words appearing in user query. Thus if a web page contains a synonym of a word in the user query, that web page is also retrieved. Concepts of implicit feedback in machine learning help to implement user preference to the search (Cunningham, Littin, & Witten, 1999).

7. EXPERIMENTAL RESULTS

An experiment was conducted on various numbers of pages. The links among the pages was taken from a data set (Carnegie Mellon University, 2012). The experiment was conducted to show the execution time of both serial rank algorithm based on sequential iteration method and MapReduce algorithm. A randomly generated dataset of up to 1 million pages was used for this purpose. The graph is shown in Figure 5. The algorithms were run on a cluster of five nodes by using Hadoop MapReduce framework. To find the execution time of sequential implementation of rank algorithm, algorithm 3 was used. The execution time for various numbers of pages is plotted in the graph as shown in Figure 5. Similarly algorithm 4 was run to get the execution time of MapReduce ranking algorithm and was plotted against the number of pages. Clearly from the graph shown in Figure 5, execution time of MapReduce ranking algorithm is smaller than that of sequential implementation of the same iterative method. While testing, damping factor was assumed to be 0.85 and the tolerance level for convergence was 10^{-5}.

An experiment was conducted on various numbers of feed urls. The experiment was conducted to show the execution time of both serial crawler algorithm based on sequential iteration method and MapReduce crawler algorithm. A data set of 500 urls has been chosen for this purpose. The graph is shown in Figure 6. The algorithms were run on a cluster of five nodes by using Hadoop MapReduce framework. To find the execution time of sequential implementation of rank algorithm, algorithm 5 was used. The execution time for various numbers of URLs is plotted in the graph as shown in Figure 6. Similarly algorithm 5 was run to get the execution time of MapReduce ranking algorithm and was plotted against the number of pages. Clearly from the graph shown in Figure 5, execution time of MapReduce ranking algorithm is smaller than that

Figure 5. Execution time of serial versus MapReduce ranking algorithm

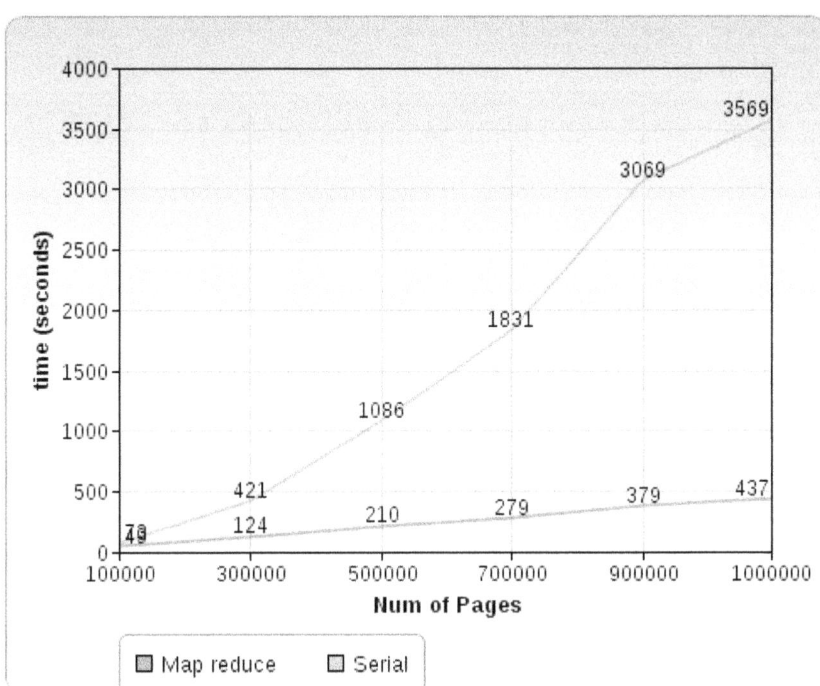

Figure 6. Execution time of serial vs. MapReduce crawler

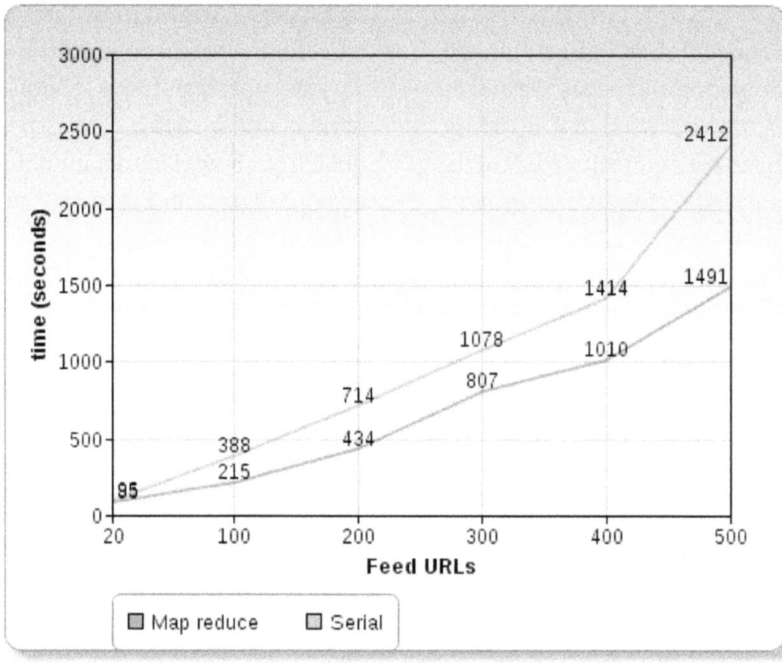

Figure 7. MapReduce crawler job

Hadoop job_201107011558_0001 on master

User: hadoop
Job Name: streamjob2584004213006662192.jar
Job File: hdfs://master:54310/home/hadoop/tmp/mapred/system/job_201107011558_0001/job.xml
Job Setup: Successful
Status: Succeeded
Started at: Fri Jul 01 16:11:49 IST 2011
Finished at: Fri Jul 01 16:15:43 IST 2011
Finished in: 3mins, 54sec
Job Cleanup: Successful

Kind	% Complete	Num Tasks	Pending	Running	Complete	Killed	Failed/Killed Task Attempts
map	100.00%	2	0	0	2	0	0 / 0
reduce	100.00%	1	0	0	1	0	0 / 0

	Counter	Map	Reduce	Total
Job Counters	Launched reduce tasks	0	0	1
	Launched map tasks	0	0	2
	Data-local map tasks	0	0	2
FileSystemCounters	FILE_BYTES_READ	0	206,194	206,194
	HDFS_BYTES_READ	5,124	0	5,124
	FILE_BYTES_WRITTEN	206,264	206,194	412,458
	HDFS_BYTES_WRITTEN	0	206,104	206,104
Map-Reduce Framework	Reduce input groups	0	3,024	3,024
	Combine output records	0	0	0
	Map input records	100	0	100
	Reduce shuffle bytes	0	101,346	101,346
	Reduce output records	0	9,276	9,276
	Spilled Records	4,638	4,638	9,276
	Map output bytes	196,870	0	196,870
	Map input bytes	3,415	0	3,415
	Map output records	4,638	0	4,638
	Combine input records	0	0	0
	Reduce input records	0	4,638	4,638

of sequential implementation of the same iterative method.

7.1. Hadoop MapReduce Web Interface

The Hadoop framework provides a web interface to monitor the MapReduce job (Figure 7). Each MapReduce job is assigned a unique job-id. The cluster consists of 2 workstation nodes. Figure 6 indicates the crawler MapReduce job which indicates the number of input records as 100, number of output records as 4638, number of map tasks as 2 and number of reduce tasks as 1. The time taken for the completion of the job is 3min, 54sec. Figure 8 indicates the rank MapReduce job which indicates the number of input records as 500000 web pages, number of map tasks as 2

Figure 8. MapReduce rank job

Hadoop job_201107011558_0002 on master

User: hadoop
Job Name: streamjob5144144907294237793.jar
Job File: hdfs://master:54310/home/hadoop/tmp/mapred/system/job_201107011558_0002/job.xml
Job Setup: Successful
Status: Succeeded
Started at: Fri Jul 01 16:58:17 IST 2011
Finished at: Fri Jul 01 17:03:18 IST 2011
Finished in: 5mins, 1sec
Job Cleanup: Successful

Kind	% Complete	Num Tasks	Pending	Running	Complete	Killed	Failed/Killed Task Attempts
map	100.00%	2	0	0	2	0	0 / 0
reduce	100.00%	1	0	0	1	0	1 / 0

	Counter	Map	Reduce	Total
Job Counters	Launched reduce tasks	0	0	2
	Rack-local map tasks	0	0	1
	Launched map tasks	0	0	2
	Data-local map tasks	0	0	1
FileSystemCounters	FILE_BYTES_READ	0	30,112,267	30,112,267
	HDFS_BYTES_READ	28,613,310	0	28,613,310
	FILE_BYTES_WRITTEN	30,112,337	30,112,267	60,224,604
	HDFS_BYTES_WRITTEN	0	15,319,663	15,319,663
Map-Reduce Framework	Reduce input groups	0	500,000	500,000
	Combine output records	0	0	0
	Map input records	500,000	0	500,000
	Reduce shuffle bytes	0	15,053,211	15,053,211
	Reduce output records	0	500,012	500,012
	Spilled Records	500,000	500,000	1,000,000
	Map output bytes	29,112,100	0	29,112,100
	Map input bytes	28,611,962	0	28,611,962
	Map output records	500,000	0	500,000
	Combine input records	0	0	0
	Reduce input records	0	500,000	500,000

and number of reduce tasks as 1. The time taken for the completion of the job is 5min, 1sec.

8. CONCLUSION

Search engine brings order to the chaotic web. It plays an important role in retrieving information. In this paper we have worked out Information Retrieval algorithms like crawlers and ranking algorithms which search engine to the greatest extent among all other techniques. Heuristics were developed to convert these algorithms into a MapReduce paradigm and was extensively tested against sequential algorithms on clusters. The significant improvement in the performance of the MapReduce framework against sequential approaches with respect to crawling and ranking the web pages was obtained. The result for the user's query was categorized into certain topics according to user interest. Implicit, explicit, relevance feedback and query expansion was also introduced to improve the search results. As a future work, we plan to develop better heuristics to deploy these algorithms on cloud and to improve the performance of these information retrieval algorithms. As a feature work, machine learning techniques can be integrated with these algorithms to improve personalized web search and can be extended to distributed data storage on cloud.

REFERENCES

Brin, S., & Page, L. (1998). The anatomy of a large-scale hypertextual Web search engine. *International Journal of Computer Networks and ISDN Systems*, *30*(7), 107–117. doi:10.1016/S0169-7552(98)00110-X

Buttcher, S., & Clarke, C. (2010). *Information retrieval and evaluating search engines*. Cambridge, MA: MIT Press.

Carnegie Mellon University. (2012). *Web graph datasets*. Retrieved from http://boston.lti.cs.cmu.edu/clueweb09/wiki/tiki-print.php?page=Web%20Graph

Cho, J., & Garcia-Molina, H. (2002). Parallel crawlers. In *Proceedings of the 11th International Conference on World Wide Web* (pp. 124-135).

Croft, B., Metzler, D., & Strohman, T. (2010). *Search engines information retrieval in practice*. Upper Saddle River, NJ: Pearson Education.

Cunningham, S. J., Littin, J., & Witten, I. H. (1999). Applications of machine learning in information retrieval. *Annual Review of Information Science & Technology*, *34*(1), 341–384.

Gleich, D., Zhukov, L., & Berkin, P. (2004). *Fast parallel PageRank: A linear system approach*. Retrieved from http://www.cs.purdue.edu/homes/dgleich/publications/gleich2004-parallel.pdf

Haveliwala, T., & Kamvar, S. (2003). *The second eigenvalue of the Google Matrix (Tech. Rep.)*. Stanford, CA: Stanford University.

Hawking, D. (2006). Web search engines – Part 1. *IEEE Computer*, *39*(6), 86–88. doi:10.1109/MC.2006.213

Hawking, D. (2006). Web search engines: Part 2. *IEEE Computer*, *39*(8), 88–90. doi:10.1109/MC.2006.286

Kim, S. J., & Lee, S. H. (2002). An improved computation of PageRank algorithm. *Journal Advances in Information Retrieval*, 341-369.

Lammel, R. (2008). *Google's MapReduce programming model—Revisited*. Redmond, WA: Data Programmability Team, Microsoft Corp.

Langville, A. N., & Meyer, C. D. (2004). Survey: Deeper inside PageRank. *Internet Mathematics*, *1*(1), 335–380. doi:10.1080/15427951.2004.10129091

Liu, T. Y. (2009). Learning to rank for information retrieval. *Foundations and Trends in Information Retrieval*, *3*(3), 225–331. doi:10.1561/1500000016

Matthew, R., & Pedro, D. (2001). The intelligent surfer: Probabilistic combination of link and content information in PageRank. In *Proceedings of the Conference on Advances in Neural Information Processing Systems* (pp. 1441-1448).

Olston, C., & Najork, M. (2010). Web crawling. *Foundations and Trends in Information Retrieval*, *4*(3), 175–246. doi:10.1561/1500000017

Pinkerton, B. (2000). *WebCrawler: Finding what people want* (Unpublished doctoral dissertation). University of Washington, Seattle, WA.

Qin, T., Liu, T.-Y., Xu, J., & Li, H. (2007). LECTOR: A benchmark collection for research on learning to rank for information retrieval. In *Proceedings of the Workshop on Learning to Rank for Information Retrieval.*

Schlatt, S. M. (2008). *The Holumbus framework: Creating scalable and highly customized crawlers and indexers.* Wedel, Germany: FH Wedel University of Applied Sciences.

Schmidt, S. (2009). *The Holumbus gramework: Distributed computing with MapReduce in Haskell* (Unpublished master's thesis). FH Wedel University of Applied Sciences, Wedel, Germany.

Shenoy, P. D., Srinivasa, K. G., Thomas, A. O., Venugopal, K. R., & Patnaik, L. M. (2004). Mining top - *k* ranked Webpages using simulated annealing and genetic algorithms. In *Proceedings of the Asian Applied Computing Conference*, Nepal (pp. 137-144).

Thorsten, J., Laura, G., Bing, P., & Helene, H. (2007). Evaluating the accuracy of implicit feedback from clicks and query reformulation in Web search. *ACM Transactions on Information Systems*, *25*(2), 1–27.

This work was previously published in the International Journal of Information Retrieval Research, Volume 1, Issue 4, edited by Zhongyu (Joan) Lu, pp. 23-37, copyright 2011 by IGI Publishing (an imprint of IGI Global).

Chapter 16
SAR:
An Algorithm for Selecting a Partition Attribute in Categorical-Valued Information System Using Soft Set Theory

Rabiei Mamat
Universiti Malaysia Terengganu, Malaysia

Tutut Herawan
Universiti Malaysia Pahang & Data Engineering Research Centre, Malaysia

Mustafa Mat Deris
Universiti Tun Hussein Onn Malaysia, Malaysia

ABSTRACT

Soft-set theory proposed by Molodstov is a general mathematic tool for dealing with uncertainty. Recently, several algorithms have been proposed for decision making using soft-set theory. However, these algorithms still concern on Boolean-valued information system. In this paper, Support Attribute Representative (SAR), a soft-set based technique for decision making in categorical-valued information system is proposed. The proposed technique has been tested on three datasets to select the best partitioning attribute. Furthermore, two UCI benchmark datasets are used to elaborate the performance of the proposed technique in term of executing time. On these two datasets, it is shown that SAR outperforms three rough set-based techniques TR, MMR, and MDA up to 95% and 50%, respectively. The results of this research will provide useful information for decision makers to handle categorical datasets.

INTRODUCTION

In today's fast moving world, decision making is a very critical issue in any organization. It is known that good decision making is supported by good information. Unfortunately, some information is uncertain. Therefore, handling uncertain data is very important since there are lots of real life problems in reality still involving uncertain data, for example in field of engineering, medical, social sciences, etc. (Maji, Roy, & Biswas, 2002). Theoretically, probabilities theories, theory of fuzzy set as well as theory of rough set can be considered as the mathematical tools for dealing with uncertainties.

DOI: 10.4018/978-1-4666-3898-3.ch016

In 1999, Molodstov proposed a theory of soft-set as a new way for managing uncertain data. Molodstov pointed out that one of the main advantages of using soft-set theory because it is free from the inadequacy of the parameterization tools, unlike in the theories mentioned above (Molodtsov, 1999). The soft-set theory uses parameterization sets, as its main solution for problem solving, which makes it very convenient and easy to apply in practice. Therefore, many applications based on soft-set theory have already been demonstrated by Molodstov, such as the smoothness of functions, game theory, operation research, Rieman integration, Perron intergration, probability theory, and measurement theory (Molodtsov, 1999).

Presently, great progress of study on soft-set theory has been achieved. Maji *et al.* (2003) firstly introduced some definitions of the related operation on soft-set. Ali *et al.* (2009) took into account some errors of formers and put forward some new operations on soft-set. The great progress has been achieved when adopting soft-set theory in applications. Maji *et al.* (2002) employed soft-set theory to solve the decision-making problem. Maji *et al.* (2001) presented a novel method of object recognition from an imprecise multi-observer data to deal with decision making based on fuzzy soft-set, which was revised by Kong *et al.* (2009). Feng *et al.* (2010) showed an adjustable approach to fuzzy soft-set based decision making by means of level soft-set. It is worthwhile to mention that some effort has been done to such issues concerning reduction of soft-set. Chen *et al.* (2005) pointed out that the conclusion of soft-set reduction offered in Maji *et al.* (2002) was incorrect, and then present a new notion of parameterization reduction in soft-set in comparison with the definition to the related concept of attributes reduction in rough set theory. The concept of normal parameter reduction is introduced in Kong *et al.* (2008), which overcome the problem of suboptimal choice and added parameter set of soft-set. An algorithm for normal parameter reduction is also presented in Kong *et al.* (2008) to overcome the problem of sub-optimal decision making in Chen *et al.* (2005). However, these soft-set-based algorithms still concern on a Boolean-valued information system.

In this paper, Support Attribute Representative (SAR), a soft-set based technique for selecting the best partitioning attribute in categorical-valued information system is proposed. The proposed technique has been tested on three datasets. Furthermore two UCI benchmark datasets are used to elaborate the performance of the proposed technique in term of executing time. It is shown that SAR outperforms three rough set-based techniques TR, MMR, and MDA. The results of this research will provide useful information for decision makers to handle categorical datasets.

The rest of the paper is organized as follows. First, we described the soft-set theory. Then, the proposed technique is described. An experiment and analysis is described afterwards. Finally, the conclusion of this work is described.

SOFT-SET THEORY

Information System

An information system is defined as a 4-tuple (quadruple)

$$S = (U, A, V, f),$$

where

$$U = \{u_1, u_2, u_3, \cdots, u_{|U|}\}$$

is a non-empty finite set of objects,

$$A = \{a_1, a_2, a_3, \cdots, a_{|A|}\}$$

is a non-empty finite set of attributes, $V = \bigcup_{a \in A} V_a$, V_a is the domain (value set) of attribute a, $f : U \times A \rightarrow V$ is an information function such that $f(u,a) \in V_a$, for every $(u,a) \in U \times A$, called information (knowledge) function. An information system can be intuitively expressed in terms of an information table (Table 1).

In many applications, there is an outcome of classification that is known. This posteriori knowledge is expressed by one (or more) distinguished attribute called decision attribute; the process is known as supervised learning. An information system of this kind is called a decision system. A is an information system of the form $D = (U, A \cup \{d\}, V, f)$, where $d \notin A$ is the decision attribute.

Let

$$S = (U, A, V, f)$$

be an information system. If $V_{\{0,1\}}$, for every $a \in A$, then

$$S = \left(U, A, V_{\{0,1\}}, f\right)$$

is called a Boolean-valued information system.

Table 1. An information system

U/A	a_1	...	a_k	...	$a_{\|A\|}$
u_1	$f(u_1, a_1)$	...	$f(u_1, a_k)$	...	$f(u_1, a_{\|A\|})$
u_2	$f(u_2, a_1)$	...	$f(u_2, a_k)$	...	$f(u_2, a_{\|A\|})$
u_3	$f(u_3, a_1)$	...	$f(u_3, a_k)$	...	$f(u_3, a_{\|A\|})$
$\vdots$	$\vdots$	$\ddots$	$\vdots$	$\ddots$	$\vdots$
$u_{\|U\|}$	$f(u_{\|U\|}, a_1)$	...	$f(u_{\|U\|}, a_k)$	...	$f(u_{\|U\|}, a_{\|A\|})$

Soft-Set Theory

Throughout this section U refers to a non empty initial universe, E is a set of parameters describing objects in U, $P(U)$ is the power set of U and $A \subseteq E$.

Definition 1: (Molodstov, 1999). A pair (F, A) is called a soft-set over U, where F is a mapping given by

$$F : A \rightarrow P(U).$$

In other words, a soft-set over U is a parameterized family of subsets of the universe U. For $\varepsilon \in A$, $F(\varepsilon)$ may be considered as the set of ε-elements of the soft-set (F, A) or as the set of ε-approximate elements of the soft-set. Clearly, a soft-set is not a (crisp) set.

As an illustration, let consider a soft-set which describes the 'attractiveness of programming language' that Mr. X is considering to use. Let assume that there are ten programming languages in the universe U that are under consideration by Mr. X such that

$$U = \begin{Bmatrix} p_1, p_2, p_3, p_4, p_5, \\ p_6, p_7, p_8, p_9, p_{10} \end{Bmatrix},$$

and is a set of decision parameter where

$$E = \{e_1, e_2, e_3, e_4, e_5, e_6, e_7\}.$$

Every $e \in E$ representing an element of attractiveness such that e_1 representing an element of 'system', e_2 representing an element of 'education,' e_3 representing an element of 'web,' e_4 representing an element of 'procedural,' e_5 representing an element of 'object oriented,' e_6 representing an element of 'reflective' and e_7 representing an element of 'functional.' Consider the mapping $F : E \to P(U)$ given by "programming language (.)", where (.) is to be filled in by one of parameters $e \in E$. Suppose that

$$F(e_1) = \{p_1, p_3, p_4, p_{10}\},$$

$$F(e_2) = \{p_2, p_7, p_8\},$$

$$F(e_3) = \{p_5, p_8, p_9\},$$

$$F(e_4) = \{p_1, p_2, p_3, p_4, p_7\},$$

$$F(e_5) = \{p_1, p_4, p_5, p_6, p_7, p_8, p_9\},$$

$$F(e_6) = \{p_5, p_8, p_9\}$$

and

$$F(e_7) = \{p_5, p_8, p_9\}.$$

As for example, $F(e_1)$ means system programming languages, whose functional value is the set $\{p_1, p_3, p_4, p_{10}\}$. Thus we can view the soft-set (F, E) as a collection of approximations as illustrated:

$$(F,E) = \left\{\begin{array}{l} e_1 = \{p_1, p_3, p_4, p_{10}\}, \\ e_2 = \{p_2, p_7, p_8\}, \\ e_3 = \{p_5, p_8, p_9\}, \\ e_4 = \{p_1, p_2, p_3, p_4, p_7\}, \\ e_5 = \{p_1, p_4, p_5, p_6, p_7, p_8, p_9\}, \\ e_6 = \{p_5, p_8, p_9\}, \\ e_7 = \{p_5, p_8, p_9\} \end{array}\right\}$$

The following proposition shows the relation between a soft-set and a Boolean-valued information system.

Proposition 1: *If* (F, E) is a soft-set over the universe U, then (F, E) is a Boolean-valued information system $S = \left(U, A, V_{\{0,1\}}, f\right)$.

Proof. Let (F, E) be a soft-set over the universe U, we define a mapping $F = \{f_1, f_2, .., f_n\}$ where

$$f_i : U \to V_i,$$

$$f_i(x) = \begin{cases} 1, & x \in F(e_i) \\ 0, & x \notin F(e_i) \end{cases}$$

for $1 \le i \le |A|$.

Hence, if $A = E$, $V = \bigcup_{e_i \in A} V_{e_i}$ where $V_{e_i} = \{0,1\}$ then the soft-set (F, E) can be considered as a Boolean-valued information system $S = \left(U, A, V_{\{0,1\}}, f\right)$.

Therefore, from Proposition 1, a soft-set (F, E) in the above example can be represented in the form of binary (Boolean) table. As can be seen in Table 2, '1' denotes the presence of the described parameters, while '0' means the parameter is not part of the description of the programming languages attractiveness.

For multi-valued information system, it needs to convert into multi-soft-sets (Herawan & Deris, 2009b; Herawan *et al.*, 2010b). It is based on the notion of a decomposition of a multi-valued information system. Let $S = (U, A, V, f)$ be a multi-valued information system and $S^i = (U, a_i, V_{ai}, f)$, $i = 1, 2, \cdots, |A|$ be a binary-

Table 2. Tabular representation of a soft-set (F,E)

U/E	e_1	e_2	e_3	e_4	e_5	e_6	e_7
p_1	1	0	0	1	1	0	0
p_2	0	1	0	1	0	0	0
p_3	1	0	0	1	0	0	0
p_4	1	0	0	1	1	0	0
p_5	0	0	1	0	1	1	1
p_6	0	0	0	0	1	0	0
p_7	0	1	0	1	1	0	0
p_8	0	1	1	0	1	1	1
p_9	0	0	1	0	1	1	1
p_{10}	1	0	0	0	1	0	0

valued information systems. From Proposition 1, we have

$$S=(U,A,V,f)=\begin{cases} S^1=\left(U,a_1,V_{\{0,1\}},f\right) & \Leftrightarrow (F,a_1) \\ S^2=\left(U,a_2,V_{\{0,1\}},f\right) & \Leftrightarrow (F,a_2) \\ \quad\vdots & \quad\vdots \quad \vdots \\ S^{|A|}=\left(U,a_{|A|},V_{\{0,1\}},f\right) & \Leftrightarrow \left(F,a_{|A|}\right) \end{cases}$$

$$=\left((F,a_1),(F,a_2),\cdots,\left(F,a_{|A|}\right)\right)$$

We define

$$(F,E)=\left((F,a_1),(F,a_2),\cdots,\left(F,a_{|A|}\right)\right)$$

as a multi-soft-set over universe U representing a multi-valued information system $S=(U,A,V,f)$.

Example 1: We consider the following data to illustrate the concept of multi-soft-set.

The dataset consist of three (3) categorical-valued attributes so-called Volume, Material and Location. Attribute Volume only has two (2) categories, i.e., High and Low. Attribute Material has three (3) categories, i.e., Hard, Medium and Soft. Meanwhile, attribute Location contains four (4) categories, i.e., Pacific, Midwest, East-Coast and Northern. The multi-soft-set representing the above information system is presented as follows.

$$(F,E)=\left\{\begin{bmatrix} \left(F,\text{Volume}_{\text{High}}\right)=\{1,2,3,4\}, \\ \left(F,\text{Volume}_{\text{Low}}\right)=\{5,6\}, \\ \left(F,\text{Material}_{\text{Hard}}\right)=\{1,2\}, \\ \left(F,\text{Material}_{\text{Medium}}\right)=\{3,6\}, \\ \left(F,\text{Material}_{\text{Soft}}\right)=\{4,5\}, \\ \left(F,\text{Location}_{\text{Pacific}}\right)=\{1,5\}, \\ \left(F,\text{Location}_{\text{Midwest}}\right)=\{2,6\}, \\ \left(F,\text{Location}_{\text{East-coast}}\right)=\{3\}, \\ \left(F,\text{Location}_{\text{Northern}}\right)=\{4\} \end{bmatrix}\right\}$$

SUPPORT ATTRIBUTE REPRESENTATIVE

In this section, we present Support Attribute Representative (SAR), a soft-set-based technique for selecting a partition attribute in a categorical-valued information system. Throughout this section a pair (F,A) refers to multi-soft-set of universe U representing a categorical-valued information system $S=(U,A,V,f)$.

Definition 2: (Support) Let (F,A) be a multi-soft-set over the universe U, where

$$(F,a_i),\cdots,\left(F,a_{|A|}\right)\subseteq(F,A)$$

and

$$\left(F,a_{i_1}\right),\cdots,\left(F,a_{i_{|a_i|}}\right)\subseteq(F,a_i)$$

The support of (F, a_{i_j}) by (F, a_{i_k}) denoted by $\text{Sup}_{(F,a_{i_k})}(F, a_{i_j})$ is defined as

$$\text{Sup}_{(F,a_{i_k})}(F, a_{i_j}) = \frac{\left|(F, a_{i_j}) \cap (F, a_{i_k})\right|}{\left|(F, a_{i_j}) \cup (F, a_{i_k})\right|},$$

$$\forall (F, a_{i_j}) \in (F, A); 1 \leq i \leq |A|; 1 \leq j, k \leq |a_i|$$

Definition 3: (Total Support) The summation of all support for (F, a_{j_k}) denoted by $\text{TSup}(F, a_{j_k})$ is defined as

$$\text{TSup}(F, a_{j_k}) = \sum_{k=1}^{|A|} Sup_{(F,a_{m_n})}(F, a_{j_k}),$$

$$\forall (F, a_{j_k}) \in (F, A);\ 1 \leq n \leq |A|;\ 1 \leq n \leq |a_m|$$

Definition 4: (Attribute Representation) The soft-set in (F, A) that have maximum total support in their domain is known as attribute representative denoted by $\text{Rep}(A_i)$ *is defined as*

$$\text{Rep}(A_i) = \text{Max}\left(\text{TSup}((F, a_{i_1}), \cdots, \text{TSup}(F, a_{i_{|A_i|}})\right)$$

Definition 5: (Mode) Mode is the number of occurrences of $\text{Rep}(A_i)$ value. If the value occurred more than one, then it is known as the multiple occurrences, otherwise, it is known as single occurrence.

Definition 6: (Support Attribute Representative) Attribute Representative with maximum value is known as Support Attribute Representative (SAR) is defined as

$$\text{SAR} = \begin{cases} \text{Max}\left\{\text{Mode}\left(\text{Rep}(A_i), \ldots, \text{Rep}(A_{|A|})\right)\right\}, \\ \text{Multiple occurences} \\ \quad \text{Max}\left\{\text{Rep}(A_i), \ldots, \text{Rep}(A_{|A|})\right\}, \\ \quad \text{Single occurence} \end{cases}$$

Next, the SAR algorithm is presented as follows.

Computational Complexity

Suppose in an information system, there are n objects, m attributes and l numbers of distinct values of each attribute. Process to determining an elementary set of all attributes needs nm. The computation of calculating the support of all subsets of U having different value of a_i is n^2l. Meanwhile, by taking the worst-case, the process to determining the SAR is 1. Therefore, the computational complexity of SAR techniques is a polynomial $O(n^2l + nm + 1)$.

Example

In this section, an example of SAR implementation will be presented. Information system in Table 3 is used as an input. All steps in this example are derived based on the algorithm shown in Figure 1. The implementation begins by computing the support for each soft-set using Defini-

Table 3. Multi-value information system

Object	Volume	Material	Location
1	High	Hard	Pacific
2	High	Hard	Midwest
3	High	Medium	East Coast
4	High	Soft	Northern
5	Low	Soft	Pacific
6	Low	Medium	Midwest

tion2.Forexample,allsupportsof $(F, \text{Volume}_{\text{High}})$ are calculated as follows:

1. Support by $(F, \text{Volume}_{\text{High}})$

$$\text{Sup}_{(F,\text{Volume}_{\text{High}})}(F, \text{Volume}_{\text{High}}) = \frac{|\{1,2,3,4\} \cap \{1,2,3,4\}|}{|\{1,2,3,4\} \cup \{1,2,3,4\}|} = \frac{4}{4} = 1$$

2. Support by $(F, \text{Volume}_{\text{Low}})$

$$\text{Sup}_{(F,\text{Volume}_{\text{Low}})}(F, \text{Volume}_{\text{High}}) = \frac{|\{1,2,3,4\} \cap \{5,6\}|}{|\{1,2,3,4\} \cup \{5,6\}|} = \frac{0}{6} = 0$$

3. Support by $(F, \text{Material}_{\text{Hard}})$

$$\text{Sup}_{(F,\text{Material}_{\text{Hard}})}(F, \text{Volume}_{\text{High}}) = \frac{|\{1,2,3,4\} \cap \{1,2\}|}{|\{1,2,3,4\} \cup \{1,2\}|} = \frac{2}{4} = 0.5$$

4. Support by $(F, \text{Material}_{\text{Medium}})$

Figure 1. SAR Algorithm for selecting partition attribute

```
Algorithm SAR
Input: Categorical-valued Dataset
Output: Partition attribute
Begin
   1. Calculate Support and Total Support
      For i = all categories
         For j=all categories

      Intersection=Sum(And(Data(:,i),Data(:,j))
            Union = Sum(Or(Data(:,i),Data(:,j)
            Support i=Intersection / Union
            Total Support I += Support i
         End
      End

   2. Determine Representative of Domain Ai
      Size(R)=[row,column]
      For i=1:row
       If Mode([Ai])
          Rep(Ai)=Large([Ai])
       else
        Rep(Ai)=large([Ai])
      End

   3. Determine SAR of Domain A
      If mode(Rep())
        SAR=SAR(Rep())
      Else
         SAR = Large(Rep())
      end
```

$$\mathrm{Sup}_{(F,\mathrm{Material}_{\mathrm{Medium}})}\left(F,\mathrm{Volume}_{\mathrm{High}}\right) = \frac{\left|\{1,2,3,4\}\cap\{3,6\}\right|}{\left|\{1,2,3,4\}\cup\{3,6\}\right|} = \frac{1}{5} = 0.2$$

5. Support by $\left(F,\mathrm{Material}_{\mathrm{Soft}}\right)$

$$\mathrm{Sup}_{(F,\mathrm{Material}_{\mathrm{Soft}})}\left(F,\mathrm{Volume}_{\mathrm{High}}\right) = \frac{\left|\{1,2,3,4\}\cap\{4,5\}\right|}{\left|\{1,2,3,4\}\cup\{4,5\}\right|} = \frac{1}{5} = 0.2$$

6. Support by $\left(F,\mathrm{Location}_{\mathrm{Pacific}}\right)$

$$\mathrm{Sup}_{(F,\mathrm{Location}_{\mathrm{Pacific}})}\left(F,\mathrm{Volume}_{\mathrm{High}}\right) = \frac{\left|\{1,2,3,4\}\cap\{1,5\}\right|}{\left|\{1,2,3,4\}\cup\{1,5\}\right|} = \frac{1}{5} = 0.2$$

7. Support by $\left(F,\mathrm{Location}_{\mathrm{Midwest}}\right)$

$$\mathrm{Sup}_{(F,\mathrm{Location}_{\mathrm{Midwest}})}\left(F,\mathrm{Volume}_{\mathrm{High}}\right) = \frac{\left|\{1,2,3,4\}\cap\{2,6\}\right|}{\left|\{1,2,3,4\}\cup\{2,6\}\right|} = \frac{1}{5} = 0.2$$

8. Support by $\left(F,\mathrm{Location}_{\mathrm{East-coast}}\right)$

$$\mathrm{Sup}_{(F,\mathrm{Location}_{\mathrm{East-coast}})}\left(F,\mathrm{Volume}_{\mathrm{High}}\right) = \frac{\left|\{1,2,3,4\}\cap\{3\}\right|}{\left|\{1,2,3,4\}\cup\{3\}\right|} = \frac{1}{4} = 0.25$$

9. Support by $\left(F,\mathrm{Location}_{\mathrm{Northern}}\right)$

$$\mathrm{Sup}_{(F,\mathrm{Location}_{\mathrm{Northern}})}\left(F,\mathrm{Volume}_{\mathrm{High}}\right) = \frac{\left|\{1,2,3,4\}\cap\{4\}\right|}{\left|\{1,2,3,4\}\cup\{4\}\right|} = \frac{1}{4} = 0.25$$

Based on the support given by each categorical soft-set, total support is computed next using Definition 3. Therefore, total support calculation for $\left(F,\mathrm{Volume}_{\mathrm{High}}\right)$ is given in Figure 2. The summary of all total support for each soft-set is shown in Table 4.

Next, the representative selection for each $\left(F,A_i\right)\in\left(F,A\right)$ is made using the formula in Definition 4. For example, representative for attribute soft-set $\left(F,\mathrm{Volume}\right)$ is determined as follows:

$$\mathrm{Rep}\left(F,\mathrm{Volume}\right) = \mathrm{Max}\begin{Bmatrix}\mathrm{TSup}\left(F,\mathrm{Volume}_{\mathrm{High}}\right), \\ \mathrm{TSup}\left(F,\mathrm{Volume}_{\mathrm{Low}}\right)\end{Bmatrix}$$

It is clear that

Figure 2. Total support calculation for soft-set $Volume_{High}$

$$\mathrm{TSup}\left(\mathrm{Volume}_{\mathrm{High}}\right) = 1 + 0 + 0.5 + 0.2 + 0.2 + 0.2 + 0.2 + 0.25 + 0.25$$

Table 4. Total support summary

Soft-Set	Total Support
$(F, \text{Volume}_{\text{High}})$	2.8000
$(F, \text{Volume}_{\text{Low}})$	2.3333
$(F, \text{Material}_{\text{Hard}})$	2.1667
$(F, \text{Material}_{\text{Medium}})$	2.3667
$(F, \text{Material}_{\text{Soft}})$	2.3667
$(F, \text{Location}_{\text{Pacific}})$	2.2000
$(F, \text{Location}_{\text{Midwest}})$	2.2000
$(F, \text{Location}_{\text{East-coast}})$	1.7500
$(F, \text{Location}_{\text{Northern}})$	1.7500

$$(F, \text{Volume}_{\text{High}}) = 2.800$$

is the representative for (F, Volume) compared to

$$(F, \text{Volume}_{\text{Low}}) = 2.3333$$

As shown in Table 4, $(F, \text{Material})$ have two sub soft-set with equal maximum value, one soft-set will be selected randomly as representative. The same step is repeated for soft-set $(F, \text{Location})$. Thus, representatives with their value of total support for all soft-set (F, A) are as follows.

$$\text{Rep}(F, \text{Volume}) = (F, \text{Volume}_{\text{High}}) = 2.8000$$

$$\text{Rep}(F, \text{Material}) = (F, \text{Material}_{\text{Medium}}) = 2.3667$$

$$\text{Rep}(F, \text{Location}) = (F, \text{Location}_{\text{Pacific}}) = 2.200$$

Finally, support attribute representative will be determined based on Definition 6. Since there is no repeat occurrence of representative values in the above case, the decision choice will be made based on second option. Therefore, in this example, attribute Volume is selected as a partition attribute.

EXPERIMENTAL RESULTS

Three simple small datasets representing Credit Card Promotion (CCP), Student Enrolment Qualifications (SEQ) and Car Evaluation (CE) have been selected. The experiment has been done using Matlab R2008a on i5 Intel CPU with 3GB Memory. The pre-processing for data cleansing and conversion to soft-set data approximation has been done using Java before this experiment takes place.

Table 5. Credit card promotion dataset

Object	MP	WP	LIP	CCI	SEX
1	Yes	No	No	No	Male
2	Yes	Yes	Yes	No	Female
3	No	No	No	No	Male
4	Yes	Yes	Yes	Yes	Male
5	Yes	No	Yes	No	Female
6	No	No	No	No	Female
7	Yes	No	Yes	Yes	Male
8	No	Yes	No	No	Male
9	Yes	No	No	No	Male
10	Yes	Yes	Yes	No	Female

Table 6. Value of attribute representative of CCP dataset

Attribute	Attribute Support Value		SAR
MP	Yes	No	MP_{Yes}=3.3388
	3.3388	1.8798	
WP	No	Yes	WP_{No}=2.9722
	2.9722	2.2833	
LIP	No	Yes	LIP_{Yes}=2.8587
	2.8178	2.8587	
CCI	No	Yes	CCI_{No}=3.5889
	3.5889	1.3619	
SEX	Male	Female	Sex_{Male}=3.0070
	3.0070	2.2500	

Experiment 1: Credit Card Promotion Dataset

The dataset shown in Table 5 contains 10 objects with five (5) categorical-value attributes, i.e., Magazine Promotion (MP), Watch Promotion (WP), Life Insurance Promotion (LIP), Credit Card Insurance (CCI) and Sex. Each attributes in the dataset contains two (2) categories.

Using SAR, as in Table 5, it is shown in Table 6 that CCI has the highest value and directly selected as the partition attribute.

Table 8. Value of attribute representative of SEQ dataset

Attribute	Attribute Support Value			SAR
Degree	Ph.D	M.Sc	B.Sc	$Degree_{M.Sc}$=4.4095
	2.9762	4.4095	3.5429	
English	Good	Medium	Bad	$English\text{-}_{Medium}$=5.3575
	1.6667	5.3575	2.0	
Experience	Medium	Good		$Experience\text{-}_{Medium}$=5.4883
	5.4883	3.5439		
IT	Good	Medium		IT_{Good}=4.5761
	4.5761	4.4095		
Mathematics	Good	Medium		$Math_{Good}$=4.5881
	4.5881	4.6714		
Programming	Good	Medium		$Prog_{Good}$=4.5881
	4.5881	4.6714		
Statistics	Good	Medium		$Stat_{Good}$=4.4502
	4.4502	4.3240		

Experiment 2: Student Enrolment Qualification (SEQ) Dataset

Table 7 shows an information system of student's enrollment qualification. There are eight (8) objects with seven categorical attributes: Degree, English, Experience, IT, Mathematics, Programming and Statistics. Note that attribute Degree and

Table 7. The student's enrollment qualification dataset

Student #	Degree	English	Exp	IT	Math	Prog	Stat
1	Ph.D	Good	Medium	Good	Good	Good	Good
2	Ph.D	Medium	Medium	Good	Good	Good	Good
3	M.Sc	Medium	Medium	Medium	Good	Good	Good
4	M.Sc	Medium	Medium	Medium	Good	Good	Medium
5	M.Sc	Medium	Medium	Medium	Medium	Medium	Medium
6	M.Sc	Medium	Medium	Medium	Medium	Medium	Medium
7	B.Sc	Medium	Good	Good	Medium	Medium	Medium
8	B.Sc	Bad	Good	Good	Medium	Medium	Good

English have three (3) categorical values and all others attributes have two (2) categorical values.

As shown in Table 8, even though attribute Exp has the largest value compare to others, but attribute Exp is not the partition attribute since there are exist two (2) attributes with two (2) equal values; Math and Programming. As a result, SAR technique chooses this two attributes as the partition attributes.

Experiment 3: Car Evaluation (CE) Dataset

Car evaluation dataset consist of 1728 instances with six (6) attributes plus one (1) partition attribute. Out of six (6) attributes, three (3) attributes have four (4) categorical value and the others have three (3) categorical values. Partition attribute has four (4) categorical values defined as accepted, unaccepted, very-good and good. Using this dataset, the two cases of experiments have been evaluated: with partition attribute (supervised) and without partition attribute (unsupervised). For the experiment with partition attribute, SAR technique had chosen the partition attribute as the partition attribute.

Table 9 shows the summary of the total support for the first case and how partition attribute has been obtained. Obviously from Table 9, attribute 'Buying' is represented by category 'Low', attribute 'Maint' is represented by category 'Low,' attribute 'Door' is represented by category 'Door-4' or 'Door-5-more', attribute 'Person' is represented by category 'Person-3,' attribute 'Lug-Boot' is represented by category 'Lug-Boot-Big,' attribute 'Safety' is represented by category 'Safety-Big' and attribute 'Decision' is represented by category 'Decision-accept' with total support value of 4.1379, 4.1212, 4.0812, 4.7797, 4.7411, 4.8150 and 6.4139 respectively. It is proved that attribute 'Decision' will be selected as the partition attribute since it has the larger total support value as compare to other total support attribute representative.

Experiment for the second case is implemented by removing partition attribute from the

Table 9. Result summary for car data evaluation dataset with partition attribute

Attribute	Total Support for Category				Attribute Representative
Buying	V-High	High	Med	Low	(Low)=4.1379
	4.0204	4.0412	4.1052	4.1379	
Maint	V-High	High	Med	Low	(Low)=4.1212
	4.0204	4.0538	4.1052	4.1212	
Door	2	3	4	5-More	(4)(5-More)=4.0812
	4.0521	4.0728	4.0812	4.0812	
Person	2	3	4-More		(3)=4.7797
	4.6760	4.7797	4.7719		
Lug-Boot	Small	Median	Big		(Big)=4.7411
	4.6932	4.7240	4.7411		
Safety	Small	Median	Big		(Big)=4.8150
	4.6760	4.7449	4.8150		
Decision	Accept	UnAccept	VeryGood	Good	(Accept)=6.4139
	6.4139	4.0690	1.7399	1.7782	

Table 10. Result summary for car data evaluation dataset without partition attribute

Attribute	Total Support for Category				Attribute Representative
Buying	V-High	High	Med	Low	3.6428
	3.6428	3.6428	3.6428	3.6428	
Maint	V-High	High	Med	Low	3.6428
	3.6428	3.6428	3.6428	3.6428	
Door	2	3	4	5-More	3.6428
	3.6428	3.6428	3.6428	3.6428	
Person	2	3	4-More		4.2
	4.2000	4.2000	4.2000		
Lug-Boot	Small	Median	Big		4.2
	4.2000	4.2000	4.2000		
Safety	Small	Median	Big		4.2
	4.200	4.200	4.200		

dataset. Table 10 shows the summary of the second case experiment. In this case, results are very identical. But as shows in the table, attribute Person, Lug-Boot and Safety can be chosen as the partition attribute.

PERFORMANCE ANALYSIS

Two large UCI benchmark datasets with different properties have been selected for the performance analysis. First selected dataset is a mushroom dataset which is large in size. It is consists of 8124 instances with 22 attributes. Out of 22 attributes, six (6) attributes have two (2) categorical values; four (4) attributes have four (4) categorical values and nine (9) categorical values respectively. Other than that, there are one attribute correspondingly has three (3) categorical values, seven (7) categorical values, ten (10) categorical values and twelve (12) categorical values. Second selected dataset is lung cancer dataset which is large in dimensional. It is consists of thirty-two (32) instances with fifty-six (56) attributes. All attributes in this dataset have a nominal value range from zero (0) to three (3).

Comparisons is being made against three previous rough set based techniques called Total Roughness (TR) by Mazlack *et al.* (2000), Min-Min Roughness (MMR) by Parmar *et al.* (2007) and Maximum Attribute Dependency (MDA) by Herawan and Deris (2009a) and Herawan *et al.* (2010a). Mean execution time for each technique is collected by executing each technique 15 times using each dataset.

Mushroom Dataset (http://archive.ics.uci.edu/ml/datasets/Mushroom)

For processing time on mushroom dataset, TR technique requires in average 168.25 seconds of execution times. However, another two techniques, MMR and MDA, does not show a significant improvement of execution times, both techniques required in average 167.46 seconds and 158.11 seconds respectively. On the other hand, SAR techniques only requires in average 8.10 seconds of execution time and shows an improvements up to 95% when comparison has been made with MDA's technique. The summary of the results is shown in Figure 3. The result indicates that SAR technique is better when working with large size of dataset.

Figure 3. Mean execution time comparisons using mushroom dataset

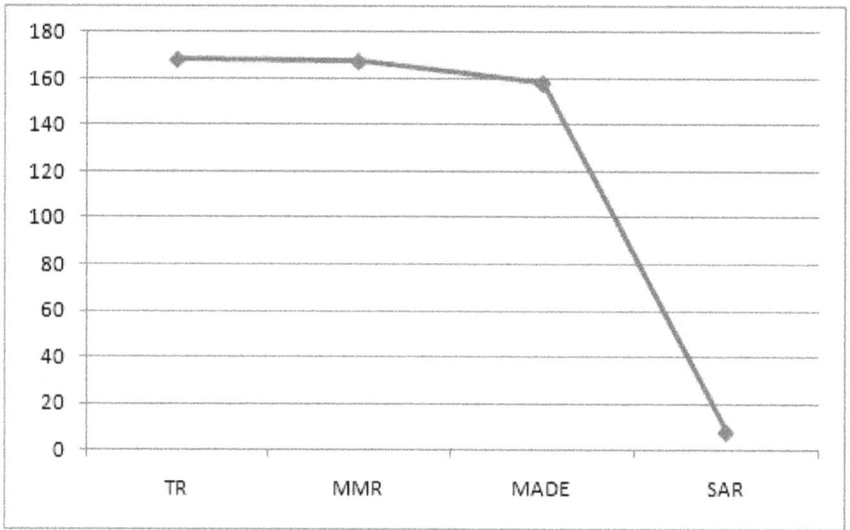

Figure 4. Mean execution time comparisons using lung cancer dataset

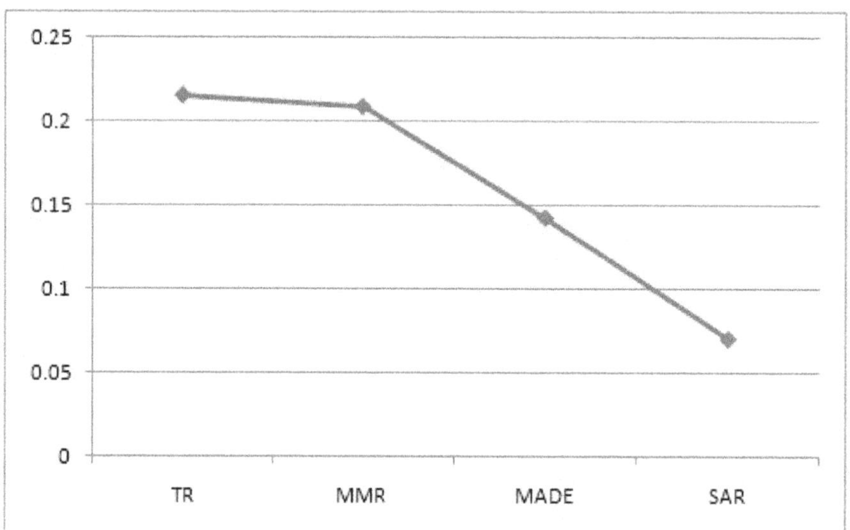

Lung Cancer Dataset (http://archive.ics.uci.edu/ml/datasets/Lung+Cancer)

Using this dataset TR, MMR and MDA techniques need in average 0.25 seconds, 0.20 seconds and 0.14 seconds of execution time, respectively. But, SAR techniques only needs in average 0.07 seconds of execution time to process the dataset. It is clear, as shown in Figure 4, SAR technique improves the execution time up to 50% faster than nearest fastest technique in study; MDA's technique.

CONCLUSION

In this paper, Support Attribute Representative (SAR), a soft-set based technique for selecting a partition attribute in categorical-valued information system has been proposed. In this technique, comparisons at the attribute level is firstly made before representative for each attributes and finally compared to each other. By using this technique, the execution time on selecting a decision can be reduced. In term of executing time, a comparison test on two UCI benchmark datasets shown that SAR outperforms three rough set-based techniques TR, MMR, and MDA up to 95% and 50%, respectively. The results of this research will provide useful information for decision makers to handle categorical-valued information system.

ACKNOWLEDGMENT

An early version of this paper appeared in the Proceeding of the 2nd International Conference on Software Engineering and Computer System (ICSECS) 2011, Kuantan, Pahang, Malaysia, June 27-29th 2011, Communications in Computer and Information Science Volume 180, Part 1, 137-147, Springer-Verlag Berlin Heidelberg 2011.

REFERENCES

Ali, M. I., Feng, F., Liu, X., Min, W. K., & Shabira, M. (2009). On some new operations in soft set theory. *Computers & Mathematics with Applications (Oxford, England)*, *57*(9), 1547–1553. doi:10.1016/j.camwa.2008.11.009

Chen, D., Tsang, E. C. C., Yeung, D. S., & Wang, X. (2005). The parameterization reduction of soft-set and its applications. *Computers & Mathematics with Applications (Oxford, England)*, *49*(5-6), 757–763. doi:10.1016/j.camwa.2004.10.036

Feng, F., Jun, Y. B., Liu, X. Y., & Li, L. F. (2010). An adjustable approach to fuzzy soft-set based decision making. *Journal of Computational and Applied Mathematics*, *234*, 10–20. doi:10.1016/j.cam.2009.11.055

Herawan, T., & Deris, M. M. (2009a). A framework on rough set-based partitioning attribute selection. In D.-S. Huang, K.-H. Jo, H.-H. Lee, H.-J. Kang, & V. Bevilacqua (Eds.), *Proceedings of the 5th International Conference on Emergent Intelligent Computing Technology and Applications* (LNCS 5755, pp. 91-100).

Herawan, T., & Deris, M. M. (2009b). On multi-soft sets construction in information systems. In D.-S. Huang, K.-H. Jo, H.-H. Lee, H.-J. Kang, & V. Bevilacqua (Eds.), *Proceedings of the 5th International Conference on Emergent Intelligent Computing Technology and Applications* (Eds.), (LNCS 5755, pp. 101-110).

Herawan, T., Deris, M. M., & Abawajy, J. H. (2010a). A rough set approach for selecting clustering attribute. *Knowledge-Based Systems*, *23*(3), 220–231. doi:10.1016/j.knosys.2009.12.003

Herawan, T., Deris, M. M., & Abawajy, J. H. (2010b). Matrices representation of multi soft-sets and its application. In D. Taniar, O. Gervasi, B. Murgante, E. Pardede, & B. O. Apduhan (Eds.), *Proceedings of the International Conference on Computational Science and its Applications* (LNCS 6018, pp. 201-214).

Kong, Z., Gao, L., Wang, L., & Li, S. (2008). The normal parameter reduction of soft-set and its algorithm. *Computers & Mathematics with Applications (Oxford, England)*, *56*(12), 3029–3037. doi:10.1016/j.camwa.2008.07.013

Kong, Z., Gao, L. Q., & Wang, L. F. (2009). Comment on "A fuzzy soft-set theoretic approach to decision making problems." . *Journal of Computational and Applied Mathematics*, *223*, 540–542. doi:10.1016/j.cam.2008.01.011

Maji, P. K., Biswas, R., & Roy, A. R. (2001). Fuzzy soft-set. *Journal of Fuzzy Mathematics*, *9*(3), 589–602.

Maji, P. K., Biswas, R., & Roy, A. R. (2003). Soft-set theory. *Computers & Mathematics with Applications (Oxford, England)*, *45*, 555–562. doi:10.1016/S0898-1221(03)00016-6

Maji, P. K., Roy, A. R., & Biswas, R. (2002). An application of soft-set in a decision making problem. *Computer and Mathematics with Application*, *44*, 1077–1083. doi:10.1016/S0898-1221(02)00216-X

Mazlack, L. J., He, A., Zhu, Y., & Coppock, S. (2000). Rough set approach in choosing partitioning attribute. In *Proceedings of the International Chinese Statistical Association 13th International Conference on Computer Applications in Industry and Engineering* (pp. 1-6).

Molodstov, D. (1999). Soft-set theory-first results. *Computers & Mathematics with Applications (Oxford, England)*, *37*(45), 19–31.

Parmar, D., Wu, T., & Blackhurst, J. (2007). MMR: An algorithm for clustering categorical data using rough set theory. *Data & Knowledge Engineering*, *63*(3), 879–893. doi:10.1016/j.datak.2007.05.005

This work was previously published in the International Journal of Information Retrieval Research, Volume 1, Issue 4, edited by Zhongyu (Joan) Lu, pp. 38-52, copyright 2011 by IGI Publishing (an imprint of IGI Global).

Chapter 17
XRecursive:
Connecting XML with Relational Databases

Mohammed Adam Ibrahim Fakharaldien
Universiti Malaysia Pahang, Malaysia

Norrozila Sulaiman
Universiti Malaysia Pahang, Malaysia

Jasni Mohamed Zain
Universiti Malaysia Pahang, Malaysia

Tutut Herawan
Universiti Malaysia Pahang, Malaysia

ABSTRACT

Storing XML documents in a relational database is a promising solution because relational databases are mature and scale very well. They have the advantages that in a relational database XML data and structured data can coexist making it possible to build application that involve both kinds of data with little extra effort. This paper proposes an alternative method named Xrecursive for mapping XML (eXtensible Markup Language) documents to RDB (Relational Databases). The Xrecursive method does not need a DTD (Document Text Definition) or XML schema. Further, it can be applied as a general solution for any XML data. The steps and algorithm of Xrecursive are given in details to describe how to use the storing structure to storage and query XML documents in relational database. The authors report their experimental results on a real database, showing that the performance of their Xrecursive algorithm achieves better results in terms of storage size, insertion time, mapping time, and reconstruction time as compared with that SUCXENT and XParent methods. In overall, Xrecursive performs better in term of query performances as compared to the both methods.

INTRODUCTION

The eXtensible Markup Language (XML) is used for representing data through the internet, but this technology needs a suitable medium for storing these data. At present, three common technologies can be used to store and retrieve XML documents, i.e., native XML database, Object Oriented Database (OODB) and Relational Database (RDB).

DOI: 10.4018/978-1-4666-3898-3.ch017

With the trend of increasing amount of XML documents on the World Wide Web, it is critical to have efficient mechanism to store and query XML documents to exploit the full power of this technology. Now day' XML emerged as a major standard for representing data on the World Wide Web while the dominant storage mechanism for structured data is the relational databases, which has been an efficient tool for storing, searching, retrieving data from different collection of data. The ability to map XML data in relational databases is difficult mission and challenging in the world of all IT organization so there is a need to develop an interfaces and tools for mapping and storing XML data in relational databases.

The extensible Markup Language (XML) is quickly becoming the de facto standard for data exchange over the Internet (Zafari, Hasami, & Shiri, 2010) and now it plays a central role in data management, transformation and exchange. Since its introduction to industry in the late 1990s, XML (Grandi, Mandreoli, Tiberio, & Bergonzini, 2003) has achieved widespread support and adoption among all the leading software tools, server, and database vendors. As importantly, XML has become the lingua franca for data by lowering the cost of processing, searching, exchanging, and re-using information. XML provides a standardized, self-describing means for expressing information in a way that is readable by humans and easily verified, transformed, and published, the hot topic is to seek the best way for storing XML documents in order to get high query processing efficiency (Sainan, Caifeng, & Liming, 2009). In addition, data can be transmitted to remote services anywhere on the Internet using XML-based Web services to take advantage of the new ubiquity of connected software applications. The openness of XML (Augeri, Bulutoglu, Mullins, Baldwin, & Baird, 2007) allows it to be exchanged between virtually any hardware, software, or operating system. Simply put, XML opens the door for information interchange without restriction. Today, the dominant storage mechanism for structured enterprise data is the relational database, which has proven itself an efficient tool for storing, searching for, and retrieving information from massive collections of data. Relational databases specialize in relating individual data records grouped by type in tables. Developers can join records together as needed using SQL (Structured Query Language) and present one or more records to end-users as meaningful information. The relational database model revolutionized enterprise data storage with its simplicity, efficiency, and cost effectiveness. Relational databases have been prevalent in large corporations since the 1980s, and they will likely remain the dominant storage mechanism for enterprise data in the foreseeable future. Despite these strengths, relational databases lack the flexibility to seamlessly integrate with other systems, since this was not historically a requirement of the database model (Reed, 2008). In addition, although relational databases share many similarities, there are enough differences between the major commercial implementations to make developing applications to integrate multiple products difficult. Among the challenges are differences in data types, varying levels of conformance to the SQL standard, proprietary extensions to SQL, and so on. For the storage of XML document, the key issue is transforming the tree structure of an XML document into tuples in relational tables (Yue, Ren, & Qian, 2008). Nowadays, there are more and more data presented as XML document, the need of storing them persistently in a database has increased rapidly while the native–XML databases usually have limited support for relational databases. In recent years, with the popularity of relational databases (RDB), approaches based on RDB (Sybase Corporation, 1999; Yoshikawa, Amagasa, Shimura, & Uemura, 2001 Jiang, Lu, Wang, & Yu, 2002a, 2002b; Kyung-Soo, 2001; Rys, 2000) to store and manipulate XML data as relational tables but still there is need to manage XML data and relational data seamlessly with similar storage and retrieval efficiencies simultaneously. XML and Relational databases cannot be kept separately because XML is becoming the universal standard data format for the representation and exchanging the information whereas most existing data lies in RDBMS and their power of data capabilities cannot be degraded so the solution to this problem a new efficient methods for storing XML documents in relational database is required. A new efficient method for storing XML document in relational database is proposed in this paper to face these problems.

The rest of this paper is organized as follows. First, we review the XML databases. Then, we describe the proposed XRecursive algorithm. Afterwards, we describe the experimental and comparison results. Finally the conclusion of this work is described.

RELATED WORK

There have been a number of different techniques for storing XML documents into database (RDB). These techniques can generally be classified into three tracks: in semi-structured databases (Goldman, McHugh, & Widom, 1999) in object-oriented databases (Bancihon et al., 1998) and in relational systems (Shanmugasundaram, Tufte, Zhang, He, DeWitt, & Naughton, 1999; Yoshikawa, Amagasa, Shimura, & Uemura, 2001; Jiang, Lu, Wang, & Yu, 2002a; Florescu & Kossman, 1999; Ramanath, Freire, Haritsa, & Roy, 2003; Bohannon, Freire, Roy, & Simeon, 2002; Tatarinov, Viglas, Beyer, Shanmugasundaram, Shekita, & Zhang, 2001; Zhang, Naughton, Dewitt, Luo, & Lohmann, 2002). Among these approaches, the relational storage approach has attracted considerable interest with a view to leveraging their powerful and reliable data management services. The aim of mapping XML documents into relational database is to utilize relational database power capabilities in indexes, triggers, data integrity, security, and query optimization by SQL. In order to store an XML document in a relational database, the tree structure of the XML document must first be mapped into an equivalent, flat, and relational schema. XML documents are then shredded and loaded into the mapped tables. Finally, at runtime, XML queries are translated into SQL, submitted to the RDBMS, and the results are then translated into XML. There is a rich literature addressing the issue of managing XML documents in relational back-ends (Shanmugasundaram, Tufte, Zhang, He, DeWitt, & Naughton, 1999; Yoshikawa, Amagasa, Shimura, & Uemura, 2001; Jiang, Lu, Wang, & Yu, 2002a; Florescu & Kossman, 1999; Ramanath, Freire, Haritsa, & Roy, 2003; Bohannon, Freire, Roy, & Simeon, 2002; Tatarinov, Viglas, Beyer, Shanmugasundaram, Shekita, & Zhang, 2001; Zhang, Naughton, Dewitt, Luo, & Lohmann, 2002). These approaches can be classified into two major categories as follows:

Schema-Conscious Approach

This method firstly creates a relational schema based on the DTD/schema of the XML documents. First, the cardinality of the relationships between the nodes of the XML document is established. Based on this information a relational schema is created. The structural information of XML data is modeled by using primary-key foreign-key joins in relational databases to model the parent–child relationships in the XML tree. Examples of such approaches are Shared-Inlining (Shanmugasundaram, Tufte, Zhang, He, DeWitt, & Naughton, 1999) LegoDB (Ramanath, Freire, Haritsa, & Roy, 2003; Bohannon, Freire, Roy, & Simeon, 2002). Note that this approach depends on the existence of a schema describing the XML data. Furthermore, due to the heterogeneity of XML data, in this approach a simple XML schema/DTD often produce a relational schema with many tables.

Schema-Oblivious Approach

This method maintains a fixed schema which is used to store XML documents. The basic idea is to capture the tree structure of an XML document. This approach does not require existence of an XML schema/DTD. Also, number of tables is fixed in the relational schema and does not depend on the structural heterogeneity of XML documents. Some examples of schema-oblivious approaches are Edge approach (Florescu & Kossman, 1999), XRel (Yoshikawa, Amagasa, Shimura, & Uemura, 2001), XParent (Jiang, Lu, Wang, & Yu, 2002a), and SUCXENT (Prakash, Bhowmick, & Mardia, 2004). Schema-oblivious approaches have obvious advantages such as the ability to handle XML schema changes better as there is no need to change the relational schema and a uniform query translation approach. Schema-conscious approaches, on the other hand, have the advantage of more efficient query processing (Tian, DeWitt, Chen, & Zhang, 2002). Also, no special relational schema needs to be designed for schema-conscious approaches as it can be generated on the fly based on the DTD of the XML document(s).

THE PROPOSED METHOD

XML Document

The data structure of XML document is hierarchical, consist of nested structures. The elements are strictly marked by the beginning and ending tags, for empty elements by empty-elements tags. Character data between tags are the content of the elements. It is an instance of XML document contains information about an employee as follows.

The Tree Structure Representation of XML Document

In this section, the structure independent mapping approach is explained with a sample XML document shown in Figure 1.

Figure 1. XML document

```
<? Xml version="1.0" encoding="UTF-8"?>
<Personnel>
<Employee type="permanent">
<Name>Seagull</Name>
<Id>3674</Id>
<Age>34</Age>
</Employee>
<Employee type="contract">
<Name>Robin</Name>
<Id>3675</Id>
<Age>25</Age>
</Employee>
<Employee type="permanent">
<Name>Crow</Name>
<Id>3676</Id>
<Age>28</Age>
</Employee>
</Personnel>
```

XRecursive Structure

Each and every XML can be describing as a XML tree. In Figure 2 the squares are the elements and the ovals are the attributes of the elements. A generated XML tree has been shown in the Figure 2. Every element or attributes are identified by a signature (number).

Definition 1: XRecursive Structure.

XRecursive is a storage structure for storing XML documents where each path is identified by its parent from the root node in a recursive manner.

Definition 2: All nodes.

Let

$$N = \{n_1, n_2, \cdots, n_k\}$$

be a set of all nodes (id) in XML and

$$B = \{np_1, np_2, \cdots, np_k\}$$

be a set of parent nodes (pid) and

$$D = \{nl_1, nl_2, \cdots, nl_k\}$$

be a set of parent nodes (tagid), then

1. $\forall np_i \in B$, $np_i \in A$
2. $\forall nl_i \in D$, $nl_i \in A$
3. $\forall np_i \in B$, $np_i \notin D$ and $\forall np_i \in A \setminus D$
4. $\forall nl_i \in D$, $\forall nl_i \notin B$ and $\forall nl_i \in A \setminus B$

Algorithm

XML document can be stored in relational database, in this paper, MYSQL by use of Figure 1 and 2 the proposed algorithm of Xrecursive to map XML document into relational database is described in Figure 3.

Figure 2. Tree structure of XML document with XRecursive labeling

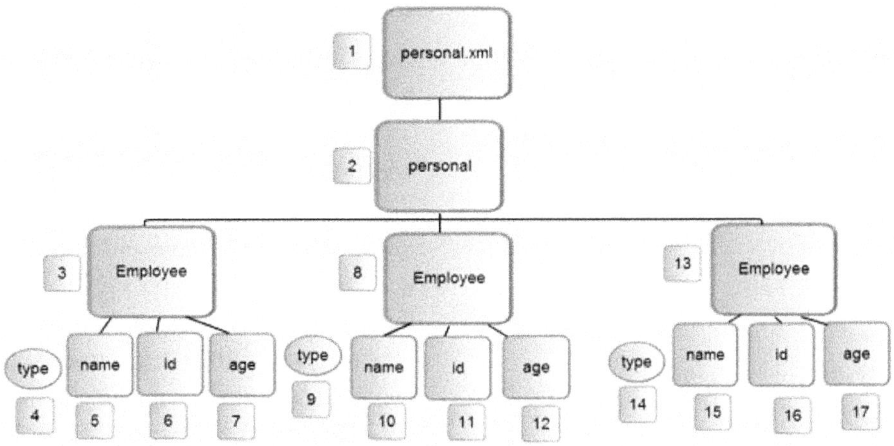

Figure 3. Xrecursive for mapping XML to RDB algorithm

Algorithm: Xrecursive for Mapping XML to RDB

00 Algorithm process XMLFile(XML as a document)

```
01  Begin
02 Let tag_structure represents the list of the nodes of the XML file
03 Let tag_value represents the list of the values of the nodes
04 Let filename=null as string and parentid=1 as integer
05 Let nodecounter=1 as integer
06 filename=read xml document name
07 Add filename, nodecounter, parentid to tag_structure
08 Recursivexmlnode(XmlDocRootNode,parentid,nodecounter)
09  store tag_structure into database
10  store tag_value into database
11  End  Algorithm
```

00 Procedure Recursivexmlnode(xmlnode, parentid, nodecounter)

```
01  Begin
02  if xmlnode is not text node then
03  Begin
04  tagstructure(xmlnode, parentid, nodecounter)
05  if xmlnode has childnodes then
06  for each xmlattribute in xmlnode attributes
07  Begin
08  set parentid=nodecounter
09  while xmlnode has childnodes do
10  tagstructure(xmlnode, parentid, nodecounter)
11  End while
12  tagstructure(xmlnode, parentid, nodecounter)
13  tagvalue(nodecounter, value, type)
14  If xmlnode.next=true then go to 09 End
    if
15  End for
16  Else
17  tagvalue(nodecounter, value, type)
18  End if
19  Else
20  tagvalue(nodecounter, value, type)
21  End if
22  End
```

00 procedure tagvalue(nodecounter, value, type)

```
01 Begin
02 Read xmlattribute value as attributevalue
03 Add nodecounter, attributevalue, type to tagvalue
04 End
```

Definition 3: (Node Id).

Let $N = \{n_1, n_2, \cdots, n_k\}$ be a set of all nodes in XML tree such that preorder $n_i <$ preorder n_{i+1}, for $1 \le i \le k$, then node Id is defined as follow

$$node\, Id(n_i) = \begin{cases} 1 & , \; for \; i = 1 \\ node\, Id(n_{i-1}) + 1, & for \; 1 < i \le k \end{cases}$$

Proposition 4: (Parent Node Id).

Let $P = \{p_1, p_2, \cdots, p_k\}$ be a set of parent node (pId) in XML tree such that preorder $n_i <$ preorder n_{i+1}, for $1 \le i \le k$, then parent node is defined as follow

$$parent(Id_i) = \begin{cases} 1 & , \; for \; i = 1 \\ parent(Id_i) < parent(Id_i), & for \; 1 < j \end{cases}$$

Example 1: In this structure when an element or type associates with its signature it also represents its parent element. We add document name in association with the id to be able to add multiple XML file in the storage. Figure 2 represents the storage of the XML file associated with its signature. For every element there will have a signature associated with it and there will also have a parent's signature associated with it. In Table 1 tagName represents the name of the node; id represents the id of the node which is the Primary Key. And finally pId represents the parent id of the node. As document name don't have any parent id so the id of the document name and parent id of the document name is same that has been shown in the Figure 2.

Definition 5: (tagId).

Let $T = \{t_1, t_2, \cdots, t_k\}$ be the list of leaf nodes in XML tree such that preorder $n_i <$ preorder n_{i+1}, for $1 \le i \le k$, then node Id is defined as follow

$$tag\, Id(n_i) = tag\, Id(n_{i-1}) + 1, \; for \; 1 < i \le k$$

In Table 2, we represent the value associated with the elements or type. In XRecursive structure there is no need to store the path value or path structure as it will be determine recursively by its parent id. In Table 1 tagName is the name of the tag, where Id is the parent key. In Table 2 tagId presents the Table 1 id thus tagId is the foreign key. In Table 2 tagId only represents the elements which contain a value and the value represents on the value column. And the type 'A' denoted to the attribute and 'E' denoted to the element.

ANALYSIS OF EXPERIMENT

We ran experiments using our XML document in Figure 1. Our experiment was performed on 3.00 GHz Pentium 4 processor with 4GB RAM, 240

Table 2. Tag_value

tagId	Value	Type
4	Permanent	A
5	Seagua11	E
6	3674	E
7	34	E
9	Contract	A
10	Robin	E
11	3675	E
12	25	E
14	Permanent	A
15	Crow	E
16	3676	E
17	28	E

Table 1. Tag_structure

tagName	Id	pId
Personal.xml	1	1
Personal	2	1
Employee	3	2
Type	4	3
Name	5	3
Id	6	3
Age	7	3
Employee	8	2
Type	9	8
Name	10	8
Id	11	8
Age	12	8
Employee	13	2
Type	14	13
Name	15	13
Id	16	13
Age	17	13

GB of hard disk running on windows XP system, we used MySQL v5.01 as the database for storing XML document and java language (Version jdk6) for parsing the XML document and then save it in MySQL. The experiments are conducted using the XML benchmark. The experiment evaluates the efficiency of storing XML document in relational database based on the XRecursive structure. Further, we compare the performance of XRecursive with SUCXENT (Prakash, Bhowmick, & Mardia, 2004) and XParent (Jiang, Lu, Wang, & Yu, 2002a). The experiment is made with respect to the following four factors:

Database Size

In term of database size from Figure 1, XRecursive has lesser storage requirement than that the SUCXENT (Prakash, Bhowmick, & Mardia, 2004) and XParent (Jiang, Lu, Wang, & Yu, 2002a), as XRecursive only uses two tables to store the XML data whereas SUCXENT uses five tables and XParent uses four tables. Comparison result can be seen in the Figure 4 which shows that by this storage method, we can reduce not only the size of database requirement of the labeling of node, but also the number of tables.

Table 3 shows the improvement of SUCXENT and XParent methods by XRecursive method in terms of database size.

Insertion Time

Figure 5 shows a comparison of the document's insertion time from Figure 1, XRecursive method faster than that the SUCXENT and XParent

Figure 4. Database Size in MB

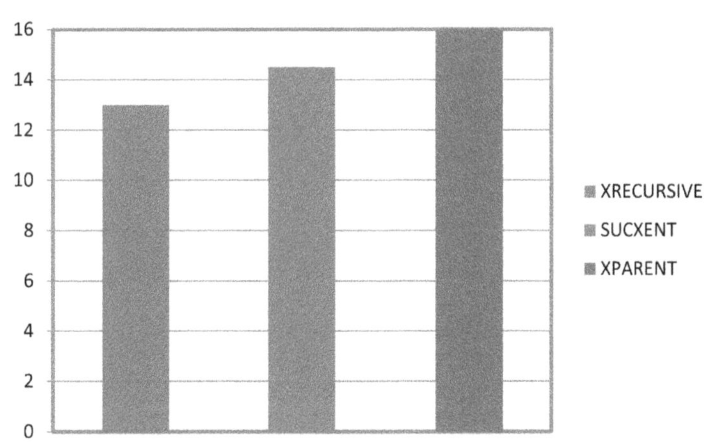

Table 3. Mapping time improvement by Xrecursive

Algorithm	Database Size	Improvement by XRecursive
Sucxent	14.5	11.5%
XParent	16	23%
Xrecursive	13	

Table 4. Insertion time improvement by Xrecursive

Algorithm	Insertion time (second)	Improvement by XRecursive
Sucxent	240	9%
XParent	250	13.6%
Xrecursive	220	

methods. The reason because XRecursive only uses two tables whereas SUCXENT and XParent, respectively use five and four tables which requires some more processing time during the filing the contents of tuples in each table.

Table 4 shows the improvement of SUCXENT and XParent methods by XRecursive method in terms of insertion time.

Further experiment in terms of mapping time and reconstructing time, we elaborate them on three different document sizes, i.e., 4KB, 28KB, and 64 KB.

Figure 5. Insertion time in second

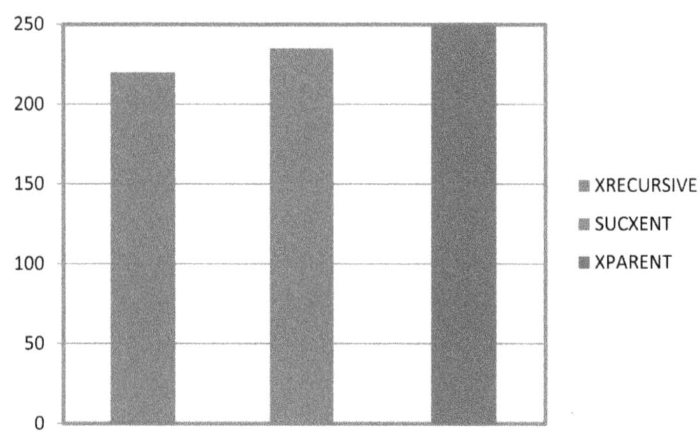

Table 5. Mapping time improvement by Xrecursive

Algorithm	Mapping time (second)		
	4KB	28KB	64KB
Sucxent	0.035	0.16	0.44
XParent	0.05	0.27	0.53
XRecursive	0.03	0.15	0.36
Average Improvement by XRecursive	0.416	0.433	0.347

Mapping Time

Figure 6 shows comparison results of the document's mapping time, XRecursive method still provide faster mapping time as compared to SUCXENT and XParent methods. Following the insertion time from previous section that XRecursive only uses two tables whereas SUCXENT and XParent, respectively use five and four tables which require some more processing time during mapping the contents of tuples in each table.

Table 5 shows the improvement of SUCXENT and XParent methods by XRecursive method in terms of mapping time.

Reconstructing Time

The results in Figure 7 shows that the time for mapping XML document to RDB is acceptable

Figure 6. Mapping time comparison

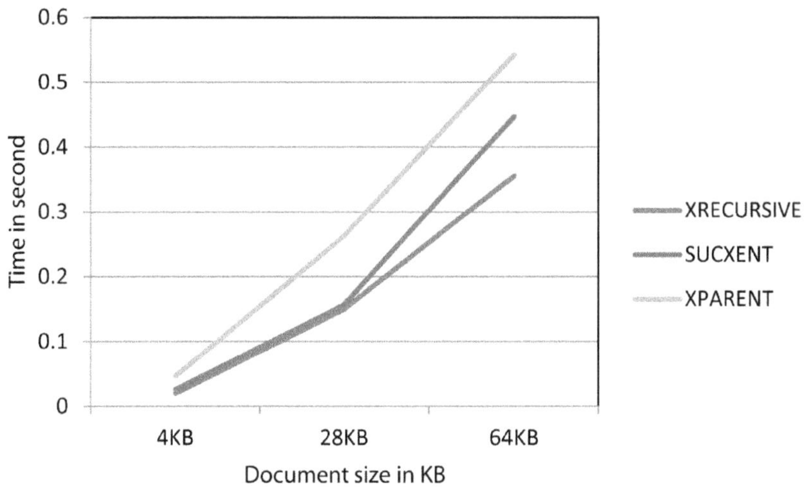

Figure 7. Reconstruction time comparison

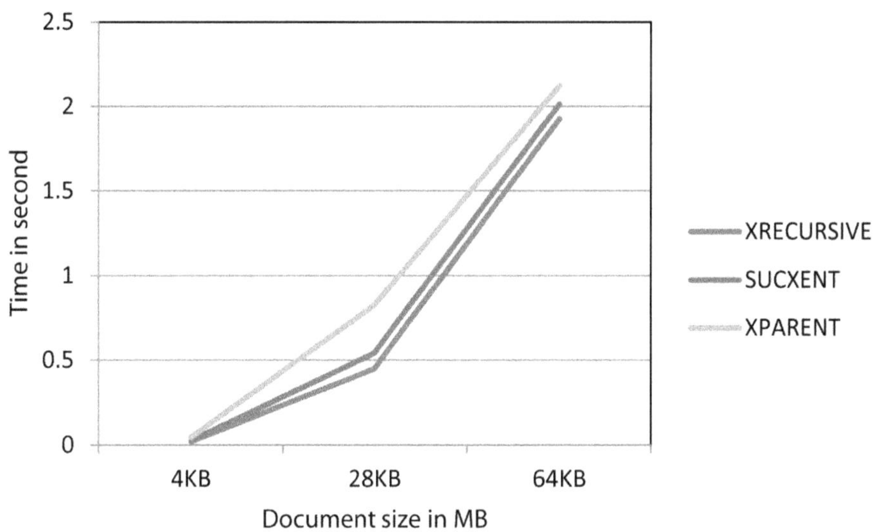

and the relation is linear between the document size and the mapping time.

Table 6 shows the improvement of SUCXENT and XParent methods by XRecursive method in terms of reconstruction time.

The overall query performance comparison is described in the following section.

Query Performance Comparison

Figure 8 shows the query performance comparisons, which compare four queries Q1, Q2, Q3, and Q4 on the three methods. With regard to the performance of queries, some points should be taken into account as described in Table 7.

From Figure 8, it is shown that Q1: Query b is a short XPath query. So there are not many joins

Table 6. Reconstruction time improvement by Xrecursive

Algorithm	Reconstruction time (second)		
	4KB	28KB	64KB
Sucxent	0.01	0.51	2.05
XParent	0.015	0.57	2.15
XRecursive	0.01	0.49	1.59
Average Improvement by XRecursive	0.25	0.102	0.32

in the SQL statement for the Edge method. Their response times are very close as expected.

Meanwhile Q2: Query requires one join in each step in the XPath query using the XRecursive method, however the SUCXENT and XParent use the path information in the path table. As result XRecursive is faster in the long XPath query as expected. Finally, for Q3 and Q4: The execution time is comparable.

Table 7. Samples query features

Query number	Query feature
Q1	Simple short path
Q2	Simple long path
Q3	Use one axis
Q4	Use two axis

CONCLUSION

XRecursive, a general storage method for XML document using relational database is proposed in this paper. XRecursive adopts the model-mapping method to store XML document in relational database, to decompose the tree structure into nodes and store all information of nodes in relational database according to the node types by recursive way. It can deal with any documents no matter whether it has fixed schema or not. By using this method we can reduce the database size require to store the XML document into relational database. The storing algorithm of XML document into relational database was also given in the paper,

Figure 8. Query performance comparison

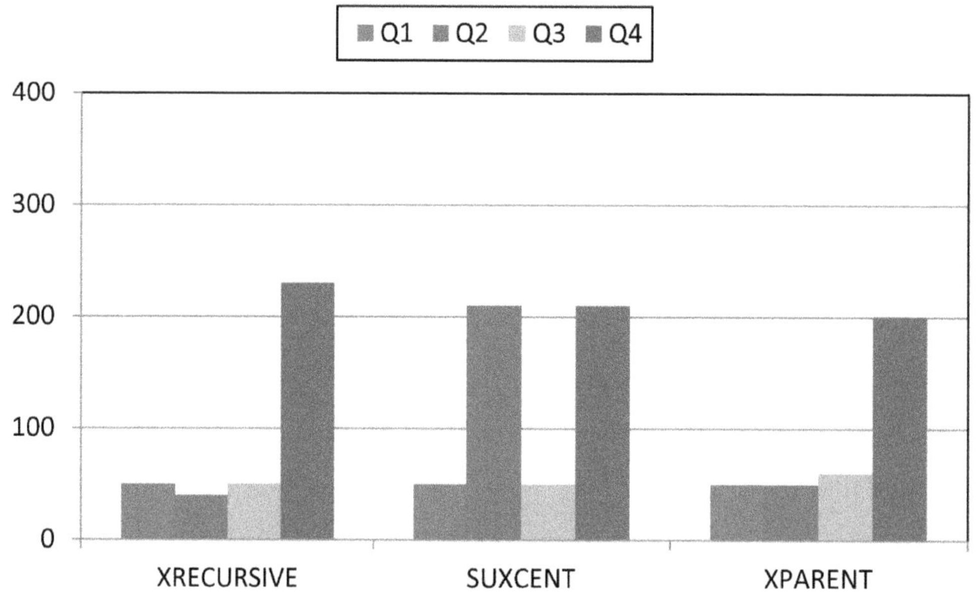

and examined the accuracy of it by using the XML document in performance section. Utilizing the actual XML document evaluated the performance of storing XML document into relational database by using our method.

ACKNOWLEDGMENT

An early version of this paper appeared in the Proceeding of the 2nd International Conference on Software Engineering and Computer System (ICSECS) 2011, Kuantan, Pahang, Malaysia, June 27-29th 2011, Communications in Computer and Information Science Volume 180, Part 2, 460-469, Springer-Verlag Berlin Heidelberg 2011.

REFERENCES

Augeri, C. J., Bulutoglu, D. A., Mullins, B. E., Baldwin, R. O., & Baird, L. C. (2007). An analysis of XML compression efficiency. In *Proceedings of the Workshop on Experimental Computer Science* (pp. 1-12).

Bancihon, F., Barbedette, G., Benzaken, V., Delobel, C., Gamerman, S., & Lécluse, C. (1988). The design and implementation of o2, an object-oriented database system. *Advances in Object Oriented Database Systems*, *6*(1), 1–22. doi:10.1007/3-540-50345-5_1

Bohannon, P., Freire, J., Roy, P., & Simeon, J. (2002). From XML schema to relations: A cost-based approach to XML storage. In *Proceedings of the IEEE International Conference on Data Engineering* (pp. 64-75).

Florescu, D., & Kossman, D. (1999). Storing and querying XML data using an RDBMS. *A Quarterly Bulletin of the Computer Society of the IEEE Technical Committee on Data Engineering*, *22*(3), 27–34.

Goldman, R., McHugh, J., & Widom, J. (1999). From semi structured data to XML: Migrating the lore data model and query language. In *Proceedings of the 2nd International Workshop on the Web and Databases* (pp. 25-30).

Grandi, F., Mandreoli, F., Tiberio, P., & Bergonzini, M. (2003). A temporal data model and management system for normative texts in XML format. In *Proceedings of the 5th ACM International Workshop on Web Information and Data Management* (pp. 29-36).

Jiang, H., Lu, H., Wang, W., & Yu, J. X. (2002a). Path materialization revisited: An efficient storage model for XML data. In *Proceedings of the 13th Australasian Database Conference* (pp. 85-94).

Jiang, H., Lu, H., Wang, W., & Yu, J. X. (2002b). XParent: An efficient RDBMS-based XML database system. In *Proceedings of the 18th International Conference on Data Engineering* (pp. 335-336).

Kyung-Soo, J. (2001). A design of middleware components for the connection between XML and RDB. In *Proceedings of the IEEE International Symposium on Industrial Electronics* (pp. 1753-1756).

Prakash, S., Bhowmick, S., & Mardia, S. (2004). SUCXENT: An efficient path-based approach to store and query XML documents. In F. Galindo, M. Takizawa, & R. Traunmüller (Eds.), *Proceedings of the 15th International Conference on Database and Expert Systems Applications* (LNCS 3180, pp. 285-295).

Ramanath, M., Freire, J., Haritsa, J., & Roy, P. (2003). Searching for efficient XML-to-relational mappings. In Z. Bellahsène, A. B. Chaudhri, E. Rahm, M. Rys, & R. Unland (Eds.), *Proceedings of the First International XML Database Symposium on Database and XML Technologies* (LNCS 2824, pp. 19-36).

Reed, D. (2008). Take a good look. *Data Strategy*, *2*(4), 24–29.

Rys, M. (2000). *Microsoft SQL server 2000 XML enhancements*. Redmond, WA: Microsoft Support Webcast.

Sainan, L., Caifeng, L., & Liming, G. (2009). Storage method for XML document based on relational database. In *Proceedings of the IEEE International Symposium on computer Science and Computational Technology* (pp. 127-131).

Shanmugasundaram, J., Tufte, K., Zhang, C., He, G., DeWitt, D. J., & Naughton, J. F. (1999). Relational databases for querying XML documents: Limitations and opportunities. In *Proceedings of the International Conference on Very Large Data Base* (pp. 302-314).

Sybase Corporation. (1999). *Using XML with the Sybase adaptive server SQL databases*. Berkeley, CA: Author.

Tatarinov, I., Viglas, S., Beyer, K., Shanmugasundaram, J., Shekita, E., & Zhang, C. (2001). Storing and querying ordered XML using a relational database system. In *Proceedings of the ACM SIGMOD International Conference on Management of Data* (pp. 204-215).

Tian, F., DeWitt, D., Chen, J., & Zhang, C. (2002). The design and performance evaluation of alternative XML storage strategies. *SIGMOD Record*, *31*(1), 5–10. doi:10.1145/507338.507341

Yoshikawa, M., Amagasa, T., Shimura, T., & Uemura, S. (2001). XRel: A path-based approach to storage and retrieval of XML documents using relational databases. *ACM Transactions on Internet Technology*, *1*(1), 110–141. doi:10.1145/383034.383038

Yue, L., Ren, J., & Qian, Y. (2008). Storage method of XML documents based-on pre-order labeling schema. In *Proceedings of the IEEE International Workshop on Education Technology and Computer Science* (pp. 50-53).

Zafari, H., Hasami, K., & Shiri, M. E. (2010). Xlight: An efficient relational schema to store and query XML data. In *Proceedings of the IEEE International Conference in Data Store and Data Engineering* (pp. 254-257).

Zhang, C., Naughton, J., Dewitt, D., Luo, Q., & Lohmann, G. (2002). On supporting containment queries in relational database systems. In *Proceedings of the ACM SIGMOD International Conference on Management of Data* (pp. 425-436).

This work was previously published in the International Journal of Information Retrieval Research, Volume 1, Issue 4, edited by Zhongyu (Joan) Lu, pp. 53-65, copyright 2011 by IGI Publishing (an imprint of IGI Global).

Compilation of References

Abbasi, A., & Chen, H. (2005). Applying authorship analysis to Arabic Web content. In P. Kantor, G. Muresan, F. Roberts, D. D. Zeng, F.-Y. Wang, H. Chen, & R. C. Merkle (Eds.), *Proceedings of the IEEE International Conference on Intelligence and Security Informatics*, Atlanta, GA (LNCS 3495, pp. 75-93).

Abbasi, A., Chen, H., & Salem, A. (2008). Sentiment analysis in multiple languages: Feature selection for opinion classification in web forums. *ACM Transactions on Information Systems*, *26*(3), 12.

Agrahri, A. K., Divya, A. T. M., & Riedl, J. "Can people collaborate to improve the relevance of search results?" *Second ACM International Conference on Recommender Systems*. Switzerland: ACM, 2008. 283-286.

Al-Hamadani, B. T., Alwan, R. F., Lu, J., & Yip, J. (2009). Vague content and structure (VCAS) retrieval for XML electronic healthcare records (EHR). In *Proceedings of the International Conference on Internet Computing* (pp. 241-246).

Al-Harbi, S., Almuhareb, A., Al-Thubaity, A., Khorsheed, S., & Al-Rajeh, A. (2008). Automatic Arabic text classification. In *Proceedings of the 9th International Conference on Statistical Analysis of Textual Data* (pp. 77-83).

Ali, M. I., Feng, F., Liu, X., Min, W. K., & Shabira, M. (2009). On some new operations in soft set theory. *Computers & Mathematics with Applications (Oxford, England)*, *57*(9), 1547–1553. doi:10.1016/j.camwa.2008.11.009

Alistair, M., Radford, M. N., & Ian, H. W. (1998). Arithmetic coding revisited. *ACM Transactions on Information Systems*, *16*, 256–294. doi:10.1145/290159.290162

Al-Kabi, M., & Al-Mustafa, R. (2006). Arabic root based stemmer. In *Proceedings of the International Arab Conference on Information Technology*, Jordan.

Al-Kabi, M., Al-Radaideh, Q., & Akawi, K. (2011). Benchmarking and assessing the performance of Arabic Stemmers. *Journal of Information Science*, *37*(2), 1–12. doi:10.1177/0165551510392305

Al-Khalifa, S., Jagadish, H., Patel, J., Wu, Y., Koudas, N., & Srivastava, D. (2002). Structural joins: A primitive for efficient XML query pattern matching. In *Proceedings of the 8th International Conference on Data Engineering*, San Jose, CA (pp. 414-152).

Allemang, D., & Hendler, J. (2011). *Semantic Web for the Working Ontologist. Second*. USA: Morgan Kaufmann, Elsevier.

Al-Radaideh, Q. (2008). The impact of classification evaluation methods on rough sets based classifiers. In *Proceedings of the International Arab Conference on Information Technology*, Sfax, Tunisia.

Al-Shammari, E. (2008). Towards an error free stemming. In *Proceedings of the International Conference on Data Mining*, Amsterdam, The Netherlands.

Al-Shammari, E. T., & Lin, J. (2008). A new Arabic stemming algorithm. In *Proceedings of the 2nd ISCA Workshop on Experimental Linguistics*, Athens, Greece.

Al-Shargabi, B., Al-Romimah, W., & Olayah, F. (2011). A comparative study for Arabic text classification algorithms based on stop words elimination. In *Proceedings of the International Conference on Intelligent Semantic Web-Services and Applications*, Amman, Jordan.

Al-Shawakfa, E., Al-Badarneh, A., Shatnawi, S., Al-Rabab'ah, K., & Bani-Ismail, B. (2010). A comparison study of some Arabic root finding algorithms. *Journal of the American Society for Information Science and Technology*, *6*(5), 1015–1024. doi:10.1002/asi.21301

Altinel, M., & Franklin, M. J. (2000). Efficient filtering of XML documents for selective dissemination of information. In *Proceedings of the 26th International Conference on Very Large Databases* (pp. 53-64).

Araujo, L. (1998). Knowing and learning as networking. *Management Learning*, *29*, 317–336. doi:10.1177/1350507698293004

Ardichvili, A., Page, V., & Wentling, T. (2003). Motivation and barriers to participation in virtual knowledge -sharing communities of practice. *Knowledge Management*, *7*, 64–77. doi:10.1108/13673270310463626

Arenas, M., & Libkin, L. (2004). A normal form for XML documents. *ACM Transactions on Database Systems*, *29*(1), 195–232. doi:10.1145/974750.974757

Arion, A., Bonifati, A., Manolescu, I., & Pugliese, A. (2007). XQueC: A query-conscious compressed XML database. *ACM Transactions on Internet Technology*, *7*, 10. doi:10.1145/1239971.1239974

Arroyuelo, D., Claude, F., Maneth, S., Maakinen, V., Navarro, G., Nguyen, K., et al. (2010). Fast in-memory XPath search using compressed indexes. In *Proceedings of the IEEE Twenty-Sixth International Conference on Data Engineering* (pp. 417-428).

Athanassopoulos, A. D. (2000). Customer satisfaction cues to support market segmentation and explain switching behavior. *Journal of Business Research*, *47*(3), 191–207. doi:10.1016/S0148-2963(98)00060-5

Atilgan, D., & Bayram, O. G. (2006). An evaluation of faculty use of the digital library at Ankara University, Turkey. *Journal of Academic Librarianship*, *32*, 86–93. doi:10.1016/j.acalib.2005.10.009

Augeri, C. J. (2008). *On some results in unmanned aerial vehicle swarms*. Unpublished doctoral dissertation, Air Force Institute of Technology, San Diego, CA.

Augeri, C. J., Bulutoglu, D. A., Mullins, B. E., Baldwin, R. O., Leemon, C., & Baird, I. (2007). An analysis of XML compression efficiency. In *Proceedings of the Workshop on Experimental Computer Science*, San Diego, CA (p. 7).

Babcock, B., Babu, S., Datar, M., Motwani, R., & Widom, J. (2002). Models and issues in data stream systems. In *Proceedings of the International Conference on Management of Data and Symposium on Principles of Database Systems* (pp. 1-16).

Babu, G. P., & Murty, M. N. (1993). A near-optimal initial seed value selection for k-means algorithm using genetic algorithm. *Pattern Recognition Letters*, *14*, 763–769. doi:10.1016/0167-8655(93)90058-L

Baeza-Yates, R., Hurtado, C., & Mendoza, M. (2004). Query recommendation using query logs in search engines. In W. Lindner, M. Mesiti, C. Turker, Y. Tzitzikas, & A. Vakali (Eds.), *Proceedings of International Workshop on Current Trends in Database Technology* (LNCS 3268, pp. 395-397).

Baeza-Yates, R., & Ribeiro-Neto, B. (1999). *Modern Information Retrieval*. Boston, MA: Addison-Wesley Longman.

Bagirov, A. M., & Mardaneh, K. (2006). Modified global k-means algorithm for clustering in gene expression datasets. In *Proceedings of the AI Workshop on Intelligent Systems of Bioinformatics*, Hobart, Australia (pp. 23-28).

Bagirov, A. M. (2008). Modified global k-means algorithm for sum-of-squares clustering problem. *Pattern Recognition*, *41*, 3192–3199. doi:10.1016/j.patcog.2008.04.004

Bagirov, A. M., Ugon, J., & Dean, W. (2011). Fast modified global k-means algorithm for incremental cluster construction. *Pattern Recognition*, *44*, 866–876. doi:10.1016/j.patcog.2010.10.018

Baldwin, C. (1999). *Super journal project*. Retrieved from http://www.superjournal.ac.uk/sj

Bancihon, F., Barbedette, G., Benzaken, V., Delobel, C., Gamerman, S., & Lécluse, C. (1988). The design and implementation of o2, an object-oriented database system. *Advances in Object Oriented Database Systems*, *6*(1), 1–22. doi:10.1007/3-540-50345-5_1

Bandyopadhyay, S., & Maulik, U. (2001). An evolutionary technique based on k-means algorithm for optimal clustering in RN. *Information Sciences--Applications, 146*, 221-237.

Bandyopadhyay, S., & Maulik, U. (2001). Non-parametric genetic clustering: Comparison of validity indices. *IEEE Transactions on Systems, Man and Cybernetics. Part C, Applications and Reviews, 31*, 120–125. doi:10.1109/5326.923275

Barrona, T. M., Chiang, R. H. L., & Storey, V. C. (1999). A semiotics framework for information systems classification and development. *Decision Support Systems, 25*, 1–17. doi:10.1016/S0167-9236(98)00088-8

Barry, S. (1996). Mereotopology: A theory of parts and boundaries. *Data & Knowledge Engineering, 20*, 287–303. doi:10.1016/S0169-023X(96)00015-8

Bedi, P. Hema. Banati, and Anjali. Thukral. "Social semantic retrieval and ranking of eResources." *Second International Conference on Advances in Recent Technologies in Communication and Computing,* Kerela, India: ACEEE, 2010. 343 - 347.

Bedi, P., Banati, H., & Thukral, A. "Use of ontology for reusing web repositories for eLearning." Edited by Khaled Elleithy et al. *Technological Developments in Networking, Education and Automation.* Netherlands: Springer Netherlands, 2010. 97-101.

Beeferman, D., & Berger, A. (2000). Agglomerative clustering of a search engine query log. In *Proceedings of the Sixth ACM SIGKDD International Conference on Knowledge Discovery and Data Mining* (pp. 407-416).

Berglund, A., Boag, S., Chamberlin, D., Fernández, M. F., Kay, M., Robie, J., & Siméon, J. (2007). *XML path language (XPath) 2.0.* Retrieved from http://www.w3.org/TR/xpath20/

Bhargava, H. K., & Feng, J. (2005). America OnLine's Internet access service: How to deter unwanted customers. *Electronic Commerce Research and Applications, 4*(1), 35–48. doi:10.1016/j.elerap.2004.10.008

Bhuyan, J. N., Raghavan, V. V., & Venkatesh, K. E. (1991). Genetic algorithm for clustering with an ordered representation. In *Proceedings of the 4th International Conference on Genetic Algorithms* (pp. 408-415).

Bischoff, K., Firan, C. S., Nejdl, W., & Paiu, R. "Can all tags be used for search?" *Seventeenth ACM Conference on Information and Knowledge Management.* New York, USA: ACM, 2008. 193–202.

Bohannon, P., Freire, J., Roy, P., & Simeon, J. (2002). From XML schema to relations: A cost-based approach to XML storage. In *Proceedings of the IEEE International Conference on Data Engineering* (pp. 64-75).

Bonifati, A., Lorusso, M., & Sileo, D. (2009). XML lossy text compression: A preliminary study. In Z. Bellahsène, E. Hunt, M. Rys, & R. Unland (Eds.), *Proceedings of the International Symposium on Database and XML Technologies* (LNCS 5679, pp. 106-113).

Borrego, A., Anglada, L., Barrios, M., & Comellas, N. (2007). Use and users of electronic journals at Catalan Universities: The result of a survey. *Journal of Academic Librarianship, 33*(1), 67–75. doi:10.1016/j.acalib.2006.08.012

Bradley, P., & Fayyad, U. (1998). Refining initial points for k-means clustering. In *Proceedings of the 15th International Conference on Machine Learning.*

Branson, S., & Greenberg, A. (2002). *Clustering web search results using suffix tree methods.* Retrieved from http://www.stanford.edu/class/cs276a/projects/reports/arigreen-sbranson.pdf

Brenes, D., & Gayo-Avello, D. (2009). Stratified analysis of AOL query log. *Information Sciences, 179*, 1844–1858. doi:10.1016/j.ins.2009.01.027

Brin, S., & Page, L. (1998). The anatomy of a large-scale hypertextual Web search engine. *International Journal of Computer Networks and ISDN Systems, 30*(7), 107–117. doi:10.1016/S0169-7552(98)00110-X

Brown, J., & Vetter, R. (2010). *Mobile education home page.* Retrieved from http://www.mymobed.com/

Brown, J., Velado, C., & Vetter, R. (2010a, July 12-15). XML Interactive: A software framework for developing interactive SMS applications. In *Proceedings of the International Conference on Internet Computing*, Las Vegas, NV (pp. 216-224).

Brown, J., Velado, C., & Vetter, R. (2010). *Take text poll home page.* Retrieved from http://www.taketextpoll.com/

Brown, J., Shipman, B., & Vetter, R. (2007). SMS: The short message service. *Computer*, *40*(12), 106–110. doi:10.1109/MC.2007.440

Buneman, P., Davidson, S., Fan, W., Hara, C. S., & Tan, W. C. (2002). Keys for XML. *Computer Networks*, *39*(5), 473–487. doi:10.1016/S1389-1286(02)00223-2

Burez, J., & Van den Poel, D. (2008). Separating financial from commercial customer churn: A modeling step towards resolving the conflict between the sales and credit department. *Expert Systems with Applications*, *35*, 497–514. doi:10.1016/j.eswa.2007.07.036

Burez, J., & Van den Poel, D. (2009). Handling class imbalance in customer churn prediction. *Expert Systems with Applications*, *36*, 4626–4636. doi:10.1016/j.eswa.2008.05.027

Buttcher, S., & Clarke, C. (2010). *Information retrieval and evaluating search engines*. Cambridge, MA: MIT Press.

Cai, K., Spangler, S., Chen, Y., & Zhang, L. (2008). Leveraging sentiment analysis for topic detection. In *Proceedings of the International Conference on Web Intelligence and Intelligent Agent Technology*, Sydney, Australia (pp. 265-271).

Cambazoglu, B. B. (2010). Review of search engines: Information retrieval in practice by Croft, Metzler And Strohman. *Information Processing & Management*, *46*, 377–379. doi:10.1016/j.ipm.2009.12.009

Caramia, G. F., & Pezzoli, A. (2004). Improving search results with data mining in a thematic search engine. *Computers & Operations Research*, *31*, 2387–2404. doi:10.1016/S0305-0548(03)00194-1

Carnegie Mellon University. (2012). *Web graph datasets*. Retrieved from http://boston.lti.cs.cmu.edu/clueweb09/wiki/tiki-print.php?page=Web%20Graph

Carusi, A. (2006). A comparison of hypertext theory and phenomenology of reading. *Arts and Humanities in Higher Education*, *5*(2), 163–180. doi:10.1177/1474022206063652

Catherine, C. M., Shipman, F. M. III, & Raymond, J. M. (2000). Making large-scale information resources serve communities of practice. *Journal of Management Information Systems*, *11*, 65–86.

Chaffey, D., Ellis-Chadwick, F., Mayer, R., & Johnston, K. (2006). *Internet marketing strategy, implementation and practice*. Upper Saddle River, NJ: Prentice Hall.

Chang, D., Xian, D., & Chang, W. Z. (2009). A genetic algorithm with gene rearrangement for K-means clustering. *Pattern Recognition*, *42*, 1210–1222. doi:10.1016/j.patcog.2008.11.006

Charalampidis, D. (2005). A modified K-means algorithm for circular invariant clustering. *IEEE Transactions on Pattern Analysis and Machine Intelligence*, *27*(12), 1856–1865. doi:10.1109/TPAMI.2005.230

Chatzopoulou, G., Eirinaki, M., & Polyzotis, N. (2009). Query recommendations for interactive database exploration. In *Proceedings of the 21st International Conference on Scientific and Statistical Database Management*, New Orleans, LA (pp. 3-18).

Chawla, S., & Bedi, P. "Query expansion using Information Scent." *International Symposium on Information Technology.* Kuala Lumpur, Malaysia: IEEE Press, 2008. 1-8.

Chen, D., Tsang, E. C. C., Yeung, D. S., & Wang, X. (2005). The parameterization reduction of soft-set and its applications. *Computers & Mathematics with Applications (Oxford, England)*, *49*(5-6), 757–763. doi:10.1016/j.camwa.2004.10.036

Cheng, J., & Ng, W. (2004). XQZip: Querying compressed XML using structural indexing. In *Proceedings of the International Conference on Extending Data Base Technology* (pp. 219-236).

Chen, L.-C. (2010). Using a new relational concept to improve the clustering performance of search engines. *Information Processing & Management*, 1–13.

Chen, P. P. (1976). The entity-relational model: Towards a unified view of data. *ACM Transactions on Database Systems*, *1*(1), 9–36. doi:10.1145/320434.320440

Chi, E. H., & Mytkowicz, T. (2008). Understanding the efficiency of social tagging systems using information theory. In *Nineteenth ACM Cconference on Hypertext and Hypermedia* (pp. 81–88). Pittsburgh, PA, USA: ACM. doi:10.1145/1379092.1379110

Chim, H., & Deng, X. (2007). A new suffix tree similarity measure for document clustering. In *Proceedings of the 16th International Conference on World Wide Web*, Banff, AB, Canada (pp. 121-130).

Cho, J., & Garcia-Molina, H. (2002). Parallel crawlers. In *Proceedings of the 11th International Conference on World Wide Web* (pp. 124-135).

Clark, J., & Makoto, M. (2001). *RELAX NG specification*. Retrieved from http://relaxng.org/spec-20011203.html

Clarke, A. (2001). *Designing computer- based learning materials*. London, UK: Gower.

Cleary, J., & Witten, I. (1984). Data compression using adaptive coding and partial string matching. *IEEE Transactions on Communications*, *32*, 396–402. doi:10.1109/TCOM.1984.1096090

Cochenour, D., & Moothart, T. (2003). E-journal acceptance at Colorado State University: A case study. *Serials Review*, *29*, 16–25. doi:10.1016/S0098-7913(02)00267-8

Codd, E. (1972). A relational model of data for large shared data banks. *Communications of the ACM*, *13*(6), 377–387. doi:10.1145/362384.362685

Cohen, S., Mamou, J., Kanza, Y., & Sagiv, Y. (2003). XSEarch: A semantic search engine for XML. In *Proceedings of the 29th International Conference on Very Large Databases* (pp. 45-56).

Connell, T. H., Rogers, S. A., & Diedrichs, C. P. (2005). OhioLINK electronic journal use at Ohio State University. *Libraries and the Academy*, *5*, 371–390. doi:10.1353/pla.2005.0033

Coussement, K. F., Benoit, D., & Van den Poel, D. (2010). Improved marketing decision making in a customer churn prediction context using generalized additive models. *Expert Systems with Applications*, *37*, 2132–2143. doi:10.1016/j.eswa.2009.07.029

Coussement, K. F., & Van den Poel, D. (2008). Churn prediction in subscription services: An application of support vector machines while comparing two parameter-selection techniques. *Expert Systems with Applications*, *34*, 313–327. doi:10.1016/j.eswa.2006.09.038

Coussement, K., & Van den Poel, D. (2008). Integrating the voice of customers through call center emails into a decision support system for churn prediction. *Information & Management*, *45*, 164–174. doi:10.1016/j.im.2008.01.005

Coussement, K., & Van den Poel, D. (2009). Improving customer attrition prediction by integrating emotions from client/company interaction emails and evaluating multiple classifiers. *Expert Systems with Applications*, *36*, 6127–6134. doi:10.1016/j.eswa.2008.07.021

Cox, A. (2005). What are communities of practice? A comparative review of four seminal works. *Journal of Information Science*, *31*, 527–540. doi:10.1177/0165551505057016

Crestani, F., Landoni, M., & Melucci, M. (2006). Appearance and functionality of electronic books. *International Journal on Digital Libraries*, *6*(2), 192–209. doi:10.1007/s00799-004-0113-9

Croft, B., Metzler, D., & Strohman, T. (2010). *Search engines information retrieval in practice*. Upper Saddle River, NJ: Pearson Education.

Cufoglu, A., Lohi, M., & Madani, K. (2008). A comparative study of selected classifiers with classification accuracy in user profiling. In *Proceedings of the 7th International Conference on Machine Learning and Application*, San Diego, CA (pp. 787-791).

Cui, H., Mittal, V., & Datar, M. (2006). Comparative experiments on sentiment classification for online product reviews. In *Proceedings of the 21st National Conference on Artificial Intelligence* (Vol. 2, pp. 1265-1270).

Cunningham, S. J., Littin, J., & Witten, I. H. (1999). Applications of machine learning in information retrieval. *Annual Review of Information Science & Technology*, *34*(1), 341–384.

Curtis, D. (2005). *E-journals: A how-to-do-it manual for building managing, and supporting electronic journal collections*. London, UK: Facet.

Cutting, D. R., Karger, D. R., Pedersen, J. O., & Tukey, J. W. (1992). Scatter/Gather: A cluster-based approach to browsing large document collections. In *Proceedings of the 15th International ACM SIGIR Conference on Research and Development in Information Retrieval* (pp. 318-329).

Davis, J., Tierney, A., & Chang, E. (2005). *A user adaptable user interface model to support ubiquitous user access to EIS style applications*. Paper presented at the Computer Software and Applications Conference

De Stefano, D., & LeFevre, J. (2007). Cognitive load in hypertext reading: A review. *Computers in Human Behavior*, *23*, 1616–1641. doi:10.1016/j.chb.2005.08.012

Diab, M. (2009). Second generation tools (amira 2.0): Fast and robust tokenization, pos tagging, and base phrase chunking. In *Proceedings of the Second International Conference on Arabic Language Resources and Tools* (pp. 285-288).

Diao, Y., Altinel, M., Franklin, M., Zhang, H., & Fischer, P. (2003). Path sharing and predicate evaluation for high-performance XML filtering. *ACM Transactions on Database Systems*, *28*(4), 467–516. doi:10.1145/958942.958947

Dilek-Kayaoglu, H. (2008). Use of electronic journals by faculty at Istanbul University, Turkey: The result of a survey. *Journal of Academic Librarianship*, *34*(3), 239–247. doi:10.1016/j.acalib.2008.03.007

Dillon, A. (2001). *Designing usable electronic text: ergonomic aspects of human information usage*. London, UK: Taylor & Francis.

Dobbie, G., & Xiaoying, W. Ling. T. W., & Lee, M. L. (2000). *ORA-SS: An object-relationship-attribute model for semi-strucured data*. Unpublished doctoral dissertation, National University of Singapore, Pulau Bukom.

Dumais, S., Platt, J., Heckerman, D., & Sahami, M. (1998). Inductive learning algorithms and representations for text categorization. In *Proceedings of the Seventh International Conference on Information and Knowledge Management*, Bethesda, MD.

Dunham, M. H. (2003). *Data mining: Introductory and advance topics*. Upper Saddle River, NJ: Prentice Hall.

Duwairi, R., Al-Refai, M., & Khasawneh, N. (2007). Stemming versus light stemming as feature selection techniques for Arabic text categorization. In *Proceedings of the 4th International Conference on Innovations in Information Technology*, Dubai, UAE.

Duwairi, R. (2007). Arabic text categorization. *International Arab Journal of Information Technology*, *4*(2), 125–132.

Dyson, M. C. (2004). How physical text layout affects reading from screen. *Behaviour & Information Technology*, *23*(6), 377–393. doi:10.1080/01449290410001715714

El-Halees, A. (2006). Mining Arabic association rules for text classification. In *Proceedings of the First International Conference on Mathematical Sciences*, Gaza, Palestine.

El-Halees, A. M. (2010). Arabic text classification using maximum entropy. [Series of Natural Studies and Engineering]. *The Islamic University Journal*, *15*(1), 157–167.

El-Kourdi, M., Bensaid, A., & Rachidi, T. (2004). Automatic Arabic document categorization based on the Naïve Bayes Algorithm. In *Proceedings of the 20th Workshop on Computational Approaches to Arabic Script-based Languages*, Geneva, Switzerland.

Ellis, David. "The dilemma of measurement in information retrieval research." *Journal of the American Society for Information Science- Special issue: evaluation of information retrieval systems* (John Wiley & Sons, Inc) 47, no. 1 (January 1996): 23 - 36.

Embley, D., & Mok, W. Y. (2001). Developing XML documents with guaranteed "good" properties, In *Proceedings of the 20th International Conference on Conceptual Modeling* (pp. 426-441).

Erat, P., Desouza, K. C., Schäfer-Jugel, A., & Kurzawa, M. (2006). Business customer communities and knowledge sharing: Exploratory study of critical issues. *European Journal of Information Systems*, *15*, 511–524. doi:10.1057/palgrave.ejis.3000643

Fader, P. S., & Hardi, B. G. S. (2009). Probability models for customer-base analysis. *Journal of Interactive Marketing*, *23*, 61–69. doi:10.1016/j.intmar.2008.11.003

Fang, Y., Parthasarathy, S., & Schwartz, F. (2001). Using clustering to boost text classification. In *Proceedings of the IEEE International Conference on Data Mining* (pp. 123-127).

Fayyad, U. M., Piatetsky, G., Smyth, P., & Uthurusamy, R. (1996). *Advances in knowledge discovery and data mining*. Cambridge, MA: MIT.

Feldman, R., Fresko, M., Goldenberg, J., Netzer, O., & Ungar, L. (2008). Using text mining to analyze user forums. In *Proceedings of the International Conference on Service Systems and Service Management*, Melbourne, Australia (pp. 1-5).

Feng, F., Jun, Y. B., Liu, X. Y., & Li, L. F. (2010). An adjustable approach to fuzzy soft-set based decision making. *Journal of Computational and Applied Mathematics*, *234*, 10–20. doi:10.1016/j.cam.2009.11.055

Feng, L., Chang, E., & Dillon, T. (2002). A semantic network-based design methodology for XML documents. *ACM Transactions on Information Systems*, *20*(4), 390–421. doi:10.1145/582415.582417

Ferragina, P., Luccio, F., Manzini, G., & Muthukrishnan, S. (2006). Compressing and searching XML data via two zips. In *Proceedings of the 15th International Conference on World Wide Web*, Edinburgh, Scotland (pp. 751-760).

Firan, C. S., Nejdl, W., & Paiu, R. "The benefit of using tag-based profiles." *Latin American Web Conference.* Santiago de Chile: IEEE, 2007. 32-41.

Florescu, D., & Kossman, D. (1999). Storing and querying XML data using an RDBMS. *A Quarterly Bulletin of the Computer Society of the IEEE Technical Committee on Data Engineering*, *22*(3), 27–34.

Fonseca, B., Golgher, P., De Moura, E., & Ziviani, N. (2003, November). Using association rules to discovery search engines related queries. *In Proceedings of the First Latin American Web Congress*, Santiago, Chile (p. 66). Washington, DC: IEEE Computer Society.

Fox, M. S. (1992). The Tove project: Towards a common-sense model of the enterprise. In *Proceedings of the 5th International Conference on Industrial and Engineering Applications of Artificial Intelligence and Expert Systems* (pp. 25-34).

Franceschet, M. (2005). XPathMark: Functional and performance tests for XPath. In S. Bressan, S. Ceri, E. Hunt, Z. G. Ives, Z. Bellahsène, M. Rys, & R. Unland (Eds.), *Proceedings of the Third International Conference on Database and XML Technologies* (LNCS 3671, pp. 129-143).

Frenckner, K. (1990). *Legibility of continuous text on computer screens -- a guide to the literature* (Tech. Rep. No. TRITA-NA-P9010). Stockholm, Sweden: Royal Institute of Technology.

Garcia, E. "Cosine similarity and term weight." *Information Retrieval Tutorials.*http://www.miislita.com/information-retrieval-tutorial/cosine-similarity-tutorial.html, 2006a.

Garcia, E. "The classical vector space model." *Term Vector Theory and Keyword Weights Tutorial.*http://www.miislita.com/term-vector/term-vector-3.html, 2006b.

Gasevic, D., Devedzic, V., & Djuric, D. (2006). *Model driven architecture and ontology development.* Berlin, Germany: Springer-Verlag.

Gayo-Avello, D. (2009). A survey on session detection methods in query log and a proposal for future evaluation. *Information Sciences*, *179*(12), 1822–1843. doi:10.1016/j.ins.2009.01.026

Gharib, T. F., Habib, M. B., & Fayed, Z. T. (2009). Arabic text classification using support vector machines. *International Journal of Computers and their Applications*, *16*(4), 192-199.

Ghawanmeh, S., Al-Shalabi, R., Kanaan, G., Khanfar, K., & Rabab'ah, S. (2005). An algorithm for extracting the root for the Arabic Language. In *Proceedings of the 5th International Business Information Management Association Conference*, Cairo, Egypt.

Ghawanmeh, S., Al-Shalabi, R., Kanaan, G., Khanfar, K., & Rabab'ah, S. (2009). Enhanced algorithm for extracting the root of Arabic words. In *Proceedings of the Sixth International Conference on Computer Graphics, Imaging and Visualization*, China (pp. 388-391).

Giacometti, A., Marcel, P., & Negre, E. (2009). Recommending multidimensional queries. In T. Pedersen, M. Mohania, & A. M. Tjoa (Eds.), *Proceedings* of *the 11th International Conference on Data Warehousing and Knowledge Discovery,* Linz, Austria (LNCS 5691, pp. 453-466).

Girardot, M., & Sundaresan, N. (2000). Millau: An encoding format for efficient representation and exchange of XML over the web. *Computer Networks*, *33*, 747–765. doi:10.1016/S1389-1286(00)00051-7

Glady, N., Baesens, B., & Croux, C. (2009). Modeling churn using customer lifetime value. *European Journal of Operational Research*, *197*, 402–411. doi:10.1016/j.ejor.2008.06.027

Gleich, D., Zhukov, L., & Berkin, P. (2004). *Fast parallel PageRank: A linear system approach.* Retrieved from http://www.cs.purdue.edu/homes/dgleich/publications/gleich2004-parallel.pdf

Godoy, D., Schiaffino, S., & Amandi, A. (2004). Interface agents personalizing web-based tasks – special issue on intelligent agents and data mining for cognitive systems. *Cognitive Systems Research*, *5*, 207–222. doi:10.1016/j.cogsys.2004.03.003

Goldman, R., McHugh, J., & Widom, J. (1999). From semi structured data to XML: Migrating the lore data model and query language. In *Proceedings of the 2nd International Workshop on the Web and Databases* (pp. 25-30).

Gòmez-Pérez, A., Fernandez-Lopez, M., & Corcho, O. (2004). *Ontological engineering: With examples from the areas of knowledge management, e-commerce and the semantic web*. New York, NY: Springer.

Gomez, R. (1998). The nostalgia of virtual community: A study of computer- mediated communications use in Colombian non- governmental organisation. *Information Technology & People*, *11*, 217–234. doi:10.1108/09593849810228020

Gong, X., Qian, W., Yan, Y., & Zhou, A. (2005). Bloom filter-based XML packets filtering for millions of path queries. In *Proceedings of the 21st International Conference on Data Engineering* (pp. 890-901).

Gourlay, S. (2001). Knowledge management and Hrd. *Human Resource Development International*, *4*, 27–46. doi:10.1080/13678860121778

Grandi, F., Mandreoli, F., Tiberio, P., & Bergonzini, M. (2003). A temporal data model and management system for normative texts in XML format. In *Proceedings of the 5th ACM International Workshop on Web Information and Data Management* (pp. 29-36).

Greg, Pass, Abdur Chowdhury, and Cayley Torgeson. "A picture of search." *1st international conference on Scalable information systems*. Hong Kong Spink: ACM, 2006. Article No.: 1.

Gruber, T. R. (1993). Toward principles for the design of ontologies used for knowledge sharing. In Guarino, N., & Poli, R. (Eds.), *Formal ontology*. Boston, MA: Kluwer Academic.

Grust, T. (2002). Accelerating XPath location steps. In *Proceedings of the ACM SIGMOD International Conference on Management of Data*, Madison, WI (pp. 109-120).

Gungo, Z., & Alper, U. (2008). K-Harmonic means data clustering with tabu-search method. *Applied Mathematical Modelling*, *32*, 1115–1125. doi:10.1016/j.apm.2007.03.011

Guo, L., Shao, F., Botev, C., & Shanmugasundaram, J. (2003). XRANK: Ranked keyword search over XML documents. In *Proceedings of the ACM SIGMOD International Conference on Management of Data* (pp. 16-27).

Guruninger, M., & Fox, M. S. (1995). Methodology for the design and evaluation of ontologies. In *Proceedings of the Workshop on Basic Ontological Issues in Knowledge Sharing*, Montreal, QC, Canada (pp. 6.1-6.10).

Gustas, R. (2010). A look behind conceptual modelling constructs in information system, analysis and design. *International Journal of Information System Modeling and Design*, *1*(1), 79–108. doi:10.4018/jismd.2010092304

Halpin, T. (2010). Object role modelling: Principle and benefit. *International Journal of Information System Modeling and Design*, *1*(1), 33–55. doi:10.4018/jismd.2010092302

Halverson, A., Burger, J., Galanis, L., Kini, A., Krishnamurthy, R., Rao, A., et al. (2003). Mixed mode XML query processing. In *Proceedings of the 29th International Conference on Very Large Data Bases*, Berlin, Germany (pp. 225-236).

Hammouda, K. M., & Kamel, M. S. (2004). Efficient phrase-based document indexing for web document clustering. *IEEE Transactions on Knowledge and Data Engineering*, *16*(10), 1279–1296. doi:10.1109/TKDE.2004.58

Han, J., & Kamber, M. (2006). *Data mining concepts and techniques*. San Francisco, CA: Morgan Kaufmann.

Hansen, P., Ngai, E., Cheung, B. K., & Mladenovic, N. (2005). Analysis of global k-means, an incremental heuristic for minimum sum-of-squares clustering. *Journal of Classification*, *22*(2), 287–310. doi:10.1007/s00357-005-0018-3

Harold, R. S. (2000). *Shakespeare*. Retrieved from http://www.cafeconleche.org/examples/shakespeare/

Hartmann, N. (1952). *The new ways of ontlogy*. Westport, CT: Greenwood Press.

Haveliwala, T., & Kamvar, S. (2003). *The second eigenvalue of the Google Matrix (Tech. Rep.)*. Stanford, CA: Stanford University.

Hawking, D. (2006). Web search engines – Part 1. *IEEE Computer, 39*(6), 86–88. doi:10.1109/MC.2006.213

Hawking, D. (2006). Web search engines: Part 2. *IEEE Computer, 39*(8), 88–90. doi:10.1109/MC.2006.286

He, J., Tan, A. H., & Tan, C. L. (2000). A comparative study on Chinese text categorization methods. In *Proceedings of the PRICAI International Workshop on Text and Web Mining*.

Hearst, M. A., & Pedersen, J. O. (1996). Reexamining the cluster hypothesis: Scatter/Gather on retrieval results. In *Proceedings of the 19th Annual International ACM SIGIR Conference on Research and Development in Information Retrieval,* Zurich, Switzerland (pp. 76-84).

Hearst, M. A. (1992). Direction-based text interpretation as an information access refinement. In Jacobs, P. (Ed.), *Text-based intelligent systems: Current research and practice in information extraction and retrieval*. Mahwah, NJ: Lawrence Erlbaum.

Herawan, T., & Deris, M. M. (2009). A framework on rough set-based partitioning attribute selection. In D.-S. Huang, K.-H. Jo, H.-H. Lee, H.-J. Kang, & V. Bevilacqua (Eds.), *Proceedings of the 5th International Conference on Emergent Intelligent Computing Technology and Applications* (LNCS 5755, pp. 91-100).

Herawan, T., & Deris, M. M. (2009). On multi-soft sets construction in information systems. In D.-S. Huang, K.-H. Jo, H.-H. Lee, H.-J. Kang, & V. Bevilacqua (Eds.), *Proceedings of the 5th International Conference on Emergent Intelligent Computing Technology and Applications* (Eds.), (LNCS 5755, pp. 101-110).

Herawan, T., Deris, M. M., & Abawajy, J. H. (2010). Matrices representation of multi soft-sets and its application. In D. Taniar, O. Gervasi, B. Murgante, E. Pardede, & B. O. Apduhan (Eds.), *Proceedings of the International Conference on Computational Science and its Applications* (LNCS 6018, pp. 201-214).

Herawan, T., Deris, M. M., & Abawajy, J. H. (2010). A rough set approach for selecting clustering attribute. *Knowledge-Based Systems, 23*(3), 220–231. doi:10.1016/j.knosys.2009.12.003

Herre, H. (2010). The ontology of mereological systems: A logical approach. In Poli, R., & Seibt, J. (Eds.), *Theory and applications of ontology: Philosophical perspectives*. London, UK: Springer. doi:10.1007/978-90-481-8845-1_3

Höchstötter, N., & Lewandowski, D. (2009). What users see – structures in search engine results pages. *Information Sciences, 179*, 1796–1812. doi:10.1016/j.ins.2009.01.028

Hong, J. L., Siew, E.-G., & Egerton, S. (2010). Information extraction for search engines using fast heuristic techniques. *Data & Knowledge Engineering, 69*, 169–196. doi:10.1016/j.datak.2009.10.002

Hosseini, M., & Abolhassani, H. (2007). Hierarchical co-clustering for web queries and selected URLs. In B. Benatallah, F. Casati, D. Georgakopoulos, C. Bartolini, W. Sadiq, & C. Godart (Eds.), *Proceedings of the 8th International Conference on Web Information Systems Engineering* (LNCS 4831, pp. 653-662).

Hosseini, M., & Abolhassani, H. (2008). Clustering search engines log for query recommendation. In Sarbazi-Azad, H., Parhami, B., Miremadi, S.-G., & Hessabi, S. (Eds.), *Advances in computer science and engineering (Vol. 6*, pp. 380–387). Berlin, Germany: Springer-Verlag. doi:10.1007/978-3-540-89985-3_47

Hristidis, V., Papakonstantinou, Y., & Balmin, A. (2003). Keyword proximity search on XML graphs. In *Proceedings of the 19th International Conference on Data Engineering* (pp. 367-378).

Hristidis, V., Koudas, N., Papakonstantinou, Y., & Srivastava, D. (2006). Keyword proximity search in XML trees. *IEEE Transactions on Knowledge and Data Engineering, 18*(4), 525–539. doi:10.1109/TKDE.2006.1599390

Hu, M., & Liu, B. (2004). Mining and summarizing customer reviews. In *Proceedings of the Tenth ACM Conference on Knowledge Discovery and Data Mining*, Seattle, WA (pp. 168-171).

Huang, B., Buckley, B., & Kechadi, T. (2010). Multi-objective feature selection by using NSGA-II for customer churn prediction in telecommunications. *Expert Systems with Applications, 37*, 3638–3646. doi:10.1016/j.eswa.2009.10.027

Hung, P. C. K. (2009). *Services and business computing solution with XML*. Hershey, PA: IGI Global. doi:10.4018/978-1-60566-330-2

Husserl, E. (1970). *Logical investigations*. London, UK: Routledge and Kegan Paul.

Jain, A. K., & Dubes, R. C. (1988). *Algorithms for clustering data*. Upper Saddle River, NJ: Prentice Hall.

Jain, A. K., Murty, M. N., & Flynn, P. J. (1999). Data clustering: a review. *ACM Computing Surveys*, *31*(3). doi:10.1145/331499.331504

Jamali, H. R., Nicholas, D., & Huntington, P. (2005). The use and the users of the scholarly e-journals: A review of log analysis studies. *Aslib Proceedings*, *57*, 554–571. doi:10.1108/00012530510634271

Jansen, B. J. (2000). The effect of query complexity on web searching results. *Information Research, 6*(1).

Jansen, D., Spink, A., Bateman, J., & Saracevic, T. (1998). Real life information retrieval: A study of user queries on the web. *ACM SIGIR Forum, 32*(1), 5–17. doi:10.1145/281250.281253

Jansen, W., & Jagers, H. P. M. (2002). Knowledge management and virtual communities. In White, S. (Ed.), *Knowledge mapping and management*. Hershey, PA: Irma Press.

Jarvelin, K., & Kekalainen, J. (2002). Cumulated gain-based evaluation of IR techniques. *ACM Transactions on Information Systems*, *20*(4), 422–446. doi:10.1145/582415.582418

Jiang, H., Lu, H., Wang, W., & Yu, J. X. (2002). Path materialization revisited: An efficient storage model for XML data. In *Proceedings of the 13th Australasian Database Conference* (pp. 85-94).

Jiang, H., Lu, H., Wang, W., & Yu, J. X. (2002). XParent: An efficient RDBMS-based XML database system. In *Proceedings of the 18th International Conference on Data Engineering* (pp. 335-336).

Jiang, H., Yi, S., Li, J., Yang, F., & Hu, X. (2010). Ant clustering algorithm with K-harmonic means clustering. *Expert Systems with Applications*, *37*, 8679–8684. doi:10.1016/j.eswa.2010.06.061

Jones, D., & Beltramo, M. A. (1991). Solving partitioning problems with genetic algorithms. In *Proceedings of the 4th International Conference on Genetic Algorithms* (pp. 442-449).

Jones, M. A., Mothersbaugh, D. L., & Beatty, S. E. (2000). Switching barriers and repurchase intentions in services. *Journal of Retailing*, *76*(2), 259–374. doi:10.1016/S0022-4359(00)00024-5

Josifovski, V., Fontoura, M., & Barta, A. (2005). Querying XML streams. *International Journal on Very Large Data Bases*, *14*(2), 197–210. doi:10.1007/s00778-004-0123-7

Jovanović, J., Gašević, D., Torniai, C., Bateman, S., & Hatala, M. (2009). The social semantic web in intelligent learning environments: state of the art and future challenges. [Roughtledge]. *Interactive Learning Environments*, *17*(4), 273–309. doi:10.1080/10494820903195140

Kadri, Y., & Nie, J. Y. (2006). Effective stemming for Arabic information retrieval. The challenge of Arabic for NLP/MT. In *Proceedings of the International Conference at the British Computer Society* (pp. 68-74).

Kalyani, S., & Swarup, K. S. (2011). Particle swarm optimization based K-means clustering approach for security assessment in power systems. *Expert Systems with Applications*, *38*, 1083–10846. doi:10.1016/j.eswa.2011.02.086

Kanaan, G., Al Shalabi, R., Ghwanmeh, S., & Al Ma'adeed, H. (2009). A comparison of text classification techniques applied to Arabic text. *Journal of the American Society for Information Science and Technology*, *60*(9), 1836–1844. doi:10.1002/asi.20832

Kanungo, T., Mount, D., Netanyahu, N. S., Piatko, C., Silverman, R., & Wu, A. (2002). An efficient K-means clustering algorithm: analysis and implementation. *IEEE Transactions on Pattern Analysis and Machine Intelligence*, *24*(7), 881–892. doi:10.1109/TPAMI.2002.1017616

Karahoca, A., & Karahoca, D. (2011). GSM churn management by using fuzzy c-means clustering and adaptive neuro fuzzy inference system. *Expert Systems with Applications*, *38*(3).

Kazunari, S., Kenji, H., Masatoshi, Y., & Shunsuke, U. "Refinement of TF-IDF schemes for web pages using their hyperlinked neighboring pages." *Fourteenth ACM conference on Hypertext and hypermedia.* Nottingham, United Kingdom: ACM, 2003. 198-207.

Kekalainen, Jaana, and Kalervo Jarvelin. "Using graded relevance assessments in IR evaluation." *Journal of the American Society for Information Science and Technology* (John Wiley & Sons) 53, no. 13 (2002): 1120–1129.

Khan, S. S., & Ahmad, A. (2004). Cluster center initialization algorithm for K-means clustering. *Pattern Recognition Letters*, *25*, 1293–1302. doi:10.1016/j.patrec.2004.04.007

Khoja, S. (2011). *Personal web page.* Retrieved May 15, 2011, from http://zeus.cs.pacificu.edu/shereen/research.htm

Khoja, S., & Garside, R. (1999). *Stemming Arabic text.* Lancaster, UK: Lancaster University. Retrieved September 22, 1999, from http://www.comp.lancs.ac.uk/computing/users/khoja/stemmer.ps

Khreisat, L. (2006). Arabic text classification using N-gram frequency statistics a comparative study. In *Proceedings of the International Conference on Data Mining*, Las Vegas, NV.

Kim, S. J., & Lee, S. H. (2002). An improved computation of PageRank algorithm. *Journal Advances in Information Retrieval*, 341-369.

Kim, S., Han, K., Rim, H., & Myaeng, S. (2006). Some effective techniques for Naive Bayes text classification. *IEEE Transactions on Knowledge and Data Engineering*, *18*(11), 1457–1466. doi:10.1109/TKDE.2006.180

Kleinberg, J. M. (1999). Authoritative sources in a hyperlinked environment. [ACM]. *Journal of the ACM*, *46*(5), 604–632. doi:10.1145/324133.324140

Koch, M. (2000). *Learning from civilization.* Retrieved from http://www.linezine.com/3.1/features/mklic.htm

Kolahi, S. (2007). Dependency-preserving normalization of relational and XML data. *Journal of Computer and System Sciences*, 636–647. doi:10.1016/j.jcss.2006.10.014

Kong, Z., Gao, L. Q., & Wang, L. F. (2009). Comment on "A fuzzy soft-set theoretic approach to decision making problems.". *Journal of Computational and Applied Mathematics*, *223*, 540–542. doi:10.1016/j.cam.2008.01.011

Kong, Z., Gao, L., Wang, L., & Li, S. (2008). The normal parameter reduction of soft-set and its algorithm. *Computers & Mathematics with Applications (Oxford, England)*, *56*(12), 3029–3037. doi:10.1016/j.camwa.2008.07.013

Krishna, K., & Murty, M. N. (1999). Genetic k-means algorithm. *IEEE Transactions on Systems, Man, and Cybernetics*, *29*(3), 433–439. doi:10.1109/3477.764879

Kurata, K., Matsubayashi, M., Mine, S., Muranushi, T., & Ueda, S. (2007). Electronic journals and their unbundled functions in scholarly communication: View and utilization by scientific, technological and medical researchers in Japan. *Information Processing & Management*, *43*, 1402–1415. doi:10.1016/j.ipm.2006.01.006

Kyung-Soo, J. (2001). A design of middleware components for the connection between XML and RDB. In *Proceedings of the IEEE International Symposium on Industrial Electronics* (pp. 1753-1756).

Lad, A. (1995). *User study of Armament Research and Development Establishment (ARDE) library* (Unpublished master's thesis). University of Pune, Pune, India.

Lai, J. Z. C., & Huang, T.-J. (2010). Fast global k-means clustering using cluster membership and inequality. *Pattern Recognition*, *43*, 1954–1963. doi:10.1016/j.patcog.2009.11.021

Lai, J. Z. C., Liaw, Y. C., & Lo, W. (2002). Artifact reduction of JPEG coded images using mean-removed classified vector quantization. *Signal Processing*, *82*(10), 1375–1388. doi:10.1016/S0165-1684(02)00277-3

Lammel, R. (2008). *Google's MapReduce programming model—Revisited.* Redmond, WA: Data Programmability Team, Microsoft Corp.

Landoni, M. (1997). *The visual book system: a study of the use of visual rhetoric in the design of electronic books.* Glasgow, UK: University of Strathclyde.

Langville, A. N., & Meyer, C. D. (2004). Survey: Deeper inside PageRank. *Internet Mathematics*, *1*(1), 335–380. doi:10.1080/15427951.2004.10129091

Largeron, C., Moulin, C., & Gery, M. (2011). Entropy based feature selection for text categorization. In *Proceedings of the ACM Symposium on Applied Computing*, TaiChung, Taiwan.

Larkey, L. S., & Connell, M. E. (2001). Arabic information retrieval at UMass in TREC-10. In *Proceedings of the Text Retrieval Conference*, Gaithersburg, MA.

Larose, D. (2005). *Discovering knowledge in data: An introduction to data mining*. Hoboken, NJ: John Wiley & Sons.

Last, M., Markov, A., & Kandel, A. (2008). Multi-lingual detection of Web terrorist content. In H. Chen, F.-Y. Wang, C. C. Yang, D. Zeng, M. Chau, & K. Chang (Ed.), *Proceedings of the International Conference on Intelligence and Security Informatics* (LNCS 3917, pp. 16-30).

Laszlo, M., & Mukherjee, S. (2007). A genetic algorithm that exchanges neighboring centers for k-means clustering. *Pattern Recognition Letters, 28*, 2359–2366. doi:10.1016/j.patrec.2007.08.006

Lavanya, D., & Usha, K. R. (2011). Performance evaluation of decision tree classifiers on medical datasets. *International Journal of Computers and Applications, 26*(4).

Lawvere, W. (1969). Adjointness in foundations. *Dialectica, 23*, 281–296. doi:10.1111/j.1746-8361.1969.tb01194.x

League, C., & Eng, K. (2007). Schema-based compression of XML data with Relax NG. In *Proceedings of the IEEE Data Compression Conference* (pp. 9-17).

Lee, G., & Lee, G. G. (2004). MMR-based feature selection for text categorization. In *Proceedings of the HLT-NAACL: Short Papers*, Boston, MA.

Lee, S. Y., Lee, M. L., Ling, T. W., & Kalinichenko, L. A. (1999). Designing good semi-strucutred databases. In J. Akoka, M. Bouzeghoub, I. Comyn-Wattiau, & E. Metais (Eds.), *Proceedings of the 18th International Conference on Coneptual Modeling* (LNCS 1728, p. 767).

Lee, D. L., Chuang, H., & Seamons, K. (1997). Documents ranking and the vector space model. *IEEE Software, 14*(2), 67–75. doi:10.1109/52.582976

Leuski, A., & Allan, J. (2000). Improving interactive retrieval by combining ranked list and clustering. In *Proceedings of the RIAO Conference,* Paris, France (pp. 665-681).

Li, L., Otsuka, S., & Kitsuregawa, M. (2008). Query recommendation using large-scale web access logs and web page archive. In S. Bhowmick, J. Kung, & R. Wagner (Eds.), *Proceedings of the 19th International Conference on Database and Expert Systems Applications* (LNCS 5181, pp.134-141).

Li, Y., Yu, C., & Jagadish, H. V. (2004). Schema-free Xquery. In *Proceedings of the 30th International Conference on Very Large Databases* (Vol. 30, pp. 72-83).

Liefke, H., & Suciu, D. (2000). XMill: An efficient compressor for XML data. *SIGMOD Record, 29*(2), 153–164. doi:10.1145/335191.335405

Likas, A., Vlassis, M., & Verbeek, J. (2003). The global k-means clustering algorithm. *Pattern Recognition, 36*, 451–461. doi:10.1016/S0031-3203(02)00060-2

Lin, C. Y., Liu, J., Cao, Y., Huang, Y., & Zhou, M. (2007). Low-quality product review detection in opinion summarization. In *Proceedings of the Joint Conference on Empirical Methods in Natural Language Processing and Computational Natural Language Learning* (pp. 334-342).

Lin, C. S., Tzeng, G. H., & Chin, Y. C. (2011). Combined rough set theory and flow network graph to predict customer churn in credit card accounts. *Expert Systems with Applications, 38*, 8–15. doi:10.1016/j.eswa.2010.05.039

Ling, T. W. (1985). A normal form for entity-relationship diagram. In *Proceedings of the 4th International Conference on Entity-Relationship Approach* (pp. 24-35).

Ling, T. W., Lee, M. L., & Dobbie, G. (2005). *Semi structured database design*. New York, NY: Springer.

Liu, B., Chin, C. W., & Ng, H. T. (2003). Mining topic-specific concepts and definitions on the web. In *Proceedings of the Twelfth International World Wide Web Conference*, Budapest, Hungary (pp. 251-260).

Liu, D., & Kubala, F. (2004). Online speaker clustering. In *Proceedings of the IEEE Conference on Acoustics, Speech, and Signal Processing* (Vol. 1, pp. 333-336).

Liu, F., Yu, C., Meng, W., & Chowdhury, A. (2006). Effective keyword search in relational databases. In *Proceedings of the ACM SIGMOD International Conference on Management of Data* (pp. 563-574).

Liu, Z., Walker, J., & Yichen, Y. (2007). Xseek: A semantic XML search engine using keywords. In *Proceedings of the 33rd International Conference on Very Large Databases* (pp. 1330-1333).

Liu, T. Y. (2009). Learning to rank for information retrieval. *Foundations and Trends in Information Retrieval, 3*(3), 225–331. doi:10.1561/1500000016

Liu, X. (2005). Reading behaviour in the digital environment: changes in reading behaviour over the past ten years. *The Journal of Documentation*, *61*(6), 700–712. doi:10.1108/00220410510632040

Li, Y., Chung, S. M., & Holt, J. D. (2008). Text document clustering based on frequent word meaning sequences. *Data & Knowledge Engineering*, *64*(1), 381–404. doi:10.1016/j.datak.2007.08.001

Lu, J., & Cripps, N. (2005). *Impact of XML applications on interdisciplinary and multidisciplinary applications.* Paper presented at the International Conference on Systemics, Cybernetics and Informatics.

Lu, J., & Fox, R. (2007). Effectively storing and querying XML. In *Proceedings of International Conference on Internet Computing and Conference on Computer Games Development* (pp. 311-317).

Lu, Y., Zhai, C. X., & Sundaresan, N. (2009). Rated aspect summarization of short comments. In *Proceedings of the 18th International Conference on World Wide Web*, Madrid, Spain, (pp. 131-140).

Lu, J. (2005). A survey of XML applications on scientific technology. *International Journal of Software Engineering and Knowledge Engineering*, *1*, 1–33. doi:10.1142/S0218194005001902

Lu, J., & Rahman, U. (2007). Semantic search technology for information retrieval on the web. *International Internet Journal of Agent Oriented Software Engineering*, *1*(2), 225–243. doi:10.1504/IJAOSE.2007.014408

Lv, T., Gu, N., & Yan, P. (2004). Normal forms for XML documents. *Information and Software Technology*, 839–846.

MacQueen, J. B. (1967). Some methods for classification and analysis of multivariate observations. In *Proceedings of the 5th Berkeley Symposium on Mathematical Statistics and Probability*, Berkeley, CA (pp. 281-297).

Madden, S., Shah, M., Hellerstein, J., & Raman, V. (2002). Continuously adaptive continuous queries over streams. In *Proceedings of the ACM SIGMOD International Conference on Management of Data* (pp. 49-60).

Maji, P. K., Biswas, R., & Roy, A. R. (2001). Fuzzy soft-set. *Journal of Fuzzy Mathematics*, *9*(3), 589–602.

Maji, P. K., Biswas, R., & Roy, A. R. (2003). Soft-set theory. *Computers & Mathematics with Applications (Oxford, England)*, *45*, 555–562. doi:10.1016/S0898-1221(03)00016-6

Maji, P. K., Roy, A. R., & Biswas, R. (2002). An application of soft-set in a decision making problem. *Computer and Mathematics with Application*, *44*, 1077–1083. doi:10.1016/S0898-1221(02)00216-X

Maneth, S., Mihaylov, N., & Saker, S. (2008). XML tree structure compression. In *Proceedings of the 19th International Conference on Database and Expert Systems Application* (pp. 243-247).

Mani, M., Lee, D., & Muntz, R. R. (2001). Semantic data modeling using XML schemas. In H. Kunii, S. Jajodia, & A. Solvberg (Eds.), *Proceedings of 20th International Conference on Conceptual Modeling,* Yokohama, Japan (LNCS 2224, pp. 149-163).

Manning, C. D., Raghavan, P., & Schütze, H. (2008). *Introduction to information retrieval.* Cambridge, UK: Cambridge University Press.

Markowetz, A., Yang, Y., & Papadias, D. (2007). Keyword search on relational data streams. In *Proceedings of the ACM SIGMOD International Conference on Management of Data* (pp. 605-616).

Masoom Raza, M., & Upadhyay, A. K. (2006). Usage of e-journals by researchers in Aligarh Muslim University: A study. *The International Information & Library Review*, *38*, 170–179. doi:10.1016/j.iilr.2006.06.009

Matsuo, Y., & Ishizuka, M. "Keyword extraction from a single document using word co-occurrence statistical information." *Sixteenth Interational Florida AI Research Society Conference.* St. Augustine, Florida: AAAI, 2003. 392--396.

Matthew, R., & Pedro, D. (2001). The intelligent surfer: Probabilistic combination of link and content information in PageRank. In *Proceedings of the Conference on Advances in Neural Information Processing Systems* (pp. 1441-1448).

Maulik, U., & Bandyopadhyay, S. (2000). Genetic algorithm-based clustering technique. *Pattern Recognition*, *33*, 1455–1465. doi:10.1016/S0031-3203(99)00137-5

Mazlack, L. J., He, A., Zhu, Y., & Coppock, S. (2000). Rough set approach in choosing partitioning attribute. In *Proceedings of the International Chinese Statistical Association 13th International Conference on Computer Applications in Industry and Engineering* (pp. 1-6).

Melville, P., Gryc, W., & Lawrence, R. D. (2009). Sentiment analysis of blogs by combining lexical knowledge with text classification. In *Proceedings of the 15th ACM SIGKDD International Conference on Knowledge Discovery and Data Mining* (pp. 1275-1284).

Mesleh, A. (2007, December 29-31). Support vector machines based Arabic language text classification system: feature selection comparative study. In *Proceedings of the 12th WSEAS International Conference on Applied Mathematics*, Cairo, Egypt.

Mesleh, A. M., & Kanaan, G. (2008). Support vector machine text classification system: Using ant colony optimization based feature subset selection. In *Proceedings of the International Conference on Computer Engineering & Systems* (pp. 143-148).

Miall, D. S., & Dobson, T. S. (2001). Reading hypertext and the experience of literature. *Journal of Digital Information, 2*(1).

Min, J.-K., Park, M.-J., & Chung, C.-W. (2003). XPRESS: A queriable compression for XML data. In *Proceedings of the ACM SIGMOD International Conference on Management of Data*, San Diego, CA (pp. 122-133).

Min, J.-K., Park, M.-J., & Chung, C.-W. (2009). *U.S. Patent No. 5956724: Method of performing queriable XML compression using reverse arithmetic encoding and type inference engine.* Washington, DC: United States Patent and Trademark Office.

Ming, C. C., Tsai, C. W., & Yang, C. S. (2011). A time-efficient pattern reduction algorithm for k-means clustering. *Information Sciences, 181*, 716–731. doi:10.1016/j.ins.2010.10.008

Mitra, V., Wang, C.-J., & Banerjee, S. (2007). Text classification: A least square support vector machine approach. *Applied Soft Computing, 7*(3), 908–914. doi:10.1016/j.asoc.2006.04.002

Moffat, A. (1990). Implementing the PPM data compression scheme. *IEEE Transactions on Communications, 38*(11), 1917–1921. doi:10.1109/26.61469

Mohan, A., Chen, Z., & Weinberger, K. "Web-search ranking with initialized gradient boosted regression trees." Edited by Olivier Chapelle, Yi Chang and Tie-Yan Liu. *JMLR: Workshop and Conference Proceedings of the Yahoo! Learning to Rank Challenge.* Haifa, Israel: Microtome Publishing, 2011. 77-89.

Mohd, W. M. W., Mohd Zain, J., & Embong, A. (2007, November 12-15). Parameterless K-Means: Auto-generation of centroids and initial number of cluster based on distance of data points. In *Proceedings of the Malaysia-Japan International Symposium on Advanced Technology*, Kuala Lumpur, Malaysia.

Molodstov, D. (1999). Soft-set theory-first results. *Computers & Mathematics with Applications (Oxford, England), 37*(45), 19–31.

Mounissamy, P., & Rani, S. (2005). Evaluation of usage and usability of electronic journals. *SRELS Journals of Information Management, 42*(2), 189–205.

Murty, T. A. V., & Devi, T. S. (2008). Access of e-journals in the institute of higher education through UGC-info net e-journal consortium. In Nigam, B. S., & Kataria, S. (Eds.), *Digital libraries* (pp. 151–160). New Delhi, India: Mahamaya.

Mustafa, S., & Al-Radaideh, Q. (2001, November 13-15). Arabic word stemming using letter successor and predecessor variety. In *Proceedings of the International Arab Conference on Information Technology*, Jordan (pp. 216-222).

Muter, P. (1996). *Interface design and optimization of reading of continuous text.* Retrieved from http://www.psych.utoronto.ca/users/muter/pmuter1.htm

National Chemical Laboratory. (2007). *59th annual report (2006-2007).* Pune, India: Author.

Naughton, M., Stokes, N., & Carthy, J. (2010). Sentence-level event classification in unstructured texts. *Information Retrieval, 13*(2), 132–156. doi:10.1007/s10791-009-9113-0

Neslin, S. A., Gupta, S., Kamakura, W., Lu, J., & Mason, C. (2006). Defection detection: Measuring and understanding the predictive accuracy of customer churn models. *JMR, Journal of Marketing Research*, *43*(2), 204–211. doi:10.1509/jmkr.43.2.204

Nicholas, D., Rowlands, I., Clark, D., Huntington, P., Jamali, H. R., & Olle, C. (2008). UK scholarly e-book usage: A landmark survey. *Aslib Proceedings*, *60*(4), 311–334. doi:10.1108/00012530810887962

Nigam, K., & Hurst, M. (2004). Towards a robust metric of opinion. In *Proceedings of the AAAI Spring Symposium on Exploring Attitude and Affect in Text: Theories and Applications*.

Nirenberg, J. (1995). From team building to community building. *National Productivity Review*, 51-62.

Nwesri, A. F. A., Tahaghoghi, S. M. M., & Scholer, F. (2006, July 22-23). Capturing out-of-vocabulary words in Arabic text. In *Proceedings of the Conference on Empirical Methods in Natural Language Processing*, Sydney, Australia (pp. 258-266).

Olston, C., & Najork, M. (2010). Web crawling. *Foundations and Trends in Information Retrieval*, *4*(3), 175–246. doi:10.1561/1500000017

Omer, M. A. H., & Ma, S. (2010). Stemming algorithm to classify Arabic documents. *Journal of Communication and Computer*, *7*(9).

Owczarczuk, M. (2010). Churn models for prepaid customers in the cellular telecommunication, industry using large data marts. *Expert Systems with Applications*, *37*, 4710–4712. doi:10.1016/j.eswa.2009.11.083

Page, L., & Brin, S. (1998). The anatomy of a search engine. In *Proceedings of the 7th International WWW Conference*, Brisbane, Australia.

Panteli, N., & Duncan, E. (2004). Trust and temporary virtual teams: Alternative explanations dramaturgical relationships. *Information Technology & People*, *17*, 423–441. doi:10.1108/09593840410570276

Paparizos, S., Al-Khalifa, S., Chapman, A., Jagadish, H. V., Lakshmanan, L. V. S., Nierman, A., et al. (2003). TIMBER: A native system for querying XML. In *Proceedings of the ACM SIGMOD International Conference on Management of Data*, San Diego, CA.

Parmar, D., Wu, T., & Blackhurst, J. (2007). MMR: An algorithm for clustering categorical data using rough set theory. *Data & Knowledge Engineering*, *63*(3), 879–893. doi:10.1016/j.datak.2007.05.005

Pass, G., Chowdhury, A., & Torgeson, C. (2006). A picture of search. In *Proceedings of the First International Conference on Scalable Information Systems* (pp. 1-7).

Pelleg, D., & Moore, A. W. (2000). X-means: extending k-means with efficient estimation of the number of clusters. In *Proceedings of the Seventeenth International Conference on Machine Learning* (pp. 727-734).

Pendharkar, P. (2009). Genetic algorithm based neural network approaches for predicting churn in cellular wireless network services. *Expert Systems with Applications*, *36*, 6714–6720. doi:10.1016/j.eswa.2008.08.050

Peng, J., Yang, D., Tang, S., Gao, J., Zhang, P., & Fu, Y. (2007). A concept similarity based text classification algorithm. In *Proceedings of the Fourth International Conference on Fuzzy Systems and Knowledge Discovery* (pp. 535-539).

Peng, F., & Chawathe, S. (2005). XSQ: A streaming XPath engine. *ACM Transactions on Database Systems*, *30*(2), 577–623. doi:10.1145/1071610.1071617

Pinkerton, B. (2000). *WebCrawler: Finding what people want* (Unpublished doctoral dissertation). University of Washington, Seattle, WA.

Pomikálek, J., & Rehurek, R. (2007). The influence of preprocessing parameters on text categorization. *International Journal of Applied Science Engineering and Technology*, *1*(4), 430–434.

Popescu, A. M., & Etzioni, O. (2005). Extracting product features and opinions from reviews. In *Proceedings of the Conference on Human Language Technology and Empirical Methods in Natural Language Processing*, Vancouver, BC, Canada (pp. 339-346).

Porter, M. F. (1980). An algorithm for suffix stripping. *Program*, *14*(3), 130–137.

Powell, G. (2007). *Beginning XML databases*. Inidianapolis, IN: Wiley Publishing.

Prabowo, R., & Thelwall, M. (2009). Sentiment analysis: A combined approach. *Journal of Informatrics*, *3*(2), 143–157. doi:10.1016/j.joi.2009.01.003

Prakash, S., Bhowmick, S., & Mardia, S. (2004). SUCXENT: An efficient path-based approach to store and query XML documents. In F. Galindo, M. Takizawa, & R. Traunmüller (Eds.), *Proceedings of the 15th International Conference on Database and Expert Systems Applications* (LNCS 3180, pp. 285-295).

Qin, T., Liu, T.-Y., Xu, J., & Li, H. (2007). LECTOR: A benchmark collection for research on learning to rank for information retrieval. In *Proceedings of the Workshop on Learning to Rank for Information Retrieval.*

Qiu, L. Q., Zhao, R. Y., Zhou, G., & Yi, S. W. (2008). An extensive empirical study of feature selection for text categorization. In *Proceedings of the 7th IEEE/ACIS International Conference on computer and Information Science.*

Quinlan, J. R. (1993). *C4.5: Programs for machine learning*. San Francisco, CA: Morgan Kaufmann.

Rahman, C. N., Sohel, F. A., Naushad, P., & Kamruzzaman, S. M. (2003). Text classification using the concept of association rule of data mining. In *Proceedings of the International Conference on Information Technology*, Kathmandu, Nepal (pp. 234-241).

Rajeshwari, D. (2005). Use of information sources in digital environment: A case study. In *Proceedings of the 3rd International CALIBER INFLIBNET on Multilingual Computing and Information Networked Digital Environment*, Kochi, India (pp. 705-711).

Ramanath, M., Freire, J., Haritsa, J., & Roy, P. (2003). Searching for efficient XML-to-relational mappings. In Z. Bellahsène, A. B. Chaudhri, E. Rahm, M. Rys, & R. Unland (Eds.), *Proceedings of the First International XML Database Symposium on Database and XML Technologies* (LNCS 2824, pp. 19-36).

Ramesh, D. B. (2008). Emergence of electronic journals. In Nigam, B. S., & Kataria, S. (Eds.), *Digital libraries* (pp. 259–268). New Delhi, India: Mahamaya.

Ray, E. T. (2001). *Learning XML guide to creating self-describing data.* Sebastopol, CA: O'Reilly Media.

Redmond, S. J., & Heneghan, C. (2007). A method for initializing the K-means clustering algorithm using kd-trees. *Pattern Recognition Letters*, *28*, 965–973. doi:10.1016/j.patrec.2007.01.001

Reed, D. (2008). Take a good look. *Data Strategy*, *2*(4), 24–29.

Remenyi, D., Williams, B., Money, A., & Swartz, E. (1998). *Doing research in business and management: an introduction to process and method.* London, UK: Sage.

Riloff, E., Patwardhan, S., & Wiebe, J. (2006). Feature subsumption for opinion analysis. In *Proceedings of the Conference on Empirical Methods in Natural Language Processing*, Sydney, Australia (pp. 440-448).

Roberts, J. (2006). Limits to communities of practice. *Journal of Management Studies*, *43*, 624–639. doi:10.1111/j.1467-6486.2006.00618.x

Rusch-Feja, D., & Siebeky, U. (1999). Evaluation of usage of and acceptance of electronic journals. *D-Lib Magazine*, *5*(10).

Ryding, K. C. (2005). *A reference grammar of modern standard Arabic.* Cambridge, UK: Cambridge University Press.

Rys, M. (2000). *Microsoft SQL server 2000 XML enhancements.* Redmond, WA: Microsoft Support Webcast.

Said, D. A., Wanas, N. M., & Darwish, N. M. (2009). A study of text preprocessing tools for Arabic text categorization. In *Proceedings of the Second International Conference on Arabic Language* (pp. 230-236).

Sainan, L., Caifeng, L., & Liming, G. (2009). Storage method for XML document based on relational database. In *Proceedings of the IEEE International Symposium on computer Science and Computational Technology* (pp. 127-131).

Saint-Ongo, H. W. (2003). *Leveraging cops for strategic advantage.* Waltham, MA: Elsevier Science.

Sakr, S. (2009). XML compression techniques: A survey and comparison. *Journal of Computer and System Sciences*, *75*, 303–322. doi:10.1016/j.jcss.2009.01.004

Salomon, D. (2007). *Data compression: The complete reference.* New York, NY: Springer.

Salton, G. (1989). *Automatic text processing*. New York, NY: Addison-Wesley.

Salton, G., & Buckley, C. (1988). Term-weighting approaches in automatic text retrieval. *Information Processing & Management*, *24*(5), 513–523. doi:10.1016/0306-4573(88)90021-0

Sanderson, M., & Braschler, M. (2009). *Best practices for test collection creation and information retrieval system evaluation. Technical Report*. Pisa, Italy: TrebleCLEF.

Sawaf, H., Zaplo, J., & Ney, H. (2001). Statistical classification methods for Arabic news articles. In *Proceedings of the Arabic Natural Language Processing*, Toulouse, France.

Sawsaa, A., & Lu, J. (2009). A generic model of knowledge mapping through virtual communities of practice in information science. In *Proceedings of the International Conference on Internet Computing* (pp. 234-240).

Sawsaa, A., & Lu, J. (2010). Ontocop: A virtual community of practice to create ontology of information science. In *Proceedings of the International Conference on Internet Computing*.

Scane, J. L. P. R. (2003). *User interface design*. London, UK: Crucial, a division of Learning Matters.

Schlatt, S. M. (2008). *The Holumbus framework: Creating scalable and highly customized crawlers and indexers*. Wedel, Germany: FH Wedel University of Applied Sciences.

Schlemiel, A., & Teigland, R. (2008). Improved organizational performance through communities of practice. *Journal of Knowledge Management*, *12*, 106–118. doi:10.1108/13673270810852421

Schmidt, S. (2009). *The Holumbus gramework: Distributed computing with MapReduce in Haskell* (Unpublished master's thesis). FH Wedel University of Applied Sciences, Wedel, Germany.

Selim, S. Z., & Ismail, M. A. (1984). K-means type algorithms: a generalized convergence theorem and characterization of local optimality. *IEEE Transactions on Pattern Analysis and Machine Intelligence*, *6*, 81–87. doi:10.1109/TPAMI.1984.4767478

Sembok, T. M. T., Abu Ata, B. M., & Abu Bakar, Z. (2011). A rule-based Arabic stemming algorithm. In *Proceedings of the 5th European Conference on European Computing Conference.*

Shang, W., Huang, H., Zhu, H., Lin, Y., Qu, Y., & Wang, Z. (2007). A novel feature selection algorithm for text categorization. *Expert Systems with Applications*, *33*(1), 1–5. doi:10.1016/j.eswa.2006.04.001

Shanmugasundaram, J., Tufte, K., Zhang, C., He, G., DeWitt, D. J., & Naughton, J. F. (1999). Relational databases for querying XML documents: Limitations and opportunities. In *Proceedings of the International Conference on Very Large Data Base* (pp. 302-314).

Shannon, C. E. (1948). A mathematica theory of communication. *The Bell System Technical Journal*, *27*, 379–423.

Shenghua, B., Guirong, X., Xiaoyuan, W., Yong, Y., Ben, F., & Zhong, S. "Optimizing web search using social annotations." *Sixteenth international conference on World Wide Web, May08-12,2007.* Banff, Alberta, Canada: ACM, 2007. 501-510.

Shenoy, P. D., Srinivasa, K. G., Thomas, A. O., Venugopal, K. R., & Patnaik, L. M. (2004). Mining top - *k* ranked Webpages using simulated annealing and genetic algorithms. In *Proceedings of the Asian Applied Computing Conference*, Nepal (pp. 137-144).

Shwartz, S., Crammer, K., Dekel, O., & Singer, Y. (2004). Online passive-aggressive algorithms. In Thrun, S., Saul, L., & Scholkopf, B. (Eds.), *Advances in neural information processing systems* (p. 16). Cambridge, MA: MIT Press.

Skibinski, P., Grabowski, S., & Swacha, J. (2007). Effective asymmertic XML compression. *Software, Practice & Experience*, *38*(10).

Smith, B. (2003). *Ontology: An introduction: How to build an ontology.* Retrieved from http://ontology.buffalo.edu/smith/

Späth, H. (1989). *Cluster analysis algorithms*. Chichester, UK: Ellis Horwood.

Staab, S., & Studer, R. (2001). Knowledge processes and ontologies. *Knowledge Management*, 26-34.

Stewart, T. (1997). The invisible key to success. *Fortune*, 173–176.

Su, Q., Xu, X., Guo, H., Guo, Z., Wu, X., Zhang, X., et al. (2008). Hidden sentiment association in Chinese web opinion mining. In *Proceedings of the ACM Conference on World Wide Web*, Beijing, China (pp. 959-968).

Sujata, H. R., & Mudhol, M. V. (2008). Use of electronic information sources at the College of Fisheries, Mangalore, India. *Annals of Library and Information Studies, 55*, 234–245.

Sun, J., Long, C., Zhu, X., & Huang, M. (2009). Mining reviews for product comparison and recommendation. *Research Journal on Computer Science and Computer Engineering with Applications, 39*, 33–40.

Sun, Y. C. (2003). Extensive reading online: an overview and evaluation. *Journal of Computer Assisted Learning, 19*, 438–446. doi:10.1046/j.0266-4909.2003.00048.x

Supreethi, K. P., & Prasad, E. V. (2007). Web document clustering technique using case grammar structure. In *Proceedings of the International Conference on Computational Intelligence and Multimedia Applications* (pp. 98-102).

Sybase Corporation. (1999). *Using XML with the Sybase adaptive server SQL databases*. Berkeley, CA: Author.

Taghva, K., Elkhoury, R., & Coombs, J. (2005). *Arabic stemming without a root dictionary.* Paper presented at the International Conference on Information Technology: Coding and Computing.

Tan, P.-N., Steinbach, M., & Kumar, V. (2005). *Introduction to data mining*. Upper Saddle River, NJ: Pearson Education.

Tappedin. (2010). *Community of educational domain.* Retrieved from http://tappedin.org/tappedin/

Tatarinov, I., Viglas, S., Beyer, K., Shanmugasundaram, J., Shekita, E., & Zhang, C. (2002). Storing and querying ordered XML using a relational database system. In *Proceedings of the ACM SIGMOD International Conference on Management of Data* (pp. 204-215).

Tatiana Gavrilova, H. J. (2008). One approach to knowledge mapping for international student portal. In *Proceedings of the International Conference on Knowledge-Dialogue-Solution*, Varna, Bulgaria.

Tenopir, C., King, D. W., Edwards, S., & Wu, L. (2009). Electronic journals and changes in scholarly article: seeking and reading patterns. *Aslib Proceedings, 61*, 5–32. doi:10.1108/00012530910932267

Terras, M. (2005). Reading the readers: Modelling complex humanities processes to build cognitive system. *Literary and Linguistic Computing, 20*(1), 41–59. doi:10.1093/llc/fqh042

Thabet, N. (2004). Stemming the Qur'an. In *Proceedings of the Workshop on Computational Approaches to Arabic Script-based Languages*, Geneva, Switzerland.

Theodoridis, S., & Koutroumbas, K. (2003). *Pattern recognition* (2nd ed.). New York, NY: Academic Press.

Thissen, F. (2004). *Screen design manual: communicating effectively through multimedia.* New York, NY: Springer.

Thomas, J. S. (2001). A methodology for linking customer acquisition to customer retention. *JMR, Journal of Marketing Research, 38*(2), 262–268. doi:10.1509/jmkr.38.2.262.18848

Thorsten, J., Laura, G., Bing, P., & Helene, H. (2007). Evaluating the accuracy of implicit feedback from clicks and query reformulation in Web search. *ACM Transactions on Information Systems, 25*(2), 1–27.

Thukral, A., Bedi, P., & Banati, H. "Automatic organization of web resources in ontologies for lLearning purpose." *Second International Conference on e-Education, e-Business, e-Management and E-Learning (IC4E 2011).* Mumbai, India.: IEEE, 2011. 38-44.

Thukral, A., Mendiratta, V., Behl, A., Banati, H., & Bedi, P. "FCHC: a social semantic focused crawler." *International Conference on Advances in Computing and Communications.* Kochi, India: Springer, 2011. 273-284.

Thukral, A., Bedi, P., & Banati, H. (2011, April). "Architecture to organize social semantic relevant web resources in a knowledgebase." *International Journal of e-Education, e-Business, e-. Management Learning, 1*(1), 45–51.

Tian, F., DeWitt, D., Chen, J., & Zhang, C. (2002). The design and performance evaluation of alternative XML storage strategies. *SIGMOD Record, 31*(1), 5–10. doi:10.1145/507338.507341

Tjondronegoro, D., & Spink, A. (2008). Multimedia search engine functionality: An exploratory study. *Information Processing & Management*, *44*(1), 340–357. doi:10.1016/j.ipm.2007.03.004

Tolani, P. M., & Haritsa, J. R. (2000). XGRIND: A query-friendly XML compressor. In *Proceedings of the IEEE 18th International Conference on Data Engineering*, University of Washington. (2002). *Index of research/xml-datasets/data*. Retrieved from http://www.cs.washington.edu/research/xmldatasets/data/

Tompson, H. S., Beech, D., Moloney, M., & Meldensohn, N. (2004). *XML schema part 1: Structures second edition*. Retrieved from http://www.w3.org/TR/xmlschema-1

Truong, Y. (2009). An evaluation of the theory of planned behaviour in consumer acceptance of online video and television services. *Electronic Journal Information Systems Evaluation*, *12*(2), 177–186.

Tsai, C., & Lu, Y. (2009). Customer churn prediction by hybrid neural networks. *Expert Systems with Applications*, *36*, 12547–12553. doi:10.1016/j.eswa.2009.05.032

Turney, P. (1999). *Learning to extract keyphrases from text* (Tech. Rep. No. ERB-1057). Ottawa, ON, Canada: National Research Council of Canada.

University of North Dakota. (n.d.). *Cataloging electronic documents*. Retrieved from http://www.und.edu/dept/library/Departments/abc/Catedocs.html

Vadrevu, S., & Velipasaoglu, E. (2011). Identifying primary content from web pages and its application to web search ranking. In *WWW 2011* (pp. 135–136). Hyderabad, India: ACM. doi:10.1145/1963192.1963261

Variz, A. (1998). Basic problems of mereotopology. In Guarino, N. (Ed.), *Formal ontology in information systems*. Amsterdam, The Netherlands: IOS Press.

Varzi, A. (1996). Parts, wholes, and part-whole relations: The prospects of mereotopology. *Data & Knowledge Engineering*, *20*, 259–286. doi:10.1016/S0169-023X(96)00017-1

Vaughan, L. (2004). New measurements for search engine evaluation proposed and tested. [Pergamon Press]. *Information Processing and Management: an International Journal*, *40*(4), 677–691. doi:10.1016/S0306-4573(03)00043-8

Verbeke, W., Martens, D., Mues, C., & Baesens, B. (2011). Building comprehensible customer churn prediction models with advanced rule induction techniques. *Expert Systems with Applications*, *38*(3).

Vincent, M., Liu, J., & Mohania, M. (2007). On the equivalence between FDs in XML and FDs in relations. *Acta Infomatica*, 230-247.

Vincent, M., Liu, J., & Liu, C. (2004). Strong functional dependencies and their application to normal form in XML. *ACM Transactions on Database Systems*, *29*(3), 445–462. doi:10.1145/1016028.1016029

Vinod, D. (2005). *Evaluation of the use of print and electronic journals in Central Library, I.I.T. Kharagpur*. Kharagpur, India: I.I.T. Kharagpur.

Voorbij, H., & Ongering, H. (2006). The use of electronic journals by Dutch researchers: A descriptive and exploratory study. *Journal of Academic Librarianship*, *32*, 223. doi:10.1016/j.acalib.2006.02.006

W3schools. (2006). *XML examples*. Retrieved from http://w3schools.com/

Wang, J., & Topor, R. (2005). Removing XML data redundancies using functional and equality-generating dependencies. In *Proceedings of the 16th Australian Database Conference* (Vol. 39, pp. 65-74).

Weiss, G. M. (2004). Mining with rarity: A unifying framework. *SIGKDD Explorations*, *6*(1), 7–19. doi:10.1145/1007730.1007734

Wen, J., Nie, J., & Zhang, H. (2001). Clustering user queries of a search engine. In *Proceedings of the 10th International World Wide Web Conference* (pp. 162-168).

Wenger, E. (1998). *Communities of practice: Learning, meaning, identity*. Cambridge, UK: Cambridge University Press.

Wenger, R. M., & Snyder, W. (2002). *Cultivating communities of practice: A guide to managing knowledge*. Boston, MA: Harvard Business School Press.

Whitelaw, C., Garg, N., & Argamon, S. (2005). Using appraisal groups for sentiment analysis. In *Proceedings of the 14th ACM International Conference on Information and Knowledge Management*, Bremen, Germany (pp. 625-631).

Wiebe, J. (1994). Tracking point of view in narrative. *Computational Linguistics*, *20*(2), 233–287.

Wikipedia. (n.d.). *Activity diagram.* Retrieved from http://en.wikipedia.org/wiki/Activity_diagram

Wikipedia. (n.d.). *Decision tree learning*. Retrieved from http://en.wikipedia.org/wiki/Decision_tree_learning

Wikipedia. (n.d.). *Multitier architecture.* Retrieved from http://en.wikipedia.org/wiki/Three- tier_(computing)#Three-tier_architecture

Wikipedia. (n.d.). *Web application framework.* Retrieved from http://en.wikipedia.org/wiki/Web_application_framework

Wikipedia. (n.d.). *XML editor.* Retrieved from http://en.wikipedia.org/wiki/XML_editor

Wilson, R., Landoni, M., & Gibb, F. (2003). The WEB Book experiments in electronic textbook design. *The Journal of Documentation*, *59*(4), 454–476. doi:10.1108/00220410310485721

Witten, H., & Frank, E. (2005). *Data mining: Practical machine learning tools and techniques* (2nd ed.). San Francisco, CA: Morgan Kaufmann.

Witten, I., & MacDonald, B. (1998). Using concept learning for knowledge acquisition. *International Journal of Man-Machine Studies*, *29*(2), 171–196. doi:10.1016/S0020-7373(88)80045-2

Woda, M. (2006, May 25-27). Conception of composing learning content into learning tree to ensure reliability of learning material. In *Proceedings of the International Conference on Dependability of Computer Systems*, Szklarska Poreba, Poland (pp. 374-381).

Wong, T. L., & Lam, W. (2005). Hot item mining and summarization from multiple auction web sites. In *Proceedings of the Fifth IEEE International Conference on Data Mining* (pp. 797-800).

Wongpun, S., & Srivihok, A. (2008). Comparison of attribute selection techniques and algorithms in classifying bad behaviors of vocational education students. In *Proceedings of the 2nd IEEE International Conference on Digital Ecosystems and Technologies*, Australia (pp. 526-531).

Wong, T. L., & Lam, W. (2008). Learning to extract and summarize hot item features from multiple auction web sites. *Knowledge and Information Systems*, *14*(2), 143–160. doi:10.1007/s10115-007-0078-2

Wright, P., & Lickorish, A. (1988). Colour cues as location aids in lengthy texts on screen and paper. *Behaviour & Information Technology*, *7*, 11–30. doi:10.1080/01449298808901860

Wu, Y., Chang, C., & Lee, Y. (2006). A general and multi-lingual phrase chunking model based on masking method. In *Proceedings of the 7th International Conference on Intelligent Text Processing and Computational Linguistics*, Mexico City, Mexico (pp. 144-155).

Wu, X., Kumar, V., Quinlan, J., Ghosh, J., Yang, Q., & Motoda, H. (2007). Top 10 algorithms in data mining. *Knowledge and Information Systems*, *14*(1), 1–37. doi:10.1007/s10115-007-0114-2

Xie, Y., Li, X., Ngai, E., & Ying, W. (2009). Customer churn prediction using improved balanced random forests. *Expert Systems with Applications*, *36*, 5445–5449. doi:10.1016/j.eswa.2008.06.121

Xu, Y., & Papakonstantinou, Y. (2005). Efficient keyword search for smallest LCAs in XML databases. In *Proceedings of the ACM SIGMOD International Conference on Management of Data* (pp. 527-538).

Xu, R., & Wunsch, D. (2005). Survey of clustering algorithms. *IEEE Transactions on Neural Networks*, *16*(3), 645–678. doi:10.1109/TNN.2005.845141

Yang, J. W. (2004). A Chinese web page clustering algorithm based on the suffix tree. *Journal of National Sciences*, *9*(5), 817–822.

Yates, R. (2004). Query usage mining in search engines. In Scime, A. (Ed.), *Web mining: applications and techniques*. Hershey, PA: IGI Global. doi:10.4018/9781591404149.ch014

Yeung, C.-M. Au, M. G. Noll, N. Gibbins, C. Meinel, and N. Shadbolt. "SPEAR: spamming-resistant expertise analysis and ranking in collaborative tagging systems." *International Journal of Computational Intelligence* (Wiley-Blackwell) 27, no. 3 (2011): 458-488.

Yi, L., Liangjie, Z., Ruihua, S., Jian-Yun, N., & Ji-Rong, W. "Clustering queries for better document ranking." *Eighteenth ACM conference on Information and Knowledge Management.* Hong Kong, China: ACM, 2009. 1569-1572.

Yi, J., Nasukawa, T., Bunescu, R., & Niblack, W. (2003). *Sentiment analyzer: Extracting sentiments about a given topic using natural language processing techniques* (pp. 427–434). Almaden, CA: IBM Almaden Research Center.

Yoshikawa, M., Amagasa, T., Shimura, T., & Uemura, S. (2001). XRel: A path-based approach to storage and retrieval of XML documents using relational databases. *ACM Transactions on Internet Technology, 1*(1), 110–141. doi:10.1145/383034.383038

Yu, C., & Jagadish, J. H. (2008). XML schema refinement through redundancy detection and normalization. *International Journal on Very Large Data Base, 17*(2), 203–223. doi:10.1007/s00778-007-0063-0

Yue, L., Ren, J., & Qian, Y. (2008). Storage method of XML documents based-on pre-order labeling schema. In *Proceedings of the IEEE International Workshop on Education Technology and Computer Science* (pp. 50-53).

Zafari, H., Hasami, K., & Shiri, M. E. (2010). Xlight: An efficient relational schema to store and query XML data. In *Proceedings of the IEEE International Conference in Data Store and Data Engineering* (pp. 254-257).

Zaghloul, W., Lee, S. M., & Trimi, S. (2009). Text classification: Neural networks vs. support vector machines. *Industrial Management & Data Systems, 109*(5), 708–717. doi:10.1108/02635570910957669

Zaiane, O., & Strilets, A. (2002). Finding similar queries to satisfy searches based on query traces. In J.-M. Bruel & Z. Bellahsene (Eds.), *Proceedings of the International Workshop on Advances in Object-Oriented Information Systems,* Montpellier, France (LNCS 2426, pp. 349-359).

Zainol, Z., & Wang, B. (2010). GN-DTD: Graphical notations for describing XML documents. In *Proceedings of the 2nd International Conference on Advances in Databases, Knowledge, and Data Applications* (pp. 214-221).

Zamir, O., & Etzioni, O. (1998). Web document clustering: A feasibility demonstration. In *Proceedings of the 19th International ACM SIGIR Conference on Research and Development of Information Retrieval* (pp. 46-54).

Zamir, O., & Etzioni, O. (1999). Grouper: A dynamic clustering interface to web search results. In *Proceedings of the Eighth International World Wide Web Conference*, Toronto, ON, Canada (pp. 1361-1374).

Zeng, H.-J., He, Q.-C., Chen, Z., Ma, W.-Y., & Ma, J. (2004). Learning to cluster web search results. In *Proceedings of the 27th Annual International ACM SIGIR Conference on Research and Development in Information Retrieval* (pp. 210-217).

Zhang, C., Naughton, J., Dewitt, D., Luo, Q., & Lohmann, G. (2002). On supporting containment queries in relational database systems. In *Proceedings of the ACM SIGMOD International Conference on Management of Data* (pp. 425-436).

Zhang, X., & Haslam, M. (2005). Movement toward a predominantly electronic journal collection. *Library Hi Tech, 23*(1), 82–89. doi:10.1108/07378830510586720

Zhao, Y., & Karypis, G. (2002). Comparison of agglomerative and partitional document clustering algorithms. In *Proceedings of the SIAM Workshop on Clustering High-dimensional Data and its Applications.*

Zhou, S., Ling, T. W., Guan, J., Hu, J., & Zhou, A. (2003). Fast text classification: A training-corpus pruning based approach. In *Proceedings of the Eighth International Conference on Database Systems for Advanced Applications.*

Zhuang, D., Zhang, B., Yang, Q., Yan, J., Chen, Z., & Chen, Y. (2005). Efficient text classification by weighted proximal SVM. In *Proceedings of the Fifth IEEE International Conference on Data Mining* (pp. 538-545).

Zubi, Z. S. (2009). Using some web content mining techniques for Arabic text classification. In *Proceedings of the 8th WSEAS International Conference on Data Networks, Communications, Computers,* Baltimore, MD (pp. 73-84).

About the Contributors

Zhongyu (Joan) Lu is Professor in the Department of Informatics at the University of Huddersfield (UK). Her extensive research covers information access, retrieval and visualization, XML technology, object oriented technologies, agent technology, data management system, security issues, mobile computing and Internet computing. Specifically for these areas, she has been an invited speaker for industrial-oriented events and published five books and more than 150 papers. Professor Lu has acted as the founder and a program chair for the International XML Technology workshop and XMLTech (USA) for 11 years (2003-2011). She also serves as chair of 6 international conferences, is a regular paper reviewer for international journals, a funding reviewer natioanlly and internationally and a committee member for sixteen international conferences in her subject area. Professor Lu is involved in both internal and external research projects. The EU projects she is involved in include: Edumecca, DO-IT, and DONE-IT, collaborating with partners from 5 EU countries. She specializes in XML technology, data technology, information retrieval and mobile computing with image retrieval through the latest wireless devices. Professor Lu serves as a member of the British Computer Society (BCS), BCS examiner of Database management system and Advanced Database Management Systems. She is a fellow of the Higher Education Academy (UK).

* * *

Bharghava Varun A. has completed Bachelor of Engineering degree in Computer Science and Engineering at M S Ramaiah Institute of Technology, 2011. His Interests lie in Cloud Computing and Data Mining. He is currently working as a Software Engineer at a Multinational Corporation. Amulya M. has completed Bachelor of Engineering degree in Computer Science and Engineering at M S Ramaiah Institute of Technology, 2011. Her Interests lie in Web Development and Data Mining. She is currently working as a Software Engineer at a Multinational Corporation.

Hema Banati is an associate professor of Computer Science in Dyal Singh College at University of Delhi. She has received her PhD in Computer Science from the Department of Computer Science, University of Delhi, India in 2006. Her research interests include Web engineering, software engineering and Human Computer Interfaces, multiagent systems and E-learning. She has many national/international publications to her credit.

Punam Bedi received her PhD in Computer Science from the Department of Computer Science, University of Delhi, India in 1999 and her M.Tech. in Computer Science from IIT Delhi, India in 1986. She is an Associate Professor in the Department of Computer Science, University of Delhi. She has about 25 years of teaching and research experience and has published about 110 papers in National/International Journals/Conferences. Dr. Bedi is a member of AAAI, ACM, senior member of IEEE, and life member of Computer Society of India. Her research interests include Web Intelligence, Soft Computing, Semantic Web, Multi-agent Systems, Intelligent Information Systems, Intelligent Software Engineering, Intelligent User Interfaces, Requirement Engineering, Human Computer Interaction (HCI), Trust, Information Retrieval and Personalization.

Srinivasa K. G. received his PhD in Computer Science and Engineering from Bangalore University in 2007. He is now working as a professor in the Department of Computer Science and Engineering, M S Ramaiah Institute of Technology, Bangalore. He is the recipient of All India Council for Technical Education - Career Award for Young Teachers, Indian Society of Technical Education – ISGITS National Award for Best Research Work Done by Young Teachers, Institution of Engineers (India) – IEI Young Engineer Award in Computer Engineering, IMS Singapore – Visiting Scientist Fellowship Award. He has published more than fifty research papers in International Conferences and Journals. He has visited many universities abroad as a visiting researcher, including the University of Oklahoma, USA, Iowa State University, USA, Hong Kong University, Korean University, National University of Singapore as a few prominent visits. He has authored two books namely *File Structures using C++* by TMH and *Soft Computer for Data Mining Applications* LNAI Series – Springer. He has awarded BOYSCAST Fellowship by DST, for conducting collaborative Research in University of Melbourne.

S. Hariharan has received Bachelor and Master in Computer Science Engineering from Madurai Kammaraj University and Anna University, Chennai respectively. Then he received his PhD in Computer Science Engineering in the year 2010 from Anna University, Chennai, India. He has acquired 7 years of experience in handling U.G & PG programmes in various academic affiliations. He started his career at Crescent Engineering College as Lecturer in the year 2004. Currently he is working as Associate Professor, Department of Information Technology, Pavendar Bharathidasan College of Engineering and Technology, Trichy, India. His research interests include Computer Networks, Wireless Communications, Information Retrieval, Data mining, Web Mining, and Text Analysis. He has published 45 papers in referred journals and conferences. He also serves as editor, associate editor and reviewer for several international journals and conferences.

Amulya M. has completed Bachelor of Engineering degree in Computer Science and Engineering at M S Ramaiah Institute of Technology, 2011. Her Interests lie in Web Development and Data Mining. She is currently working as a Software Engineer at a Multinational Corporation.

Anil Kumar Muppalla has completed Bachelor of Engineering degree in Computer Science and Engineering at M S Ramaiah Institute of Technology, 2011. His Interests lie in Cloud Computing and Mobile Computing. He has organised and delegated several technology symposiums. He is currently working as a Software Engineer at a Multinational Corporation.

T. Ramkumar is currently working as professor in the Department of Computer Applications, A.V.C.College of Engineering, Mayiladuthurai, Tamilnadu, India. He has received PhD degree in Computer Applications during the year December'2010 from Anna University, Chennai. His area of specialization includes Knowledge discovery from multiple databases and Object Computing. He is the fellow member of ISTE.

Anjali Thukral is an assistant professor in the Department of Computer Science at Keshav Mahavidyalaya, University of Delhi with an experience of over 10 years of teaching to undergraduate and post-graduate students. She is also a research scholar and her research interests include Information Retrieval, Knowledge Representation, Ontology, eLearning, Semantic Web and Multi Agent Systems.

Index

I

J

K

L

M

N

O

P

Q

R

S

T

V

W

X

www.ingramcontent.com/pod-product-compliance
Ingram Content Group UK Ltd.
Pitfield, Milton Keynes, MK11 3LW, UK
UKHW050951290926
15470UKWH00005B/1761

9 781466 6389